THE CRITICAL
MIDDLE SCHOOL
READER

D1566988

THE CRITICAL MIDDLE SCHOOL READER

Edited by

Enora R. Brown and Kenneth J. Saltman

Foreword by James A. Beane
Afterword by Mara Sapon-Shevin

Routledge
Taylor & Francis Group

NEW YORK AND LONDON

Published in 2005 by
Routledge
Taylor & Francis Group
270 Madison Avenue
New York, NY 10016

Published in Great Britain by
Routledge
Taylor & Francis Group
2 Park Square
Milton Park, Abingdon
Oxon OX14 4RN

Printed in the United States of America on acid-free paper
10 9 8 7 6 5 4 3 2 1

International Standard Book Number-10: 0-415-95069-4 (Hardcover) 0-415-95070-8 (Softcover)
International Standard Book Number-13: 978-0-415-95069-5 (Hardcover) 978-0-415-95070-1 (Softcover)

Library of Congress Cataloging-in-Publication Data

The critical middle school reader / edited by Enora R. Brown and Kenneth J. Saltman.
    p. cm.
  Includes bibliographical references and index.
  ISBN 0-415-95069-4 (hard : alk. paper) -- ISBN 0-415-95070-8 (pbk. : alk. paper)
  1. Critical pedagogy. 2. Middle school education. I. Brown, Enora R. II. Saltman, Kenneth J., 1969-

LC196.C753 2005
373.236--dc22

2005004838

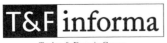

Taylor & Francis Group
is the Academic Division of T&F Informa plc.

Visit the Taylor & Francis Web site at
http://www.taylorandfrancis.com

and the Routledge Web site at
http://www.routledge-ny.com

This book is dedicated to Thora K. Brown, Barton E. Brown, Enoch U. Brown, Arthur G. Wright, and Aiesha D. Wright for just being there. And to Kathy Szybist.

Contents

Foreword

James A. Beane

Probably no level of education has seen more attention in the past few decades than the middle school. Perhaps it is something about young adolescents and the awkward place they seem to occupy in the minds of so many educators. Maybe it is the apprehension of parents when their children suddenly seem so less compliant and dependent. Maybe it is the willingness of many middle school educators to stick their professional necks out for reform. Maybe it is the young adolescents themselves who often seem so willing to point out the problems in their schools and communities. Whatever the reason, middle school reform and restructuring have been the subject of numerous reports, researches, conferences, and mainstream media analyses. The debates over what they should be for, how they should be organized, and what and how young adolescents should learn are deeply divided. This should come as no surprise. Middle level schools were set up for controversy from the start.

By the early 1900s, the upper two grades of the elementary school—grades seven and eight—had become a problem. Nearly 70 percent of those who finished sixth grade dropped out by the end of the eighth grade, not only exacerbating the growing issue of child labor, but flooding the market with unskilled workers. The elementary schools in influential metropolitan areas were overcrowded with the large influx of immigrants. In the two upper grades, increasing numbers of students were held back for academic failure in grade school.

Under the influence of Harvard President Charles Eliot, two NEA committees, the Committees of Ten and Fifteen, had already concluded in the early 1890s that the average age of students entering college (18) ought to be lower. One way of addressing that "problem" was to introduce college preparatory courses earlier than high school (National Education Association, 1893, 1895). Meanwhile, social efficiency advocates were determined to bring more vocational education into the schools so as to prepare young workers, especially immigrants, for the factory life to which their social class would assign them. In the end, removing grades seven and eight from the elementary school offered the opportunity simultaneously to relieve overcrowding and open the door for a two-track system in those two grades. This case of converging interests between classical humanists and the social efficiency advocates was conveniently bolstered (and partly defended by) the stage-related arguments of the developmentalists who, following the work of G. Stanley Hall (1908), argued that early adolescents should be segregated to accommodate their uniqueness. Out of this unusual situation came a new institution that would beat the odds against lasting reforms: the junior high school (Braun y Harycki, 2002).

Over time, the junior high school evolved to satisfy those constituencies (Briggs, 1920; Pringle, 1937). Vocational "guidance" was offered to direct young people toward college or toward work. The former were placed in college preparatory courses previously offered in the first years of the high school while the latter were placed in vocational preparation courses, along with a smattering of survey-level academic courses. All of this was done, at least theoretically, with an eye to the developmental level of young adolescence although even a close reading of junior high school literature does not always reveal exactly how that connection is made.

For the most part, though, that portrait of the junior high school and its program has persisted over time, just as its founders intended. The one serious departure occurred during the mid-century "progressive" era when proposals were made to shift at least part of the program toward a problem-centered "core" or general education curriculum more suitable than the pure subject approach for promoting democratic personal and social integration. Like other curriculum reforms associated with the progressive movement, general education "core" programs of that type dwindled rapidly amid the conservative rumblings of the 1950s and the emphasis on disciplinary structures in the 1960s (Beane, 1997). However, a lingering controversy was left over whether the original purposes of the junior high school were still pertinent or ought to be replaced with a new vision more deeply rooted in social reconstruction than adaptation.

Ironically, just as the progressive aspects of the junior high school were on their last legs, a new movement started in relation to middle level education that would eventually have major implications for the work of teachers (Alexander, 1965). As the children of the post-war "baby boom" stretched the capacity of the elementary schools in the late 1950s, many junior high school leaders began to argue for a new configuration of grades that would relieve overcrowding and, presumably, offer other important benefits. Their proposal was to remove grade six from the elementary school and combine it with grades seven and eight. In so doing, the junior high school would be replaced with the "middle school." Moreover, grade five could also be moved into the "middle school," to help end earlier the de facto racial segregation defined by neighborhood elementary schools. To make room for the elementary students, ninth graders would be moved to the high school, supposedly a more appropriate place anyway, given that the average age of achieving puberty had declined by roughly one year since the founding of the junior high school (Drasch, 1976; Tanner, 1961).

Meanwhile, advocates for the new middle schools also argued for rethinking aspects of the junior high school that contributed to a lack of alignment between the developmental characteristics of young adolescents and the organization and program of the school. Among many pervasive misalignments were the continued presence of high school–like scheduling and grouping structures that tended to make the school an impersonal and alienating place for young adolescents. In other words, advocates argued, it was finally time to change the middle level school from a "junior" version of the high school to one that would be more appropriate for what they described as the needs and interests of young adolescents. Their case was almost sure to resonate with many outside the profession, for as Charles Silberman would report after touring schools in the late 1960s, "the junior high school, by almost unanimous agreement, is the wasteland—one is tempted to say cesspool—of American education" (1970, p. 324).

Repeating history, then, the middle level of schooling was once again opened to the possibility of change by a convergence of interests, in this case those of administrative efficiency coupled with those of developmentalism. Faced with the unattractive alternative of building more and more new elementary schools as well as the intransigence of segregation in neighborhood schools, and buoyed by the arguments of middle level reformers, many school officials found the prospect of middle schools attractive enough that what is now called the "middle school movement" was soon under way and over the next several decades it would accomplish many things that its junior high school predecessor had not. In other ways, it too would fall short of the goals reformers envisioned.

More so than the junior high school movement, that of the middle school has managed to bring the concept of development to a much more visible position in policies and programs. Hardly a middle level journal or conference goes by without reiteration of the so-called "characteristics of young adolescence," a cornucopia of physical, social, and intellectual developments ostensibly describing the age group. So successful has this corner of middle school work been, that a language debate was spawned over how properly to refer to the stage. Contestants ranged from the original "early adolescence" to the invented term "transescence" (Eichhorn, 1966) to the currently popular "young adolescence." Armed with this language and the litany of supposed characteristics, advocates for middle level reform have launched an armada of widely recognized and frequently implemented structural arrangements: teaching teams to meet the "need" for close-knit community, advisory programs to meet the "need" for constant guidance, and flexible block scheduling to meet the "need" for variability in activities. And that agenda for reform has been buoyed by the considerable weight of the conference and publications of the National Middle School Association and its state and international partners.

To belittle the concern for development or the structural changes found in so many middle schools would be an absolute mistake. Research has shown them to be very successful in supporting academic and social achievement of young adolescents, including those who are poor and of color (Felner, Jackson, Kasak, Mulhall, Brand, & Flowers, 1997). Moreover, if we were to stand for something in our middle schools, we could stand for a lot worse things than the young people who attend them. We could stand for preparing youth for corporate labor needs or the narcissistic academic desires of university admission committees, for example. To its credit, the middle school movement has for the most part persisted in its rhetoric of responsiveness to the young adolescents it serves.

On the other hand, in limiting their explanation of middle school policy to the characteristics of young adolescence, middle level reformers have elevated puberty, a moment in human development, to the status of an ideology, which it clearly is not. The most obvious result is the vulnerability of the middle school philosophy to various critics. For example, critics of "child-centeredness" have had considerable success in claiming that middle schools lack academic rigor and put too much emphasis on self-esteem of students. As ell, religious neoconservatives have had a field day attacking the values education promoted in advisory programs and the devilish implication of favorite middle school methods like collaborative groups and community-building activities.

But those external critiques are only one kind of problem for the middle school movement's version of itself. From within, its major claims have been left almost completely unproblematic. The litany of presumed characteristics of young adolescents is taken to be based in physiological development with almost no attention to the possibility that is at least as much a sociohistorical and cultural construction. The litany is also taken to include all young adolescence when, in fact, it roots are almost entirely in data gathered from young adolescents who were white and lived in affluent suburban communities (Gay, 1994). And on top of all that, few middle school advocates seem to understand that by emphasizing development alone, the middle school concept fails to attach itself to any large and compelling social vision that might elevate its sense of purpose, attract more advocates, and help sustain the concept against its critics.

In this latter sense, the middle school movement reproduces (or more likely continues) the historical failure of mainstream progressives to carry their concern for children toward support for the kind of social reconstruction that would work to end the social and economic injustices that crush the spirits and aspirations of young people. Lacking that, it is little wonder the middle school has lacked a critical look. In fact, from the inside, the current movement feels like a happy story complicated by the external politics of neoconservative education policies. The response to those complications has largely been a matter of seeking ways to protect the middle schools from those policies without necessarily engaging in any resistance to them. Hence we now find an emerging middle school literature dominated mostly by ways to work with (in), adapt to, or address things like standardized testing, scripted curriculum packages, overly prescriptive content standards and other policies that are actually antithetical to a progressive vision of middle level education. In short, the middle school is in a kind of malaise, a condition Dickinson (2001) aptly calls "arrested development."

What is needed instead is a reexamination of the middle school concept to see where it has the strength to sustain itself, where it must finally face up to persistent contradictions, and how it might be pushed to a stronger, more complete, and more compelling vision of its possibilities. And that is exactly where Enora Brown and Kenneth Saltman's *Critical Middle School Reader* is a timely and desperately needed addition to the literature on middle level education. As they put it in their introduction to the volume, "The history of advocacy in the middle school movement for progressive changes puts it in a good position to extend the work done over the past 40 years, reexamine current ideas and practices in the middle school canon, and stand up to be heard, in this current national climate of standardization, accountability, and privatization."

To that end, Brown and Saltman have assembled a range of essays and papers that show just how we might begin to take another and better look at middle level claims and policies. Their selections show that while a critical view has only occasionally surfaced from within popular middle school literature, it has meanwhile been going on all around it. But they do not accomplish this by rejecting the middle school movement or its reform platform out-of-hand. To do so would not only be alienating to many advocates, but also deny the many achievements of the movement. Instead, they place samples of the most progressive literature from inside the movement alongside examples of critical theory and cultural studies, some of which are undoubtedly unknown to those educators who have not strayed beyond the boundaries of middle level studies. The result is a provocative and stimulating mix.

From a personal standpoint I welcome this volume to the middle school literature. I have spent nearly 40 years advocating for middle school reform inside the movement while also maintaining ties to larger progressive, democratic, and critical movements. One of the greatest frustrations of that professional dual identity has been trying to convince colleagues in each arena to take those in the other one seriously—or at least to find out what they are up to. Middle school developmentalists who have worked so hard for young adolescents and critical theorists who speak against injustice, oppression, and naïve history are not enemies. Both seek something better for young people, their schools, and the larger social world. So long as they remain out of touch with each other, both are diminished. Perhaps the first step toward an alliance is to show how the ideas of each enrich those of the other. For that reason I will recommend reading this volume to colleagues in both arenas. If necessary, I will insist that they do.

REFERENCES

Alexander, W. M. (1965). The junior high school: A changing view. In Hass, G., & Wiles, K. *Readings in curriculum*. Boston: Allyn & Bacon.

Beane, J. (1997). *Curriculum integration: Designing the core of democratic education*. New York: Teachers College Press.

Braun y Harycki, D. (2002). November 1902: Teddy bears and "lower high schools," *WAMLE Journal, 7*(1), 4–11.

Briggs, T. H. (1920). *The junior high school*. Boston: Houghton Mifflin.

Dickinson, T. (2001). Reinventing the middle school: A proposal to counter arrested development. In Dickinson, T. (Ed.), *Reinventing the middle school*. New York: Routledge.

Drasch, A. (1976). Variations in pubertal development and the school system: A problem and a challenge, *Transescence, 4*, 14–26.

Eichhorn, D. H. (1966). *The middle school*. New York: Center for Applied Research in Education.

Felner, R. D., Jackson, A. W., Kasak, D., Mulhall, P., Brand, S., & Flowers, N. (1997). The impact of school reform for the middle years, *Phi Delta Kappan, 78*(7), 528–550.

Gay, G. (1994). Coming of age ethnically: Teaching young adolescents of color, *Theory Into Practice, 33*(3), 149–555.

Hall, G. S. (1908). *Adolescence,* Volumes I and II. New York: D. Appleton.

National Education Association. (1893). Report of the committee on secondary school studies. Washington, DC: U.S. Government Printing Office.

National Education Association. (1895). Report of the committee of fifteen on elementary education, with the reports of the sub-committees: On the training of teachers; On the correlation of studies in elementary education; On the organization of city school systems. New York: American Book.

Pringle, R. W. (1937). *The junior high school: A psychological approach*. New York: McGraw-Hill.

Silberman, C. E. (1970). *Crisis in the classroom*. New York: Random House.

Tanner, J. M. (1961). *Education and physical growth*. London: University of London.

Acknowledgments

We would like to thank our students for helping us to think about the issues in this book. We would also like to thank those who have been active in the field whose different perspectives have pushed us to question our own presumptions about middle school as well as the presumptions of others. We would also like to especially thank James Beane and Mara Sapon-Shevin for contributing to this volume. Routledge editor Catherine Bernard not only enthusiastically embraced the idea for this book but she played an active and invaluable role in shaping it. For this we are extremely grateful. We also thank our colleagues in the Educational Policy Studies and Research Department at DePaul University for their collegiality and support. In particular we are grateful for the input and ongoing dialogue of Pauline Lipman and Stephen Haymes. Finally, we thank our friends and family for their support.

Introduction

ENORA R. BROWN

We believe especially that businesses, in their role as employers, should be much more involved in the process of setting goals for education in America. If the business community gets more involved in both the design and delivery of education, we are going to become more competitive as an economy. (Carnegie, 1983, p. 18)

"Education must no longer serve social structures and unjust power arrangements.... As John Dewey, George Counts, and other educators insisted in the early twentieth century, society must be the function of education. In other words, improving society and creating a just, caring, and ecologically sustainable community must be a primary focus of education. Middle schools must adopt this vision or they will ... reproduce modern hierarchical and unjust power structures that will never have the effect of empowering students and teachers." (Slattery, 1999, p. 29)

This *Critical Middle School Reader* was created to fill a void in the academic texts for pre-service teachers and teacher educators in the area of middle school education. It is the first compilation of both critical and traditional readings on the theory and practice of education at the middle level. By critical, we mean texts that challenge oppression and promote emancipation by examining the values, beliefs, and assumptions that undergird particular bodies of knowledge. By traditional, we refer to those texts that are complicit in reinforcing existing relations of power, by blindly accepting and transferring unexamined bodies of knowledge as factual information. It is also an interdisciplinary reader—with texts from the social, psychological, and biological sciences, the humanities, and cultural studies—designed to prompt questions and reframe basic assumptions about youth development and public education, which undergird the middle school concept and related educational policies and practices. *The Critical Middle School Reader* is the first collection of essays that presents multiple critical perspectives on adolescence and middle level education, including critical theory and pedagogy, cultural studies of youth, critical psychology, postmodernism, and contemporary feminism. These critical perspectives are presented along with excerpts from "the classics," e.g., across the disciplines of psychology, education, political economy, which reflect the disciplines' interdependent role in the historical construction of adolescence and creation of middle level education.

The idea for *The Critical Middle School Reader* grew out of our interest in examining the confluence of sociological, psychological, historical, and political economic origins of middle level education, and out of the glaring absence of a critical reader for student inquiry in the middle school endorsement courses that we taught. Most textbooks on middle school education are not interdisciplinary and are grounded in traditional psychology. As such, they tend to reaffirm G. Stanley Hall's recapitulationist view of the pubertal child/early adolescence. In this view, the pubertal child—that is, a White middle class boy—relives the evolutionary development of his primitive "savage" ancestors in order to attain the height of his "racially proscribed" intellectual and physical development during early adolescence. Thus, it was in the interests of society in the early 20th century, for educators to "inoculate" White boys against modern society and pubescent sexuality, and to utilize their primitive urges in order to build powerful men, promote racial improvement, and preserve civilization. Traditional textbooks did not challenge these beliefs and other underlying assumptions about youth that provided the rationale and goals for middle level education. To this day, in the 21st century, the implicit assumption in the bank of traditional research that anchors human development textbooks is that the "normal child" is white, middle class, and preferably male, against which all "others" are judged and ultimately are relegated to the ranks of "the deficient" or "the exotic." Nancy Lesko's pivotal book, *Act Your Age: A Cultural Construction of Adolescence* (2001), is one of the few books that draws on interdisciplinary, critical perspectives in this area, and that examines the beliefs and assumptions about youth that have been "naturalized" and rendered primitive the characteristics of adolescence. In addition, the need for a critical reader became more acute with the adoption and subsequent revision of the Carnegie Council's *Turning Points* report (1989/2000) that ushered in a new wave of middle school reform, mandated middle school endorsements through more than 33 state board of education systems across the country, and the subsequent increases in preservice teachers' demands for courses leading to the endorsement in schools of education nationwide.

The interdisciplinary texts in this volume address the significant role that structural and ideological shifts in society play in the human processes of development, in particular, in the emergence of the construction of adolescence as a stage in the lifespan. With attention to the changes in economic and civic life in the United States, these texts facilitate a critique of the normalized characterizations of youth as "troubled," "impulsive," "underdeveloped," "hormones-with-legs," and they provide closer examination of the explicit and tacit goals of middle level education. These readings contribute to the argument that major cycles of economic, sociocultural, and political change in the 19th to 21st century have defined and repositioned youth in society, ushered in public education policy and disciplinary practices that control and harness the strivings of youth, and promote race, class, and gender identities to sustain the emergent social order.

For example, it was during the advent of industrial capitalism that grassroots and philanthropic efforts fought for and won universal public education. This social victory secured an educated workforce for a newly mechanized, labor-saving economy, and increased the competitiveness of burgeoning capitalists both here and abroad. The race- and class-stratified nature of public education, however, also by design maintained a divided working class on the factory floor and bolstered racial privilege among White workers (Anderson, 1988). Similarly, the educational reform for junior high schools in the early 20th century paralleled widespread social and economic upheaval as rural dwellers, immigrants, and their families became urban, factory town dwellers in search of work. Increasing dropouts among youth, the "need" to socialize the growing immigrant population, and concerns over the vagaries and proclivities of itinerant youth catalyzed this educational reform. Junior high schools were designed to redirect the energies of youth, socialize them, and prepare poor youth for work and the wealthy for further education.

Parallel processes are evident in recent educational reforms that seem responsive to major economic shifts in today's global economy. As the world economy shifts from an industrial, electromechanical to a microelectronic technology—that is, from labor-saving to labor-replacing devices—so have there been commensurate, widespread reforms in public education to "accommodate" capital interests. Social and economic imperatives of a changing economy and increasing dropouts forged the educational rationale for middle level education in the 1960s and for middle school reform in the late 1980s, to "prepare" students for their contributions to economic growth in the new millennium (Spring, 1998). Current depictions of adolescent youth, which locate social problems in the youth rather than in the social order, are reminiscent of those proffered in the late- 19th century as justifications for the educational reform that accompanied industrial capitalism (Carnegie, 1989).

The "business of education" is alive and well today, just as it was at the turn of the 20th century. In 1905, Andrew Carnegie, steel magnate and leading advocate of vocational training, founded the Carnegie Foundation, began to provide major funding for "intelligence" and educational testing, and in 1906 created the Carnegie Unit, a standardized measure for high school credit required for colleges' participation in the foundation's pension plan. These initiatives reflected Carnegie's view that education should uplift "deserving and qualified" male youth and solve the social ills that accompanied the influx of immigrants to the United States. To this day, the Carnegie Foundation's belief that business should guide education is reflected in its lucrative creation of the Educational Testing Service (ETS) and investment in standardized testing, its founding of the Teachers Insurance Annuity Association (TIAA) (Bowles & Gintis, 1976; www.carnegiefoundation.org/aboutus/history.htm), and in their renewed interest in middle school reform and "concerns" about the waywardness of youth gone "adrift," as presented in the *Turning Points* report (1989).

The standards, accountability, and privatization of the education movement glaringly reveals corporate involvement in the current drive to further stratify education in a climate of dwindling economic opportunities for most and an increasing gap between the poor and the wealthy. The tracking and socializing function of schools has reached an all-time high with this new corporate-induced "educational reform," and the creation of organizations such as the National Center on Education and the Economy (NCEE), well-funded by Carnegie and other corporations, "philanthropies," and government agencies. As stated by Marc Tucker, president of the NCEE, "It is clear that business has an open door to the top policy makers, including the President, in a way that professional educators would envy" (Spring, 1998, p. 152). "Now more than ever, what you earn is a function of what you know and can do, or we condemn them [to] working ever longer hours for ever lower pay.... [We must give] our young people the world-class skills and knowledge they need to compete in a swiftly integrating world economy ... [through an] education [that] is standards-based ...

and … coherent." (NCEE, 2004). The interdisciplinary readings in this volume highlight the relationship among the economy, educational reform, and the need for social consciousness directed toward social change. They also illuminate the pivotal role that corporations like Carnegie have historically played and continue to play in shaping education for economic gain, either directly by educating or socializing the workforce for employment and by assessing education based on its economic productivity, or indirectly by engendering workers' ideological support for corporations' masked, profit-driven endeavors and simultaneously blaming growing economic inequality on prospective workers' failure to embrace lifelong learning (Carnegie, 1989; Goodman & Saltman, 2002; Spring, 1998). By illuminating the role of business in middle school education, we hope to support educators' emergent efforts to engage in transformative practice.

While all of the chapters are not directly related to middle level education, they contribute to the ultimate goal of this edited volume: to explore the implications of divergent perspectives on the "pubertal child" and the "nature" of adolescence for the middle school concept and curriculum, and to consider the pedagogical goals and practices that will promote the overarching democratic purpose of education not only for early adolescents, but for all youth growing up in this global era.

CRITICAL THEORY AND TRADITIONAL APPROACHES

As the title states and as we've been reiterating throughout this introduction, this is a *critical* middle school reader. But what do we mean by the term "critical"? The term *critical* has a specific historical meaning, which originated in the domain of social philosophy and sociology known as critical theory. Stephen Bronner and Douglas Kellner (1989) explain that critical theory "maintains a nondogmatic perspective which is sustained by an interest in emancipation from all forms of oppression, as well as by a commitment to freedom, happiness, and a rational ordering of society." That is, critical theory acknowledges that there are multiple contextually derived perspectives and sources of truth, many of which have been and are subjugated in order to maintain existent relations of power along the lines of race, class, and gender. Critical theory deals explicitly with asymmetrical relations of power and is a form of knowledge, an analytical tool, an approach, or way of coming to know the world, with the aim of uncovering, interpreting, or examining reality in the pursuit of emancipation. It differs from other forms of knowledge production and acquisition that deny the role of power in constructing knowledge, like positivism, which claims "objectivity" in its goal to prove or verify truth and tends to deny the values, assumptions, and interpretations that create the "facts" that grow out of and undergird empirical research; it also differs from hermeneutics, which utilizes interpretive techniques to unearth and understand unveiled phenomena, as in psychoanalysis. Critical theory relies on *both* empirical and interpretive knowledge, is multidisciplinary, and open to the process of questioning taken-for-granted assumptions in the interests of exposing oppression. It does not separate "facts" or knowledge from the interests served by or values informing the selection and organization of "factual" knowledge, in its effort to emancipate or attain depth of understanding.

The term critical, within educational theory, is drawn from this tradition and extends to the theoretical and practical concerns expressed in critical pedagogy. Like critical theory, critical pedagogy aims at emancipation and, specifically, raises questions about the ways that education, broadly conceived, has contributed to or can oppose oppression.

Within the tradition of critical pedagogy, critical thinking does not mean principally helping students to develop problem-solving or higher-order thinking skills. Rather, the goal of "being critical" or critical thinking is to learn to connect knowledge to broader social, political, cultural, and economic forces and struggles. It highlights the relationships among knowledge, authority, politics, and power. In other words, in the context of hierarchical societal relations, the question must be posed: Who produced this knowledge in this particular way and who benefits from having this body of knowledge, with its omissions and commissions, framed and guided by these particular values and beliefs? Simply put, whose knowledge is this and whose interests does it serve?

Critical pedagogy is based on the premise that since all knowledge is value laden in the context of political and economic relations of power, there are multiple sources of "truth," which must be examined, understood, and constructed for the particular interests that they serve. Critical pedagogy makes struggles over values, history, and authority central to human-centered, democratic, and ethical education. This tradition encourages praxis or reflective practice, the process of theorizing or making sense of experience to inform future action. Such reflective action that continually questions the source and meanings embedded in knowledge, language, meaning, and representations seeks to challenge the ways that educative forces become complicit with oppression. Within this view, teachers, students, and other knowledge producers can engage in critical practice to produce meanings that are more liberatory and egalitarian, and that strive toward more just social relations in the future.

One of the central distinctions between critical and traditional approaches in education is that critical pedagogy has a vision of challenging oppression. Traditional approaches are, for example, rote learning, standardized assessments, unexamined knowledge and assumptions, omissions of historical social inequality in curriculum, pedagogy, assessments, and textbooks, as well as educators' pedagogical claims or insistence on "objective" "nonpolitical" curriculum, textbook, or instructional methods. These approaches to teaching and learning do not have the explicit intention or vision of challenging oppression or working toward democracy. Rather than aiming for social and individual transformation, they aim for individual accommodation to the way things are. This is not to suggest in an essentialist manner that any particular teaching method is inherently complicit with oppression. Some are, while others are not and can be judiciously and critically used toward the goal of equality and social justice. The key is to examine the underlying values, knowledge, beliefs, and goals that these and other practices have, as they either promote or oppose the aim of emancipation. However, traditional pedagogical approaches to the construction of knowledge—such as the banking method or teaching to the test—tend to be more adaptive, with an emphasis on constructing knowledge or "transferring information" that does not challenge, but maintains current ways of thinking or being in the world. Traditional approaches avoid, ignore, and deny the profound role of unexamined beliefs, values, and institutionalized structural inequalities in contributing to the "official knowledge" in textbooks, or "best practices" for teacher education. Official knowledge in textbooks is exemplified in history textbooks replete with omissions in historical accounts that masquerade as truth, distort the past, and contribute to the construction of particular social identities along race, class, and gender lines. Similarly, "best practices" for teacher education mathematics has relied on the teaching algorithms or rules to students that eclipse and replace the intuitive, creative problem-solving capacities of youth, deny them the deeper understanding of mathematical processes, and deny them the opportunity to learn mathematical skills through practices of social criticism, interpretation, and intervention. The adaptive perspective is at odds with thinking of students as learners, not simply to be governed but rather capable of learning the skills and dispositions to govern with others. The adaptive perspective fails to consider that the core principles of democracy require informed citizens capable of engaging in democratic deliberation toward a richer life for all of humanity.

In search of a quick fix and maintenance of the status quo, traditional approaches avoid, ignore, or explain away the role of society and its structures of power in emergent social ills, while more comfortably placing the blame on the individual child or family as the source of educational failure or other social problems. Such an approach has been used, for example, to explain away racial or ethnic differences in achievement, school failure, dropout patterns, among others. Unexamined traditional approaches ultimately reproduce and exacerbate existing societal inequalities and reaffirm errant understandings or presumptions about the source and hence the solution to a given social ill. Traditional approaches tend to encourage students not to question, but to merely learn or "bank" certain "facts," skills, and dispositions to accommodate and adapt to the world *as it is*. They do not encourage or help students to understand or consider the ways in which they are capable of acting to transform the world in ways that are more just, free, and democratic. While the traditional view minimally emphasizes the acquisition or demonstration of competencies such as literacy and numeracy, the transformative perspective views the acquisition of functional skills as inseparable from transformative skills of critical thinking that link learning to broader social problems and concerns.

So what does this have to do with middle school education? We think that it has everything to do with the middle school. We need to think critically about middle school education, just as we do about all levels of education, for youth and adults. No area or arena of education should be exempt. The history of advocacy in the middle school movement for progressive changes puts it in a good position to extend the work done over the past 40 years, to reexamine current ideas and practices in the middle school canon, and to stand up to be heard, in this current national climate of standardization, accountability, and privatization. We need to think critically in order not only to generate new ideas and new solutions, but also to understand the political and social consequences of certain perspectives that we cherish. Ultimately, we need to strive to align our practice with our new understandings. Toward that end, we as educators can do more and better for the education of youth, that is, *all* youth. Because the youth are our future, both literally and figuratively, then it would behoove us to enhance their ability to make a difference, as well as our own.

As we have taught prospective middle school teachers over the years, various questions on the nature of youth, middle school, and liberatory education have arisen for us over and over again: Are middle schools in concept or practice liberatory, and if so, for whom? Does the middle school concept, policy, and practice strive to transform social inequality in schools and society? What is our construction of adolescence and how does it inform our work and the place of youth in society? Are our pedagogical and curricular approaches "adaptive" or do they promote critical thinking, analysis, and questioning in youth so that they can embrace the challenges of both personal and social transformation? Does our work take us closer to a more just society and how do we resist, in classrooms and other arenas, the retrograde national policies, practices, and justificatory rationale that threaten this possibility? We welcome the readers of this volume to add their questions to this preliminary list.

GLOBALIZATION

Another of our underlying aims in this volume is to make explicit the link between the construction of adolescence, middle level education, and globalization. Why? What is globalization? What does it have to do with middle school? Globalization is a hotly contested term. It is commonly used to refer descriptively at the very least to heightened global economic integration along with the cultural and political effects accompanying it. Globalization is more frequently prescriptively invoked in very different ways. Advocates of corporate globalization (neoliberals) tend to see the global expansion of markets as inevitably benefiting the world's population. For advocates, the policy goals involve lessening any perceived opposition or constraint on the free flow of capital, trade, and markets, and it involves political and cultural agendas that are consistent with this. Hence, advocates argue for government and organization regulations that favor business and that privatize public goods and services. Advocates of globalization put a great deal of faith in markets to "naturally" accomplish human priorities. Opponents of this business-based version of globalization refer to their version of globalization as the Global Justice Movement. Advocates of the Global Justice Movement recognize increasing global integration and believe that such integration needs to be managed not principally by the private for-profit sector but by the global public in a democratic fashion. Meetings of the World Social Forum have been held for several years. People involved in social movements for various struggles for justice, human rights, and democracy have convened to discuss how global development can benefit the bulk of the world's public. World Social Forum convening meetings developed as a response to neoliberal meetings such as the World Economic Forum, where the rich and powerful have met to plan their vision for the future. For advocates of the Global Justice Movement such neoliberal versions of globalization are a means for the most powerful people on the planet to secure their continued economic dominance at the expense of everyone else. They point to the failure of free trade and privatization to benefit the majority of people it was alleged to benefit in the past. For example, the North American Free Trade Agreement allowed U.S. companies greater ease in industrial production in Mexico. Global Justice advocates point to the fact that, while U.S. corporations involved in production in the border *Maquilladoras* (industrial corridor on the border) have profited greatly from the new rules, the people living and working there have continued to suffer terrible poverty. Advocates of the Global Justice Movement see the necessity of public sector protections to raise standards of living, and they see the necessity of developing mechanisms to redistribute political, economic, and cultural power toward the bulk of the world's population.

But again, what does this have to do with adolescence or middle school? Many writers on middle school address the purposes and function of middle schools as "serving" their constituents or responding to the "needs" of the learner. Commonly, such writing is framed through the market metaphors of consumption or marketing demographics originating in advertising. Some address how effective middle school instruction ideally prepares the student for competition in the national economy and even to contribute to global economic competition (Carnegie, 1983, 1989; Jackson & Davis, 2000). These ways of thinking about middle school share an accommodationist view that middle schools provide tools for students to fit into the world the way it is. The accommodationist view can be seen as highly compatible with the corporate version of globalization because it assumes that public schools have a largely economic function of preparing students as workers and consumers. A transformative view that sees students as developing principally as critical citizens capable of future deliberation, debate, and self- and social governance appears far more compatible with the global justice perspective. Indeed, as critics of public school privatization have discussed, the extent to which U.S. public schools and policy debates have been increasingly overtaken by business language and models has been a major threat to the public purposes and priorities of public schooling for a democratic society. The question of how public and democratic forms of education, at the elementary, middle school, and secondary level can be expanded on a national and global level is of tantamount importance for a future that puts humanity, equality, freedom, and justice as animating goals. Middle school education and the ongoing movement have a pivotal role to play in preparing youth to become those critical citizens capable of forging paths toward democracy in local and global contexts. It is in this context that questions emerged for the editors: How does globalization inform middle school policy, reform, and the future of middle level education? What is significant about corporate involvement in middle school curriculum, in the funding of charter and other forms of privatized education, in developing policy for public education? Join us in examining these and other questions of relevance.

This volume of critical and traditional readings was created out of our desire to share these questions and to generate new ones. Our intent is to create a space for dialogue and thinking about the origins of, goals of, and assumptions about the middle school concept, about youth, and about the future direction for an educational process that can and should promote personal, social, and societal transformation. This book is a starting point, since it is the *first* critical middle level reader, and we hope that it will inspire a broader conversation about the future of middle school and the possibilities for it to be reconceptualized through hopeful social ideals. Our goal is not to "throw the baby out with the bath water" nor to just raise criticisms and questions with no end in mind. Rather, it is to stimulate thinking about issues, concerns, and questions that are explicitly addressed in the readings and, more importantly, to stimulate thinking about issues, concerns, and questions that emerge for the reader from the texts and from ensuing dialogue about them. Ultimately, in the critical tradition, we hope that this text will inspire not just thought but reflective action as well that could involve reforming and reimagining middle school practice as well as teacher education.

PURPOSE OF AND USE FOR THE READER

The array of essays in this reader should achieve a number of important aims. First, we have chosen selected excerpts of traditional thought from primary sources, in psychology, sociology, and education *to examine the historical construction of adolescence* as a biological, maturational process and to examine its relationship to the resultant creation of middle level education for this "special population." These texts illustrate the origins and evolution of the concept of adolescence as a "cultural invention" (Beane & Brodhagen, 2001; Stone & Church, 1957/1975), its identification as a distinct period in the lifespan, and the *separate* educational and social institutions designed for this particular group, adolescents. These texts support our efforts to "denaturalize" (Lesko, 1996) and demystify adolescence, to place the evolution of the concept of adolescence in its historical context, and to understand its role as a pivotal rationale for middle level education, both past and present. We are not suggesting that the biological, psychological, and other maturational processes that accompany the onset of puberty are insignificant. Rather, we want to reaffirm that the social meanings constructed around the developmental processes that define "adolescence," and educational reforms that were and are instituted should be understood, examined, and critiqued within the larger social and historical contexts from which they emerged.

Second, these primary sources are juxtaposed against critical perspectives in order *to examine and illuminate the sociocultural, economic, and political origins of the "stage of adolescence."* These readings were chosen to raise questions about the past and present function and purpose of the middle school within the context of the emergent industrial economy of the late 19th century and the post-industrial, global economy of the 21st century. These texts address the role of societal inequality, along race, class, and gender lines, in structuring public education, in charting the life trajectories and constructing the social identities of youth in different communities, and in shaping the curricular experiences and educational goals of schools. They reveal the complex ways in which different class-based groupings come together as stakeholders with disparate interests (e.g., education, business, social), around a common reform (e.g., advent of universal public education in the 1800s, middle school education in the 1960s, and standardized, privatized education in 2001). The new reform that emerges has both liberatory and constraining possibilities (e.g., public education used to secure social mobility and maintain social inequality). The critical texts reveal the disparities between the dominant culture's espoused educational and psychological rationale for educational reform and the powerful social and economic motivations for reforms that will sustain or realign structural hierarchies of power in society. We chose these readings to illustrate ways in which educational structures, curricular content, and educational reforms in the dominant culture have grown out of and are organically connected to existing societal relationships of inequality, and in turn, the ways in which educational policies, practices, and reforms may reproduce or contest existing social arrangements. In addition, these readings underscore the view that schools are not institutions that stand above the fray of social problems, and that the teaching-learning process, i.e., content, construction, and use of knowledge can either reaffirm existent social realities or acknowledge, question, and contest social issues that exist in students' daily lives.

Third, collectively, these traditional and critical readings were chosen *to problematize "common sense" notions about early adolescence and middle level education.* The critical readings, adjacent to traditional texts, offer alternatives to dominant discourse about youth development, the construction of social identities, institutionalized curricular models and pedagogical practices, and the purpose and goals of education. We compiled this *Critical Middle School Reader* as a valuable resource to educators, preservice teachers, and others concerned about the future of youth, to analyze, understand, and solve the thorny problems in social life. All of the readings, whether historical, theoretical, or research-based analyses, whether critical or traditional, are accessible to students at introductory and advanced levels of study, and are appropriate for undergraduate and graduate students. These varied texts differ in length and difficulty. As such, they support educators' pedagogical flexibility in teaching courses in middle level education, and provide room for preservice teachers to grow in their thinking and analysis across different conceptual texts. Teacher educators may introduce their students to a range of perspectives on adolescence and education in this volume, guide them through thoughtful analyses and critique of the ideas and assumptions in both "classical" and critical texts, and create opportunities and set the stage for teachers–learners to imagine, envision, and create truly democratic and liberatory possibilities in schools and the larger social order for youth.

This reader is timely in light of recent research indicating that middle schools in their design and implementation are not a good "fit" for the stated needs of youth. This has prompted closer examination and a rethinking of the goals, curricular design, and pedagogical approaches previously recommended for middle level education (Beane & Brodhagen, 2001), particularly in the current climate of standardization and accountability.

ORGANIZATION OF THE BOOK

The sections in the *Critical Middle School Reader* are organized around key thematic concerns that seek to address some differences between traditional and critical approaches. The reader contains four major sections: section I: The Social Construction of Adolescence; section II: The Middle School Concept and the Purpose of Education; section III: The Construction of Identity; and section IV: Curriculum, Assessment, and Critical Pedagogy. Each section begins with an introduction and overview of the texts, explaining the relationships among them and their implications for middle level academic discourse and pedagogical practice. The first readings in each section tend to be traditional or classical texts, followed by readings from varying critical perspectives. Each section introduction ends with a collection of Discussion Questions and each section ends with Recommended Readings for Future Study.

Section I, The Social Construction of Adolescence, focuses on the biological versus sociological "roots" of adolescence. This section opens with texts that demonstrate the continuity and changes in normative thinking about adolescence over the past century: an excerpt by G. Stanley Hall, the "father of adolescence," and a reading by Jeanne Brooks-Gunn and Edward O. Reiter, that addresses pubertal processes and current-day conceptions of adolescence. Critical psychological and social historical texts by Gail Bederman, Nancy Lesko, and Mike Males challenge Hall's recapitulationist theory and resultant negative constructions of youth that emerge. Readings by William Kessen, Jeffrey Moran, and Henry Giroux illuminate the origins and functions of particular cultural constructions of youth that were/are forged in the context of social, economic, and political changes in the dominant society. These readings facilitate an examination of biological versus social constructivist views of adolescence, their implications for the stratified social position of adolescents and race- and class-based ideological justifications, and their relationship to the tacit assumptions that undergird educational policies and practices in middle schools.

Section II, The Middle School Concept and Purpose of Education, addresses the founding principles and conceptual rationale for middle level education policy, including perspectives that challenge the traditional view of adolescent youth and tacit goals of public education at all levels. The readings by William Alexander and colleagues, The Carnegie Corporation's *Turning Points* report, and text by John Lounsbury and Gordon Vars capture the origins of and rationale for the middle school reform movement and consider possibilities for future directions. Critical texts by Nancy Lesko, Samuel Bowles and Herbert Gintis, Robin Goodman and Kenneth Saltman, and Paolo Freire challenge common underlying assumptions and implicit goals of education embodied in the *Turning Points* report. The divergent perspectives in this section should serve as a means to raise questions about the middle school movement, in particular, and public education reform movement, in general, as they support or thwart efforts to realize truly democratic visions for the future.

Section III, The Construction of Identity, focuses on the concept and process of identity formation and construction and the ways in which race, class, gender, and sexual identities of youth are negotiated both subjectively and socially. Texts by Erik Erikson and Stuart Hall provide convergent and divergent psychoanalytic and critical views of identity. They lay the foundation for the ethnographic and conceptual texts by Janie Ward, Enora Brown, Ann Ferguson, Julia Hall, Angela Valenzuela, Stacey Lee, Dennis Anderson, and Donaldo Macedo that provide powerful insights into the social identities that youth negotiate, within complex historical, cultural, and economic relations. These texts provide insight into the intersubjective meanings and social dynamics that are created in educational settings, that bracket the social identities and life trajectories of middle school youth, and that reproduce societal structures of inequality.

Section IV, Curriculum, Assessment, and Critical Pedagogy, focuses on the construction and use of knowledge, as it informs middle school curricular and assessment processes. Conceptual texts are accompanied by readings that examine the implementation of innovative, integrated curricula in middle school classrooms and provide a vision for transformative educational processes. Recommendations from Carnegie Corporation's revised *Turning Points* report (Jackson & Davis, 2000) reflect the pervasive impact that corporate-sponsored national educational "reforms" on standards and accountability has had on current middle school policy and practice. Texts by James Beane and Peter McLaren are grounded in critical constructivist conceptions of knowledge and promote the liberatory democratic possibilities in education and in society through curriculum integration and critical pedagogy. Readings by Jean Anyon, Eric Gutstein, Melinda Fine, and Kathe Jervis illustrate the ways in which the class- and race-based ideology in the dominant culture pervades standard curriculum, and demonstrate the impact that integrated, problem-focused, social justice curricula has had on students and teachers. The chapter by Linda McNeil addresses the destructive effects of national reforms for standardization on public education and on the quality and nature of teaching and learning in classrooms. Despite the challenges, all authors argue for educators' civic and ethical commitment to and social action directed toward social justice and other democratic goals. This compilation of readings provides insights into the complex and subtle relationships that exist between curricula, pedagogy, and the construction of youth identities, as well as the role of education in promoting student learning for social change.

With a wealth of critical and traditional material on a wide range of themes about youth and middle school education available, there were other texts we would have liked to include in this volume. However, with the limitations of space before us, we had to cut or omit texts and limit the size of certain excerpts. There were choices made about the topical content of the book as well as reluctant omissions made due to space limitations. We chose not to organize the reader around common themes of development, i.e., social, emotional, cognitive, and physical, or concerns and "problems" about adolescents, such as sexual activity, teenage pregnancy, HIV/AIDS, violence, drug use, suicide, gangs, health and mental health issues, cognitive development, or employability, because those topics are covered extensively elsewhere. Although there is an array of traditional and critical readings in the "problem" areas, we did not want to contribute to the dominant discourse that locates unexamined social problems *in* or projects them *onto* the youth, by organizing the *first* dialogue among traditional and critical views around "youth problems."

In addition, there are omissions in some areas of the book that are important. Although we wanted a *Critical Reader* with breadth and relevance for a wide audience, the editors did not want to create a book that superficially represented every possible social identity, along the lines of race, ethnicity, and sexuality, just to have "an article by or about them" in the book. While such identity politics was not the editors' aim, we wanted balance, we wanted to address multiple dimensions of identity, and we wanted to examine issues about marginalized youth in schools and society. We had some, but not enough. For example, we were not able to include additional critical texts about Native American youth (Dehyle, 1995, 1998), construction of girlhood (Driscoll, 2002; Henry, 1998; McRobbie, 1991), critical race theory (Ladson-Billings, 2003), sexuality (Bickmore, 1999; Eder & Parker, 1987; McLaren, 1995), and others on youth in middle schools (Gay, 1994; Sipe, 2004). Any development of a critical perspective on middle school must take these up.

Similarly, there were articles by advocates from the middle school movement that we wanted to include. Some are readily available and may be used in conjunction with the *Critical Reader*, e.g., *This We Believe* (2003). However, other topical texts would have made important contributions, for example: cooperative learning (Sapon-Shevin, 1994), or team teaching (Erb & Dickinson, 1997; Kasak, 2001; Erb & Doda, 1989), teacher preparation (Cochran-Smith, 1995; McEwin & Dickinson, 1997; Scales & McEwin, 1994), administration (Clark & Clark, 1994; Erb, 2001), alternatives to standardized testing (Hilliard, 2000; Peterson & Neill, 2000), early research review (Lipsitz, 1977), gender differences in middle schools (Butler & Manning, 1998), girls and mathematics (Walkerdine, 1998), curriculum and instruction (Stevenson, 1998), history, math, science, literacy, and other disciplines (Edelsky, 1996; Gutierrez, 2000; Khisty, 1995; Schaafsma, 1993; Spring, 1994; Zinn, 1995).

However, while we hope to initiate expanded dialogue about broad issues that we wanted to address, we invite all who are concerned and interested to join in and contribute to the ongoing conversation, inquiry and efforts toward social change in middle schools and in other social institutions.

REFERENCES

Anderson, J. (1988). *The education of Blacks in the south, 1860–1935*. Chapel Hill, NC: University of North Carolina Press.

Beane, J., & Brodhagen, B. (2001). Teaching in middle schools. In V. Richardson (Ed.) *Handbook of research on teaching* (4th ed., pp. 1157–1174). Washington, DC: American Educational Research Association.

Bickmore, K. (1999). Why discuss sexuality in elementary school? In W. Letts, IV, & J. Sears (Eds.) *Queering elementary education: Advancing the dialogue about sexualities and schooling.* Lanham, MA: Rowman & Littlefield.

Bowles, S., & Gintis, H. (1976). *Schooling in capitalist America: Educational reform and the contradictions of economic life.* New York: Basic Books.

Bronner, S., & Kellner, D. (1989). *Critical theory and society.* New York: Routledge.

Butler, D., & Manning, M. (1998). *Addressing gender differences in young adolescents.* Olney, MD: Association for Childhood Education International.

Carnegie Council on Adolescent Development (1989). *Turning Points: Preparing American youth for the 21st century.* New York: Carnegie Corporation of New York.

Carnegie Foundation Task Force on Education for Economic Growth (1983). *Action for excellence.* Denver: Education Commission of the States.

Clark, S., & Clark, D. (1994). *Restructuring the middle level school.* Albany: State University of New York.

Cochran-Smith, M. (1995). Color-blindness and basket-making are not the answers, *American Educational Research Journal, 32*(3), 493–522.

Dehyle, D. (1995). Navajo youth and Anglo racism: Cultural integrity and resistance, *Harvard Educational Review, 65*(3), 403–445.

Dehyle, D. (1998). From break dancing to heavy metal: Navajo youth, resistance, and identity, *Youth and Society, 30*(1), 3–32.

Driscoll, C. (2002). *Girls: Feminine adolescence in popular culture and cultural theory.* New York: Columbia University Press.

Edelsky, C. (1996). *With literacy and justice for all: Rethinking the social in language and education.* Bristol, PA: Taylor & Francis.

Eder, D., & Parker, S. (1987). The cultural production and reproduction of gender: The effect of extracurricular activities on peer-group culture, *Sociology of Education, 60*(July), 200–213.

Erb, T. (2001). *This we believe … and now we must act.* Westerville, OH: National Middle School Association.

Erb, T., & Dickinson, T. (1997). *The future of teaming.* Columbus, OH: National Middle School Association.

Erb, T., & Doda, N. (1989). *Team organization: Promise, practices and possibilities.* Washington, DC: National Education Association.

Gay, G. (1994). Coming of age ethnically: Teaching young adolescents of color, *Theory Into Practice, 33*(3), 149–155.

Goodman, R., & Saltman, K. (2002) *Strangelove: Or how we learn to stop worrying and love the market.* Lanham, MD: Rowman & Littlefield.

Gutierrez, K. (2000). Teaching and learning in the 21st century, *English Education, 32*(4), 290–298.

Henry, A. (1998). "Speaking up" and "speaking out": Examining "voice" in a reading/writing program with adolescent African Caribbean girls, *Journal of Literacy Research, 30*(2), 233–252.

Hilliard, A. (2000). Standards: Decoy or quality control. In B. Swope & B. Miner (Eds.). *Failing our kids: Why the testing craze won't fix our schools* (pp. 64–69). Milwaukee, WI: Rethinking Schools.

Jackson, A., & Davis, G. (2000). *Turning Points 2000: Educating adolescents in the 21st century.* New York: Teachers College Press.

Kasak, D. (2001). Flexible organizational structures. In T. Erb (Ed.). *This we believe and now we must act* (pp. 90–98). Columbus, OH: National Middle School Association.

Khisty, L. (1995). Making inequality: Issues of language and meanings in mathematics teaching with Hispanic students. In W. Secada, E. Fennema, & L. Adajian (Eds.). *New directions for equity in mathematics education* (pp. 279–297). New York: Cambridge University Press.

Ladson-Billings, G. (Ed.) (2003). *Critical race theory perspectives on social studies: The profession, policies, and curriculum.* Greenwich, CT: Information Age Publishing.

Lesko, N. (1996). Denaturalizing adolescence: The politics of contemporary representations, *Youth and Society, 28*(2), 139–161.

Lesko, N. (2001). *Act your age: A cultural construction of adolescence.* New York: RoutledgeFalmer.

Lipsitz, J. (1977). *Growing up forgotten: A review of research and programs concerning early adolescence.* Lexington, MA: Lexington Books.

McEwin, C. K., & Dickinson, T. (1997). Middle level teacher preparation and licensure, In J. Irvin (Ed.). *What current research says to the middle level practitioner.* Westerville, OH: National Middle School Association.

McLaren, P. (1995). Moral panic, schooling, and gay identity, In G. Unks (Ed.). *The gay teen.* New York: Routledge.

McRobbie, A. (1991/2000). *Feminism and youth culture.* New York: Routledge.

National Middle School Association (2003). *This we believe: Successful schools for young adolescents.* Westerville, OH: National Middle School Association.

NCEE (2004). NCEE's mission: A message from Marc Tucker, President [online]. Available: www.ncee.org/ncee/mission.

Peterson, B., & Neill, M. (2000). Alternatives to standardized tests. In B. Swope & B. Miner, *Failing our kids: Why the testing craze won't fix our schools* (pp. 96–101). Milwaukee, WI: Rethinking Schools.

Sapon-Shevin, M. (1994). Cooperative learning in middle schools: What would it take to really do it right? *Theory Into Practice, 33*(3), 183–190.

Scales, P., & McEwin, C. (1994). *Growing pains: The making of America's middle school teachers.* Columbus, OH: National Middle School Association.

Schaafsma, D. (1993). *Eating on the street: Teaching literacy in a multicultural society.* Pittsburgh, PA: University of Pittsburgh Press.

Sipe, P. (2004). Newjack: Teaching in a failing middle school, *Harvard Educational Review, 74*(3), 330–339.

Slattery, P. (1999). The excluded middle: Postmodern conceptions of the middle school. In C. Walley & W. Gerrick (Eds.). *Affirming middle grades education.* Boston: Allyn & Bacon.

Spring, J. (1994). *Deculturalization and the struggle for equality: A brief history of the education of dominate cultures in the United States* (4th ed.). Boston: McGraw-Hill.

Spring, J. (1998). *Education and the rise of the global economy.* Mahwah, NJ: Lawrence Erlbaum Associates.

Stevenson, C. (1998/2002). *Teaching ten to fourteen year olds* (3rd ed.). Boston, MA: Allyn & Bacon.

Stone, L., & Church, J. (1957/1975). Adolescence as a cultural invention. In A. Esman (Ed.). *The psychology of adolescence* (pp. 7–11). New York: International Universities Press/New York: Random House.

Walkerdine, V. (1998). *Counting girls out: Girls and mathematics.* London: Falmer Press.

Zinn, H. (1995). Why students should study history: An interview with Howard Zinn, In D. Levine, R. Lowe, B. Peterson, & R. Tenorio (Eds.) Rethinking schools: An agenda for change (pp. 89–99). New York: The New Press.

I

THE SOCIAL CONSTRUCTION OF ADOLESCENCE

Kenneth J. Saltman

The whole future of life depends on how the new powers now given suddenly and in profusion are husbanded and directed.... Never has youth been exposed to such dangers of both perversion and arrest as in our own land and day. (Hall, 1904, xv)

Today's adolescents face similar but more complex challenges. The dilemma of a spin-the-bottle kiss or clandestine petting is apt to be in terms of sexual experimentation in the form of "life-and-death" risk-taking. Although they may be presented with information about AIDS and other sexually transmitted diseases, they are no less prone to experimenting. And today's adolescents are less likely to have that "inner voice" that encourages them to do the right thing." (Simpson, 1999, 6)

What does it mean to say that adolescence is a "social construct"? To claim that adolescence is a social construction is to call into question more common claims that the nature of adolescence can be understood principally through the sciences of biology and psychology. Instead, adolescence as a social construction suggests that adolescence is a cultural and social category within which facts about youth are interpreted and made meaningful. In chapter 1, the excerpt from G. Stanley Hall's Adolescence presents the rationale and early psychological meanings that informed the creation of this new stage in human development. Although the above quotes by G. Stanley Hall and Sue Simpson were written almost a century apart, they are indicative of the continuity, persistence, and embedded-ness of meanings about the incompetencies, hazards, and liabilities of adolescence, pre-sented as if they were "inherent," irreversible, and biologically driven characteristics. It is crucial to emphasize that to claim that adolescence is a social construction is not to deny biological or psychological characteristics pertaining to youth of a particular age. As chapter 2 in this section by Brooks-Gunn and Reiter explains, youth in a certain age range do tend to have common biological developmental characteristics. The authors examine the pubertal experience of middle-class white youth, including the physiological changes that occur, the meanings of puberty for youth and adults in industrial and non-industrial countries, and varied cultural rites of passage that mark the onset of adolescence or transition to adulthood. They consider the implications of these pubertal processes for health and academic education programs.

To claim that adolescence is a social construction is not to say, for example, that puberty is a fiction or merely a narrative with no natural scientific content. However, to recognize that adolescence is a social construction is to recognize, as Kessen argues in chapter 3, that the meaning of biological or psychological realities do become meaningful or relevant in different ways in different social contexts. His historical analysis focuses on the culturally laden construction of childhood in the U. S. that accompanies the emer-gence of industrial capitalism. Similarly, Margaret Mead's pivotal work in Samoa (1928) illustrates the varied cultural meanings that are ascribed to the onset of puberty and atten-dant rites of passage. Kessen's insight does not challenge biological or psychological insights about adolescence but rather encourages a perspective that views the scientific and cultural as intertwined.

The meaning of adolescence is different in different cultures and at different historical moments. In the early 20th century, for example, informed by selective evolutionary and psychoanalytic ideas of Darwin and Freud, G. Stanley Hall posited that adolescence was a crucial period of individual development in which the individual's development replayed the development of the human species from primitive savage early humans to civilized White Europeans. As Gail Bederman details in chapter 4, within Hall's view only White middle-class boys were capable of fully reaching individual development necessary to bear on the burden of carrying civilization forward. Girls and non-Whites could never hope to reach the developmental level of White boys. Hall worried that modern industrial society threatened White middle-class boys who might succumb to the nervous order of the day called "neurasthenia." In order for these boys to succeed individually and carry on the White man's burden of civilization, boys, during adolescence, would need to become toughened up by drawing on their primitive evolutionary past. For Hall, the future of the human race depended on the successful rearing of middle-class White boys who needed to carry civilization forward. The stresses of modern industrial life and emergent sexuality (as Moran and Bederman discuss) were thought to threaten the development of White boys who could be strengthened by drawing on the power of primitives who could never hope to reach the same developmental heights as White boys. White boys would need to become toughened up by going back to nature, learning woodcraft, building fires, and banging drums. (The Boy Scouts and the YMCA originated with common concerns of Hall's.) Only if White boys were toughened up by drawing on the lower stage of human evolution could they and all of "the human race" hope to evolve by overcoming the crisis of adolescence. Such ideas were implicated in the imperial thought exemplified by Theodore Roosevelt who would embrace White man's burden to "civilize the savages" in Puerto Rico, the Philippines, and Haiti.

The point here is, to say that adolescence is a social and cultural construction is to recognize, first of all, that adolescence meant something very different in the past and that it may mean something very different in the future. It is also to recognize that the meanings assigned to adolescence are not arbitrary but rather relate to broader material and symbolic power struggles. Social meanings embedded in the construction of adolescence grow out of the particular sociohistorical, economic, and political realities from which they emerged. A brief history clarifies this point.

Adolescence was emerged as a distinct period in the lifespan under a number of unique social conditions at the advent of industrialism. First, advances in medicine and science extended the lifespan and enhanced the quality of life, which allowed enough "time" in one's life for education, personal discovery, and vocational exploration to be a designated developmental task. Second, the introduction of mechanized labor-saving devices, a cornerstone of modern industrial capitalism, created social and economic upheaval and displacement, as adults and youth migrated en masse to cities for work. Third, as mechanization generated this massive influx of farmers, artisans, and immigrant families to the industrial centers, and as scores of unwelcome, "roving" youth came in search of "adult" factory work to support their families, the school dropout rate increased severely despite the spread of statewide compulsory education.

Concurrently, Hall published his two-volume tome, *Adolescence* (1904), creating a body of biological and psychological-based knowledge that codified the "natural characteristics" of these age-designated youth from this growing immigrant and rural population, who were displaced by industrialization and began to cohere as a "group" in the context of changing social and economic conditions. The social dislocation and repositioning of youth contributed to Hall's and others' emerging ideological view that youth would succumb to their "natural proclivities" and thus needed moral direction, needed for their new-found powers to be "husbanded," needed to be socialized for civic life, and needed unique educational experiences to channel their energies in productive ways for society.

Ultimately, growing elitist concerns about the need to "tame" immigrant youth and socialize them to U.S. work life and culture prompted social efficiency advocates and developmentalists to forge educational reforms that would begin to reposition youth outside of the labor force and inside of public schools and other "socializing" organizations, like Settlement Houses, etc. They rallied to create in 1910 the "segregated" junior high school for pubescent youth, an educational reform that would reduce the dropout rate and channel working class and affluent youth "earlier" into their respective tracks of vocational training or higher education (Beane & Brodhagen, 2001; Bowles & Gintis, 1976; Lipsitz, 1977; Spring, 1972) and their ascendance into adulthood. The commensurate passage of progressive measures, such as child labor, compulsory education, and other laws, also began to forge a distinct youth population, culture, and separate sphere of activity. This confluence of social, economic, political, and ideological factors codified the construct of adolescence and lines of demarcation between adults and youth. Adolescent "characteristics" became imbued with "inherent meanings" that, in fact, reflected the social dislocation of youth and the dynamics of a social order that was changing from an agricultural economy to an industrial-based capitalist economy. Adolescence became the projective site and repository for social, sexual, and moral anxieties that were rooted in American society.

As the history of the origins of adolescence illustrates, the truths of adolescence, adolescent development, and the way adolescence is understood in its relation to middle level education and reform can only be understood as part of the social order in which such claims about youth are made. It is crucially important to recognize the fact that if the meaning of claims about youth and adolescence is inextricably linked to the social order, then any claim about youth and adolescence is both a historical and a political claim in that it presumes particular social values, hierarchies, and conflicts.

For example, lingering claims found in original literature on adolescence by Hall (1904) and contemporary writing on adolescence and middle level pedagogy suggest that adolescents are plagued by "storm and stress" and "raging hormones." Although the historical origins of such claims can be located in late 19th century and early 20th century biology, psychology, and evolutionary science that are today recognized as "bad science," in the form of recapitulation theory, this "bad science" continues to inform the way adolescence is thought about. Such "bad science," for example, held that adolescents in their individual development recapitulated (performed) the development of the human race. To recognize that adolescence is a social construction is to ask crucial political questions about knowledge of adolescence such as: "How did these ideas about adolescence come into being? When? By whom? And to whose advantage and at whose expense?" In this view the naturalizing of adolescence with recourse to psychology or biology covers over such crucial political questions and thus also commits the political act of denying the politics of childhood.

As selections from Hall, Gail Bederman, and Nancy Lesko explain, adolescent development was not race or gender or class neutral. From different perspectives in chapters 4 and 5, Bederman and Lesko counter the underlying premises presented by Hall, and challenge the extension of that reasoning in current formulations. While Bederman illustrates how the meanings of adolescence have historically been wrapped in broader struggles over race, gender, and sex, Lesko shows how these struggles to define adolescence by different competing interests relate to policy initiatives regulating youth and informing middle level thought and practice.

Although middle level scholars today might be inclined to laugh off the "bad science" of Hall as no longer relevant, as the selections in this section and others illustrate, this thinking about adolescents in pathological terms can be found centrally in middle level literature today as adolescents continue to be described as naturally and universally characterized as "adrift," "awkward," "scraggly cygnets" (Carnegie, 1989; Simpson, 1999). In the tradition of Hall, adolescents today continue to be stigmatized as naturally pathological, exemplified by the quotes at the beginning of this section. There are concrete political implications of such framings of youth. Chapters 6, 7, and 8 address the social and political origins of particular characterizations of youth in the 19th and 20th century. In chapter 6, Moran chronicles Hall's invention of and need to manage the sexual adolescent, which coincided with society's cultural anxieties about sex and the press to forge "a new morality"/social mores concordant with social reorganization ushered in by industrial capitalism. Further, as the selections from Mike Males and Henry Giroux in chapters 7 and 8 explain, in current popular and academic discourse youth are framed as both innocent and culpable—that is, simultaneously incapable of making decisions about their own well-being and yet excluded from political participation while they are scapegoated for a number of social ills, from poverty and crime to childbirth that are the principal responsibility of those who do hold political power—namely, adults. Such framings of youth justify unjust regulation of youth while concealing the origins of the systemic inequalities oppressing youth and adults, including a hierarchical economic system that in turn is interwoven with racial and gender/ sex hierarchy.

As well, the racial and masculinist evolutionary "bad science" of Hall's day continues to inform thought in multiple social spheres. For example, the U.S. military names high-technology weapons that will enforce "our civilized way" after iconry of tough savage primitivism, genocided native American tribes, and extinct animals—tomahawk missiles, raptor planes, Apache helicopters—while sports teams in schools are named after and continue to refer to the "savage nature" of animals and tribes, etc. The significance of this for the construction of adolescence and for middle level education is that contemporary categorizations, definitions, and claims about adolescence are imbricated in broader his-torically informed cultural realities, sets of ideas, values, and meanings.

These facts point to a central concern of the editors. The emphasis on the social con-struction of youth and adolescence needs to be understood as part of a critical approach that views the study of middle level education as ideally furthering the goals of a more substantive democratic society. Naturalized biological and psychological claims about adolescence and youth are at odds with a critical approach to adolescence and youth in which the meanings of youth are questioned with an end of fostering more equal social relations. Such a critical approach encourages us to ask how it is, for example, that ado-lescents are expected not to know about political realities yet these same political reali-ties keep roughly 40 million youth in the United States living in dire poverty with the average age of a homeless person in America standing at 9. The unequal conditions suf-fered by youth today are not principally the result of the biological or psychological dis-positions of those youth. Nor will biological and psychological study of youth that denies the social contribute to the goal of a more democratic, ethical, or humane society. This social, historical, and political approach to the study of youth emphasizes that the meaning of youth like the meaning of democracy itself is in play and is struggled over by different groups with competing material and ideological interests. The social construc-tion of adolescence is of prime importance to those involved in and concerned about middle school.

Even if partially based on erroneous assumptions, it is important to unearth the mis-conceptions that have and continue to inform the ways in which we structure education for "young adolescents," and inadvertently subvert liberatory possibilities in middle school education. In part, the value of recognizing that adolescence is a social construc-tion is that it encourages middle level educators and others to think about how claims about youth are linked to historical and present-day power-struggles. If the meaning and reality of adolescence is struggled over rather than fixed permanently by scientific reality, then the "truth" of adolescence is less a matter of discovering the eternal nature of it than it is a matter of engaging in dialogue, debate, and deliberation about what adolescence can mean for a society theoretically committed to democratic ideals. Such debate also would challenge the extent to which youth have been blamed for social ills instead of addressing broader structural inequalities. This would also ideally mean that adults take responsibility for social problems, and identify sources of problems in social structures rather than projecting them onto the youth. Seeing adolescence as a social construction means debating what adolescence means. And debating what adolescence means grows out of the recognition that social, political, and economic conditions made adolescence what it has become today. Such a view is radically hopeful because it suggests potentially re-imagining not only what adolescence can become but also what society can become.

QUESTIONS FOR REFLECTION AND DIALOGUE

1. How is thinking of adolescence as a social construct different from the legacy of thought about adolescence as biologically and psychologically based?
2. What does it mean to say that adolescence is a construction?
3. How have views of adolescence changed over history?
4. How have different perspectives about adolescence been related to political interests, economic interests, or symbolic interests of different groups making claims about adolescence?
5. How do the chapters in this section contribute to an understanding of adolescence as a social construct?
6. How does adolescence being a social construct relate to a critical form of middle school?

REFERENCES

Beane, J., & Brodhagen, B. (2001). Teaching in middle schools, In V. Richardson (Ed.). *Handbook of research on teaching* (pp. 1157–1174). Washington, DC: American Educational Research Association.

Bowles, S., & Gintis, H. (1976). *Schooling in capitalist America.* New York: Basic Books.

Carnegie Council on Adolescent Development (1989). *Turning Points report: Preparing American youth for the 21st century,* Executive Summary (pp. 8–17). New York: Carnegie Corporation of New York.

Hall, G. S. (1904). *Adolescence.* New York: D. Appleton & Co.

Lipsitz, J. (1977). *Growing up forgotten: A review of research and programs concerning early adolescence.* Lexington, MA: Lexington Books.

Mead, M. (1928). *Coming of age in Samoa.* Ann Arbor, MI: Morrow.

Simpson, S. (1999). Early adolescent development, In C.W. Walley & W.G. Gerrick (Eds.). *Affirming middle grades education.* Needham Heights, MA: Allyn & Bacon.

Spring, J. (1972). *Education and the rise of the corporate state.* Boston: Beacon Press.

1

From *Adolescence*

G. STANLEY HALL

THE YEARS FROM about eight to twelve constitute an unique period of human life. The acute stage of teething is passing, the brain has acquired nearly its adult size and weight, health is almost at its best, activity is greater and more varied than ever before or than it ever will be again, and there is peculiar endurance, vitality, and resistance to fatigue. The child develops a life of its own outside the home circle, and its natural interests are never so independent of adult influence. Perception is very acute, and there is great immunity to exposure, danger, accident, as well as to temptation. Reason, true morality, religion, sympathy, love, and esthetic enjoyment are but very slightly developed. Everything, in short, suggests the culmination of one stage of life as if it thus represented what was once, and for a very protracted and relatively stationary period, the age of maturity in some remote, perhaps pigmoid, stage of human evolution, when in a warm climate the young of our species once shifted for themselves independently of further parental aid. The qualities now developed are phyletically vastly older than all the neo-atavistic traits of body and soul, later to be superposed like a new and higher story built on to our primal nature. Heredity is so far both more stable and more secure. The elements of personality are few, but are well organized and on a simple, effective plan. The momentum of the paleopsychic traits is great, and they are often clearly distinguishable from those to be later added. Thus the boy is father of the man in a new sense in that his qualities are indefinitely older and existed well compacted untold ages before the more distinctly human attributes were developed. Indeed, there are a few faint indications set forth in the text of a yet earlier age nodality or meristic segmentation, as if amid the increased instabilities of health at the age of about six we could still detect the ripple-marks of an ancient public beach now lifted high above the tides of a receding shore-line as human infancy has been prolonged. I have also given reasons that lead me to the conclusion that, despite its dominance, the function of sexual maturity and procreative power is peculiarly mobile up and down the age-line independently of many of the qualities usually so closely associated with it, so that much that sex created in the phylum now precedes it in the individual.

Rousseau would leave prepubescent years to nature and to these primal hereditary impulsions and allow the fundamental traits of savagery their fling till twelve. Biological psychology finds many and cogent reasons to confirm this view if only a proper environment could be provided. The child revels in savagery, and if its tribal, predatory, hunting, fishing, fighting, roving, idle, playing proclivities could be indulged in the country and under conditions that now, alas! seem hopelessly ideal, they could conceivably be so organized and directed as to be far more truly humanistic and liberal than all that the best modern school can provide. Rudimentary organs of the soul now suppressed, perverted, or delayed, to crop out in menacing forms later, would be developed in their season so that we should be immune to them in maturer years, on the principle of the Aristotelian catharsis for which I have tried to suggest a far broader application than the Stagirite could see in his day.

These nativistic and more or less feral instincts can and should be fed and formed. The deep and strong cravings in the individual to revive the ancestral experiences and occupations of the race can and must be met, at least in a secondary and vicarious way, by tales of the heroic virtues the child can appreciate, and these proxy experiences should make up by variety and extent what they lack in intensity. The teacher art should so vivify all that the resources of literature, tradition, history, can supply which represents the crude, rank virtues of the world's childhood that, with his almost visual imagination, reenforced by psychonomic recapitulatory impulses, the child can enter upon his full heritage, live out each stage of his life to the fullest, and realize in himself all its manifold tendencies. Echoes only of the vaster, richer life of the remote past of the race they must remain, but just these are the murmurings of the only muse that can save from the omnipresent dangers of precocity. Thus we not only rescue from the danger of loss, but utilize for further psychic growth the results of the higher heredity, which are the most precious and potential things on earth. So, too, in our urbanized hot-house life, that tends to ripen everything before its time, we must teach nature, although the very phrase is ominous. But we must not, in so doing, wean still more from, but perpetually incite to visit field, forest, hill, shore, the water, flowers, animals, the true homes of childhood in this wild, undomesticated stage from which modern conditions have kidnapped and transported him. Books and reading are distasteful, for the very soul and body cry out for a more active, objective life, and to know nature and man at first hand. These two staples, stories and nature, by these informal methods of the home and the environment constitute fundamental education.

But now another remove from nature seems to be made necessary by the manifold knowledges and skills of our highly complex civilization. We should transplant the human sapling, I concede reluctantly, as early as eight, but not before, to the schoolhouse with its imperfect lighting, ventilation, temperature. We must shut out nature and open books. The child must sit on unhygienic benches and work the tiny muscles that wag the tongue and pen, and let all the others, which constitute nearly half its weight, decay. Even if it be prematurely, he must be subjected to special disciplines and be apprenticed to the higher qualities of adulthood, for he is not only a product of nature, but a candidate for a highly developed humanity. To many, if not most, of the influences here there can be at first but little inner reponse. Insight, understanding, interest, sentiment, are for the most part only nascent, and most that pertains to the true kingdom of mature manhood is embryonic. The wisest requirements seem to the child more or less alien, arbitrary, heteronomous, artificial, falsetto. There is much passivity, often active resistance and evasion, and perhaps spasms of obstinacy, to it all. But the senses are keen and alert, reactions immediate and vigorous, and the memory is quick, sure, and lasting, and ideas of space, time, and physical causation, and of many a moral and social licit and non-licit, are rapidly unfolding.

Never again will there be such susceptibility to drill and discipline, such plasticity to habituation, or such ready adjustment to new conditions. It is the age of external and mechanical training. Reading, writing, drawing, manual training, musical technic, foreign tongues and their pronunciation, the manipulation of numbers and of geometrical elements, and many kinds of skill have now their golden hour, and if it passes unimproved, all these can never be acquired later without a heavy handicap of disadvantage and loss. These necessities may be hard for the health of body, sense, mind, as well as for morals, and pedagogic art consists in breaking the child into them betimes as intensively and as quickly as possible with minimal strain and with the least amount of explanation or coquetting for natural interest and in calling medicine confectionery. This is not teaching in its true sense so much as it is drill, inculcation, and regimentation. The method should be mechanical, repetitive, authoritative, dogmatic. The automatic powers are now at their very apex, and they can do and bear more than our degenerate pedagogy knows or dreams of. Here we have something to learn from the schoolmasters of the past back to the middle ages, and even from the ancients. The greatest stress, with short periods and few hours, incessant insistence, incitement, and little reliance upon interest, reason, or work done without the presence of the teacher, should be the guiding principles for pressure in these essentially formal and, to the child, contentless elements of knowledge. These should be sharply distinguished from the indigenous, evoking and more truly educational factors described in the last paragraph, which are meaty, content-full, and relatively formless as to time of day, method, spirit, and perhaps environment and personnel of teacher, and possibly somewhat in season of the year, almost as sharply as work differs from play, or perhaps as the virility of man that loves to command a phalanx, be a martinet and drill-master, differs from femininity which excels in persuasion, sympathetic insight, storytelling, and in the tact that discerns and utilizes spontaneous interests in the young.

Adolescence is a new birth, for the higher and more completely human traits are now born. The qualities of body and soul that now emerge are far newer. The child comes from and harks back to a remoter past; the adolescent is neo-atavistic, and in him the later acquisitions of the race slowly become prepotent. Development is less gradual and more saltatory, suggestive of some ancient period of storm and stress when old moorings were broken and a higher level attained. The annual rate of growth in height, weight, and strength is increased and often doubled, and even more. Important functions previously non-existent arise. Growth of parts and organs loses its former proportions, some permanently and some for a season. Some of these are still growing in old age and others are soon arrested and atrophy. The old moduli of dimensions become obsolete and old harmonies are broken. The range of individual differences and average errors in all physical measurements and all psychic tests increases. Some linger long in the childish stage and advance late or slowly, while others push on with a sudden outburst of impulsion to early maturity. Bones and muscles lead all other tissues, as if they vied with each other, and there is frequent flabbiness or tension as one or the other leads. Nature arms youth for conflict with all the resources at her command—speed, power of shoulder, biceps, back, leg, jaw—strengthens and enlarges skull, thorax, hips, makes man aggressive and prepares woman's frame for maternity. The power of the diseases peculiar to childhood abates, and liability to the far more diseases of maturity begins, so that with liability to both it is not strange that the dawn of the ephebic day is marked at the same time by increased morbidity but diminished rates of morality. Some disorders of arrest and defect as well as of excessive unfoldment in some function, part, or organ may now, after long study and controversy, be said to be established as peculiar to this period, and diseases that are distinctly school- and city-bred abound, with apparently increasing frequency. The momentum of heredity often seems insufficient to enable the child to achieve this great revolution and come to complete maturity, so that every step of the upward way is strewn with wreckage of body, mind, and morals. There is not only arrest, but perversion, at every stage, and hoodlumism, juvenile crime, and secret vice seem not only increasing, but develop in earlier years in every civilized land. Modern life is hard, and in many respects increasingly so, on youth. Home, school, church, fail to recognize its nature and needs and, perhaps most of all, its perils. The cohesions between the elements of personality are loosened by the disparities of both somatic and psychic development, and if there is arrest at any stage or in any part before the higher unity is achieved there is almost sure to be degeneration and reunion on a lower level than before. One of the gravest dangers is the persistent ignoring by femininists of the prime importance of establishing normal periodicity in girls, to the needs of which everything else should for a few years be secondary.

The functions of every sense undergo reconstruction, and their relations to other psychic functions change, and new sensations, some of them very intense, arise, and new associations in the sense sphere are formed. Haptic impressions, appetite for food and drink, and smell are most modified. The voice changes, vascular instability, blushing, and flushing are increased. Sex asserts its mastery in field after field, and works its havoc in the form of secret vice, debauch, disease, and enfeebled heredity, cadences the soul to both its normal and abnormal rhythms, and sends many thousand youth a year to quacks, because neither parents, teachers, preachers, or physicians know how to deal with its problems. Thus the foundations of domestic, social, and religious life are often most undermined. Between religion and love God and nature have wrought an indissoluble bond so that neither can attain normality without that of the other. Secondary sexual qualities are shown to have an ever-widening range, and parent-hood to mean more with every upward step of development. The youth craves more knowledge of body and mind, that can help against besetting temptations, aid in the choice of a profession, and if his intellect is normal he does not vex this soul overmuch about the logical character of the universe or the ultimate sanction of either truth or virtue. He is more objective than subjective, and only if his lust to know nature and life is starved does his mind trouble him by in-growing. There are new repulsions felt toward home and school, and truancy and runaways abound. The social instincts undergo sudden unfoldment and the new life of love awakens. It is the age of sentiment and of religion, of rapid fluctuation of mood, and the world seems strange and new. Interest in adult life and in vocations develops. Youth awakes to a new world and understands neither it nor himself. The whole future of life depends on how the new powers now given suddenly and in profusion are husbanded and directed. Character and personality are taking form, but everything is plastic. Self-feeling and ambition are increased, and every trait and faculty is liable to exaggeration and excess. It is all a marvelous new birth, and those who believe that nothing is so worthy of love, reverence, and service as the body and soul of youth, and who hold that the best test of every human institution is how much it contributes to bring youth to the ever fullest possible development, may well review themselves and the civilization in which we live to see how far it satisfies this supreme test.

Never has youth been exposed to such dangers of both perversion and arrest as in our own land and day. Increasing urban life with its temptations, prematurities, sedentary occupations, and passive stimuli just when an active, objective life is most needed, early emancipation and a lessening sense for both duty and discipline, the haste to know and do all befitting man's estate before its time, the mad rush for sudden wealth and reckless fashions set by its gilded youth—all these lack some of the regulatives they still have in older lands with more conservative traditions.

2

The Role of Pubertal Processes

JEANNE BROOKS-GUNN AND EDWARD O. REITER

IN NEGOTIATING THE phase of life between childhood and adulthood, adolescents face a number of developmental challenges, many of them involving reproductive events. As young people's bodies develop, they begin to incorporate such changes into their construction of self and must learn to cope with others' responses to their mature bodies. They also must learn how to respond to feelings of sexual arousal and, for many, questions about when and with whom to have sexual intercourse.[1]

Puberty itself is a key developmental challenge for adolescents. They must accommodate to the physical changes in a cultural milieu that, for girls, values the prepubertal over the mature female body. They must negotiate the loosening of childhood ties to parents and the move toward greater psychological and physical autonomy. As they do so, they must deal with sexual arousal and the beginning of relationships with members of the opposite sex, even as they are trying to develop a stable and cohesive personality structure for the regulation of mood, impulse, and self-esteem. How do boys and girls experience the social and biological changes that occur as they become reproductively mature? What does this experience mean to them and to others? How does it alter self-definitions and relationships? What are the effects on subsequent development in a variety of domains, including competence, psychopathology, and deviant behavior?

Of particular interest is the vulnerable youth, for whom the onset of puberty may herald overwhelming challenges because of difficulties in coping with all the concurrent changes of early adolescence. To identify vulnerable youth, we look at predisposing factors such as culturally mediated beliefs about puberty, family circumstances, patterns of parental interaction, personality characteristics, and earlier preadolescent patterns of negotiating developmental challenges. Other contextually mediated factors include school transition, peer relations, and the "fit" between one's developing body and expectations about attractiveness or skill at sports.

Pubertal experiences, then, are part of the larger context of the life course. They occur most prominently in early adolescence (23), but pubertal growth often extends into middle adolescence as well (13). Behavioral changes may be influenced directly by physical processes, may be more generally related to the effects of age and grade in school, or may be linked to pubertal growth through social or contextual factors. Specific models have been developed to consider such possible interactions (23, 24, 76, 128).[2] Generally, more interactive models are replacing ones that were either mainly environmental or biological. Until fairly recently research focused on a limited set of biological and social changes as being age related and characteristic of all adolescents. That focus is changing. In addition to life events themselves, the timing and sequencing (tempo) of those events that mark the progression toward adulthood are now seen as critical in the definition of this particular phase of life and in our understanding of how the individual adapts to life changes.[3]

Finally, researchers in this area have been remiss in considering situational factors when comparing experiences and outcomes in different social classes and ethnic groups (and, in some cases, even boys and girls). In this sense pubertal research reflects the history of other rapidly evolving areas of human development (for example, early research on mother-infant interaction and peer relationships). White middle-class individuals are the first group to be studied, with more situationally based and culturally sensitive work following. We regret that we are able to say little about the pubertal experience of groups other than middle-class white youth, but we are hopeful that, with the next generation of studies, more may be said in the near future. Also, this chapter, unlike the others in this volume, will provide more information about girls' than boys' experiences. Generally the only topics for which this occurs are those having to do with reproduction, including parenthood. This bias probably reflects societal beliefs that childrearing and family roles are more important for females than males and, by inference, that pubertal change has more of an impact on girls than on boys (16). As Simone de Beauvoir so eloquently states:

> The young boy, be he ambitious, thoughtless, or timid, looks toward an open future; he will be a seaman or an engineer, he will stay on the farm or go away to the city, he will see the world, he will get rich; he feels free, confronting a future in which the unexpected awaits him. The young girl will be a wife, grandmother; she will keep house just as her mother did, she will give her children the same care she herself received when young—she is twelve years old and already her story is written in the heavens. She will discover it day after day without ever making it. (44, p. 278)

HISTORY OF PUBERTAL RESEARCH

Before turning to these topics, as well as describing the pubertal processes themselves, we must place pubertal research in a short-term historical context (15). Essentially until the 1980s almost no developmental work on the meaning or effects of puberty had been conducted (the notable exceptions are the California and the Fels Longitudinal Growth Studies). Two seminal works appearing in the 1970s highlighted both a lack of systematic study and the vital role of this life phase in healthy development (79, 104). At the same time, researchers examined whether "storm and stress" was an appropriate characterization of the experience and behavior of young adolescents, and whether changes in self-image during early adolescent transitions were best seen as continuous or discontinuous (117, 120). These studies seemed to assume that alterations in self-image and emotionality, if they occurred, would be due in part to pubertal changes as well as to the context in which these physical transformations occurred. Somewhat surprisingly, then, pubertal processes were not a subject of study in the 1970s. Then in the 1980s, starting with a 1981 conference on girls at puberty (23), this topic came into its own. During that decade at least six conferences were held on early adolescence, with the topic of puberty having a prominent place in each (24, 25, 76, 90, 101, 111).

Why did pubertal research languish? After all, the father of adolescent psychology, G. Stanley Hall, was writing on the subject in the early 1900s. Documenting pubertal rituals was a time-honored tradition in anthropology (113, 122). Physicians and physical anthropologists were busy cataloguing physical growth in a number of cultural settings, and endocrinologists were exploring the hormonal underpinnings of many of these changes (75, 153). While this is speculative, we believe that the lackluster response of behavioral scientists to the quite obvious manifestations of the transition from childhood to adulthood had to do with how pubertal changes are perceived and presented in our society.

First, many adults seem uncomfortable discussing puberty themselves and, by inference, believe that young people feel the same way. As Weideger recounts, many adult women report having been very upset about menarche ("I was afraid to tell my mother or friends; I was so ashamed," 166 p. 169). It is a short step from one's own discomfort to the belief that pubertal children do not talk about the changes and that puberty is a private, not a public (or at least a highly salient), event. Many investigators have found it difficult, if not sometimes impossible, to work with or recruit potential subjects from schools for their research on puberty (17). In Brooks-Gunn's original early adolescent work, she had to contact the Central New Jersey Girls Scouts, since only a handful of public schools had granted permission to ask teenage girls about their menarcheal experiences and feelings (27). In her more recent studies concerning pubertal processes other than menarche (growth of breasts and pubic hair, weight spurts), she has collaborated with private schools because of the reluctance and discomfort of some public school administrators when faced by such topics (16).

Second, at a more individual level many parents, particularly fathers, report being uneasy about raising the subject of puberty with their offspring (the exception being mothers and daughters discussing menarche). Such feelings may be one reason why so many parents favor sex education in the schools (three-fourths to four-fifths, according to various national opinion surveys). In part, parents are prisoners of their own experiences. The number of women who report having been unprepared for menarche increases dramatically with age cohort (100): cultural beliefs handed down to immigrants from Europe often forbade such preparation (1); and sexual squeamishness may be as much or more a part of the American as the Western European experience, as demonstrated by differences in societal regulation of fertility (19, 92).

Third, even educational materials reflect society's ambivalence toward puberty. Much more explicit information is given to teenagers in many Western European countries than in the United States (92). In West Germany, for example, the health-education pamphlet published by the Johnson & Johnson Company describes the pubertal process by showing photographs of girls in the five Tanner stages, just as medical texts do. In contrast, such graphic information is not included in any of the comparable health-education pamphlets published for American teenage girls; it is considered too controversial. In addition, pamphlets given to girls in the 1970s and earlier focus on concealment, reflecting societal beliefs (20). According to one booklet, menstruation is "a natural, normal part of life. Treat it naturally, normally, and you won't be embarrassed or upset each time it comes" (2). Another booklet states, "It's absolutely impossible for anyone to know you are menstruating unless of course you act stupid about the whole thing" (73). More recent materials are much less judgmental, perhaps reflecting changes in attitudes.

Such cultural messages are absorbed very quickly by our youth. Boys almost never talk about pubertal changes with their parents. One small study by Brooks-Gunn of pubertal boys found that only one had discussed first ejaculation with his father (62). None of the boys had told their friends that they had had an ejaculation (whether through nocturnal emission or masturbation). Indeed, for over four-fifths of the boys the study interview was the first time they had discussed this topic (information is typically transmitted via locker-room jokes and magazines). As one of the few scientists who have studied the topic explains: "Imagine an American boy coming to the breakfast table exclaiming, 'Mom, guess what? I had my first wet dream last night. Now I'm a man.' It is not without significance that such an imaginary episode is greeted in American culture with laughter" (141, pp. 333–334).

This cultural milieu has influenced the type of research that is conducted and perhaps the amount of useful work that is done (given the time and effort needed to obtain cooperation from the schools), as well as the responses of the pubertal child and significant others to physical change (17). It also attests to the significance of these changes.

PHYSIOLOGICAL CHANGES OF PUBERTY

Pubertal maturation is controlled by the reproductive endocrine system, which first operates in the fetal period. Events are controlled largely by complex interactions among the brain, the pituitary gland, and the gonads (ovaries in females and testes in males). The pituitary is a small organ at the base of the brain that receives signals from the brain and releases hormones into the bloodstream. These hormones, in turn, influence organs throughout the body, regulating growth and many other aspects of normal body function. Signals back to the brain, either through nerve pathways or by way of hormones in the blood, complete the circuit. Two systems of particular relevance to adolescent development are the hypothalamus-pituitary-gonadal axis, which regulates sexual maturation and reproduction, and the hypothalamus-pituitary-adrenal axis, which controls many aspects of the body's response to stress.

Before birth, gonads develop in males and begin to secrete hormones called androgens. Androgens set in motion a series of events that result in the development of male internal and external sex organs, and specifically in the formation of the hypothalamus-pituitary-gonadal axis. This process results in the birth of a boy; if it does not occur, the child is a girl. After what appears to be a short burst of sex steroid activity in the first few months of life, this hormonal system then operates at a fairly low level until middle childhood (135, 136).

Two independent processes, controlled by different mechanisms but closely linked in time, are involved in the increase of sex steroid secretion in the prepubertal and pubertal periods. One process, adrenarche, involves production of androgens by the adrenal gland; this precedes by about two years the second event, gonadarche, which involves reactivation of the quiescent hypothalamic-pituitary-gonadotropin-gonadal system.

Physical Changes

Growth occurs during childhood and adolescence because of a complicated, harmonious interaction of multiple and diverse factors. Genetic influences, nutritional status, hormonal changes, and the presence or absence of diseases modulate the growth process both qualitatively and quantitatively during adolescence. The physical changes of puberty, extending from the preteenage years to the end of the second decade, have been carefully described (109, 110). In girls, breast development is divided into five stages. In boys, genital development is also divided into five stages. Five stages of pubic hair growth have also been described for both girls and boys.

Development of secondary sexual characteristics in girls. Breast budding, typically the first sexual characteristic to appear in girls, occurs at approximately 10.5 years. In one-fifth of girls, the appearance of pubic hair occurs prior to breast buds. The interval between breast budding and adult breast configuration is about 4.5 years and is similar whether girls mature at a younger or older age. Menarche (the first menses) occurs at approximately 12.5 years in the United States, about two years after breast buds appear. Menarche follows the peak height velocity, the age at which the most rapid growth occurs; in fact the time of maximum deceleration of growth in height is most closely associated with menarche. The peak height velocity occurs before development of pubic hair in one-fourth of girls and in the initial stage of, or probably before, breast development in one-fourth of girls. The growth spurt begins approximately six to twelve months before breast budding, at a mean age of 9.6 years. A wide variation exists in the sequence of events involving the growth of breasts and pubic hair and genital maturation, with a standard deviation of approximately one year for the onset of each given stage.

Development of secondary sexual characteristics in boys. The initial sign of sexual development is the onset of testicular growth, which occurs at about 11 to 11.5 years (Tanner stage 2). The bulk of testicular volume is attributable to the sperm-producing tubules, the mass of which is considerably greater than that of the sparse androgen-producing Leydig cells. In almost no cases does visible pubic hair develop during Tanner genital stage 2; 41% of boys are in Tanner genital stage 4 by the time pubic hair growth is first observed. Approximately three years pass between the first signs of genital growth and the development of adult male genitalia, but a lapse of almost five years is still within the normal range. The peak height velocity is achieved by only a few boys by Tanner genital stage 3 but by 76% by genital stage 4. In boys the mean age at initiation of the adolescent height spurt is approximately 11.7 years—thus beginning shortly after the first evidence of gonadal maturation. The age of peak height velocity is between 13 and 14 years.

Spermarche, which is the onset of the release of spermatozoa, has been estimated on the basis of age at finding spermaturia, determined by longitudinal assessment of urinary samples (99). Spermarche occurs between 12 and 14 years, at a rather early stage of pubic hair growth and within an extremely wide variation of testicular volume. Peak height velocity and maximum levels of testosterone production follow spermarche. Despite considerable variability of detectable spermaturia, this event does appears to be relatively early. Most boys reach spermarche by age 14, despite the often sparse degree of systematic virilization.

Sex and ethnic differences in pubertal growth. The initiation of the pubertal growth spurt may be the earliest measurable physical feature in girls, occurring, as we have seen, about year before breast budding. The growth spurt in boys does not begin until considerable gonadal development has occurred. This is why girls in the earlier stages of adolescence are taller than boys. Boys are on the average about two years older than girls at the age of their maximum growth spurt, but the amount of height attained (10–14 inches, or 25–35 cm) and the velocity of the spurt (2–3 inches per year, or 5–8 cm per year) does not differ substantially between boys and girls. The height growth spurt typically lasts about four years, with growth ceasing in girls at about 17 and in boys at about 20 years of age. The female growth spurt slows at menarche in midpuberty. In general, a girl can expect to grow 1 to 3 inches (3 to 7 cm) after menarche, and considerable pubertal sexual development may yet occur in almost fully grown girls. In contrast, a pubescent boy may not achieve his maximum growth until he has developed nearly adult genitalia. Pubic hair growth may also occur from midpuberty to late puberty in boys, while the process generally appears throughout the pubertal years in girls. The progression of pubertal growth is the same across ethnic groups.

Tempo or timing of pubertal change. Tanner has extensively described the substantial variations that occur in growth patterns—both the tempo of growth and the speed with which children carry out the entire growth process (155).[4]

Maturational timing seems to be the same across ethnic groups, provided nutrition is adequate. It is widely believed, however, that puberty occurs later among Asians than among whites. Brooks-Gunn completed a comparative study of dancers with national ballet companies in the United States, Western Europe, and the People's Republic of China, and found that the mean age of menarche was quite late for dancers, in comparison to population norms. The manuscript was criticized during the review process on the grounds that Asians have a later mean menarcheal age than whites. During a visit to China, however, she learned that the age reported in journals available to Western scientists was verified by several Chinese physicians and experts on sports medicine: menarche occurs at the same age in China for the population at large (at least in urban areas where nutrition is good and reporting of health statistics is extensive) as in the United States (81). The erroneous belief that it does not may be due in part to the fact that Asian females are generally lighter and smaller than their American counterparts;[5] therefore it is assumed that their physical development is delayed. This is an example of ethnocentrism that one might expect to see applied to psychological events but not biological ones. Controversy also exists with respect to whether Africans and African-Americans develop earlier than other ethnic groups (57).

Brain Growth

Growth in brain weight proceeds through periods of varying velocity, with specific regions of the brain growing at different times in a pattern related in a complex way to the evolutional age of the brain region (97). Early data suggested that brain cells increase in number from birth through age 2 or 3, after which little or no growth occurs. Later evidence suggests that brain growth extends well into adolescence and perhaps even further; questions as to amount, region, timing, and synchrony remain (46, 70). More recent qualitative studies demonstrate progressive differential maturation of nerve cells throughout childhood and adolescence (134). Sophisticated studies with magnetic resonance imaging confirm continuing changes in the structural functioning of the brain through midadolescence (89).

With respect to puberty and brain growth, Epstein (54, 55) has posited that while brain cell growth is essentially complete after the first two years of life, peaks and troughs in brain growth across regions occur throughout childhood and adolescence. Changes in head circumference over time are used as his proxy for brain weight and hence growth. He reports increases in head circumference around ages 10 to 12, after which a steep decline is seen for girls and a more gradual one for boys. These data have been criticized on several grounds, including analytic procedures (108), lack of replication (112), and lack of a sex difference, which would be expected if the changes had anything to do with puberty since boys develop later than girls (52, 126). It is more likely that "while discrete brain regions definitely progress through something like 'spurts,' in terms of such processes as the generation of nerve cells and of connections between them, different brain regions do so out of synchrony and in a reliable developmental sequence" (70, p. 552).[6]

Studies of EEG activity from childhood to young adulthood have demonstrated a continuous process of growth, best described by an exponential growth function, along with discrete spurts in specific parts of the brain (157).[7] The sophisticated technological assessment of brain maturation is providing dramatic new descriptive data of brain growth and maturation; the relevance for hormonal, cognitive, and psychological changes still needs to be clarified, however.

The Endocrine System at Puberty

Hormonal control of pubertal growth. The endocrine system mediates interactions between nutrition and genetic makeup to influence growth and physical changes in puberty. Before secondary sex characteristics develop, concentrations of the pituitary hormones called gonadotropins—luteinizing hormone (LH) anf follicle-stimulating hormone (FSH)—increase. Also noteworthy are the pulsating patterns in which the pituitary secretes these hormones over a twenty-four-hour period. Appropriate "bursts" or pulses, induce the ovaries and testes to produce increased levels of estrogens and androgens, which in turn stimulate physical growth. In addition, they stimulate the gonads to produce sperm in males and mature ova in females.

At about the same time, levels of growth hormones and a family of growth-hormone-dependant factors (the somatomedins) increase. Near the end of the pubertal process, perhaps in response to rising hormone levels, the production of these growth hormones seems to diminish. These growth factors are produced throughout the body by all dividing cells and act not only by classical endocrine hormonal means, having circulated to the site, but also locally on neighboring cells or even on the cell that produces them.

It remains unclear how the hormonal, nutritional, and energy regulators of pubertal growth act together to initiate puberty. The associations between the sex hormones and the growth hormone—peptide growth factor system are being studied, especially connections between the growth factors and production of sperm or ova, and the role of local production and action of peptide growth factors in diverse tissues—skeletal and other—relative to material brought from distant sites.

Regulatory systems that control the reproductive endocrine system. Maturation of the reproductive endocrine system, which normally culminates in the production of sex steroids and sperm or ova by fertile adults, is regulated at multiple sites. Parts of the brain, including the cortex, limbic system, and complex neurotransmitter systems, modulate hypothalamic function. These influence the *hypothalamus*, which directly controls the pituitary by producing gonadotropin-releasing hormone (GnRH), which it secretes in rhythmic pulses. The *pituitary* synthesizes, stores, and secretes LH and FSH in response to continued stimulation by GnRH. And the *gonads* (ovaries or testes) respond by synthesizing and secreting sex steroid (androgens and estrogens) and producing sperm or ova. The hypothalamus also stimulates the pituitary to produce adrenocorticotropic hormone (ACTH), which causes the adrenal glands to increase androgen production (135, 136).

As we stated earlier, the hypothalamic-pituitary-gonadal system first functions during fetal life and early infancy (certainly in males and probably in females). It is then suppressed to a low level of activity for almost a decade and is reactivated during late childhood (94). Studies of newborn primates have suggested that this system may already be fully mature in males, but that its maturation in the female may extend into early childhood (130, 131). Such processes may operate in humans as well, although data are sparse. The role of the fetal gonads in producing androgens that alter maturity of the hypothalamus is currently under study.

Experimental and clinical studies support the hypothesis that the brain, not the pituitary gland or gonads, restrains the activity of the reproductive endocrine system in prepubertal children. This inhibition appears to be mediated through suppression of GnRH production and secretion (136). The number of hypothalamic GnRH cells and the production of GnRH do not differ in juvenile and adult monkeys, suggesting that the quiescent phase of reproductive function is mediated by some type of inhibitory mechanism (3). Intermittent, rather nonspecific excitation of hypothalamic GnRH-secreting neurons in prepubertal monkeys prematurely activates the pubertal process, providing strong evidence for regulation of the GnRH pulse generator and its secretory products by brain structures that regulate the hypothalamus (66).[8]

Neuroendocrine Control of the Onset of Puberty

Temporal definitions of pubertal events. As we have noted, the earliest manifestation of pubertal development in the male is enlargement of the testes, whereas in the female acceleration of height growth and breast budding are the first physical indications of puberty. In boys, increased evidence of testicular growth (or any other pubertal manifestation) prior to age 9 is viewed as being precocious and absence of any changes after age 14 as being delayed. In girls, onset of breast budding prior to age 8 or evidence of initiation of the pubertal growth spurt prior to age 7 is considered sexually precocious and the absence of these changes after age 13 to be delayed.

Extensive endocrinologic assessments of syndromes of sexual precocity and of delayed adolescent maturation have been undertaken. Of ongoing research interest are several relatively recent treatment approaches. The hypothalamic-pituitary-gonadal axis, prematurely reactivated in the syndrome of sexual precocity, is silenced by treatment with potent agonists of endogenous GnRH (74). These analogues of GnRH mimic the action of constant infusions of the native material on pituitary gonadotropin release; a process of "receptor down regulation" leads to an impairment of LH and FSH secretion (74). In the syndrome of delayed sexual maturation, therapy with replacement GnRH given in pulses has been effected (132). Accordingly, exploration of the regulation of hypothalamic, pituitary, and gonadal function is being undertaken in which administration of pulsatile GnRH has replaced the usual hypothalamic secretion profile. The recognition and study of such chemical manipulation of pituitary function has enabled investigators to inhibit selectively the reproductive endocrine axis in animals and assess varied growth and hormonal events at different stages of the pubertal process.

Timing of the onset of puberty. The average age at onset of puberty shows a secular trend over the past century toward earlier occurrence; the trend cuts across geographic and ethnic lines (154). This progressive decline in the age of puberty is thought to be due to improvements in socioeconomic conditions; such a trend appears to have slowed or ceased over the last twenty years (154). Nutrition and weight early in life (the fetal and infancy periods) as well as nutrition and weight at the age of puberty may influence the onset of puberty (102). A critical amount of body weight or fat has been thought to trigger the onset (60), but much research does not support this hypothesis (43, 98, 146).

Although menarche is a relatively late pubertal event and is removed from those neural factors that influence both the production of gonadotropin-gonadal sex steroid and physical changes at the initiation of puberty, the possibility exists that some alteration of body metabolism, including the ratio of fat to lean body mass (somatometer), may affect central nervous system (CNS) restraints on the onset of puberty. Studies have characterized potential metabolic signals during maturation in monkeys (37, 150). Earlier use of alternative energy stores (amino acids and fatty acids) by the fasting juvenile primate, unlike the adult primate, perhaps related to increased rates of energy consumption or diminished availability of energy substrate, led Steiner and his co-workers to consider the linkage between metabolic alterations during maturation and the timing of the onset of puberty. Production of insulin, ketone bodies, and free fatty acids, along with alterations in the neural uptake of tryptophan and tyrosine, with consequent altered neurotransmitter synthesis, may be metabolic signals that affect the brain and, thus, temporally modify the onset of puberty.

Central nervous system control of the timing of puberty. Two mechanisms have been invoked to explain the prepubertal restraint by the central nervous system of gonadotropin secretion. One is a sex-steroid–dependent mechanism, a highly sensitive hypothalamic-pituitary-gonadal negative feedback system. The other is a sex-steroid-independent mechanism that can be ascribed to "intrinsic" CNS inhibitory influences. In all likelihood both the inhibition of gonadotropin secretion in a highly sensitive manner by low levels of sex steroid throughout the pre-pubertal years and inhibitory action intrinsically mediated by the central nervous system, perhaps based on metabolic, body weight or composition, or other energy signals, interact to maintain the decadelong quiescence of the reproductive endocrine system.[9]

CURRENT ISSUES

The central questions around which much of the current research revolves are relevant to matters of policy. These include: What is the pubertal experience like for teenagers today, and how does it differ from that in the past, both in the United States and in other cultures? How do pubertal experiences, in some circumstances and for some subgroups, trigger maladaptive responses? How may puberty, in conjunction with other events occurring during early adolescence, influence the emergence of developmental psychopathology? Can puberty (and in what circumstances and for what subgroups) rightfully be considered stormy and stressful, as it has been described since the dawn of adolescent psychology (77)? Does puberty herald an intensification of gender roles, and with it a truncation of role options and aspirations for girls, and is it thus more of a crisis for girls than for boys? And do changes in parental relationship with pubertal children have anything to do with subsequent differences in autonomy and achievement between male and female youth?

Meaning of Pubertal Change

Puberty may elicit a wide array of emotions. The child may feel alternately excited and frightened, pleased and dismayed, by the changes, and, given the rapidity with which they occur, bewildered as well. Physical change may be viewed as a cultural event that marks a transition. In nonindustrialized societies, where educational demands do not postpone work and parenthood, the transition is made directly into adulthood. In developed countries, where educational trends delay entry into the work force, the transition is not to adulthood per se but to the intermediate phase that we call adolescence. Thus, the timing of taking on adult roles is associated with the way puberty is construed across cultures. When youth are expected immediately to become parents and working members of the community, puberty is often treated as a rite of passage, with various celebrations and ceremonies. Among the Arapesh of New Guinea,

> a girl's first menstruation and the accompanying ceremonial take place in her husband's home. But her brothers must play a part in it and they are sent for; failing brothers, cousins will come. Her brothers build her a menstrual hut, which is stronger and better constructed than are the menstrual huts of older women …The girl is cautioned to sit with her legs crossed. Her woven arm and leg bands, her earrings, her old lime gourd and lime spatula are taken from her. Her woven belt is taken off. If these are fairly new they are given away; if they are old they are cut off and destroyed. There is no feeling that they themselves are contaminated, but only the desire to cut the girls' connection with her past.
>
> The girl is attended by older women who are her own relatives or relatives of her husband. They rub her all over with stinging nettles. They tell her to roll one of the large nettle-leaves into a tube and thrust it into her vulva: This will ensure her breasts growing large and strong. The girl eats no food, nor does she drink water. On the third day, she comes out of the hut and stands against a tree while her mother's brother makes the decorative cuts upon her shoulders and buttocks. This is done so gently, with neither earth nor lime rubbed in—the usual New Guinea method for making scarification marks permanent—that it is only possible to find the scars during the next three or four years. During that time, however, if strangers wish to know whether a girl is nubile, they look for the marks. Each day the women rub the girl with nettles. It is well if she fasts for five or six days, but the women watch her anxiously, and if she becomes too weak they put an end to it. Fasting will make her strong, but too much of it might make her die, and the emergence ceremony is hastened. (113, pp. 92–93)

The Mano of Liberia have a pubertal ceremony for boys:

> The boys went through a ceremonial "death." In the old days they were apparently run through with a spear and tossed over the curtain. Onlookers heard a thud as he was supposed to hit the ground inside, dead. Actually, the boy was protected by a chunk of plantain stalk tied on under his clothes. Into this the spear was thrust. A bladder of chicken's blood at the right spot was punctured and spilled to make it all very realistic to other boys and women

who could not resist the desire to see their sons, perhaps for the last time. Inside the fence *sa yi ge* (a ritual personage) and two assistants, all masked, caught the boys in mid-air, and dropped a heavy dummy to complete the delusion. The boys were actually unharmed and were quickly carried away into the deep forest which is the Poro grove. (83, pp. 13–14).

When puberty is not a rite of passage, the community typically does not acknowledge the event; instead, more private responses seem to be emphasized. In less industrial settings the advent of puberty may be seen as an economic and political event, in that marriage, which is expected to follow, may cement already existing interfamilial alliances or promote new ones. In addition, the girl's reproductive ability may be perceived as an asset by the father, who wishes to trade on her potential fertility. This fertility, which is inferred from the onset of menstruation, is important in societies where high birth rates are necessary, given labor-intensive agricultural methods and high rates of childhood mortality. It has been posited that chaperonage, bride-price, seclusion, and residence with the bridegroom's family before puberty are all means of regulating fertility prior to marriage and of realizing the economic value of the daughter to the family (122). Indeed, pubertal rituals are more likely to be celebrated in societies in which fraternal interest groups are absent and subsistence economic conditions prevail; in both instances alliances among kin are weak, increasing the value of using daughters as bargaining chips to strengthen them (122).[10]

Regardless of the context and the form of the ceremony, puberty is celebrated in many world cultures. Somewhat surprisingly, then, either not much is said about puberty in developed societies, or else, at least until recently, it was cast in negative terms. As we have noted, the literature on menarche as recently as the early 1970s perceived the onset of menstruation as a crisis for the pubertal girl. This model was based on retrospective reports by adults of their pubertal experience rather than on prospective studies of girls themselves. Here is a typical adult report: "I had no information whatsoever, no hint that anything was going to happen to me … I thought I was on the point of death from internal hemorrhage … What did my highly educated mother do? She read me a furious lecture about what a bad, evil, immoral thing I was to start menstruating at the age of eleven! So young and so vile! Even after thirty years, I can feel the shock of hearing her condemn me for 'doing' something I had no idea occurred" (166, p. 169). In addition, the focus was on negative consequences, not on the fact that puberty is a part of growing up for all humans. Perhaps this reflected the psychodynamic and medical perspectives of most of the extant literature. Nonetheless, a reader might have found this view puzzling. After all, menarche was a mark of becoming an adult female. Was this necessarily negative? Did all girls resist growing up? Weren't there positive aspects to becoming mature? The crisis model was subsequently reframed as an examination of the *meaning* of menarche to girls as well as the transition from child to adult (27, 139).

A review of the early literature by Brooks-Gunn indicated that the adult psychoanalytic sources most often characterized menarche as anxiety producing and distressing (26, 45). Her subsequent research, along with that of others, aimed to determine how traumatic menarche actually was for girls, rather than relying on retrospective reports from clinical adult samples (see 11 and 71 for reviews of this literature of the 1970s and early 1980s). In general these studies suggested that girls experience an array of feelings—positive, negative, and ambivalent—as illustrated by a passage from Anne Frank's diary: "Each time little excited, I mean it's her first bra.

The father's probably feeling a little embarrassed, and maybe a little down that his daughter's growing up so fast.

And the story ends, the daughter gets the bra, and everybody lives happily ever after.

Story 3

She like went shopping with her mom or something, she got a bra.

Her dad is wondering what they got.

She doesn't want her dad to see.

Her mom took it out, and she was totally humiliated and embarrassed.

Her dad understood and stuff like that, but um, she thought it was really rude of her mother to do that, because, ya know, her mother was sort of teasing her and joking her and so was the dad.

And she was very embarrassed.

Finally, the fact that many adults were unprepared for puberty and did not discuss it with their parents may add to their discomfort, as we suggested earlier.

Timing of maturation. We know much more about the effects of maturational timing on the adolescent than we do about the meaning of pubertal changes. This is somewhat surprising since to understand the relative effect of puberty (that is, timing vis-à-vis one's peers), it would seem necessary to know how individuals generally incorporate societal and personal experiences of this universal set of events into their self-definitions. Again, we believe that ambivalence about puberty, in a society that attempts to ignore adolescent sexual arousal and has not come to grips with the short-term historical changes in sexual behavior, may in part determine the content of research. Hence, this ambivalence helps explain the focus on individual differences rather than the universal experience as well as determining what questions are more "acceptable" ("Are you early, on-time, or late with respect to your peers?" rather than "How physically developed are you, and how do you feel about breast growth, hair development, menarche, and so on?").

The question usually asked has to do with potential negative consequences of being "off-time" with respect to maturation, whether early or late. (This issue is investigated only for timing, although individual differences in duration or sequence may be significant as well). Girls' and boys' progression through puberty is different, as we showed earlier in this chapter: girls typically have their growth spurt sooner and at different points in the process of developing secondary sexual characteristics than do boys (girls prior to menarche and breast stage 4 and boys after genital stage 4). Early-maturing girls and late-maturing boys are posited to be at greater risk for adjustment problems than other groups, given that they are the two most off-time groups, given relative gender differences in maturation (24).

Early-maturing boys seem to have an advantage relative to late maturers in many aspects of socioemotional and academic functioning, and some of these effects persist into adulthood (116, 125). Some seem to be more pronounced for boys of lower socioeconomic status (SES), for whom early maturation may confer greater prestige in athletics, but this focus may also have the effect of moving them away from academics (41). Thus, late-maturing low-SES boys are at a particular disadvantage with respect to self-esteem and popularity, given the value placed on physical strength, sports, and macho behavior. Interestingly, later in life the popular early-maturing boys may be at a disadvantage, given that the very attributes that increased their adolescent prestige also may tend to result in rigid, sex-stereotyped attributes in middle age rather than more flexible characteristics (125).

Early maturation does not seem to be an advantage for girls, even for a short time. The influence of maturational timing can be seen in physical development, preparation for and feelings about menarche, body image and self-image, and deviant behavior and relationships with parents and peers (girls have been studied more extensively in recent years, given conflicting results in the early longitudinal growth studies; see 24).[11]

Early maturers weigh more and are slightly shorter "than are late..." maturers when pubertal growth is complete, and this difference persists throughout life. Early maturers may not be as well prepared for pubertal change as are late maturers. Early maturers are less likely to report that their father knew about their menarche and are less likely to tell their fathers about it directly (12). Since girls seem to choose girlfriends in part on the basis of physical status, early-maturing girls may have a smaller network of intimate friends (although we have little data directly addressing this theory.) Early maturers seem to have a poorer body image than on-time or late maturers, at least when general measures of body image and weight-related indexes are used (9, 51). This is true of girls in elementary, junior, and senior high school. In addition, more eating problems, lasting throughout adolescence, are found among early-maturing girls compared to on-time and late maturers (29). In part, such differences may result because body build is associated with popularity; being thin is a desirable condition for almost all adolescent girls, and dieting is a common response to the current cultural demands for thinness. Early maturers, by virtue of being somewhat heavier than average, do not conform to the cultural values favoring thinness and the prepubertal figure. Thus it is not surprising that they may have a less positive body image (related to weight) and are more concerned about dieting than are later maturers, just as late-maturing boys are concerned about not having large enough muscles.

Early maturers, both boys and girls, may exhibit poorer emotional health than late maturers (14, 129). In addition, early-maturing girls who experience negative events at home and in school are more likely to exhibit depressive affect than later-maturing girls who experience similar events (33). Girls also seem to be more negatively affected than boys by the confluence of events occurring during adolescence (128).

Early maturers, both boys and girls, may engage in adult behaviors (such as smoking, drinking, and sexual intercourse) at an earlier age than later maturers. They also seem to be somewhat more advanced with respect to dating than on-time or late maturers, at least in middle school. Actual pubertal status, however, does not seem to be associated with dating behavior (47, 63, 143); dating seems to be heavily age related and associated with peer behavior. By late adolescence differences between early and late maturers in dating and sexual behavior disappear for both boys and girls (91).

We know very little about the effects of maturational timing on parent-child relationships. Hill has reported stress in parent-child relationships for seventh-grade girls who had been menstruating for over a year (86), suggesting that some early-maturing girls may, at least in the short run, have difficulties with their parents (and vice versa). In addition, Steinberg and Hill report that boys at the apex of puberty experience more conflict with their parents than at other times during the pubertal sequence, although how timing enters the equation is not known (149).

[While carving the roast, my father] leaned over and dropped the first hacked slice of meat onto my plate. Then, on his way back up, he began to scrutinize my nearby face. With more disapproval than curiosity he suddenly said, "What's that?"

"What's what?"

"That on your cheek—there." He pointed at me with the carving knife.

I winced away. I knew perfectly well what he was talking about. What he had picked out publicly to confront me with was something that, after causing me no end of anguish that afternoon I decided was simply a pimple—a round, brown, ephemeral blemish which I had clumsily tried to cover up with dabs of my mother's make-up snitched from the jars lined up on her crowded dressing table. But, a novice in such methods, I had succeeded only in altering its color. It was no disguise for my father's eagle eye, though it might easily have hidden the imperfection from Alan Steiger, the young lawyer. (142, pp. 84–86).

He wouldn't ask anyone else, he knew. It was too close to the prom. He put another piece of meat into his mouth. *Oh, God, what was wrong with him?* He thought everything had been going along fine. He would've asked her to go steady. Maybe that's why she broke the date, he thought. She knew they were getting to that point. Perhaps someone else had asked her. Perhaps she had just been using him all these months, just waiting for someone else to come along. Anybody. Anybody was better than Dennis Holowitz. *I'm so ugly, he thought, grinding the meat between his teeth. Ugly, I'm sick. I'm ashamed. My clothes are ugly. My face is ugly. My body is ugly. What am I doing alive? I always come back to this point. It's always there. This ugliness. I can't fight it. I'm running out of strength.* (168, pp. 82–83).

Brooks-Gunn and her colleagues asked adolescent girls to tell a story about a picture of a young girl standing in front of a mirror:

Story 1

She just took a shower and she wants to see if she is growing and all, and I guess she's just like seeing what she looks like. She's growing and she's just like looking at herself in the mirror.

Story 2

She probably thought, you know, she looked bad or something. So she looked in the mirror to see how she looked.

Story 3

She's wondering about what she should wear, and whether she should leave her hair like that, I mean it really looks like a really conservative type of cut.

She gets dressed, she goes to school, and after school she goes to a haircutter and gets her head shaved.

Story 4

She's looking at her face. And she's thinking, um, am I pretty. Um, and um, she's not really. She doesn't know really if she's pretty or not. She's kind of confused.

Professional and athletic demands. One of the possible negative outcomes of both physical development and its timing has to do with the expectations that adolescents have for their eventual appearance. The adolescent may perceived physical growth to be a sort of lottery, an outcome that cannot be known beforehand (80). That is, what will the ultimate shape and appearance of various body parts be? Looking at one's parents may give some hints but not the complete picture (correlations for heritability estimates for mother-daughter menarcheal age are in the 40s and 50s, for parent-offspring height in the 80s, and for parent-offspring weight in the 90s; see 64, 151). Expectations are not always fulfilled; such "mismatches" may set the stage for subsequent maladaptation. This is particularly true for those adolescents engaged in athletic or professional endeavors that require a particular body shape. Brooks-Gunn compared girls in dance company schools with girls in the general population in order to determine how the requirements of a particular social situation match up with individual physical and behavioral characteristics. With respect to dancers the demands are clear: they must maintain a low body weight in order to conform to professional standards and must devote a great deal of time to practice. Dancers are more likely to be late maturers than nondancers (61, 163). Being a later maturer may be particularly advantageous (as well as normative) for dancers, even though it has not been shown to be so for nondancers (30, 129, 143). In keeping with her premise, dancers who matured on time had poorer emotional health and body images and more eating problems than did the later-maturing dancers. Some sports also require (or prefer) particular body types, with similar results for athletes when the requirements call for thinness (18).

School and peer influences. Peer situations other than athletics, in conjunction with pubertal growth, may render an adolescent vulnerable to problem behavior. An example is the finding that, among sixth-grade girls, maturing early influences body image differently depending on whether they are in elementary or middle school (9, 144). A Swedish study found that, while early-maturing girls were more likely to drink and be sexually active than later maturers, the effect was related to having older friends, a phenomenon that was more prevalent among early than among late maturers (105). Presumably, early maturers actively sought or were sought by older adolescents as friends.

Parent-child relationships. Particular parent-child situations that may be sources of conflict are being studied; researchers want to know more about the intensity, meaning, and timing of conflict. Conflict and disagreement seem to be almost universal, though not intense (147). Such conflict is typically seen as temporary, as Hill's term "perturbation" implies (86). Parent-child relations are generally thought to be transformed as both parents and young adolescents renegotiate their relationship (72). While research has documented the nature of early adolescent relationships, discussion is sparse on actual developmental changes (from late childhood through late adolescence) and on the processes underlying them (14, 147).

Changes in parents' and children's expectations for one another may be as significant as changes in actual interaction patterns, although much less research has centered on the former. Children who are tall for their age group are expected by adults to perform more socially mature tasks (10). The fact that leadership and school achievement have been associated with children's and adolescents' height to a small degree (50) suggests the social stimulus value of physical characteristics (the role parents may play in the acquisition of such values has not been specified, however). As children enter puberty, parents may expect better-developed children to exhibit more socially adult behavior. For example, girls who are more physically mature than their peers may elicit more freedom from parents, thus making it likely that they will engage in dating earlier than other girls. These expectations may result in changes in interactions, although the process by which this may occur has not been studied.

Intensification of Gender Roles

Why is puberty seen as negative for girls while no mention of a similar crisis is found for boys? For boys, puberty is believed to expand role possibilities into the realm of work and achievement; for girls, roles are believed to be confined. In Chodorow's terms, boys are characterized as "doing" and girls as "being" (40). These distinctions, while believed to exist prior to puberty as a result of socialization, are thought to become pronounced at puberty, when gender-role divisions become apparent (possibly because of reproductive differences; see 87). Little research exists, however. Does gender-role intensification occur at puberty, and do girls really redefine themselves primarily in terms of reproductive roles while boys do not? If so, what are the processes underlying such self-definitional changes, and how do parents and peers contribute (16)?

Evidence that gender roles intensify at puberty is found in expectations for more "adult" behavior from pubertal children and increasing parental vigilance over girls after puberty. The author of *Kinflicks* gives us a vivid example of gender-role ideology for the pubertal female: "No more football? She might as well have told Arthur Murray never to dance again … I went upstairs, and as I exchanged my shoulder pad for a sanitary pad and elastic belt, I knew that menstruation might just as well have been a gastrointestinal hemorrhage in terms of its repercussions on my life" (4, p. 33).

Let us now consider how boys and girls also differ in terms of autonomy, intimacy, and emotional health.

Autonomy. As Erikson has suggested, girls may be more vulnerable to problems with autonomy than boys. Girls are believed to be more emotionally focused on and less individuated from their mothers than are boys (40, 93). Such differences may explain, in part, why girls are believed to speak "in a different voice" —more interpersonal, intimate, and relationally focused (67). Perhaps parent-child interactions occurring in early adolescence are different for boys than for girls. For example, observational studies suggest that girls are interrupted more and ignored more while boys assert themselves more as puberty progresses (86). That mothers seem to exert more power over their postmenarcheal than premenarcheal daughters, and that their use of power is associated with their daughters' compliance, suggests a partial explanation for the nonassertive behavior of girls in family interactions (34). More work on the process of autonomy for girls and boys, as well as on the antecedents for and consequences of parental behavior, is obviously called for.

Intimacy. At the same time, boys may be more vulnerable to lack of intimacy. Girls tend to have a smaller number of best friends, to whom they tell everything, while boys tend to have larger groups of friends with whom they engage in activities. While friendship patterns are being studied, intimacy is not always the focus. Gilligan's work underscores the importance of intimacy to females (67); its lack in men is left to novelists and popular psychologists, who decry men's ability to form close relationships. Boys may be more vulnerable to intimacy problems that emerge, or become more salient, at the time of puberty.

While this is speculative, the fact that it is culturally unacceptable to talk about male pubertal changes and the feelings they engender may be a pivotal issue in how males structure their friendships. In contrast, almost all girls today talk over pubertal changes with their mothers and their close girlfriends. Whether and how such differences influence disclosure and intimacy is not known, however.

Emotional health. Three of the best-studied and most prevalent psychiatric problems (and their less severe forms) are depression (depressive affect), conduct disorders (aggressive behavior and affect), and eating disorders (compulsive eating). All three are linked to gender, become more prevalent after puberty, and are associated with personality factors and situational events.

Perhaps the most alarming outcome associated with the pursuit of thinness through dieting is the rising incidence of weight-related clinical syndromes among adolescent and young adult females (5, 6). Anorexia nervosa is an eating disorder characterized by behavior directed toward weight loss, by peculiar attitudes toward food, by distorted body image, and by an implacable refusal to maintaining body weight. Occurring predominantly in females (90% to 95% of all cases), it is one of the few psychiatric disorders that can follow an unremitting course resulting in death. It is most likely to occur just after the pubertal weight spurt (78). Bulimia is an eating disturbance characterized by episodes of uncontrollable overeating, usually followed by vomiting, exercise, or laxative abuse to prevent food absorption. It occurs most frequently in late adolescence and early adulthood.

Severe depression is more likely to occur after puberty than before (38, 133). In addition, postpubertal girls are much more likely to be diagnosed as depressed than are boys, with these differences continuing into adulthood (140). Hormonal, sex role, and situational factors have been posited to account for these difference (25, 68, 119).

Conduct disorders and aggression are more prevalent among boys than girls from early childhood on, although they increase dramatically in early adolescence, suggesting that pubertal factors may exacerbate existing predispositions (which themselves are probably both biologically and socially mediated). In addition, younger boys with severe acting-out behavior problems are at much higher risk than girls for conduct disorders in adolescence and later in adulthood (53, 137).[12]

IMPLICATIONS FOR EDUCATION AND FUTURE DIRECTIONS
Studying the role of pubertal processes in the early adolescent transition has several implications for health and academic education. Pubertal children are not well educated about reproductive changes (19, 22, 84, 95). Courses in sex education and family life are not offered in all school districts, and in those that do offer them (about three-quarters nationally), education is not provided in fifth and sixth grade, the time when the majority of children are beginning to develop secondary sexual characteristics. Furthermore, existing programs are often brief and not particularly extensive. Programs have been shown to increase knowledge about reproduction without resulting in an earlier initiation of sexual intercourse (88). The specter of HIV infection may alter sex education in the schools. The fact that 94% of all parents want their schools to provide information to their children on the spread of HIV infection and AIDS (82) may offer an opportunity to expand the health-education curriculum more generally (18).

The off-time maturer, particularly the early-maturing girl, is currently provided little information about her maturational status. While children who mature extremely early or late are likely to come to the attention of a physician, early or late maturers within the normal range are not. These children may nonetheless have some concerns about being abnormal. A brief discussion outlining the sequence and timing of an event and the wide range of variations may be all that is needed to reassure many off-time maturers.

Parents, teachers, and school nurses could benefit from information about the potential pressures to date and to engage in adultlike behavior that pubertal children often face. Also, the knowledge that conflicts often surround the process of growing up may reassure parents and adolescents who find these altercations stressful. Finally, we need to let adults and teenagers know that some youths respond negatively to puberty and that certain factors and situations render them vulnerable to problems associated with pubertal change, such as the dieting and binging behavior seen in many segments of our society. Decreases in certain nutrients (for example, iron and calcium) at puberty may have long-term health implications, including bone weakness and hormonal problems (165).

With regard to academic achievement, we have said little about the role of puberty in cognitive development. It is clear, however, that puberty may influence school achievement in a variety of indirect ways. Depressive affect and low self-esteem are generally associated with poor school performance; factors that increase the likelihood of poor emotional health may thus diminish academic achievement (128). Making the transition to middle school, a time at which academic demands increase, may be difficult for pubertal children, especially if the middle school begins in sixth grade (143). The confluence of multiple biological and social events seems to presage an increase in school problems and depressive affect (7, 145). Coping with family problems at the time of puberty may be especially difficult for girls, setting in motion a pattern of low self-esteem and school failure (127). Maturing early, for both girls and boys, may lead to a focus on dating and peer relationships, to the detriment of school achievement (106). While such factors have been shown to have short-term effects, little research addresses long-term school problems or factors that can either maintain a negative pattern or act as self-righting mechanisms.

While by no means exhaustive, this chapter sets out current approaches to the study of puberty as well as recommendations for future directions. In the biological realm we still do not understand fully the physiological mechanisms responsible for initiating and regulating neuroendocrine maturation and somatic growth, nor do we know how environmental factors may interact with biological ones to enhance or impede maturation. From a clinical perspective, the biological and social markers for severe problems such as depression, conduct disorders, and eating disorders are not well understood, nor are the reasons for their emergence or increase following the transition to adolescence. Few investigators have examined the role pubertal processes may play in cognitive change or the role of cognition in the emergence of negative emotions. Social-cognition perspectives are just beginning to be applied to the transition to adolescence, with this work being directed toward attributions and rule setting in the conventional, social, and moral realm. Other processes possibly associated with pubertal change (self-definition, social comparison, and so on) await investigation. Psychodynamic perspectives are regrettably rare in our research, even though clinical theorizing has been the basis for much of the current thinking on parent-child relationships, storm and stress, identity formation, and gender-role intensification, all topics of considerable interest. Not enough attention is being given to the progression from pubertal growth to sexuality. Across all topics too few cross-cultural and multiethnic studies have been conducted. Finally, the long-term implications of pubertal change and pubertal influences on behavior are just beginning to be studied.

NOTES

We wish to thank the National Institutes of Health, the W. T. Grant Foundation, and the Russell Sage Foundation for their support. We are grateful for the comments of Michelle Warren and James Tanner. The help of Rosemary Deibler and Florence Kelly in manuscript preparation was appreciated.

1. According to a study of four groups of American teenagers, 60% had had intercourse by the following ages: white males, age 18; white females, age 19; black males, age 16; black females, age 18 (88).
2. The proclivity to make inferences about direct biological effects in the absence of appropriate designs is great, however, and some of the pubertal research fails to use sufficient caution. This is also true of the literature on menstruation (31, 124, 138). The specification of models testing direct and indirect biological effects of puberty would be extremely helpful.
3. Examining sequences of events, however, does not mean that their temporal ordering is invariable across individuals. The young adolescent may move into a middle school in sixth or seventh grade. She may begin to date as early as fifth grade, as late as twelfth grade, or not at all. Interindividual differences in the onset (and cessation) of pubertal processes are found, as is intraindividual variability in the timing and sequence of pubertal events.
4. Tanner developed "tempo-conditional" standard growth curves in which individuals' growth curves may be expressed on a set of curves with varying rates, all derived from normal children. Despite being at the same height and weight at the initiation of puberty, and perhaps also at the conclusion of pubertal change, individuals experience the process at rates that vary dramatically.
5. Indeed, different weight norms (for height and age) have to be used to calculate weight percentiles for Chinese and American youth, given these differences. More generally, ethnic differences have been reported in weight, height, leg and arm length (proportional to overall length), skin-fold thickness, and possibly fat distribution. These differences have been reported in relatively well-nourished populations (57).
6. Different developmental patterns for the two cerebral hemispheres are apparent. We wish to suggest that specific age-linked patterns parallel the cognitive developmental sequence described by Piaget. Few data exist on how such changes might be associated with Piagetian stages in early adolescence (69). More generally, a great deal of research on hemispheric specialization and how it may be influenced by puberty has been conducted on spatial abilities. This work is attempting to explain the sex differences seen in spatial abilities by positing that boys, by virtue of experiencing a later puberty, have a longer period of functional lateralization (161, 162). Yet striking sex differences are found in only one aspect of spatial ability, that of mental rotations (103), and gender effects are seen prior to puberty (118). Many have tested the hypothesis that late-maturing girls have better spatial scores than their early-maturing peers, following Waber's premise and initial confirmatory findings. Effects, when found, tend to be small and are most likely to occur in studies using extreme samples (69, 118).
7. Of particular concern to students of puberty is Epstein's thesis (54) that acceleration of head circumference (and presumably brain growth) is associated with intelligence, which has not been found to be true (112). Epstein has gone on to suggest that learning is accelerated during periods of brain growth, and that middle school, a time when students are in a trough as to brain growth, may not be a particularly good time for learning new skills (56). Others have studied possible disruptions in cognition during early adolescence; while the ability to recognize unfamiliar faces may be lower in children aged 12 to 14 than in younger or older children (39), pubertal "dips" are not seen in any other of a number of cognitive abilities studied (see, for a review of this literature, 69; also 49).
8. The intimate ultrastructural and immuno-histochemical analysis of the arcuate nucleus and surrounding area of the hypothalamus remains to be carried out. The neuropharmacologic control of pulse generator function, whether by neural, neurohumoral, peripheral metabolic, or genome-determined circadian (or circhoral) periodicity is unresolved. Continuing assessment of this region of the

brain with the application of DNA probes will lead to further definition of hypothalamic peptides involved with reproductive endocrine function.

9. The physiological translation of the nutritional, sociological, and exertional influences on the reproductive endocrine system is obscure. Extensive studies of neuropharmacologic mediation of these modulators of pubertal onset, along with intrinsic (possibly genetic) CNS factors, remain to be carried out. Plant states that "the mechanisms that dictate the arrest and reawakening of the hypothalamic GnRH pulse generator remain a fundamental problem of developmental neurobiology" (131, p. 1782).

10. Other, intrapsychic and status-role explanations have been offered for the frequency with which puberty is celebrated in many non-Western societies (35).

11. While we know a great deal about the effects of being an early maturer (24), the literature suffers from various problems: different measures of pubertal status being used to classify individuals' timing (for example, bone age, menarcheal age, peak height velocity, secondary sexual characteristic development); the use of different percentile cutoffs to define early and late maturers (that is, across studies, between 15% and 30% of individuals may be defined as early or late); the use of normative or criterion-based classifications; and the use of age or grade distributions for pubertal events. In addition, comparisons between more deviant groups of off-time maturers (defined statistically, such as two standard deviations away from the norm, making up 1% to 2% of the population, or clinically, such as those children with precocious puberty), and less deviant groups (defined statistically, such as one standard deviation away from the norm, making up one-third of the population) are not made; almost all research focuses on the latter group, the more normative group of off-time maturers. Finally, with the exception of the California Longitudinal Growth Studies, little attention has been given to the possible long-term effects of being an off-time maturer (see, for exceptions, 106).

12. Prospective studies are necessary in order to understand the antecedents of theses disorders, and, in a more normative sense, the less severe problems, as well as to see how the antecedents may differ for pubertal males and females. In addition, comparative studies of different sets of factors that may predispose a boy to be prone to aggression and a girl to depression, for example, are needed. Almost none exist.

REFERENCES

Abel, T., & Joffe, N. F. (1950). Cultural background of female puberty. *American Journal of Psychotherapy*, 4, 90–113.

Adams, L. A., Vician, L., Clifton, D. K., & Steiner, R. A. (1987). Gonadotropin-releasing hormone (GnRH) mRNA content in GnRH neurons is similar in the brains of juvenile and adult male monkeys. In *Macaca fascicularis*. Proceedings of the 69th Annual Meeting of the Endocrine Society, 1987.

Alther, L. (1976). *Kinflicks*. New York: Knopf.

Attie, I., & Brooks-Gunn, J. (1987). Weight-related concerns in women: A response to or a cause of stress? In R. C. Barnett, L. Biener, & G. K. Baruch, eds., *Gender and stress*. New York: Free Press, pp. 218–254.

Attie, I., & Brooks-Gunn, J. (1989). The development of eating problems in adolescent girls: A longitudinal study. *Developmental Psychology*, 25(1), 70–79.

Baydar, N., Brooks-Gunn, J., & Warren, M. P. (in press). Determinants of depressive symptoms in adolescent girls: A four-year longitudinal study. *Developmental Psychology*.

Beach, F. A. (1975). Behavioral endocrinology: An emerging discipline. *American Scientist*, 63, 178–187.

Blyth, D., Simmons, R., & Zakin, D. (1985). Satisfaction with body image for early adolescent females: The impact of pubertal timing within different school environments. *Journal of Youth and Adolescence*, 14(3), 207–225.

Brackbill, Y., & Nevill, D. (1981). Parental expectations of achievement as affected by children's height. *Merrill-Palmer Quarterly*, 27, 429–441.

Brooks-Gunn, J. (1984). The psychological significance of different pubertal events to young girls. *Journal of Early Adolescence*, 4(4), 315–327.

Brooks-Gunn, J. (1987). Pubertal processes and girls' psychological adaptation. In R. Lerner & T. T. Foch, eds., *Biological-psychosocial interactions in early adolescence: A life-span perspective*. Hillsdale, N.J.: Erlbaum, pp. 123–153.

Brooks-Gunn, J. (1988a). Transition to early adolescence. In M. Gunnar & W. A. Collins, eds., *Development during transition to adolescence: Minnesota symposia on child psychology*. Vol. 21. Hillsdale, N.J.: Erlbaum, pp. 189–208.

Brooks-Gunn, J. (1988b). Antecedents and consequences of variations in girls' maturational timing. *Journal of Adolescent Health Care*, 9(5), 1–9.

Brooks-Gunn, J. (1989a). Pubertal processes and the early adolescent transition. In W. Damon, ed., *Child development today and tomorrow*. San Francisco: Jossey-Bass, pp. 155–176.

Brooks-Gunn, J. (1989b). Adolescents as children and as parents: A developmental perspective. In I. E. Sigel & G. H. Brody, eds., *Family Research*. Vol. 1. Hillsdale, N.J.: Erlbaum, pp. 213–248.

Brooks-Gunn, J. (1990). Barriers and impediments to conducting research with young adolescents. *Journal of Youth and Adolescence*, 19(5).

Brooks-Gunn, J., Boyer, C. B., & Hein, K. (1988). Preventing HIV infection and AIDS in children and adolescents: Behavioral research and intervention strategies. *American Psychologist*, 43(II), 958–964.

Brooks-Gunn, J., & Furstenberg, F. F., Jr. (1989). Adolescent sexual behavior. *American Psychologist*, 44(2), 249–257.

Brooks-Gunn, J., & Matthews, W. (1979). *He and she: How children develop their sex-role identity*. Englewood Cliffs, N.J.: Prentice-Hall.

Brooks-Gunn, J., Newman, D., & Warren, M. P. (1989). Significance of breast growth. Unpublished manuscript.

Brooks-Gunn, J., & Paikoff, R. L. (in press). Taking no chances: Teenage pregnancy prevention programs. *American Psychologist*.

Brooks-Gunn, J., & Petersen, A. C., eds. (1983). *Girls at puberty: Biological and psychosocial perspectives*. New York: Plenum Press.

Brooks-Gunn, J., Petersen, A. C., & Eichorn, D. (1985). The study of maturational timing effects in adolescence. Special issue. *Journal of Youth and Adolescence*, 14(3, 4).

Brooks-Gunn, J., & Petersen, A. C. (1991). Studying the emergence of depression and depressive symptoms during adolescence. Special issue. *Journal of Youth and Adolescence*, 20(2), 115–120.

Brooks-Gunn, J., & Ruble, D. N. (1980). Menarche: The interaction of physiology, cultural, and social factors. In A. J. Dan, E. A. Graham, & C. P. Beecher, eds., *The menstrual cycle: A synthesis of interdisciplinary research*. New York: Springer, pp. 141–159.

Brooks-Gunn, J., & Ruble, D. N. (1982). The development of menstrual related beliefs and behaviors during early adolescence. *Child Development*, 53, 1567–77.

Brooks-Gunn, J., Samelson, M., Warren, M. P., & Fox, R. (1986). Physical similarity of and disclosure of menarcheal status to friends: Effects of age and pubertal status. *Journal of Early Adolescence*, 6(1), 3–14.

Brooks-Gunn, J., & Warren, M. P. (1985a). Measuring physical status and timing in early adolescence: A development perspective. *Journal of Youth and Adolscence*, 14(3), 163–189.

Brooks-Gunn, J., & Warren, M. P. (1985b). Effects of delayed menarche in different contexts: Dance and nondance students. *Journal of Youth and Adolescence*, 14(4), 285–300.

Brooks-Gunn, J., & Warren, M. P. (1988). The psychological significance of secondary sexual characteristics in 9- to 11-year-old girls. *Child Development*, 59, 161–169.

Brooks-Gunn, J., & Warren, M. P. (1989). Biological contributions to affective expression in young adolescent girls. *Child Development*, 60, 372–385.

Brooks-Gunn, J., Warren, M. P., & Rosso, J. T. (1991). The impact of pubertal and social events upon girls' problem behavior. *Journal of Youth and Adolescence*, 20(2), 115–120.

Brooks-Gunn, J., & Zahaykevich, M. (1989). Parent-child relationships in early adolescence: A developmental perspective. In K. Kreppner & R. M. Lerner, eds., *Family systems and life-span development*. Hillsdale, N.J.: Erlbaum, pp. 223–246.

Brown, J. K. (1963). A cross-cultural study of female initiation rites. *American Anthropologist*, 65, 837–853.

Bruch, H. (1978). *The golden cage*. Cambridge, Mass.: Harvard University Press.

Cameron, J. L., Koerker, D. J., & Steiner, R. A. (1985). Metabolic changes during maturation of male monkeys: Possible signals for onset of puberty. *American Journal of Physiology*, 249, 385–391.

Cantwell, D. P., & Baker, L. (1991). Manifestations of depressive affect in adolescence. *Journal of Youth and Adolescence*, 20(2), 121–134.

Carey, S., Diamond, R., & Woods, B. (1980). Development of face recognition—a maturational component? *Developmental Psychology*, 16, 257–269.

Chodorow, N. (1978). *The reproduction of mothering: Psychoanalysis and sociology of gender.* Berkeley: University of California Press.

Clausen, J. A. (1975). The social meaning of differential physical and sexual maturation. In S. E. Dragastin & G. H. Elder, Jr., eds., *Adolescence in the life cycle: Psychological change and the social context.* New York: Halstead.

Conel, J. L. (1939–1967). *The postnatal development of the human cerebral cortex.* Vols. 1–87. Cambridge, Mass.: Harvard University Press.

Crawford, J. D., & Osler, D. C. (1975). Body composition at menarche: The Frisch-Revelle hypothesis revisited. *Pediatrics,* 56(3), 449–458.

de Beauvoir, S. (1968). *The second sex.* New York: Knopf.

Deutsch, H. (1944). *The psychology of women.* Vol. 1. New York: Grune & Stratton.

Dobbing, J., & Sands, J. (1973). Quantitative growth and development of the human brain. *Archives of Diseases in Childhood,* 48, 757–767.

Dornbusch, S. M., Carlsmith, J. M., Gross, R. T., Martin, J. A., Jennings, D., Rosenberg, A., & Duke, P. (1981). Sexual development, age, and dating: A comparison of biological and social influences upon one set of behaviors. *Child Development,* 52, 179–185.

Dornbusch, S. M., Carlsmith, J. M., Duncan, P. D., Gross, R. T., Martin, J. A., Ritter, P. L., Siegel-Gorelick, B. (1984). Sexual maturation, social class, and the desire to be thin among adolescent females. *Developmental and Behavioral Pediatrics,* 5(6), 308–314.

Dubas, J. S., Crockett, L. J., & Petersen, A. C. (1990). Longitudinal investigation of sex and individual differences in cognitive abilities during early adolescence: The role of personality and the timing of puberty. Manuscript submitted for publication.

Duke, P. M., Jennings, D. J., Dornbusch, S. M., & Siegel-Gorelick, B. (1982). Educational correlates of early and late sexual maturation in adolescence. *Journal of Pediatrics,* 100(4), 633–637.

Duncan, P. D., Ritter, P. L., Dornbusch, S. M., Gross, R. T., & Carlsmith, J. (1985). The effects of pubertal timing on body image, school behavior, and deviance. *Journal of Youth and Adolescence,* 14, 227–235.

Eichorn, D. H., & Bayley, N. (1962). Growth in head circumference from birth through young adulthood. *Child Development,* 33, 257–271.

Elliot, D. S., & Voss, H. L. (1974). *Delinquency and dropout.* Lexington, Mass.: D. C. Heath.

Epstein, H. T. (1974). Phrenoblysis: Special brain and mind growth periods. Pt. 2. Human mental development. *Developmental Psychobiology,* 7, 217–224.

Epstein, H. T. (1986). Stages in human brain development. *Developments in Brain Research,* 30, 114–119.

Epstein, H. T., & Toepfer, C. F. (1978). A neuroscience basis for reorganizing middle grades education. *Educational Leadership,* 35, 656–660.

Eveleth, P. B., & Tanner, J. M. (1976). *Worldwide variation in human growth.* London: Cambridge University Press.

Faust, M. S. (1983). Alternative constructions of adolescent growth. In J. Brooks-Gunn & A. C. Petersen, eds., *Girls at puberty: Biological and psychosocial perspectives.* New York: Plenum, pp. 105–125.

Frank, A. (1972). *The diary of a young girl.* New York: Pocket Books.

Frisch, R. E. (1984). Body fat, puberty, and fertility. *Biology Review,* 59(2), 161–188.

Frisch, R. E., Wyshak, G., & Vincent L. (1980). Delayed menarche and amenorrhea in ballet dancers. *New England Journal of Medicine,* 303(1), 17–19.

Gaddis, A., & Brooks-Gunn, J. (1985). The male experience of pubertal change. *Journal of Youth and Adolescence,* 14(1), 61–69.

Gargiulo, J., Attie, I., Brooks-Gunn, J., & Warren, M. P. (1987). Dating middle-school girls: Effects of social contest, maturation, and grade. *Developmental Psychology,* 23(5), 730–737.

Garn, S. M. (1980). Continuities and change in maturational timing. In O. Brim & J. Kagan, eds., *Constancy and change in human development.* Cambridge, Mass.: Harvard University Press, pp. 113–162.

Garwood, S. G., & Allen, L. (1979). Self-concept and identified problem difference between pre- and post-menarcheal adolescents. *Journal of Clinical Psychology,* 35, 527–528.

Gay, V. L., & Plant, T. M. (1987). N-methyl-D, L aspartate elicits hypothalamic gonadotropin-releasing hormone release in prepubertal male rhesus monkeys *(Macaca mulatta). Endocrinology,* 120, 2289–96.

Gilligan, C. (1982). *In a different voice.* Cambridge, Mass.: Harvard University Press.

Gjerde, P. F., & Block, J. (1991). Preadolescent antecedents of depressive symptomatology at age 18: A prospective study. *Journal of Youth and Adolescence*, 20(2), 217–232.

Graber, J. A., & Petersen, A., eds. (1991). Cognitive changes at adolescence: Biological perspectives. In K. Gibson & A. C. Petersen, eds., *Brain matruation and cognitive development: Comparative and cross-cultural perspectives (foundations of human behavior)*. New York: Walter de Gruyter.

Greenough, W. T., Black, J. E., & Wallace, C. S. (1987). Experience and brain development. *Child Development*, 58, 539–559.

Grief, E. B., & Ulman, K. J. (1982). The psychological impact of menarche on early adolescent females: A review of the literature. *Child Development*, 53, 1413–30.

Grotevant, H. D., & Cooper, C. R. (1986). Individuation in family relationships. *Human Development*, 29, 82–100.

Growing up and liking it. (1976). Milltown, N. J.: Personal Products.

Grumbach, M. M. (1985). True or central precocious puberty. In D. T. Kriegerr & C. W. Barden, eds., *Current therapy in endocrinology and metabolism*. Philadelphia: B. C. Decker, pp. 4–8.

Grumbach, M. M., & Sizonenko, P. C., eds. (1986). *Control of the onset of puberty*. Vol. 2. New York: Academic Press.

Gunnar, M. A., & Collins, W. A. (1988). *Development during the transitions in adolescence: Minnesota symposia on child psychology*. Vol. 21, Hillsdale, N. J.: Erlbaum.

Hall, G. S. (1904). *Adolescence: Its psychology and its relation to psychology, anthropology, sociology, sex, crime, religion, and education*. Englewood Cliffs, N. J.: Prentice-Hall.

Halmi, K. A. (1980). Eating disorders. In H. I. Kaplan, A. M. Freedom, & B. J. Sadock, eds., *Comprehensive textbook of psychiatry*. Vol. 3. Baltimore: Williams and Wilkins.

Hamburg, B. A. (1974). Coping in early adolescence. In S. Arieti, ed., *American handbook of psychiatry*. 2nd ed. New York: Basic Books, pp. 212–236.

Hamburg, B. A. (1980). Early adolescence as a life stress. In S. Levine and H. Ursin, eds., *Coping and health*. New York: Plenum Press, pp. 121–143.

Hamilton, L. H., Brooks-Gunn, J., Warren, M. P., & Hamilton, W. G. (1988). The role of selectivity in the pathogenesis of eating disorders. *Medicine and Science in Sports and Exercise*, 20(6), 560–565.

Harris Poll. (1988). Report card for parents: When AIDS comes to school. *Children's Magazine*, pp. 1–8.

Harley, G. W. (1941). Notes on the Poro in Liberia. In B. B. Sommer, ed., *Puberty and adolescence*. New York: Oxford University Press, p. 24.

Hayes, C. D., ed. (1987). *Risking the future: Adolescent sexuality, pregnancy, and childbearing*. Vol. 1. Washington, D.C.: National Academy of Sciences Press.

Hill, J. P. (1982). Early adolescence. Special issue. *Child Development*, 53(6).

Hill, J. P. (1988). Adapting to menarche: Familial control and conflict. In M. R. Gunnar & W. A. Collins, eds., *Development during the transition to adolescence*. Vol. 21. Hillsdale, N. J.: Erlbaum, pp. 43–77.

Hill, J. P., & Lynch, M. E. (1983). The intensification of gender-related role expectations during early adolescence. In J. Brooks-Gunn & A. C. Petersen, eds., *Girls at puberty: Biological and psychosocial perspectives*. New York: Plenum, pp. 201–228.

Hofferth, S. L., & Hayes, C. D., eds. (1987). *Risking the future: Adolescent sexuality, pregnancy, and childbearing*. Vol. 2. Washington, D.C.: National Academy of Sciences Press.

Holland, B. A., Haas, D. K., Norman, D., Brant-Zawadzki, M., & Newton, T. H. (1986). MRI of normal brain maturation. *American Journal of Neuroradiology*, 7, 201–208.

Irwin, C., ed. (1987). *New directions for child development*. San Francisco: Jossey-Bass.

Jessor, S. L., & Jessor, R. (1975). Transition from virginity to nonvirginity among youth: A social-psychological study over time. *Developmental Psychology*, 11(4), 473–484.

Jones, E., Forrest, J. D., Henshaw, S. K., Silverman, J., & Torres, A. (1988). Unintended pregnancy, contraceptive practice, and family planning services in developed countries. *Family Planning Perspectives*, 20(2), 53–67.

Josselson, R. L. (1980). Psychodynamic aspects of identity formation in college women. *Journal of Youth and Adolescence*, 2, 3–52.

Kaplan, S. L., Grumbach, M. M., & Aubert M. L. (1976). The ontogenesis of pituitary hormones and hypothalamic factors in the human fetus: Maturation of the central nervous system regulation of anterior pituitary function. *Recent Progress in Hormone Research*, 32, 161–243.

Kirby, D. (1984). *Sexuality education: An evaluation of programs and their effects.* Santa Cruz: Network Publications.

Koff, E., Rierdan, J., & Silverstone, E. (1978). Changes in representation of body image as a function of menarcheal status. *Developmental Psychology,* 14, 635–642.

Kretschmann, H. J., Kammradt, G., Krauthausen, I., Sauer, B., & Wingert, F. (1986). Brain growth in man. *Bibliotheca Anatomica,* 28, 1–26.

Kulin, H. E., Buibo, N., Mutie, D., & Sorter, S. (1982). The effect of chronic childhood malnutrition on pubertal growth and development. *American Journal of Clinical Nutrition,* 36, 527–536.

Laron, Z., Arad, J., Gurewitz, R., Grunebaum, M., & Dickerman, Z. (1980). Age at first conscious ejaculation: A milestone in male puberty. *Helvetica Paediatrica Acta,* 5, 13–20.

Larsen, V. L. (1961). Sources of menstrual information: A comparison of age groups. *Family Life Coordinator,* 10, 41–43.

Lerner, R. M., & Foch, T. T., eds. (1987). *Biological-psychosocial interactions in early adolescence: A life-span perspective.* Hillsdale, N.J.: Erlbaum Associates.

Liestol, K. (1982). Social conditions and menarcheal age: The importance of the early years of life. *Annals of Human Biology,* 9, 521–536.

Linn, M. C., & Petersen, A. C. (1985). Emergence and characterization of sex differences in spatial ability: A meta-analysis. *Child Development,* 56, 1479–98.

Lipsitz, J. (1977). *Growing up forgotten: A review of research and programs concerning young adolescents.* Lexington, Mass.: D. C. Heath.

Magnusson, D., Strattin, H., & Allen, V. L. (1985). Biological maturation and social development: A longitudinal study of some adjustment processes from midadolescence to adulthood. *Journal of Youth and Adolescence,* 14(4), 267–283.

Magnusson, D. (1988). *Individual development from an interactional perspective: A longitudinal study.* Hillsdale, N.J.: Erlbaum.

Malina, R. M. (1983). Menarche in athletes: A synthesis and hypothesis. *Annals of Human Biology,* 10(1), 1–24.

Marsh, R. W. (1985). Phrenoblysis: Real or chimera? *Child Development,* 56, 1059–61.

Marshall, W. A., & Tanner, J. M. (1969). Variations in pattern of pubertal changes in girls. *Archives of Diseases in Childhood,* 44, 291–303.

Marshall, W. A., & Tanner, J. M. (1970). Variations in the pattern of pubertal changes in girls. *Archives of Diseases in Childhood,* 45, 13–23.

McArnery, E. R., & Levine, M., eds. (1987). *Early adolescent transitions.* New York: Health Publications.

McCall, R. B., Meyers, E. C., Jr., Hartman, J., & Roche, A. F. (1983). Developmental changes in head-circumference and mental-performance growth rates: A test of Epstein's hypothesis. *Developmental Psychobiology,* 16, 457–468.

Mead, M. (1935). *Sex and temperment.* New York: William Morrow and Co.

Money, J., & Ehrhardt, A. A. (1972). *Man and woman, boy and girl.* Baltimore: Johns Hopkins University Press.

Morris, N. M., & Udry, J. R. (1980). Validation of a self-administered instrument to assess stage of adolescent development. *Journal of Youth and Adolescence,* 9, 275–276.

Mussen, P. H., & Jones, M. C. (1957). Self-conceptions, motivations, and interpersonal attitudes of late- and early-maturing boys. *Child Development,* 28, 243–256.

Nesselroade, J. R., & Baltes, P. B. (1974). Adolescent personality development and historical change: 1970–1972. *Monographs of the Society for Research in Child Development,* 39(1), ser. no. 154.

Newcombe, N., & Dubas, J. S. (1987). Individual differences in cognitive ability: Are they related to timing of puberty? In R. M. Lerner & T. T. Foch, eds., *Biological-psychosocial interactions in early adolescence.* Hillsdale, N.J.: Erlbaum.

Nolen-Hoeksema, S., Girgus, J. S., & Seligman, M. E. P. (1991). Sex differences in depression and explanatory style in children. *Journal of Youth and Adolescence,* 20(2), 233–246.

Offer, D. (1987). In defense of adolescents. *Journal of the American Medical Association,* 257(24), 3407–8.

Olweus, D. (1984). Stability in aggressive and withdrawal inhibited behavior patterns. In R. Kaplan, V. Konecni, & R. Novaco, eds., *Aggression in children and youth.* Boston: Martinus Nijhoff Publishers, pp. 162–174.

Paige, K. E. (1983). A bargaining theory of menarcheal responses in preindustrial cultures. In J. Brooks-Gunn & A. C. Petersen, eds., *Girls at puberty: Biological and psychosocial perspectives.* New York: Plenum Press, pp. 301–322.

Paikoff, R. L., & Brooks-Gunn, J. (1989). Physiological processes: What role do they play during the transition to adolescence? In R. Montemayor, G. Adams, & T. Gullotta, eds., *Advances in adolescent development.* Vol. 2. *The transition from childhood to adolescence.* Beverly Hills: Sage Publications, pp. 63–81.

Parlee, M. B. (1973). The premenstrual syndrome. *Psychological Bulletin,* 80(6), 454–465.

Peskin, H. (1967). Pubertal onset and ego functioning. *Journal of Abnormal Psychology,* 72, 1–15.

Petersen, A. C. (1983). Pubertal change and cognition. In J. Brooks-Gunn & A. C. Petersen, eds., *Girls at puberty: Biological and psychosocial perspectives.* New York: Plenum, pp. 179–198.

Petersen, A. C. (1987). The nature of biological-psychosocial interactions: The sample case of early adolescence. In R. M. Lerner & T. T. Foch, eds., *Biological-psychosocial interactions in early adolescence: A lifespan perspective.* Hillsdale, N.J.: Erlbaum, pp. 35–61.

Petersen, A. C. (1988). Adolescent development. In M. R. Rosenzweig, ed., *Annual review of psychology.* Palo Alto: Annual Reviews, pp. 583–607.

Petersen, A. C., & Crockett, L. (1985). Pubertal timing and grade effects on adjustment. *Journal of Youth and Adolescence,* 14(3), 191–206.

Plant, T. M. (1986). Gonadal regulation of hypothalamic-gonadotropin releasing hormone release in primates. *Endocrine Review,* 7, 75–88.

Plant, T. M. (1988). Puberty in primates. In E. Knobil and J. Neill, eds., *The Physiology of Reproduction.* Vol. 2, New York: Raven Press, pp. 1763–88.

Pratt, D. I., Finkelstein, J. S., O'Dey, St. L., Badger, T. M., Rau, P. N., Campbell, J. D., & Crowley, W. F. (1986). Long-term administration of gonadotropin-releasing hormones in men with idiopathic hypogonadotropic hypogonadism. *Annals of Internal Medicine,* 105, 848–855.

Puig-Antich, J. (1987). Affective disorders in children and adolescents: Diagnosis validity and psychobiology. In H. Meltzer, ed., *Psychopharmacology: The third generation of progress.* New York: Raven Press.

Rabinowicz, T. (1986). The differentiated maturation of the cerebral cortex. In F. Falkner & J. M. Tanner, eds., *Human growth: A comprehensive treatise.* Vol. 2. New York: Plenum, pp. 385–410.

Reiter, E. O. (1987). Neuroendocrine control process: Pubertal onset and progression. *Journal of Adolescent Health Care,* 8, 479–491.

Reiter, E. O., & Grumbach, M. M. (1982). Neuroendocrine control mechanisms and the onset of puberty. *Annual Review of Physiology,* 44, 595–613.

Robins, L. N. (1966). *Deviant children grown up: A sociological and psychiatric study of sociopathic personality.* Baltimore: Williams and Wilkins.

Ruble, D. N., & Brooks-Gunn, J. (1979). Menstrual symptoms: A social cognitive analysis. *Journal of Behavioral Medicine,* 2, 171–194.

Ruble, D. N., & Brooks-Gunn, J. (1982). The experience of menarche. *Child Development,* 53, 1557–66.

Rutter, M.; Graham, P.; Chadwick, O. F.; & Yule, W. (1976). Adolescent turmoil: Fact or fiction. *Journal of Child Psychology and Psychiatry,* 17, 35–56.

Shipman, G. (1971). The psychodynamics of sex education. In R. E. Muuss, ed., *Adolescent behavior and society: A book of readings.* New York: Random House, pp. 326–336.

Shulman, A. K. (1976). *Memoirs of an ex-prom queen.* New York: Bantam Books.

Simmons, R. G., & Blyth, D. A. (1987). *Moving into adolescence: The impact of pubertal change and school context.* New York: Aldine-De Gruyter.

Simmons, R. G., Blyth, D. A., & Mckinney, K. L. (1983). The social and psychological effects of puberty on white females. In J. Brooks-Gunn & A. C. Petersen, eds., *Girls at puberty: Biological and psychosocial perspectives.* New York: Plenum, pp. 229–272.

Simmons, R. G., Burgeson, R., & Reef, M. J. (1988). Cumulative change at entry to adolescence. In M. A. Gunnar & W. A. Collins, eds., *Development during transition to adolescence: Minnesota symposia on child psychology.* Vol. 21. Hillsdale, N.J.: Erlbaum, pp. 123–147.

Sisk, C. L., & Bronson, F. H. (1986). Effects of food restriction and restoration on gonadotropin and growth hormone secretion in immature female rats. *Biological Reproduction,* 35, 554–561.

Smetana, J. G. (1988). Concepts of self and social convention: Adolescents' and parents' reasoning about hypothetical and actual family conflicts. In M. A. Gunnar & W. A. Collins. eds., *Development during transition to adolescence: Minnesota symposia on child psychology.* Vol. 21. Hillsdale, N.J.: Erlbaum, pp. 79–119.

Steinberg, L. (1988). Reciprocal relation between parent-child distance and pubertal maturation. *Developmental Psychology,* 24(1), 122–128.

Steinberg, L. D., & Hill, J. P. (1978). Patterns of family interaction as a function of age, the onset of puberty, and formal thinking. *Developmental Psychology,* 14, 683–684.

Steiner, R. A., Cameron, J. L., McNeill, T. H., et al. (1983). Metabolic signals for the onset of puberty. In R. L. Norman, ed., *Neuroendocrine aspects of reproduction.* New York: Academic Press, pp. 183–227.

Stunkard, A. J., Sorensen, T. I. A., Hanis, D., Teasdale, T. W., Chakraborty, R., Schull, W. J., & Schulsinger, F. (1986). An adoption study of obesity. *New England Journal of Medicine,* 314, 193–198.

Susman, E. J., Inoff-Germain, G., Nottelmann, E. D., Loriaux, D. L., Cutler, G. B., & Chrousos, G. P. (1987). Hormones, emotional dispositions, and aggressive attributes in young adolescents. *Child Development,* 58, 1114–34.

Tanner, J. M. (1962). *Growth at adolescence.* New York: Lippincott.

Tanner, J. M. (1981). *A history of the study of human growth.* Cambridge: Cambridge University Press.

Tanner, J. M., & Davies, P. S. W. (1985). Clinical longitudinal standards for height and height velocity for North American children. *Journal of Pediatrics,* 107, 317–329.

Tanner, J. M., Whitehouse, R. H., & Takaishi, M. (1966). Standards from birth to maturity for height, weight, height velocity, and weight velocity: British children, 1965. *Archives of Disease in Childhood,* 41, 454–471, 613–635.

Thatcher, R. W., Walker, R. A., & Giudice, S. (1987). Human cerebral hemispheres develop at different rates and ages. *Science,* 236, 1110–13.

Thornberry, O. T., Wilson, R. W., & Golden, P. (1986). Health promotion and disease prevention provisional data from the National Health Interview Survey: United States, January–June 1985. *Vital and Health Statistics of the National Center for Health Statistics,* 119, 1–16.

Udry, J. R., Richard, L. T., & Morris, N. M. (1986). Biosocial foundations for adolescent female sexuality. *Demography,* 23(2) 217–230.

Udry, J. R., Billy, J. O., Morris, N. M., Groff, T. R., & Raj, M. H. (1985). Serum androgenic hormones motivate sexual behavior in adolescent boys. *Fertility and Sterility,* 43(1), 90–94.

Waber, D. P. (1976). Sex differences in cognition: A function of maturation rate? *Science,* 192, 572–574.

Waber, D. P. (1977). Sex differences in mental abilities, hemisphere lateralization, and rate of physical growth at adolescence. *Developmental Psychology,* 13, 29–38.

Warren, M. (1980). The effects of exercise on pubertal progression and reproductive function in girls. *Journal of Clinical Endocrinology and Metabolism,* 51, 1150–57.

Warren, M. P. (1985). When weight loss accompanies amenorrhea. *Contemporary Obstetrics and Gynecology,* 28(3), 588–597.

Warren, M. P., Brooks-Gunn, J., Hamilton, L. H., Hamilton, W. G., & Warren, L. F. (1986). Scoliosis and fractures in young ballet dancers: Relation to delayed menarche and secondary amenorrhea. *New England Journal of Medicine,* 314, 1348–53.

Weideger, P. (1975). *Menstruation and menopause.* New York: Knopf.

Wooley, S. C., & Wooley, O. W. (1985). Intensive outpatient and residential treatment for bulimia. In D. M. Garner & P. E. Garfinkel, eds., *Handbook of psychotherapy for anorexia nervosa and bulimia.* New York: Guilford Press, pp. 391–430.

Zindel, P. (1971). *My darling, my hamburger.* New York: Bantam.

3

The American Child and Other Cultural Inventions

WILLIAM KESSEN

THE THEME OF the child as a cultural invention can be recognized in several intellectual and social occasions. Ariès' (1962) commentary on the discovery and transformation of childhood has become common knowledge; there is an agitated sense that American children are being redefined by the present times (Lasch, 1978); there is a renewed appreciation of the complexity of all our children (Keniston, 1977); and ethnographic and journalistic reports tell us of the marvelous departures from our own ways of seeing children that exist in other lands (Kessen, 1975). In simple fact, we have recently seen a shower of books on childish variety across cultures and across the hierarchies of class and race.

We could have just as readily discovered commanding evidence of the shifting nature of childhood by a close look at our own history. Consider just three messages drawn haphazardly from the American past. To the parents of the late 18th century:

> The first duties of Children are in great measure mechanical: an obedient Child makes a Bow, comes and goes, speaks, or is silent, just as he is bid, before he knows any other Reason for so doing than that he is bid. (Nelson, 1753).

Or to our parents and grandparents:

> The rule that parents should not play with their children may seem hard but it is without doubt a safe one. (West, 1914)

Or hear a parent of the 1970s speak of her 6-year-old:

> LuAnn liked the school in California best—the only rules were no chemical additives in the food and no balling in the hallways. (Rothchild & Wolf, 1976)

And we cannot escape the implications of an unstable portrait of the child by moving from folk psychology to the professional sort. On the contrary, a clear-eyed study of what experts have said about the young—from Locke to Skinner, from Rousseau to Piaget, from

Comenius to Erikson—will expose as bewildering a taxonomy as the one provided by preachers, parents, and poets. No other animal species has been cataloged by responsible scholars in so many wildly discrepant forms, forms that a perceptive extraterrestrial could never see as reflecting the same beast.

To be sure, most expert students of children continue to assert the truth of the positivistic dream—that we have not yet found the underlying structural simplicities that will reveal the child entire, that we have not yet cut nature at the joints—but it may be wise for us child psychologists in the International Year of the Child to peer into the abyss of the positivistic nightmare—that the child is essentially and eternally a cultural invention and that the variety of the child's definition is not the removable error of an incomplete science. For not only are American *children* shaped and marked by the larger cultural forces of political maneuverings, practical economics, and implicit ideological commitments (a new enough recognition), *child psychology* is itself a peculiar cultural invention that moves with the tidal sweeps of the larger culture in ways that we understand at best dimly and often ignore.

To accept the ambiguity of our task—to give up debates about the fundamental nature of the child—is not, however, a defeatist or unscientific move. Rather, when we seriously confront the proposition that we, like the children we study, are cultural inventions, we can go on to ask questions about the sources of our diversity and, perhaps more tellingly, about the sources of our agreements. It is surely remarkable that against the background of disarray in our definition of the child, a number of ideas are so widely shared that few scholars question their provenance and warrant. Paradoxically, the unexamined communalities of our commitment may turn out to be more revealing than our disagreements. Within the compass of the next several pages, I point toward disagreements that were present at the beginnings of systematic child study, and then turn in more detail to the pervasive and shared themes of American childhood in our time, themes that may require a more critical review than we have usually given them.

PRESENT AT THE BIRTH

When child psychology was born, in a longish parturition that ran roughly from Hall's first questionary studies of 1880 (Hall, 1883) to Binet's test of construction of 1905 (Binet & Simon, 1916), there were five determining spirits present. Four of them are familiar to us all; the fifth and least visible spirit may turn out to be the most significant. One of the familiars was in the line of Locke and Bain, and it appeared later for Americans as John Broadus Watson; the line has, then and now, represented behavior, restraint, clarity, simplicity, and good news. Paired in philosophical and theoretical opposition was the spirit that derived from Rousseau, Nietzsche, and Freud, the line that represented mind, impulse, ambiguity, complexity, and bad news. The great duel between the two lines has occupied students of children for just under 300 years.

The third magus at the beginning was the most fully American; Williams James can stand as the representative of the psychologists whose central concern was with sensation, perception, language, thought, and will—the solid, sensible folk who hid out in the years between the World Wars but who have returned in glory. It is of at least passing interest to note that the cognitivists participated lightly in the early development of child study; James and, even more, Munsterberg and, past all measure, Titchener found results from the study of children too messy for the precision they wanted from their methods.

The godfather of child psychology, the solidest spirit of them all, was Charles Darwin, foreshadowing his advocates and his exaggerators. His contemporary stand-in, G. Stanley Hall, was the first in a long and continuing line that has preached from animal analogues, has called attention to the biological in the child, and has produced a remarkably diverse progeny that includes Galton, Gesell, and the ethologists.

I rehearse (and oversimplify) the story of our professional beginnings to call attention to how persistent the lines have been, how little they have interpenetrated and modified one another, and how much their contributions to our understanding of the child rest on a network of largely implicit and undefended assumptions about the basis of human knowledge, social structures, and ethical ascriptions. The lines of the onlooking spirits are themselves historical and cultural constructions that grew, in ways that have rarely been studied analytically or biographically, from the matrix of the larger contemporaneous culture.[1]

And so to the fifth circumnatal spirit, the one that knew no technical psychology. In the middle 50 years of the 19th century, the years that prepared the United States for child psychology, dramatic and persistent changes took place in American society. I could sing the familiar litany of urbanization, industrialization, the arrival of the first millions of European immigrants (another strand of diversity among children that requires a closer look). We know that the Civil War transformed the lives of most American families, white and black (although we still know remarkably little about the daily lives of children during and after the war). The United States developed, and *developed* is the word of choice, from an isolated agricultural dependency to an aggressive and powerful state. Technology and science joined the industrial entrepreneurs to persuade the new Americans, from abroad and from the farm, that poverty was an escapable condition if one worked hard enough and was aggressively independent. But there were other changes that bore more immediately on the lives of American children; let me, as an example of cultural influences on children and child psychology rather than as a worked-through demonstration of my thesis, extract three interwoven strands of the changes that touched children.

The first, and the earliest, was the evolving separation of the domain of work from the domain of home. When women left or were excluded from the industrial work force in the 1830s and 1840s, the boundary marked by the walls of home became less and less penetrable. First for the white, the urban, the middle-class, the northeastern American, but enlisting other parts of the community as time went on, work (or *real work* as contrasted with *homework*, the activity of women and schoolchildren) was carried on in specialized spaces by specialized people, and home became the place where one (i.e., men) did not work (Cott, 1977; Lasch, 1977).

The second and entailed change was the radical separation of what a man was from what a woman was. Colonial and early Federal society, like all other cultures, had stable and divergent visions of the proper sphere of male and female. But in the half century under our present consideration, something of a moral metamorphosis occurred in the United States (and in large measure, in England, too) and one of modern history's most eccentric arrangements of human beings was put in place. The public world of men was seen as ugly, aggressive, corrupting, chaotic, sinful (not an altogether regretted characteristic), and irreligious. The increasingly private world of women was, in inevitable antithesis, sweet, chaste, calm, cultured, loving, protective, and godly. The muscular Christianity of the Mathers and Edwardses became the feminized Christianity of matrons and pastors; the caretaking of culture became the task of women's groups (Douglas, 1978). So dramatic a statement of the contrast is hardly an exaggeration of the facts. And the full story remains to be told; historians of medical practice, for example, are just beginning to reveal the systematic attempt to desex American and British women in the 19th century with methods that ranged from sermons to surgery (Barker-Benfield, 1977).

The third change in American life that set the cultural context for child psychology followed on the first two. Children continued to be cared for by women at home, and in consequence, they took on the coloration of mother, hearth, and heaven. The early American child, who was told, "consider that you may perish as young as you are; there are small Chips as well as great Logs, in the Fire of Hell" (18th-century primer, quoted by Johnson, 1904), became Little Eva, Huckleberry Finn, and eventually Peter Pan. The sentimentalization of children—caught for tombstones and psychology books best by Wordsworth's "Heaven lies about us in our infancy!"—had implications for family structure, education, and the definition of the child in expert writings that we have not yet, nearing the end of the 20th century, fully understood or confronted.

Thus it was that American child psychology began not only under the conflicting attention of Locke, Rousseau, James, and Darwin, but with the progressivist, sexist, and sentimental expectation of the larger culture standing by.

THE COMMON THEMES OF AMERICAN CHILD PSYCHOLOGY

Are we now free of our origins? It would be both unhistorical and undevelopmental to believe so, in spite of all we have learned about research and about children over the last 100 years. The positivist promise of pure objectivity and eternal science has been withdrawn. Therefore, it may be methodologically therapeutic to glance, however briefly, at several common themes of our field that seem dependent, in the usually complicated way of human history, on the story I have sketched thus far. All of the themes may be ready for a thoughtful new evaluation.

The Commitment to Science and Technology

The notable success of the physical sciences in the 19th century, the elation that followed on the Darwinian revolution, and the culture's high hopes for a technological utopia joined at the end of the 19th century to define child psychology as scientific and rational. The vagaries of casual stories about children, the eccentricities of folk knowledge, and the superstitions of grandmothers were all to be cleansed by the mighty brush of scientific method (Jacoby, 1914; Watson, 1928). The conviction that we are scientists remains one of the heart beliefs of child psychology, and in its humane and sensible forms, the commitment to a systematic analytic examination of the lives of children and their worlds is still the unique and continuing contribution of child psychology to American culture.

But some less obvious and perhaps less defensible consequences of the rational scientific commitment were pulled along into child psychology by the high hopes of its founders. Perhaps the one that we have had the most difficulty in handling as a profession is the implication *in all theories of the child* that lay folk, particularly parents, are in need of expert guidance. Critical examination and study of parental practices and child behavior almost inevitably slipped subtly over to advice about parental practices and child behavior. The scientific statement became an ethical imperative, the descriptive account became normative. And along the way, there have been unsettling occasions in which scraps of knowledge, gathered by whatever procedures were held to be proper science at the time, were given inordinate weight against poor old defenseless folk knowledge. Rigorously scheduled feedings of infants, separation of new mothers from their babies, and Mrs. West's injunction against playing with children can stand as examples of scientism that are far enough away not to embarrass us enlightened moderns.

More, I risk the guess that the sentimental view of the child that prevailed at the beginnings of child psychology—a vision which, let it be said, made possible humane and appropriate reforms in the treatment of children—was strongly influential in what can only be called a salvationist view of children. Child psychologists, again whatever their theoretical stripe, have taken the Romantic notion of childish innocence and openness a long way toward the several forms of "If only we could make matters right with the child, the world would be a better place." The child became the carrier of political progressivism and the optimism of reformers. From agitation for child labor reform in the 1890s to Head Start, American children have been saviors of the nation. The romantic inheritance of purity and perfectibility may, in fact, have misled us about the proper unit of developmental study and about the major forces influencing human growth and change. I will return to the consideration of our unit of study shortly.

There has often also been a socially hierarchical message in our scientific-normative interactions with the larger culture. Tolstoy said that there is no proletarian literature; there has been no proletarian child psychology either, and the ethically imperative forms of child psychology, our messages to practice, have ranged from pleas for equitable treatment of all children to recipes for forced assimilation to the expected forms of child behavior. Once a descriptive norm has been established, it is an antique cultural principle to urge adherence to it.

Finally, for some eras of child study, there has been an enthusiastic anticipation that all problems are reducible by the science of the moment; intellectual technology can succeed (and imitate) the 19th century's commercial and industrial technology in the progressive and ultimate betterment of humankind. The optimism of the founders of child study and their immediate successors is dimmer today— "The sky's the limit" may be replaced by "You win a few, you lose a few"—and serious questions have been posed even for the basic assumptions underlying the scientific analysis of human behavior (Barrett, 1978). Child psychology may soon have to face anew the question of whether or not a scientific account of human development can be given without bringing in its wake the false claims of scientism and the arrogance of an ethic based on current findings.

The Importance of Mothers, Early Experience, and Personal Responsibility

Strangely at odds with the theme of rational scientific inquiry has been the persistence of the commitment to home and mother in otherwise varying portraits of the child. Some child psychologists have been less than laudatory about the effectiveness of particular mothering procedures (Watson dedicated his directive book on child rearing to the first mother who raises a child successfully), but critics and praisers alike have rarely doubted the basic principle that children need home and mother to grow as they should grow (again, the normative injunction enters). I do not mean to dispute the assumption here; I want only to suggest its connection with the mid-19th-century ideology that long preceded systematic child psychology and to point out several riders on the assumption that have, in the past, been less vividly visible.

Two riders on the home-and-mother position are under active debate and study nowadays—the irrelevance of fathers and the critical role of early experience. The cases represent with the starkness of a line drawing the influence of contemporaneous cultural forces on the definition of psychology's child. It would be difficult to defend the proposition that the recent interest in the place of fathers or the possibilities of out-of-home child rearing grew either from a new theory of development or from striking new empirical discoveries. Rather, for reasons too elaborate to explore here, fewer and fewer American women have been willing or able to devote all of their work time to the rearing of children. It will be instructive to see how much the tasks assigned fathers and day-care centers reflect the old ascriptions to essential maternity. Psychology follows culture, but often at a discreet distance.

The blending of new social requirements into old ideology is precisely demonstrated by the incorporation of fathers and day-care workers into the premise that what happens to the child in the first hours, weeks, months of life holds an especially determining position in human development. Proclaimed on epistemological grounds by Locke, gathered into the American ethos in part because it so well fit the perfectionist argument, elevated to scientific status by evolutionary theory, the doctrine of the primacy of early experience has been an uncontested part of American culture and American child psychology throughout the history of both. Only in the last several years has the premise been called seriously into question (Kagan, Kearsley, & Zelazo, 1978) and, even then, at a time when ever more extravagant claims are being made about the practical necessity of safeguarding the child's first hours (Klaus & Kennell, 1976).

The assumption of essential maternity and the assumption of the determining role of early experience join to support yet another underdebated postulate of child psychology. If something goes wrong in the course of a child's development, it is the primary responsibility of the mother (or whoever behaves as mother), and once more in echo of the salvationist view, if a social problem is not repaired by modification of the child's first years, the problem is beyond repair. The working of the postulate has produced ways of blaming mothers that appear in all theoretical shapes and, more generally, ways of blaming other victims of social injustice because they are not readily transformed by the ministrations of the professionals (Ryan, 1971).

The tendency to assign personal responsibility for the successes and failures of development is an amalgam of the positivistic search for causes, of the older Western tradition of personal moral responsibility, and of the conviction that personal mastery and consequent personal responsibility are first among the goals of child rearing. It is difficult to imagine an American child psychology without a core commitment to the proposition that someone is responsible for what happens in the course of development.

The Belief in the Individual and Self-Contained Child
Hovering over each of the traditional beliefs mentioned thus far is the most general and, in my view, the most fundamental entanglement of technical child psychology with the implicit commitments of American culture. The child—like the Pilgrim, the cowboy, and the detective on television—is invariably seen as a free-standing isolable being who moves

through development as a self-contained and complete individual. Other similarly self-contained people—parents and teachers—may influence the development of children, to be sure, but the proper unit of cultural analysis and the proper unit of developmental study is the child alone. The ubiquity of such radical individualism in our lives makes the consideration of alternative images of childhood extraordinarily difficult. We have never taken fully seriously the notion that development is, in large measure, a social construction, the child a modulated and modulating component in a shifting network of influences (Berger & Luckmann, 1966). The seminal thinkers about children over the past century have, in fact, been almost undeviating in their postulation of the child as container of self and of psychology. Impulses are in the child; traits are in the child; thoughts are in the child; attachments are in the child. In short, almost every major theory of development accepts the premises of individualism and takes the child as the basic unit of study, with all consequences the choice has for decisions that range from selecting a method of research to selecting a therapeutic maneuver.

Uniform agreement on the isolable child as the proper measure of development led to the research paradigms that have dominated child psychology during most of its history; basically, we have observed those parts of development that the child could readily transport to our laboratories or to our testing sites. The use of isolated preparations for the study of development has, happily, been productive of remarkable advances in our knowledge of children, but with the usual cost of uniform dogma, the commitment to the isolable child has occasionally led child psychology into exaggerations and significant omissions.

There are signals now aloft that the dogma of individualism, both in its claim of life-long stability of personality and in its claim that human action can be understood without consideration of context or history, is under severe stress. The story that Vygotsky (1978) told 50 years ago, the story of the embeddedness of the developing mind in society, has finally been heard. The image of the child as an epigenetic and continuous creation of social and biological contexts is far more ambiguous and more difficult to paint than the relative simplicities of the traditional and culturally justified self-contained child; it may also illuminate our understanding of children and of our science.

THE PRESENT MOMENT

The cultural epigenesis that created the American child of the late 20th century continues, and so does the epigenesis that created child psychology. Necessarily, there is no end of the road, no equilibrium. Rather, the transformations of the past 100 years in both children and child psychology are a startling reminder of the eternal call on us to be scrupulous observers and imaginative researchers; they may also serve to force our self-critical recognition that we are both creators and performers in the cultural invention of the child.

NOTE

1. It has become a cliché to speak of psychoanalysis as an out-growth of Jewish intellectual culture in turn-of-the-century Vienna (a shallow summary at best), but no corresponding common saying exists for, say, Watson's growing up in postwar Carolina, or Hall's curious combination of *odium sexicum* and *odium theologicum* in Victorian times, or Binet's history as an apostate continental associationist.

REFERENCES

Ariès, P. *Centuries of childhood*: *A social history of family life* (R. Baldick, Trans.). New York: Knopf, 1962.

Barker-Benfield, G. J. *Horrors of the half-known life*. New York: Harper & Row, 1977.

Barrett, W. *The illusion of technique*. Garden City, N.Y.: Doubleday, 1978.

Berger, P. L., & Luckmann, T. *The social construction of reality*: *A treatise in the sociology of knowledge*. Garden City, N.Y.: Doubleday, 1966.

Binet, A., & Simon, T. Upon the necessity of establishing a scientific diagnosis of inferior states of intelligence (E. S. Kite, Trans.). In A. Binet & T. Simon, *The development of intelligence in children*. Baltimore, Md.: Williams & Wilkins, 1916. (Originally published, 1905.)

Cott, N. F. *Bonds of womanhood*: *Women's sphere in New England, 1780–1835*. New Haven, Conn.: Yale University Press, 1977.

Douglas, A. *The feminization of American culture*. New York: Avon Books, 1978.

Hall, G. S. The contents of children's minds. *Princeton Review*, 1883, *11*, 249–272.

Jacoby, G. W. *Child training as an exact science: A treatise based upon the principles of modern psychology, normal and abnormal*. New York: Funk & Wagnalls, 1914.

Johnson, C. *Old-time schools and schoolbooks*. New York: Macmillan, 1904.

Kagan, J., Kearsley, R. B., & Zelazo, P. R. (With the assistance of C. Minton). *Infancy*: *Its place in human development*. Cambridge, Mass.: Harvard University Press, 1978.

Keniston, K., & Carnegie Council on Children. *All our children*: *The American family under pressure*. New York: Harcourt Brace Jovanovich, 1977.

Kessen, W. (Ed.). *Childhood in China*. New Haven, Conn.: Yale University Press, 1975.

Klaus, M. H., & Kennell, J. H. *Maternal-infant bonding*. Saint Louis: Mosby, 1976.

Lasch, C. *Haven in a heartless world*: *The family besieged*. New York: Basic Books, 1977.

Lasch, C. *The culture of narcissism*: *American life in an age of diminishing expectations*. New York: Norton, 1978.

Nelson, J. *An essay on the government of children under three general heads*: *Viz., health, manners, and education*. London: (no publisher), 1753.

Rothchild, J., & Wolf, S. B. *The children of the counterculture*. Garden City, N.Y.: Doubleday, 1976.

Ryan, W. *Blaming the victim*. New York: Random House, 1971.

Vygotsky, L. S. *Mind in society*: *The development of higher psychological processes* (M. Cole, V. John-Steiner, S. Scribner, & E. Souberman, Eds.). Cambridge, Mass.: Harvard University Press, 1978.

Watson, J. B. *Psychological care of infant and child*. New York: Norton, 1928.

West, M. *Infant care* (Publication No. 8). Washington, D.C.: U.S. Children's Bureau, 1914.

4

"Teaching Our Sons"

Gail Bederman

HALL'S NEW MASTER NARRATIVE: RECAPITULATION THEORY

In the late nineteenth century, recapitulation theory was scientific orthodoxy among most American biologists. Medelian genetic theory was not known, even to most embryologists, until about 1900. Instead, scientists believed in Lamarck's theory that acquired traits could be inherited. Recapitulation theory provided scientists with a persuasive explanation of the mechanism by which an individual offspring could inherit its parents' learned traits. An individual would follow the developmental path its forebears took. Its ontogeny would recapitulate its phylogeny. As a child or young animal matured, it precisely repeated the evolutionary path its ancestors had taken, from the most distant protozoan upward. Thus, a human embryo could be seen to develop gills and would gradually ascend the evolutionary ladder. The newest advanced evolutionary traits, developed by the child's parents or grandparents, were simply added on at the very end of the child's growth period. Thus, human evolution could be consciously aided by making certain that each generation of boys was developed to its highest potential, so that this generation, in turn, could pass its racial improvement on to its sons.[1]

Advanced intelligence was the highest, final evolutionary development, and it came last, in adolescence. However, it could only come to members of advanced races whose forebears had ascended to the top of the evolutionary ladder, and thus added the most advanced stage to the end of their particular phylogenetic path. Scientists believed that until adolescence, Negro children were often as bright or brighter than white children. At adolescence, however, Negro children stopped developing, because their ancestors had never gone on to evolve a higher intelligence. Black adults were believed to be roughly as intelligent as Anglo-Saxon children, precisely because their intellectual development stopped in the evolutionary stage corresponding to white childhood. Hall was in the best scientific company, then, in believing that white children were the evolutionary equivalents of "primitive" savages.[2]

Although some historians have spoken of recapitulation theory as if it were metaphoric, the big distinction between recapitulation theory and previous notions of primitive immaturity is recapitulation theory's absolute literalness. Recapitulation theory held that children actually, physically relived the adult development of their primitive ancestors. From at least the sixteenth century, advocates of hierarchical rankings like the Great Chain of

Being had written of "lesser races" as if they were children, but they rarely argued that nonwhites actually had children's morphological traits. Colonial New Englanders, for example, had believed that children had primitive, animalistic urges which needed to be tamed, just as wild animals or Indians needed to be tamed. According to recapitulation theory, however, children were not merely metaphoric savages; their somatic makeup made children physically recapitulate primitive evolutionary stages. You could no more train a child to perform tasks evolutionarily beyond him than you could train an adult savage. Both had the same biological capacity, because both were at the same evolutionary level. Following this logic, one must not only give up the idea of racial egalitarianism as unscientific—after all, lower races literally were children compared to whites—one must also recognize that children acted "savage," not because they were bad or willful, but because that was their nature at that stage of evolution.[3]

Although Hall was not the first to use recapitulation theory to link child study to the study of savages, his recapitulation-based theories were surely among the most ambitious. He believed that by applying Darwinism to the study of human development, he could do for psychology what Darwin had done for biology: he could bring psychology out of the rigid formal categories of the nineteenth century and make it more dynamic.[4]

It is impossible to overstate how literally Hall applied recapitulation theory to his theories of psychology and education. For him, the key to understanding child nature was to recognize that children grew up repeating the actual psychological experiences of their primitive adult ancestors. Child development, down to the most specific detail, could be explained by looking for correlations in the distant evolutionary past. For example, he suggested that modern children's tendency to pick scabs stemmed from their primitive ancestors' propensity to pick lice.[5] Civilized children laughed at human pain, even at death, because they were like men in primitive times, when one person's death meant more food for the rest.[6] Children feared animals with big teeth, big eyes, and rough fur because, only recently, their savage ancestors had been eaten by such creatures.[7] These examples could be multiplied almost indefinitely.[8] Hall even suggested that anthropologists should extrapolate from studies of civilized children to reconstruct the cultures of lost primitive races.[9] For example, he believed that the relative independence of modern children eight to twelve years old corresponded to a lost primitive "pigmoid" race, "when in a warm climate the young of our species once shifted for themselves independently of further parental aid."[10] Just as studying primitive savages could explain child development, so studying modern children could provide knowledge about lost stages and "missing links" in human evolutionary history.

Yet Hall's interest in recapitulation theory was more than scholarly. Hall believed his psychology was the basis of a practical pedagogy which would solve the neurasthenic paradox by building powerful manhood out of the primitive impulses of young boys. Hall described two ways that educators could build young boys into powerful men. First, by taking advantage of little boys' natural reliving of their ancestors' primitive evolutionary history, educators could "inoculate" them against the weakness of excessive civilization. Second, by taking advantage of the flood of inherited primitive traits which crowded in on young men at sexual puberty, educators could move them closer to being the "super-man." And, as valuable as this primal manhood would be for individual men, Hall believed more was at stake, here, than personal male power. By shoring up the collective masculine power of the civilized races, Hall believed he could not only save civilization from degenerating; he could help move civilization toward a millennial perfection.

LEADING AMERICAN MEN TOWARD A MORE PERFECT CIVILIZATION: THE SAVAGE BOY AS "A PILLAR OF SMOKE BY DAY, AND FIRE BY NIGHT"

Deeply ambivalent about manly self-restraint, Hall still believed in the manly power which stemmed from an iron will and a strong character. Yet in the light of the neurasthenic paradox, self-restraint seemed to stem less from an iron will than from a paucity of nervous force. Even the masculine passions their own grandfathers had safely enjoyed exhausted neurasthenic modern man. Men could no longer drink, love, or fight without suffering nervous exhaustion. Passion—sexual or otherwise—became the issue for Hall. It was both deeply desirable and dangerous. It made for manliness but could unman a neurasthenic. Hall began to look for ways to revitalize passionate and powerful manhood within advanced civilization.

Recapitulation theory allowed Hall to suggest ways to rear men with the strength to be both highly civilized and deeply passionate. The key was to take advantage of recapitulation and small boys' natural reliving of their ancestors' primitive emotionality. Children's "instincts and feelings ... are reverberations from the remote ancestral past."[11] Civilized boys, unlike their fathers, still had access to the powerful emotions of their savage ancestors. By fully reliving their ancestors' vibrant passions, Hall suggested, little boys could incorporate a primitive's emotional strength into their adult personalities.[12]

Hall eloquently described this problem of overcivilized male passionlessness in 1903. In "our day and civilization," he lamented, "the hot life of feeling is remote and decadent. Culture represses, and intellect saps its root. The very word passion is becoming obsolete." What could civilized men, with their overdeveloped intellects and their weak and neurasthenic bodies, know of primitive passions, "of hate that makes men mad or bestial, of love that is not only uncalculating but is stronger than life, of fear that shakes the pulses and courage that faces death in its cruelest forms unflinchingly, of the wager of battle where men fight beasts or each other with teeth and knives and spitting revolvers, of torture, of joy that threatens sanity?" Lost was the passion which moved barbarians to fight "with teeth and knives and spitting revolvers." Men's hearts were "parched and bankrupt," and their "refined sensibilities" undermined their manhood.[13]

Yet just when the "hot life of feeling" seemed lost to civilized men forever, racial recapitulation restored it to them. Civilized men could rediscover their lost passions in the primitive emotions of their sons: "Happily for our craft, the child appears at the truly psychological moment, freighted as it is, body and soul, with reminiscences of what we were so fast losing. It is abandoned to joy, grief, passion, fear and rage. It is bashful, shows off, weeps, laughs, desires, is curious, eager, regrets and swells with passion, not knowing that these last two are especially outlawed by our guild." "Freighted body and soul" with "reminiscences" of the evolutionary past, children became men's safe island of primitive passion in civilization. "Despite our lessening fecundity, our over-schooling, city-fication and spoiling, the affections we instill and the repressions we practice, they are still the light and hope of the world."[14]

Children's primitivism was "the light and hope" of the overcivilized world, not only because they were the next generation but because children's reliving of their evolutionary past provided an unfailing guide toward man's true evolutionary destiny. Here, Hall was drawing on the millennial subtext inherent in "civilization." To nineteenth-century Americans, "the advancement of civilization" always connoted a secularized version of

Protestant millennialism: as the most civilized races advanced, they grew ever closer to human perfection on earth, ever closer to the highest evolutionary destiny.[15] Hall believed that racial recapitulation allowed psychologists to study the trajectory of this natural evolution toward human perfection, from the savage past toward the glorious future.

Child development thus had an oracular function, which Hall likened to the biblical image of God leading the children of Israel out of Egypt. Just as God had taken the form of a pillar of smoke by day and a pillar of fire by night for the Israelites journeying toward the promised land, so he had provided racial recapitulation as an infallible guide for man's evolutionary journey toward racial perfection. "Childhood and youth in their best impulses of development are not perverse but point more infallibly than anything else to the constant pole of human destiny. *Das ewige Kindliche* [the eternal child] is now taking its place beside, if not in some respects above, *Das ewige Weibliche* [the eternal feminine] as man's pillar of smoke by day and fire by night to lead him on."[16] Victorian society had revered the eternal feminine as the source of religion and morality. As Hall saw it, however, Victorian feminized religion had grown effeminate and empty.[17] The eternal child was a far surer source of a higher morality because he was rooted in the holy truths of evolution. The eternal child—eternal both in the divine truths he held and in the evolutionary trajectory he embodied—could become "man's pillar of cloud by day and fire by night" to lead him out of his overcivilized wilderness and into the promised land of racial advancement and powerful manhood.

Yet the most perfect civilization and the highest racial perfection could never be attained if civilized men remained weak and neurasthenic. Here Hall's interest in the savage little boy became a matter of practical pedagogy. By encouraging small boys to embrace their primitive passions instead of repressing them, educators could "inoculate" boys with the primitive strength they would need to avoid developing neurasthenia. As adults they could be safely civilized, refined, and cultured—but only if they had fully lived and outgrown a temporary case of savagery as small boys.

Hall described this reliving of primitive emotions as a sort of vaccination process.[18] In the same way that vaccination allowed people to resist smallpox by giving them a mild and controllable dose of the disease, reliving their ancestors' primitivism would allow boys to carry a weakened case of "savagery" in their systems and thus give them the primitive masculine strength to avoid neurasthenic breakdown and overcivilized effeminacy. Or, as Hall put it, the boy should have "been exposed to and already recovering from as many forms of ethical mumps and measles as, by having in mild form now he can be rendered immune to later when they become far more dangerous."[19] This bad childhood behavior denoted not moral weakness but moral development. A boy who misbehaves "is not depraved but only in a savage or half-animal stage." By allowing him to be true to his evolutionarily primitive nature, he would develop the antibodies necessary to render him "immune" to moral illnesses which could unman him later in life.

Hall specifically associated this childhood savagery with boys, not girls. Girls, he wrote, were more governed by adult motives, whereas "boys are nearer to primitive man."[20] Both boys and girls were buffeted by powerful feelings, but boys' emotions approached "savagery," whereas girls' emotions were characterized by "sentiment." This sexual difference in childhood emotion was even reflected in the difference between boys' and girls' preferred reading materials: "The boy who reads frontier stories till he is almost persuaded to be an 'Injun' is merely being vaccinated against savagery later in life." Girls, on the other hand, were more tame and tractable, so they read love stories.[21] Girls did not have this special link with savagery; nor did their feminine natures require such "inoculations." Only boys had the potential or need to be "vaccinated against savagery later in life" by reliving the moral savagery of their ancestors.

Of course, Hall didn't want little boys to actually *become* savages, any more than doctors wanted those they inoculated to die of smallpox. He merely wanted little boys to let their natural primitive tendencies express themselves fully so that, at the proper developmental stage, their savage tendencies could be replaced by the strongest, healthiest possible civilized traits. Eventually, at the proper recapitulatory moment (about age nine), boys would need to learn discipline.[22] Nor did Hall want small boys' savage tendencies to lead to dangerous violence. Boys simply needed to be encouraged to read bloody stories and engage in fisticuffs when necessary, in order to get the full benefit of racial recapitulation, and to avoid exacerbating civilization's excess of manly self-restraint.

To some extent, then, Hall's focus on boyhood savagery stemmed directly from his strategies of representation. In order to solve the neurasthenic paradox, he needed to represent the power of civilized manliness as developing naturally out of a pure, primal boyhood. Thus, for Hall, boyhood savagery was not a pedagogical end in itself. It was simply a means to allow young men to grow up masculine enough to avoid neurasthenia and other effeminizing tendencies of advanced civilization.

Yet although Hall intended to strengthen manly "civilization" by encouraging boyhood "savagery," at first some of his contemporaries found this distinction hard to understand. As we saw, when Hall opened a highly publicized 1899 education conference by calling on Chicago's kindergarten teachers to let small boys express their savage impulses, a minor scandal erupted. Addressing the teachers, Hall argued that educators should actively cultivate not only civilized emotions like love and virtue but also "primitive" emotions like anger, sin and pain.[23] Little boys who experienced only pleasure missed out on the healthful benefits of racial recapitulation, and lost the vital experience of repeating the savage experiences of the race. Lacking the ability to repeat evolution's advance, boys suffered evolutionary decay. Such boys were like the nautilus. Originally the nautilus had been a crab but, due to its excessively easy life, the species had degenerated into a helpless parasite. Now it had lost the use of its legs, eyes, skeleton, even its "reproductive apparatus."[24] In other words, the nautilus now had life so easy that it had —literally—lost its balls.

Civilized boys could avoid this horrifying emasculation by being exposed to judicious amounts of savagery. Hall condemned educators who never allowed boys "to fight, or to hear or read stories with bloodshed in them," who prevented them from learning "how it feels at the painful end of the rod," or from experiencing the "hard conditions of life, under which savage developed into civilized man." Hall, at base a partisan of civilization, conceded that pleasure was essential too. But, he argued, modern middle- and upper-class children got enough pleasure as it was. (Poor boys, he conceded parenthetically, needed more pleasure and less pain—again, "civilization's" larger emphasis on race allowed Hall to minimize the importance of class differences.)[25]

Underlying all these violent suggestions lay Hall's theories of racial recapitulation. Hall's speech is packed with images of little boys reliving the violent life of primitive man.

> The child is in the primitive age. The instinct of the savage survives in him, just as the physical peculiarities of the aquatic stage survive in his body and determine its conformations…. Boys are naturally robbers; they are bandits and fighters by nature. A scientific study has been made of boys' societies…. In every instance these societies have been predatory. All of the members thirsted for blood, and all of their plans were for thievery and murder. I recite these facts because they go to show, with many other facts, that a child repeats the history of his race.[26]

Boys must embrace primitive violence if they were to develop moral manliness. "Unless you want to make a selfish, knock-kneed weakling of him, teach him to double up his fist and strike back…. Physical courage is the foundation for moral courage later in life. One is to the child and the savage what the other is to the grown and cultured man."[27] Although Hall sometimes spoke of "the child," the context of his remarks makes it clear that he was really discussing only boys. He had no desire to see little girls engaged in fisticuffs. Boys, alone, must be little savages.

Hall objected strenuously to the sloppy effeminate sentimentality in current kindergartens: "All that rot they teach to children about the little raindrop fairies with their buckets washing down the windows must go." But he predicted that a virile reaction against effeminacy was setting in. "We shall go back to reading the old, bloody stories to children, and children will like to hear them because they are healthy little savages."[28] Once women stopped teaching boys about fairies and started teaching them about blood and guts, their innate savagery could blossom, and the little boys would grow up strong and manly enough to withstand the emasculating tendencies of civilization.[29]

Hall anticipated a cool reception from the organizers of the Kindergarten College, for he had frequently asserted that the kindergarten movement was degenerating into a sea of effeminate sentiment.[30] Yet although he was trying to be inflammatory, the lady teachers he wished to provoke listened politely, offering not a single dissenting opinion.[31] According to a local paper, "Dr. Hall, when he had concluded, confessed himself disappointed that he had not been more criticized, and he admitted having 'flaunted' some of his beliefs, as it were, in the hope of meeting with opposition."[32]

The editors of Chicago's daily newspapers soon provided all the "opposition" Hall could stand, however. In 1899, much of the middle class was still too enmeshed in Victorian culture to understand Hall's primitivist solution to the neurasthenic paradox.[33] The *Chicago Times Herald* called Hall a "preacher of pain and pessimism" and suggested that his message "sounds more like a disordered liver than psychology."[34] The *Chicago Evening Post* rejected Hall's insistence that civilization could be strengthened by a dose of savagery. "The whole training of early childhood is an attempt to turn the child from the savage instincts that are born in it, and to reverse the procedure would be to turn our faces again to the barbaric past."[35]

Moreover, some middle-class men—fearful of working-class men's challenges to their authority—cared more about taming potentially disruptive working-class boys in the public schools than about combating overcivilized effeminacy. The Chicago Board of Education, charged with running orderly schools, objected to Hall's violent methods of promoting "virility in education." As Chairman Brenan explained, "We do not believe it will benefit the public school teachers to attend a convention where the speakers advocate teaching prize-fighting and bullying as an art. The boys will learn that fast enough without being taught." He therefore revoked the permission he had previously granted Chicago's teachers to dismiss classes early in order to attend the Kindergarten College.[36] To the Board, class war probably loomed as a more imminent danger than neurasthenia.

By the end of the conference, Hall had received all the opposition he could stomach and complained bitterly that he had been badly used by the press and the school board.[37] Hall was trying to rescue civilized manhood by infusing it with a dose of virile savagery. The press, however, accused Hall of attacking the civilized values he was trying to save. Small wonder Hall felt unjustly attacked and abused!

Yet not everyone misunderstood or attacked Hall. Several prominent men responded enthusiastically to Hall's message about boyhood primitivism. For example, Episcopal Bishop Samuel Fallows endorsed Hall's defense of boyish pugilism, claiming that without reenacting his violent "inherited proclivities," a boy could not grow into a strong man, ready for manly moral battle.[38] Most notably, Theodore Roosevelt wrote Hall a flattering letter agreeing that "the *barbarian virtues*" could keep civilized boys from becoming effeminate "milksops": "Over-sentimentality, over-softness, in fact washiness and mushiness are the great dangers of this age and of this people. Unless we keep the *barbarian virtues*, gaining the civilized ones will be of little avail."[39] These men, like Hall, believed that overcivilized decadence could be held at bay, and overcivilized boys could be masculinized by embracing the primitive.

In glorifying the middle-class little boy as a savage, Hall was suggesting a solution to the neurasthenic paradox. By fully reliving their forebears' primitive passions, boys could grow up strong enough to survive the effeminizing tendencies of higher civilization. Boys must fight, bully, and dream of massive bloodshed. This juvenile savagery would "vaccinate" them with a controlled dose of the primitivism which would allow them to retain their virility as civilized adults. Combining the civilized power of higher races, with the masculine strength of primitive man, they would have the vitality to move humanity closer to millennial human perfection.

But reliving the savage emotions of boyhood was not the only strategy Hall found to remasculinize the civilized man. Adolescence, too, gave Hall a way to resolve the neurasthenic paradox by using recapitulation theory. And if the key for childhood was the figure of the savage little boy, the key for adolescence was the figure of the racially mutable adolescent boy.

PERFECTING MANHOOD: APPROACHING THE "SUPER-MAN" THROUGH THE RACIALLY MUTABLE ADOLESCENT BOY

Adolescence was a very different stage of development than boyhood, as Hall saw it—a stage of far greater danger. Adolescent boys (those between the ages of fourteen and twenty–four) were especially vulnerable to civilization's two greatest energy-draining forces: neurasthenia and masturbation. On the one hand, the intellectual demands of high school and college were likely to drain an overstudious adolescent boy's nerve force and render him neurasthenic. On the other hand, with sexual puberty came the capacity for masturbation, which could lead to a host of physical and mental debilities. Moreover, neurasthenia and masturbation were both diseases of civilization: Both struck down highly evolved adolescent boys who overdrew their limited capital of nervous or sexual energies. Masturbation was "far more common among civilized than among savage races."[40] Neurasthenia was the quintessential disease of overcivilization. If the best of civilized adolescent boyhood was so vulnerable to neurasthenic weakness and masturbatory enervation, how could they develop the evolutionary vitality necessary to advance their race toward a perfect civilization?

Here, again, racial recapitulation allowed Hall to solve the neurasthenic paradox by representing his culture's dualistic formulations as merely different stages in an ongoing evolutionary process. Both masturbation and neurasthenia had gained their power by mobilizing a set of linked opposites to depict civilized men's nervous energies as endangered. Through that linked set of opposites, physicians like Beard had given men a choice: they could either be civilized, manly, and undervitalized or they could be primitive, masculine, and passionate. They couldn't be both. Hall rejected these dualistic formulations and represented them as different developmental stages of the same process. In his writings on childhood, Hall had represented the little boy as primitive, passionate, and masculine—and thus the larva of a civilized man strong enough to withstand the enervation of modern civilization. In his writings on adolescence, too, Hall dismantled the neurasthenic paradox by redefining neurasthenia's linked opposites as merely different developmental stages. Here, too, the key was to tie male power to racial power through the processes of evolution and racial recapitulation.

Hall began by assuming the central importance of sexual puberty to male adolescence. This focus on adolescent male sexuality was, of course, nothing new. Parents and educators, including Hall, had long warned that puberty was a uniquely dangerous time. Puberty predisposed young men to a precocious sexual expression which would exhaust their sexual "capital," leaving them too weak to develop into powerful men. Yet while Hall continued to believe that masturbation would lead to illness and neurasthenic collapse, in the 1890s he began to welcome the onset of male adolescent sexuality as a positive good instead of a danger.

On the one hand, Hall suggested, if channeled properly into nonsexual pursuits, a young man's nascent sexuality could give him renewed access to a powerful and manly vitality. When boys reached sexual awakening at puberty, according to Hall, they were suddenly flooded with sexual energy. This sexual energy was a valuable legacy: it was "capital" which, if carefully hoarded, would richly provide for a boy throughout his manhood. As Hall wrote in 1882 (drawing on a pervasive economic imagery comfortable to his class), "between the ages of twelve and sixteen ... the young adolescent receives from nature a new capital of energy ... and success in life depends upon the care and wisdom with which this energy is husbanded."[41] Hall had been raised and educated to assume that if this sexuality were carefully husbanded and a boy built a strong character by willfully suppressing his desires, he would develop into a manly and powerful man. If he squandered his sexual energy through masturbation or promiscuity, however, this expenditure of his "capital" would stunt the growth of true, virile manhood. His sexual growth would stop, and he would suffer premature degeneration.

By 1894, however, eager to solve the neurasthenic paradox by substituting developmentalism for dualism, Hall had begun to suggest that young men's new sexual energy could provide a healthful substitute for their scarce nervous energy. Educators need not concentrate on *repressing* adolescent boys' sexual energy; instead they could *channel* it into education. This would have the dual advantage, first, of keeping youths safe from sexual dissipation and, second, of giving them more energy to devote to higher education without becoming neurasthenic. "Every intellectual interest has some value as a palliative or alternative, or psycho-kinetic equivalent of inebriation or degraded love," Hall maintained.[42] By transforming young men's sexual passions into a source of scarce nervous energy, Hall was able both to mitigate the danger of neurasthenia and to reconstruct adolescent male sexuality in ways which did not stress self-restraint.

Hall did not believe the sexual maturity of puberty offered the same educational benefits to adolescent girls, however. He accepted Dr. Edward H. Clarke's widely held view that excessive education would divert necessary energies away from girls' developing reproductive systems, rendering them ill or even sterile.[43] Whereas boys protected their limited supply of sexual force by channeling it into their studies, girls would destroy their sexual force if they likewise channeled it into studies—they would permanently damage their reproductive capacities.[44] Thus, when Hall spoke of the regenerative opportunities of puberty, he was implicitly discussing only boys.

In embracing adolescent male sexuality as a positive good, Hall did more than merely suggest pubertal boys sublimate their new sexual energy. Hall described adolescent boys' sexual awakening as a spiritual awakening in the Protestant tradition of religious conversion, or "second birth." Among American Protestants, adolescence was the traditional age when young Christians experienced the spiritual "second birth" of religious conversion and became full-fledged church members.[45] Hall repeatedly insisted that puberty was a "physiological second birth," the moment of his physical development when the individual was born again as a full-fledged member of his race. Receiving the biological capacity to become a father constituted rebirth as a full member of the race, according to Hall, because now a youth could compete with other men to father the most superior offspring, and thus contribute to the ongoing evolutionary life of the race.

As Hall understood it, the "physiological second birth" of sexual maturity linked each individual boy to his race and the evolution of a perfect civilization, just as the spiritual second birth of reborn Protestants had linked each Christian to the true church and to the cosmic progress toward the millennium. Hall believed it was "no accidental synchronism of unrelated events that the age of religion and that of sexual maturity coincide" for Protestants as well as more primitive religions.[46] This was simply a religious reflection of the high and holy truths embedded in the evolutionary process. At sexual maturity, when a boy received the capacity for paternity, he ceased to exist merely for himself, and began to exist as a potential contributor to the divine process of racial evolution and the advancement of civilization. Adolescence was thus a holy time, when sexuality and spirituality burst upon a young man simultaneously, through the physiological second birth.[47]

Here, then, Hall had found a solution to the problem of manly self-restraint, which had tormented him since his own adolescence. Sex was not dirty; it was holy. It was God's means of creating healthier human specimens and more advanced races.[48] In *Adolescence*, Hall waxed lyrical about the ecstatic, almost holy, pleasures of sex and orgasm, which he described as "the sacred hour of heredity": "In the most unitary of all acts, which is the epitome and pleroma [abundance; plenitude] of life, we have the most intense of all affirmations of the will to live, and realize that the only true God is love, and the center of life is worship.... This sacrament [sex] is the annunciation hour, with hosannas which the whole world reflects.... Now the race is incarnated in the individual and remembers its lost paradise."[49] Hall believed that for healthy, married adults, God was love, and love was Godly. Sex was designed for procreation; procreation was the mechanism of evolution; and evolution was God's way of progressing toward the millennium. "Nor is religion degraded by the recognition of this intimate relationship, save to those who either think vilely about sex or who lack insight into its real psychic nature and so fail to realize how indissoluble is the bond that God and nature have wrought between religion and love."[50] All these delicious pleasures were aspects of the holy evolutionary process.

Adolescent boys' new sexual maturity tied them in mystic and powerful ways to the entire sweep of evolution, and gave them special racial gifts, gifts which could regenerate a decadent civilization. On the one hand, puberty linked a youth, via racial recapitulation, to his savage ancestors. On the other hand, puberty linked a youth, as a potential father, to the race's evolutionary future. By taking advantage of both factors, educators could bring American boys ever closer to the "super-man that is to be."

Racial recapitulation was the key factor which could help educators evolve this super-man. With the onset of physiological second birth at puberty, boys were suddenly flooded with ancestral tendencies and inheritances. As Hall put it, when a child reaches puberty, "very many of the remote ancestral strains of the blood appear. Blood from many different ancestral stocks is poured into the veins at once. We ... each have some twenty million ancestors, if we reckon back to the time of William the Conqueror. These hereditary traits, then, are poured in, and appear at this time."[51] This onrush of atavistic ancestral traits fragmented an adolescent's personality and was the cause of adolescents' characteristic emotional turmoil.[52]

White American adolescents were at greater risk than Europeans because, the more ethnically diverse a child's ancestors, the more different primitive pasts he would relive and the more turbulent his adolescence would be. "The more mongrel the stock or the more numerous the strains of bloods of which it is composed, and the more unsettled the body of ethnic or national customs, traditions, and beliefs, the more critical does the whole adolescent period become."[53] (Note that Hall is talking about clashes not of environmentally based cultures, but of biological races—"numerous strains of blood" and "mongrel stocks.") Since each individual repeated the history of the race and since adolescence was a period when distant racial influences were particularly intense, it followed that any individual who was forced to repeat the histories of several races at once would be subjected to a severe multiplication of the normal stresses of adolescence. "Pure stocks with settled ways and ideals, which pass this ferment safely and quickly, are at one extreme, and a composite nation like our own, with new and diverse models of thought and life, and everything unsettled, is open to unparalleled dangers of arrested development."[54] White American youths' unstable racial inheritance (English, French, Dutch, German, and so on) threatened them with "arrested development."

Yet although American adolescents were in especial danger from their "mongrel" racial stock, Hall believed their very racial mix made it possible for them to achieve the most complete manhood ever evolved—to become, in fact, the "super-men" who could lead the nation to a millennial future: "In this country, with all its excitements and precocities, and especially with our mongrel blood ... the seething is not only greater, but longer. But if there is increased danger of both stunting and collapse, there is also the possibility of later but higher and more complete unity in the 'cosmic, super-man' of the future."[55] White

Americans' "mongrel blood" made their adolescence far more dangerous than that of more homogeneous races. Yet, precisely because of their racial liminality, American boys could develop into the cosmic super-man of the future.

Evolution's Lamarckian mechanism was what would make it possible for educators to help America's youths evolve toward super-men. If civilization's most gifted youths were properly educated to their full potential, they would pass their educational advancement on to their offspring genetically, thus raising the next generation to a higher evolutionary plane. As Hall informed the National Educational Association in 1894, "Evolution has taught the teacher that he or she is to be its chief agent in the march of progress…. In the vision of the super-man, if it is ever to be realized, it will be because the school, the college and university will succeed in bringing childhood to more complete maturity."[56]

The key in moving white American boys toward the super-man was to prolong their adolescence so that they could slowly and safely relive all the many competing primal pasts their multiple racial heritage was thrusting upon them. Educators must carefully allow boys to fully reexperience all the final stages from all their racially diverse ancestors, whether English, German, or Scandinavian. Recapitulation theory held that an organism's last developmental stages were the most advanced, because evolution's most recent beneficial adaptations were simply added on to the end of the growth process. By slowly and fully reliving this plethora of racially inherited stages, mongrel white adolescents could make the highest stages of *all* their racial ancestors fully their own. At the same time, they could move their racial inheritance to an even higher plane through their own advanced education. As fathers, they would pass this advancement on to their own children via Lamarckian inheritance, and this process could be repeated, ad infinitum. Thus, by slowly and carefully taking advantage of racial recapitulation, racially liminal adolescents could move the race ever closer to evolutionary perfection and the super-man.

But only *white* American mongrels could evolve into the super-man. The lower races simply did not have the white races' advanced final stages, so their adolescence was far shorter and there was no point prolonging it. "Colored children and those of low stock are often as bright as others, if not more so; but at from six to twelve they fall behind, and their educational period closes."[57] White "mongrel" adolescents, on the other hand, did inherit these advanced final stages. Indeed, those with an ethnically diverse heritage inherited several of them. The longer the adolescence, the more completely the child could relive, and thus make his own, his ancestors' evolutionary advancements. Scientists agreed that evolutionarily advanced species needed extended childhoods in order to fully assimilate all their ancestors' latest evolutionary advances: the longer a creature's immaturity, the more evolutionarily advanced the species. Because so many white American youths were of racially mixed European descent, Hall theorized, their adolescence could be almost infinitely extended, as they fully relived the most advanced stages of a profusion of highly evolved races. As Hall put it, even "if this period of adolescent immaturity is exceptionally prolonged and dangerous here, the possibilities of ultimate and complete manhood are correspondingly greater."[58] By taking advantage of their multiple racial heritage, and of adolescents' direct ties to all their primitive ancestors, American young men could bypass current threats to masculinity and develop the "ultimate and complete manhood" of the "cosmic super-man of the future."

When Hall prophesied the development of the "super-man" he did indeed mean *man*. Girls, unlike boys, could not develop into the super-man. Adolescent girls could develop their best potential; they could become excellent mothers and nurture the future race; they might even be flooded with racial memories when they hit puberty. Yet women's education could never bring about the super-man or advance the race.

Here, Hall based his theories on the biological axiom that females were generic, while males were variable.[59] According to contemporary science, only men had the evolutionary function of variability—of developing advantageous variations which they could pass on to their offspring. Sexual selection was driven by males' competing with one another in order to win females. Males needed to develop a multiplicity of attractive variations to please females. Thus men, being variable, were the only beings capable of becoming scientific geniuses and advancing civilization by passing this genius on to their children. Females, on the other hand, were generic. They were sexually passive and thus lacked the need to compete for their mates. Females therefore varied far less than males. This conservative, generic nature meant that women more rarely became idiots or degenerates, according to scientists; but they were also constitutionally unable to become geniuses. As respected British psychiatrist Harry Campbell put it in 1891, "Genius of the highest order is practically limited to the male sex."[60]

Hall's aim of prolonging adolescence in order to allow youths to take advantage of their ancestors' varied racial gifts was designed to encourage favorable variation, and thus referred only to males. When the most elite young men were given this opportunity to fully develop their potential, they would be able to pass their advancement on to their offspring (according to Lamarckian theory), who would start from a higher evolutionary stage and be able to develop even further. They were thus, in a very real sense, advancing the race toward the super-man. Women, on the other hand, could not take advantage of this evolutionary mechanism of variability. Even if educators slowed girl's development, allowing them to relive their primitive evolutionary heritage, girls were biologically unable to develop inheritable genius. Moreover Hall believed that too much educational development could make a woman sterile, killing instead of improving her offspring.[61] The only being who could develop or pass on newly developed, evolutionarily advanced traits was the properly educated, slowly matured, racially liminal adolescent *boy*. Educating young women could not lead to the evolution of the super-man.

The racially liminal adolescent boy—the larva of the super-man—embodied traits which had previously seemed impossibly dualistic and mutually contradictory. By reconciling these dualisms, Hall further resolved his neurasthenic paradox. For one thing, the "physiological second birth" combined sexuality with spirituality. Having just received his "capital" of sexual energy, the pubertal adolescent boy fairly glowed with virile sexual energy—no neurasthenic decadent, he! Yet as virile as he was, Hall's properly reared adolescent boy was perfectly pure, sublimating all his energy in his education. By constructing puberty as a physiological second birth, Hall allowed his adolescent boy to be both stainlessly virtuous and powerfully sexual. This let Hall abandon dualistic constructions of manly power which were based on unsatisfactory codes of self-restraint and repression.

Similarly, the racially mongrel adolescent boy combined the primitive and the civilized—qualities which had always seemed mutually exclusive. On the one hand, he was the future of civilization—part of the next wave of experts, businessmen, and scientists, and the father of future generations. On the other hand, despite his ties to advanced civilization, the adolescent boy was the heir of his primitive ancestors. Awash with the primal traits and memories of a profusion of distant racial ancestors, he had the strength to withstand the degenerative tendencies of modern civilization.

Hall was extremely serious about evolving the super-man. In article after article between 1894 and 1901, he invoked the vision of a perfectible man whom educators could develop by applying recapitulation theory to education. In 1896, Hall closed an article in the *Christian Register* by quoting Tertulian: "Stand forth, O soul of man, naked, genuine, real, just as thou dost come into the world from the hand of God, and having stood forth, grow to thy full perfection!"[62] In 1897, he insisted in a scholarly psychology article, "Man is not the larva of an angel, but of a higher superman that is to be."[63] In 1899, he enthused to the New Jersey Association for the Study of Children and Youth, "You and I are 'poor critturs,' We are limited in action, knowledge and thought…. Let us say, All hail to the hereafter! The superman is yet to come."[64]

Hall repeatedly hinted at the earthshaking importance of his theories and at their revolutionary ability to contribute to human evolutionary advancement. He insisted that his evolutionary psychology had "begun a movement bigger than Darwinism,"[65] and predicted that in a few years the entire world would recognize its cosmic importance. In 1894, for example, he prophesied that within ten years his theories would have begun to completely regenerate the human race, leading to "a scientific reconstruction that aims at the top and is the salvation and ultimate development and end and aim of creation and of history."[66] Over the next ten years, Hall repeatedly claimed that by applying his theories to adolescent boys' education, he was finding a way to perfect the race, and to help turn white American boys into super-men.

Alas, Hall's grandiose ambitions of ushering in the evolutionary millenium—"the salvation and ultimate development and end and aim of creation and of history"—were thwarted. Ten years after Hall made his stirring prediction of future success, he had abandoned his plan to turn racially liminal adolescents into super-men. Between 1894 and 1904, Lamarckian theories of racial recapitulation had begun to be deeply discredited. August Weissman's theory that inheritance was determined by chromosomes, not by parental behavior, was on its way to becoming the standard scientific interpretation. With chromosomes as evolution's method of inheritance, scientists soon abandoned their belief that racial recapitulation was the way one generation's evolutionary advancement was passed on to the next.[67]

Thus, by 1904, when Hall published his magnum opus, the two volume, fourteen-hundred-page *Adolescence,* he was faced with a dilemma. It was his first major book and, at age sixty, he intended it to be the scholarly masterpiece which would cement his academic reputation.[68] He had been working on *Adolescence* since 1894 and was loathe to abandon ten years of work. Yet he knew his theory of the racially liminal adolescent would not be accepted by cutting-edge scholars because it was based almost entirely on the increasingly dubious theory of recapitulation. Therefore, although Hall expressed his continuing belief in the psychological applications of racial recapitulation, he took a cagey and defensive tone. "Realizing the limitations and qualifications of the recapitulation theory in the *biologic* field, I am now convinced that its *psychogenetic* applications have a method of their own," he insisted.[69] He even included a brief, half-hearted discussion of his theory's relevance to a Weismannist biological framework.[70]

After Lamarckianism was discredited, Hall, like many of his contemporaries, became discouraged about the possibility of engineering human racial improvement. If human evolution occurred, not through education passed down genetically to the next generation, but over long and dismal eons of genetic mutations, the development of superior individuals had no evolutionary utility at all. Educators could build better citizens or better people, but they lacked any power to engineer a better race. Thus, after 1903 Hall no longer argued publicly that educators could turn American boys into "supermen."[71]

Nonetheless, Hall remained committed to the millennial mission of furthering human evolutionary advancement. Although the demise of Lamarckianism doomed his theories of allowing racially liminal adolescents to evolve into super-men, Hall cast about for other methods of working toward racial perfection. By 1911 Hall, like many of his contemporaries, would find such a method in eugenics, arguing that severe "defectives" should be discouraged from reproducing and healthy people encouraged.[72] Yet in 1904 Hall remained skeptical of eugenics as a means of large-scale racial engineering, both for moral reasons (he believed in marriage for love, not breeding) and because he believed the scientific study of heredity was still too rudimentary.[73]

ADOLESCENT RACES

Between 1903 and 1911, Hall explored a different avenue toward human evolutionary perfection which he, as an educator, could further. He continued to devote most of his efforts to educating white adolescents; but rather than placing his millennial faith in their racial perfectibility, Hall began to find new hope in the evolutionary potential of primitive peoples, whom he saw as "adolescent races." As Hall himself put it in his introduction to *Adolescence,* man was "an organism in a very active stage of evolution.… Perhaps other racial stocks than ours will later advance the kingdom of man as far beyond our present standpoint as it now is above that of the lowest savage or even animals."[74] Primitive races themselves, who embodied savage traits more fully and completely than the racially recapitulating adolescent could ever do, temporarily became Hall's hope for human perfection in the distant future.

This was not Hall's only public cause during these years. Hall was working to safeguard and remake the power of manhood on a variety of different fronts. For example, at the same time that he was focusing on "adolescent races," he was also spending a great deal of effort on combating coeducation and the educational "sissification" of American boys. But through 1911 Hall's identity as a strong manly expert, bravely defending childish, weak primitives against the dangers of civilization, gave him a public platform to demonstrate his own manly power and authority as well as a way for him to work toward the "super-man that is to be."

This shift from racially mutable white adolescents to mutable nonwhite adolescent races as the millennial hope of the future was not as big a change as it might seem. Recapitulation theory held that as children's bodies developed, they actually repeated the evolutionary physical development of their forebears. American adolescents (on the brink of civilization) and primitive races (of all age groups) had long been, for Hall, precise equivalents. Substituting "races with adolescent characteristics" for "adolescents with racial characteristics" as candidates for bringing mankind toward the "super-man that is to be" was fully in keeping with Hall's overall theories. Thus, Hall came full circle in his use of race to vitalize—and virilize—effeminate civilization.

While most of *Adolescence* pulls together Hall's long-standing theories about white youths, the final chapter, entitled "Ethnic Psychology and Pedagogy, or Adolescent Races and Their Treatment," outlines Hall's vision of the evolutionary promise of primitive, non-white races.[75] Hall believed that "savages"—of all ages—were actually "adolescent races" who should be educated according to his larger principles of adolescent psychology. "Most savages in most respects are children, or, because of sexual maturity, more properly, ado-lescents of adult size.... Their faults and their virtues are those of childhood and youth. They need the same careful and painstaking study, lavish care, and adjustment to their nature and needs."[76] These adult primitives required the same educational care that young white adolescent boys did.

"Racial pedagogy" was simply Hall's program of adolescent white education applied to the education of adults of these "adolescent" races. As he described it, imperialists who forced primitive races to accommodate themselves to Western civilization were precisely analogous to teachers who overpressured civilized white adolescents. In both cases forcing the "adolescents" to become prematurely civilized left them weak and neurasthenic. "The inexorable laws of forcing, precocity, severity, and overwork, produce similarly disastrous results for both" children and savages.[77] Like overpressured children, these primitive adults were able to learn highly civilized skills. Yet because adolescent races had not evolved to a mature evolutionary stage, they lacked the moral and intellectual capacity to use these skills. "The whole history is summed up in a 'a swift adoption of the externals of civiliza-tion going hand in hand with a steady physical decline, and a promising but suddenly arrested moral development.'"[78] Like a dissipated neurasthenic adolescent, overpressured adolescent races soon became sick and morally decadent.

Yet, like adolescent boys, adolescent races had the millennial capacity to evolve, some-day, into super-men. Hall offered his readers a vision of the future greatness of some unknown, primitive adolescent race.

> In later ages other stocks now obscure, and perhaps other tongues now unstudied will occupy the center of the historic stage, appropriating the best we achieve, as we learn from Semites, Greeks, and Romans. If this be true, every vigorous race, however rude and undeveloped, is, like childhood, worthy of the maximum of reverence and care and study, and may become the chosen organ of a new dispensation of culture and civilization. Some of them now obscure may be the heirs of all we possess and wield the ever-increasing resources of the world for good or evil somewhat perhaps as we now influence their early plastic stages, for they are the world's children and adolescents.[79]

Hall reminded his civilized readers that their own age was not "the culminating period of history." The "best and greatest things have not happened yet." To nurture mankind's mil-lennial future, civilized man must nurture the world's adolescent races. One day these primitive "stocks" could be the world's super-men.

It was thus crucial that civilized men protect the world's primitive races, just as enlight-ened educators protected adolescent boys. And, for a few years, Hall put his theories into practice by taking up the cause of antiimperialism.[80] Having lost the possibility of building American adolescents into super-men, the only way Hall could continue his mission to perfect civilization was by safeguarding "adolescent races." In the process, however, Hall continued to reconstruct the power of middle-class white manhood.

Between 1903 and 1911, Hall actively set himself up as a professional expert on "racial pedagogy." This racial expertise allowed Hall to position himself as especially powerful and manly. By insisting that the world's non-white races were children who needed his enlightened protection, Hall constructed himself as a sort of racial pedagogue, a strong and manly civilized expert who must exercise paternal care over his weak charges. Savages, like children, were weak and vulnerable, and required the manly supervision of powerful civilized men like himself. As a racial pedagogue, Hall's manly strength and authority stood in stark contrast to the weakness and dependence of the "primitive" races he championed.

Hall's incarnation as racial pedagogue took a number of forms, both academic and political. He founded and coedited the *Journal of Race Development*. He established and taught a course entitled "Racial Pedagogy" at Clark University, where he was college president.[81] He organized a series of yearly conferences on the social problems of Asia, Africa, and the Near East.[82] He also set himself up as an authority on the education of African Americans and American Indians.[83]

Nor did Hall confine himself to the academic arena. His identity as manly racial pedagogue actually spurred him into temporarily becoming a leader in the anti-imperialist movement. Hall's somewhat short-lived (1905–8) public political activism was completely out of character—he usually confined his politicking to professional disagreements within the halls of academe. Most notable was Hall's public opposition to King Leopold's brutal regime in the Congo Free State. The Belgian king had annexed the Congo as his personal possession and had virtually enslaved the entire population. After 1905, horrifying reports of atrocities in the Congo were widely reported in the press. These reports galvanized the manly racial pedagogue. From early 1906 through late 1908, Hall served as president of the National Congo Reform Association. In this capacity, the scholarly academic took on the unfamiliar persona of the man of affairs, granting newspaper interviews, preparing position papers for the *Congressional Record,* and even traveling to Washington to meet with President Theodore Roosevelt.

Hall's speeches on behalf of the Congolese suggest that his desire to see "primitives" as unmanly children was at the heart of his anti-imperialism. A colonizer, he insisted, had a fatherly duty to treat its childish "wards" more as "its children, and less as its slaves."[84] Rather than being a manly protector of his African "children," Leopold was plundering the Congo and brutalizing its people. In numerous speeches, Hall luridly reported the evolutionary backsliding—Congolese men's indulgence in rape and cannibalism—which had resulted from Leopold's abdication of manly paternalistic responsibility. Hall's descriptions of "photographs of cannibal feasts and of bodies of women being salted" for food simultaneously reinforced both contemporary myths of African men as unmanly primitives and Hall's own manly position as heroic protector of dependent and unmanly "adolescent races."[85]

Hall even suggested, in his persona as racial pedagogue, that the Congo situation provided a good opportunity for white men like himself to inculcate manliness in America's own "adolescent races"—in African American men. "What the black man here chiefly needs is self-respect: to be taught to be a manly negro … he needs a great cause such as interest in his brethren in the dark continent.… It is no argument against such a policy that the negro himself has not yet seen the full significance of this opportunity." Again, Hall holds himself up as a model of superior manhood, here in contradistinction to African American men, who (whether they recognized it or not) needed to learn about true manliness by emulating white men like himself.[86]

In constructing himself as the manly racial pedagogue, Hall was upholding a traditional view of manliness that encompassed the gentlemanly protection of the weak and dependent. Yet, ironically, in his advocacy of racial pedagogy, Hall was simultaneously reinforcing a contradictory view of manhood—one tied, not to self-restrained "manliness," but to newer formulations of passionate "masculinity." For, as Hall described it, the only reason racial pedagogy was needed was that evolution "naturally" spurred racially superior men to annihilate racially inferior men. In other words, Hall's identity as manly protector of inferior "adolescent races" depended on the idea that " masculinity" naturally predisposed men toward racial violence. We have previously encountered this view in journalists' discussions of the "natural man's" predilection for lynching. By insisting that men of superior races naturally desired to attack men of inferior races, Hall was reinforcing this new construction of "the natural man," with its passionate, primitive masculinity.

As Hall explained in *Adolescence,* from the moment of man's evolutionary origin, he had a passionate desire to eradicate all lower forms of life, whether animal or human. "Man early became the wanderer and destroyer par excellence. Less than any other animal, can man tolerate rivals in the struggle for existence."[87] As soon as man emerged as a species, he systematically set about destroying all his close evolutionary competitors.

This genocidal urge was a masculine impulse: Hall explicitly made men, and not women, the engines of this destructive evolutionary fury. He stressed the masculinity of "the hunting passion" that in prehistoric times drove man to exterminate numerous animals in his "long hot struggle… [to become] the lord of the animal creation." Like all "masculine" passions, this "hunting passion" was shared by all men; and civilized men, like their "savage" ancestors, still decorated their social clubs with their dismembered trophies. In contrast, the few animals who could coexist with man, then as now, were all domesticated by women. "Only the few score of animals which primitive woman domesticated for food or service can thrive beside him, and his clubrooms and dwellings are still decorated with the products of his head-hunting prowess."[88] Hall's figure of man the destroyer thus referred explicitly to men and to masculinity.

This instinctive masculine violence, a legacy of the Stone Age, was today leading civilized men to engage in imperialism, with its massive racial genocide. The contemporary masculine instinct for imperialistic racial extermination was

the same instinct which in pre-historic times destroyed … the gigantic extinct mammals, and has forever scarred man's soul with fear, anger, and wanton cruelty. The same enmity against the lower races, which in our day has exterminated forever the Boethuks, the Tasmanians, and is reducing so many lower human ethnic stocks to make way for favored races, is but a relic of the rage which exterminated the missing links and made man for ages the passionate destroyer.[89]

Violence was the birthright of man the destroyer, the masculine exterminator who slaughtered animals and primitive men.

In this ostensible opposition between the benevolent racial pedagogue and man the bloodthirsty destroyer, Hall once again used race to rewrite problematic Victorian ideologies of manly self-restraint. The racial pedagogue was framed in terms of Victorian traditions of self-restrained manliness. Just as the boy Stanley had been taught to restrain his sexual passions—to allow his willful manliness to contain his masculine desires—so the adult Hall depicted the manly racial pedagogue restraining the violent masculine passions of man the destroyer.

Yet by making these masculine passions racial instead of sexual, their implications changed. As a boy Hall had learned that unbounded masculine passions—masturbatory desires or sexual dissipations—were a source of unmanly weakness. As a man, however, he depicted unbounded masculine passion —genocidal fury—as the evolutionary force which propelled the white races to their current position of racial supremacy. Like sexual passion, this racial passion was immoral. Yet it was precisely this masculine passion for racial violence that had allowed the white race to win the Darwinistic struggle for racial primacy, in the person of man the destroyer, enraged and cruel, who decimated all his racial competitors.

Thus, although self-restrained manliness and passionate masculinity remained at odds for Hall, they were also—paradoxically—linked. Civilized, manly man had achieved his self-restrained evolutionary eminence precisely because, in the past, he had shown his capacity for savage, passionate, violent masculinity. Ostensibly Hall was trying to discredit imperialistic racial violence. In spite of his good intentions, however, Hall nonetheless reinforced the increasingly prevalent idea that the capacity for "primitive" racial violence was an inherent part of masculinity.

After 1909, Hall began to concentrate his energies on Freudian psychology, and his interest in race gradually faded.[90] But although Hall concentrated less on the linkages between racial dominance and masculinity, many of his contemporaries retained their interest. The final word about Hall, race, and masculinity must be an extraordinary article in the *Boston Sunday American* of 1915, in which the newspaper's illustrator and editors directly translated Hall's use of racial primitivism into images of violent, aggressive masculinity.[91]

The text of the article, excerpted from a scholarly address Hall gave on anger, was a typical Hallian argument that primitive emotions (in this case, anger), when repressed and channeled, gave civilized people vitality enough to withstand the enervating effects of civilization. But the editor seems to have understood and approved Hall's subliminal message about the revitalization of overcivilized masculinity and presented it in a way his readers could understand more directly.

The newspaper fortified Hall's relatively tame article with headlines and illustrations which made primitive masculinity (though never directly referred to) the centerpiece. "How Rage, Anger and Hatred Help Us to Success. Why It is ANGER and NOT LOVE that 'Makes the World Go Round,' and Is the Secret of the Progress of Men and Nations," blared the headline. The gendered subtext would have been readily apparent to readers: where Victorians had counseled their sons to restrain their passions—to develop high-minded manliness—now experts believed "Rage, Anger, and Hatred" would lead "Men" to "Progress." Feminized Victorian morality was giving way to masculine aggression as the "Secret" which superior men needed to get ahead.

The three illustrations and their quoted captions drove the point home.[92] Violent, aggressive emotion, as experienced by primitive men, was the source of power and masculinity. Two illustrations depicted angry, naked, black-skinned men in threatening postures. A hairy anthropoid, half man and half ape, shows his teeth and grasps a club as the caption announces "One Philosopher Argues That It was Anger that Made Primitive Man Lord of Creation by Inspiring Him to Fight." Above him, five glowering, war-painted black men crouch beside a howling man who clutches a spear in his clenched fists, as the caption explains, "Savages Work Themselves Into Frenzied Rage in Order to Fight Their Enemies." And, lest the reader miss the point that manly self-mastery and protection of the weak is not the sort of manhood that "anger" engenders, the illustrator depicts these "savages" working themselves into a frenzy over an enemy that has the rounded breasts and hips of a woman—no overcivilized manliness here!

The top illustration also depicts a naked man—but here, he is not black and angry but white and dying. Marat lays pitifully in his bath, having been murdered by the glaring virago, Charlotte Corday. Marat, like the savage naked men in the other illustrations, makes a fist. Yet Marat's first impotently clutches not a club or spear but a bed sheet. We can read this illustration as a parable about the anemic weakness of civilized manliness and the need for the "Force-Creating Emotion" which would provide masculinity. Decimated by a too-strong woman—a feeling that in effeminate modern civilization, male power has evaporated—the old self-restrained manliness, like Marat, teeters on the brink of expiring. Yet male power can be rescued by something new—the primitive anger and raw quest for dominance echoed by bushmen in the neighboring illustration, who shake their fists over what appears to be the bound and helpless image of a naked woman. This racially based imagery, like Hall's figure of man the destroyer, was essential to the construction of new middle-class ideologies of violent, passionate "masculinity."

NOTES

1. Stephen Jay Gould, *Ontogeny and Phylogeny* (Cambridge, Mass.: Harvard University Press, 1977); Carl Degler, *In Search of Human Nature: The Decline and Revival of Darwinism in American Social Thought* (New York: Oxford University Press, 1991), 4–47. For an excellent discussion of the interactions between cultural developments and Darwin's own writings, including a discussion of recapitulation, see Gillian Beer, *Darwin's Plots: Evolutionary Narrative in Darwin* (London: Routledge and Kegan Paul, 1983), esp. 104–45.
2. Gould, *Ontogeny and Phylogeny*, 69–166; Russett, *Sexual Science*, 49–77, esp. 53–4.
3. Gould, *Ontogeny and Phylogeny*, 69–114; 135–55.
4. See, for example, G. Stanley Hall, "Child Study and Its Relation to Education," *Forum 29* (August 1900): 694, 696; Hall, *Adolescence,* 1:v.
5. G. Stanley Hall and Arthur Allin, "The Psychology of Tickling, Laughing, and the Comic," *American Journal of Psychology 9* (October 1897): 12–13.
6. Ibid., 20.
7. G. Stanley Hall, "Heirs of the Ages," *Proceedings N.J. Association for the Study of Children and Youth* (March 1899): 10.
8. For example, see also G. Stanley Hall, "A Study of Fears," *American Journal of Psychology 8* (January 1897): 147–249.
9. G. Stanley Hall, "Student Customs," *Proceedings, American Antiquarian Society* 141 (October 1900): 84–5.
10. Hall, *Adolescence,* 1:x-xi; see also 1:45.

11. G. Stanley Hall, "Pedagogical Methods in Sunday School Work," *Christian Register 74* (November 1895): 719–20.

12. Of course, Hall didn't need recapitulation to associate boyhood with savagery. Middle-class culture already associated boyhood with the primitive. See Rotundo, *American Manhood*, 30, 36. However, when Hall put these older ideas about boyhood savagery in the context of recapitulation and of civilization's movement toward the millennium, he was able to imbue them with a much larger—even cosmic—cultural significance. For the cultural context of the late-century interest in "bad boys," see Steven Mailloux, *Rhetorical Power* (Ithaca, N.Y.: Cornell University Press, 1989), 100–29.

13. G. Stanley Hall and Theodate L. Smith, "Showing Off and Bashfulness As Phases of Self-Consciousness," *Pedagogical Seminary 10* (September 1903): 97. This whole passage reappears almost verbatim in Hall, *Adolescence,* 2:59–60.

14. Hall and Smith, "Showing Off," 97–8.

15. See chapter 1.

16. G. Stanley Hall, "Some Fundamental Principles of Sunday School and Bible Teaching," *Pedagogical Seminary 8* (December 1901): 463. See also Hall, "Child Study and Its Relation to Education," 700.

17. On the wider cultural rejection of this feminized religion, see Bederman, "The Women Have Had Charge."

18. Hall saw this vaccination process as one whereby actual "rudimentary organs" were temporarily developed, allowing boys to repeat the savage emotions of their primitive ancestors. These primitive emotional organs needed to be actively used so that they could later atrophy and make way for more evolutionarily advanced powers to develop. Hall and Allin, "The Psychology of Tickling," 17.

19. Hall, *Adolescence,* 2:452.

20. Ibid., 2:398.

21. G. Stanley Hall, "Address at the Dedication of the Haston Free Public Library Building, N. Brookfield Mass. September 20, 1894," in *The Haston Free Public Library Building* (Brookfield, Mass.: Lawrence, 1894), 20.

22. G. Stanley Hall, "The Ideal School as Based on Child Study," *Forum 32* (September 1901): 27–32.

23. G. Stanley Hall, "The Education of the Heart (Abstract)," *Kindergarten Magazine 2* (May 1899): 592–4.

24. Ibid., 593.

25. Ibid.

26. G. Stanley Hall, "Corporal Punishments," *New York Education 3* (November 1899): 163, 164.

27. Ibid., 164.

28. Ibid., 165.

29. Months later, stung by the ridicule in Chicago, Hall denied that he had ever made the extreme statements reported in this transcript; but at the same time, he refused to repudiate them. Instead, he hedged on his precise position and seemed to wish the whole thing had never happened. Based on careful reading of his other works at the time, I believe Hall did make these statements, but tried to take them back when the newspapers made a fuss. He didn't want to sound like a crank or be ridiculed by the press; but he believed in the savage little boy. See C. E. Franklin, "Dr. G. Stanley Hall on Training of Children," *New York Education 3* (December 1899): 226.

30. G. Stanley Hall, "The Kindergarten," *School and Home Education 18* (June 1899): 508. See also G. Stanley Hall, "Some Defects of the Kindergarten in America," *Forum 28* (January 1900): 582–3.

31. "Boxing for Babies," *Chicago Record,* 4 April 1899, 7.

32. "Defends Small Boys," *Chicago Inter-Ocean,* 4 April 1899, 3.

33. See Mailloux, *Rhetorical Power,* 100–29.

34. "A Preacher of Pain and Pessimism," *Chicago Times Herald,* 5 April 1899, 6.

35. "Dr. Hall's Ultra Views," 4.

36. "Ban on Dr. Hall's Idea," *Chicago Tribune,* 6 April 1899, 7. See also "Frowns on Pugilism," *Chicago Record,* 6 April 1899, 6.

37. "Made Up of Sarcasm," *Chicago Times Herald,* 7 April 1899, 3.

38. "Seconds Dr. Hall's Opinion," *Chicago Record,* 10 April 1899, 8. See also "School of Psychology a Center Point of Interest," *Chicago Times-Herald,* 7 April 1899, 3, for Rev. Jenkin Lloyd Jones' approving comments.

39. Theodore Roosevelt to G. Stanley Hall, 29 November 1899, reprinted in Ross, *G. Stanley Hall,* 318; emphasis in original.

40. Hall, *Adolescence,* 1:452–3.

41. G. Stanley Hall, "The Moral and Religious Training of Children," *Princeton Review* 10 (January 1882): 43.

42. G. Stanley Hall, "Universities and the Training of Professors," *Forum 17* (May 1894): 302–3.

43. Hall, *Adolescence,* 1:511–2, 2:568–612. On Clarke, see Russett, *Sexual Science,* 116–8.

44. Hall, *Adolescence,* 2:590–612.

45. Joseph F. Kett, *Rites of Passage: Adolescence in America 1790 to the Present* (New York: Basic, 1977), 62–85.

46. Hall, *Adolescence,* 2:292–3.

47. G. Stanley Hall, "Child Study: The Basis of Exact Education," *Forum 17* (May 1894): 439. See also Hall, "Universities and the Training of Professors," 302.

48. For a more in-depth picture of Hall's revised, adulatory views of sex, circa 1904, see *Adolescence,* 2:281–362 and G. Stanley Hall and Theodate L. Smith, "Curiosity and Interest," *Pedagogical Seminary* 10 (September 1903): 338–42. For an insightful analysis of the broader middle-class move to reclaim male sexuality as a positive good, see also Christina Simmons, "Modern Sexuality and the Myth of Victorian Repression," in *Passion and Power: Sexuality in History,* ed. Kathy Peiss and Christina Simmons (Philadelphia: Temple University Press, 1989), 157–77.

49. Hall, *Adolescence,* 2:123.

50. Ibid., 2:292–3.

51. Hall, "Pedagogical Methods in Sunday School Work," 719–20. Hall's assumptions about what race was the closest to becoming the "super-man" are manifest in his reckoning from the time of William the Conqueror—a date of importance only to the history of Anglo-Saxons.

52. Hall, "Universities and the Training of Professors," 302.

53. G. Stanley Hall, "On the History of American College Text-Books and Teaching in Logic, Ethics, Psychology and Allied Subjects," *Proceedings of the American Antiquarian Society,* n.s. 9 (April 1894): 154–5.

54. Hall, "On the History of American College Text-Books," 155.

55. Hall, "Universities and the Training of Professors," 302.

56. G. Stanley Hall, "Remarks on Rhythm in Education," *Proceedings of the National Education Association* (1894): 85.

57. Hall, "Universities and the Training of Professors," 303.

58. Hall, "On the History of American College Text-Books," 155.

59. For a detailed discussion of principles of male variability and female conservatism, see Russett, *Sexual Science,* 92–100. For Hall's explicit statement of these principles, see, e.g., G. Stanley Hall, "Normal Schools, especially in Massachusetts," *Pedagogical Seminary* 9 (June 1902): 183–4.

60. Harry Campbell, *Differences in the Nervous Organisation of Man and Woman* (London: Lewis, 1891), 173; quoted in Russett, *Sexual Science,* 95.

61. Hall, *Adolescence,* 2:569–610.

62. G. Stanley Hall, "Modern Methods in the Study of the Soul," *Christian Register 75* (February 1896): 133.

63. Hall and Allin, "Psychology of Tickling," 30.

64. Hall, "Heirs of the Ages," 13. For other examples, see also Hall, "Some Fundamental Principles of Sunday School," 464; and Hall, "Child Study and Its Relation to Education," 702.

65. G. Stanley Hall, "Results of Child Study Applied to Education," *Transactions of the Illinois Society for Child Study 1* (1895): 13.

66. G. Stanley Hall, "Child Study in Summer Schools," *Regents' Bulletin 28,* University of the State of New York (July 1894): 336.

67. Gould, *Ontogeny and Phylogeny,* 167–206; Russett, *Sexual Science,* 155–80.

68. Ross, *G. Stanley Hall,* 325.

69. Hall, *Adolescence,* 1:viii; emphasis added.

70. Ibid., 1:50.

71. His letters suggest that he continued to hold his old recapitulation-base theories privately, however. For Hall's continuing, embittered, and embattled belief in racial recapitulation, see G. Stanley Hall to William A. White, 11 December 1912, in Hall Papers, box 26, folder 9, and G. Stanley Hall to Robert M. Yerkes, 18 May 1915 in Hall Papers, box 26, folder 10.

72. See, for example, G. Stanley Hall, "Eugenics: Its Ideals and What It Is Going To Do," *Religious Education 6* (June 1911): 152–9, and "Make Humanity Better by Controlling Unfit, Says President Hall," *Boston Sunday Post,* 29 October 1911.

73. Hall, *Adolescence*, 2:722.

74. Ibid., 1:vii–viii.

75. Ibid., 2:648–748. See also G. Stanley Hall, "The Relations between Lower and Higher Races," *Proceedings of the Massachusetts Historical Society*, 2d ser., 17 (January 1903): 4–13, much of which Hall incorporated into *Adolescence.*

76. Hall, *Adolescence*, 2:649.

77. Ibid.

78. Ibid., 2:659–60.

79. Ibid., 2:748.

80. Ibid., 2:714–9.

81. Memo of courses taken by Grace Lyman, written by G. Stanley Hall, in Hall Papers, box 25, folder 8.

82. Programs in Hall Papers, box 16.

83. See, for example, G. Stanley Hall, "The Undeveloped Races in Contact with Civilization," *Bulletin of the Washington University Association 4* (1906): 145–50; G. Stanley Hall, "How Far Are the Principles of Education along Indigenous Lines Applicable to American Indians?" *Pedagogical Seminary 15* (1908): 365–9; and G. Stanley Hall, "A Few Results of Recent Scientific Study of the Negro in America," *Proceedings, Massachusetts Historical Society*, 2d ser., 19 (1905): 95–107.

84. "Stanley Hall to Sec. Root," *Boston Transcript* (7 March 1906).

85. "Final Word is Not Yet, *Worcester Telegram*, (18 March 1906). For a collection of news clippings on Hall's activities with the Congo National Reform Association, see his Collected Works at Clark University.

86. Quoted in "Opens Field of Thought," *Worcester Telegram*, (21 January 1906).

87. Hall, *Adolescence*, 2:651; on woman the domesticator of feral man, see also 1:224–5 and 2:116–7, 299, 372–3, and 375.

88. Hall, *Adolescence*, 2:93.

89. Ibid., 2:93.

90. Stephen Jay Gould has noted strong connections between recapitulation theory and Freud's ideas, which may well have made them especially interesting to Hall. Freud was himself a recapitulationist, and his ideas of children's developmental stages were surely influenced by recapitulation. See Gould, *Ontogeny and Phylogeny,* 155–64; for Hall's interest in Freud, see Ross, G. *Stanley Hall*, 368–94; and Saul Rosenzweig, *Freud, Jung, and Hall the King Maker: The Historic Expedition to America (1909)* (Seattle: Hogrefe and Huber, 1992).

91. G. Stanley Hall, "How Rage, Anger and Hatred Help Us to Success," *Boston Sunday American*, 15 August 1915, Feature section, p. 4.

92. It's not clear whether two of the captions were quotes from Hall. I cannot find them in the accompanying newspaper article. They certainly sound like Hall, however, and are probably in the complete address from which the newspaper article is excerpted, G. Stanley Hall, "Anger as a Primary Emotion and the Application of Freudian Mechanisms to Its Phenomena," *Journal of Abnormal Psychology* 10:81–87. The third quote is from this address.

5

Denaturalizing Adolescence: The Politics of Contemporary Representations

NANCY LESKO

There is really no clue by which we can thread our way through all the mazes of culture and the distractions of modern life save by knowing the true nature and needs of childhood and adolescence.... Other oracles may grow dim, but this one will never fail.

—G. STANLEY HALL (1900, P. 701)

G. Stanley Hall had a noble goal for re-capitulation in education—to reconstruct the grammar-school course: scientifically, so that school-hours, curricula, exercise, buildings, etc., shall all be ... in accordance with child-nature, the true norm.

—STEPHEN JAY GOULD (1977, P. 154)

ADOLESCENTS, WHETHER EMBODIED as television's stars of *Beverly Hills 90210, Fresh Prince of Bel-Air*, or *The Wonder Years*, as pregnant teenagers on the cover of *Time* magazine, or as the ubiquitous knots of teenagers at shopping malls and video arcades, are a familiar and seemingly fixed element of the social, cultural, and economic landscape. Similarly, the knowledge about adolescents' characteristics—that they are hormonally driven, peer oriented, and identity seeking—is accepted as fact, established by empirical research. Even the idea that a population can be identified by age, massed together as distinctive on that single criterion, is unremarkable. Adolescence is natural and naturally occurring.

However, historians of childhood and youth argue that conceptions of young people are social categories and, therefore, subject to historical processes. Youth is not an immutable stage of life, free from the influence of historical change (Haws & Hiner, 1985).

Author Note: This research was supported, in part, by grants from the Spencer Foundation and the Proffitt Foundation, Indiana University. The author is solely responsible for the ideas expressed. Correspondence can be sent to Nancy Lesko, School of Education, Indiana University, Bloomington, IN 47405; e-mail: nlesko@indiana.edu.

Rather, adolescence can be seen as the *effects* of certain sets of social practices across numerous domains of contemporary legal, educational, family, and medical domains (Walkerdine, 1990). This conceptualization highlights the constructedness and mutability of what are assumed to be natural and naturally occurring teenagers. Certainly, a full archaeology of adolescence beyond the scope of this article. However, this article initiates a critique of several taken-for-granted views of adolescents. This "denaturalizing" of conceptions of adolescents involves calling into question key assumptions through rhetorical, historical, and feminist rereadings of the production of particular knowledge about adolescents.

This deconstruction of natural adolescents is called for by both practical and theoretical events. First, educators currently are involved in restructuring secondary schools to make a variety of school programs both more humane and worthwhile learning environments. A failure to examine the commonsense assumptions regarding students may undermine educational reform efforts. Policies grounded in static ideas of adolescence will likely reproduce, albeit with small changes, current educational practices. Thus a piece of school reform left unexamined is the implicit and explicit assumptions that teachers have regarding adolescents. For example, literature on middle school practices so heavily emphasizes the physiological turmoil of young adolescents that self-esteem issues and hormones appear to consume them. Such an emphasis positions teachers to question whether such hormonally burdened young people can respond capably or successfully to substantive intellectual tasks. In this way, unexamined conceptions of the nature of adolescents undeniably contribute to decisions about feasible school curricula and policies.

From a theoretical perspective, there is likewise a need to examine underlying conceptions of students in empirical and theoretical literature on youth. Walkerdine (1990) explains that "the purpose of examining the conceptualizations which form the bedrock of modern practices is to draw out the key terms to the regime of truth which is constituted in and by the practices" (p. 137). Walkerdine's argument accepts Foucault's characterization of the modern period in which social control changed from being wielded through repressive practices to practices of normalization. The creation of normal adolescents occurred along the same lines as did the demarcation of wayward girls (Schlossman & Wallach, 1978), juvenile delinquency (Platt, 1977), and White trash (Rafter, 1988). Populations were identified, usually as problems and with alleged defining characteristics, to be measured against *others* on the basis of physical, mental, and/or moral traits. The middle to late 1800s and early 1900s witnessed the steady production of knowledge in social sciences, medicine, education, and social work, among others, regarding normal individuals and groups.[2] Deviance was identified and studied, and professions and institutions were developed to respond to deviants (Macleod, 1983; Richardson, 1989). Buoyed by the knowledge of the new sciences of psychology, physical anthropology, biology, and sociology (Cravens, 1978), populations were labeled and treated as feeble-minded, morally disordered, wayward, and/or lacking parental guidance (Richardson, 1989). In defining and measuring the deviant populations such as the precocious and the laggards, the new researchers, social workers, and educators legitimated and enhanced their own positions as socially useful experts but also constructed scientifically grounded normalities. For example, as psychologists discussed the sources and hazards of both precocious and wayward youths, a normative unproblematic youth was constructed simultaneously.

To disavow the racist and classist attitudes of the new experts of the late 1800s but to continue to use their assumptions and conceptualizations, despite noble intentions, perpetuates their regime of truth. The interconnections between regulation of behavior and knowledge construction and use in the social sciences and in education are central to Fouaultian theory. Thus theories must be seen as part of interactional social practices, with particular effects in and on the ways in which adolescence and adolescents exist and mean. From this perspective, retheorizing is crucial to the construction of new social practices in and outside of schools.

This article is premised on connections between scientific research findings and socially regulative practices and asks how scientific knowledge about adolescent nature, located primarily in the field of psychology, participates in constructing and maintaining the boundaries for what may count as normal and deviant teenagers. However, I posit that adolescence has multiple registers of meaning and effects (Haraway, 1991) and functions as defining and limiting what counts as normal (and socially desirable) in the domains of civilized/uncivilized, sexual/asexual, rational/irrational, and manly/unmanly. Talk about adolescents—their problems, characteristics, and needs—is a central arena for talking about social expectations for productive, rational, independent adults.

When we specify the end product of the transition to adulthood as unified, self-reflective people with coherent identities and emotional control, we are specifying a normal developmental outcome that is gender, race, and class specific although masquerading as universal and neutral (Henriques, Hollway, Urwin, Venn, & Walkerdine, 1984; Walkerdine, 1990). In turn, the nature of adolescence is connected through a "chain of needs" (Fraser, 1989) to specific policies and practices. Along with the power to define nature and needs is the power to specify the response to that nature and needs. For example, when educators define young adolescents as having a need for close relationships with adults, curricular practices that provide homerooms or other types of mentoring or counseling opportunities are constructed simultaneously. To define, with empirical evidence, that adolescents have a particular nature and thus specific needs is to scientifically construct educational practices (Walkerdine, 1990). As Hall (1900) clearly understood, scientists who define youths' nature have enormous influence over all aspects of scientific pedagogy.

STRUGGLES TO DEFINE NATURE
According to Haraway (1989), nature in the last instance grounds identity: "A kind of being grounds a kind of knowledge, i.e., ontology grounds epistemology" (p. 417). Haraway (1991) maintains that knowledge in any scientific field contests for how to construct "what can authoritatively count as the case about the world" (p. 310). The present analysis challenges the reigning authoritative knowledge about adolescents and asks, What kind of being is the adolescent who grounds particular kinds of knowledge about adolescence?

The reigning conception of adolescents is that of a natural being, outside of specific historical time and place (Lipsitz, 1991).[3] The social processes through which teenagers are produced are removed in this view of adolescence, leaving a naturally occurring adolescent who are simultaneously defined as problematic, out of control (Walkerdine, 1990; Macleod, 1983), and, concomitantly, needing control by others (Haraway, 1991). If adolescents are portrayed as universal and ahistorical, then their characteristics are immutable. Consequently, they must be constrained by adults rather than by changes in the social and organizational practices that helped create them.

Feminist scholars in various fields have noted the politics of representing social constructions as natural objects. For example, anthoropologists Yanigasako and Collier (1990) argue that inquiries into childbearing and child rearing as socially constructed in particular historical situations are fundamentally undermined by the assumed natural biological division between women who bear children and men who do not. Yanigasako and Collier discuss how an acceptance of the nature/culture division in anthropological theory and research is concomitant with an acceptance of biology as universal, outside of cultural influences, and with inevitable social consequences for gendered division of labor. They argue that in not examining how biological sex differences are socially constructed, feminist theory ultimately is undermined by these biological differences. In a similar vein, Fausto-Sterling's (1985) critique of research on sex differences in intelligence and hormones amply illustrates the social consequences of empirical research on natural, or biological, differences as they have implications for educational policy and employment practices. Thus it is not enough to study the cultural or social aspects of adolescents, allowing the biological processes to stand as real truths outside of social processes. We must examine the ontological assertions regarding adolescence and the biological research that establishes them as natural and inevitable.

Understanding that scientific truths—whether theory or empirical findings—are the effects of sets of assumptions and practices, this article examines the "social being of truth" (Taussig, 1987, p. xiii) around adolescence. By examining the rhetoric and content of selected contemporary truths about adolescence and the contexts of their initial articulation during the late 1800s in the United States, I investigate the politics of a particular representation and interpretation of adolescence. The method of analysis is a montage of historical, rhetorical, and feminist analyses across the domains of the emerging disciplines of psychology, anthropology, and pedagogy (Taussig, 1987).

CONTEXTS OF THE MODERN DISCOURSE ON ADOLESCENCE

Although conceptions and representations of adolescence existed prior to the late 1800s, in that time period youth became an object of the emerging sciences of psychology, anthropology, and pedagogy (Walkerdine, 1990). That scientific conception of adolescence, articulated most effusively by the "father of adolescence," G. Stanley Hall, in his two-volume *Adolescence: Its Psychology and Its Relations to Physiology, Anthropology, Sociology, Sex, Crime, Religion, and Education* (Hall, 1905), was produced during a historical period characterized by broad social, economic, and scientific change. The scientific discourse on adolescence was constructed in the contexts of urbanization, industrialization, nationalism, colonization, domestic changes in family relations, and bureaucratization.[4] Thus scientific adolescents came into existence when the United States itself was a *young* modern nation and, in the eyes of certain groups, in turbulence, adrift, or, in the contemporary jargon, at risk. Wiebe (1967) characterizes that perplexity as follows:

> Americans in a basic sense no longer knew who or where they were. The setting had altered beyond their power to understand it, and within an alien context they had lost themselves. In a democratic society, who was master and who servant? In a land of opportunity, what was success? … The apparent leaders were as much adrift as their followers. For lack of anything that made better sense of their world, people everywhere weighed, counted, and measured it. (pp. 42–43)

Historians such as Wiebe (1967) and Platt (1977) argue that the sense of social confusion of that time period cannot be overstated; similarly strong was the belief among nativists that the United States had a clear choice between ordering the new disorderly immigrants (e.g., Catholics, Eastern Europeans, Blacks from the South) or being overtaken by socialist and ethnic demands. Historical accounts portray these decades as fateful, where America would prosper or decline, a clear turning point in the nation's history. I read the emergent discourse on adolescence as speaking with and to the (primarily) White, middle-class, nativist concerns about social order and progress during those turning-point years (Cravens, 1978; Macleod, 1983; Franklin, 1986).

The emergent discourse on adolescence also spoke with and to concerns about manliness, strength, and dominance. The concerns about order and progress were connected to a "nervous masculinity" (Macleod, 1983, p. 46) in which concerns about civilization and economic progress were interwoven with gender and dominance issues in families, workplaces (Smith-Rosenberg, 1985), and scientific research (Russett, 1989). Thus social and economic progress was seen as a problem of virility, strength, and/or dominance (Haraway, 1989; Macleod, 1983; Smith-Rosenberg, 1985), and adolescent development was a vehicle through which to discuss the means to secure strong wills and disciplined bodies among middle-class White males (Macleod, 1983). One sees this dimension of concern over boys in the spectacular growth of character-building organizations such as the Boy Scouts and youth programs of the YMCA during these years; these were conscious movements to get boys out of the hands of mothers and female teachers into comradeship with males (Macleod, 1983). Concerns about feminized boys were acute, especially in the Northeast, where the number of middle-class White youths had declined substantially. The precious resource of future leaders for America needed to be managed closely; to ensure potency, males needed to control against feminizing, that is, weakening influences. This move for remasculinization of youths was supported by viewing adolescence as a pivotal and problematic life stage and by scientific conceptions of development that defined middle-class White male characteristics as normative for adulthood and denigrated characteristics and behaviors identified as feminine or childish. A third context in which concerns of dominance and masculinity arose was the international. One sees this concern in Lord Baden-Powell's founding of the Boy Scouts, which was an outgrowth of his experiences in the Boer War and his resultant fears for the British Commonwealth's strength and viability. As a career officer, he wanted to promote early and continuous training of boys to be nationalistic, disciplined, and obedient to orders (Macleod, 1983; Rosenthal, 1984), and he packaged this regimen with the playfulness and camaraderie of camping, woodcraft, and nature lore. During the late 1800s, the United States emerged as a colonial power, and the connections between colonialist expansion and the new disciplines of psychology and anthropology are marked.[5]

Many scientists, working from a recapitulationist perspective, believed that inquiry into lower species such as women, savages, and children would illuminate the evolutionary progression of the race and factors contributing to or blocking such progress. If individual lives recapitulated the history of human evolution, they by studying those persons at lower evolved stages, scientists and educators could minimize the number of White males who were *arrested* at the lower stages of development. Thus greater contact among the United States, European nations, and savages through colonialism provoked scholarly interest in establishing scientifically the differences between civilized and uncivilized peoples and in securing the continued progress and dominance of the civilized (Haraway, 1989; Stocking, 1982). Anthropology and psychology were concerned with investigating differences between males and females, between adults and children, and between civilized peoples and savages. Psychologists of adolescence, such as Hall and his students and colleagues at Clark University, situated their inquiries within and across psychology and anthropology, explicitly drawing analogies across women, savages, and youths (Russett, 1989). Thus recapitulation theory is crucial for understanding the link among conceptions of adolescence, developmental psychology, and cultural anthropology because it established child development and human evolution as mirrors of one another. The identifiable stages of child development replicated the identified stages of the development of civilizations (savagery, barbarism, feudalism, constitutional government). The objects of study in psychology, anthropology, and child study were women, natives, and youths, and numerous parallels were established across the three natures. All three shared an otherness from middle-class White men, as well will see, in their emotionality, weakness, and failure to be disciplined individuals. The norm for development was constructed within and against the undeveloped, inferior, and/or arrested characteristics of women, natives, and children (Haraway, 1989; Walkerdine, 1990).

The discourse on adolescence during the late 1800s and early 1900s participated in three broad social arenas: the changes in the U.S. economic, urban, domestic, and corporate life; the struggle for masculine control within the new families, institutions, and industries; and the colonialist and nationalist concern for progress and domination. In this view, adolescence spoke about controlled change and development, reason, potency, and discipline, and it linked these positive attributes with Euro-American middle-class masculinity. Adolescence is positioned to discuss and mark boundaries for proper development, civilized thought and behavior, productivity, reason, and masculine virility. Thus adolescence, situated across the academic questions (and social conflicts) of race and ethnicity in anthropology and the questions of gender and normality in psychology, spoke with and to concerns for establishing intellectual and social boundaries between normal/abnormal, civilized/savage, masculine/feminine, and sexual/nonsexual.

But to stipulate in this brief way the social and scientific contexts in which adolescence emerged is insufficient to the task of denaturalizing adolescence. In addition to drawing the contexts in which scientific findings were produced, we must investigate the scientific truths regarding adolescence for the presence of these histories (Smith, 1990). The following sections pursue that aim by examining the "confident characterizations" (Trinh, 1989) of adolescence for how anxieties about control, normality, masculinity, and sexuality, among others, are reproduced in contemporary visions of youth.

COMING OF AGE

Adolescents *come of age* into adulthood. Adolescents are *at the threshold* of adulthood. Adolescence is also referred to as the *transition to adulthood*. Gould (1991) suggests that these terms have an evolutionary connection, a sense of coming into an enlightened period after a long darkness. Hall was an evolutionary psychologist (Curti, 1959; Gould, 1977), and he believed that adolescence was a time of an evolutionary leap of individuals and of the race. If the species, and individual young men, were not to be arrested at the gang stage (boys from the ages of 8–11 years), then adolescents must be helped to develop.

Coming of age participates in what Wood (1984) characterizes as an "ideology of emergence" (p. 73). Wood found that adults in secondary schools considered teenagers, but specifically the sex drive of young males, as naturally emerging, outside of social influences or relations, and this allowed adults in schools to turn their backs on sexist practices. Wood's analysis of an ideology of emergence points to a conception of adolescence as outside of society, just emerging from within, rather than socially constituted and constituting.[6] Coming of age locates the force of the arrival in youths as natural creatures, arriving at age akin to how spring arrives each year with the swelling of tree buds. Natural and portentious, coming of age signifies an important, powerful, and uncontrollable change.

Chudacoff (1989) demonstrates how industrial capitalism, technological advances, medicine, and education all operated during the late 1880s and early 1900s to develop an age-conscious America. Schools began age grading (Kett, 1977), and psychologists provided tests for mental age as well (Richardson, 1989). Hand in hand with the identification of distinctive and narrowly age-bounded peer groups, norms for behavior were articulated. Coming age also carries norms for behavior, which provide standards by which deviance can be identified. Age became a major factor in the normalizing of populations. Youths in age-graded and mentally measured school classrooms could be identified as age appropriate, as "on time," precocious, or slow (Macleod, 1983). Similarly, pedagogies could be evaluated for their age appropriateness (Walkerdine, 1990). Chudacoff carefully describes how narrow bands of age peers became normed by specific expectations for behavior and accomplishments in health, in schooling, and in play. Thus the terms coming of age and at the threshold identify youths at the turn of a new normative period of life.

Trinh (1989) terms language such as coming of age and at the threshold as "homiletic,"[7] capturing the mix of patriarchal preaching and scientific gospel found in much scientific rhetoric (Brumberg, 1988; Haraway, 1989). Trinh demonstrates how such homiletic language appears to give the subject—adolescents—importance but really confers greater authority on the author of the homily. If a scientist proclaims the potentials and problems of coming age, then the scientist who is defining the not yet of age is positionally superior. Being in the state of coming of age erases the ability of those in the state to describe or know themselves and places the privilege and responsibility on adult experts to explain adolescents. Anthropologist Victor Turner used the term "liminality" to describe the position of persons between states, in the midst of a rite of passage, outside of social positions and power (Turner, 1969). Trinh's (1989) critique of colonialist anthropology also applies to youth; she writes that the natives (or adolescents) are the "handicapped who cannot represent themselves and have to either be represented or learn how to represent themselves" (p. 59). Adolescents are similar to colonized natives when scientists declare them to be coming of age, a rhetorical move my which the experts "strip their identity off and paste it back on" (p. 12). Adolescents are emptied out, made liminal, and then reconstituted by scientific descriptors and schooling practices.

To mass youths together with the terms coming of age and at the threshold sets up a clear positional superiority of adults over adolescents based on age. Age is a positional superiority in which adults always come out better, no matter what the particular issues or behaviors. Coming of age reduces human subjectivity to one dimension—age—accompanied by shadowy evolutionary images of animal, savage, and civilized societies.

What sources, functions, and effects might such a positional massification of youths have? Haraway (`1989) writes that massification, or dehumanization, needs a story.[8] What is the story that allows us to reduce adolescents to a one-dimensional mass on the basis of age? Spacks (1981) argues that "our psychology confirms our sociology" (p. 290). The old have power in our society, and it follows that our psychology illuminates how the undeveloped—the young—are lacking. Other scholars point to the economic conditions of industrial capitalism during the late 1800s, which diminished work opportunities such as apprenticeships. As a result, middle-class youths remained economically dependent on families longer, and extended schooling became more normative in securing jobs in the changing economy (Kett, 1977; Modell & Goodman, 1990; Ryan, 1981). However, if Haraway (1989) is correct, then neither the sociological nor the economic analysis alone helps understand the story that supports the massification of adolescents into the liminal coming of age.

To inquire further into the massification of adolescence and adolescents' scientifically based inferiority, I turn to the other two confident discourses on adolescence: that adolescents are hormone driven and that teenagers are overwhelmingly influenced by peers. Being teenaged locates a young person in a liminal state, but the hormonal and peer-oriented descriptors provide the action and problems of the naturalized story of adolescence.

BIOLOGY IS DESTINY: THE ADOLESCENT BODY

> Sex asserts its mastery in field after field, and works its havoc in the form of secret vice, debauch, disease, and enfeebled heredity, cadences the soul to both its normal and abnormal rhythms. … Thus the foundations of domestic, social and religious life are oftenest undermined. (Hall, 1905, p. xii)

The second confident characteristic of adolescents declares that they are controlled by hormones and, therefore, dangerously out of control.[9] The onset of pubertal growth sets in motion hormonal changes that determine physiological growth and affect emotions. The image of a storm-tossed land is invoked; the adolescent body is tormented by the physiological and emotional storm of hormonal changes. Hall also wrote of adolescent disorientation stemming from being driven from the Garden of Eden of childhood. Both metaphors link images of nature with crisis.

In a recent comprehensive anthology of research on adolescence in the developmental framework, the editors write that "biological processes drive many aspects of adolescence, although social contexts shape the expression of biological imperatives to a remarkable degree" (Feldman & Elliott, 1990, p. 1). The chapter on adolescent sexuality in the same collection opens by stating that "reproductive maturation is the most distinctive feature of the transition from childhood to adulthood. It is also potentially the most problematic" (Katchadourian, 1990, p. 330). Read together, these statements identify biology, or reproductive maturation, as driving many aspects of adolescence.[10]

The medical model of the human being is invoked here, "the belief that biology is primary, that hormonal changes cause behavioral ones, but not vice versa" (Fausto-Sterling, 1985, p. 100). This is the paradigm of biological causation, a linear, unicausal model of human behavior. Fausto-Sterling analyzes how this model leads to a set of beliefs, supported by problematic studies, about menstruation and menopause. When biology is viewed as the sole cause of behavior, "the hormonal renders the social inevitable" (Goldberg, 1973, p. 93).

"The idea that women's reproductive systems direct their lives is ancient" (Fausto-Sterling, 1985, p. 91). The fluctuations of women's systems (naturally abnormal women) render them untrustworthy in positions of responsibility.

> Their dangerous, unpredictable furies warrant control by the medical profession, while ironi-cally, the same "dangerous" females also need protection because their reproductive systems, so necessary for the procreation of the race, are vulnerable to stress and hard work. (pp. 91–92)

We know that thoughts, mind-sets, and emotions can affect a woman's menstrual cycle; for example, exhaustion, travel, illness, and/or stress can alter the timing of a menstrual flow, change the number and intensity of premenstrual signals, and influence discomfort. These all are variations in the physiological monthly cycle, influenced by a woman's emo-tional state and, in turn, by social and economic situations. The biological primacy model, also called the "normative disease-model framework," ignores historical and cultural con-texts, as it also pathologizes changeableness or rhythmicity as either "inherently unhealthy" or judged according to appropriate norms for change (Koeske, 1980, p. 8).

Adolescence is similarly conceived from the biological causation model, with biological changes being primary and unidirectional, resulting in disequilibration—the storms of hormones and moods. The quotes at the beginning of this section assert that adolescence, with its fluctuations, charges, and unpredictability, is attributed to "biological impera-tives" or "reproductive [sic] maturation." Context is only *grafted on* and shapes the expres-sion of the biological forces (James & Prout, 1990).[11]

Fausto-Sterling (1985) argues that a simple linear model of biological causation is inad-equate for theory and research on hormones in women and men and that we must strug-gle for a complex conceptualization in which mind, body, and culture depend on one another inextricably. Similarly, adolescence requires a conceptualization in which physical changes are viewed as interrelated with mind and feeling in specific situations. Such a con-ceptualization would contribute to a view of youth as socially constructed, within particu-lar contexts and discourses, rather than universal, timeless, and massified.

A related problem in the discourse on adolescents as body out of control is the objecti-fied, developing body. Leder (1990) writes,

> Since the seventeenth century, the body has been primarily identified with its scientific description, that is, regarded as a material object whose anatomical and functional properties can be characterized according to general scientific law. The human body is taken as essen-tially no different from any other physical object. (p. 5)

This scientific account emphasizes the body as experienced from a third-person rather than from a first-person perspective.

Leder (1990) proposes investigating the "lived body" rather than the physical body. The lived body is the locus of experience, not just a constellation of hormones that get "expressed" in different social contexts. The lived body is the embodied self that lives and breathes, perceives and acts, speaks and reasons. The lived body is not a located thing but rather is a path of access, a being in the world.

Leder (1990) illustrates the concept of the lived body with a discussion of what it means to learn how to swim, which is not merely a physical skill comprised of mechanical movements. In Leder's view, the skill of swimming is *incorporated*. When Leder learned to swim, his relationship to the world also changed: "I operate from that new skill upon the world.... For example, the lake looks different than in my pre-swimming days, when it could not be crossed and offered no access" (p. 32). Perspective and perception changed with physical ability. Incorporation of new skills is the result of a "rich dialectic wherein the world transforms my body, even as my body transforms its world" (p. 34). This is an investigation of the body from the first-person perspective, an approach that could provide a socially located understanding of pubertal changes that included physical, mental, and emotional dimensions.

Adolescent bodies in this second confident characterization of physical and hormonal changes are objectified as things that are out of control. A denaturalizing of adolescence must include both a view of body in interaction with the world and a first-person, lived body perspective.

PEER CULTURES AND PEER PRESSURE

The third confident characterization about adolescents is that they are strongly peer oriented. Coleman's (1961) study, *The Adolescent Society,* is the cornerstone of the contemporary sociological evidence for this aspect of adolescent nature. In a study of student attitudes in 10 high schools, Coleman found that being popular was more important than getting good grades. Although Coleman's findings have been critiqued (Brown, 1990), numerous other field studies[12] confirm the conclusions (or begin with the assumptions) that friends are more important to teenagers than is anything else. By examining similar strains in Victorian psychology's view of women and savages, I show how this taken-for-granted view is a demeaning one, a term that again massifies and positions its objects as immature, dangerous, and needing to be controlled. Some feminist and cultural critiques of psychological and social psychological research[13] characterize the bias against peer-oriented social relations in work like Coleman's as evidence of the dominant White, middle-class, male perspective throughout the sciences. Whose lives and values are supported in the demeaning of peer orientations? Does the pathologizing of peer orientation exhalt individual autonomy as a primary characteristic of adulthood?

Victorian psychologists studied and pronounced on the natures of women, savages, and children. All three were "undeveloped men," that is, seen as deficient against the norm of middle-class European men. Men were believed to be stronger intellectually, creatively, in will, and in achievement drives. Two characterizations of women and savages by the Victorian psychologists relate to peer orientation.

First, the undeveloped men were less individuated.

> Endowed with less measure of individuality, women resembled one another more than did men. Women's nature was more generic and less specific. Each woman is a more adequate representative of her sex than a man is of his. (Russett, 1989, pp. 74–75)

Russett translates this assertion into the colloquialism, If you've seen one, then you've seen them all. Thus women were seen as uniform.

Second, the psychological correlate of this uniformity of women was conformity. "Women go in flocks, and in social matters are less prone to stand out with salient individuality"(Russett, 1989, p. 75).

Both of these characteristics are regularly attributed to adolescents, who are characterized as succumbing to peer pressure and being part of peer cultures, which socialize them to peer norms. Whether it be middle-class youths with norms of sexuality or drug use or studies of gangs or of high school groups, friends are the most important and influential people in adolescents' lives. The linking of uniformity and conformity among adolescents in relation to strong peer orientation persists in current research, with some modifications.[14] This conceptualization establishes teenagers as dangerous *others*, not as individuated adults. Fabian (1983) notes how the term "culture" historically has been used as part of the description of and distancing from others. The application of the term culture to youth (e.g., youth subculture or peer culture) helps create conceptual distance between the activities and perspectives of those with a culture and those with "practical reason" (Sahlins, 1976).

This third characterization of adolescents as excessively peer oriented is also portrayed as naturally occurring. When youths reach the age of puberty, they long for only the companionship of other youths. However, little attention is given to the impact of social practices and attitudes on youths' peer orientation. The separation of youths in age-segregated middle and high schools for 6 hours each day must have a strong impact on looking to other youths for norms, approval, and companionship. The sociological work of Eisenstadt (1964) suggests that in a highly competitive, production-oriented society, youth friendships may be the sole arena for affirmation as a person without evaluation by external standards. Corroborating the social structural seclusion of youths, Greenberger and Steinberg's (1986) study of teenagers' waged labor shows that even in contemporary jobs, youths work primarily with peers and have little interaction with or supervision by adults. These studies suggest that peer orientation is as likely to be an effect of social and institutional arrangements as it is a foundational element of adolescent nature.

To identify adolescents as succumbing to peer pressure and, therefore, as insufficiently individuated also contributes to the expecting adults to act as autonomous individuals, a norm that has been analyzed and critiqued by scholars in several fields (e.g., Bellah, Madsen, Sullivan, Swidler, & Tipton, 1985; Gilligan, 1982; Varenne, 1977). To demean peer pressure has the effect of privileging an individualism that historically is associated with middle-class White males and largely alien to the experiences of many people of color and women. Thus this aspect of the discourse on adolescence validates individual autonomy as the superior mode of being in the world, a position that is problematic for contemporary economic, environmental, and family situations.

AGE DUALISM: ADOLESCENT/ADULT

The scientific view of adolescents, as examined through three of its most confident characteristic discourses, draws from and contributes to a series of binary oppositions that include adolescent/adult, feminine/masculine, savage/civilized, emotions/reason, body/mind, massed/individuated, and culture/practical reason. Adolescence participates in multiple registers of meaning in social, cultural, and economic life. One result of these multiple binary oppositions is to reify age in a way that appears completely natural. People between the ages of 12 and 17 years are believed to naturally and inevitably possess certain characteristics and behaviors that correspond with essentially different natures than those of adults. The set of binary oppositions cements adults in positions of superiority, regardless of the topic. Adolescents have been constructed and problematized in a way similar to the modern conception of the elderly (Cole, 1984), with the effect of making youthfulness the problem of adolescents and denying a basic human solidarity in growing up. When groups such as the elderly or the young are constructed as other and problematic, social regulation of these others is supported and specified by the social science experts who represent them.

By examining the confident characterizations regarding adolescence, I have endeavored to call into question the naturalness of the hierarchy of adult over youth that is part of the modern scientific discourse on adolescence. Historian Joan Scott summarizes the aims of such denaturalizing:

> We must find ways (however imperfect) continually to subject our categories to criticism, our analyses to self-criticism. If we employ Derrida's definition of deconstruction, this criticism means analyzing in context the way any binary opposition operates, reversing and displacing its hierarchical construction, rather than accepting it as real or self-evident or in the nature of things. (Scott, 1988, p. 41)

CONCLUSION

I have articulated a critique of the reigning conceptions of adolescence as twice naturalized in that they portray particular characteristics of youths between the ages of 12 and 17 years as naturally occurring and as having natures that essentially are distinct from those of adults and children. In critiquing the naturalized status of adolescence, I seek to contest for the scientific account of what counts as knowledge about adolescence and to establish the social nature of adolescents over the abstracted, ahistorical, individualized view that ends up confirming, backed by scientific evidence, that teenagers need to be controlled.

The analytical approach employed here first examined the rhetorical construction of adolescence in the continuing use of terms such as coming of age and at the threshold. This homiletic style helps establish the age as important but also as indecipherable by those undergoing the portentious changes. Teenagers are massed together on the single criterion of age.

Feminist critiques of research on hormones provide a model for scrutinizing assumptions of a biologically driven view of human beings. Because adolescence is defined on the basis of biological changes of puberty, which are presumed to be disruptive and destabilizing, this characterization of adolescence also contributes to a view of teenagers as dangerous and out of control. Because teenagers are biologically (and thus inevitably) unstable, adult control is a logical and necessary response. This characterization has important consequences for school practices and curriculum; adolescents are considered under the control of hormones and unavailable for serious (i.e., critical) school tasks and responsibilities.

The third confident characterization of teenagers is that they are peer oriented or prone to cliques and gangs. This characterization provides further evidence of their irresponsibility and untrustworthiness; bolsters the White, middle-class, male norm of individual autonomy as synonymous with maturity; and supports adult control of youths' lives. No attention is given to the sociohistorical segmentation of teenagers into organizations with narrow age bands and the lessening of contact with adults or children as the contexts for turning toward age mates. Peer orientation has been naturalized as a universal, naturally occurring characteristic of teenagers. The deconstructive moves of this analysis are initial steps in a larger examination of the production of adolescence in sciences, schools, and popular culture. Assumptions regarding the distinctive nature of youths and the acceptance that adolescence unfolds of its own accord in the individual teenaged body, triggered by hormones, are significant effects of social practices and scientific discourses. I believe that a view of teenagers as essentially out of control due to hormonal storms plays an important part in maintaining control of youths as the highest value in secondary schools and simultaneously legitimates a dumbing down of the curriculum. Only those youths who demonstrate how reason, rather than hormones, rules their lives (e.g., youths who are compliant with and successful in meeting educators' demands for how, when, and what to learn and accept as important) are deemed mature and given some small measures of freedom and responsibility. In the interest of changing widely held conceptions of teenagers as disequilibrated, out of control, and requiring continual surveillance, I have begun these critiques of how social scientists and educators contribute to the construction of adolescents as natural and problematic.

NOTES

1. Of course, reformers moving toward more humane or liberatory practices are joined by reformers interested in producing more orderly, regulated, predictable workers (Labaree, 1992).
2. See, for example, Henriques, Hollway, Urwin, Venn, and Walkerdine (1984), Luke (1989), Rafter (1988), Richardson (1989), and Walkerdine (1990).
3. I am not ignoring the scholarship on the history of childhood, which clearly locates youth in specific historical and social situations. Nevertheless, the concept of adolescence carries modernist baggage of ahistorical, asocial subjectivity. However, for recent work that attempts to rectify this, see Elder, Modell, and Parke (1993) and James and Prout (1990).
4. For elaboration on the turn-of-the-century period, see Gay (1984), Kett (1977), Macleod (1983), Ryan (1981), Schlossman (1977), Smith-Rosenberg (1985), and Wiebe (1967).
5. For examining connections among the new sciences and colonialist expansion, three very important works are Cravens (1978), Haraway (1989), and Stocking (1982). However, this is by no means a definitive list of useful scholarship on this topic.
6. The conception of youth as outside of society is also visible in scholarship on peer sexual harassment in schools and its accepted status as natural, as "boys being boys" (see Stein, 1993).
7. Speier (1976) terms this perspective an "adult ideological" perspective, whereas Alanen (1988) critiques it as elitist. Each characterization captures a different dimension of its social relations.
8. See Haraway's (1989, p. 231) *Primate Visions*. Haraway's actual words are that "sadism demands a story," a quote from Laura Mulvey. However, I think that the sense in which she invokes sadism can be broadened to dehumanization.
9. Hall's (1905) quote refers to some of the social fears of his and our time: national, economic, and social decline due to failure to control sexuality. The bodies of Black youths, especially Black girls, are central to these anxieties in both Hall's time and in the present. Space does not permit a discussion of the racialization of sexuality issues that are encoded in the problems of teenage sexuality. For an introduction to those issues, see Lesko (1995) and Solinger (1992).
10. I have selected particular quotations that support my argument from the lengthy and varied Feldman and Elliott (1990) anthology. At numerous points in the anthology, authors state that the unilinear biological approach to conceptualizing youth is inadequate. Nevertheless, I argue that in a fundamental way, developmental perspectives are grounded in biology and can be faulted in the way Fausto-Sterling (1985) does. In arguing this point, I also rely on the critique that psychology is grounded on a humanistic view of human beings as autonomous individuals outside of society (Henriques et al., 1984). The biological view of youth participates in that modernist, asocial definition of human beings. Two recent volumes that will be helpful on denaturalizing biological characterizations, but that arrived too late for use in this analysis, are Oudshoorn (1994) and Tiefer (1995).

11. Zuckerman (1993) claims that historical analysis of children and youths often is used as a prologue to the "real" data, presided over by developmental psychologists (p. 231). This is a different way of characterizing the failure to contextualize.

12. For example, see Brake (1985), Cusick (1973), Dunphy (1969), Larkin (1979), Hammersley and Woods (1984), and Willis (1977).

13. In psychology, see Gilligan (1982) and Hare-Mustin and Marecek (1990). In anthropology, see Heath (1983), Lubeck (1985); Stack (1974), and Varenne (1977).

14. For example, see Brown (1990). Schwartz (1987) portrays the dualism attendant in this conformity view. When teenagers (or women or natives) are not oversocialized, they are undersocialized or rebellious. Neither the conforming nor the rebelling position of youth gathers much positive support, although both are generally thought to be in the nature of adolescents.

REFERENCES

Alanen, L. (1988). Rethinking childhood. *Acta Sociologica, 31*, 53–67.

Bellah, R. N., Madsen, R., Sullivan, W. M., Swidler, A., & Tipton, S. M. (1985). *Habits of the heart: Individualism and commitment in American life.* Berkeley: University of California Press.

Brake, M. (1985). *Comparative youth culture.* London: Routledge and Kegan Paul.

Brown, B. B. (1990). Peer groups and peer cultures. In S. S. Feldman & G. R. Elliott (Eds.), *At the threshold: The developing adolescent* (pp. 171–196). Cambridge, MA: Harvard University Press.

Brumberg. J. J. (1988). *Fasting girls: The emergence of anorexia nervosa as a modern disease.* Cambridge, MA: Harvard University Press.

Chudacoff, H. P. (1989). *How old are you? Age consciousness in American culture.* Princeton, NJ: Princeton University Press.

Cole, T. R. (1984). The prophecy of *Senescence*: G. Stanley Hall and the reconstruction of old age in America. *The Gerontologist, 24*, 360–366.

Coleman, J. S. (1961). *The adolescent society.* New York: Free Press.

Cravens, H. (1978). *The triumph of evolution: American scientists and the heredity-environment controversy, 1900–1911.* Philadelphia: University of Pennsylvania Press.

Curti, M. (1959). *The social ideas of American educators.* Paterson, NJ: Littlefield. Adams.

Cusick, P. (1973). *Inside high school.* New York: Holt, Rinehart & Winston.

Dunphy, D. (1969). *Cliques, crowds, and gangs.* Melbourne, Australia: Cheshire.

Eisenstadt, S. N. (1964). *From generation to generation: Age groups and social structure* (2nd ed.). New York: Free Press.

Elder, G. H., Jr., Modell, J., & Parke, R. D. (Eds.). (1993). *Children in time and place: Developmental and historical insights.* New York: Cambridge University Press.

Fabian, J. (1983). *Time and the other: How anthropology makes its object.* New York: Columbia University Press.

Fausto-Sterling, A. (1985). *Myths of gender: Biological theories about women and men.* New York: Basic Books.

Feldman, S. S., & Elliott, G. R. (Eds.). (1990). *At the threshold: The developing adolescent.* Cambridge, MA: Harvard University Press.

Franklin, B. (1986). *The struggle for the American community.* London: Falmer.

Fraser, N. (1989). *Unruly practices: Power, discourse and gender in contemporary social theory.* Minneapolis: University of Minnesota Press.

Gay, P. (1984). *The bourgeois experience, Victoria to Freud* (Vol. 1). New York: Oxford University Press.

Gilligan, C. (1982). *In a different voice.* Cambridge, MA: Harvard University Press.

Goldberg, S. (1973). *The inevitability of patriarchy.* New York: William Morrow.

Gould, S. J. (1977). *Ontogeny and phylogeny.* Cambridge, MA: Belknap.

Gould, S. J. (1991). *Bully for the brontosaurus.* New York: Basic Books.

Greenberger, E., & Steinberg, L. D. (1986). *When teenagers work.* New York: Basic Books.

Hall, G. S. (1900). Child study and its relation to education. *Forum, 29*, 688–693, 696–702.

Hall, G. S. (1905). *Adolescence: Its psychology and its relations to physiology, anthropology, sociology, sex, crime, religion, and education* (Vol. 1). New York: Appleton.

Hammersley, M., & Woods, P. (Eds.). (1984). *Life in school.* Milton Keynes, England: Open University Press.

Haraway, D. J. (1989). *Primate visions: Gender, race, and nature in the world of modern science.* New York: Routledge.

Haraway, D. J. (1991). *Simians, cyborgs, and women: The reinvention of nature.* New York: Routledge.

Hare-Mustin, R. T., & Marecek, J. (Eds.). (1990). *Making a difference.* New Haven, CT: Yale University Press.

Hawes, J. M., & Hiner, N. R. (Eds.). (1985). *American childhood: A research guide and historical handbook.* Westport, CT: Greenwood.

Heath, S. B. (1983). *Ways with words.* New York: Cambridge University Press.

Henriques, J., Hollway, W., Urwin, C., Venn, C., & Walkerdine, V. (1984). *Changing the subject: Psychology, social regulation, and subjectivity.* London: Methuen.

James, A., & Prout, A. (1990). *Constructing and reconstructing childhood: Contemporary issues in the sociological study of childhood.* London: Falmer.

Katchadourian, H. (1990). Sexuality. In S. S. Feldman & G. R. Elliott (Eds.), *At the threshold: The developing adolescent* (pp. 330–351). Cambridge, MA: Harvard University Press.

Kett, J. (1977). *Rites of passage: Adolescence in America, 1790 to the present.* New York: Basic Books.

Koeske, R. (1980). Theoretical perspectives on menstrual cycle research. In A. Dan, E. Graham, & C. P. Beecher (Eds.), *The menstrual cycle* (Vol. 1, pp. 8–24). New York: Springer.

Labaree, D. (1992). Doing good, doing science: The Holmes Group reports and the rhetorics of educational reform. *Teachers College Record, 93,* 628–640.

Larkin, R. W. (1979). *Suburban youth in cultural crisis.* New York: Oxford University Press.

Leder, D. (1990). *The absent body.* Chicago: University of Chicago Press.

Lesko, N. (1995). The "leaky needs" of school-aged mothers: An examination of U.S. programs and policies. *Curriculum Inquiry, 25*(2), 25–40.

Lipsitz, J. (1991). Public policy and young adolescents: A 1990s context for researchers. *Journal of Early Adolescence, 11,* 20–37.

Lubeck, S. (1985). *Sandbox society.* London: Falmer.

Luke, C. (1989). *Pedagogy, printing, and Protestantism: The discourse on childhood.* Albany: State University of New York Press.

Macleod, D. I. (1983). *Building character in the American boy: The Boy Scouts, YMCA, and their forerunners, 1870–1920.* Madison: University of Wisconsin Press.

Modell, J., & Goodman, M. (1990). Historical perspectives. In S. S. Feldman & G. R. Elliott (Eds.), *At the threshold: The developing adolescent* (pp. 93–122). Cambridge, MA: Harvard University Press.

Oudshoorn, N. (1994). *Beyond the natural body: An archeology of sex hormones.* London: Routledge.

Platt, A. M. (1977). *The child savers: The invention of delinquency.* Chicago: University of Chicago Press.

Rafter, N. H. (Ed.). (1988). *White trash: The eugenic family studies. 1877–1919.* Boston: Northeastern University Press.

Richardson, T. (1989). *Century of the child: The mental hygiene movement and social policy in the U.S. and Canada.* Albany: State University of New York Press.

Rosenthal, M. (1984). *The character factory: Baden-Powell and the origins of the Boy Scout movement.* New York: Pantheon Books.

Russett, C. E. (1989). *Sexual science: The Victorian construction of womanhood.* Cambridge, MA: Harvard University Press.

Ryan, M. P. (1981). *Cradle of the middle class: The family in Oneida County. New York, 1790–1865.* New York: Cambridge University Press.

Sahlins, M. (1976). *Culture and practical reason.* Chicago: University of Chicago Press.

Schlossman, S. (1977). *Love and the American delinquent: The theory and practice of "progressive" juvenile justice, 1825–1920.* Chicago: University of Chicago Press.

Schlossman, S., & Wallach, S. (1978). The crime of precocious sexuality: Female juvenile delinquency in the Progressive Era. *Harvard Educational Review, 48,* 65–94.

Schwartz, G. (1987). *Beyond conformity or rebellion: Youth and authority in America.* Chicago: University of Chicago Press.

Scott, J. W. (1988). *Gender and the politics of history.* New York: Columbia University Press.

Smith, D. E. (1990). *The conceptual practices of power: A feminist sociology of knowledge.* Boston: Northeastern University Press.

Smith-Rosenberg, C. (1985). *Disorderly conduct: Visions of gender in Victorian America.* New York: Oxford University Press.

Solinger, R. (1992). *Wake up little Susie: Single pregnancy and race before Roe v. Wade.* New York: Routledge.

Spacks, P. M. (1981). *The adolescent idea: Myths of youth and the adult imagination.* New York: Basic Books.

Speier, M. (1976). The adult ideological viewpoint in studies of childhood. In A. Skolnick (Ed.), *Rethinking childhood* (pp. 175–192). Boston: Little, Brown.

Stack, C. (1974). *All our kin.* New York: Harper & Row.

Stein, N. D. (1993). It happens here, too: Sexual harassment and child sexual abuse in elementary and secondary schools. In S. K. Biklen & D. Pollard (Eds.), *Gender and education* (pp. 191–203. Chicago: National Society for the Study of Education.

Stocking, G. W. (1982). *Race, culture, and evolution: Essays in the history of anthropology* (2nd ed.). Chicago: University of Chicago Press.

Taussig, M. (1987). *Shamanism, colonialism, and the wild man: A study in terror and healing.* Chicago: University of Chicago Press.

Tiefer, L. (1995). *Sex is not a natural act and other essays.* Boulder, CO: Westview.

Trinh, T. M. (1989). *Woman, native, other.* Bloomington: Indiana University Press.

Turner, V. (1969). *The ritual process.* Ithaca, NY: Cornell University Press.

Varenne, H. (1977). *Americans together.* New York: Teachers College Press.

Walkerdine, V. (1990). *Schoolgirl fictions.* London: Verso.

Wiebe, R. (1967). *The search for order, 1877–1920.* Westport, CT: Greenwood.

Willis, P. (1977). *Learning to labor: How working class kids get working class jobs.* London: Columbia University Press.

Wood, J. (1984). Groping towards sexism: Boys' sex talk. In A. McRobbie & M. Nava (Eds.), *Gender and generation* (pp. 54–84). London: Macmillan.

Yanigasako, S. J., & Collier, J. F. (1990). The mode of reproduction in anthropology. In D. L. Rhode (Ed.), *Theoretical perspectives on sexual difference* (pp. 131–144). New Haven, CT: Yale University Press.

Zuckerman, M. (1993). History and developmental psychology, a dangerous liaison: A historian's perspective. In G. H. Elder, Jr., J. Modell, & R. D. Parke (Eds.), *Children in time and place: Developmental and historical insights* (pp. 230–240). New York: Cambridge University Press.

6

The Invention of the Sexual Adolescent

JEFFREY P. MORAN

The most rigid chastity of fancy, heart and body is physiologically and psychologically as well as ethically imperative until maturity is complete on into the twenties, nor is it hard if continence is inward.

—G. STANLEY HALL, *ADOLESCENCE* (1904)

AT THE DAWN of the twentieth century, a sixty-year-old man invented adolescence. After decades of vocational uncertainty and then years of frenetic research in child study, philosophy, psychology, and the social sciences, G. Stanley Hall, a psychologist and president of Clark University, published in 1904 a two-volume work devoted to the special situation and needs of young people who had reached puberty but were still too young to marry. Only with the publication of *Adolescence*, Hall's masterpiece of research and creative interpretation, did Americans begin to speak of that new category of being, the Adolescent.

The new word signified deep changes. For decades—even centuries—before, Americans had considered young people to be more like inchoate, inferior adults than a separate class unto themselves. But by the late nineteenth century this older view was fading, gradually being eclipsed by a vision of youth as a unique period of life, with its own dynamic and its own demands. A great many Americans were growing vaguely aware of this shift, and young people were becoming increasingly conscious of their separateness as a group from adult culture, but overt recognition of youth's new position awaited Hall's investigations at the turn of the century. Adolescence is a modern invention.

While the American adolescent is a child of the twentieth century, Hall and his fellow popularizers of the concept invested adolescence with the moral values dear to the previous century. In particular, they built the structure of adolescence solidly upon a foundation of nineteenth-century sexual morality. Hall's plain demand for chastity in 1904, for example, seemed a fitting continuation of the warnings against "self-pollution" that pervaded mid-nineteenth-century America. This correspondence was hardly accidental, for Hall and the generation of men and women who developed the concept of adolescence were children of their times. They had grown to maturity under the public moral code that later generations would label—and libel—as "Victorianism," with its characteristic embrace of elevated sentiment and repressed sexuality.

Hall and his allies had also experienced firsthand the peculiar historical circumstances that led to the dominance of Victorianism among middle-class Americans. In the United States, the imperative for sexual self-control, which lay at the heart of Victorian morality, was rooted in a centuries-old tradition of Christian asceticism, but in the context of the unsettled American way of life early in the nineteenth century—the new excitements of democracy, an exploding economy, rapid urbanization, feminist reform—this imperative to curb one's desires grew more insistent, more dynamic, and more public. Far from a matter confined to the bedroom, sexuality and sexual control came to define the Victorian concern for the civilized self.

Although G. Stanley Hall had grown ambivalent about many aspects of this civilized sexual morality, at the beginning of the twentieth century he nevertheless tied the new concept of adolescence directly to the same tradition of sexual control that he had for years suffered from, exemplified, and, despite himself, perpetuated. Nor was Hall the only American at the time to link adolescence with sexuality, for many Americans had shared in one way or the other the experiences that led Hall to his conclusion. to understand the meaning of adolescence in the twentieth century is to come to terms with the Victorian sexual ideology of the nineteenth century and the social changes that gave this ideology such cultural force.

"I believe my whole affective life is as strong and deep, and perhaps more so, than that of most I know," wrote G. Stanley Hall as he neared eighty, "but I have never been able to entirely escape the early atmosphere of repression of sentiment."[1] Born in 1844 and reared by pious parents in rural Ashfield, Massachusetts, Hall early developed what his biographer calls an "ambivalence" between his own natural depth of feeling and his community's expectation that its citizens would suppress their emotions. As Hall's own youth and early manhood would demonstrate, nowhere was the expectation of repression stronger than in the sexual arena.

Hall's parents were farmers in Ashfield, and on their meager land Hall learned early the rudiments of sex and reproduction from observing the activities of sheep, pigs, cattle, and horses. Although that experience was undoubtedly instructive, Hall seems to have been much more struck by the unconscious and conscious sexual lessons his parents taught. When Hall was very young, he was taught to refer to his genitals only as "the dirty place," and for years he continued to believe that this was their "proper and adopted designation." Later on, his father delivered to Stanley and some other boys a brief moral about a youth who, as Hall recalled decades later, "abused himself and sinned with lewd women and as a result had a disease that ate his nose away until there were only two flat holes in his face for nostrils and who also became an idiot."[2]

The story unquestionably made an impression: for a long time afterward, every time young Stanley Hall had an erection or a nocturnal emission, he became "almost petrified" that he was growing feebleminded, and he carefully examined the bridge of his nose "to see if it was getting the least bit flat." From all that he heard and inferred from his elders and his fellow students, Hall concluded "that any one who swerved in the slightest from the norm of purity was liable to be smitten with some loathsome disease which I associated with leprosy and with the 'unpardonable sin' which my minister often dwelt on."[3]

Understandably, Hall dreaded the rather natural responses of his own body. In his early teens, he actually rigged an apparatus to prevent nocturnal erections, and further wrapped his genitals in bandages—tactics which, he recalled, "very likely only augmented the trouble." Later, fearing he was "abnormal," he consulted a physician in a neighboring town. "He examined me and took my dollar, and laughed at me," Hall noted, "but also told me what consequences would ensure if I became unchaste." Throughout his teens and on through his third decade, Hall suffered what he called "intense remorse and fear" each time he masturbated, and he prayed fervently for the strength to overcome this vice. Hall later discerned that this struggle was a primary factor in his "conversion" experience as a sophomore at Williams College, but he confessed that his new relationship with God "made the struggle for purity far more intense, though I fear but little more successful."[4]

Hall considered for years that his sexual impulses made him "exceptionally corrupt and not quite worthy to associate with girls," and he blamed his shame over these impulses for his acute shyness around women. Indeed, society's stern proscriptions against premarital sex prolonged Halls' feelings of unworthiness almost until the time he married in his early thirties. In later years, he mused about the "untold anguish of soul" he might have been spared had someone simply told him that nocturnal emissions had occasional erections were entirely common for young men.[5]

Even if one exaggerates Hall's later contributions to the concept of adolescence, his sexual experiences are of more than individual interest. These ideas about sexuality were not peculiar to him or his family or even his community, but rather were representative of broader trends in white, middle-class, American culture in the nineteenth century. The years around Hall's birth and childhood, in fact, witnessed an unprecedented rise of concern over sexual self-control. Although Michel Foucault has noted a "discursive explosion" about sex dating from around the end of the sixteenth century in Europe, in the United States it would be easier to locate an explosion of concern beginning in the 1830s and gaining in intensity over the course of the century.[6]

The increased anxiety about sex expressed itself partly through the proliferation of advice manuals. Works such as John Todd's 1837 *Student's Manual* were well within the tradition of Ben Franklin's "improving literature," but from the 1830s onward the amount of this literature mushroomed, and the tone of the advice grew edgier, more insistent on the dangers of failure and the need for strict conformity.[7] A small group of writers stood ready to provide their readers guidance in sexual matters and, by extension, in the mastery of the unruly self. Books are not the same as behavior, of course, and the spokesmen for Victorian morality often complained bitterly that their advice went unheeded, but even if Victorian respectability was only a "heroic ideal," an "ideology seeking to be established," it nevertheless provides a window onto the values of nineteenth-century America.[8] These writers reflected changing sexual mores at midcentury and also earnestly tried to shape those values to conform to their own peculiarities.

The unruly self of their concern was primarily a *male* self. Although our dominant image of Victorian sexuality has been formed by the era's severe condemnations of female sexual activity and desire, the sexual advisers typically addressed themselves to a male audience. As part of the general Victorian idealization of women as vessels of purity, moralists maintained that women suffered less than men of all ages from insistent sexual urges—indeed, "good" women were often considered to harbor no sexual feelings at all, and they were expected to raise husbands and children to their own elevated plane. Any woman who transgressed the narrow boundaries of purity found herself ostracized and severely punished, but these advisers claimed that women were quite unlikely to succumb to overwhelming sexual desire.

Not so with young men, who suffered particularly from imperious carnal urges. They needed all the help they could get to maintain mastery over their own bodies. Further, unlike young women, young men could not expect a smooth transition to adulthood. These writers expected that girls and women would be passed directly from their parents' house to their husband's, but they feared that boys growing to manhood were left to discover their own path to maturity. Thus, although their advice often applied to girls and women as well, the moral advisers of the mid-nineteenth century directed the bulk of their exhortations toward young men.

The young men who heeded this advice—as Hall was to do—embarked on a strenuous mission. Ministers, physicians, and occasional "unscrupulous quacks" brought moral perfectionism to the physical plane and demanded that readers gain complete self-mastery over their body and their mind. It would not be enough simply to avoid carnal acts; they must banish lust from their thoughts and even from their dreams. In this new literature, there was no reason a thirty-year-old man could not be as chaste as an infant, if only he would learn to educate his will and exercise that chief bourgeois virtue, self-control. Any falling away from this rigid self-government would be a perversion of the sexual instinct, bringing in its train dire consequences.

Built around the axis of self-control was a range of sexual prescriptions that partook of the biblical tradition of mortification of flesh, but these intensified the self-denial beyond what earlier Americans would have recognized. Sexual intercourse, the advisers insisted, existed solely for procreation; to use it for mere pleasure was supremely selfish and betrayed the continued presence of the brute within the man. Outside of marriage, of course, full chastity was the only proper course of behavior. But even within marriage, partners were not to allow bestial lust to distort their relations.

For all Victorians, chastity extended not simply to the body but also to the mind: a lustful imagination was in many ways just as evil as carnal activity. In keeping with the need for mental purity, Victorians decried references to most bodily functions as "vulgar" —Hall was not the only child taught to refer to his genitals as "the dirty place." Activists in later generations—including a mature G. Stanley Hall—were to denounce this "conspiracy of silence" regarding sexuality, but Victorians felt that a prudent avoidance of such topics safeguarded them from the dangers of an inflamed imagination. Sexuality in this view was indeed a powerful force, but it was a subject to be cloaked in euphemism and silence, and its dynamic power existed to be contained.

Given this idealization of sexual reticence, it is ironic indeed that we understand the contours of Victorian sexual morality only because contemporary writers on the subject proclaimed the need for silence and control so insistently and conspicuously. These Victorian authors were adamant, however, that they broke their silence reluctantly and only to support more fully the other elements of the sexual and moral code.

The authors of advice manuals concerned themselves not solely with sex but with the entire constellation of values that made up Victorian respectability.[9] Social responsibility, personal discipline, moral rectitude—these were the hallmarks of the successful, respectable citizen. Sexuality was only the stubborn local dimension of a generally rigid self-government, for in no area of life did the Victorians condone selfishness and immediate gratification. Nevertheless, these authors were preoccupied with carnality, and their almost obsessive return to the theme of sexual control makes clear that meeting the challenge of sexual temptation was not only critical for social respectability but also central to the development of a person's very character.

Victorians did not conceive of moral development as a natural process. Recognizing only the rational will as sovereign, moral advisers were adamant that character was to be *created*. The idea of "finding yourself" —finding beneath the accretions of civilization a fixed self with its own integrity—is much more a product of the twentieth century and would have made little sense to Victorians, who found in "natural" impulses only a sordid animality. In the highly gendered world of Victorian ideology, character was primarily a male ideal. It connoted a sturdy independence in thought and deed; the man of character possessed a rational will, and with the certitude of this God-given faculty he could stand against the shifting winds of public opinion. And just as he stood firm against the public, so the man of character held his ground against his own baser desires.

Indeed, controlling the instinctual urges was itself the foundation of character. "You cannot give way to any appetite, without feeling instant and constant degradation," warned a New England minister, John Todd, in a manual printed and reprinted at midcentury, *The Young Man: Hints Addressed to the Young Men of the United States.* "Conscience can be deadened and murdered in no way so readily as by such indulgence."[10] The ambitious young man must not give in to selfish, "natural" desires. He must control not only his sexual drive but also his taste for strong drink and rich, spicy food. In most medical theories of the era, beginning with Benjamin Rush in the late eighteenth century and continuing through Sylvester Graham's interpretations in the 1830s, these three appetites had a reciprocal influence on one another. Highly spiced foods, too much meat, certain kinds of shellfish, and all forms of alcohol could inflame the system and stir up the embers of lust.[11] Indulging in such victuals was both sign and cause of weakening discipline. In addition to suggesting that these stimulants be avoided, the concept of self-regulation called for a young man not to be lazy and not to squander his time and energy on such useless activities as light reading and frivolous conversation. The young Victorian created character by mastering in all areas of life his too-human propensity for the easy path and immediate gratification.

Sexual regulation could be just another aspect of the general imperative to control one's impulses. But lust was more than just one appetite among equals; nobody warned that laziness or creamy sauces would inevitably lead to death. Sexuality became a metaphor for all of the appetites to be regulated, but it was supremely momentous.[12] Controlling his insistent carnality was the young man's greatest exercise of his sovereign will. After winning the battle with lust, the growing youth would find other temptations comparatively easy to master.

In the stadium of sexual temptation, the greatest foe was masturbation, and so writers of the time returned almost obsessively to the dangers of "self-abuse," as it was euphemistically known.[13] This seemed peculiarly a masculine vice: according to writers at the time, girls who fell prey to self-abuse were clearly aberrant, while so many boys wrestled with the temptation that the struggle was well-nigh universal among them. The pervasiveness of masturbation, however, was hardly an argument for its acceptance. Of all the animalistic urges the young man faced, masturbation threatened most powerfully to overrun the boundaries of civilized restraint: "I have had boys come to me, with complaints of ill health," wrote the antebellum health reformer Sylvester Graham, "who, on being closely questioned on this point, have confessed that they had indulged in this vice as often as three times in twenty-four hours; and sometimes thrice in a single night."[14] The moral writers' preoccupation with this constant temptation, which needed only privacy and ignorance to work its harm, lay in masturbation's symbolic representation of an entire flood of desires and indulgences; once a young man touched himself in that way, he threatened the entire structure of Victorian character. Self-discipline, social responsibility, character—masturbation symbolically toppled all of the pillars.

Happily, science combined with morality to condemn the private sensualist to lasting debility unto death. With some exceptions, experts in the nineteenth century adhered to a physiology in which the body was largely a fixed-energy system; vital strength invested in private sensuality was energy drained from the rest of the organism, and sometimes the loss was permanent. Thus, the masturbator first grew weak, less resistant to further indulgence. If he continued in the habit—and by the nature of the vice, he probably would—he risked far more than his moral standing. "Few of my own sex wholly escape this snare," maintained the phrenologist Orson S. Fowler, "while thousands on thousands die annually from this one cause!"[15]

Some doctors had derived from the eighteenth-century French physician Samuel August Tissot the idea that spermatic fluid was a concentrated form of the body's liquors: one ounce of sperm was thought to equal forty ounces of blood, so ejaculation was inherently a perilous business. But even those who rejected Tissot's hydraulic calculus retained the general notion that sexual expenditure was particularly draining.[16] In a trend that was to have far-reaching consequences, many Americans increasingly justified the ethical conventions of society with appeals not to God but to medical science or future success in the world.

Combatting the attractiveness of self-indulgence, moral advisers had faith in the young man's ability to avoid masturbation and kindred temptations, if only he knew the consequences. Advice manuals therefore contained scenes of Hogarthian damnation to warn the youth away from danger. One man whose mother had given him such a pamphlet when he was eleven vividly remembered the descriptions of "feeble mindedness, insanity, [and] early failing general health." "At this age I was not very critical and swallowed this garbage completely," recalled W.O. Frick, a physician, some sixty years later. "All during later adolescence I had intense guilt and became shy and somewhat withdrawn."[17] Frick was, in fact, a success story. Properly enlightened as to the results of sensuality, the young man rationally subjugated his passions under an iron will. By cultivating a sense of shame and morality, by exercising constantly and avoiding aphrodisiacal edibles, he found he could control his sexual urges and, by extension, all aspects of his self. In the crucible of this struggle he would forge a character that contained no trace of the baser human elements.

At the height of its effectiveness, moral willpower could prevent not only voluntary acts of debauchery but also actions that seemed to be involuntary. Nocturnal emissions seemed at first an unfortunate consequence of waking chastity, but Dr. Thomas Nichols, a "water-cure" specialist in the mid- to late nineteenth century, believed that the will, strengthened by conscience and religion, could curtail even this debilitating expenditure. The English physician William acton was not alone in his belief that the individual could keep his dreams pure.[18] Again and again, Victorians trumpeted the efficacy of the rational, moral will.

If this willpower failed, however, "respectable" physicians were as ready as quacks to advocate more coercive methods of sexual suppression. Doctors did not offer a blanket endorsement of these mechanical aids, however. Despite his sympathy for their function, Dr. George Napheys felt that "spermatorrhoeal rings" used to prevent nocturnal emissions were both inconvenient *and* in lamentably short supply, while "cauterization" had perhaps been overemployed. Paralleling Stanley Hall's nocturnal experiments with a binding apparatus and bandages, Napheys noted with approbation a Dr. Wood's practice of applying strips of plaster along the back of the male member to prevent spermatorrhoea (or accidental spermatic discharge) and "self-pollution." In extreme cases, Napheys did not hesitate to recommend repeated blisterings and "infibulation," or suturing closed the female labia or male foreskin.[19] Such draconian measures, along with tying an offender's hands or performing a clitoridectomy, were better geared toward subjects, such as children and women, who were thought to have less willpower to begin with and, quite obviously, less power to resist being "cured," but moral and medical experts also recommended these treatments for the many adult males who took seriously the warnings about the dangers of indulgence.[20] Clearly, sexual control by one method or another was a critical value for many Victorians.

Physicians and ministers justified these drastic treatments and their overheated rhetoric with an appeal to the fixed-energy conception of human physiology, but the campaign for sexual control did not grow simply out of a new medical theory. Indeed, Tissot and Benjamin Rush had formulated the medical basis for the war on lust decades earlier without immediately inciting their fellows to join the crusade, and physicians had added little to this field of medicine in the intervening years. Rather, the ideology of sexual respectability that appeared quite notably around the 1830s arose in response to new cultural needs. More than an ideal imposed from above by physicians and other authorities, sexual respectability grew out of men and women's everyday needs, and its tenets in turn gave texture to their daily lives and desires and conceptions of themselves.

As a central expression of the evangelical revivals that began to sweep the nation in the 1820s, Victorian morality represented the quest for stability and certainty in the midst of an unsettled, industrializing, urbanizing America. The expanding capitalist economy, for example, demanded of its actors a certain amount of self-denial and delayed gratification. One could easily reduce this entire genre of advice literature to the terms of economic functionalism—the connections to Max Weber's depiction of the Protestant, capitalist spirit are obvious—except that the moral writers were often extremely anxious about capitalism's capacity to unleash selfishness and monomaniacal individualism—vices exemplified, in their minds, by the habits of masturbation and visiting with prostitutes.[21] Nevertheless, moral advisers still held out the promise that sexual respectability, temperance, and piety could lead to significant earthly rewards.

Moral character performed other functions in a nation that lacked a hereditary aristocracy and, by the 1830s, supported near-universal white male suffrage. Moral character was particularly important in the American democracy, Sylvester Graham maintained in an 1834 lecture, "where the aggregate of individual character and individual will, constitutes the foundation and efficiency of all our civil and political institutions."[22] In a nation with no hereditary elite, political virtue could grow only out of personal virtue. Perhaps paradoxically, personal virtue could also serve to recreate boundaries of status in an antiaristocratic nation. In the 1830s, families of merchants, shopkeepers, master artisans, and other aspiring men increasingly used their higher regard for religion, temperance, self-control, and sexual respectability to distinguish themselves from common laborers and the rising tide of Irish immigrants.[23]

For many middle-class women, sexual respectability not only helped to signify their family's status but also played a role in their strategy for domestic relations. Although many historians have treated middle-class, white women as the victims of Victorian respectability, elements of the system made a great deal of sense in their lives. For a woman in the nineteenth century, fear of sex was in part a rational response, for almost every act of intercourse could potentially result in pregnancy, and every pregnancy bore the risk of great suffering and even death.[24] This individual hostility toward sex became part of a broader "feminist" strategy to attack male sexual prerogative as a means to reform male behavior. Many female sexual reformers decried the male propensity for unleashed sexuality, as exemplified by what one historian, following the Victorian activist Lucinda Chandler, has called "the delirium of masturbatory orgies, uncontrolled marital 'carnalism,' and the 'furious' expression of 'selfish propensities.'"[25] In contrast to these bestial tendencies, respectable women could gain a certain amount of moral stature through their alleged freedom from carnal desire.[26] Sexual respectability also gave women a vocabulary to use in their struggle for the right to place limits on the husband's sexual demands. Victorian sexual respectability could be for women a tactic in personal and political negotiations.

As this interpretation suggests, the central target of this prescriptive literature was young men. The unsettled nature of American society in the early nineteenth century affected them perhaps most of all. With the transportation revolution that began around 1815, young men were increasingly abandoning agriculture for commercial and industrial occupations.[27] They fled not only their parents' traditional occupation but also the adult community's supervision and protection. Thus, the literature of Victorian morality was in many respects the expression of an older generation's uneasiness in contemplating the independence of male youth—indeed, the existence of the literature itself implied that the traditional mechanisms of cultural transmission had broken down.[28] Recognizing that young men were now less bound by traditional community restraints, advisers hoped their prescriptive literature would help youths internalize these inhibitions.[29] This argument might also explain why the moral writers directed their work more at young men than at young women, for girls were never given the liberty allowed to boys and hence seemed to have less need to internalize the moral code. By placing the proper books and pamphlets in the hands of their departing children, parents could perhaps assuage some of their own anxieties.

The arguments from women's concerns and parental fear, however, should not overshadow the primary object of concern in the Victorian advice literature. These sexual ideals had less to do with social control than with *self*-control, and young men, especially, demanded help in negotiating their own path through the twisting streets and dark alleys of an industrializing, urbanizing America.[30] The household economy and the system of apprenticeship in many trades were in decline throughout the century, and many white, middle-class young people who lived in the cities or left home for the cities were increasingly cut off from extended contact with their elders. Expected to leave for school or employment before their character was fully molded, these young American men had to "tread over quicksands that are to be found in the country," mourned John Todd, "and the breathing-holes of hell which fill the great city." Tempted by "panders, and seducers," perhaps in league with a woman who "exults in being a successful recruiting-officer of hell!" the independent boy also faced his own weaknesses, such as light and foolish reading and "reveries of imagination," which might call up lurid scenes of debasement.[31]

If the hazards of vice were not great enough, competitors and Herculean tasks obstructed the path to success. "Strong and mighty are the men who are to be swimmers with you in the stream of life," Todd continued, "—high the waves which you are to buffet,—swift the currents which are set against you, and fearful will be the results."[32] The author's tidal metaphors captured well the sense of helplessness that could come over an individual trying to make his way in the city, and his book offered hope that the reader, through habit, industry, and discipline, could himself become one of the strong swimmers. In a disrupted environment, the young man could control little other than his own self; perhaps the rigidity of his self-control was proportionate to the chaos that surrounded him.

Upwardly mobile young men in midcentury America purchased dozens of elevating books, attended scores of lectures at that urban haven, the Young Men's Christian Association (its first American branches sprang up in the 1850s), and in seeking advice on how to behave, they did not particularly care if the answers were medical or theological or, as most often, a great stew of both.[33] They wanted reassurance that they could somehow swim clear of the dangerous waves. Interlaced with John Todd's medical and moral advice were pertinent observations on the usefulness of conversation, so long as it was not idle, and other fortifications for the young man, perhaps fresh from the country, entering a sophisticated metropolis. Todd spent fifteen pages, for example, furnishing arguments for the reader to use if he should happen to meet an atheist while at school. Cut off from their parents and the community in which they grew up, many young men sought guidance where they could find it.

Sexual respectability therefore was an integral element of nineteenth-century middle-class life. It served as a stern guide to personal comportment, a necessary foundation for proper maturation, and a weapon in sexual negotiation. Indeed, the boundaries of civilized sexual morality gave shape even to those acts that men and women intended as transgressions of its borders. G. Stanley Hall's youthful terrors notwithstanding, perhaps the code's rigidity even added savor to its violation.[34] Although its ideological dominance did not necessarily compel Victorians to behave as they were supposed to at all times, this code of sexual morality nevertheless gave meaning to men and women's desires and daily acts. Such a powerful system of belief did not simply fade away as the nineteenth century shaded into the twentieth. On the contrary, as a code of behavior for young people, in particular, Victorian sexual respectability found renewed life at the dawn of the new era.

As the nineteenth century drew to a close, G. Stanley Hall had left his youthful contest with temptation far behind. His shame and shyness had largely dissolved in the face of his experiences in Germany's less puritanical atmosphere and his marriage, in 1879, to Cornelia Fisher. In the meantime, Hall had earned a doctorate at Harvard University and become an academic psychologist, specializing first in laboratory research and then, eventually, in the study of youth and education. It was in his role as a man of science, representative of a type that was rising to prominence late in the nineteenth century, that Hall began to investigate more intensively the feelings and experiences that had proved so central to his own development, and sought to reconcile them with Darwinian thought. Shortly after the turn of the century, Hall gathered the phenomena he and his students were studying into one unitary concept, inventing for the first time the discrete, observable stage of life they dubbed "adolescence." Just as sexuality was central to the Victorian moralists' hazy, undefined notion of "youth," so was it a critical component of the new, scientific concept of adolescence.

The category was new, but Sylvester Graham and John Todd would have recognized the content of Hall's definition. Although Hall hung the concept of adolescence on a novel evolutionary framework, he employed almost exclusively the traditional materials of Victorian sexual respectability. Channeling both his own idiosyncrasies and the general currents of thought around him into one enormously influential book, *Adolescence*, Hall placed chastity and self-denial directly at the center of the interpretation.[35] Indeed, adolescence was precisely that period of chastity between puberty, or sexual awakening, and marriage, when the young man or woman's sexual impulses could finally be expressed. Without the demand for sexual repression and sublimation, the modern concept of adolescence made no sense at all.

The invention of adolescence rested on three important material changes in the nineteenth century. First, as the end of the nineteenth century approached, young people were increasingly segregated and sorted by age, especially in the rapidly expanding public schools—by 1900, well over half of school-age Americans were enrolled in public or private schools at some point during the year.[36] Their separation from the adult world was thus sharper and more visible than before. Hall's work in child study and adolescent psychology both responded to and reinforced this trend toward segregation and age-grading. Second, due perhaps to nutritional changes, the average age at puberty declined over the course of the century, so young people were becoming sexually mature earlier in life. Finally, at the same time, the period of training and education for young men, especially, grew longer. So men and women increasingly delayed marriage until they were on a secure financial footing, even as they were physiologically prepared for matrimony earlier and earlier.[37] Toward the end of the nineteenth century, the median age at first marriage had risen to 26.1 years for men, 22 years for women; after the age at marriage dropped in the first years of the twentieth century, the nineteenth-century averages would not be approached again until the 1970s.[38] The contrast was more striking for the "better" sorts that Hall would have considered his social peers: the average age at marriage for graduates of Harvard and Yale Colleges was 29 to 31.[39] Many Americans at the turn of the century commented that this extended period of forbidden sexuality was a garden of temptation, an almost cruel prolongation of youthful Sturm und Drang.[40] Nevertheless, wrote Hall, "The ideals of chastity are perhaps the very highest that can be held up to youth during this ever lengthening probationary period."[41]

Chastity, for Hall, possessed evolutionary as well as moral significance. Hall dreamed of becoming the "Darwin of the mind," and as this would suggest, he was greatly taken with evolutionary theory. He interpreted the prolonged period of adolescent chastity in the United States not as a mere social convention but as a factor in the evolution of "civilized" races. Others agreed. "No one need be told how dependent all human social elevation is upon the prevalence of chastity," wrote William James, Hall's mentor at Harvard, at the turn of the century. "Hardly any factor measures more than this the difference between civilization and barbarism."[42]

The association between sexual control and social evolution at the turn of the century was not arbitrary. The Victorian ethnographers who were coming into prominence late in the century concentrated particularly on the sexual morality of "savage" cultures. These gentleman-anthropologists argued that polygamy, promiscuity, and incest were rife among the "lower races" as well as in the Anglo-Saxon's own racial history, but noted with relief that the progress of Anglo-Saxon civilization had educated its members in sexual control, elevating them above the immediate sensuality of the primitive races.[43] This sense of race consciousness and racial superiority grew sharper in the United States toward the end of the nineteenth century as hundreds of thousands of "new" immigrants arrived yearly from eastern and southern Europe, threatening the "old stock" Americans with their sheer numbers and their unfamiliar habits. Many "old stock" Americans commented with disdain on the distance between what they saw as the newcomers' degraded sexual habits and the native Anglo-Saxon's sexual purity. Thus, the moral code that originated as a highly personal response among middle-class whites to the disorder of American life in the early to mid-nineteenth century gradually came to be thought of as a group characteristic, even a racial trait. To young American men making their way in the world, the code of civilized sexuality still offered personal guidance, but it also functioned to signify the crucial distance between cultured Anglo-Saxons and the "primitive" races.

In Hall's formulation, adolescent chastity not only signified the social distance between "civilized" and primitive" races, it *created* this distance through a complex biological process known as recapitulation. Like many educated observers in this first flush of Darwinism, Hall conflated cultural differences with biological differences: the different pattern of adolescence among the western European peoples, he argued, separated them from the savages biologically as well as socially. Hall and his many students postulated that the fetus first recapitulates its phylogeny—that is, the human fetus as it grows repeats all the stages of human ancestry, from the single-celled origins of life through a semiaquatic stage and an "apelike" stage, before emerging as an evolutionarily complete *Homo sapiens*. After birth, Hall argued, the growing child then recapitulates all the human stages of social or racial evolution: "The child comes from and harks back to a remoter past; the adolescent is neo-atavistic, and in him the later acquisitions of the race slowly become prepotent."[44] "Reason, true morality, religion, sympathy, love, and esthetic enjoyment" were some of the later acquisitions entirely absent in primitive races and in all children, but gradually appearing in the civilized adolescent.[45]

The differences between races developed out of the divergent paths taken by youths after puberty. In lesser races, noted Hall's colleague in psychology, Sanford Bell, "Pubescence marked the beginning of the distinctively sexual experience of both sexes."[46] The civilized youth, in contrast, also felt a surge of sexual feeling at puberty, but was gradually differentiated from his primitive brothers by "the system of sex inhibitions that are considered an essential part of the ethical habits of our young people."[47] In other words, a "savage" youth was considered fully mature, sexually active, at an age when the "civilized" adolescent was just beginning his most strenuous period of mental and spiritual growth.

Rather than indulging his sexual desires in the interval between puberty and marriage, the civilized adolescent devoted his energies to developing those qualities, such as reason and true morality, that marked his race's advancement over the lesser peoples. As civilization advanced, so did the probationary period increase to allow the individual time to develop the newer, higher evolutionary traits. This interval of chastity husbanded vitality for physical and mental growth and was the crucible that formed a disciplined character. Again, sexual control was the preeminent arena for the exercise of the will. In contrast to this male agon, Hall argued, the adolescent girl's chief developmental task was to avoid the kinds of mental and physical exertions that might deplete her reproductive capacity—he felt that too much education, for example, might have a sterilizing effect on a young woman.

After his own titanic struggles with sexual temptation, Hall never claimed that the storm and strife of male adolescence was easy. Hall romanticized the excitement and intensity of the struggle and waxed rapturous about the adolescent's potential to sublimate desire into religion or athletics or art, but he remained aware that the fight against temptation might involve much guilt and anguish as well. Indeed, the struggle might even go horribly wrong at some key moment. As the modern science of sexology publicized the existence of such sexual "perversions" as homosexuality, masochism, pederasty, and a Latinate list of variations on these themes, Hall and Sanford Bell argued that these deviations were themselves the consequences of civilized chastity.[48] As the "social inhibitions" tried to establish themselves during adolescence, the adolescent's thwarted heterosexual impulses sometimes were not sublimated into civilized characteristics but instead flowed into other sexual channels.[49] Despite his recognition of this danger, Hall refused to condemn repression: "This is the hard price that man must pay for full maturity."[50]

More broadly, repression was the price that the race had to pay to retain its superiority. Civilized sexual tension, the strain of "strong passions held in strong control," was as necessary for the race as for the individual, according to Hall.[51] He asserted that a sexually mature parent—one who had successfully sublimated during adolescence—would beget healthier offspring, who would perhaps repeat this cycle, until the race itself was composed of more intelligent, more moral, more advanced persons. The cumulative effect of this inheritance was the racial progress and racial differentiation that lay at the heart of Hall's recapitulation theory.

At the same time, just as an extended period of chastity could foster racial progress, premature sexuality could lead to racial decline. If Hall's adolescent did not advance past the stage of primitiveness before reproducing, he or she could not pass on the "later acquisitions of the race," and the child would be marked by atavism. Similarly, parents who had misspent their adolescence sexually risked passing on the consequences of vice to their children[52] Citing Auguste Morel's "pessimistic vaticinations" that the European race may someday degenerate, Hall maintained that this decline "will be by the progressive failure of youth to develop normally and to maximal maturity and sanity."[53] In the charged racial atmosphere at the turn of the century, these warnings of Anglo-Saxon decline coursed with the energy of scientific "truth" and deep cultural anxiety.[54] Adolescents struggled for sexual control not just for their own sake but for the sake of society and their race.

Hall was not the first observer to claim that what we call adolescence exists as a separate stage of life, or even the first to claim the primacy of sexual urges during this period—Rousseau's *Emile* had already covered this territory—but *Adolescence* was the first sustained, systematic examination of the theme, and it arrived at a propitious moment of harmony between Hall's national position and the country's broader social needs.

Although Hall's theory of race and recapitulation was destined to have a very short life, the concept of adolescence quickly became so popular that many Americans accepted it as common sense, and it became part of the culture's mental furniture. Hall's reputation and extensive network of colleagues certainly played a role in obtaining a general hearing for the new concept. As a professor at Johns Hopkins and at Clark University, Hall had trained a significant proportion of all the nation's academic psychologists, and he exercised considerable sway over a number of disciplinary journals. Hall's history as a founder and leader of the "child study" movement at the end of the nineteenth century extended his influence still further over the nation's teachers and interested parents.

But the popularity of adolescence as a concept did not depend on one man. Rather, it owed its positive reception chiefly to its explanatory power, its usefulness in clarifying the meaning of confusing everyday phenomena so that they suddenly made sense. For one, young people as a group were becoming more visible: native-born parents, especially, were having fewer children and spacing them more closely in age, and youths were increasingly segregated by age into schools or supervised activities.[55] Earlier puberty and later marriage highlighted still further this awkward age between sexual maturity and legitimate sexual expression. In the 1890 census, 80 percent of men between the ages of twenty and twenty-four were still single, and over half of the women their age were as well; young men and women living in the largest cities were more likely yet to remain single well into their twenties.[56] Young people, in turn, began to be more conscious of their own separateness. Although a "youth culture" in some senses awaited the coming of the 1920s youths at the turn of the century were already taking more of their social and sartorial cues from one another than from their elders. As adolescents became more visible, so did their peculiar characteristics, such as gang activity, the rage for religious conversion, overwhelming sentimentality, and, especially, sexual urges. Where these once seemed like individual, if common, idiosyncrasies, they could now be explained as the adolescent's "natural" impulses, subject to explanation and scientific investigation. As science continued its ascent to cultural preeminence, the aura of scientific truth that surrounded adolescence helped ensure the new concept's acceptance.

The wide range of adolescence's explanatory power, however, should not obscure its fundamental components and their implications. A great many forces were at work in the creation of adolescence, but in the final analysis, a combination of Hall's personal history, the Victorian moral inheritance, and racial fears at the turn of the century led to sexuality's taking center stage in the drama of adolescence. With this heritage, adolescence was from the beginning not simply an explanatory concept but a summons to action.

By defining adolescence as a sexually tempestuous period and making sexual control and sublimation the keystone of the maturation process, Hall and his fellow investigators set themselves a mighty task. By their very definition, adolescence demanded careful and sustained external control. Proper sexual adjustment was critical to a successfully resolved adolescence, and yet it was constantly endangered, both by the adolescent's own unruly impulses and by the American environment's corrupting energies. Although Hall waxed eloquent about the glories of the youthful sexual instinct, even he ultimately came down more on the side of suppression and sublimation than freedom. Few Americans went even as far as he toward embracing adolescent sexuality, but many agreed with Hall on one central point: young men and women could not be left to face this crucial struggle against temptation on their own. The question to be answered in the first two decades of the twentieth century was, Who would help them?

The perceived power of the adolescent's sexual drive was itself sufficient to demand external aid in mastering it, but this impulse seemed to investigators like Hall even less manageable in the context of American life at the turn of the century. As many contemporaries saw the problem, urbanization was a major culprit. From the beginning of the Civil War to the turn of the century, America's urban population had increased almost fivefold, from 6.25 million to just over 30 million, with 8 million people living in metropolises with 500,000 or more inhabitants; in contrast, the rural population, while larger in absolute numbers, had not even doubled during the same period, increasing from 25 million to 45 million.[57] G. Stanley Hall was utterly typical in fearing that the "contagion of vice" was most virulent in the burgeoning cities of the United States.[58] "At its best," he wrote, "metropolitan life is hard on childhood and especially so on pubescents, and children who can not pass these years in the country are robbed of a right of childhood that should be inalienable."[59] Although Hall grounded his animosity toward urban life in recapitulation theory—the urban youth's precocious sexual experiences disrupted the gradual unfolding of the stages of growth—he partook of the common nostalgia of a people born in the country and transplanted to the city. As more and more Americans moved to the city, they increasingly feared that the allure of urban excitement would pull adolescents from the proper path to maturity.

Even without being familiar with all the tenets of the new "adolescence" as Hall defined it, many parents at the turn of the century had good reason to fear the effects of their children's sexual awakening. Disease, exploitation, and unwanted pregnancies were common dangers, and soon reformers would make society much more aware of the health threats that premarital sex could pose. As always, adolescent sexuality also aroused deeper parental fears of separation. Whatever its other associations, a child's sexual activity connotes at some level a new independence, a rechanneling of intense emotion away from the parents and onto another object. Always a tension in family life, such sexual independence became at the turn of the century a more critical blow against many families, especially in the cities, where fertility rates for the native born were falling and family size had been contracting through the late nineteenth century. Rather than producing a large crop of children, parents had fewer children and made a larger investment of resources in each one. Adolescent independence, or simply sexual experimentation, could have a greater impact in a family of four than in a family of ten. Many parents, especially among the educated middle class, were increasingly receptive to the idea that their adolescent children needed help regulating their desires.

To control youthful sexuality, the nineteenth century offered a handful of methods that students of adolescence judged, in the end, insufficient. Hall, for example, placed the storm and strife of adolescent sexuality at the service of the religious impulse, hoping that a religious conversion experience would eventually grow out of the adolescent's sexual struggle and in turn make that struggle easier to bear.[60] Conversion, however, was no longer the common experience that it had been in Hall's youth, and laments about the general decline of religious sentiment grew increasingly loud after the turn of the century. Similarly, the ability of the community to police its young seemed in decline because of the perceived anonymity of modern city life. Finally, the family still had a role to play in fostering self-control among its children, but academic experts, public schools, and youth agencies increasingly sought to assert authority over the growing youth.

Meeting the needs of the modern adolescent required a modern method. Medicine, eugenics, psychology, education—all of these modern fields promised to help the adolescent meet the inevitable struggle with sexuality. Their successes and failures form a major part of the story of adolescence in the twentieth century. For Hall and the hundreds of men and women allied with his project, doing nothing was never an option. Having created adolescence, they were bound to manage it.

NOTES

1. G. Stanley Hall, *Life and Confessions of a Psychologist* (New York: D. Appleton and Co., 1923), p. 589.
2. Ibid., pp. 131–132.
3. Ibid.
4. Ibid.
5. Ibid.
6. Michel Foucault, *The History of Sexuality*, vol. 1: *An Introduction*, trans. Robert Hurley (New York: Vintage Books, 1990); Ronald G. Walters, *Primers for Prudery: Sexual Advice to Victorian America* (Englewood Cliffs, N. J.: Prentice-Hall, 1974), p.10. See John D' Emilio and Estelle B. Freedman, *Intimate Matters: A History of Sexuality in America* (New York: Harper and Row, 1988); Peter Gay, *The Bourgeois Experience: Victoria to Freud*, vol. 1: *Education of the Senses* (New York: Oxford University Press, 1984); and Carl Degler, "What Ought to Be and What Was: Women's Sexuality in the Nineteenth Century," in Michael Gordon, ed., *The American Family in Social-Historical Perspective* (New York: St. Martin's Press, 1978), pp. 403–425.
7. John Todd, *The Student's Manual: Designed, by Specific Directions, to Aid in Forming and Strengthening the Intellectual and Moral Character and Habits of the Student* (Northampton, Mass.: J. H. Butler, 1837).
8. "Ideology seeking to be established" is a phrase Degler applies to William Acton's view of women as "passionless" in Degler, "What Ought to Be and What Was," p. 406.
9. George H. Napheys, *The Transmission of Life: Counsels on the Nature and Hygiene of the Masculine Function* (Philadelphia: H. C. Watts Co., 1877), pp 263–264.
10. John Todd, *The Young Man: Hints Addressed to the Young Men of the United States* (Northampton, Mass.: J. H. Butler, 1845), p. 368.
11. For a moderate view, see Napheys, *Transmission of Life*, pp. 47–48; also Orson S. *Fowler, Amativeness: Embracing the Evils and Remedies of Excessive and Perverted Sexuality, Including Warning and Advice to the Married and Single* (New York: 1889), in Charles Rosenberg and Carroll Smith-Rosenberg, eds., *Sex and Science: Phrenological Reflections on Sex and Marriage in Nineteenth Century America* (New York: Arno Press, 1974), pp. 53–55; Sylvester Graham, *A Lecture to Young Men* (1834; repr. New York: Arno Press, 1974).
12. Peter Cominos, "Late-Victorian Sexual Respectability and the Social System," *International Review of Social History* 8, nos. 1 and 2 (1963): 18–8 and 216–250.
13. E. H. Hare, "Masturbatory Insanity: The History of an Idea," *Journal of Medical Science* 108 (Jan. 1962): 1–25.
14. Graham, *A Lecture to Young Men*, p. 44.
15. Fowler, *Amativeness*, p. 14.
16. Samuel A. A. D. Tissot, *Onanism* (orig. English trans., 1766; repr., New York: Garland Publishing, 1985); see also Eliza B. Duffey, *The Relations of the Sexes* (1876; repr., New York Arno Press, 1974), p. 179.
17. W. O. Frick, Pasadena, California, communication with the author, 13 Oct. 1995.
18. Cominos, "Late-Victorian Sexual Respectability," 32–33.
19. Napheys, *Transmission of Life*, p. 83, 90–92.
20. Gail Pat Parsons, "Equal Treatment for All: American Medical Remedies for Male Sexual Problems: 1850–1900," *Journal of the History of Medicine and Allied Sciences* 32 (Jan. 1977): 55–71.

21. Max Weber, *The Protestant Ethic and the Spirit of Capitalism,* trans. Talcott Parsons (New York: Charles Scribner, 1958); also Stephen Nissenbaum, *Sex, Diet, and Debility in Jacksonian America: Sylvester Graham and Health Reform* (Westport, Conn.: Greenwood Press, 1980).

22. Graham, *Lecture to Young Men,* p. 7.

23. Paul E. Johnson, *A Shopkeeper's Millennium: Society and Revivals in Rochester, New York, 1815–1837* (New York Hill and Wang, 1978).

24. Linda Gordon, *Woman's Body, Woman's Right: A Social History of Birth Control in America* (New York: Grossman Publishers, 1976), pp. 105–106.

25. William Leach, *True Love and Perfect Union: The Feminist Reform of Sex and Society,* 2nd ed., (Middletown, Conn.: Wesleyan University Press, 1989), p. 91.

26. Nancy F. Cott, "Passionlessness: An Interpretation of Victorian Sexual Ideology, 1790–1850," in Nancy F. Cott and Elizabeth H. Pleck, eds., *A Heritage of Her Own* (New York: Simon and Schuster, 1979), pp. 162–181.

27. Joseph Kelt, *Rites of Passage: Adolescence in America 1790 to the Present* (New York: Basic Books, 1977), pp. 30–31; also John Demos, *Past, Present, and Personal: The Family and the Life Course in American History* (New York: Oxford University Press, 1986), pp. 99–100.

28. R. P. Neuman, "Masturbation, Madness, and the Modern Concepts of Childhood and Adolescence," *Journal of Social History* 8 (Spring 1975): 1–27.

29. See Anthony Comstock, *Traps for the Young* (1883), new ed., ed. Robert Bremner (Cambridge, Mass.: Belknap Press of Harvard University Press, 1967).

30. On the infrastructure supporting this rapid social change, see, for example, George R. Taylor, *The Transportation Revolution, 1815–1860* (New York: Rinehart, 1951); also Nissenbaum, *Sex, Diet, and Debility in Jacksonian America,* preface.

31. Todd, *The Young Man,* pp. 118–120, 142.

32. Ibid., 354.

33. Peter Gay, "Victorian Sexuality: Old Texts and New Insights," *American Scholar* 49 (Summer 1980): 374–375.

34. See Karen Lystra, *Searching the Heart: Women, Men, and Romantic Love in Nineteenth-Century America* (New York. Oxford University Press, 1989).

35. G. Stanley Hall, *Adolescence: Its Psychology and Its Relations to Physiology, Anthropology, Sociology, Sex, Crime, Religion and Education,* 2 vols. (1904; new ed., New York: D. Appleton and Co., 1908). Neuman cautions against confusing the universal biology of puberty with the socially determined period of adolescence, in "Masturbation," 23.

36. U.S. Department of Commerce, Bureau of the Census, *Historical Statistics of the United States: Colonial Times to 1970,* Part 1 (White Plains, N.Y.: Kraus International Publications, 1989), p. 369.

37. Neuman, "Masturbation," 6–7.

38. *Historical Statistics of the United States,* p. 19.

39. Dorothy Ross, *G. Stanley Hall: The Psychologist as Prophet* (Chicago: University of Chicago Press, 1972), p. 338n.

40. Sanford Bell, "A Preliminary Study of the Emotion of Love between the Sexes," *American Journal of Psychology* 13 (July 1902): 327–328.

41. Hall, *Adolescence,* **2**: 453.

42. William James, *Principles of Psychology,* 1: 22–23; quoted in Nathan G. Hale, Jr., *Freud and the Americans: The Beginnings of Psychoanalysis in the United States, 1876–1917* (New York: Oxford University Press, 1971), p. 110.

43. Herbert Spencer, *The Principles of Sociology,* 3rd ed. (1885; repr., New York: D. Appleton and Co., 1925), 1: 621–622.

44. Hall, *Adolescence,* 1: xiii; George W. Stocking, Jr., *Race, Culture, and Evolution: Essays in the History of Anthropology* (Chicago: University of Chicago Press, 1982), pp. 110–132.

45. Hall, *Adolescence,* 1: x.

46. Bell, "Emotion of Love," 327.

47. Ibid.

48. George M. Beard, *American Nervousness: Its Causes and Consequences* (New York: G.P. Putnam's Sons, 1881), p. 26; George M. Beard, *Sexual Neurasthenia: Its Hygiene, Causes, Symptoms and Treatment*, ed. A. D. Rockwell (5th ed., New York: E. B. Treat and Co., 1902); see also Barbara Sicherman, "The Uses of a Diagnosis: Doctors, Patients, and Neurasthenia," *Journal of the History of Medicine* 32 (Jan. 1977): 33–55.
49. Bell, "Emotion of Love," 328; Hall, *Adolescence*, 1: 285–286.
50. Bell, "Emotion of Love," 327–328; Hall, *Adolescence*, 1: 453. For a less sanguine evaluation of civilized repression before Freud, see Charles W. Page, "The Adverse Consequences of Repression," *American Journal of Insanity* 49 (Jan. 1893): 372–390.
51. Hall, *Adolescence*, 1: 322.
52. Stocking, *Race, Culture, and Evolution*, p. 242.
53. Hall, *Adolescence*, 1: 324.
54. On racial thought, see John S. Haller, *Outcasts from Evolution: Scientific Attitudes of Racial Inferiority, 1859–1900* (Chicago: University of Illinois Press, 1971).
55. See Demos, *Past, Present, and Personal*, pp. 104–105.
56. U.S. Bureau of the Census, *Eleventh Census, 1890, Population*, 1: clxxix–clxxxvi.
57. *Historical Statistics of the United States*, pp. 11–12.
58. G. Stanley Hall, "The Moral and Religious Training of Children and Adolescents," *Pedagogical Seminary* 1 (1891): 196.
59. Hall, *Adolescence*, 1: 321.
60. Ross, *G. Stanley Hall*, pp. 330–332.

7

"Bashing Youth" and "Wild in Deceit"

MIKE MALES

BASHING YOUTH: MEDIA MYTHS ABOUT TEENAGERS

"Unplanned pregnancies. HIV infection and AIDS, other sexually transmitted diseases. Cigarettes, alcohol and drug abuse. Eating disorders. Violence. Suicide. Car crashes."

THE 21-WORD lead-in to a *Washington Post* (12/22/92) report sums up today's media image of the teenager: 30 million 12- through 19-year-olds toward whom any sort of moralizing and punishment can be safely directed, by liberals and conservatives alike. Today's media portrayals of teens employ the same stereotypes once openly applied to unpopular racial and ethnic groups: violent, reckless, hypersexed, welfare-draining, obnoxious, ignorant.

And like traditional stereotypes, the modern media teenager is a distorted image, derived from the dire fictions promoted by official agencies and interest groups.

During the 1980s and 1990s, various public and private entrepreneurs realized that the news media will circulate practically anything negative about teens, no matter how spurious. A few examples among many:

- In 1985, the National Association of Private Psychiatric Hospitals, defending the profitable mass commitment of teenagers to psychiatric treatment on vague diagnoses, invented the "fact" that a teenager commits suicide "every 90 minutes"—or 5,000 to 6,000 times every year. Countless media reports of all types, from the Associated Press (4/4/91) to *Psychology Today* (5/92), continue to report this phony figure, nearly three times the true teen suicide toll, which averaged 2,050 per year during the 1980s (Vital Statistics of the United States).
- In a 1991 campaign to promote school-based clinics, the American Medical Association (AMA) and the National Association of State Boards of Education published a report that inflated the 280,000 annual births to unmarried teenaged mothers into "half a million," and claimed a "30-fold" increase in adolescent *crime* since 1950. In fact, 1950 youth crime statistics are too incomplete to compare, and later, more comprehensive national reports show no increase in juvenile crime rates in at least two

decades. (Contrast, for example, the FBI Uniform Crime Reports for 1970 and 1992.) The facts notwithstanding, the national media (e.g., AP, 6/8/90) dutifully publicized the organizations' exaggerations.

- In the early '80s, officials hyping the "war on *drugs*" orchestrated media hysteria about "skyrocketing" teenage drug abuse at a time when, in fact, teenage drug death rates were plummeting (down 70 percent from 1970 to 1982). In the late '80s, the same media outlets parroted official claims of a drug-war "success" when, in reality, youth drug death rates were skyrocketing (up 85 percent from 1983 to 1991—see *In These Times*, 5/20/92).

Today, official and media distortions are one and the same. Who's to blame for poverty? Teenage mothers, declares Health and Human Services Secretary Donna Shalala in uncritical news stories (see *Los Angeles Times*, 12/12/93) that fail to note that teenage mothers on welfare were poor before they became pregnant.

Who's causing violence? "Kids and guns," asserts President Clinton, favorably quoted by reporters (AP, 11/14/93) who neglect to mention that six out of seven murders are committed by adults. Who's dying from drugs, spreading AIDS, committing suicide? Teenagers, teenagers, teenagers, the media proclaim at the behest of official sources, even though health reports show adults much more at risk from all of these perils than are adolescents.

Media Myth: "Teenage" Sex

The strange logic of the modern media's attack on adolescents is nowhere stranger than its portrayal of "teen" sexuality. Consider its jargon: When a child is born to a father over age 20 and a teenage mother (which happened 350,000 times last year), the phenomenon is called "children having children." When an adult pays a teenager for sex, it is "teenage prostitution."

Some 2 million sexually transmitted diseases and a quarter-million abortions that result from adult/teen sex every year are headlined as "teenage" VD, AIDS and abortion. The causes of these "epidemic social problems" are teenage immaturity, risk-taking, and peer pressure. Their cure is more preaching, programming and punishment aimed at "teenage sex."

According to U.S. Public Health Service reports, 71 percent of all teenage parents have adult partners over age 20. California and U.S. vital statistics reports show that men over age 20 cause five times more births among junior high-age girls than do boys their own age, and 2.5 times more births among high school girls than high school boys do. Even though many more pregnancies among teenage females are caused by men older than 25 than by boys under 18, media reports and pictures depict only high schoolers. By their choice of terms and images, the media blame the young and female while giving the adult and male a break.

This is exactly the image desired by thousands of agencies and programs who profit politically and financially from the issue—such as the Centers for Disease Control, which blames "teenage AIDS" on promiscuous "kids … playing Russian roulette." (AP, 4/10/92) The media have followed the official lead: The three leading newsweeklies have all run cover stories featuring the same formulaic reporting.

Newsweek's "Teens and AIDS" (8/3/92), *Time*'s "Kids, Sex, & Values" (5/24/93) and *U.S. News & World Report*'s "Teenage Sex: Just Say Wait" (7/26/93) all featured surveys of "kids," photos of suburban schools, sidebars lambasting sexy movies, and dire commentary on sexual irresponsibility among schoolboys and girls. Time and U.S. News both blamed "teenage sex" on "confused" kids, and held up sex and abstinence education as the cure.

Imagine how different these stories would be if the media told the decidedly un-sexy truth about pregnant teens: the large majority are impoverished girls with histories of physical, sexual and other abuses by parents and other adults, and most are impregnated by adult men. When the *L.A. Times*, in an exceptional report (3/14–15/93), actually showed the bleak childhoods of pregnant, disadvantaged teens, the accompanying official rhetoric blaming MTV and "peer pressure" looked silly.

Media Myth: "Teenage" Violence

On "teenage" violence, the media picture is similarly skewed: "Teen Violence: Wild in the Streets" (*Newsweek*, 8/2/93), "Kids and Guns" (*Newsweek*, 3/9/92), "When Killers Come to Class" (*U.S. News*, 11/8/93), and "Big Shots" (*Time*, 8/2/93) all follow a standard format. The lead-in details the latest youth mayhem, followed by selected "facts" on "the causes of skyrocketing teen violence": adolescent depravity, gun-toting metalheads, TV images, rap attitude, gang culture, lenient youth-court judges. And perhaps (in a few well-buried sentences) such small matters as poverty, abuse, racial injustice, unemployment and substandard schools.

Given the emphasis on "teen" violence, a California Department of Justice report (8/13/93) comes as a shock: It found that 83 percent of murdered children, half of murdered teenagers and 85 percent of murdered adults are slain by adults over age 20, not by "kids"—or, in President Clinton's stock phrase (AP, 11/14/93), "13-year-olds … with automatic weapons." In fact, FBI reports show 47-year-olds (people Clinton's age) are twice as likely to commit murder than are 13-year-olds.

But while the media champion official rhetoric on violence by youth, they rarely provide similar attention to the epidemic of adult violence against youth. The National Center on Child Abuse and Neglect (5/93) reported that at least 350,000 children and teenagers are confirmed victims of sexual and other violent abuses every year by adults whose average age is 32 years. Comparison of these figures with crime reports shows that for every violent and sexual offense committed by a youth under 18, there are three such crimes committed by adults against children and teens.

The reporting of the 1992 National Women's Study of 4,000 adult women (AP, 5/22/92) is a case study in media bias. The Rape in America report found that 12 million American women have been raped; of these, 62 percent were raped before age 18. The half-million-plus children and teenagers victimized every year averaged 10 years of age; their rapists' average age was 27.

The media unrelentingly headline "children having children" and "killer kids," and endlessly wonder what is "out of control when it comes to the way many teens think" (*U.S. News*, 7/26/93). Surely the widespread adult violent and sexual attacks against youths are a compelling answer. Consistent research shows such abuses are the key factors in violence, pregnancy, drug abuse and suicide among teenagers (see *Family Planning Perspectives*, 1–2/92).

But the same media outlets with plenty of space to dissect sexy videos and dirty rap lyrics couldn't find room to examine the real rapes of hundreds of thousands of children and teenagers every year. *Time* gave it three paragraphs (5/4/92), while *U.S. News* didn't mention it at all. Neither did *Newsweek*, although in four years it has devoted five cover stories to the dangers of rock and rap music (3/19/90, 7/2/90, 6/29/92, 11/2/92, 11/29/93). Similarly, the media have largely ignored the rising number of prison studies (including those at the Minnesota State Prison and the Massachusetts Treatment Center for Sexually Dangerous Persons) which show 60 percent to 90 percent of all inmates—and nearly all of those on death row—were abused as children. The most conservative study, by the National Institute of Justice, projects that 40 percent of all violent crimes (some half-million every year) result from offenders being abused as children (*In These Times*, 9/20/93).

In a similar vein, news outlets (other than a flurry of coverage of the National Commission on Children's report) have generally failed to examine the enormous increase in youth and young-family poverty, which rose by 50 percent from 1973 to 1991 (U.S. Census Bureau, Poverty in the United States). Nor have mainstream media seriously addressed the devastating effects of racism, rising poverty and unemployment on a generation of young people of color.

The media portrait reflects politicians' unadmitted priorities: Condemning violence by youth is a guaranteed crowd-pleaser; focusing on adult violence against kids isn't as popular. (Most news consumers are adults, and kids can't vote.)

In a rare exception—a report that devoted more space to poverty and child abuse than to TV sex—*Time*'s Oct. 8, 1990 cover article pointed out a truth long known to prison wardens and juvenile court judges: "If children are not protected from their abusers, then the public will one day have to be protected from the children." But most outlets continue to treat violent youth as mysterious freaks of nature: The lead headline in the Sunday *Los Angeles Times* (12/9/93) opinion section blared: "Who are our children? One day, they are innocent. The next, they may try to blow your head off."

Perhaps the *L.A. Times* (whose landmark 8/25/85 survey indicated that childhood sexual abuse is epidemic, affecting one-fifth of all Americans) should instead question its own media escapism. From July through September 1993, that newspaper carried 34 articles and commentaries on the effects of violent media, rap and video games on youth—but not one inch on the effects of child abuse in promoting youth violence.

While the *L.A. Times* gives prominent coverage to charges of child abuse involving the rich and famous—like singer Michael Jackson and the Beverly Hills Menendez brothers—when the L.A. Council on Child Abuse and Neglect reported 140,000 children abused in the county in 1992, the *Times* (11/4/93) relegated the story to an inside section with no follow-up or comment.

Two Sides, Same Bias
The extraordinary lack of context and fairness in media coverage of youth stems from two elemental difficulties. First, the standard media assumption is that fairness is served by quoting "both sides"—but on youth issues, "both sides" frequently harbor adult biases against teenagers.

In the much-publicized debates over school programs to reduce "teen" pregnancy, for example, the press quoted "liberal" sources favoring condom handouts balanced by "conservative" sources demanding abstinence education (e.g. *USA Today*, 11/19/91). However, both lobbies based their arguments on the same myth—that heedless high school boys are the main cause of "teen" pregnancy—and avoided the same disturbing fact: that even if every high school boy abstained from sex or used a condom, most "teen" pregnancies would still occur.

The second difficulty is that "teenage" behavior is not separate from "adult" behavior. Such hot topics as "teen pregnancy," "teen suicide," and "youth violence" are artificial political and media inventions. In real-world environments, teenagers usually act like the adults of their family, gender, race, class, location and era, often because their behaviors occur with adults.

For example, Vital Statistics of the United States shows that white adults are twice as likely to commit suicide as black adults, and white teens are twice as likely to commit suicide as black teens. From 1940 to 1990, unwed birth rates rose 4.7 times among teenage women and 4.6 times among adult women. The FBI's 1992 Uniform Crime Reports show that men commit 88 percent of all adult violent crime; boys commit 88 percent of all juvenile violent crime.

Why are adult contexts, common to media reports on youth prior to the 1970s, only rarely cited today? Because that would prevent adolescents from serving as the latest scapegoats for problems that affect society in general.

And there is a subtler reason: the interests circulating negative images of teens want the source of malaise located within youth, where it can be "treated" by whatever solutions the publicizing interest groups profit from, rather than in unhealthy environments whose upgrading will require billions of dollars in public spending. Thus short-term political and corporate profit lies not in fixing environments, but in fixing kids.

The treatment industry's message is clear: "Our teenagers have lost their way," declares the AMA. The press has been a key element in the campaign to persuade the public that the cause of youth pregnancy, violence, suicide, and drug addiction lies within the irrational psychologies and vulnerabilities of adolescents.

A standard news and documentary feature is the "troubled teen" rescued by the teamwork of "loving parents" and "get-tough" professionals. (For an example justifying the abduction of youth by "therapeutic programs," see the Los Angeles Times, 6/2/93). Despite melodramatic media splashes advertising the "success" of this program or that therapy (often based on testimonials or the promoter's own "study"), controlled, long-term research finds efforts to "cure" troubled teenagers generally ineffective.

On the other hand, the publicity campaigns for such treatments—disguised as news—have been quite successful. During the 1980s, the number of teens forced into intensive psychiatric treatment quadrupled, while adolescent commitments to drug and alcohol treatment tripled. If institution and treatment industry claims are valid, we should have seen dramatic improvements in youth behavior.

Exactly the opposite is the case. In the last five to 10 years, intense media and government attacks on various behaviors—chiefly drug abuse, violence and pregnancy—have been followed by rapidly rising problems among teenagers. Stable violence rates and rapidly declining birth rates and drug death levels prior to 1985 have suddenly reversed: All three rose rapidly from the mid-1980s to the early 1990s. The media's unwillingness to question official policy and its failures helped make these reverses possible.

Beyond Youth-Bashing

A few journalists refuse to kowtow to official myths, and instead publicize the enormous racial imbalances inherent in "youth violence," the fundamental sexism of the current debate over "teen" pregnancy, the realities of millions of raped, beaten and neglected children, the skyrocketing rates of youth poverty imposed by ever-richer American elites, and the futility of modern behavior modifications, laws and treatments aimed at forcing the young to "adjust" to intolerable conditions.

Ron Harris's *Los Angeles Times* series on juvenile crime (8/22–25/93) analyzed the crucial factors of racism, poverty and abuse in creating today's youth violence, and exploded the popular fiction of lenient sentencing. (Teens, in fact, serve prison terms 60 percent longer than adults for equivalent crimes.) Kevin Fedarko's perceptive eulogy (*Time*, 1/20/92) to post-industrial Camden, New Jersey, "a city of children" relinquished to poverty and prostitution, may stand as the decade's finest illustration of 1990s America's abandonment of its young.

J. Talan's expose (*Newsday*, 1/7/88) of the profiteering behind the skyrocketing rate of fraudulent adolescent psychiatric commitments to "fill empty beds" in "overbuilt hospitals" was one of the few to question official "treatment" claims. Time's indictment of the "shameful" selfishness, abuses and uncaring attitudes of adults toward "America's most disadvantaged minority: its children" (10/8/90) also stands as an indictment of today's media obsequiousness.

These articles' debunking of conventional wisdom does not stop the same children-blaming myths from showing up in day-to-day coverage of youth problems. But these occasional exceptions do suggest how media responsibility could halt today's political assault on youth and heal spreading intergenerational hostilities.

WILD IN DECEIT: WHY "TEEN VIOLENCE" IS POVERTY VIOLENCE IN DISGUISE
In previous decades, American politicians and social scientists predicted waves of violence stemming from "impulsive" blacks, volatile Eastern European immigrants, "hot-blooded" Latin Americans, and other groups "scientifically" judged to harbor innately aggressive traits. In each case, the news media joined in vilifying whatever temporarily unpopular minority that politicians and pseudo-science had flocked to blame.

And in each case, the branding of disfavored population groups as inherently violent has been disproven. (See Stephen Jay Gould's *The Mismeasure of Man* for examples.) In each case, violence has been found to be a straightforward function of poverty, income disparity.

Here we go again.

Experts have identified a 1990s demographic scapegoat for America's pandemic violent crime: our own kids. A mushrooming media scare campaign about the coming "storm" of "teenage violence" waged by liberal and conservative politicians and experts alike is in full roar.

Teenage Time Bombs
Blaming "a ticking demographic time bomb," *U.S. News & World Report* (12/4/95) warns of "scary kids around the corner." The "troublesome demographic trends" are a growing adolescent population.

"A Teenage Time Bomb," *Time* announced (1/15/96), quoting Northeastern University criminologist James Alan Fox's view of teenagers as "temporary sociopaths—impulsive and immature." Added *Time*: "If [teens] also have easy access to guns and drugs, they can be extremely dangerous."

Other top-quoted criminologists, like UCLA's James Q. Wilson and former American Society of Criminology president Alfred Blumstein, are in full agreement with Fox: Young equals violent. And top political officials concur. The *Los Angeles Times* (12/18/95) noted FBI Director Louis Freeh and other authorities' alarm over "the fact that the crime-prone 16-to-24 year-old group will grow dramatically over the next decade—which Freeh cited as "an alarming indicator of future trends."

The trendiest demographic scapegoater is the centrist Brookings Institution's John DiIulio Jr., anointed "The Crime Doctor" and "one of Washington's in-vogue thinkers" by the *L.A. Times* (5/2/95). "More male teenagers, more crime. Period," is his message. A new breed of youthful "super-predators" menace the nation, so vicious even hardened adult convicts are scared of them, DiIulio said.

Journalists ought to be aware they are pouring gasoline on a fire they have already fanned. A 1994 Gallup Poll (*Gallup Poll Monthly*, 9/94) found that American adults already hold "a greatly inflated view of the amount of crime committed by people under the age of 18," with the most salient reason "news coverage of violent crime committed by juveniles." The average American adult believes that youths commit 43 percent of all violent crime in the U.S., three times the true figure of 13 percent—and, as a result, a large majority is eager to harshly punish juveniles.

Responsible journalists would be looking to reverse this dangerous misimpression they have helped create. Just the opposite is occurring.

In the scare campaign against adolescents, the news media not only uncritically repeat official claims, they actively embellish them with sinister cover stories and apocalyptic tales of suburban mayhem. The message is screamed from headlines, magazine covers, and network specials: Adolescents are "wild in the streets" (*Newsweek*, 8/2/92); teens everywhere are "killer kids" (*Reader's Digest*, 6/93).

Though casting a few paeans to details like poverty, discrimination and abuse, the media scare campaign declares that violence is innate to teenagers and coming mayhem is inevitable. Therefore, the only real solution, articulated by former Robert Kennedy aide Adam Walinsky (*Atlantic*, 7/95), is spending tens of billions to hire five million more police officers and suspending basic civil rights to combat the "epidemic of teen violence."

Unnatural Aggression

The problem with the 1990s teen-violence scare campaign is not that its prediction of a more violent future is wrong—it may well be correct. The problem is its wrongheaded explanation for why violence is rising.

There is no such thing as "youth violence," any more than there is "black violence" or "Italian violence." The recent rise in violent crime arrests among youths is so clearly founded in social conditions, not age-group demographics, that experts and officials have had to strain mightily to ignore or downplay them.

The social scientists receiving the most media attention "argue that teenage aggression is natural." (*Newsweek*, 8/2/92) If it is, we would expect teens all over the world to be violent. That is far from the case.

Murder, the most reliably reported crime around the world, is typically committed by killers very close in age to their victims (unless the victims are children or the elderly). In the 19 largest industrial nations outside the U.S., the 40 million young males aged 15 to 24 committed just 800 murders in the most recent reporting year (World Health Organization, *World Health Statistics Annual*, 1994). In these other Western nations, which have a total of 7,100 murders a year, the typical killer is age 30 or older, far beyond the teen years.

In stark contrast, the U.S.'s 18 million 15-to-24-year-old males accounted for 6,800 murders in 1992. American murder peaks at age 19. U.S. 15-to-24-year-olds are 16 times more likely to be murdered than their counterparts in other Western nations. (U.S. adults have a seven times' greater murder risk.)

U.S. experts, politicians, and their media parroters couldn't be more wrong: There is nothing innately violent about teenagers. There is something extremely violent—hysterically so—about the United States. Not even similar "frontier cultures" such as Canada and Australia have murder tolls remotely approaching ours.

Clearly, there are reasons other than "teen age" that explain why nine out of 10 young men murdered in the world's 20 largest Western countries are Americans. Here American social scientists and the media dispense some of the most absurd escapisms as "explanations."

Favorite Villains

The favorite conservative and pop-psychology villain (from right-wing media critics like Michael Medved and William Bennett to officials of the Clinton administration) is media violence, and the cure-all is more restrictions on TV, movies, books and music available to youths. But the media in most other Western nations are as violent as America's or more so. Efforts by U.S. experts to explain why Japan has extraordinarily violent media but extraordinarily low societal violence (9 million Japanese teens accounted for just 35 murders in 1992) are the essence of lame. (See James Q. Wilson's illogic in the *Los Angeles Times*, 6/25/95.)

The favorite liberal scapegoat is America's gun proliferation. "Whereas illegal firearms were not easily available to 12 year-olds just a few years back, guns can now be obtained in any neighborhood by almost any youngster who has a yen for one," the *L.A. Times* reported (9/9/95), summing up expert opinion. The panacea is another age-based restriction: tougher laws to keep guns away from youths.

True, Europeans and Japanese do not routinely pack heat. And Californians, in a state with 4,000 murders in 1994, purchase 300,000 to 400,000 handguns every year.

But if violent media and guns "in every neighborhood" were the reasons for teen violence, we would expect affluent white families to have the most murderous kids. White households are nearly twice as likely to harbor guns, and one-third more likely to subscribe to blood-dripping cable TV channels, than black and other nonwhite households (*Statistical Abstract of the U.S. 1995*). Yet in California, where whites are the plurality race, nonwhites account for 87 percent of all teen homicides and 80 percent of all teen arrests for violent crimes. How do those who blame media violence, gun availability, and/or "inherent teenage aggression" explain that?

Poverty Violence

The major factor, buried in teen-violence stories and rarely generating any remedies, is poverty. The biggest differences between the U.S. and the 19 other relatively peaceful industrial nations cited above are youth poverty and extreme disparities in income between rich and poor. The 1995 Luxembourg Income Study found the U.S. raises three to eight times more children in poverty than other Western nations. The U.S. has the largest and fastest-growing gap in income between its richest 5 percent and poorest 5 percent of any industrial society (*U.S. News*, 8/28/95).

One figure summarizes the real U.S. violence issue. In 1993, 40 million Americans lived below the official poverty line (which itself understates the true rate of poverty). Half of these are children, and six in ten are non-white. While most impoverished people are not violent, there is no question among criminologists that the stresses of poverty are associated with much higher violent crime levels among all races and ages.

(That poverty is linked to crime should not come as a great surprise. After all, during the Great Depression murder spiraled upward—peaking in 1933 with a rate of 9.7 murders per 100,000, higher than 1993's 9.5 per 100,000 rate. See U.S. Census Bureau, *Historical Statistics of the United States*.)

If you divide the number of violent crimes by the number of people living in destitution, the phenomenon of "teenage violence" disappears: Adjusted for poverty, 13-to-19-year-olds have almost the same crime rate as people in their 40s, and have a crime rate well below that of those in their 20s and 30s. (Bureau of Justice Statistics, *Sourcebook of Criminal Justice Statistics 1994*; U.S. Census Bureau, *Poverty in the United States*, 1993).

The same adjustment for poverty sheds light on an issue that moderates and liberals seem afraid to discuss—the disproportionate amount of crime committed by non-white teens. "It's increasingly clear that everyone's kids are at risk," the Rand Corporation's Peter Greenwood told the *L.A. Times* (9/6/95)—which reprinted the meaningless comment under the blaring headline, "A New Wave of Mayhem."

Neither Greenwood nor the *Times* explained why, if "everyone's kids are at risk," a black youth is 12 times more likely to be murdered than a white youth, or why 31 California counties with a combined population of 2.5 million reported zero teen murders in 1993 (California Center for Health Statistics, 1995).

In fact, teen murder rates for whites are low and falling; non-white teen murder rates are high and rising. In 1975, 97 white youths and 240 nonwhite (including Hispanic) youths were arrested for homicide in California. In 1994, homicide arrests among white youths had fallen to 60, but among non-white youths had doubled to 482 (*Crime & Delinquency in California*, 1975–1993, and 1994 printout).

But notwithstanding Charles Murray's racist *Bell Curve* theories, non-white "dysgenics" is not the explanation for the disparity. If one adjusts the racial crime rate for the number of individuals living in extreme poverty, non-whites have a crime rate similar to that of whites at every age level.

The raging anecdotal campaign to portray affluent youths as out of control (see *New York Times Magazine*, 10/8/95; *Los Angeles Times*, 9/6/95), and the far-out-of-proportion hype accorded the pathetic suburban Lakewood Spur Posse, are attempts to hide the fact that the issue is the same as it always has been: poverty and racism.

Masking the Issues

Why is "teen violence" deployed by politicians and experts through a compliant media to mask the real issue of "poverty violence"? Because in Washington, as *U.S. News & World Report* notes (11/6/95), "reducing child poverty, much less eradicating it, is no longer a paramount priority for either political party."

Instead, the focus is on the sort of proposals put forward by the conservative Council on Crime in America (Reuters, 1/16/96): more police, more prisons, longer sentences imposed at younger ages. That states like California, Texas and Oklahoma have imposed exactly such get-tough measures for two decades and suffered record increases in violent crime appears to have little impact on the debate.

We don't want to spend the money to reduce youth poverty. But blaming concocted "innate" teenage traits for violence opens up a wide array of political and agency profiteering to "treat" the problem. Admitting that the issue might be that 45 percent of black youth, and 40 percent of Hispanic youth, grow up in poverty is not on the official agenda—so it is not on the news media's, either.

SIDEBAR: KILLER ADULTS

There's a statistic in the FBI's *Uniform Crime Reports* 1994 that shatters the emotional mythology surrounding "children killing children." It shows that for the 1,268 murder victims under age 18 whose killers' ages were known, 889 (or 70 percent) of the murderers were adults—not other youths. Of the 9,004 adult murder victims, 91 percent of the killers were adults.

The media did headline—for one day—the report by the U.S. Advisory Board on Child Abuse and Neglect that found that 2,000 children/youths were murdered and 140,000 seriously injured in abuses inflicted by their parents and caretakers in 1993 (Associated Press, 4/26/95). But none of the media appeared to make the connection between violent abuse of children and later violent crime by teenagers.

Little press attention was afforded a National Institute of Justice report (*The Cycle of Violence*, October 1992) that found that child abuse "begets violence," increased the number of violent criminals by 38 percent, and raised the national violent crime volume by over 60 percent; or a Bureau of Justice Statistics report (*Murder in Families*, 1994) showing that within families, parents are six times more likely to murder their teenage children than the other way around.

And no one has commented on the irony of two 1993 figures: 350,000 juveniles were arrested for violent felonies and misdemeanors (*Uniform Crime Reports*, 1993), while 370,000 children and youths were confirmed victims of violent and sexual offenses perpetrated by their parents or caretakers (*Statistical Abstract of the U.S.*, 1995).

8

Nymphet Fantasies: Child Beauty Pageants and the Politics of Innocence

Henry A. Giroux

Only in a climate of denial could hysteria over satanic rituals at daycare centers coexist with a failure to grasp the full extent of child abuse. (More than 8.5 million women and men are survivors.) Only in a culture that represses the evidence of the senses could child pageantry grow into a $5 billion dollar industry without anyone noticing. Only in a nation of promiscuous puritans could it be a good career move to equip a six-year-old with bedroom eyes.

—Richard Goldstein, Village Voice, June 24, 1997

THE DISAPPEARING CHILD AND THE POLITICS OF INNOCENCE

The notion of the disappearing child and the myth of childhood innocence often mirror and support each other. Within the myth of innocence, children are often portrayed as inhabiting a world that is untainted, magical, and utterly protected from the harshness of adult life. In this scenario, innocence not only erases the complexities of childhood and the range of experiences different children encounter, but it also offers an excuse for adults to evade responsibility for how children are firmly connected to and shaped by the social and cultural institutions run largely by adults. Innocence in this instance makes children invisible except as projections of adult fantasies—fantasies that allow adults to believe that children do not suffer from their greed, recklessness, perversions of will and spirit and that adults are, in the final analysis, unaccountable for their actions.[1]

If innocence provides the moral ethos that distinguishes children from adults, the discourse that deals with the disappearance of childhood in our culture signals that it is being threatened by forces that tend to collapse that distinction. For example, in cultural critic Neil Postman's thoroughly modernist view of the world, the electronic media, especially television, presents a threat to the existence of children and the civilized culture bequeathed to the West by the Enlightenment.[2] Not only does the very character of television—its fast-paced format, sound-byte worldview, information overload, and narrative organization—undermine the very possibility for children to engage in critical thinking, but its content works to expel images of the child from its programming by both "adultifying" the child and promoting the rise of the "childfied" adult.[3] But Postman is quick to extend his thesis to other spheres, noting, for example, the disappearance of children's clothing and children's games, the entry of children into professional sports, and the increasing willingness of the criminal justice system to treat children as miniature adults. Postman's lament represents less a concern with preserving childhood innocence than a cry for the passing of a world in which popular culture threatens high culture, and the culture of print loses its hold on a restricted and dominant notion of literacy and citizenship training. The loss of childhood innocence in this scenario marks the passing of a historical and political time in which children could be contained and socialized under the watchful tutelage of such dominant regulatory institutions as the family, school, and church.

Many politicians eager to establish themselves as protectors of childhood innocence also have appropriated the specter of the child as an endangered species. In their rush to implement new social and economic policies, numerous politicians hold up children as both the inspiration for and prime beneficiaries of their reforms. Lacking opportunities to vote, mobilize, or register their opinions, young children become an easy target and referent in discussions of moral uplift and social legitimation. They also become pawns and victims. Far from benefiting children, many of the programs and government reforms enacted by Clinton and the Republican-led Congress represent what Senator Edward Kennedy (D-MA) has called "legislative child abuse."[4] Protecting the innocence of children appears to have a direct connection with the disappearing child, although not in the sense predicted by Neil Postman. The draconian cuts in welfare reform enacted in the 1996 Personal Responsibility and Work Opportunity Reconciliation Act are having a devastating effect on a great number of poor families and their children. While welfare roles have declined since 1996, a report released by the National Conference of State Legislatures indicated that 40 to 60 percent of the poor people who leave welfare obtain employment but often at below-poverty-level wages. Moreover, assistance has been terminated for substantial numbers of children with disabilities. Meanwhile, thousands of families are losing welfare aid because of penalties for noncompliance with new welfare reform rules, and many of those who lose benefits do not find work. Harsh compliance measures, inadequate child care, marginal employment, low wages, and lack of adequate transportation for poor families all combine to make a mockery of welfare reform.[5] In this instance, children are indeed disappearing—right into the hole of poverty, suffering, and despair.[6] In short, the language of innocence suggests a concern for all children but often ignores or disparages the conditions under which many of them are forced to live, especially those who are generally excluded because of race or class from the privileging and protective invocation of innocence.

Politicians have little interest in the welfare of kids who are poor and nonwhite. In view of this fact, innocence emerges less as a term used to highlight the disappearance of kids than as a metaphor for advancing a conservative political agenda based on so-called family values, in which middle-class white children are viewed as more valued and deserving of the material resources and cultural goods of the larger society than are poor and nonwhite children.[7] In this selective appropriation, innocence turns with a vengeance on its humanitarian impulse: The everyday experience of childhood is held hostage to the realities of power and the disingenuous rhetoric of political pragmatism.

As the rhetoric of child welfare heats up in the public consciousness, innocence is increasingly being redeployed by politicians, journalists, and media pundits to rearticulate which specific children are deserving of entitlements and adult protection and what forces pose a threat to them. Imbued with political and ideological values, innocence as used by the popular press is not merely selective about which children are endangered and need to be protected; it also is used to signal who and what constitutes a threat to children.

As politicians, the popular press, and the media increasingly use "the child" as a moral yardstick it becomes more difficult for adults to fail to take responsibility for what they do to kids. Consequently, childhood innocence appears both threatened and threatening. According to popular wisdom, the enemies of children are not to be found in the halls of Congress, in the poisonous advertisements that commodify and sexualize young children, or even in the endless media bashing that blames children for all of society's ills.[8] On the contrary, the child molesters, pedophiles, abductors, and others who prey on children in the most obscene ways imaginable are the biggest threat to children. Here the notion of childhood innocence does more than produce the rhetoric of political opportunism; it also provides the basis for moral panic. Both conservatives and liberals have fed off the frenzy of fear associated with a decade of revelations of alleged child abuse. Starting with the 1987 McMartin preschool case, a wave of fear-inspired legislation has swept the nation to protect children from endophilies, child molesters, predatory priests and teachers, and anyone else who might be labeled as a sexual deviant who poses a treat to the innocence of children.[9] Child abuse in this scenario is reduced to the individual pathology of the molester and pedophile; the fear and anger it arouses are so great that the Supreme Court is willing to suspend certain constitutional liberties in order to keep sexual predators locked up even after they finish serving their sentences.[10]

But the issue of widespread child abuse has done more than inspire a national fear of child molesters. It points beyond the language of individual pathology to the more threatening issue of how society treats its children, exposing the degree to which children have not been provided with the security and resources necessary to insure their safety and well-being. While the most disturbing threat to innocence may be child abuse, this form of abuse cannot be assessed only through the horrible behaviour of sexual predators. Such abuse needs to be situated within a broader set of political, economic, and social considerations; such considerations probe deeply into the cultural formations that not only make children visible markers of humanity and public responsibility but also see them as a menacing enemy or as merely a market to be exploited. The social investment in children's innocence may be at the center of political rhetoric in the halls of Congress, but other forces in American society aggressively breed a hatred and disregard for young people, especially those who are excluded because of their class, race, gender, or status as non-U.S. citizens.

Here I argue that the central threat to childhood innocence lies not in the figure of the pedophile or sexual predator but in the diminishing public spheres available for children to experience themselves as critical agents. Children must be able to develop their capacities for individual and social development free from the debilitating burdens of hunger, poor healthcare, and dilapidated schools, while simultaneously being provided with fundamental social services such as state protection from abusive parents. As cities become increasingly ghettoized because of the ravaging effects of deindustrialization, loss of revenue, and white flight, children are left with fewer educational, social, and economic services to fulfill their needs and desires. As public schools are abandoned or surrendered to the dictates of the market, children increasingly find themselves isolated and removed from the discourses of community and compassion. As the state is hollowed out and only its most brutal apparatuses—police, prisons, etc.—remain intact, children have fewer opportunities to protect themselves from an adult world that offers them dwindling resources, dead-end jobs, and diminished hopes for the future.[11] At the same time, children are increasingly subjected to social and economic forces that exploit them through the dynamics of sexualization, commodification, and commercialization.[12]

JONBENET RAMSEY, RACE, AND THE PERILS OF HOME

While the concept of innocence may incite adults to publicly proclaim their support for future generations, more often than not it protects adults from the reality of society and the negative influence they have in contributing to the ever-increasing impoverishment of children's lives. Of course, flash points in a society often signal that children are in danger and that certain elements in the cultural pose a threat to their innocence. Conservatives, for example, have focused on the dangers presented by rap music, cinematic violence, and drugs to launch an attack on Hollywood films, the fashion world, single teen moms, and what it calls the cultural elite. But rarely do conservative and liberal critics focus on the ongoing threats to children at the center of dominant economic, political, and cultural relations—the dismantling of welfare benefits for poor children, particularly cuts in health insurance, food stamps, and housing allowances; the growing assault on young black males through an ever-expanding criminal justice system, and the increasing demonization of young teens in the media.

Poverty, racism, sexism, and the dismantling of the welfare state do great harm to children, but the press does not report most of the stories exemplifying the effects of these social conditions; if it does, little public discussion or self-examination follows.

One recent exception can be found in the case of JonBenet Ramsey, the six-year-old who was found strangled in her wealthy parents' Boulder, Colorado home the day after Christmas in 1996. Throughout the first half of 1997, the press fixated on the case. Major media networks, newspapers, and tabloids besieged the public with photographs and television footage of JonBenet, dubbed the slain little beauty queen, posing coquettishly in a tight dress, wearing bright red lipstick, her hair bleached blond. The case revealed once again that the media gravitate toward victims that fit the dominant culture's image of itself. Not only are children who are white, blond, and middle class invested with more humanity, they become emblematic of a social order that banishes from consciousness any recognition of abused children who "don't fit the image of purity defiled."[13]

Consider the case of a nine-year-old African American child, labeled in the press Girl X. Girl X was raped, beaten, blinded, murdered, and dumped in a stairwell in the rundown Cabrini Green Housing Project in Chicago. The brutal murder aroused a great deal of publicity in Chicago but was virtually ignored by the national media. Race and poverty relegated Girl X to a nonentity. Innocence is applied primarily to children who are white and middle class, often tucked away in urban townhouses and the safe sanctuaries of segregated suburban America. But there is something equally disturbing about the JonBenet Ramsey case. Innocence also masks the sexualization and commodification of young girls who are taught to identify themselves through the pleasures and desires of the adult gaze. The child becomes the principal incitement of adult desire, but the educational and commercial practices at work remain unexamined because they take place within acceptable cultural forms such as children's beauty pageants. This murder also challenges the assumption that privileged families are immune to accusations of child abuse or neglect. The death of the young beauty queen raises serious questions about the cultural practices and institutions of everyday life that shape children's lives, often in ways that undermine children's chances of entering adulthood free from violence, intimidation, and abuse.

I argue that by critically examining the beauty pageant we can begin to see how the language of innocence obscures from the public's view the appropriation, sexualization, and commercialization of children's bodies. In pursuing this argument, I examine how the culture of child beauty pageants functions as a site where young girls learn about pleasure, desire, and the roles they might assume in an adult society. I also examine how such pageants are rationalized, how they are upheld by commercial and ideological structures within the broader society, and how they are reproduced, reinforced, and sustained in related spheres such as advertising and fashion photography—spheres that also play an important role in marketing children as objects of pleasure, desire, and sexuality. Here I attempt to challenge the concept of such rituals as innocent, to reconsider the role they play as part of a broader cultural practice in which children are reified and objectified. This is not meant to suggest that all child beauty pageants constitute a form of child abuse. Pageants vary both in the way they are constructed and in how they interact with local and national audiences. Moreover, their outcomes are variable and contingent. But beauty pageants, as sites of representation, identity formation, consumption, and regulation, have to be understood in terms of how they articulate and resonate with other cultural sites engaged in the production and regulation of youth, the packaging of desire, and the sexualized body.

BEAUTY PAGEANTS AND THE SHOCK OF THE REAL
The Ramsey case challenges and disrupts ideological conventions that typically apply to narratives of childhood innocence. The blitz media coverage following the brutal murder of six-year-old JonBenet Ramsey gives evidence to that fact. On one level, Jon-Benet's case attracted national attention because it fed into the frenzy and moral panic Americans are experiencing over the threat of child abuse—fueled by horrific crimes like the kidnap and murder of Polly Klaas in California. Similarly, it resonated with the highly charged public campaigns of various legislators and citizen groups calling for the death penalty for sex offenders such as Jesse Timmendequas, the child molester who killed seven-year-old Megan Kanka. On another level, it opened to public scrutiny another high-profile example of a child succeeding at the make-believe game of becoming an adult. Not unlike Jessica Dubroff, the seven-year-old would-be Amelia Earhart who, while attempting to be the youngest pilot to cross the United States, died in a plane crash, JonBenet Ramsey also projected the uncanny ability to present herself as an adult. But if the boundary between innocence and impurity, child and adult, became blurred in both cases, JonBenet's notoriety as an object of public fascination revealed a dark and seamy element in American culture.

Night after night the major television networks aired videotapes of little JonBenet Ramsey in a tight, off-the-shoulder dress, bright red lipstick, and teased, bleached blond hair pulling a feathered Mardi Gras mask coyly across her eyes as she sashayed down a runway. Playing the role of an alluring sex kitten, JonBenet seemed to belie the assumption that the voyeuristic fascination with the sexualized child was confined to the margins of society, inhabited largely by freaks and psychopaths.

The JonBenet Ramsey case revealed not only how regressive notions of femininity and beauty are redeployed in this conservative era to fashion the fragile identities of young girls but also how easily adults will project their own fantasies onto children, even if it means selling them on the beauty block. The JonBenet case offered the public a spectacle in which it became both a voyeur and a witness to its own refusal to address the broader conditions that contribute to the sexualization and commercialization of kids in the culture at large. The general public has come to recognize that child abuse often takes place at home and that the conventional image of the molester as an outsider is less than credible thanks to the recent attention given to child abuse by celebrities such as Roseanne Barr and Oprah Winfrey. The view of the home as a safe space for children also became questionable, as it became clear that the Ramseys imposed their own strange fantasies on their daughter and in doing so denied her an identity suitable for a six-year-old. Instead, they positioned her within a child beauty pageant culture that stripped her of her innocence by blurring the boundary between child and adult. Not allowed to be a child, JonBenet was given the unfortunate job of projecting herself through a degrading aesthetic that sexualized and commodified her. Collapsing the (hardly clear-cut) boundaries between the protective parental gaze and the more objectified adult gaze, JonBenet's parents appear to have stripped their daughter of any sense of agency, independence, or autonomy in order to remake her in the image of their own desires and pleasures. Parental "care" in this case appears to have been wielded tyrannically to prevent JonBenet from experiencing childhood pleasures and needs outside the gaze of pleasure-seeking, narcissistic adults.

Images of six-year-olds cosmetically transformed into sultry, Lolita-like waifs are difficult to watch. They strike at the heart of a culture deeply disturbed in its alleged respect for children and decency. Whereas the blame for the often-violent consequences associated with this eroticized costuming is usually placed on young women, it is hard to blame JonBenet Ramsey for this type of objectification. The public's usual attacks on kids suggesting that they are responsible for society's ills breaks down in this case as it becomes more difficult for adults to evade responsibility for what they do to children—their own and others.[14] JonBenet's image violently transgresses a sacred responsibility associated with protecting the innocence of children. Writ large across the media coverage of the JonBenet case was the disturbing implication and recognition that childhood innocence is tarnished when children can no longer expect "protection … consistency and some sort of dignity" from adults.[15]

The JonBenet Ramsey case prompted an unusual debate in the media and national press. Lacking the theoretical tools or political will to analyze the institutional and ideological forces in the culture that generate such disregard for children, the media focused on what was often termed "the strange subculture of child beauty pageants." More often than not it suggested that the abuse children suffered in such pageants was due to overbearing mothers trying to control their daughters' lives. It seems that if young girls are unavailable for scapegoating, their mothers will suffice. Rarely did the media raise the larger issue of how young girls are being educated to function within such a limited sphere of cultural life or how such a regressive education for young girls is more often the norm rather than the exception.

The traditional moral guardians of children's culture who would censor rap lyrics, remove "dangerous" videos and CDs from public circulation, boycott Disney for pro-gay and lesbian labor practices, and empty school libraries of many classic texts have had little to say about the sexualization of young children in children's beauty pageants, a social form as American as apple pie. Nor are they willing to acknowledge that such pageants must be considered within a broader set of practices which increasingly includes youth sport events that appeal to middle- and upper-class parents who seem willing to sacrifice their children's welfare to the imperatives of success and celebrity. Amid the silence of conservatives and the family values crowd, liberal and progressive reporters have begun to raise some important questions. For example, CBS anchorman Dan Rather criticized the television networks for running the Jon-Benet tapes, claiming that they amounted to nothing less than kiddy porn. Columnist Frank Rich wrote a courageous piece in the *New York Times* in which he argued that the "strange world of kids' pageantry is not a 'subculture'—it's our culture. But as long as we call it a subculture, it can remain a problem for somebody else."[16] Reporter Richard Goldstein followed up Rich's insights with a three-part series in *The Village Voice* in which he argued that the marketing of the sexual child has a long history in the United States and that the JonBenet case "brings to the surface both our horror at how effectively a child can be constructed as a sexual being and our guilt at the pleasure we take in such a sight."[17] For Goldstein, the JonBenet case challenges the American public to confront the actual nature of child abuse, which is all too often a part of family life and is further legitimated by a culture willing to capitalize on children as the new arena for the production of pleasure and commercial exploitation.

All of these critiques raise valid concerns about the role of child beauty pageants and how they produce particular notions of beauty, pleasure, and femininity that are as culturally gender-specific as they are degrading. Such criticisms also prompt a debate about the nature of adult needs and desires that push kids into pageants, and how such pageants correspond with other social practices that "silently" reproduce roles for children that undermine the notion of child innocence and reinforce particular forms of child abuse. In what follows, I examine these issues in detail by focusing on the scope and popularity of children's beauty pageants, what they attempt to teach young girls, and the broader commercial forces that sustain them. I also locate the phenomenon of child beauty pageants within a broader, related set of cultural practices, especially the world of high-fashion advertising and the rise of the teenage model.

BEAUTY AND THE BEAST: A GENEALOGY OF CHILD BEAUTY PAGEANTS

Frank Rich is on target in arguing that child beauty pageants represent more than a subculture in American society. Ted Cohen, President of World Pageants Inc., which publishes an international directory of pageants, estimates that the pageantry industry represents a billion-dollar-a-year industry, with sponsors such as Procter and Gamble, Black Velvet, and Hawaiian Tropics.[18] An estimated 3,000 pageants a year are held in the United States in which more than 100,000 children under the age of twelve compete.[19] In some cases, girls as young as eight months are entered in pageants. California, Florida, and

New York hold the most pageants, and the number of pageants in the United States appears to be growing, despite the fact that many contests, especially at the national level, charge entrants between $250 and $800.[20] Most contestants who enter local pageants are from working-class families driven by mobility fantasies and the lure of a small cash prize. The larger and more expensive pageants appear to be dominated by middle- and upper-class parents like the Ramseys, who have lots of money and resources to spend on costly voice and dance lessons, pageant coaches, expensive costumes, and entry fees.[21]

Pageants are a lucrative business. Promoters market prurient pleasure and rake in big dividends, with some making as much as $100,000 on each event. In addition, child beauty pageants have produced a number of support industries, including costume designers, grooming consultants, interview coaches, photographers, and publishers,[22] not to mention the cosmetics, weight reduction, and other "beauty-aid industries." Trade magazines such as *Pageant Life,* which has a circulation of 60,000, offer their readers images and advertisements celebrating ideals of femininity, glamour, and beauty while marketing young girls in the image of adult drives and desires. In some cases, parents invest big money for makeup artists, hairstylists, and coaches to teach prepubescent kids particular "pro-am modeling styles and tornado spins."[23] A story that appeared in *Life* magazine in 1994 featuring Blaire, an eleven-year-old seasoned beauty pageant performer, documented this trend. Blaire's fortunes at winning got better when her mom and dad hired Tony, a voice coach and makeup artist, who charges $40 an hour, to completely redesign her. When Blaire's father was asked why he was so involved with entering Blaire in child beauty pageants, he answered: "I am a plastic surgeon only from the neck up. I enjoy the beauty of the face. No doubt that's why I am so involved with Blaire." The article reports that "Bruce is captivated by his daughter's beauty but prefers it enhanced: He apologizes to strangers when she is not wearing makeup. Some parents have accused Bruce of enhancing Blaire's looks with surgery." Blaire indicates that she loves pageants; they are all she is interested in. The article ends by pointing out that Blaire lacks a child's spontaneity and then conjectures that she "shows so little offstage emotion because she's so busy editing herself with adults."[24]

Blaire's case may appear to some a caricature of pageant life, narrowly depicting parents who push their kids too hard and who impose their own interests and desires on children too young to decide whether they actually want to participate in the pageants. But the popular literature is replete with such stories. Many parents involved in these pageants do not seem concerned about the possible negative consequences of dressing their children in provocative clothing, capping their teeth, putting fake eyelashes on them, and having them perform before audiences in a manner that suggests a sexuality well beyond their years.

The popular literature that supports the child beauty pageant culture fails to acknowledge that "sexualized images of little girls may have dangerous implications in a world where 450,000 American children were reported as victims of sexual abuse in 1993."[25] Trade magazines such as *Pageant Life* and *Babette's Pageant and Talent Gazette* are filled with ads in which toddlers strike suggestive poses. Full-page spreads of contest finalists depict contestants ranging in age from two to twenty-four years. All of the entrants are defined by the same aesthetic: the makeup, pose, smile, and hairstyles of the six-year-olds are no different from those of the young women. Within the beauty pageant aesthetic, the line between children and adults is blurred; all of the images depict the cool estrangement of sexual allure that has become a trademark of the commodities industry. In addition, the magazines are full of ads hawking outfits from companies called, for example, "Hollywood Babe" and "Little Starlet Fashions"—with many ads invoking the warning "Don't Be Left Behind."[26] One even gushes that contestants may enter a particular pageant for the fee of only $1.00 per pound. Success stories for the younger-age set (four- to eight-year-olds) consistently focus on the thrill of competition, on winning titles, and on the successful modeling careers of the pageant winners.

Parents and pageant sponsors often respond to public criticisms by arguing that the press overreacted to JonBenet Ramsey's death by unfairly focusing on beauty pageants as somehow being implicated in her murder. Others legitimate the child beauty pageant culture as a route to get their kids into lucrative careers such as modeling or to win college scholarships, financial awards, and other prizes. The most frequently used rationale for defending pageants is that they build self-esteem in children, "help them to overcome shyness, and [teach them how] to grow up."[27] One pageant director in Murrieta, California, refuted the criticism that pageants are detrimental for young girls, arguing that "many young girls look at pageants as a protracted game of dress up, something most young girls love."[28] Pam Griffin, another pageant proponent, whose daughter trained JonBenet Ramsey, remarked that "more girls are trying pageants after seeing how much fun JonBenet had."[29] Even *Vogue* reporter Ellen Mark concluded that most kids who participate in beauty pageants end up as success stories. The reason for their success, according to Mark, is that "pageants made them feel special.... Little girls like to look pretty."[30]

This argument, in appropriating the ideology of liberal feminism, emphasizes that girls gain affirming self-direction, autonomy, and a strong competitive spirit through their participation in pageants. But such critiques often fail to recognize that self-esteem is actually being defined within a very narrow standard of autonomy, one that is impervious to how gender is continually made and remade within a politics of appearance that is often reduced to the level of a degrading spectacle. Self-esteem in this context means embracing rather than critically challenging a gender code that rewards little girls for their looks, submissiveness, and sex appeal. Coupled with the ways in which the broader culture, through television, music, magazines, and advertising, consistently bombards young girls with a sexualized ideal of femininity "from which all threatening elements have been purged,"[31] self-esteem often becomes a euphemism for self-hatred, rigid gender roles, and powerlessness.

There is a certain irony in appropriating the language of self-esteem to defend child beauty pageants, especially since the pageants provide young children with standards of beauty that 1 of 40,000 young women will actually meet. Must we ask what is wrong with young girls wanting to become fashion models who increasingly look as if they will never grow up (e.g., Kate Moss), and for whom beauty is not only defined by the male gaze but appears to be one of the few requisites to enter "into the privileged male world."[32] Feminist theorist Naomi Wolf is right in arguing that the problem with linking standardized notions of sexualized beauty to self-esteem is that it does not present young girls or adult women with many choices. This is especially true when issues regarding sexual pleasure and self-determination are held hostage to notions of femininity in which it becomes difficult for women to move beyond such infantilized representations in order to express themselves in ways that are empowering.[33] Moreover, on the other side of the cheap glamorization of the waif-child as the fashion icon of beauty is the reality of a patriarchal society in which the nymphet fantasy reveals a "system by which men impose their authority on women and children alike."[34]

In short, rarely do the defenders of child beauty pageants address the consequences of stealing away a child's innocence by portraying her as a sexualized nymphet. Once again, they have little to say about what children are actually learning in pageants, how a child might see herself and mediate her relationship to society when her sense of self-worth is defined largely through a notion of beauty that is one-dimensional and demeaning. Nor do parents and other pageant participators seem to question the wisdom of allowing children to be sponsored by corporations. The message that often informs such relations is that the identities of the young girls who enter the pageants become meaningful only when tied to the logic of the market. What a young girl learns is that "in order to enter [the] contest she must represent someone other than herself."[35]

Unlike contests that took place ten or fifteen years ago, pageants, especially the national ones, now offer bigger prizes and are backed by corporate sponsors. Moreover, as the commercial interests and level of investment have risen, so have their competitive nature, hype, and glitz. V.J. LaCour, publisher of *Pageant Life Magazine* and a firm supporter of child beauty pageants, thinks that many parents have resorted to makeup and other "extreme" measures because "the parents are trying to get a competitive edge."[36] In some cases, parents resort to mentally punitive and physically cruel practices to get their kids to perform "properly." Lois Miller, owner of the Star Talent Management in Allentown, Pennsylvania, reports that she has "seen parents who have pinched their children for messing up their dress or not looking appropriate or not wiggling enough or not throwing kisses."[37] Parents often respond to such criticisms by claiming that their kids are doing exactly what they want to do and that they enjoy being in the pageants. This argument is strained when parents enter children as young as eight months into pageants, or when parents decide, as reported in *Money* magazine, that their four-year-old child needed a talent agent to make the "right connections" outside of the beauty pageants.

Sixty Minutes, the television program highly acclaimed for its investigative reporting, aired a segment on child beauty pageants on May 18, 1997, in the aftermath of the Jon-Benet Ramsey controversy. The premise of the program, announced by commentator Morley Safer, was to explore whether "child beauty pageants exploit children to satisfy ambitions of parents." To provide a historical perspective on such pageants, *Sixty Minutes* aired cuts from child beauty pageants that had been seen on the program in 1977 and then presented videotaped shots of JonBenet and other children performing in a recent pageant. The contrast was both obscene and informative. The children in the 1977 pageants wore little-girl dresses and ribbons in their hair; they embodied a childlike innocence as they displayed their little-girl talents—singing, tap, and baton twirling. Not so with the more recent pageant shots. The contestants did not look like little girls but rather like coquettish young women whose talents were reduced to an ability to move suggestively across the stage. Clearly, as Morley Safer indicated, "By today's beauty pageant standards, innocence seems to have vanished." When he asked one of the stage mothers who had appeared in the 1977 program what she thought of today's pageants, she responded that she recently went to a child beauty pageant and "walked in the door and walked out. It was disgusting to see the beaded dresses and blown-up hair on kids." The program's take on child beauty pageants was critical, yet it failed to consider the broader social practices, representations, and relations of power that provide the context for such pageants to flourish in the United States. Nor did it analyze the growing popularity of the pageants as part of a growing backlash against feminism reproduced in the media, culture, and fashion industries as well as in a growing number of conservative economic and political establishments.[38] Morley Safer was, however, clear about the assumption that the root of such abuse toward children was to be placed squarely on the shoulders of overly ambitious and exploitative mothers.

The feminist backlash has not stopped more informed criticisms from emerging. For example, some child psychologists argue that the intense competition at pageants compounded with the nomadic lifestyle of traveling from one hotel to another when school is not in session make it difficult for young children to make friends, putting them at risk for developing problems in social interactions with other children. Other child specialists argue that it is as developmentally inappropriate to "teach a six-year-old to pose like a twenty-year-old model as it is to allow her to drive [and] drink alcohol."[39] Of course, there is also the stress of competition and the danger of undermining a child's self-confidence, especially when she loses, if the message she receives is that how she looks is the most important aspect of who she is. Psychologist David Elkind argues that parents used to be concerned with the ethical behavior of kids. A decade ago, when kids got home from school, their parents asked them if they were good. Now, because of the new economic realities of downsizing and deindustrialization, parents are fearful that their kids will be losers.[40] Parents, too often, now focus on how well their kids are competing. Journalist Marly Harris writes that the "massive restructuring of the economy creates a winner-take-all society in which parents believe that if kids don't end up as one of the few winners they will join the ranks of the many losers."[41] Thus the question kids get when they come home in the 1990s is no longer "Have you been good?" but "Did you win?" The message here is did you get the highest grades? Harris also believes that the money spent on child pageants by parents, up to $10,000 per child a year in some cases, could be invested in more productive ways, say in savings plans to help them finance the cost of a college education. But the attributes that are accentuated when defining their identities and self-esteem offer them limited opportunities to develop and express themselves.[42]

In spite of such criticisms, child beauty pageants are enormously popular in the United States, and their popularity is growing. Moreover, they have their defenders.[43] In part, such popularity can be explained, as I mentioned previously, by their potential to make money for promoters, but there is more to the story. Children's beauty contests also represent places where the rituals of small-town America combine with the ideology of mass consumer culture. Pageants with titles such as "Miss Catfish Queen," "Miss Baby Poultry Princess," and "The Snake Charmer Queen Ritual Competition" suggest that such rituals are easily adapted to "local meanings and familiar symbols, values, and aesthetics—those relevant to the producers, performers, and consumers of the contest."[44] Such rituals are easy to put on; are advertised as a legitimate form of family entertainment; resonate powerfully with dominant Western models of femininity, beauty, and culture; and play a crucial role at local and national levels of reproducing particular notions of citizenship and national identity. Child beauty pageants are often embraced as simply good, clean entertainment and defended for their civic value to the community. Moreover, while adult beauty contests, such as the annual Miss America pageant, have been the target of enormous amounts of feminist criticism,[45] few academics and cultural critics have focused on child beauty pageants as a serious object of cultural analysis.[46]

BEYOND THE POLITICS OF CHILD ABUSE

Any attempt to challenge the sexist practices and abuses at work in children's beauty pageants must begin with the recognition that pageants represent more than trivial entertainment. Educational theorist Valerie Walkerdine argued that forms of popular culture such as the beauty pageant offer a way for working-class girls to escape the limiting discourses and ideologies found in schools and other institutions. Popular culture becomes a realm of fantasy offering the promise of escape, possibility, and personal triumph. Desire in this instance gains expression through an endless parade of highly sexualized images and narratives that not only provide the promise of erotic fantasies that "belong to them" but also constitute for these young girls an important strategy for survival.[47] According to Walkerdine, popular cultural forms such as child beauty pageants occupy a reputable public space in which preadolescent working-class girls are offered forms of identification they can appropriate as survival practices in a society stacked against them. But what Walkerdine ignores is that such fantasies often are founded on forms of identification and hope that offer nothing more than the swindle of fulfillment, providing limited choices and options to young girls. Moreover, while such strategies cannot be dismissed as politically incorrect but must be considered within a broader understanding of how desire is both mediated and acted upon, the social costs for such identifications go far beyond the benefits they provide as a buffer against hard times. In the long run, such investments serve to limit, often exploit, and disrupt working-class lives. At the same time, the emergence of cultural forms such as the child beauty pageant makes clear the degree to which viable public spheres are diminishing for children. As public funding decreases, support services dry up, and extracurricular activities are eliminated from schools because of financial shortages, society contains very few noncommercial public spaces for young people to identify with and experience. As market relations expand their control over public space, corporations increasingly provide the public spheres for children to experience themselves as consuming subjects and commodities with limited opportunities to learn how to develop their full range of intellectual and emotional capacities to be critical citizens.

While many progressives are well aware that the struggle over culture is tantamount to the struggle over meaning and identity, it is also important to recognize that any viable cultural politics also must locate specific cultural texts within wider relations of power that shape everyday life. Understood within a broader set of relations, child beauty pageants become an important object of critical analysis for a number of reasons. First, the conservative and rigid gender roles that are legitimated at many child beauty pageants must be analyzed both in terms of the specific ideologies they construct for children and how these ideologies find expression in other parts of the culture. What I want to suggest is that the values and dominant motifs that shape beauty pageants gain their meaning and appeal precisely because they find expression in related cultural spheres throughout American society. For instance, by examining advertising campaigns such as those produced by Calvin Klein or in the increasing use of advertising that depicts the ideal modern American female as young, extremely thin, sexually alluring, and available, it becomes clear that the processes at work in the objectification of young children are not altogether different from the social relations that take place in other sites. All of these sites use the bodies and body parts of young girls to market desire and sell goods. What often makes such connections untenable in the public eye is that beauty pageants appropriate innocence as a trope for doing what is best for children, often in the name of dominant family values. And yet, it is precisely in the name of innocence that practices that might be seen in other contexts as abusive to children are defined within the dominant culture as simply good, clean, family entertainment.

In advertisements for Calvin Klein's Obsession perfume and in his more recent jeans ads, innocence becomes a fractured sign and is used unapologetically to present children as the objects of desire and adults as voyeurs. Innocence in this instance feeds into enticing images of childlike purity as it simultaneously sexualizes and markets such images. Sexualizing children may be the final frontier in the fashion world, exemplified by the rise of models such as Kate Moss who represent the ideal woman as a waif—sticklike, expressionless, and blank-eyed.[48] Or it simply makes celebrities out of teenage models such as Ivanka Trump, who in their waning teen years are left wondering if they are too old to have a career in those culture industries that reduce a woman's talents to elusive and short-lived standards of desire, sexuality, and beauty. What connects the beauty pageants to the world of advertising and fashion modeling is that young girls are being taught to become little women, while women are being taught to assume the identities of powerless, childlike waifs. In this instance, Lolita grows up only to retreat into her youth as a model for what it means to be a woman.[49] Here innocence reveals a dark quality; not only are youth being assaulted across a variety of public spaces but their identities, especially those of young women, are being appropriated in different ways in diverse public sites for the high pleasure quotient they evoke in satisfying adult desires and needs.

As an ethical referent, innocence humanizes children and makes a claim on adults to provide them with security and protection. But innocence gains its meaning from a complex set of semiotic, material, and social registers. And what is happening to children in many cultural spheres as seemingly unrelated as child beauty pageants and the world of advertising and fashion modeling suggests how vulnerable children actually are to learning the worst social dimensions of our society: misogyny, sexism, racism, and violence. Innocence needs to be understood as a metaphor that is open to diverse uses and whose effects can be both positive and devastating for children. If innocence is to become a useful category for social analysis, the term must be understood politically and ethically only through the ways in which it is represented and used within everyday life, shaped by language, representations, and the technologies of power. Central to analyzing a politics of innocence the need to address why, how, and under what conditions the marketing of children's bodies increasingly permeates diverse elements of society. Likewise, educators and others must uncover not only the political and ideological interests and relations of power at work in the construction of innocence but also the actual ways in which cultural practices are deployed to influence how children and adults learn about themselves and their relationships to others.

Innocence becomes both a mystifying ideology and a vehicle for commercial profit. In the first instance, innocence is a highly charged term that points to pedophiles and sexual perverts as the most visible threats to children in our society. Such a restricted notion of innocence fails to understand how child abuse connects to and works its way through the most seemingly benign of cultural spheres such as the beauty pageant. Thus beauty pageants are not only ignored as serious objects of social analysis but are dismissed as simply a subculture. Here innocence protects a particular notion of family values that is class specific and racially coded. In a society in which working-class youth and youth of color are represented as a threat and menace to public order, innocence becomes an ideological trope defined through its contrast with children who are constructed as "other." Innocence as ideological trope reinforces a politics of innocence that legitimates the cultural capital of children who are largely white, middle class, and privileged. Moreover, the discourse of innocence provides little understanding of how the conditions under which children learn in specific places resonate and gain legitimacy through their connection to other cultural sites.

In the second instance, innocence falls prey to the logic of the market and the successful teaching operations of consumerism. The myth of innocence is increasingly appropriated through a glitzy aesthetic in which children provide the sexualized bait that creates images and representations that tread close to the border of pornography. In this scenario, children's sense of play and their social development are transformed through marketing strategies and forms of consumer education that define the limits of their imaginations, identities, and sense of possibility while simultaneously providing through the electronic media a "kind of entertainment that subtly influence[s] the way we see [children], ourselves, and our communities."[50]

Concerned educators, parents, and activists must begin to challenge and counter such images, ideologies, and social practices as part of a cultural politics that makes issues of teaching and power central to its project. This means taking seriously how beauty pageants and other popular cultural sites teach children to think of themselves through the representations, values, and languages offered to them.[51] It also means expanding our understanding of how education is played out on the bodies of young children in pageants and how this practice resonates with what children are taught in other cultural spheres. Schools and other educational sites must treat popular culture as a serious area of analysis. This suggests teaching kids and adults how to read popular culture critically. It also means teaching them how to be cultural producers capable of using new technologies to create texts that honor and critically engage their traditions and experiences. In strategic terms, students must be offered texts, resources, and strategies that provide a complex range of subject positions that they can address, inhabit, mediate, and experiment with. Students and adults also should be taught how to organize social movements at the local and national levels to pressure and boycott companies that engage in abusive practices toward children. Underlying this merging of the political and the educational is the overt political goal of "enabling people to act more strategically in ways that may change their context for the better"[52] and the educational goal of finding ways for diverse groups of children and adults to work together to transform popular public spheres into sites that address social problems by way of democratic, rather than merely market, considerations.[53]

In short, the socialization of children must be addressed within a larger discussion about citizenship and democracy, one that resists what philosopher Theodor Adorno calls the "obscene merger of aesthetics and reality."[54] What Adorno means here is precisely the refutation of those ideologies and social practices that attempt to subordinate, if not eliminate, forms of identity fundamental to public life, to an economy of bodies and pleasures that is all surface and spectacle. Such a discussion not only calls into question the conditions under which kids learn, what they learn, and how this knowledge shapes their identities and behavior, it also raises questions about the material and institutional relations of power that are fundamental for maintaining the integrity of public life—a condition that is essential for all children to learn in order to be critical participants in the shaping of their lives and the larger social order. Child abuse comes in many forms, and it has become a disturbing feature of American society. The current assault being waged on children through retrograde policy, the dismantling of the welfare state, and the pervasive glut of images that cast them as the principal incitements to adult desire suggest that democracy is in the throes of a major crisis. If democracy is to carry us forward into the next century, surely it will be based on a commitment to improving the lives of children, but not within the degrading logic of a market that treats their bodies as commodities and their futures as trade-offs for capital accumulation. On the contrary, critical educators and other progressives need to create a cultural vision and a set of strategies informed by "the rhetoric of political, civic, and economic citizenship."[55] The challenge to take up that commitment has never been so strained nor so urgent.

NOTES

1. Marina Warner, *Six Myths of Our Time* (New York: Vintage, 1995), esp. chap. 30. Of course, the concept of childhood innocence as a historical invention has been pointed out by a number of theorists. See, for example, Philip Aries, *Centuries of Childhood* (Harmondsworth: Penguin, 1979); Lloyd de Mause, ed., *The Evolution of Childhood* (New York: Psychohistory Press, 1974).
2. Neil Postman, *The Disappearance of Childhood* (New York: Vintage, 1994).
3. See ibid., esp. chap. 8. The notion that television and popular culture represent the main threat to childhood innocence is central to the conservative call for censorship, limiting sex education in the schools, restricting AIDS education, redefining the home as the most important source of moral education, and the "Gumping" of American history (in which the 1960s often are seen as the source of the country's current social ills). The quintessential expression of this position can be found in the speeches, press releases, and writing of former secretary of education and "drug czar" William Bennett. It can also be found in legislation supported by groups such as the Christian Coalition, especially the Parental Rights and Responsibilities Act of 1995. Examples of the conservative position on child abuse, the loss of innocence, and the "poisonous" effects of popular culture abound in the popular press. See, for example, Jeff Stryker, "The Age of Innocence Isn't What It Once Was," *New York Times*, July 13, 1997, p. E3.
4. Cited in Peter Edelman, "The Worst Thing Bill Clinton Has Done," *The Atlantic Monthly* 279 (March 1997), p. 45.
5. All of these figures are taken from two articles on the Children's Defense Fund web site (www.childrensdefense.org/): "The New Welfare Law: One Year Later," October 14, 1997, pp. 1–5, and "CDF, New Studies Look at Status of Former Welfare Recipients," May 27, 1998, pp. 1–4. See also Jennifer Wolch, "American's New Urban Policy: Welfare Reform and the Fate of American Cities," *Journal of American Planning Association* 54:N1 (Winter 1998), pp. 8–11.
6. For specific statistics on the state of youth in the United States, see Children's Defense Fund, *The State of America's Children Yearbook 1998* (Boston: Beacon Press, 1998); Ruth Sidel, *Keeping Women and Children Last* (New York: Penguin, 1996).

7. For an analysis of the ideological underpinnings of the right-wing family values crusade, see Judith Stacey, *In the Name of the Family: Rethinking Family Values in the Postmodern Age* (Boston: Beacon Press, 1996).

8. For an analysis of the widespread assault currently being waged against children, see: Henry A. Giroux, *Channel Surfing: Race Talk and the Destruction of Today's Youth* (New York: St. Martin's Press, 1997); Mike A. Males, *The Scapegoat Generation: America's War on Adolescents* (Monroe, ME: Common Courage Press, 1996); Charles R. Acland, *Youth, Murder, Spectacle: The Cultural Politics of "Youth in Crisis"* (Boulder, Colo.: Westview Press, 1995); Holly Sklar, "Young and Guilty by Stereotype," *Z Magazine* (July-August 1993): 52–61; Deena Weinstein, "Expendable Youth: The Rise and Fall of Youth Culture," in Jonathan S. Epstein, ed., *Adolescents and Their Music* (New York: Garland, 1994), pp. 67–83; and various articles in *Microphone Fiends*, ed. Andrew Ross and Tricia Rose (New York: Routledge, 1994); Lawrence Grossberg, *We Gotta Get Outta Here* (New York: Routledge, 1992).

9. For a brilliant analysis of how the image of the sexual predator is used to preclude from public discussion the wide range of social factors at work in causing child abuse, see James R. Kincaid, *Child-Loving: The Erotic Child and Victorian Culture* (New York: Routledge, 1992).

10. For an analysis of the Supreme Court's decision, see Linda Greenhouse, "Likely Repeaters May Stay Confined," *New York Times*, June 24, p. A19.

11. The concept of the hollow state comes from Stanley Aronowitz, *The Death and Birth of American Radicalism* (New York: Routledge, 1996).

12. The literature on advertising and the marketing of children's desires is too extensive to cite, but one of the best examples is Stephen Kline, *Out of the Garden: Toys, TV, and Children's Culture in the Age of Marketing* (London: Verso Press, 1993).

13. Richard Goldstein, "The Girl in the Fun Bubble: The Mystery of JonBenet," *Village Voice*, June 10, 1997, p. 41.

14. For a sustained treatment of the current assault on kids, especially those who are poor, nonwhite, and urban, see Henry A. Giroux, *Fugitive Cultures* (New York: Routledge, 1996). See also Angela McRobbie, *Postmodernism and Popular Culture* (New York: Routledge, 1994).

15. Annie Gottlieb, "First Person Sexual," *The Nation*, June 9, 1997, p. 26.

16. Frank Rich, "Let Me Entertain You," *New York Times*, January 18, 1997, section 1, 23.

17. Goldstein, "The Girl in the Fun Bubble," p. 41.

18. Cited in Karen de Witt, "All Dolled Up," *New York Times*, January 12, 1997, p. D4.

19. While the statistics on children's beauty pageants vary, a number of sources cite similar figures to the ones I cite here. See, for example, Rich, "Let Me Entertain You"; Ellen Mark, "Pretty Babies," *Vogue* (June 199), p. 240; Beverly Stoeltje, "The Snake Charmer Queen Ritual Competition, and Signification in American Festival," in Colleen Ballerino, Richard Wilk, and Beverly Stoeltje, eds., *Beauty Queens* (New York: Routledge, 1996), p. 13.

20. Cited in Part Jordan, "The Curious Childhood of an Eleven-Year-Old," *Life* (April 1994), p. 38.

21. In the wake of JonBenet's death, a sharp decline in the popularity of child beauty pageants has resulted in a rise in entry fees. Fees that were once $200 are now $500, thus weeding out all but the most wealthy contestants. See Alex Kuczynski, "Tough Times on the Children's Pageant Circuit," *New York Times*, September 13, 1998, Section 9, p. 1,8.

22. Mark, "Pretty Babies," p. 240.

23. Linda Caillouet echoes a point made by many academics and journalists across the country: "Pageants have changed over the past 30 years. Grade-schoolers are wearing makeup, modeling swim wear and sashaying down runways. Today's little girls' parents often invest big money in coaches to teach the children the pro-am modeling style and tornado spins. They pay for makeup artists and hair stylists to accompany the children to pageants. Some of the kids use tanning beds. Seven-years olds have reportedly worn false teeth, false eyelashes, and colored contact lenses." Cited in Linda Caillouet, "Slaying Has Child Pageants on Defensive," *Arkansas Democrat-Gazette*, April 14, 1997, p. 1A.

24. Jordan, "Curious Childhood," pp. 62, 68.

25. Michael F. Jacobson and Laurie Ann Mazur, *Marketing Madness* (Boulder, Colo.: Westview, 1995), p. 79.

26. Cited in ad for "Debbrah's: Nation's Top Pageant Designers," *Pageant Life* (Winter 1996), p. 26.

27. Elliot Zaren, "Eyebrows Lift at Child Strutting in Sexy Dresses, Makeup," *Tampa Tribune*, January 14, 1997, p. 4.

28. Cited in Jodi Duckett, "In the Eyes of the Beholder: Child Beauty Pageants Get Mixed Reviews," *Morning Call*, April 6, 1997, p. E1.

29. Ibid.

30. Mark, "Pretty Babies," p. 283.

31. Susan Bordo, *Unbearable Weight: Feminism, Western Culture, and the Body* (Berkeley: University of California Press, 1993), p. 162.

32. Ibid., p. 179.

33. Naomi Wolf, *The Beauty Myth* (New York: Anchor Books, 1992).

34. Richard Goldstein, "Nymph Mania: Honoring Innocence in the Breach," *Village Voice*, June 17,1997, p. 71. This is not to suggest that women and children do not mediate and resist such domination as much as to make clear the determinate relations of power that lie behind the resurrection of the nymphet in the culture.

35. Stoeltje, "The Snake Charmer," p. 23.

36. Cited in Caillouet, "Slaying Has Child Pageants on Defensive," p. 1A.

37. Cited in Duckett, "In the Eyes," p. E1.

38. See, for example, Susan Faludi, *Backlash: The Undeclared War Against American Women* (New York: Anchor Books, 1991).

39. This paragraph relies heavily on comments by pediatric psychologists cited in Rebecca A. Eder, Ann Digirolamo, and Suzanne Thompson, "Is Winning a Pageant Worth a Lost Childhood?" *St. Louis Post-Dispatch*, February 24, 1997, p. 7B.

40. David Elkind, "The Family in the Postmodern World," *National Forum* 75 (Summer 1995), pp. 24–28.

41. Marly Harris, "Trophy Kids," *Money Magazine* (March 1997), p. 102.

42. As Annette Corrigan points out, "Young girls should have the freedom to explore the unlimited possibilities of their humanity and to be valued, as men are, for much more than how they look or their capacity to stimulate desire in the opposite sex," Annette Corrigan, "Fashion, Beauty, and Feminism," *Meanjin* 51:1 (1992), p 108.

43. For an academic defense of beauty pageants as simply an acting out of community standards, see Michael T. Marsden, "Two Northwestern Ohio Beauty Pageants: A Study in Middle America's Cultural Rituals," in Ray B. Browne and Michael T. Marsden, eds., *The Cultures of Celebration* (Bowling Green, Ohio: Bowling Green State University Press, 1994), pp. 171–180. Marsden is so intent in seeing pageants as ritualistic performances that he does not notice how ideological his own commentary is when focusing on some of the most sexist aspects of the pageant practices. Hence, for Marsden, bathing suit competitions simply prove that "beauty can be art." For a more complex analysis see Robert H. Lavender, "'It's Not a Beauty Pageant!' Hybrid Ideology in Minnesota Community Queen Pageants," in *Beauty Queens*, pp. 31–46. See also Susan Orlean's insipid defense of child beauty pageants as public rituals that offer mothers pride when their daughters win and provide pageant contestants the comfort of a family "in which everyone knows each other and watches out for each other." Susan Orlean, "Beautiful Girls," *The New Yorker*, August 4, 1997, pp. 29–36.

44. Stoeltje, "The Snake Charmer Queen Ritual Competition," p. 13.

45. For an important analysis of the different critical approaches to beauty and the politics of appearance that feminists have taken since the appearance of the first Miss America pageant in 1968, see Corrigan, "Fashion, Beauty, and Feminism," pp. 107–22. What is so interesting about this piece is that nothing is said about child beauty pageants. This is especially relevant since many of the conceptual approaches dealing with the politics of appearance simply do not apply to six-year-olds. For instance, the notion that beauty can be appropriated as an act of resistance and turned against the dominant culture seems a bit far-fetched when talking about children who can barely read.

46. One exception can be found in the collection of essays in Cohen et al., ed., *Beauty Queens*.

47. Valerie Walkerdine, *Daddy's Girl: Young Girls and Popular Culture* (Cambridge, Mass: Harvard University Press, 1997), p. 166.

48. While I have not developed in this chapter the implications such depictions have for women, many feminists have provided some excellent analysis. See especially Bordo, *Unbearable*. For a shameful defense of thinness as an aesthetic in the fashion industry, see Rebecca Johnson, "The Body," *Vogue* (September 1997), pp. 653–658. Johnson goes a long way to legitimate some of the most misogynist aspects of the beauty industry, but really reaches into the bottom of the barrel in claiming resentment

is the primary reason that many women criticize the image of waiflike models permeating the media. Claiming that thinness is only an aesthetic and not a morality, Johnson seems to forget that within the dominant invocation of thinness as a standard of beauty is the suggestion that overweight women are slovenly, older women are ugly, and nonwhite women are not as beautiful as the ever-present blonde waifs who populate the media.

49. The classic work on this issue is Mary Pipher, *Reviving Ophelia: Saving the Selves of Adolescent Girls* (New York: Ballantine Books, 1994). See also Nicole Peradotto, "Little Women: A New Generation of Girls Growing Up Before Their Time," *Buffalo News*, January 26, 1997, p. 1F.

50. Cohen et al., eds., Introduction to *Beauty Queens*, 10.

51. For a critical analysis of how young girls are represented in popular culture and what is learned by them, see Walkerdine, *Daddy's Girl*; see also McRobbie, *Postmodernism and Popular Culture*.

52. Lawrence Grossberg, "Toward a Genealogy of the State of Cultural Studies," in Cary Nelson and Dilip Parameshwar Gaonkar, eds., *Disciplinarity and Dissent in Cultural Studies* (New York: Routledge, 1996), p. 143.

53. This suggests that adults not only take responsibility for how children's identities are constructed within oppressive social relations but also that such adults support those youth such as Free Children, a youth group consisting of kids between ten and sixteen years of age who are organizing at the national and international level to "help children being abused and exploited, but to also empower young people to believe in themselves and to believe that they can play an active role as citizens of this world." Craig Kielburger, "Children Can Be Active Citizens of the World," *Rethinking Schools* (Summer 1997), p. 19.

54. Adorno cited in Geoffrey Hartman, "Public Memory and Its Discontents," *Raritan* 8:4 (Spring 1994), p. 27.

55. Stanley Aronowitz, "A Different Perspective on Inequality," in Henry A. Giroux and Patrick Shannon, eds., *Education and Cultural Studies* (New York: Routledge, 1998), p. 193.

Suggested Readings
for Further Study

Blos, P. (1962). *On adolescence: A Psychoanalytic interpretation*. New York: Free Press.

Engels, F. (1884/1972). *Origin of the family, private property, and the state*. New York: Penguin Books.

Esman, A. (Ed.) (1975). *The Psychology of adolescence: Essential readings*. New York: International Universities Press, Inc.

Feagin, J., & VanAusdale, D. (2001). *The first R: how children learn race and racism*. Lanham, MD: Rowman & Littlefield.

Feldman, S., & Elliott, G. (Eds.) (1990). *At the threshold: The developing adolescent*. Cambridge, MA: Harvard University Press.

Freud, S. (1962). *Three essays on the theory of sexuality*. New York: Basic Books.

Gaines, D. (1990). *Teenage wasteland: Suburbia's dead end kids*. New York: HarperPerennial.

Giroux, H. (1999). *The mouse that roared: Disney and the end of innocence*. New York: Routledge.

Jenkins, H. (1998). *Children's culture reader* (pp. 1–40). New York: New York University Press.

Lesko, N. (1996). *Act your age! A social construction of adolescence*. New York: RoutledgeEalmer.

Lipsitz, J. (1977). *Growing up forgotten: A review of research and programs concerning early adolescents*. Lexington, MA: Lexington Books.

Lipsitz, J. (1984). *Successful schools for young adolescents*. New Brunswick, NJ: Transaction Books.

Males, M. (1996). *Scapegoat generation*. Monroe, ME: Common Courage Press.

Males, M. (1998). *Framing youth: Ten myths about the next generation*. Monroe, ME: Commin Courage Press.

Moran, J. (2000). *Teaching sex: The shaping of adolescence in the 20th century*. Cambridge, MA: Harvard University Press.

Prout, A., & James, A. (1997). A new paradigm for the sociology of childhood? Provenance, promise, and problems. In A. James & J. Prout, *Constructing and reconstructing childhood* (pp. 7–23). Washington, DC: Falmer Press.

Wallis, C. (May, 2004). What makes teens tick. *Time Magazine*, New York: Time Inc.

Williams, P. (May 24, 1999). The auguries of innocence, *Nation, 9*.

II

THE MIDDLE SCHOOL CONCEPT AND THE PURPOSE OF EDUCATION

Enora R. Brown

That the [junior high] school system [should] check the physical, mental, and moral evils that accompany and grow out of adolescence. (Bennett, 1919, p. 3, cited in Lipsitz, 1977, p. 89)

Young adolescents are far more at risk for self-destructive behaviors—educational failure, drug and alcohol abuse, school age pregnancy, contraction of sexually transmitted diseases, violence—than their age group ever was before.… In groping for a solid path toward a worthwhile adult life, adolescents can grasp the middle grade school as the crucial and reliable handle. (Carnegie, 1989, p. 13).

A latter day effort to correct the flaws of junior highs through the middle school movement shows little change over the original design. (Cuban, 1992, p. 227)

In relation to other world economies, "the key to both productivity and competitiveness is the skills of our people and our capacity to use highly educated and trained people to maximum advantage in the workplace" (Marshall & Tucker, 1992, p. 82—In Jackson & Davis, 2000, p. 15).… "As the American population ages and becomes increasingly dependent on today's youth to ensure its own economic well-being … young adolescents [must] develop the capacity to contribute to the country's economic future." (Jackson & Davis, 2000, p. 15)

The major function of the school was to guide the student into his proper place in the corporate structure but also that the school should be organized along lines of a corporation … that this would give the student a good introduction into the workings of the industrial community. (Spring, 1972, p. 97)

The chapters in this section address various dimensions of the Middle School Concept, based on the "founding fathers" early conceptualizations. As the opening quotes indicate, this section also addresses the role of corporate interests in a changing economy and the institutionalized goals of public education. Critical readings examine the genesis and evolution of the Middle School Concept and challenge some of the basic underlying assumptions about youth and the purpose of education that guide current middle level policy and practices. In 2003, the National Middle School Association, the professional organization committed to the support of young adolescents and the middle school movement, released its official position paper, *This We Believe*, and posited the following 14 characteristics that constitute the culture and programmatic qualities of successful middle schools:

The National Middle School Association *believes* that: *Successful schools* for young adolescents are characterized by *a culture* that includes: 1) educators who value working with this age group and are prepared to do so, 2) courageous, collaborative leadership, 3) a shared vision that guides decisions, 4) an inviting, supportive, and safe environment, 5) high expectations for every member of the learning community, 6) students and teachers engaged in active learning, 7) an adult advocate for every student, and 8) school-initiated family and community partnerships.

Therefore, successful schools for young adolescents *provide*:

1) Curriculum that is relevant, challenging, integrative, and exploratory, 2) multiple learning and teaching approaches that respond to their diversity, 3) assessment and evaluation programs that promote quality learning, 4) organizational structures that support meaningful relationships and learning, 5) school-wide efforts and policies that foster health, wellness, and safety, and 6) multifaceted guidance and support services. (National Middle School Association, 2003, p. 7)

These tenets of the Middle School Concept are an outgrowth of the work of William M. Alexander, the "father of the middle school," who coauthored chapter 9, the first chapter of this section in 1963, from "The Emergent Middle School." Alexander coined the term "middle school," conceptualized the developmental, programmatic, and organizational aims of the "emergent middle school" for pubescent youth, as distinct from its predecessor, the junior high school, and laid the foundation for a national effort to implement these programs for 10- to 14-year-olds. His work paved the way for the key components of middle school education: (1) heterogeneous grouping and cooperative learning vs. "ability grouping," (2) integrated/core curriculum vs. separate subject study, (3) teacher–student/advisor–advisee relationship vs. separate guidance counselor, (4) block schedule vs. multiple periods, and (5) interdisciplinary team teaching vs. individual instruction. Grounded in G. Stanley Hall's conception of adolescence, Alexander and his colleagues highlight the physical, intellectual, and psychosocial "needs" of the transescent "in-between-ager," and argue for a change from the 6-3-3 grade structure in schools and "bridge" curriculum to facilitate students' transition from elementary to high school. This text illustrates the persistence of the foundational premise regarding special education for the pubertal child from the junior high to the middle school concept: that as youth reach puberty with its attendant developmental changes, a new educational program and organization was needed to manage a "social concern"—how to harness, redirect, and control the vagaries of youth in transition.

Chapter 10 is the Executive Summary from the Carnegie Corporation's *Turning Points Report*, a landmark publication in 1989. It launched the corporation's Middle Grade School State Policy Initiative (MGSSPI), implemented nationally in 225 schools. This national policy elaborates the principles developed by Alexander, with attention to emergent technological and social changes that were revamping the job market prompting corporate attention to changes in education for youth that would promote economic growth in the upcoming new millennium. (Spring, 1998). While the report reflects Carnegie's current motivation for spearheading and funding this educational reform—the "waywardness" and "unreadiness" of the youth as their prospective workforce, it also instantiates the corporation's century-long role in the "business of education" (Bowles & Gintis, 1976; Saltman, 2000; Spring, 1998). The *Turning Points* report represents the converging interests and concerns of developmentalists, educators, and corporate leaders, whose view of youth locates the source and solution of social and economic ills within the youth, rather than in the larger social order. In 1989, it foreshadows the growing role of corporate business in education, which threatens the survival of public education and the equitable provision of quality education for youth across race and class lines in 2004.

Chapter 11, "The Future of Middle Level Education: Optimistic and Pessimistic Views" is written by respected leaders in the National Middle School Association, John Lounsbury and Gordon Vars. The authors' historical perspective of the middle school reform movement chronicles its accomplishments over the past 115 years and the current threats to middle school education posed by the standards movement and privatization of public education. This reading reveals the difficulties that arise in the middle school reform movement as it comes up against conservative corporate-driven national policies, and must consider ways to resist or accommodate the effects of these destructive trends and protect or relinquish the stated goals of middle level education. As one of the few traditional texts that mentions the threat posed by corporate-led "educational reforms" to public education, it may prompt middle school advocates to take social action and overcome what Dickinson (2001) has called "arrested development" in middle school education.

In chapter 12, Nancy Lesko presents the first critical perspective in this section, entitled "Back to the Future: Middle Schools and the *Turning Points* Report." She challenges the Victorian era–based assumptions and beliefs about adolescents in the *Turning Points* report that inform organizational structures, curriculum design, and teacher–student relationships in schools, and posits that middle school policies and practices, in fact, "produce" adolescence. She argues against the report's assertions that middle schools stabilize youth, that "youth deficiencies" contribute to social and economic uncertainties in society, and that school personnel's tacit affectional ties with youth are supportive rather than controlling. Lesko deconstructs the report to reveal its curricular focus on behavioral control, health embedded in Victorian morality, and learning factual knowledge, rather than on its espoused focus on critical thinking (MacIver & Epstein, 1993). Her critical discursive analysis of the *Turning Points* report reveals the continuity of thought about youth throughout the 20th century, despite educators' reform efforts, and the historically embedded, institutionally sanctioned, and normalized practices and meanings that frame constructions of youth and attendant educational structures and processes. Lesko provides an invaluable lens for examining other "naturalized" processes of human development in relation to the economic and ideological contexts in which they occur.

In Samuel Bowles and Herbert Gintis's time-honored classic, "Schooling in Capitalist America," the authors analyze the organic relationship between capitalist relations of production and the structure and culture of public education. The authors argue in chapter 13 that a bureaucratic, repressive, and authoritarian climate is created in public education with a top-down, teacher-focused learning process, consciously designed as a "hidden curriculum" that prepares students, organizationally and socially, for their subordinate positions as employees and sources of profit in the workplace. They assert that the social regulatory function of schools is to promote students' docility, obedience, punctuality, industriousness, and cultural capital (Bourdieu & Passeron, 1977/1994) to prepare them for their commensurate place in the workforce and position in society, and that schools "perpetuate, legitimate, and reproduce" social inequality, mirroring the societal disparities along race, class, and gender lines. While schools promote social control, simultaneously, education may inadvertently heighten social consciousness and resistance against oppression. Bowles and Gintis's analysis is indispensable to an understanding of the structural and ideological function of public schools in maintaining the social order, and to ongoing inquiry into the role that major shifts in the economy play in generating substantive educational reforms toward the preservation of existing relations of power. As such, it provides a perspective for understanding the significance of the Carnegie Corporation's leading role in middle level education reform efforts in both the early and late 20th century.

Robin Goodman and Kenneth Saltman analyze multinational corporate investment in producing school curricula, commodifying youth, and privatizing education, in chapter 14, "Rivers of Fire: Amoco's iMPACT on Education and Other Corporate Incursions." The authors examine the implications of Amoco's producing middle school science curriculum, Rivers of Fire, and omitting Amoco's support of U.S. foreign military intervention for global capital expansion, their human rights violations, economic exploitation and rampant incursion of "collateral damage," and capricious ecological destruction, all in the pursuit of oil. In the curriculum, these "covert operations" are masked behind the image of Amoco, as a "responsible corporate citizen" that tames nature, fosters democracy, and spreads the "joys of capitalism" to the "underdeveloped" world, and is presented to the captive audience of adolescent population, subject to an affectively disarming ideological worldview (Lesko, chapter 12), marketed to them through the latest technology and the glitz of fun-filled, engaging cartoons and other educational materials. Youth are being wooed for their ideological support of future ventures of corporate capital, when they become adults.

This section illustrates the profound, ostensibly benign relationship that exists between corporate capital and educational reform, as corporations, e.g., Amoco, Carnegie, etc., invest in education (divest through government-sponsored tax evasion) and fund the "public good" in order to protect and extend the private aims of corporate capital, e.g., socialization of the workforce, creation of a captive consumer audience, ideological conversion. Goodman and Saltman's analysis exposes the unbridled expansion of global capital and search for profits in local home markets of privatized health care, patented scientific discovery, educational curricula, educational reform, and ultimately, public education itself. Focusing on global capital, this chapter extends Bowles and Gintis's analysis in chapter 13 of this section and suggests that the corporate agenda to maximize profits has the unintended effect of sowing the seeds of resistance in the schools and other sites in the global arena.

This section concludes with a chapter by Paolo Freire, the renowned Brazilian scholar and activist, whose internationally acclaimed work has transformed education at all levels. In chapter 15, from *Pedagogy of the Oppressed*, Freire carves out the principles of critical pedagogy and the purpose of education: consciencization, that is, to raise the consciousness of the oppressed and, thereby, transform their own lives and society. Freire criticizes the pervasive "banking method" of education and explains the destructive consequences of this pedagogical approach, separating knowledge from discovery, for the student or the oppressed, in fostering complicity and discipline. He examines the ways in which this approach constructs the learner and teacher and its implications in the context of hierarchies of power in society and in schools. His analysis is consonant with Lesko's and Bowles and Gintis's in describing schools as means to maintain social control, quell social unrest, and subvert the learners' critical analysis of their own oppressed conditions under capitalism.

Rather, Freire argues for "problem-posing," a liberatory educational process that fosters conscious critical thinking about one's immediate conditions. Problem-posing alters the teacher–student relationship, creates a consensual, dialogic process for the knowledge construction, and fosters new consciousness to change reality. As such, education becomes a "practice of freedom" through which students can invest in creating their own knowledge, embrace new perceptions and understandings that emerge, and transform their ways of being and acting on the world in order to change their own material conditions. Problem-posing as liberatory pedagogy acknowledges the history of teachers–learners and the mutability of circumstances, the ongoing process of change, and the capacity for teachers–learners to collaboratively create their own future in the ongoing pursuit of becoming fully human. From this perspective, education is a life-long human process, ever disrupting false perceptions of reality, reaching toward the revolutionary … the ongoing transformation of humanity.

Freire's view diametrically opposes the dominant culture's institutionalization of the banking method in public education, which is most poignantly characterized by the corrosive resurgence of the standards-accountability movement and the flattening of human learning, potential, and spirit. It vehemently opposes the resultant increasing emphasis on classroom discipline and growing trend to militarize schools in poor communities. As teachers teach to the test, students are narcotized into complacency and failure, with no active role in the learning process and educators are demoralized as this process of deintellectualization in education stifles their own and their students' creativity and thoughtful inquiry. Freire's view has implications for the middle school movement: Should middle schools "take two steps backwards" and follow the retrograde policy change on the part of *Turning Points* 2000, which altered its 14 points to coincide with the national standards movement, or strive to implement integrated, problem-focused curriculum? Can educators take a reflective step back, employ Freire's problem-posing model, and examine the assumptions that guide our constructions of, work with, and expectations for adolescents? Can we allow ourselves to engage in the process of critically thinking about the relationship between education and society, so that we too may take up the challenges that face us, intellectually and in social action? Freire's work reveals the pressing need for educators to examine, analyze, and deconstruct the multitude of educational reforms that surface in order to determine who benefits in the short run, and whose interests are served in the long-run.

QUESTIONS FOR REFLECTION AND DIALOGUE

1. What is William Alexander's rationale for the new middle school? How are his arguments for middle school education the same or different from those in the *Turning Points* report? What social and economic developments in the United States provided a context for the creation of the junior high school, the middle school movement, and current educational reforms?

2. How does *Turning Points* "naturalize" assumptions about adolescents and provide the rationale for the report's plans and recommendations? How might recommendations for middle school education be different if they were not based on the naturalization of adolescence?

3. What are Lesko's primary criticisms of the *Turning Points* report with regard to the depictions of young adolescents, school organization, and curriculum? What are the implications of her criticisms for the education of youth in middle schools? What should change?

4. What is the purpose of schooling in capitalist America? How do the relations of production shape the organization and climate in public education and foster resistance to oppression?

5. What is the history and function of multinational corporations in various aspects of educational reform? What are the immediate and long-term consequences Amoco's science and other curricula, i.e., the hazards for the youth and society in general? What should be the response to their role in education?

6. What is the purpose of schooling according to Freire and how does it differ from traditional models? Why does Freire call problem-posing education a liberatory process? What are the implications of his conception of education for teachers and students, for education of youth in middle schools?

REFERENCES

Bennett, G. V. (1919). *The junior high school.* Baltimore: Warwick & York. In Lipsitz, J. (1977). *Growing up forgotten: A review of research and programs concerning early adolescence.* Lexington, MA: Lexington Books.

Bourdieu, P., & Passeron, J. (1977/1994). *Reproduction in education, society, and culture.* London: Sage Publications.

Bowles, S., & Gintis, H. (1976). *Schooling in capitalist America: Educational reform and the contradictions of economic life.* New York: Basic Books.

Carnegie Council on Adolescent Development (1989). *Turning points: Preparing American youth for the 21st century.* New York: Carnegie Corporation of New York.

Cuban, L. (1992). What happens to reforms that last? The case of the junior high school, *American Educational Research Journal, 29*(2), 227–251.

Dickinson, T. (2001). *Reinventing the middle school.* New York: RoutledgeFalmer.

Jackson, A., & Davis, G. (2000). *Turning points 2000: Educating adolescents in the 21st century.* New York: Teachers College Press.

MacIver, D. J., & Epstein, J. L. (1993). Middle grades research: Not yet mature, but no longer a child. *The Elementary School Journal, 93*, 519–533.

National Middle School Association (2003). *This we believe: Successful schools for young adolescents.* Westerville, OH: National Middle School Association.

Saltman, K. (2000). *Collateral damage: Corporatizing public schools: A threat to democracy.* Lanham, MD: Rowman & Littlefield.

Spring, J. (1972). *Education and the rise of the corporate state.* Boston, MA: Beacon Press.

Spring, J. (1998). *Education and the rise of the global economy.* Mahwah, NJ: Lawrence Erlbaum Associates.

9

From *The Emergent Middle School*

William M. Alexander

Paul Woodring's statement that "it now appears that the 6-3-3 plan, with its junior high school, is on the way out"[1] seemed in October 1965, to be an exaggeration of the facts. Even two years later, however, as this book is in press, Woodring's prediction seems less extreme. There definitely appears to be a rather widespread interest in reorganizing especially the middle division of the 6-3-3 plan into some type of middle or intermediate school different from the traditional grade 7–9 junior high school.

This chapter reviews the rationale, status, and direction of the movement in the 1960s toward a new middle school. Thus it serves also as an overview of the emergent middle school to which this book is devoted.

WHAT IS THE EMERGENT MIDDLE SCHOOL?

The use of the adjective "new" or "emergent" before "middle school" is deliberate and essential. Clearly the junior high school Americans have known in the twentieth century was intended to be a "middle" school. Indeed Samuel Popper's work on *The American Middle School* declares that "what over the years we have come to know as the Junior High School *is* institutionally America's Middle School."[2] To Popper, "What is at issue now in professional dialogue is not whether there shall be a junior high school or a "middle" school, a semantic distinction without a difference, but rather which grades are functionally appropriate for this unit of public school organization."[3]

But to many educators, including the present authors, the issue seems rather to be whether a new program and organization would serve the function of a middle school better than those of the traditional school structures, especially of the upper elementary grades and the grade 7–9 junior high school. The function itself does seem to remain that ascribed by Popper to the pioneers of the junior high school:

> Its pioneers in the United States meant the middle school to serve as a transitional unit between childhood education in the elementary school and later adolescent education in the high school. Pupils between these two stages of maturation, standing at the threshold of puberty, were to be assigned to a middle school.[4]

In our judgment, today's interest in a new middle school stems in part from dissatisfaction with what the junior high school has become, not with original conception of function. Along with Popper, we would agree that "its unhappy past can well serve as a prologue to a brighter future, provided we cast out from the middle school what has become functionally obsolescent." However, we cannot fully accept as adequate what he proposes (still a grade 7–9 organization, without adequate ties to the levels below and above, we fear) as "a revitalization program" for "the middle school of tomorrow."[5]

The emergent middle school is more than merely a reorganized junior high school. In fact, considerable impetus to a new type of middle school comes from dissatisfaction with the program and organization of the upper years of the elementary school. Too, there is much support for a four-year high school including the ninth grade. Thus the new middle school should be seen more as an effort to reorganize the total school ladder than just one of its levels. It is the 6-3-3 plan, not just one or more of its divisions, that is being reorganized, that may indeed be, as Woodring observed, "on its way out."

We do not conceive of the middle school as serving only early adolescents, unless "early" be regarded as synonymous with the "in-between years." "Middle" here is believed to have two significant connotations which should help to define the scope and limitations of the middle school. In the first place, the youth served are in the "middle," between childhood and adolescence. In the second place, the schools serving them should be in the "middle," between schools for childhood and for adolescent education. Since individual children vary widely in the age at which they attain full adolescence, and since schools are not uniformly and precisely identified as being for childhood or adolescence, overlappings are inevitable and approximations essential.

Thus there is a very real dilemma as to the placement of the middle school in the school organizational plan. The dilemma is heightened by the diverse factors operating in American school districts, which have created every variety of graded structures, including (without reference to pre-grade 1, community junior college, and ungraded structures) such organizations as 1-12, 8-4, 6-6, 6-3-3, 6-2-4, 5-3-4, 4-4-4, 7-5, 7-2-3, and others. Nevertheless, it is clear that before 1960 the most popular organization had become the 6-3-3 one (a reversal in forty years from the 8-4 plan equally popular in 1920) and that the current reorganization movement is one that modifies this pattern. Specifically, the emergent middle school combines into one organization and facility certain school years, usually those in grades 5–8 or 6–8, that have been separated by elementary and junior high organizations under the 6-3-3 plan.

What, then, is the emergent middle school? To us, it is *a school providing a program planned for a range of older children, preadolescents, and early adolescents that builds upon the elementary school program for earlier childhood and in turn is built upon by the high school's program for adolescence.* Specifically, it focuses on the educational needs of what we have termed the "in-between-ager," although its clientele inevitably includes a few children for whom puberty may arrive before or after the middle school period. It is a school having a much less homogeneous population, on the criterion of developmental level, than either the elementary or high school, with their concentration on childhood or adolescence.

Thus, the emergent middle school may be best thought of as *a phase and program of schooling bridging but differing from the childhood and adolescent phases and programs.* This conception assumes that schooling is planned from school exit to school termination with three closely articulated phases or levels: childhood, middle, and adolescent. The decision as to what grades and ages, if any, are to be assigned to specific levels must be, we believe, a decision to be reached within each school district on the basis of local data and experience as to developmental levels of children, existing graded school organizations, and school facilities. We ourselves are inclined to believe that the school level for childhood should generally be designed to serve children until about age ten, and the level for adolescence those who are about fourteen and older, with the middle school designed for those in between these years. We fully recognize, however, both the wisdom and the necessity of disregarding such theoretical norms in a particular situation. The essential point is that there be a planned program of schooling giving due consideration to these three levels of growth and development.

• • •

AIMS OF THE EMERGENT MIDDLE SCHOOL: SUMMARY

The aims of the emergent middle school, as we have defined it, have been stated or implied, at least in general terms, throughout the previous sections of this chapter. We now summarize these aims, as identified and accepted by the authors:

1. To serve the educational needs of the "in-between-agers" (older children, preadoles-cents, early adolescents) in a school bridging the elementary school for childhood and the high school for adolescence.
2. To provide optimum individualization of curriculum and instruction for a popula-tion characterized by great variability.
3. In relation to the foregoing aims, to plan, implement, evaluate, and modify, in a con-tinuing curriculum development program, a curriculum which includes provision for: (a) a planned sequence of concepts in the general education areas; (b) major emphasis on the interests and skills for continued learning; (c) a balanced program of exploratory experiences and other activities and services for personal development; and (d) appropriate attention to the development of values.
4. To promote continuous progress through and smooth articulation between the sev-eral phases and levels of the total educational program.
5. To facilitate the optimum use of personnel and facilities available for continuing improvement of schooling.

• • •

INCREASING KNOWLEDGE ABOUT THE TRANSITION FROM CHILDHOOD TO ADOLESCENCE

Fortunately, many more validated facts about the genetic, physiological, psychological, and cultural dynamics acting in and upon children going through major transition to adolescence are now available. When the junior high schools were set into motion more than fifty years ago, available facts were of a highly generalized nature. Research data gave the average height and weight, together with standard deviations, of children and youth at each chronological age covered by elementary and secondary education. This succession of averages made growth appear both gradual and even throughout childhood and adolescence. On the basis of these data so fine a scholar as Alexander Inglis,[6] for example, advanced the thesis that gradual and even development of individuals was the factual and reasonable basis for planning the work of both the junior and senior high schools. Inglis' interpretations assumed that normal individual development followed the averages of growth shown by large samples of children and youth at each successive chronological age.

A quarter century before, G. Stanley Hall[7] had studied a relatively small number of persons as they passed from childhood into adolescence. His penetrating observations indicated that this period was one of swiftly accelerated growth, followed by equally swift deceleration of the growth rate. He gathered case data which showed that many young people suffered considerable anxiety about their growth and about their new organic functions during this period. He claimed that his subjects went through times of emotional turbulence, erratic behavior, and independent assertiveness during this transition period. All of these insights were repudiated by educators during the two decades when junior high schools were in their formative period. It was felt that research had validated the idea that transition from childhood to adolescence posed no special problems for the pupils, except as individuals lacked intellectual capacity or carried special personal adjustment problems. A counselor or two could take care of pupils "who had problems."

In the 1920s and 1930s, anthropologists, physiologists, psychologists, and sociologists began new studies of human growth and development. Multidiscipline, longitudinal studies began. Data of many different kinds were gathered about the same individuals through a period of years. The physical and organic development, the development of interpersonal relationships among peers, the evolution of relationships with families, the learning of reading, languages, and arithmetic skills, the development of intelligence, the expression of emotions, and the evolution of concepts of self-all these kinds of changes in human beings were studied by teams of specialists who gathered data about the same individuals through periods of from eight to thirty-five years. These records of how *individuals* grow, develop, and evolve are now available to us. These records make it possible for us to see how individual persons vary from each other as they go through their transition from childhood to adolescence.

As happens too often in education, there is a twenty-five year lag between the availability of valid scientific knowledge and its functional application in the educative process. This is particularly true if the new information requires a fundamental rethinking of factors that influence learning with consequent changes in ways the learning process is organized, stimulated, and guided. For example, between 1936 and 1966, a number of definitive longitudinal studies of the growth of boys and girls and of concomitant physical, social, and psychological phenomena were published. Almost no perceptible impact on education occurred until the emergence of ungraded, flexibly scheduled and individual progress oriented experimental schools within recent years.

What has gradually become apparent is that childhood is a well-marked period in human development. During this period growth is rather steady in pace, marked by the gradual increase in capacities to learn and to do. The growth and developmental processes impose no dramatic changes in behaviors expected of youngsters and therefore no pressing adjustment problems. Rather, our society imposes the learning tasks. The adjustment problems met are due more to illness, to organic defects, learning limitations, culturally imposed learning demands that are inappropriate to the child's background and capacities, familial disorders, and societal disorders such as social class and caste discriminations.

While all these bases for adjustment problems persist through the period of transition from childhood into adolescence, other very significant behavioral requirements and developmental adjustment problems are imposed unavoidably by the growth process itself and by its outcomes. These new developmental tasks and adjustment problems are caused by physiological changes in the functioning of the body, by changes in perceptions of the self that inevitably accompany these growth and physiological alterations of the body dynamics, by changes in modes of cognitive functioning, and by ways in which home, school, and other social institutions view the individual and deal with these changes.

The transitional period, usually of from a three- to five-years duration, is marked by:

1. Differences in physical maturity levels within each sex and between sexes, as well as changes in physiological functioning, which are greater than those occurring at any other time during the growth cycle.
2. The gradual emergence of a more adult-like mode of intellectual functioning.
3. Psychological and social reorientation more traumatic than that of any similar period of growth.

• • •

THE TURBULENT EMOTIONS

As the individual matures, emotional behavior become more mature. The transitional period, according to Gesell, Ilg, and Ames,[8] is marked by the end of one cycle of emotional organization and the beginning of another. The child is changing from emotional behavior which can be described as contended and amiable to that displayed by an often aggressive, belligerent, and argumentative individual. At times he may seem hurt, sad, jealous, or competitive; at other times, worried, cheerful, affectionate, or timid. The anger of the pre-adolescent is more intense and deeper than that of the younger child, and he may strike out with more fervor. It takes him longer than the younger child to recuperate from emotional outbursts.

During the years of ages ten to fourteen, the emotional development of the child, if plotted on a line graph, would show many minor peaks and valleys. According to Gesell, Ilg, and Ames:

> The twelve-year-old tends to be outgoing, exuberant, enthusiastic. At the thirteen level there is a calming down.... Thirteen is more withdrawn and more thoughtful both about himself and others.... His great sensitiveness and even his secretiveness indicate that his emotions are deepening and refining.... The full blown fourteen-year old is a spontaneous extrovert. He does not hold back and brood or feel sorry for himself. He is full of laughter, jokes, and humor....[9]

The full adolescent is quite different—an evident calming down can be observed. He may be very enthusiastic toward school or show resistance. He is beginning a period of self-awareness which continues through the teens.

Learning to cope with his changing body, a new mode of intellectual operations, and the desire to be a person in his own right—independent of familial, and especially maternal, dominance—presents a tremendous problem of adjustment for youngsters during this transitional period. Behavior of an emotional nature can be traced to one or several of these changes. If the transitional years are years of turbulent emotions (and evidence supports the notion that they are just that—turbulent), is it any wonder? During no other period of human growth and development are youngsters required to adjust themselves to so many changes simultaneously.

YOUNG PEOPLE IN TRANSITION: SUMMARY

The physical, intellectual, and psycho-social development of youngsters during the transitional period have been presented in separate sections of this chapter. The following summary of characteristics of young people during this period is an attempt to demonstrate the interrelatedness of these components and return the reader's attention to the concept of the whole child:

1. The transition period is marked by the necessity for relearning to manage the body skillfully during a period of rapid change in body dimensions and general awkwardness.
2. The transition period is marked by the onset and gradual regularization of menstruation in girls and of nocturnal emissions and more frequent erections in boys. These new physical phenomena bring about the need for learning to maintain standards of health and hygiene. They set up new concepts of self and new problems of social behavior.
3. The transition period is marked by a beginning awareness of new erotic sensations in both boys and girls. It is also marked by an awakening interest in persons of the opposite sex and by the necessity for learning to manage these sensations without undue brashness or embarrassment.
4. The transition period is marked by the necessity for developing many social skills in interacting with persons of the opposite sex. These skills run the gamut—from learning to use cosmetics, or to choose and wear clothing that will attract the opposite sex, to learning how to receive and give caresses related to the erotic drive and to manage and check one's partner in these activities.
5. The transition period is marked by dramatic changes in the activities of the peer group and in what is required to maintain belonging to the peer group. Learning to dance, to talk the current slang, "to kid" and to accept "kidding," to joke and to accept practical jokes played on one, and perhaps to drive a car are examples of peer group activities during this period.[10]
6. The transition period is marked by an important evolution in relationships with parents. These include the ways in which love is expressed between the young person and the parents, the assertion by the rapidly developing person of his right to make many more decisions about his own behavior, his own social life, his own management of money, his own choice of companions, and so on. Some psychologists consider this as rebellion, or a drive for independence. It seems more likely to be an attempt by the youth to secure for himself the right to make more decisions about his own behavior. It is not a desire to be free of parents but the need to have them accord him the right to test his own choice-making under the new circumstances in which he is living.

7. The transition period is marked by a tremendous change in the individual's perception of himself and, consequently, in a quest for a satisfying concept of himself. Who am I? What am I able to do? Where do I fit into the social world? Into the vocational world? Into the spiritual world? Into the political world? Where do I belong? What do I believe about life and death? If finding the answers to these questions are required of the developmental periods of adolescence and adulthood, the framing of the questions and the exploration of where and to whom to look for answers are among the requirements of persons in transition from childhood into adolescence. Sometimes this is done overtly. More often, perhaps, the young people reveal what is on their minds by frank criticism of adult behavior, by challenges to established mores and ideas. Some show it by quiet withdrawal that finds the teacher or parent suddenly aware that this person has asked no sincere or penetrating questions for some months. For before the affirmation of a new concept of self-becoming can be made, there is the period of uncertain fumbling, the period of confusion about what the right questions are.

8. The transition period often is marked by the necessity of redefining what is right and what is wrong. Evidence of organic maturation confronts the individual with many complex choices about how to behave. Are the next-older peer group, the young post-pubescent adolescents, right or wrong in what they do, or claim to do? Is what a person feels as conscience only the memory of what parents and teachers told him when he was too young to be able to decide for himself? How can a person tell? Many a parent thinks of his child in transition as an "innocent child" and is horribly shocked to discover that he has been exploring some undesirable behavior "to find out whether it is really wrong or not."

9. The transition period is marked by the development of a new mode of intellectual operations—a movement away from a dependence upon what can be perceived in the immediate environment to a level of hypothesizing and dealing with abstractions. It is an establishment of a level of adult-like thought (when the adult is his logical best) and a willingness and desire to test ideas. It is manifested in a youngster's dealings not only with what is normally conceived to be activities directly related to so-called school work but also with all facets of his everyday life.

These changes that occur during the period of transition from childhood to adolescence should be reflected, we believe, in a transitional school program. The program for the "in-between-ager" should be developed with direct concern for his characteristics as just summarized. This transitional period is unique in the developmental sequence—a uniqueness which renders children and young people at this stage of development as quite different from those in the first few years of school and those in the high school years.

Does the present school program reflect our knowledge about the transition from childhood to adolescence? As we shall note in Chapter 3, the organization breaks sharply from grade 6 to grade 7, in the very middle of the transitional period of most children's lives. Indeed, Dacus' study[11] of social, emotional, and physical maturity, and opposite sex choices of pupils in grades 5 through 10, found that the differences were *least* between pupils in grades 6 and 7 and pupils in grades 9 and 10—the present break points! The present organization tends to be based on the scientific data related to human growth and development which was available more than fifty years ago. Furthermore, the program of present schools, however organized, rarely focuses during the in-between years on these developmental characteristics, which would seem to be logical priorities. In chapter 3 the present program provided for youngsters during this transitional period will be critically examined, as a further justification for a new program in the emergent middle school.

EVOLUTION OF THE PLAN

The predominant pattern of school organization in the United States today is the six-year elementary school, the three-year junior high school, and the three-year senior high school. It is a product of twentieth-century America. The elementary and high schools had European antecedents and were largely the result of an American effort to pattern our educational system after European plans—specifically, the Prussian system. The junior high school is, however, uniquely American and renders the 6-3-3 plan uniquely American. The present 6-3-3 plan had its beginning some three score years ago with the establishment of the first junior high school.[12]

SUMMARY

The 6-3-3 plan as it exists today does not seem to meet adequately the needs of the in-between-aged student. The upper elementary program tends to be a patchwork of separate subjects, usually under the guise of the self-contained classroom, where the teacher is required to provide instruction in subject fields for which he may have had little preparation. It treats fifth- and sixth-grade youngsters in very much the same way it provides for the first-grader. The junior high school is, in many ways, a mimic of the senior high school. Its program is fragmented and rigid. Its teachers and administrators too often feel they are there on a temporary basis and have received little or no training specifically designed for teaching at that level. The high school impinges on the program of the ninth grade because of the requirements of the Carnegie unit schedule.

The purposes of the 6-3-3 plan as viewed in the literature have been eclipsed by administrative efficacy. The group which suffers most by this inadequacy is the in-between-aged students. They have been forced to the background in the planning of the school program.

We view the 6-3-3 plan in modern education as an anachronism analogous to the horseless carriage in a time of focus on a race for space. It is time to change to an organization and a program designed to care for *youngsters in the middle years*, too, as well as the younger and older ones.

NOTES

1. Paul Woodring, "The New Intermediate School," *Saturday Review*, 48:77 (October 16, 1965).
2. Samuel H. Popper, *The American Middle School: An Organizational Analysis* (Waltham, Mass.: Blaisdell Publishing Company, 1967), p. xi.
3. Popper.
4. Popper, p. xii.
5. Popper.
6. *The Secondary School* (Boston: Ginn & Company, 1921).
7. *Adolescence* (2 vols.; New York: Appleton-Century-Crofts, 1904).
8. Arnold Gesell, Frances L. Ilg, and Louise B. Ames, *Youth: The Years From Ten to Sixteen* (New York: Harper & Row, Publishers, 1956).
9. Gesell, Ilg, and Ames, p. 333.

10. Caroline Tryon, "Summary of Material Presented to Members of the Collaboration Center by Herbert R. Stolz," in summaries of Presentations of Consultants to the Collaboration Center, Vol. 9 (mimeographed, [Chicago: Division of Child Development and Teacher Personnel, Commission on Teacher Education, American Council on Education, October 15–December 11, 1939]).

11. Wilfred P. Dacus, "A Study of the Grade Organizational Structure of the Junior High School as Measured by Social Maturity, Emotional Maturity, Physical Maturity, and Opposite-Sex Choices" (doctoral dissertation, University of Houston, Abstract; *Dissertation Abstracts,* 24: 1461–1462, 1963).

12. See William Van Til, Gordon F. Vars, and John H. Lounsbury, *Modern Education for the Junior High School Years* (Indianapolis: The Bobbs-Merrill Company, Inc., 1967), pp. 5–21.

10

Turning Points: Preparing American Youth for the 21st Century

CARNEGIE COUNCIL ON ADOLESCENT DEVELOPMENT

YOUNG ADOLESCENTS FACE significant turning points. For many youth 10 to 15 years old, early adolescence offers opportunities to choose a path toward a productive and fulfilling life. For many others, it represents their last best chance to avoid a diminished future.

Early adolescence is characterized by significant growth and change. For most, the period is initiated by puberty, a period of development more rapid than in any other phase of life except infancy. Cognitive growth is equally dramatic for many youth, bringing the new capacity to think in more abstract and complex ways than they could as children. Increased sense of self and enhanced capacity for intimate relationships can also emerge in early adolescence. All of these changes represent significant potential in our young people and great opportunity for them and the society.

Unfortunately, by age 15, substantial numbers of American youth are at risk of reaching adulthood unable to meet adequately the requirements of the workplace, the commitments of relationships in families and with friends, and the responsibilities of participation in a democratic society. These youth are among the estimated 7 million young people—one in four adolescents—who are extremely vulnerable to multiple high-risk behaviors and school failure. Another 7 million may be at moderate risk, but remain a cause for serious concern.

During early adolescence, youth enter a period of trial and error during which many first experiment with alcohol and drugs and risk permanent addiction. More and more adolescents 15 years old and younger are becoming sexually active, risking sexually transmitted diseases or pregnancy and the birth of unhealthy, low-birthweight babies.

The conditions of early adolescence have changed dramatically from previous generations. Today, young people enter a society that at once denounces and glorifies sexual promiscuity and the use of illicit drugs. They live in urban neighborhoods and even in some rural towns where the stability of close-knit relationships is rare, where the sense of community that shapes their identity has eroded. They will seek jobs in an economy that will require virtually all workers to think flexibly and creatively as only an elite few were required, and educated, to do in the past.

In these changed times, when young people face unprecedented choices and pressures, all too often the guidance they needed as children and need no less as adolescents is withdrawn. Freed from the dependency of childhood, but not yet able to find their own path to adulthood, many young people feel a desperate sense of isolation. Surrounded only by their equally confused peers, too many make poor decisions with harmful or lethal consequences.

Middle grade schools—junior high, intermediate, and middle schools—are potentially society's most powerful force to recapture millions of youth adrift, and help every young person thrive during early adolescence. Yet all too often these schools exacerbate the problems of young adolescents.

A volatile mismatch exists between the organization and curriculum of middle grade schools and the intellectual and emotional needs of young adolescents. Caught in a vortex of changing demands, the engagement of many youth in learning diminishes, and their rates of alienation, substance abuse, absenteeism, and dropping out of school begin to rise.

As the number of youth left behind grows, and opportunities in the economy for poorly educated workers diminish, we face the specter of a divided society: one affluent and well-educated, the other poorer and ill-educated. We face an America at odds with itself.

RECOMMENDATIONS FOR TRANSFORMING MIDDLE GRADE SCHOOLS

The recommendations contained in this report will vastly improve the educational experiences of all middle grade students, but will most benefit those at risk of being left behind. The Task Force calls for middle grade schools that:

- *Create small communities for learning* where stable, close, mutually respectful relationships with adults and peers are considered fundamental for intellectual development and personal growth. The key elements of these communities are schools-within-schools or houses, students and teachers grouped together as teams, and small group advisories that ensure that every student is known well by at least one adult.
- *Teach a core academic program* that results in students who are literate, including in the sciences, and who know how to think critically, lead a healthy life, behave ethically, and assume the responsibilities of citizenship in a pluralistic society. Youth service to promote values for citizenship is an essential part of the core academic program.
- *Ensure success for all students* through elimination of tracking by achievement level and promotion of cooperative learning, flexibility in arranging instructional time, and adequate resources (time, space, equipment, and materials) for teachers.
- *Empower teachers and administrators to make decisions about the experiences of middle grade students* through creative control by teachers over the instructional program linked to greater responsibilities for students' performance, governance committees that assist the principal in designing and coordinating school-wide programs, and autonomy and leadership within sub-schools or houses to create environments tailored to enhance the intellectual and emotional development of all youth.
- *Staff middle grade schools with teachers who are expert at teaching young adolescents* and who have been specially prepared for assignment to the middle grades.
- *Improve academic performance through fostering the health and fitness* of young adoles-

cents, by providing a health coordinator in every middle grade school, access to health care and counseling services, and a health-promoting school environment.

- *Reengage families in the education of young adolescents* by giving families meaningful roles in school governance, communicating with families about the school program and student's progress, and offering families opportunities to support the learning process at home and at the school.
- *Connect schools with communities*, which together share responsibility for each middle grade student's success, through identifying service opportunities in the community, establishing partnerships and collaborations to ensure students' access to health and social services, and using community resources to enrich the instructional program and opportunities for constructive after-school activities.

A PLAN FOR ACTION

The early adolescent years are crucial in determining the future success or failure of millions of American youth. All sectors of the society must be mobilized to build a national consensus to make transformation of middle grade schools a reality. The Task Force calls upon all sectors that care about youth to form partnerships that will create for young adolescents a time of purposeful exploration and preparation for constructive adulthood.

The Task Force calls upon the education sector to start changing middle grade schools now. Teachers and principals are at the center of this process. We urge superintendents and boards of education to give teachers and principals the authority to make essential changes, and work collaboratively to evaluate student outcomes effectively.

We ask leaders in higher education to focus immediately on changes needed in the preparation of middle grade teachers and in ways of collaborating with middle schools to support their reform.

We urge health educators and health care professionals to join with schools to ensure students' access to needed services and to the knowledge and skills that can prevent health-damaging behaviors.

We call upon youth-serving and community organizations, many with significant experience in working with young adolescents, to develop or strengthen their partnerships with middle grade schools.

We call upon states to convene statewide task forces to review this report and systematically examine its implications for their communities and schools. We ask states to consider new mechanisms for providing the incentives that will be required to bring about local collaboration between schools and community agencies.

We urge the President and other national leaders to study the recommendations of this report with a view to establishing a comprehensive federal policy for youth development, including funds for research and demonstration projects; support for pre- and in-service teacher education; full funding for successful existing programs serving middle grade students, such as the Chapter I program for disadvantaged youth; and, along with states and local school districts, relief from compliance with nonessential regulations that inhibit experimentation within individual schools willing to test the ideas contained in this report.

We call upon the private and philanthropic sectors, including foundations, to continue to support new ideas and expand their efforts in the implementation of policies designed to render early adolescence a fruitful period for every young person. The Task Force recommends the establishment of a national forum, with regional equivalents, to monitor the development of new approaches and share information with those interested in transforming middle grade schools. We also recommend the creation of trusts, supported through private and public funds, to support experiments in middle grade innovations in states and communities.

We call upon parents to become involved in defining goals, monitoring their children's studies, and evaluating the progress of the entire school. We urge parents to bring pressure for change in education, health care, and school-community partnerships. We urge parents, and other tax-payers, to support public schools and to demand from schools far better performance than schools now deliver.

Finally, we call upon all those deeply concerned about young adolescents' future, and the future of this nation, to begin now to create the nationwide constituency required to give American young adolescents the preparation they need for life in the 21st century.

The work of all these sectors will be necessary to transform middle grade schools. Through their efforts, a community of learning can be created that engages those young adolescents for whom life already holds high promise, and welcomes into the mainstream of society those who might otherwise be left behind.

WHAT IS THE PROBLEM?

The world is being rapidly transformed by science and technology in ways that have profound significance for our economic well-being and for a democratic society. One upshot is that work will require much technical competence and a great deal of flexibility; not just one set of skills acquired early and essentially good for life, but adaptability to an evolving body of knowledge and new opportunities calling for greatly modified skills. Successful participation in a technically based and interdependent world economy will require that we have a more skillful and adaptable workforce than ever before—at every level from the factory floor to top management.

In the years immediately ahead, the national cohort of young people will be smaller than in recent decades. Fewer college-age students will enter the workforce. By the year 2000, about one-third of these young people will be Black or Hispanic, the groups now at the bottom of the educational and economic ladder. We need to develop the talent of *all* our people if this nation is to be economically competitive and socially cohesive in the different world of the next century.

To do so, we must take advantage of the neglected opportunity provided by the fascinating period of early adolescence, ages 10 to 15 years. This is a time not only of inordinate vulnerability, but also of great responsiveness to environmental challenge. So it provides an exceptional chance for constructive interventions that can have lifelong influence.

The onset of adolescence is a critical period of biological and psychological change for the individual. Puberty is one of the most far-reaching biological upheavals in the life span. For many young adolescents, it involves drastic changes in the social environment as well, foremost among them the transition from elementary to secondary school. These years are highly formative for behavior patterns in education and health that have enduring significance. Adolescence is typically characterized by exploratory behavior, much of which is developmentally appropriate and socially adaptive for most young people. However, many of these behaviors carry high risks. The adverse effects may be near-term and vivid, such as school dropout or alcohol-related accidents. Or they may be long-term, such as bad health habits that lead to heart disease and cancer.

There is a crucial need to help adolescents at this early age to acquire durable self-esteem, flexible and inquiring habits of mind, reliable and relatively close human relationships, a sense of belonging in a valued group, and a sense of usefulness in some way beyond the self. They need to find constructive expression of their inherent curiosity and exploratory energy; and they need a basis for making informed, deliberate decisions—especially on matters that have large consequences, such as educational futures and drug use.

The challenge for educational and related institutions is thus to help provide the building blocks of adolescent development and preparation for adult life. Yet most American junior high and middle schools do not meet the developmental needs of young adolescents. These institutions have the potential to make a tremendous impact on the development of their students—for better or for worse—yet they have been largely ignored in the recent surge of educational reform. As currently organized, these middle grades constitute an arena of casualties—damaging to both students and teachers. Recent research notes a range of negative indicators—all of which have alarming implications for students' engagement and satisfaction with education—around the time that most children move from elementary to either a junior high or middle school.

Most young adolescents attend massive, impersonal schools, learn from unconnected and seemingly irrelevant curricula, know well and trust few adults in school, and lack access to health care and counseling. Millions of these young people fail to receive the guidance and attention they need to become healthy, thoughtful, and productive adults.

We have tolerated this situation for many years, but now our society is changing dramatically. Young adolescents are far more at risk for self-destructive behaviors—educational failure, drug and alcohol abuse, school age pregnancy, contraction of sexually transmitted diseases, violence—than their age group ever was before. Our schools are simply not producing young adolescents who have learned to adopt healthy lifestyles. Moreover, our schools are producing all too few young adolescents with higher skill levels and problem-solving abilities that the economy increasingly needs. The time has come for a fundamental reassessment of this pivotal institution in the lives of these young people.

TASK FORCE REPORT FILLS A GAP

Carnegie Corporation of New York established the Carnegie Council on Adolescent Development in 1986 to place the compelling challenges of the adolescent years higher on the nation's agenda. In 1987, as its first major commitment, the Council established the Task Force on Education of Young Adolescents under the chairmanship of David W. Hornbeck, former Maryland Superintendent of Schools and a nationally recognized leader in education. Members were drawn from education, research, government, health, and the non-profit and philanthropic sectors. The Task Force commissioned papers, interviewed experts in relevant fields, and met with teachers, principals, health professionals, and leaders of youth-serving community organizations. It examined, first-hand, promising new approaches to fostering the education and healthy development of young adolescents.

The result is a ground-breaking report that fills a serious gap in reports on education reform in the 1980s. The report reinforces an emerging movement, still relatively unrecognized by policymakers, to build support for and educate young adolescents through new relationships between schools, families, and health and community institutions.

The recommendations in this report engage people at all levels of society in this movement: the President and the Congress; officials of state and local governments; members of boards of education, superintendents, administrators, principals, and teachers; health professionals and leaders of youth-serving and community organizations; and parents and students themselves. The report indicates ways in which these groups can help accomplish a fundamental upgrading of education and adolescent development.

The emerging adolescent is caught in turbulence, a fascinated but perplexed observer of the biological, psychological, and social changes swirling all around. In groping for a solid path toward a worthwhile adult life, adolescents can grasp the middle grade school as the crucial and reliable handle. Now, the middle grade school must change, and change substantially, to cope with the requirements of a new era, to give its students a decent chance in life and to help them fulfill their youthful promise. This is a daunting task but a feasible one. This report will be a great help to those who wish to make this goal a practical reality.

David A. Hamburg
President, Carnegie Corporation of New York
Chair, Carnegie Council on Adolescent Development
New York
June 1989

DEMANDING THE VERY BEST FOR AND FROM YOUNG ADOLESCENTS

This report examines the condition of America's young adolescents and how well middle grade schools, health institutions, and community organizations serve them. The Task Force makes recommendations for new structures for middle grade education, which the Task Force believes will help to preserve a strong and vital America.

Before proceeding, however, it is useful to consider our goal. What qualities do we envision in the 15-year-old who has been well served in the middle years of schooling? What do we want every young adolescent to know, to feel, to be able to do upon emerging from that educational and school-related experience?

Our answer is embodied in five characteristics associated with being an effective human being. Our 15-year-old will be:

- An intellectually reflective person;
- A person enroute to a lifetime of meaningful work;
- A good citizen;
- A caring and ethical individual; and
- A healthy person.

AN INTELLECTUALLY REFLECTIVE PERSON

The young adolescent is maturing intellectually at a significant rate. Our youth will be able to analyze problems and issues, examine the component parts, and reintegrate them into either a solution or into a new way of stating the problem or issue. In developing thinking skills, the youth will master self-expression and be able to "hear" others' expressions through diverse media. These skills of self-expression and hearing include persuasive and coherent writing, articulate verbal expression, and familiarity with symbols and basic vocabularies of the arts, mathematics, and the sciences. Moreover, the student will be able to appreciate and absorb the perspectives of cultures (and languages) different from his or her own.

A PERSON ENROUTE TO A LIFETIME OF MEANINGFUL WORK

Our young adolescent will begin to understand work as both the means of economic survival and an important source of one's identity. The youth will be increasingly aware of career and occupation options, not feeling bound by restrictions of race, gender, or ethnicity. Each will understand that high school graduation is a prerequisite to being competitive in the adult workforce and will begin to understand the advantages of postsecondary education. Perhaps most importantly, the youth will have learned to learn, a critically important capacity because of the rapidly changing nature of occupations and jobs. Finally, the youth will have pursued a course of study and developed cognitively in a manner that maintains all career options.

A GOOD CITIZEN

Our young adolescent will be a good citizen in three ways. First, our 15-year-old will accept responsibility for shaping and not simply being shaped by surrounding events. Central to demonstrating good citizenship is a youth who is a doer, not just an observer. The youth will, for example, demonstrate good citizenship by helping to determine the nature and character of his or her own school community.

A second reflection of the young adolescent's good citizenship will be an understanding of the genesis and history of the United States and its basic values, such as the principles of democracy upon which the nation is built. In understanding these values, the youth will be able to assess the degree to which the nation practiced those values historically and practices them today. The youth will understand the way government in the United States functions at the local, state, and federal levels and will participate in appropriate ways in creating and maintaining a healthy community.

Finally, our young adolescent's good citizenship will be embodied in a positive sense of global citizenship. That involvement will reflect an appreciation of both the Western and non-Western worlds. The youth will possess a feeling of personal responsibility for and connection to the well-being of an interdependent world community.

A CARING AND ETHICAL INDIVIDUAL

Our 15-year-old will not only have developed the capacity to think clearly and critically, but will also have learned to act ethically. The youth will recognize that there is good and bad and that it is possible and important to tell the difference. The youth will exhibit the courage to discern the difference as a normal part of daily life and to act on the conclusions reached.

The young person will embrace many virtues such as courage, acceptance of responsibility, honesty, integrity, tolerance, appreciation of individual differences, and caring about others. The young person will demonstrate all these values through sustained service to others.

Finally, our 15-year-old will understand the importance of developing and maintaining close relationships with certain other people, including friends and family, relationships of the character that require great effort and even sacrifice, but without which life is filled with insecurity and loneliness.

A HEALTHY PERSON

The 15-year-old we envision will be physically and mentally fit. Exercise, diet, and proper health consultation and care will nurture a youth whose physical and mental health needs have been understood and met. Equally important, our young adolescent will have a self-image of competence and strength. This self-image will be based on the fact that the youth will be at least very good at something, because success is critical to a positive self-image. The youth's field of success may be academic or extracurricular, vocational or avocational, community or familial.

In addition, our young person will have developed self-understanding, rejoicing in the knowledge of personal strengths and enroute to overcoming weaknesses. A combination of self-understanding and a positive self-image, taken with other skills in the individual's repertoire, will equip the youth with appropriate coping skills.

We have described the young adolescent we envision. Our vision is of such an outcome for *every* youth of the nation, not just for those more advantaged than others. Every human being has the capacity to achieve significant success, not just minimum competence, in each of the five areas.

Our 15-year-old is a thinking, productive, caring, and healthy person who takes seriously the responsibility of good citizenship. The challenge of the 1990s is to define and create the structures of teaching and learning for young adolescents 10 to 15 years old that will yield mature young people of competence, compassion, and promise.

David W. Hornbeck
Chair, Task Force on Education of Young Adolescents
Baltimore
June 1989

11

The Future of Middle Level Education: Optimistic and Pessimistic Views

JOHN H. LOUNSBURY AND GORDON F. VARS

AGE, IT IS commonly assumed, enhances perspective. And likewise, it is generally held that those who can look back the furthest are in the best position to predict the future. One might well assume, then, that based on our collective 100 plus years of experience with middle level education, the co-authors of this article are well-equipped for the task given us by the guest editor—to look back and then to look ahead. One of us, an eternal, but often naïve optimist, sees the glass as now half full; while the other, a seasoned veteran always close to the classroom, is keenly conscious of current conditions that would quell almost anyone's optimism about the future of middle level education and so views the glass as half empty. But first, consider the following.

MIDDLE LEVEL EDUCATION IN CHRONOLOGICAL PERSPECTIVE

- **115 years** have passed since Charles W. Eliot, the president of Harvard University, kicked off the movement to reorganize secondary education with his call for school programs "to be shortened and enriched."
- **94 years** have passed since the Indianola Junior High School, generally regarded as the first junior high school, was established in Columbus, Ohio.
- **85 years** have passed since the Commission on the Reorganization of Secondary Education (1918) in its famous report *Cardinal Principles of Secondary Education* recommended the 6-3-3 form of organization.
- **58 years** have passed since the 6-3-3 pattern became majority practice in America's school districts, with most pupils going through a junior high school on the way to high school graduation.
- **40 years** have passed since William Alexander, in a speech at Cornell University, first used and advocated the term *middle school*. (Gordon Vars was present).
- **30 years** have passed since National Middle School Association (NMSA) was launched.

- **18 years** have now passed since the 6-8 middle school became the centerpiece of the 5-3-4 pattern that is, by far, the most common form of school organization in the United States.

About the *organizational* success of the movement to reorganize secondary education, which began in the last decade of the 19th century, there can be little doubt. The face of American education has been remade twice during the last century as a result of this effort. First, the junior high school replaced the traditional 8-4 pattern with the 6-3-3 plan. More recently, the 5-3-4 arrangement with the middle school in the center has become the most common pattern of school organization.

The middle school entered the educational arena, overtook, and passed the 7-9 junior high school to become the dominant form of school organization in little more than 20 years! This is a truly remarkable achievement by any standard, particularly when it is realized that no single government agency operates our public schools; rather, in just two decades 50 independent states, each in its own way, adopted the middle school idea. And now in the intervening years, the junior high school seems to be approaching extinction.

The true goal of the middle school movement, however, has never been organizational, but rather programmatic; and so there is another side to the story—one much more complicated and, unfortunately, much less successful. The way public education is operated at the school and classroom levels is the result of many interacting factors and conditions, most old but some new. There are vested interests and deeply institutionalized practices. Always present is the human inclination to resist change. Economic and political factors are constantly at work. Resolving conflicting demands and expectations of various stakeholders is a never-ending challenge (Vars, 2000).

Into such a complex entity the middle school concept charged, seeking to do essentially what the junior high school sought to do (but was unable), to make fundamental changes in the way schools operate and instruct. No easy victory should have been anticipated—and none has been achieved. But efforts to institute middle schools that are developmentally responsive have been widespread for several decades. It may be a good time to take stock and predict the future—from two perspectives.

A GLASS HALF FULL

Certainly the middle school movement has already had a major impact on American education and seems ready to exert further influence. Optimism about the future of middle level education seems, then, justified on several counts:

Early Adolescence Has Gained Recognition as a Distinct Developmental Period

Children do not leave childhood one year and become adolescents the next; but rather there is between the two this major period of transition covering roughly ages 10 to 15. Scholarly consideration of early adolescence has advanced dramatically in the last few decades. And although the general public has not yet come to recognize fully the special and enduring importance of early adolescence, the topic has been addressed on many fronts and was helped considerably by the Carnegie Corporation's widely distributed report, *Turning Points: Preparing America's Youth for the 21st Century* (Carnegie Council on

Adolescent Development, 1989), and the follow-up report *Turning Points 2000: Educating Adolescents in the 21st Century* (Jackson & Davis, 2000).

In addition to the burgeoning body of professional literature covering early adolescence, there is now a good supply of books for the general public dealing with what has been well characterized as "the roller coaster years" (Giannetti & Sagarese, 1997). Newspaper stories and popular magazine articles also frequently feature these years when youth come of age. Although this attention is late in coming and is still incomplete, it is building a knowledge base of understanding about young adolescents to guide sound educational practices.

A Third Level of Education Has Been Established

Traditionally, public education was comprised of elementary education for children and secondary education for adolescents. Now, however, the middle level has claimed a place as a third level. Teacher education and licensure are gradually coming to recognize middle level teaching as distinctive and calling for specially designed preparation programs. While progress has been discouragingly slow, a handful of states have put in place non-overlapping certification, while many others have created endorsements; and almost all states have under consideration some proposals that would recognize the middle level in licensure. Colleges and universities have instituted middle level programs that often precede state licensure, and a few universities have independent middle level departments.

Professional Associations Exist to Support Middle Level Education

The existence of professional associations is a major factor supporting an optimistic outlook. The junior high schools had no voice compared to that now present in National Middle School Association. As the fastest-growing professional association in recent decades, NMSA has achieved a place of prominence at the table with other national associations and is able to exercise considerable influence. NMSA's middle school message and materials are extended immeasurably through its 58 state, regional, and provincial affiliates. The conferences and the publications of NMSA are recognized for their excellence and their value in influencing classroom instruction and school reform. The Month of the Young Adolescent, an NMSA initiative, is co-sponsored by more than 40 other national youth-serving agencies and organizations, and this annual celebration has given greatly increased public attention to young adolescents and the schools that serve them.

In addition to National Middle School Association, the National Association of Secondary School Principals and the National Association of Elementary School Principals both have commitments to middle level education and offer services to administrators of schools enrolling middle grades. Both associations also collaborate with NMSA.

Particularly important in advancing middle level education in recent years has been the support offered by foundations. The Carnegie Corporation and the Edna McConnell Clark Foundation are two prime examples. The creation of the National Forum to Accelerate Middle-Grades Reform is another platform that has given a boost to middle level education. This alliance of educators, researchers, national associations, and officers of professional organizations is committed to promoting the academic performance *and* healthy development of young adolescents. One of the Forum's initiatives was the creation of "Schools to Watch." This program was extended to Georgia, North Carolina, and California in 2003. As a result, 10 good schools that have achieved gains in student performance beyond what might be expected in light of their demographics have been spotlighted. The program will be implemented in four additional states in 2004.

Research Findings Give Validity to the Middle School
Although the movement thrived in its early years, it did so more on faith than on the findings of research. Middle school advocates had, and still have, deeply held convictions about what is best for young adolescents. Their experiences when working with kids confirmed the validity of their positions. Now, however, research is able to provide hard evidence that the middle school does in fact work.

When the tenets of the concept are implemented fully over time, student achievement and development increase markedly (Felner et al., 1997)! While research in education can never be as definitive as in other fields, there has been accumulating in the last decade the results from a number of carefully designed studies that strengthen immeasurably the case for middle school practices, and additional evidence is forthcoming. At the same time, it might be noted, there are no studies appearing to show the effectiveness of traditional junior high practices!

Research and Resources in Support of This We Believe (Anfara, 2003) summarizes research findings. A companion to *This We Believe*: *Successful Schools for Young Adolescents* (National Middle School Association, 2003), this publication documents the results of research studies showing the success of middle school practices.

Classroom Teachers by the Hundreds Are Doing Good Things for Kids Day In and Day Out
Fifth and finally, optimism for the future is fueled by what can be witnessed in middle level schools all across America. The middle school movement has given conscientious, professional teachers and principals opportunities and encouragement for breaking the mold rather than perpetuating traditional ways and for assuming leadership as team leaders and administrators. Although most come from elementary or high school backgrounds and usually lack middle level preservice education, a new breed of courageous, caring teachers has implemented more effective learning strategies, ones that lead to improved student achievement and personal development—and their numbers are growing. If one wants to see cutting edge professional practices, increased student involvement, student-centered classrooms, teachers working together as collegial professionals, go to a middle school. If one is looking for examples of student-led conferences wherein students have assumed responsibility for their own learning, curriculum-based service learning programs, problem-centered learning that cuts across subject lines, or school-initiated parent involvement programs, go to a middle school.

Despite a climate that gives little support or recognition, there are legions of genuinely good teachers both touching lives and successfully teaching skills and content in hundreds of middle schools. They give life at the grass roots level to a movement that is firmly based on human growth and development. The best examples of what the art and craft of teaching can be when practiced fully are more often than not found at the middle level. A recognition of this reality surfaced in Georgia. The 2000 Georgia Teacher of the Year was a middle school teacher. The 2002 Georgia Teacher of the Year, although a high school teacher in a rural North Georgia school, was and is an open advocate for student-centered classrooms and integrated learning. The 2003 Georgia Teacher of the Year was a middle school teacher. And, you guessed it, the 2004 Georgia Teacher of the Year is a middle school teacher, as were two of the other three finalists for the 2004 award.

Middle school teachers are influencing the lives of young adolescents daily, providing models, and teaching lessons of life, as well as preparing them academically. While many parents are aware of this, the general public somehow seems oblivious to this important aspect of teaching at the middle level as the media and the politicians focus on test scores.

A GLASS HALF EMPTY

Pessimism about the future of middle level education is justified when one bears in mind the current educational reform efforts that run directly counter to the unique characteristics, needs, and concerns of young adolescents. Consider four important aspects of young adolescents and the ways that current reforms impact them.

Individual Differences

Human beings differ in many ways, and these differences are magnified during the middle school years. Individuals go through the massive physical, social, emotional, and intellectual changes of puberty at different times and at different rates. Middle level classes are made up of men, women, and children, plus those who are at various points in between!

Yet young people dealing with these most profound changes are now confronted by demands that they all measure up to some adult-determined "standards." They, their teachers, and their schools are punished if students do not attain a certain score on a paper-and-pencil test, which may or may not be aligned with the standards. Little or no allowances are made for differences in social background, innate academic ability, handicapping conditions, or even students' command of the English language. When applied strictly, high-stakes testing dooms numbers of students to failure even before they take part in an assessment.

Mental Development

One of the most exciting aspects of working with middle level youth is their rapidly developing ability to think more abstractly. The human brain is truly one of the great miracles of the universe, and its role in all of life's processes is becoming clearer, offering educators powerful new ways to promote intellectual development.

Yet at this very time, most of the mandated assessments being used to determine students' attainment of the standards focus heavily on recall of facts, one of the lowest forms of thinking. Moreover, the high stakes attached to student test scores coerce schools and teachers into spending an inordinate amount of time drilling students on facts and skills deemed most likely to be on those tests. Teachers, have little time to follow up on students' interests, to say nothing of inviting them to share in planning learning experiences that address their personal and social concerns.

Some effects of this pressure were revealed in the nationwide survey reported by McEwin, Dickinson, and Jenkins (2003). They found that middle schools had increased the time devoted to "direct instruction" and decreased time for electives, and in some schools even the advisory period, supposedly set aside to give students a place to deal with some of their needs and concerns, was being used for test-prep. Is it too extreme an exaggeration to suggest that high-stakes testing may be lobotomizing an entire generation of young people?

Socialization

Heightened sensitivity to acceptance by the peer group also distinguishes the middle school years. Parents sometimes feel that they no longer have much influence on their children who seem so wrapped up in interactions with other young people. Although peers may provide wholesome models for young people, wanting to be accepted by "the gang" may lead them into exceedingly risky behavior: smoking, drinking, drugs, sex, crime, and violence. Unfortunately the desire to be in with the crowd is continuously being exploited by media and commercial interests to the tune of millions of dollars every year.

Some of the anxieties experienced by adolescents may be ameliorated if they are shared with others going through the same period of life in advisory programs or other student-centered activities. Wholesome socialization also can be promoted in such student activities as intramural athletics, performance groups, clubs, and electives minicourses. Cooperative learning is a research-proven strategy that increases academic achievement, and it also meets a socialization need. Yet the percent of middle schools using cooperative learning "regularly" increased only moderately between 1993 and 2001 (McEwin, Dickinson, & Jenkins, 2003, pp. 32–33), and in 37% to 41% of the schools it was used only "occasionally" or "rarely."

At the very time when students are seeking to develop bonds with others, stress in schools and in the broader society is on individual achievement. The few states that once included group problem solving as part of student assessment have had to bow to dictates imposed by the *No Child Left Behind Act* (Arhar, 2003). Our entire culture is increasingly driven by stress on individual success, measured primarily in terms of money. Sports heroes, rock stars, and CEOs receive millions of dollars, while more and more people sink deeper into poverty and lack needed social services. Sociologists decry the loss of genuine community in our society, as symbolized in the title of Putnam's (2002) research report *Bowling Alone*.

Independence

Throughout their middle school years, young people seek increasing independence from adults. Making the transition from a heavily dependent child to a fully independent adult is difficult even under the best of circumstances. Adults who work with youth know that the best way to avoid outright rebellion is to gradually reduce restrictions, negotiate honestly, and be prepared for some lapses as young people assume more responsibility. Middle level schools are uniquely situated to help both students and families deal wisely and compassionately with young adolescents' struggle for independence. Understanding teachers and parents offer young people many choices, nonjudgmentally guide them toward reasonable choices, and help them learn from the consequences of choices that prove unwise.

Moreover, a basic principle of democracy is that those who will be affected by a decision should share in making that decision. Cooperative teacher-student planning has long been advocated by progressive educators (Giles, 1941; Miel, 1952; Parrish & Waskin,

1967), and is a key element of the integrative/core curriculum advocated by some middle level specialists (Beane, 1993, 1997; Lounsbury & Vars, 1978, Vars, 1993). Middle school teachers sometimes involve students in determining such things as appropriate classroom rules and scheduling options, even if they do not invite students to participate fully in deciding what is studied, how it will be studied, and how it will be evaluated.

Now, however, the dominant approach to educational reform is top-down dictation from bureaucrats at federal, state, and district levels, leaving teachers no choice but to submit to high-stakes tests that they know many students will fail. Schools have resorted to various ways of minimizing the negative consequences of low test scores, including the "encouragement" of students who do not do well on tests to be absent on the test day. Unreasonable requirements that schools post arbitrary gains every year make the pressure even worse, leading some teachers and principals to unethically give students help on the tests. Many parents fall prey to the offerings of various for-profit test-prep corporations. In such a coercive environment, neither students nor their teachers dare take the time needed to learn and practice democratic principles.

GREATER THREATS
Thus far some current educational reforms that seem designed to thwart healthy development of middle level youth have been examined. Serious as these may be, they appear to be driven by forces that pose threats to our entire society as well as to our middle schools.

Attacks on the Public Schools
The *Nation at Risk* pronouncement (National Commission on Excellence in Education, 1983) has been viewed by some as the opening gun of a systematic effort by wealthy corporate interests and their political allies to replace public education with for-profit institutions. Berliner and Biddle (1995) documented how these organizations created a "manufactured crisis" in education and used it to push for vouchers, charter schools, for-profit school management, and the like. Since then other educators have added their voices to the warning. Boutwell (1997) called attention to *Corporate America's Agenda for Schools*. Ohanian (1999) pointed out how the "military-industrial-infotainment complex" influences politicians at all levels to impose impossible demands on public schools, measure compliance with inappropriate, poorly designed, and often incorrectly scored tests, then punish schools that do not measure up. Unfortunately, the major brunt of the punishment is borne by school districts already saddled with high concentrations of students living in poverty, a meager tax base, and state budgeting that does little to equalize per-pupil resources for education.

Rampant Commercialism
Time was when public schools were considered "off-limits" to advertising. It was assumed that since young people were required to attend, they should be protected from commercial interests. But by the year 2000, Molnar and Morales (2000) could say "Commercial activities now shape the structure of the school day, influence the content of the school curriculum, and determine whether children have access to a variety of technologies" (p. 43). School districts strapped for funds too often enter into one-sided "partnerships" with businesses that then use the schools to "make a buck." It is ironic that corporate

interests, seemingly bent on destroying the public schools from the outside through government-imposed high-stakes testing, are simultaneously exploiting the children held captive in those same schools for commercial gain (See Kohn, 2002).

Media Consolidation

The same military-industrial-infotainment complex also controls the major public information sources—newspapers, radio, television, magazine and book publishing. The situation was already serious when Berliner and Biddle published their analysis in 1995. Since then global giants have tightened their grip on the media, leaving few outlets for the voices of dissent. On top of that, some of their former executives are now setting federal policy. Indeed, the fox is now guarding the henhouse!

Economic Inequities

Unequal support for public schools in most states reflects a gross and increasing gap between the rich and the poor. Globalization and the stagnant U.S. economy are putting severe strains on public school budgets, while tax breaks and loopholes in tax laws allow wealthy individuals and corporations to avoid paying their fair share. The proportion of our citizens living in poverty is increasing, and most of them are children. The direct correlation between a school district's wealth and its school "effectiveness" is revealed every time a state publishes comparative ratings—the wealthy are at the top, the poor are at the bottom. The "Savage Inequalities" that Kozol (1991) railed against are still with us and getting worse.

At one time public schools were viewed as "the bulwark of democracy." Now we are faced with seemingly deliberate attempts to destroy public schools, throttle free speech, and put more and more wealth and power into fewer and fewer hands.

TOMORROW—AND THE DAY AFTER TOMORROW

Having looked at the status of middle level education from two perspectives, what hope is there for the advancement of student-centered, democratic education at the middle level? It is difficult to implement the middle school envisioned in *This We Believe* (National Middle School Association, 1995, 2003) in the current hostile environment, and some of the most dedicated and creative teachers are abandoning the field altogether. Others are holding on until retirement, doing the best they can for the children they teach. There is good reason for pessimism.

Surely, however, as the obsession with standardized tests runs its course, America and her policymakers will come to realize the obvious limitations of current reform efforts and recognize that the full education needed by today's young adolescents requires much, much more than that which is assessed by tests. Gains in test scores, when and if achieved, will have no immediate impact on the serious problems that beset our society. The greater need is to guide the overall development of young adolescents in ways that will equip them with the behavioral attributes, attitudes, and values they need to make wise choices in all aspects of their lives. Success in doing so will in no way handicap the school's clear responsibility for the intellectual development of students but will, in fact, fulfill that responsibility more effectively.

In the final analysis the future of middle level education, of public schooling, indeed, of all life on this planet depends on the human spirit. Survivors of the Nazi concentration camps reported that even under those incredibly brutal circumstances the spirit of many people was not completely crushed. The love of children and youth that motivates parents, teachers, and other caring adults seems to be inherent in human nature (Clark, 2002). Middle school educators have correctly been recognized for the degree to which that spirit characterizes their work.

In retrospect, both views are sound; one is not right and the other wrong. The resolution of this dilemma may be a matter of time. The pessimistic view is probably valid for tomorrow, while the optimistic view should be valid for the day after tomorrow. Eventually, the positive view ought to prevail, for it has the realities of human growth and development on its side and is in keeping with the democratic way of life that, while threatened, still characterizes our society. But we must take to heart the admonition of Edmund Burke issued in 1795, "The only thing necessary for the triumph of evil is for good men to do nothing."

Using *This We Believe: Successful Schools for Young Adolescents* (National Middle School Association, 2003) as a tool, good middle level educators should work with new vigor, individually and in collaboration with professional colleagues, to bring about the day after tomorrow. Holding, as only middle level educators do, the very best opportunity to influence not only the future of individuals but of society itself, we can make the critical difference.

REFERENCES

Anfara, V. A., Jr., (2003). *Research and resources in support of* This We Believe. Westerville, OH: National Middle School Association.

Arhar, J. M. (2003). No child left behind and middle level education: A look at research, policy, and practice. *Middle School Journal, 34*(5), 46–51.

Beane, J. A. (1993). *A middle school curriculum: From rhetoric to reality* (2nd ed.). Columbus, OH: National Middle School Association.

Beane, J. A. (1997). *Curriculum integration: Designing the core of democratic education.* New York: Teachers College Press.

Berliner, D. C., & Biddle, B. J. (1995). *The manufactured crisis: Myths, fraud, and the attack on America's public schools.* Reading, MA: Addison-Wesley.

Boutwell, C. E. (1997). *Shell game: Corporate America's agenda for the schools.* Bloomington, IN: Phi Delta Kappa Foundation.

Carnegie Council on Adolescent Development. (1989). *Turning points: Preparing American youth for the 21st Century.* New York: Carnegie Corporation.

Clark, M. E. (2002). *In search of human nature.* London & New York: Routledge.

Commission on the Reorganization of Secondary Education. (1918). *Cardinal principles of secondary education, Bulletin 1918, No. 35.* Washington, DC: U.S. Department of the Interior, Bureau of Education.

Felner, R. D., Jackson, A., Kasak, D., Mulhall, P., Brand, S., & Flowers, N. (1997). The impact of school reform for the middle years: Longitudinal study of a network engaged in *Turning Points*-based comprehensive school transformation. *Phi Delta Kappan, 78*(7), 528–532, 541–550.

Giannetti, C. C., & Sagarese, M. (1997). *The roller-coaster years: Raising your child through the maddening yet magical middle school years.* New York: Broadway Books.

Giles, H. H. (1941). *Teacher-pupil planning.* New York: Harper.

Jackson, A. W., & Davis, G. A. (2000). *Turning points 2000: Educating adolescents in the 21st century.* New York & Westerville, OH: Teachers College Press & National Middle School Association.

Kohn, A. (2002). *Education Inc: Turning learning into a business.* Arlington Heights, IL: Skylight.

Kozol, J. (1991). *Savage inequalities: Children in America's schools.* New York: Crown.

Lounsbury, J. H., & Vars, G. F. (1978). *A curriculum for the middle school years.* New York: Harper.

McEwin, C. K., Dickinson, T. S., & Jenkins, D. M. (2003). *America's middle schools in the new century: Status and progress*. Westerville, OH: National Middle School Association.

Miel, A., & Associates. (1952). *Cooperative procedures in learning*. New York: Bureau of Publications, Teachers College, Columbia University.

Molnar, A., & Morales, J. (2000). Commercialism @ schools. *Educational Leadership, 58*(2), 39–44.

National Commission on Excellence in Education. (1983). *A nation at risk: The imperatives for educational reform*. Washington, DC: United States Department of Education.

National Middle School Association. (1995). *This we believe: Developmentally responsive middle level schools*. Columbus, OH: Author.

National Middle School Association. (2003). *This we believe: Successful schools for young adolescents*. Westerville, OH: Author.

Ohanian, S. (1999). *One size fits few: The folly of educational standards*. Portsmouth, NH: Heinemann.

Ohanian, S. (2003). Capitalism, calculus, and conscience. *Phi Delta Kappan, 84*(10), 736–747.

Parrish, L., & Waskin, Y. (1967). *Teacher-pupil planning for better classroom learning*. New York: Harper. Reprinted by Pitman.

Putnam, R. D. (2000). *Bowling alone: The collapse and revival of American community*. New York: Simon & Schuster.

Vars, G. F. (1993). *Interdisciplinary teaching: Why and how*. Columbus, OH: National Middle School Association.

Vars, G. F. (2000). Common learnings: A 50-year quest. *Journal of Curriculum & Supervision, 16*(1), 70–89.

12

Back to the Future: Middle Schools and the Turning Points *Report*

NANCY LESKO

CONCEPTIONS OF ADOLESCENTS are a foundational element of schooling, a fact that is generally ignored. Notions of good teaching, stimulating curricula, and reasonable organizational practices in schools are all grounded on views of students, however tacit or implicit those images of youth may be. Proposed changes in school structures and definitions of teachers will be undermined if views of teenagers remain substantially those inherited from the Victorians.

This article develops this thesis of the interrelationships of conceptions of youth with curricula and school organization by examining one recent reform report on middle schools, *Turning Points: Preparing American Youth for the 21st Century* (Carnegie Council, 1989). I analyze the report with an eye to the economic and social contexts of its creation,[1] historical comparisons, and the relationships among elements of the proposed "new" middle school.

Teenagers are popularly defined by hormones and peers. This image is predominantly deficit-centered; that is, youth are people who *cannot* think abstractly, act independently, consider the consequences of their actions, or be given responsibilities. Teenagers must prove themselves as obedient, responsible, and serious before they are entrusted with decisions over anything but trivial aspects of their lives. Adolescence is tacitly portrayed as a disease, to be endured. Spacks (1981) claims that "our psychology [of adolescence] confirms our sociology" (p. 290); that is, conceptions of youths' deficiencies follow from their low social position and their lack of social power. Hormones triggered by physiological changes are the purported sources of these deficiencies, which can only be corrected by getting older.

An alternative to the biologically-determined view of adolescence emphasizes youth's social nature, in which particular physiological facts are interpreted and given meaning within particular historical and social circumstances. In this conceptual framework, the facts of pubertal development are less salient than how adults and peers interpret and interact with them, that is, the emphasis is on *what is made of* physiological differences. This article adopts this latter position in which I see school practices helping to create the nature of adolescence, rather than just responding to naturally-existing beings.

Starting with this presumption leads to a focus on the constructed nature of adolescence, and to the contribution of schools and curricular practices in the production of young adolescents. I investigate the conception of adolescence in the *Turning Points* report by looking directly at the stated description of youth but also by examining curricular and organizational practices that are described as better "matches" for young adolescents.

THE "PROBLEM" OF YOUNG ADOLESCENTS

The *Turning Points* report opens with images of young adolescents as "adrift" on seas of sexuality, peer pressure, and the use of drugs and alcohol.[2] Young adolescents are at a turning point in their lives, moving toward "a productive and fulfilling life" or taking the turn toward "a diminished future" (p. 8). The report portrays contemporary society as one in which traditional moorings (close-knit families, stable neighborhoods, plentiful low-skilled jobs) continue to erode, requiring that middle schools pick up the slack.

The authors of the report argue that the organization and curriculum of middle schools is "mismatched" (p. 8) to the intellectual and emotional needs of contemporary young adolescents. As a result, at this crucial juncture when fateful choices are being made, youth are often disengaged from school learning, absent from school, and prone to drop out. If youth are to become good workers, be in relationships with families and friends, and participate in a democratic society, middle schools' organization and curricula must be reformed (p. 8).

> In groping for a solid path toward a worthwhile adult life, adolescents can grasp the middle grade school as the crucial and reliable handle. (p. 14)

What kind of "reliable handle" is the proposed middle grade school?

MIDDLE SCHOOL ORGANIZATION

The "reliable handle" of reformed middle grades schooling is described via eight principles. Schools operating on these principles will benefit all students, but especially those "at risk of being left behind" (p. 9). The first three principles, which address organization and curriculum,[3] are:

- Large middle grade schools are divided into smaller communities for learning.
- Middle grade schools transmit a core of common knowledge to all students.
- Middle grade schools are organized to ensure success for all students. (p. 36)

These three principles reflect popular, widespread beliefs that schools should be subdivided into smaller sub-units, that a core curriculum should be taught, and that all students should be able to succeed (Newmann, 1993). Overall, the authors argue for a middle school that is nurturant: "a place where close, trusting relationships with adults and peers create a climate for personal growth and intellectual development"(p. 37). The "family" climate of middle schools will nurture the academic and psychological components of young adolescents—they will learn basic knowledge and believe that they can learn and be successful.

In these three principles, the framers of the report capsulize a slew of practices and policies, such as team teaching, mentoring, interdisciplinary curriculum, development of self-esteem and motivation, formal instruction of thinking skills, and cooperative learning. A whole rainbow of practices is explicated, although briefly, in the report under these three principles.

In order to think critically about these proposals, I situate the report in its socio-historical context and also compare its recommendations with the turn of the century problems and practices. The *Turning Points* report was issued during a historical era dominated by two concerns: economic uncertainty and population change. Schools are targeted by business leaders as the primary cause of the country's eroded competitiveness in the international economy. According to John Akers, chair of IBM, "If our students can't compete today, how will our companies compete tomorrow?" (cited in Cuban, 1993, p. 11). The blaming of the U.S. economic situation on students' inadequate knowledge, limited skills, and poor work attitudes is widespread, but the linkage is questionable (Cuban, 1993).

The second dominant context of the *Turning Points* report is the "invasion" of youth from mother-only, poor, limited English proficient, non-White families. A special issue of *Education Week,* "Here They Come, Ready or Not" (1986), exemplifies the fascination with and worry about the "browning of America" and its impact on schools. The specter of alien youth in our schools, or on our streets, connects with economic worries to produce escalating fear about the future of America.

Although the rhetoric of the *Turning Points* report emphasizes young adolescents' "needs" for intimacy and autonomy, when the historical context is added, economic and social unity concerns dominate the document. In order to see the economic and social concerns within the terminology drawn from humanistic psychology, a comparison with the turn of the century is useful.

TURN OF THE CENTURY IMAGERY AND PRACTICES
Much of the *Turning Points* imagery and organizational and pedagogical practices are borrowed from the late 1800s and early 1900s, also a period of substantial immigration and economic uncertainty (Wiebe, 1967). During this earlier period of change, the theme of community building was also popular among curriculum workers and social scientists. Curricular historian Barry Franklin (1986) sees "community" used at the turn of the century as a trope for social control, that is, as a basis for order, stability, and progress. The new class of intellectuals and professionals (e.g., the psychologist E.L. Thorndike) had grown up in small towns in the Midwest and the Northeast and believed that

> stability, order, and progress were ultimately dependent on the degree to which beliefs and attitudes were shared.... [I]f American society was to be both orderly and progressive, a homogeneous culture and a spirit of like-mindedness and cooperation had to exist within its population. (Franklin, 1986, p. 6)

This historical comparison is further borne out by the descriptions of school-communities in *Turning Points,* which strongly resemble the "affectional discipline" popular among Victorians and progressives. In this approach, love, guilt, and shame were utilized to manipulate and control children's behavior. Schlossman (1977) documents the use of "love" as control in progressive juvenile justice in the form of the "family reform school," which emphasized

> persuasion and manipulation of children's native emotional resources, especially their capacity to receive and reciprocate affection; strong maternal influence; close, frequent and informal relationships between youngsters and exemplary authority figures; isolated settings in order to avoid perverse worldly pleasures. (p. 53)

The *Turning Points* image of a good middle school emphasizes affectional ties among adults and youth who participate in close, personal communities for learning. Such relationships may seem unequivocally good to White, middle class professionals, but they are institutional creations that use emotional connections to shape behavior and thinking. I believe it is important to acknowledge the particular kinds of interpersonal power orchestrated in such settings rather than to pretend that authority and control are dissipated or absent in schools with "houses," "families," and "good feelings".

Thus, I find in the *Turning Points* recommendations a return to the answers of the late 1800s and early 1900s, also a time of population change and economic uncertainty. The first three principles for reformed middle schools emphasize school communities and close teacher-student relationships, both of which offer adults the opportunity to control youth through "affectional love" practices. The revised middle school of the *Turning Points* report aims to simulate face-to-face communities, whose stability is achieved through a common perspective and values, supported by a common core curriculum and an achievement orientation.

CURRICULUM

The three principles for transforming the middle school curriculum focus on "transmit[ting] a core of common knowledge to all students; ensur[ing] success for all students; and promot[ing] good health" (p. 36).

In the section detailing the knowledge core, the authors state:

> Every student in the middle grades should learn to think critically through mastery of an appropriate body of knowledge, lead a healthy life, behave ethically and lawfully, and assume the responsibilities of citizenship in a pluralistic society. (p. 42)

The section on critical thinking emphasizes a multidisciplinary, inquiry approach to learning, which diverse scholars and practitioners endorse (e.g. Tchudi, 1991). But if we examine the lengthy example of a "good" curriculum, there appears to be a stronger emphasis on learning factual knowledge and behavioral controls. Given the legacy of trivialized, factual knowledge in schools, changing to knowledge indepth is a major challenge (Newmann, 1993).

The "comprehensive life sciences curriculum" appears to be a centerpiece of the report.[4] The course of study integrates the biological and behavioral sciences in its focus upon the nature of adolescent development, health education, and health promotion: moving from the "biological underpinnings and social responses to puberty" and then "directly to sexuality: the reproductive system, sexual behavior, and maintaining health" (p. 46). These biological and sexuality topics occupy the first semester of the 2-year curriculum; the second semester deals with culture, including marriage and the family in comparative perspective. The second year concentrates on "the physiology of body systems, their behavioral associations, implications for good health, and societal consequences" (p. 46).

This course of study illustrates an interdisciplinary curriculum that is directly relevant and, allegedly, of high interest to most youth, and a vehicle for teaching correct behavior. This curriculum seems to be a dream come true: mixing disciplinary knowledge, high interest and relevance, and "behavioral science." However, in this "life sciences curriculum to teach healthy behavior" (p. 46), when healthy behavior for young adolescents is defined as abstaining from sex, drugs, and alcohol, the curriculum leans toward indoctrination and persuasion to "just say no."

The authors of the report never articulate the dilemmas of teaching critical thinking alongside stringent health "don'ts." This omission contributes to the conclusion that critical thinking only goes so far in health issues. The life sciences curriculum is one of numerous places in the report where knowledge appears to be a thin veneer over adult control of youth's behavior.

In the section on teaching for critical thinking, the authors state:

> A primary goal in choosing curricula and teaching methods ... should be the disciplining of young adolescents' minds, that is, their capacity for active, engaged thinking. A student with a disciplined mind can assimilate knowledge ... challenge the reliability of evidence ... recognize the viewpoint behind the words ... see relationships. (p. 43)

These examples of cognitive competencies seem reasonable and desirable at first glance but, if we look more closely, the verbs tell a different story. For example, in the section, "enroute to a lifetime of meaningful work," young adolescents will *understand, be aware, not feel bound,* and have *learned to learn.* In the section on being a good citizen, young adolescents will *accept responsibility, understand,* and *possess a feeling of responsibility.* Under goals for becoming caring and ethical people, our youth will *recognize, embrace,* and *understand.* The goals regarding becoming a healthy person are described as possessions: *will be physically and mentally fit* and *will have a self-image of competence and strength* [all italics added] (pp. 15–17).

The tone and language in these curricular sections is one of attributes that are poured into passive objects or qualities purchased whole and possessed. Although the report's ideal 15-year-old combines thinking, caring, productive work, and healthy practices, the language used to describe the feeling and bodily dimensions of this ideal person is limited to "understanding" or "accepting responsibility." Youth are vessels to be filled with predetermined feelings, understandings, and competence. This language of indoctrination strongly undercuts the rhetoric of developing critical thinking, except as pre-packaged, isolatable "skills."

In the 106-page document, the student presence is minimal: A poem about confusions and the lack of answers by an eighth grade boy from Columbia, Missouri, and the cover illustration of turbulent seas by a sixth grade girl from Washington, DC, comprise youths' contributions. Otherwise students are present only as problems to be solved or beings to be placed on the right path.

Development of "success for all students" revolves around the institution of cooperative learning and peer tutoring. Both of these strategies are widely endorsed (e.g., Heath & Mangiola, 1991; Sapon-Shevin, 1989). However, the political dimensions of redistributing school resources so that all students succeed are omitted from the report. It is as if cooperative learning and peer tutoring can be added to existing school practices without disturbing any other expectations (Sapon-Shevin, this issue).

My aim here is to make visible the uses of adult authority in the schooling of young adolescents and the near absence of authority and power shared with youth. Even though the *Turning Points* report includes many valuable, important ideas regarding changes in pedagogy, in my reading, they are framed by a primary interest in controlling and indoctrinating youth for economic viability and social unity. The emphasis on control of youth's thoughts and behavior is central to many current teenagers' disenchantment and alienation from school, since teenagers are finely tuned to adults' overt and covert messages and skeptical about the validity of adult recommendations.

CONCEPTIONS OF YOUNG ADOLESCENTS

What structure of an "object" is allowed to materialize in a discourse? (Haraway, 1989, p. 15)

Repeatedly, the *Turning Points* report states that young adolescents need guidance and attention to become healthy, thoughtful, and productive adults (p. 13). One of the eight guiding principles is that "schools promote good health; the education and health of young adolescents are inextricably linked" (p. 36). The emphasis on health in the report and its centrality in the "new" middle school curriculum is puzzling.

Historical analysis of the late 1800s also provides an interpretation of the health emphasis and its relation to economic and social agendas. Gay's (1984) analysis of the panic in the late 1800s around sex education, which sought to eradicate masturbation, emphasizes the relationship between sexuality and mastery of the world. Gay argues that sex education responded to fears of weakness, which had political, military, and biological dimensions.

> [Masturbation] ... seemed a pointless and prodigal waste of limited and valuable resources leading figuratively ... to impotence. It constituted a loss of mastery over the world and oneself. The campaign to eradicate self-abuse was ... a way of conserving strength and maintaining control, both highly cherished and maddeningly elusive goals in the 19th century. (Gay, 1984, p. 317)

The *Turning Points* interweaving of education and health seems similarly grounded upon multifaceted fears. The emphasis on protecting and preserving health also resonates with concerns about dominance and potency—economic, political, and international. Unhealthy behaviors are irresponsible and pernicious, in that they are both self-abusive and corrosive of the health of the body politic (Gay, 1984). In using imagery, language, and pedagogical strategies with roots in the late 19th and early 20th centuries, the *Turning Points* report reiterates concerns of dominance and mastery, and echoes the training of the armed forces.

In addition to the preparation of youth for domination, the report also flattens particularities and contradictions of youth and their lives in and out of school. This "sanitizing" follows from the conception of adolescents' education as a one-way socialization process. In this view, adults and organizations socialize youth; through affectional ties and cooperation, youth will internalize the values and practices of productivity and responsibility (Franklin, 1986). Youths' differences are irrelevant in such a stance.

Another consequence of this one-way view of socialization is that youth are absent from the report as active participants in education. They are present as the passive objects of teachers, administrators, and parents, but they do not actively contribute to life in schools nor to the production of the goals and aims of middle grades education. Thus, even though critical thinking, peer tutoring, and team learning receive attention in the recommendations, there is still an overriding passiveness accorded students. An especially telling sentence about inactiveness occurs in the section on teacher empowerment:

> Students who witness teachers making decisions and discussing important ideas can envision what it is like to participate in decision making. (p. 54)

This one-directional, passive conception of education is critiqued by numerous scholars who advocate for a radical, active, multicultural democracy in schools (e.g., Perry & Fraser, 1993). The diminished, flattened young adolescents in this report cannot be educated into the conflicts and contradictions of American history and society, and to the difficult public policy issues around civil rights, social welfare, jobs, and environmental concerns, to name a few, but are to be safely harbored from disputes, conflicts, and negotiations of differences. The youth who are adrift on turbulent seas are primarily to be directed—directed to understand, be responsible, and be healthy. This remains solidly the standard formulation of youth: out-of-control and needing direction, knowledge, and discipline from adults.

CONCLUSION

My reading of the *Turning Points* report emphasizes its fundamental linking of secondary school reforms with concerns for economic productivity and social unity. These economic and social contexts prompted my comparison with the ideas and practices of educators in the late 1800s and early 1900s, who also faced economic and social change. Like their counterparts a century ago, the authors of *Turning Points* offer a vision of safety and strength in the order and values of face-to-face communities and shared core knowledge, ethics, and health practices. And like numerous past theorists and practitioners with a model of socialization and education as oneway and passive, youth are seen as social problems who redeem themselves by receiving curricular knowledge and values (albeit on contemporary topics such as decision making and reflective thought).

This view of the problem and the solutions reinvigorates a view of youth as unreliable, unstable, and incapable of judgment, independence, or responsible actions. Despite the incorporation of numerous compelling contemporary practices and ideas, the report utilizes language, imagery, and pedagogical strategies that reinforce Victorian and progressive era views of youth as needing to be controlled through "love" and "communities." For these reasons, the *Turning Points* report remains an unsatisfactory trip "back to the future."

NOTES

1. The composition of the Task Force on the Education of Young Adolescents is noteworthy. In alphabetical order the members were (with their then-current positions): Bill Clinton, governor of Arkansas; James Comer, professor of psychiatry at Yale; Alonzo Crim, professor of urban educational leadership at Georgia State University; Jacquelynne Eccles, professor of psychology at the University of Colorado; Lawrence Green, vice president of the Kaiser Family Foundation; Fred Hechinger, president of the New York Times Foundation; David Hornbeck (chair), lawyer and professor of education and public policy at Johns Hopkins; Renee Jenkins, professor of pediatrics at Howard University School of Medicine; Nancy Kassebaum, U.S. senator from Kansas; Herman LaFontaine, superintendent of Hartford, CT, schools; Deborah Meier, principal, Central Park East Secondary School, New York; Amado Padilla, professor of education at Stanford; Anne Petersen, dean, College of Health and Human Development at Pennsylvania State University; Jane Quinn, director of programs for Girls Clubs of America; Mary Budd Rowe, professor of science education at University of Florida; Roberta Simmons, professor of psychiatry and sociology, University of Pittsburgh; and Marshall Smith, dean of the School of Education at Stanford. This is a distinguished list of participants. Most of the academics are in specialties of medicine, psychiatry, and psychology with applications in schooling.

2. The imagery that is intended to take our youth into the 21st century is identical to G. Stanley Hall's a century ago. Hall is often termed the "father of adolescence" for bringing adolescence into scientific and popular awareness. He saw adolescents as ships tossed on tempestuous seas of sexuality, without mooring. Hall also emphasized adolescence as an evolutionary turning point, where youth and the species could move forward or stand still. His popularizing of adolescence reiterated it as a crucial era in social and individual life: heavy with opportunity and potential disaster. And also in Hall's footsteps, schools are invoked as the powerful force to recapture youth adrift (see Strickland & Burgess, 1965).

3. The principles excluded from discussion here concern the middle school governance, preparation of teachers, and school relationships with families and communities. They are: "Teachers and principals have the major responsibility and power to transform middle grade schools. Teachers for the middle grades are specifically prepared to teach young adolescents. Families are allied with school staff through mutual respect, trust, and communication. Schools and communities are partners in educating young adolescents" (p. 36). The principle about health, "Schools promote good health; the education and health of young adolescents are inextricably linked" (p. 36) is discussed in the section (in this article) on curriculum.

4. This interpretation of the life sciences curriculum as central and illustrative of the goals of the *Turning Points* report stems from the close reading of the report and from two recent special issues of journals focused upon adolescence and including scholars involved in the *Turning Points* report (Takanishi, 1993a, 1993b). The special issues of *American Psychologist* and *Teachers College Record* both focus heavily on health issues of youth.

REFERENCES

Carnegie Council on Adolescent Development. (1989). *Turning points: Preparing American youth for the 21st century*. Washington, DC: Carnegie Corporation of New York.

Cuban, L. (1993, Summer). Are schools to blame? *Rethinking Schools*, p. 11.

Franklin, B. (1986). *The struggle for the American community*. London: Falmer Press.

Gay, P. (1984). *The bourgeois experience, Vol. I, education of the senses*. New York: Oxford University Press.

Haraway, D. (1989). *Primate visions: Gender, race, and nature in the world of modern science*. New York: Routledge.

Heath, S. B., & Mangiola, L. (1991). *Children of promise*. Washington, DC: National Education Association.

Here they come, ready or not [Special Issue]. (1986, May 14). *Education Week*.

Newmann, F. (1993). Beyond common sense in educational restructuring. *Educational Researcher, 22*(2), 4–22.

Perry, T., & Fraser, J. W. (Eds.). (1993). *Freedom's plow: Teaching in the multicultural classroom*. New York: Routledge.

Sapon-Shevin, M. (1989). Selling cooperative learning without selling it short. *Educational Leadership, 47*(4), 63–65.

Schlossman, S. L. (1977). *Love and the American delinquent: The theory and practice of "progressive" juvenile justice, 1825–1920.* Chicago: University of Chicago Press.

Spacks, P. M. (1981). *The adolescent idea: Myths of youth and the adult imagination.* New York: Basic Books.

Strickland, C. E., & Burgess, C. (Eds.). (1965). *Health, growth, and heredity: G. Stanley Hall on natural education.* New York: Teachers College Press.

Takanishi, R. (Ed.). (1993a). Adolescence [Special issue]. *American Psychologist, 48*(2).

Takanishi, R. (Ed.). (1993b). Adolescence in the 1990s [Special issue]. *Teachers College Record, 94*(3).

Tchudi, S. (1991). *Travels across the curriculum.* New York: Scholastic.

Wiebe, R. H. (1967). *The search for order, 1877–1920.* Westport, CT: Greenwood Press.

13

Schooling in Capitalist America

SAMUEL BOWLES AND HERBERT GINTIS

SINCE ITS INCEPTION in the United States, the public school system has been seen as a method of disciplining children in the interest of producing a properly subordinate adult population. Sometimes conscious and explicit, and at other times a natural emanation from the conditions of dominance and subordinacy prevalent in the economic sphere, the theme of social control pervades educational thought and policy. The forms of school discipline, the position of the teacher, and the moral conception of the child have all changed over the years, but the overriding objective has remained.

The most striking testimonial to the hegemony of the social control ideology is perhaps its clear primacy even among those who opposed such obvious manifestations of the authoritarian classroom as corporal punishment and teacher-centered discussion. The most progressive of progressive educators have shared the common commitment to maintaining ultimate top-down control over the child's activities. Indeed, much of the educational experimentation of the past century can be viewed as attempting to broaden the discretion and deepen the involvement of the child while maintaining hierarchical control over the ultimate processes and outcomes of the educational encounter. The goal has been to enhance student motivation while withholding effective participation in the setting of priorities.

Hence, like the view of the child, the concept of discipline has itself changed. Two aspects of this change are particularly important. First, the once highly personalized authority of the teacher has become a part of the bureaucratic structure of the modern school. Unlike the teachers in the chaotic early nineteenth-century district schools, modern teachers exercise less personal power and rely more heavily on regulations promulgated by higher authorities. Although frequently prey to arbitrary intervention by parents and other community members, the nineteenth-century teacher was the boss of the classroom. The modern teacher is in a more ambiguous position. The very rules and regulations which add a patina of social authority to his or her commands at the same time rigidly circumscribe the teacher's freedom of action. Second, the aim of discipline is no longer mere compliance: the aim is now "behavior modification." Prompt and obedient response to bureaucratically sanctioned authority is, of course, a must. But sheer coercion is out of keeping with both the modern educator's view of the child and the larger social needs for a self-controlled—not just controlled—citizenry and work force.

Discipline is still the theme, but the variations more often center on the "internalization of behavioral norms," on equipping the child with a built-in supervisor than on mere obedience to external authority and material sanctions.

The repressive nature of the schooling process is nowhere more clearly revealed than in the system of grading, the most basic process of allocating rewards within the school. We will have gone some distance toward comprehending the school as it is—in going behind the educational rhetoric—if we can answer the question: Who gets what and why?

Teachers are likely to reward those who conform to and strengthen the social order of the school with higher grades and approval, and punish violators with lower grades and other forms of disapproval, independent of their respective academic and cognitive accomplishments. This fact allows us to investigate exactly what personality traits, attitudes, and behavioral attributes are facilitated by the educational encounter.

Outside of gross disobedience, one would suspect the student's exhibition of creativity and divergence of thought to be most inimical to the smooth functioning of the hierarchical classroom. For the essence of the modern educational encounter is, to use Paulo Freire's words, that teaching:

> becomes an act of depositing, in which the students are the depositories and the teacher is the depositor. Instead of communicating, the teacher issues communiqués and makes deposits which the students patiently receive, memorize, and repeat. This is the "banking" concept of education.... The teacher teaches and the students are taught.... The teacher chooses and enforces his choice and the students comply.... The teacher acts and the students have the illusion of acting through the action of the teacher.[1]

Others refer to this conception as the "jug and mug" approach to teaching whereby the jug fills up the mugs.

Thus the hostility of the school system to student behavior even approaching critical consciousness should be evident in the daily lives of students. Students are rewarded for exhibiting discipline, subordinacy, intellectually as opposed to emotionally oriented behavior, and hard work independent from intrinsic task motivation. Moreover, these traits are rewarded independently of any effect of "proper demeanor" on scholastic achievement.

Conformity to the social order of the school involves submission to a set of authority relationships which are inimical to personal growth. Instead of promoting a healthy balance among the capacity for creative autonomy, diligence, and susceptibility to social regulation, the reward system of the school inhibits those manifestations of personal capacity which threaten hierarchical authority.

We have emphasized elements of the "hidden curriculum" faced in varying degrees by all students. But schools do different things to different children. Boys and girls, blacks and whites, rich and poor are treated differently. Affluent suburban schools, working-class schools, and ghetto schools all exhibit a distinctive pattern of sanctions and rewards. Moreover, most of the discussion here has focused on high-school students. In important ways, colleges are different; and community colleges exhibit social relations of education which differ sharply from those of elite four-year institutions. In short, U.S. education is not monolithic.

Why do schools reward docility, passivity, and obedience? Why do they penalize creativity and spontaneity? Why the historical constancy of suppression and domination in an institution so central to the elevation of youth? Surely this is a glaring anomaly in terms of traditional liberal educational theory. The naive enthusiasm of the contemporary free-school movement suggests the implicit assumption that no one had ever tried to correct this situation—that the ideal of liberated education is simply a new conception which has never been tried. Even sophisticated critics, such as Charles Silberman, tend to attribute the oppressiveness of schooling to simple oversight and irrationality:

> What is mostly wrong with public schools is not due to venality or indifference or stupidity but to mindlessness.... It simply never occurs to more than a handful, to ask why they are doing what they are doing—to think seriously or deeply about the purposes or consequences of education.[2]

Yet, the history of the progressive-education movement attests to the intransigence of the educational system to "enlightened change" within the context of corporate capitalism.

We believe the available evidence indicates that the pattern of social relationships fostered in schools is hardly irrational or accidental. Rather, the structure of the educational experience is admirably suited to nurturing attitudes and behavior consonant with participation in the labor force. Particularly dramatic is the statistically verifiable congruence between the personality traits conducive to proper work performance on the job and those which are rewarded with high grades in the classroom.

Capitalist production, in our view, is not simply a technical process; it is also a social process. Workers are neither machines nor commodities but, rather, active human beings who participate in production with the aim of satisfying their personal and social needs. The central problem of the employer is to erect a set of social relationships and organizational forms, both within the enterprise and, if possible, in society at large, that will channel these aims into the production and expropriation of surplus value. Thus as a social process, capitalist production is inherently antagonistic and always potentially explosive. Though class conflicts take many forms, the most basic occurs in this struggle over the creation and expropriation of surplus value.

It is immediately evident that profits will be greater, the lower is the total wage bill paid by the employer and the greater is the productivity and intensity of labor. Education in the United States plays a dual role in the social process whereby surplus value, i.e., profit, is created and expropriated. On the one hand, by imparting technical and social skills and appropriate motivations, education increases the productive capacity of workers. On the other hand, education helps defuse and depoliticize the potentially explosive class relations of the production process, and thus serves to perpetuate the social, political, and economic conditions through which a portion of the product of labor is expropriated in the form of profits.

This simple model, reflecting the undemocratic and class-based character of economic life in the United States, bears a number of central implications:

First, we find that prevailing degrees of economic inequality and types of personal development are defined primarily by the market, property, and power relationships which define the capitalist system. Moreover, basic changes in the degree of inequality and in socially directed forms of personal development occur almost exclusively—if sometimes indirectly—through the normal process of capital accumulation and economic growth, and through shifts in the power among groups engaged in economic activity.

Second, the educational system does not add to or subtract from the overall degree of inequality and repressive personal development. Rather, it is best understood as an institution which serves to perpetuate the social relationships of economic life through which these patterns are set, by facilitating a smooth integration of youth into the labor force. This role takes a variety of forms. Schools legitimate inequality through the ostensibly meritocratic manner by which they reward and promote students, and allocate them to distinct positions in the occupational hierarchy. They create and reinforce patterns of social class and racial and sexual identification among students which allow them to relate "properly" to their eventual standing in the hierarchy of authority and status in the production process. Schools foster types of personal development compatible with the relationships of dominance and subordinacy in the economic sphere, and finally, schools create surpluses of skilled labor sufficiently extensive to render effective the prime weapon of the employer in disciplining labor—the power to hire and fire.

Third, the educational system operates in this manner not so much through the conscious intentions of teachers and administrators in their day-to-day activities, but through a close correspondence between the social relationships which govern personal interaction in the workplace and the social relationships of the educational system. Specifically, the relationships of authority and control between administrators and teachers, teachers and students, students and students, and students and their workplace. Power is organized along vertical lines of authority from administration to faculty to student body; students have a degree of control over their curriculum comparable to that of the worker over the content of his job. The motivational system of the school, involving as it does grades and other external rewards and the threat of failure rather than the intrinsic social benefits of the process of education (learning) or its tangible outcome (knowledge), mirrors closely the role of wages and the specter of unemployment in the motivation of workers. The fragmented nature of jobs is reflected in the institutionalized and rarely constructive competition among students and in the specialization and compartmentalization of academic knowledge. Finally, the relationships of dominance and subordinacy in education differ by level. The rule orientation of the high school reflects the close supervision of low-level workers; the internalization of norms and freedom from continual supervision in elite colleges reflect the social relationships of upper-level white-collar work. Most state universities and community colleges, which fall in between, conform to the behavioral requisites of low-level technical, service, and supervisory personnel.

Fourth, though the school system has effectively served the interests of profit and political stability, it has hardly been a finely tuned instrument of manipulation in the hands of socially dominant groups. Schools and colleges do indeed help to justify inequality, but they also have become arenas in which a highly politicized egalitarian consciousness has developed among some parents, teachers, and students. The authoritarian classroom does produce docile workers, but it also produces misfits and rebels. The university trains the elite in the skills of domination, but it has also given birth to a powerful radical movement and critique of capitalist society. The contradictory nature of U.S. education stems in part from the fact that the imperatives of profit often pull the school system in opposite directions. The types of training required to develop productive workers are often ill suited to the perpetuation of those ideas and institutions which facilitate the profitable employment of labor. Furthermore, contradictory forces external to the school system continually impinge upon its operations. Students, working people, parents, and others have attempted to use education to attain a greater share of the social wealth, to develop genuinely critical capacities, to gain material security, in short to pursue objectives different from—and often diametrically opposed to—those of capital. Education in the United States is as contradictory and complex as the larger society; no simplistic or mechanical theory can help us understand it.

NOTES

1. Paulo Freire, *Pedagogy of the Oppressed* (New York: Herder and Herder, 1972), 58–59.
2. Charles Silberman, *Crisis in the Classroom* (New York: Vintage, 1971), 10, 11.

14

Rivers of Fire: Amoco's iMPACT on Education and Other Corporate Incursions

Kenneth J. Saltman and Robin Truth Goodman

SLICK!

This is a computer simulation of an oil spill at sea. Students must plan and implement methods of dealing with an oil spill at sea. Designed for use for individuals and groups, having two levels: beginner and expert. This resource incorporates graphics, sound effects and a range of printed materials … L20.00 … Add to Shopping Cart.…

—BP Educational Services[1]

From the two sets of three colorful Amoco-branded wall posters to the Amoco-branded curriculum box to the Amoco ads in the videos themselves, Amoco's iMPACT middle-school science curriculum provides this massive multinational oil company with what advertisers refer to as multiple "impressions" or viewing of the brand logo (Ries & Ries, 1999). The curriculum is clearly designed to promote and advertise Amoco to a "captive audience" in public schools. Brightly mottled posters show Sesame Street-style cartoon characters riding roller coasters to learn physics, a lone cartoon diver encounters a gigantic sea monster to learn biology, and an ominous black mountain explodes with molten magma. These cartoons, with more rainbow-colors than an oil slick, include scientific labels with arrows reminding kids that all of this fun is educational. Amoco stamps its corporate logo on fun and excitement, curiosity and exploration, education, nature, science, and work. By rendering its red, white, and blue logo visible in school classrooms, Amoco appears as a "responsible corporate citizen" supporting beleaguered public schools with its corporate philanthropy. Not only does the corporate sector defund the public sector by evading its tax responsibility to such public goods as public schools, but the growing trend towards privatization, for-profit charter schools, magnet schools, and commercialization redefine the public schools as sources for private profit.[2] In reality, Amoco's use of the innocent-looking aesthetics of children's culture, its appeal to fun and child-like curiosity, conceal the fact that this oil company is far from innocent of not only undermining the public sector in this country, but of outright human-rights violations, widespread environmental devastation, and the uprooting of indigenous communities globally.[3]

Like other corporate curricula, Amoco's sprightly lessons do more than provide entry for corporate advertisements into public space.[4] This curriculum functions as a diversion from what Amoco is actually doing around the world, and it functions ideologically to construct a corporate-friendly worldview, define youth identity and citizenship through consumption, and render nationality as a corporate interest rather than the public interest. Amoco's curriculum produces ideologies of consumerism that bolster its global corporate agenda, and it does so under the guise of disinterested scientific knowledge, benevolent technology, and innocent entertainment.

BPAmoco IN COLOMBIA

Separating the pedagogical from the political, Amoco's curriculum conceals how this corporation undermines democratic institutions such as public schooling and participates in the hindering of democracy and perpetration of human rights abuses and environmental destruction abroad. As Wharton economist Edward Herman and ColombiaWatch's Celia Zarate-Laun (1999) expose, the largest investor in Colombia, British Petroleum (BP; now BPAmoco), has created its own mercenary forces, but also imported British counterinsurgency professionals to train Colombians. BP gave its own intelligence reports to the Colombian military that were used to track and kill local "subversives": "Amnesty International and Human Rights Watch have documented numerous examples of collaboration between Colombian army units and brutal paramilitaries who are guilty of over 75 percent of the human rights violations that have been committed in Colombia's civil conflict" (Delacour, 2000). The other oil companies in Colombia have also "cultivated the army and police and hired paramilitaries and foreign mercenaries to protect their oil pipelines" (Herman & Zarate-Laun, 1999). BPAmoco's behavior overseas must be understood in the context of the relationship between the U.S. government's foreign policy and its support of the corporate sector.

Though said to be specifically supporting Colombia's "war on drugs" and not its militarized counterinsurgency efforts, U.S. aid to Colombia (the third highest amount of foreign military aid after Israel and Egypt) has been earmarked for specific regions of the country such as the Amazon and Orinoco basins and the Putumayo region more broadly—regions that happen to be the areas of influence of the rebel Revolutionary Armed Forces of Colombia (FARC)—while largely avoiding the northern areas of the country where the drug-trade routes are protected by paramilitaries closely allied with drug-traffickers and members of the Colombian army. Exempting and supplying arms to an important segment of the drug trade suggests that, as with anti-communism in the past, the drug-war rationale covers over the pursuit of larger objectives that can be read from what the army and paramilitaries do—remove, kill, and silence the large segments of the rural population that stand in the way of the exploitation of Colombia's resources by transnational corporations such as BPAmoco (Herman & Zarate-Laun, 1999).

Under the pretext of the drug war, the U.S. government is funding Colombia's internal war against ideologically dissenting factions such as the FARC (currently 18,000 strong) and the smaller ELN (currently counting 3,000) (Cooper, 2001, p. 14). In June of 2000, the

U.S. Congress approved a $1 billion aid package to Colombia, including military training, helicopters, and intelligence.[5] Carla Anne Robbins (2000) of *The Wall Street Journal* reports that even though the U.S. has, for the past ten years, exercised caution in extending developmental aid to Colombia because of widespread allegations of human rights abuses, the Colombian government has managed to reassure Washington that its military equipment will only be used for anti-narcotics maneuvers and not for counterinsurgency. Yet, as Justin Delacour of *Z-Net* has demonstrated, the Clinton administration was "remarkably resistant to conditions placed on the aid that require them to demonstrate that the Colombian government is vigorously rooting out complicity between the army and paramilitaries."[6] In fact, as Marc Cooper (2001) of *The Nation* remarks, "Bill Clinton's State Department, with only hours left before the Bush transition, employed a loophole in the U.S. aid package [Plan Colombia] and voluntarily' decided to 'skip' having to certify that the Colombian government has complied with U.S. human rights demands attached to Plan Colombia legislation—specifically, suppression of the paramilitary death squads" (p. 14). *The Journal* admits that unless the close ties between the FARC and the drug trade are loosened, the United States's stated intentions of bringing peace, political reform, and crop substitution to the region will surely fail. José Cuesta of the Citizens' Network for Peace in Colombia alleges, "The coca crops are nothing but a concrete response to the ravages caused by unrestrained free-market policies (Cooper, 2001, p. 16). Washington has only committed one percent of the Plan Colombia aid package to crop substitution, and this means that *campesinos* will not be able to produce even at subsistence level without sustaining coca fields: "In general a kilo of cocaine is sold at 1.5 to 1.7 million pesos (about $6,800–$7,700) and net profit per hectare is 200,000 pesos (about $90). Comparatively speaking, a carga, which is about 100 kilos of corn, is sold for 30,000 pesos, and after paying the costs the peasant is left with only 10,000 pesos (about $4.50) per carga (Zarate-Laun, 2001). Even as *The Wall Street Journal* (Robbins, 2000) professes that the problem in the FARC-controlled regions stems from drug trafficking, it also attributes the need for militarization to the FARC's economic reforms, in particular their attempts to tax the corporate sector:

> As conservatives were complaining that Bogota was selling out to the Marxists [because of the Colombian government's agreement to negotiate settlement with guerrillas], New York Stock Exchange Chairman Richard Grasso accepted an invitation to fly to the demilitarized zone to tutor the FARC on the joys of capitalism.... [Carlos Antonio] Lozada [one of the FARC's negotiators] … explains that instead of indiscriminate kidnapping, the FARC's new Law 002 will levy a tax on anyone with more than $1 million in assets (p. A12).[7]

The expansion of NAFTA into South America is being accompanied by the expansion of U.S. military presence, not only in Colombia through the provision of military attack helicopters and counterinsurgency equipment for maneuvers nominally against trafficking, but also in Ecuador and El Salvador where bases are being built. This movement of capital through military expansion illustrates concretely *New York Times* foreign correspondent Thomas Freidman's (1999, p. 309) thesis that "The hidden hand of the market will never work without the hidden fist—McDonald's cannot flourish without McDonnell Douglas, the designer of the F-15. And the hidden fist that keeps the world safe for Silicon Valley's technologies is called the United States Army, Air Force, Navy, and Marine Corps."

This militarization opens the region to U.S. investment as it destroys the fields and liveli-hoods of poor peasants, using methods as brutal as those attributed to the FARC. Along-side and contingent to militarization, education can work to open wider reaches for the neoliberal market. Wall Street's journey to the region demonstrates that investors under-stand how education in the "joys of capitalism" opens the way to corporate infiltration.[8] Clearly, the so-called "War on Drugs" is in the business of an ideological production partly installed through the very processes of militarization.

This military intervention into the political situation in Colombia owes to the fact that the United States imports more oil from the region than it does from the middle east (260,000 barrels from Colombia per day). Indeed, the claim can hardly be made that the Administration is funding drug containment policies internationally when publicly funded treatment centers have been radically cut from city, state, and federal budgets within the United States. In 1994, the White House commissioned the Rand Institution to research the most effective methods for controlling and reducing drugs. The Rand report found that treatment was seven percent cheaper and more successful than domestic enforcement, eleven percent more than interdiction, and twenty-three percent more than source-country eradication policies, the policy which this aid package embraces (Dela-cour, 2000). Clearly, therefore, the defunding of public support for treatment ultimately benefits the profit-mongering of the private sector. This is why, unlike public advocates like Noam Chomsky and Ralph Nader, private corporations like BPAmoco support the militarization of Colombia's "War on Drugs":

> [I]t's questionable whether or not it even qualifies as a drug policy at all. Several corporations whose interests have nothing to do with drug policy have been pushing the Colombia package from day one. Multinationals and U.S.-based weapons producers who are pushing the pack-age include Occidental Petroleum Corp., Enron Corp., BPAmoco, Colgate-Palmolive Co., United Technologies Corp. and Bell Helicopter Textron Inc. Occidental Petroleum's strong backing of the package derives from the fact that its extensive oil operations in Colombia have been frequently sabotaged by guerrilla groups who object to the terms of the agreement between the Colombian government and multinational oil corporations that operate in the country. Occidental Petroleum's Vice-President Lawrence Meriage was even called to testify before the House Government Reform Subcommittee on Drug Policy, leading observers to wonder how oil executives suddenly qualified as drug policy experts. (Delacour, 2000)

Ultimately, then, U.S. taxpayers are paying millions of dollars to protect the oil pipe-lines of BPAmoco, Occidental Petroleum (a strong backer of Al Gore's political career and presidential campaign), Shell, and Texaco—companies that have spilled 1.7 million barrels of oil onto the soils and into rivers in the last 12 years. At the same time, U.S. chemical companies Monsanto and Dow are being enriched by U.S.-assisted spraying of their toxic herbicides (Roundup and Spike) on coca and opium plants in Colombia:

> Monsanto's Roundup, which is the principal chemical being sprayed in Colombia to reduce the coca and poppy crops, contains phosphorus, which upon contact with water captures oxygen and destroys fish in lakes, lagoons, and marshes. Crop spraying affects food crops such as cassava, plantains, corn, and tropical fruits. Likewise, peasants exposed to the spray have

reported cases of diarrhea, fever, muscle pain, and headaches attributed to their exposure to the chemical spray. (Zarate-Laun, 2001)

Not only is this, too, endangering the world's second richest ecosystem (after that of Brazil), but the same drugs evading eradication by the chemical sprays (coca production is in fact on the rise) are being sold to the United States with the profits being used to fund both right wing death squads who work in the interests of the multinationals and the government and to fund the left wing guerillas fighting against the government and the multinationals (Zarate-Laun, 1999).

In short then, the same interests that are supporting drug trafficking are also supporting multinational corporate expansion in the region. This is not just a case of two blood-seeking powers—the government and the insurgency—fighting it out at the expense of the little guy, but rather an imperialist manipulation for economic and ideological control where corporations are winning the conflict on both sides. The entire process of corporate expansion is militarized in combination with the drug trade. However, by omitting any mention of the complex web of murder, pollution, and politics undergirding its quest for profit, Amoco lies to school kids by painting a picture of science and education as innocent and free of their motivating forces—in this case corporate greed.

THE AMOCO CURRICULUM

The Amoco curriculum is not simply about hiding the insidious operations of the company abroad under sunny pictures of smiling children playing happy games in pristine parks. The Amoco curriculum also constructs and naturalizes a worldview where public concerns are erased underneath the adventures of corporatism and the thrills of the consumer. Part of educating citizens in the "joys of capitalism" consists of, for instance, making the exploitation of other nations' natural environments, raw materials, and labor forces seem like affective friendships or even love affairs, celebrated in joyous pictures of wondering gazes at the triumphs of technological mastery. These kinds of images stage a drama of corporate excellence that overrides any possible comprehension about how exactly such curricula are remaking public schooling itself as a training ground for consumer armies:

At the primary and secondary levels, the spoils of the public school system have long been coveted by "education entrepreneurs," touting the "discipline" of the marketplace over the "inefficiency" of the public realm, and normalizing the rhetoric of corporate management—the public as customer, education as competitive product, learning as efficiency tool. Remember Lamar Alexander's declaration, shortly before becoming secretary of education, that Burger King and Federal Express should set up schools to show how the private sector would run things?… While your local high school hasn't yet been bought out by McDonalds, many educators already use teaching aids and packets of materials, "donated" by companies, that are crammed with industry propaganda designed to instill product awareness among young consumers: lessons about the history of the potato chip, sponsored by the Snack Food Association, or literacy programs that reward students who reach monthly reading goals with Pizza Hut slices. (Ross, 2000)

While Amoco seduces school kids with the allures of fun knowledge, it is also actively engaging in practices that directly undermine the public. Domestically, as Amoco was distributing its "Rivers of Fire" curriculum in Chicago, it was creating real rivers of fire in Michigan and Missouri. In River Rouge, Michigan, the city was fighting to force Amoco to stop leaking explosive petroleum products into its sewer system.[9] City leaders worried that Amoco was recreating the conditions for an explosion in 1982 that "set off fires and smaller explosions inside nearby sewer lines and blew out windows of buildings and cars (Pardo, 1999, p. D3). While the "Rivers of Fire" video was being distributed in Chicago, in Sugar Creek, Missouri, families were forced to flee their homes as Amoco's cleanup of its decades-old ground, water, and air pollution forced contaminated air into the homes of local residents. The Chappell family, advised by the EPA to find alternative lodging, had begun an investigation into unusually high incidents of cancer in their neighborhood (Pardo, 1999, p. D3). At the same time, BPAmoco plead guilty to felony charges in a case of illegal dumping of toxic chemicals.

> Alaska's North Slope is an environmentally sensitive area and BP's Endicott Island-drilling site sits on the Beaufort Sea, home to birds and marine life. Hundreds of 55-gallon barrels containing paint thinners, paints, oil and solvents were dumped, according to federal prosecutors. (D3)

The conviction followed a sixteen-month-long legal battle in which BPAmoco denied knowledge of the dumping, despite the previous conviction of their same contractor on identical dumping charges. This pollution, too, had been going on for years.

Amoco produces this science curriculum in conjunction with Scholastic, Waste Management Inc., and Public Television and freely distributes it to the Chicago Public Schools. The overwhelming corporate interest in investing in this project is far from innocent, philanthropic, or charitable, as the curriculum participates in an overall corporate strategy of producing global corporate citizens and recreating profit motives as moral values, or rather, tutoring the kids in the "joys of capitalism." As Alex Molnar has shown, Scholastic itself is one of the most aggressive and shameless cases of corralling youth into the consumer market:

> [Mark] Evans [a senior vice president of Scholastic, in his 1988 essay in *Advertising Age*] managed to paint a picture of noble purpose and business need combined in perfect harmony to advance the welfare of American students. Perhaps not wishing to seem too self-serving, he failed to mention that at the time he wrote his essay, Scholastic was in the process of establishing its educational marketing division and was looking for corporate clients. Early in his essay, Evans identified a few business-supported educational projects that, in his mind, illustrated how corporations, pursuing profits, and schools, trying to better educate their students, could work in tandem to advance the cause of social progress. Then he dispensed with the good cop fiction and came to the point: "More and more companies see education marketing as the most compelling, memorable and cost-effective way to build share of mind and market into the twenty-first century." Evans then set aside any pretense of high educational and social purpose when he chose a model for all to emulate. "Gillette is currently sponsoring a multimedia in-school program designed to introduce teenagers to their safety razors—building

brand and product loyalties through classroom-centered, peer-powered lifestyle patterning." (Molnar, 1996)

In conjunction with these company goals, the Amoco curriculum certainly shows how profits and market values are replacing social purpose in the education of citizens. The Amoco curriculum demonstrates how corporations are using schools to teach market values as a form of common sense, even fashioning them as the basis of morality. Oil companies in particular, as David Cromwell (2000, p. 8) points out, are using classroom curricula to spread propaganda that "modern civilization is dependent on the hydrocarbon business" as the popularization of this belief is essential to the survival of the industry. Specifically, as we detail in what follows, Amoco's curriculum—including videos, posters, teachers' guides—envisions nature and knowledge, as well as work, education, and science, through the imaginary of corporate culture.

Nature

Each of the videos begins and ends with advertisements for Amoco. "Major funding for The New Explorers is provided by Amoco, celebrating the adventure of scientific discovery for the year 2000 and beyond." This voice-over accompanies images of pristine nature: the moon, a bald eagle flying over a serene lake. The Amoco logo, in patriotic red, white, and blue, joins with the bald eagle in suggesting that the trademark could replace the U.S. flag. In the context of public-school classrooms (replete with a U.S. flag hanging near the VCR), such merging of these common tropes fashions the idea of national citizenship as corporate branding.

These framing advertisements present peaceful scenes of idealized yet decontextualized nature, labeled with the oil company logo and suggesting an alignment of ecological health and the Amoco corporation. The ad for Amoco is followed by a connected ad for Waste Management, Incorporated, "Helping the world dispose of its problems." Together these images and assuring voice-over present nature in a state of benevolent corporate management. The pristine horizon punctuated by a range of snow-capped mountains, pure colors, still lake waters, and soaring birds serves to Americanize the natural landscape further by placing the corporate logo in the spacious skies and mountain ranges of the beauty America sings. The pure air and stillness give a sense that time has stopped and that human hands have left nature's sublimity untouched and dazzling. The history of Waste Management, Inc., reveals, of course, quite another story, and certainly the contention that Waste Management, Inc., disposes of the world's problems is less credible than would be a contrary claim that it has created new ones. Founder and billionaire Wayne Huizenga, a hero of capitalist consolidation, mergers, and acquisitions, has come up time and again under allegations of unethical practices, illegal price-setting, stock bailings, and underworld corruption. Additionally, his profit motivations have proven far from environmentally astute, as he reneged on the waste-hauling industry's practices of breeding pigs to eat edible garbage when his own pigs developed special diseases not evident on the competitors' farms.[10] Though Huizenga has since sold the company, Waste Management, Inc., has a stake in deregulating capital and finance as well as finding ways to avoid restrictive environmental legislation. The pedagogical intent here is to show nature as self-regulating, able to revitalize and reproduce itself without human intervention or investments of any kind. The logo then serves to link the bountiful abundance and cleanliness of nature without controls to the advancement of clean, corporate, healthful capital.

The videos represent nature as not merely best served by corporate management but as an expression of corporate culture. "Rivers of Fire" opens with a drive through the jungle likened to that of a typical suburban commuter on his way to his desk job: "Except for the tropical foliage, [geologist Frank Truesdale's] routine looks like a typical suburban commute, but when he takes the first exit off the paved highway, we get a hint that he's not exactly on his way to a desk job in an office building." Frank's four-wheel-drive jostles down a dirt-paved road flanked on either side by lush vegetation. Corporations themselves thus come to seem part of nature.

Within the imaginary of the videos, nature appears alternately as dangerous and in need of control or as tamed suburban landscape. "If something goes wrong here," warns Bill Kurtis in "Dive Into Darkness," "there's no easy escape to the surface. Since cave diving took hold in the 1960s, more than 300 people have died in caves in Florida, Mexico, and the Caribbean alone. Temporary loss of air supply, temporary disorientation, temporary loss of lights—those aren't reasons to die in a cave," admits one of the experts. "The reason people die in those situations is panic, perceived stress. That's what kills people. But despite these risks," the video concludes, "not one of them [the divers] would turn back. This is not just a job for these divers. It's a mission. Like the original explorers in space. They had to send a person there to really know what's going on." "Rivers of Fire" presents scientists as adventurers, explorers, but also conquistadors driven to control an angry and unpredictable final frontier—namely, the earth itself about to spew forth burning deadly fluids. Narrator and producer Bill Kurtis kneels before a stream of magma running into the ocean as he explains the danger: "In January of 1983," a voice-over begins, "the skies were just as blue on the big island of Hawaii, the beaches just as inviting as any other day. But 30 miles beneath the crater of Kilowaya, molten lava was rising." This narration is accompanied by ominous bassy music, invoking horror movie conventions as in *Jaws* when the shark is about to attack. Continual video cross cuts intersperse the explosion of this deadly lava with shots of human technology—seismic equipment that Kurtis explains is necessary to watch, and hence control, the unpredictable earth. Lava flows "threaten homesites and other subdivisions that may be in its way." By framing nature as violent and in need of control by science and technology, "Rivers of Fire" naturalizes the role that the corporation, and more specifically Amoco, plays in protecting citizens and property from the threat of nature. The technological instruments provide "a way to prevent lava from consuming those who live around the volcanoes."

In this case, the video does more than camouflage the real role that Amoco's science and technology play in threatening citizens and nature. It also denies the history of why the volcano observatory was established in the early twentieth century and by whom. The curriculum fails to mention that the observatory was initially funded by one of the five businesspeople who overthrew the indigenous Hawaiian government and installed a plutocracy. The observatory was designed not merely to study nature but to predict volcanic flows so that other foreign investors could be convinced that their investments in development projects and industry would not be destroyed by lava. In other words, the video presents, as disinterested study of nature, a history of economic and political imperialism. When Amoco and Scholastic describe their lessons as "An Amoco Expedition with the New Explorers," they are actively excluding the history of conquest that paved the way for today's seemingly disinterested measurement of nature. The establishment of the observatory was part of settling the frontier, annexing Hawaii, and continuing the westward expansion that was part of an American history characterized by violence and exploitation and motivated by profit rather than a benevolent protection of citizens from an unruly nature:

> The entire history of this country has been driven by violence. The whole power structure and economic system was based essentially on the extermination of the native populations and the bringing of slaves. The Industrial Revolution was based on cheap cotton, which wasn't kept cheap by market principles but by conquest. It was kept cheap by the use of land stolen from the indigenous populations and then by the cheap labor of those exploited in slavery. The subsequent conquest of the West was also very brutal. After reaching the end of the frontier, we just went on conquering more and more—the Philippines, Hawaii, Latin America, and so on. In fact, there is a continuous strain of violence in US military history from "Indian fighting" right up through the war in Vietnam. The guys who were involved in "Indian fighting" are the guys who went to the Philippines, where they carried out a massive slaughter; and the same people who had just been tried for war crimes in the Philippines went on to Haiti, where they carried out another slaughter. This goes right up through Vietnam. If you look at the popular literature on Vietnam, it's full of "We're chasing Indians."[11]

In the Amoco videos, nature—rather than technology, corporations, and capitalism—appears to threaten families, consumption, and the innocent pleasures of beachcombing. Additionally, nature functions as an extension of the corporation, becomes plunderable, and substitutes as the workspace. Such an understanding of nature as the worksite serves well its oil-drilling sponsor, Amoco, who also wants students to see that nature is dangerous to civilization and in need of control, manipulation, and constant measurement by scientists. In "Dive Into Darkness" one scientist reminds viewers that nature is being destroyed: "things are disappearing so rapidly we need to document them."

Knowledge

The Amoco kit includes three videotapes, six colorful wall posters, teachers' guides, and public relations instructions for teachers and gas station owners to place promotional photos and stories about the "partnership" in local newspapers. Amoco's curriculum suggests that education must be fun, exciting, exploratory, and meaningful to students. "I think it's important that students see many things on the way home from school that they saw in the classroom," explains one of the physics teachers. And the success of such meaningful pedagogical practices is proven in the countless testimonies of students who were never interested in science before now. "Any teacher can go to college and get their degree and come in to teach and do all kinds of chalk talk," one student observes. "But Mr. Hicks comes in and makes it all fun. He basically loves every one of us… We're a family and he teaches it with love."

The Amoco curriculum draws on popularized notions of progressive pedagogy to suggest that education should derive from experience, that students be involved in "constructing" knowledge by participating in activities that are meaningful to them, and that learning must not disconnect knowledge from the world. We will provide a brief example. Middle-school pedagogue, Nancie Atwell (1998) professes to make learning meaningful by giving kids more power to decide on curriculum and on what happens in the classroom: "Together we'll enter the world of literature, become captivated, make connections to our lives, the world, and the world of other books, and find satisfaction" (p. 35). Atwell, hailed in both the popular and educational presses as an educational innovator, emphasizes hands-on learning where kids take responsibility in deciding what the curriculum will be and formulate, in discussions with their classmates, the kinds of topics they will write about. Atwell contrasts this new way of teaching middle school with a more traditional teacher-centered methodology where kids' potentials for imagination and involvement are never tapped or developed. At the same time, however, she does not talk about how this freedom for educational experimentation functions to bolster the sense of privilege of her white private-school, suburban students, nor does she address how these methods are meant to train, precisely, those in control of the future means of production.

For Atwell, "empowering" students means giving them a sense of confidence and personal power. Yet, Atwell has no sense of different levels of power, privilege, agency, and sense of entitlement experienced by different students in different social, economic, and cultural contexts. Atwell's kids are already in a class position to receive power. Atwell does not help her students see their privileges as a part of a broader system that fails to extend basic social services to students elsewhere. Nor does she offer her students the tools for challenging oppressions, such as the maintenance of a highly unequal structure of educational resource allocation. Atwell, thus, embraces a highly individualized progressive methodology divorced from any social, political referent for more just social transformation. Likewise, Amoco's "Rock n' Roll Physics" shows conventional classroom physics lessons as the height of decontextualized, abstract, and boring education, which fails because of its incapacity to engage students. A physics teacher drones on spewing formulas as students sleep, doodle, and play with chewing gum. Narrator Bill Kurtis says, "This is no way to teach physics." Cut to the class riding on a roller coaster and Kurtis yells from the roller coaster, "Now this is the way to learn physics." As Atwell states, "Learning is more likely to happen when students like what they are doing" (1998, p. 52), but there is no sense given here about what kinds of students get to experience such pleasures and under what circumstances, nor what kinds of political values, institutions, and configurations of power are being assumed and supported through such initiatives. Such pleasure is seldom innocent.

The use of adventure-thrill and high-speed derring-do in the Amoco curriculum keys in to a broader public discourse about the economy that promotes instability, fear, and physical trepidation as the goal of the good life. As the Amoco curriculum redefines the pursuit of knowledge as a dangerous game, *Time Magazine* and MTV both juxtapose high-risk sport with day trading and risky stock investment. Quitting jobs, starting businesses, and risky investment in the market are being likened to base jumping, paragliding, mountain climbing, and other adventure sports. MTV shows bungy-jumpers freaking out over whether or not to plunge while an e-trade advertisement contextualizes the situation in the lower right corner of the screen. Clearly, *Time* and MTV construct and romanticize the popular embrace of volatile and uncertain ventures. This could be viewed as simply a ploy to naturalize an increasingly unstable economy as an exciting challenge that the brave can fearlessly negotiate. Job insecurity, an uncertain financial future, and growing inequalities in wealth and income appear as exciting obstacles to brave in the new economy. The risk economy is metaphorized as a natural impulse to stand on the jagged ledge of a tantalizing mountain to climb or jump off of in the Mountain Dew commercial. In this way, we argue, adventure sports are being used by corporate mass media to naturalize economic insecurity.

The notion of hands-on learning is indebted to contemporary progressive educational methodologies of constructivism, grounded in Piagetian theory as well as the influence of the Deweyan tradition and a misguided appropriation of Paulo Freire's criticism of banking education. "Education thus becomes," Freire maintains, "an act of depositing, in which the students are the depositories and the teacher is the depositor. Instead of communicating, the teacher issues communiqués and makes deposits which the students patiently receive, memorize, and repeat" (Freire, 1970/1993, p. 53). These progressive traditions share with the Amoco curriculum an insistence on the centrality of the learner, the need for a de-centering of teacher authority in the classroom, and the importance of knowledge that is meaningful as the basis for further learning. The Amoco curriculum seems progressive by appearing to take seriously the notion that education should be meaningful to students and that the classroom structure should not treat students as depositories for rarified teacher knowledge. However, like many wrong-headed liberal appropriations of Freire, the Amoco curriculum treats progressive educational ideals instrumentally—that is, strictly as methods to increase the likelihood that students will absorb knowledge of which the justifications for its teaching remain unquestioned.[12] In the case of the Amoco videos, there are no questions raised as to why students should learn physics framed in this way, whose interests are served by the teaching of this knowledge, what is this knowledge used for in the world, and at whose expense and to whose benefit? Hence, seemingly progressive methodologies are not theoretically justified and end up being just a more efficient delivery system for accepted knowledge about science and technology.

The Amoco videos view nature as a resource. That is, nature appears as needing to be tamed and domesticated, brought within the control of scientific rationality represented in automatic machines drawing lines on graphs, making sense. Nature is out there waiting to be retrieved, transported back to laboratories, equipped with state-of-the-art technology for measurement and storage, named and labeled for future research. "Imagine a place left on earth," says Master of Ceremonies Bill Kurtis, introducing "Dive Into Darkness," "that is virtually unexplored." The underwater cave Sagitarius in Sweetings Key off the Bahamas is, he continues, an "unstudied world waiting for … discovery."

However, the pursuit of knowledge here seems like an alibi. Scattered throughout the surfaces of these environmental niches, scientists find natural holes filled with energy sources: Dr. Jill Yaeger of Antioch University swims across blue holes brimming with blue bubbles. These blue holes, the voice-over explains, give off a strong force which, when reversed by the tides, create twisting fields of force that sweep swimmers into tow without granting any path of escape or release. Searching for knowledge, the scientific exploration team is able to avoid such deep-sea traps. The energy fields themselves are resources to be used in the production of knowledge. The company that sponsors the videos does not think it worth mentioning that it is in the business of exploiting energy fields as resources for production. Acquiring knowledge of nature as energy becomes a substitute, even a cover, for exploiting natural sources of energy for company profit. Collecting bits of natural knowledge becomes a safety valve, an antidote to the destruction that natural energy would cause if left unexplored and unexploited, and a compassionate rationale for expanding technocratic controls into foreign territories. Amoco's view of nature communicates that what is important to know about nature is how it can be used for human progress and profit. "Scientists believe that sharks may hold the secrets to important medical benefits for man," "Dive Into Darkness" informs students: "They're animals in need of protection and study." The video neglects to mention that human industry in the form of commercial fishing is the primary cause of the endangerment of sharks. Instead, "humanitarian" concerns serve to justify Dr. Jill Yaeger's dives into darkness on a mission to bring back the newly discovered form of crustacia, "remipede," to her research laboratory in Ohio. These animals need to be known about, named, labeled, and catalogued in order to construct a total knowledge of life, the videos suggest, and of evolution. In fact, the sea dives themselves are depicted as travels back through evolution, into the dark origins of life at the bottom of the sea, while the precarious return to the water's surface works as a triumphant enlightenment. However, what made the journey of discovery so successful turns out to be the successful retrieval of the remipede for scientific research—in other words, the collection and acquisition of resources. The videos translate activities of collecting into the ethical entertainment of learning, knowledge acquisition, and accumulation. The idea that knowledge of nature needs to be whole and complete means here that mastery of nature leads to a greater variety of products. Amoco does not allude to the ways nature might be destroyed when its products are extracted, nor to how nature and the ecosystem are not designed simply to be exploited for human instrumental use, nor to how all nature is not passively waiting to be turned into products of consumption and objects of display.

Earthworms and Empires

Public Image: The corporate image of Monsanto as a responsible member of the business world genuinely concerned with the welfare of our environment will be adversely affected with increased publicity …

Sources of Contamination: Although there may be some soil and air contamination involved, by far the most critical problem at present is water contamination …. Our manufacturing facilities sewered a sizable quantity of PCB's in a year's time …

—MONSANTO COMMITTEE MEMO, 1969 (BEILES, 2000)

Amoco is not the only company using nature to teach kids the values and joys of capitalism. Under these types of curricula, nature is re-made to express and reflect the social relations of capital, and thereby the unequal relations of capital are made to seem part of nature. A 2000–2001 exhibit, entitled "Underground Adventure," at Chicago's Field Museum of Natural History, for example, is a spectacular trip underneath the earth's surface to explore the wonders of the soil.[13] "You will never feel the same about the soil again," are the words that welcome you into Monsanto's "fun for the whole family" learning trek. On the other side of the video-greeting room called the "base-camp," is Monsanto's magical shrinking machine that suddenly transforms all the critters around the visitors into towering monsters, gigantic plastic beetles, and bulging roots that would have made Kafka ogle and Gulliver shake his head. What is truly fantastic about the display, however, is not so much that Monsanto is hiding its own destruction of such fertility in the soil through its genetic manipulations, or its annihilation of such critters through its production of insecticides such as Roundup, or its own monopolistic stronghold of species' diversity by its horizontal control of agricultural products that create essential needs among farmers for its other exclusive products. Nor is it very surprising, after all, that Monsanto would not acknowledge, in this exhibit, its emissions of PCBs, which contaminated much farming and breeding lands in West Anniston, Alabama and caused cancer among much of the population there with the full and documented knowledge of the company itself as to the damage that PCBs cause.[14] Rather, what makes Monsanto's natural history lessons truly magical is precisely how the company manages to exhibit such unethical, unbalanced, and destructive capitalist practices as the way of nature, rather than of multinational corporations.

The aims of Monsanto's exhibit are clear from the moment the visitor enters. The first thing the visitor sees is a series of Plexiglas displays professing the importance of the soil in providing various consumer products. These are not just any consumer products, but rather major corporate trademarks. For example, one case displays an old pair of blue jeans with the glaring "Gap" label, while the sign reads: "Without soil, there would be no jeans. These jeans are made of cotton denim stitched together with cotton thread. Their blue color comes from indigo dye. Cotton and indigo come from plants that need soil to grow. No soil—no jeans." Next comes a basket of Coca-Cola cans piled on top of each other. The sign exclaims, "The aluminum in these cans has been recycled over and over again. But new aluminum starts out locked inside of soil in an ore called bauxite. No soil—no aluminum." The exhibit never admits what Monsanto or the other sponsors have at stake in displaying this particular constellation of goods—for example, Monsanto's production of Nutrasweet artificial sweetener used in Diet Coke. "Without soil there would be no penicillin," the next sign triumphantly declares. The sign does not go on to explain Monsanto's investments in the pharmaceutical industry, nor how the consolidation of large pharmaceutical companies and their lobbying of protections for global intellectual property rights is making medicine less accessible throughout the world to those who need it most. Rather, it indicates how many lives are being saved because penicillin arises fruitfully from the soil.

Monsanto is clearly telling its young patrons that, just like the mall, the soil is rich in its offerings of fun and diverse things to wear and to buy, as if multinational products emerge straight out of the earth without involving people, labor, or social relations. In other words, Monsanto seems to literalize the classical Marxist claim that naturalization erases the processes of production from the commodity. Nature is made to seem richly abundant of capitalist output. This process makes invisible the inequalities inherent in the mass manufacturing of cotton or dye, or the injustices practiced in both third- and first-world sweatshops where, for example, much of The Gap's merchandise is stitched together by the poor, the exploited, and the marginalized, or when Coca-Cola's local parent-company, Minute Maid, employs child labor for low wages in Brazil. What is not assessed, too, is how such multinationals are involved in, say, polluting the very soil they are said to enrich by distributing non-biodegradable and non-recyclable litter, or dumping their excesses in third-world markets to keep prices high, thereby making such items not truly as widely accessible as their spontaneous soil generation would imply.

Another object the visitor sees is a giant United States penny inscribed with the words, "In Soil We Trust." Indeed, the godhead capital lords over nature here. As well, Lincoln's prominent visage at the entrance invokes the authority of the state and American history to suggest an organic connection to capital growth in the former prairie-land of Chicago. More simply, first seeing a series of commodities that come from soil and then seeing money itself in the soil, the visitor is being told outright, "There is big money in the soil." To emphasize that the soil is naturally organized by the laws of capital, in the "Root Room," scientific labels mark uniform units of time along the branch of a tree, becoming farther and farther apart to demonstrate that the branch's rate of growth is accelerating. This celebration of unlimited accumulation and growth makes the project of capital seem driven by a natural propensity towards expansion, rather than, as William Greider (1997, p. 455) points out, towards depletion and non-sustainability: "The nettlesome assertion," he writes, "that governing authorities did not wish to grasp [in 1992] was that rising affluence itself, at least as it was presently defined and achieved, faced finite limits. The global system, as it generated new wealth-producing activity, was hurtling toward a wall, an unidentified point in time when economic expansion would collectively collide with the physical capacity of the ecosystem." In real terms, Monsanto's vision of unrelenting growth and monumentalized consumption can only be sacralized by forgetting the social costs of accelerated production, costs usually not accounted for on balance sheets, such as "deforestation, desertification, urbanization and other activities that, so to speak, paved over the natural world" (Greider, 1997, p. 456). Also rendered invisible are other costs attributed to the impoverishment of the places providing the raw materials, or to their domination by outside powers, like weakened institutions for justice, fiscal austerity, starvation wages, and diminished authority for taxing foreign businesses. Making capital bigger does not necessarily make the world better for most people. Moreover, the exhibit does not allude to the fact that Monsanto's own growth did not happen naturally at all. Rather, it resulted in part from a governmental action responding to pressures from big business interests: the passage of the 1996 Freedom to Farm Act, which was to phase out federal subsidies to farmers and thereby drive small farmers out of business. The legislation, however, did not work to stabilize prices or lessen the surpluses pushing prices up, but rather required an increase in government subsidies to farmers (from $16 billion in 1998 to $32 billion in 1999) as Congress enacted "emergency" relief measures. "Among the consequences," Greider (2000, p. 15) concludes, "the capital-intensive treadmill for farmers sped up, and they became even more eager to embrace whatever innovation promised to boost returns. Just as farm prices were cratering, Monsanto and others began promoting genetically altered seeds for corn and soybeans with cost-cutting promises, and this new technology swept the landscape."

Ideas about bigness and growth presented in the entryway set the standard, throughout the exhibit, for connecting consumption to the expansion of the good life promised by corporate growth. The individual museum-goer is supposed to identify with the bugs and critters and so with corporate greed, wanting to consume enough to fatten corporate bellies. Further down the path of exploration, a section is called, "Recycling Leftovers," where the sign reads: "Partnership or Parasite: Can You Tell Which is Which?" The life-size panorama shows giant worms and bugs feasting on each other in a "feeding frenzy." Across the way stands a vending machine. The first item for selection in this vending machine explains, "millipede: decomposer" while the glass screen displays a package of decaying plants. The vending machine places the viewer into the same position of the feeding critters nearby, proving that nature is but another manifestation of the kind of consumption that vending machines offer when they sell junk food and soda. Critters seem to be selecting their nutrients in the same way that shoppers do, even as some of the selected nutrients cause death and decay to others. Like Amoco, Monsanto is presenting nature as consumer relations under corporate management.

This playful cartoonishness makes violence cute, and even as the bugs chew each other to death, nobody seems to get hurt and everybody seems equally to win organic improvements and benefits. Capital competition appears as a fearless game of destruction through consumption rather than harmful, as it was, for example, to Karen McFarlane and her family in West Anniston:

> [Karen] has PCBs in her body fat. According to tests done by a local doctor, Ryan's blood has nearly triple the level considered "typical" in the United States; for Tiffany, their 6-year-old, it's double. Nathan, 8, has severe developmental problems, and everyone in the family suffers from respiratory problems and the skin rashes associated with PCB exposure. Chris, Karen's 11-year-old son, who's home from school with an upset stomach and is splayed out on the couch, lifts his Panthers basketball T-shirt to reveal brownish-red blotches up the sides of his chest. "It smells like decaying flesh," Ryan warns. "Like it's rotten." (Beiles, 2000, pp. 19–20)

Certainly for the McFarlanes, the soil where they grow their food and feed their livestock is not abundantly offering consumer items like clothes from The Gap, nor giant smiling pennies, nor the healthy promise of penicillin. Instead, the joyful critters happily participating in Anniston's consuming frenzy are increasing the McFarlanes' exposure to deadly PCBs, as the contamination's rate of growth intensifies moving up the food chain.

Not only are the McFarlancs and their neighbors now caught up in a litigation suit that will most likely take years before they see results; indeed it is clear to them that Monsanto would have been more strictly scrutinized by the government if the contamination were happening in a wealthier and whiter area. As it eats away at the shrunken bugs and worms, Monsanto's drive for unlimited growth and profitability appears no longer as a cute and childish game nor an arcade governed by nature and its laws of free competition, but instead as excessive degradation and costs to powerless citizens with the stakes unfairly and quite unnaturally set against them.

In Monsanto's display of nature, natural organisms are not only consumers but also compose the labor force. Certain critters are presented as looking for jobs, displaying their resumes, classifying their skills, like "must work well with others in grazing and/or predatory relationship," "must be energetic and willing to work overtime," or "dis-assembly line worker." In case the point still is not clear, further along there is a tilted tank of soil with water pouring in, demonstrating the way water spreads through the earth. The tank is tagged, "The Trickle-Down Effect." Referencing Reagonomics, conservative pro-corporate economic language seems here to describe relations of nature, showing—as an established fact—how everybody benefits, grows, and nourishes when the top layers get moistened.

As Donna Haraway (1997, pp. 65–66) notes about corporate-motivated representations of biotechnology and genetic fusion more generally, "The latent content is the graphic literalism that biology—life itself—is a capital-accumulation strategy in the simultaneously marvelous and ordinary domain of the New World Order, Inc …. Specifically, natural kind becomes brand or trademark, a sign protecting intellectual property claims in business transactions." As the visitor leaves the exhibit, famous quotes about the earth are painted across the wall facing a kaleidescopic, holographic projection of the world. The globe is constituted by video images of trees and clouds that merge into shots of tilled fields which, in turn, merge into housing developments. Consistent with multiple other displays, the video globe suggests a holistic endless cycle of nature within which the actions of clouds, trees, lightning, corporations, and consumers all play a role as redemptive forces of nature. Directly across from this, the wall declares in bold letters, "Plowed ground smells like earthworms and empires."

CONCLUSION

The domination of nature as a resource by multinational corporations, which the videos depict as benevolent and fun, clears the way for their domination and exploitation of peoples and nations, their violent bids to control third-world labor through militarization, and the wiping out of any local and more equitable terms of production. In other words, what they taught—through school curricula and museum exhibits—about the healthy curiosity of scientists is, in reality, the violence of colonial conquest for capitalist acquisition, or the reduction of all value to money values and the simultaneous decimation of human values. Affirms David Harvey,

> This power asymmetry in social relations [between first and third world nations] ineluctably connects to the inequities in environmental relations in exactly the same way that the project to dominate nature necessarily entailed a project to dominate people. Excessive environmental degradation and costs, for example, can be visited upon the least powerful individuals or even nation states as environmental hazards in the workplace as well as in the community. Ozone concentrations in large cities in the United States affect the poor and "people of color" disproportionately and exposure to toxins in the workplace is class-conditioned. From this arises a conflation of the environmental and the social justice issues. (1996, p. 155)

Indeed, Amoco's treatment of nature models Amoco's treatment of the people who live in the areas surrounding the sites of exploration. The black people of Sweetings Key, Bahamas, do not seem to have gainful employment; like the remipedes, they are sitting around waiting for the white scientists to put them to productive work. As picturesque backdrops, they stand by the boats, seemingly incomprehensive as the scientists explain the uses of the equipment to the video viewers. As they start to trek to the lake, the scientists seem overburdened with large and heavy tools for the dive, and Bill Kurtis explains that they have brought two of every piece of equipment in case of failings. The natives are therefore requisitioned to carry the heavy air tanks and gear on their backs, following the scientists through a wooded field in an image reminiscent of a typical colonial scene like the one Michael Taussig (1987, p. 298) describes of Colombian Indians carrying Spaniards across the Andes: "The normal load for a porter was around 100 pounds, while some were known to have carried 200. Even with these weights they were said to climb the mountains with the greatest of ease and seldom to rest." The relationship between the natives and the scientists in the Amoco video seems cordial but noncommunicative, as they silently do chores to their benefactors' bidding, expressing no will of their own, nor any sense of initiative outside of serving the needs and doing the tasks of the scientists. Though the natives in the Amoco video are indeed laboring, there is no sense here of payment, contracts, organization, conflict, possibilities of worker self-interest or of worker control over work conditions. Instead, the natives are rendered quasi-mechanical, instrumental, objectified, and vitally curious mirrors of scientific wonder, proving that the scientists' curiosity is natural, primitive and raw, the kernel of being human. The black men stare out over the waters, and the camera lingers over their profiled tense faces, creating suspense and worry about the scientists' welfare and safety in the dangerous waters. The bravery of the scientists in the pursuit of knowledge is made starkly visible as the natives sit by the waters' edge, not knowing the treasures of discovery which the white establishment, in its superiority, values so highly.

What is the "iMPACT" of such colonialist portrayals being brought into the Chicago public schools, which are disproportionately black and Hispanic? What are the videos teaching to working-class students about their relationship to the white establishment and to science? The videos all begin with a message from a light-skinned black woman named Paula Banks who is an Amoco Vice President. Banks, surrounded by countless antique and contemporary Amoco red-white-and-blue filling station signs, explains to young viewers that science should be not only educational, but fun and exciting. Distributed to largely non-white students in the Chicago Public Schools, the video suggests that alignment with the power of the corporation to control nature like the white scientists do, comes through a whitening. Aside from providing Amoco with a few solid minutes of advertising the logo, this prelude establishes the oil company as "multicultural" and hence offers promise of potential employment to young non-white viewers. Absent here are the historical facts that domestically, jobs above the level of service station "jockey" were not available to blacks during the time of the antique Amoco signs nor the fact that, globally, the history of oil company exploration and production is the history of white imperialism and enrich-ment and black subjugation and impoverishment. This is, of course, aside from recent lawsuits against oil giants such as Amoco, Texaco, and others for the maintenance of a corporate glass ceiling on promotions and racist harassment on the job and for their envi-ronmental exploitation of jungle lands inhabited by the indigenous people of Ecuador and elsewhere (Press, 1999).

More than this, the presence of a light-skinned black woman enters into a racial spec-trum manifested in the videos that mirrors that of the skin-tone hierarchy of white supremacy. Race ranges from the dark-skinned primitive natives in the Bahamas to the light-skinned black Paula Banks to the white scientific explorers. The racial as representa-tions in the film position blacks as working with nature and as a part of nature and whites as controlling, studying, and manipulating nature. Dark-skinned black Frank Truesdale, a federal forestry worker and not an Amoco employee, the only non-white scientist in the videos, who works on the volcano itself, is shown to be in a romantic relationship with a feminized moody earth. "Frank knows his volcano too well to relax," notes the voice-over. "He's seen all her moods. Serene beauty. Wonder. Anger." Unlike the white scientists,

Truesdale appears to have an intimate relationship with anthropomorphized nature. "It was the beginning of a beautiful friendship," the voice-over narrates the history of Truesdale's career, "Frank and the volcano." This intimacy establishes him as closer to nature, elided with it. Frank is not the one you see operating the high-tech equipment, the machines, the large needles and measuring rods automatically drawing minute seismatic changes on a graph. "These machines," the voice-over explicates, "could hear the volcano's heartbeat." Rather, Truesdale is the one out in the field, discovering and experiencing nature directly with a primitive metal stick that digs up the lava and a barrel of water that cools it for study. Truesdale's work shows him engulfed in nature and so, part of it, distanced from technology, which facelessly watches over him, overseeing his acquisitions and his labors while processing his collections of data reduced to numbers on a chart.

Neoliberalism envisions a world controlled by corporate power where environmental and human rights as well as democracy are marginalized, if not completely annihilated, in the pursuit of power, profit, and growth. How does such a dystopic idea about the future become widely acceptable, even the only possibility imaginable? Currently, schools are often the ideological mechanisms where the values of international capitalist relations are being diffused. As Henry Giroux (2001) notes, "In this scenario, public education is replaced by the call for privately funded educational institutions or for school-business partnerships that can ignore civil rights, exclude students who are class and racially disenfranchised, and blur the lines between religion and state" (pp. 22–23). In other words, students are learning to see their interests coinciding with those of global capital, even and especially in those places where they are fundamentally at odds. Schools need to become, instead, places where students learn to renegotiate their relationships to corporate-sponsored ideologies and to formulate possibilities for oppositional political agency.

As Amoco and other corporate curricula continue to turn schooling into a propaganda tool for their own destructive interests, one solution is clearly to stop using them. Another is to provide teachers with resources for researching the agendas of the corporations that finance and distribute such products in public schools and museums so that the ideological functions of the curricula can be turned against themselves and the corporations' global agendas will be shown as contextualized and centered within the curricula. In this way, students can be shown how their interests and worldviews actually differ from the way their interests and worldviews are constructed in the curricula. However, in the face of, for example, classroom overcrowding, the growing bureaucratization of teacher tasks and paperwork, and the cutting of public supports, equipment, programs, and infrastructures in schools, teachers are still prone and even sometimes compelled to use the preparation short-cuts that corporate curricula offer free of charge. Public actions like the anti-World Trade Organization and anti-World-Bank-and-International Monetary-Fund protests in Seattle and Washington D.C. mainstream information about how corporations are operating against the public interest; these are instrumental in exposing human rights and environmental abuses, the exploitation of cheap labor abroad by destroying environmentally-sustaining and economic infrastructures in already poor nations, and the weakening of democracy on a world-level as capital gains power over civil governing. This type of counter-hegemonic education of the public serves as a counterpoint to the seamlessly happy world ensconced in the pleasures of pure knowledge promised by Amoco and Monsanto and starts on the difficult, up-hill path of demanding that corporations be held responsible for their crimes against nature and humanity. The adoption of global capitalist interests into school curricula cannot be countered simply by teaching students to read critically. Additionally, the school needs to be revitalized as a public power that holds out against private interests. As in South Africa in the 1970s, schools need to therefore be linked to other battlegrounds fighting for democratic values and human liberation as well as to those popular forces now producing counter-scenarios to the lie of disinterested satisfaction in a corporate-controlled public sphere.

NOTES

1. BP Educational Services, <http://www.bpes.com/default.asp.>
2. For example, AOL Time Warner's weekly advertisement for all things corporate, *Time Magazine*, informs readers that they should be principally concerned with Wall Street's profit from privatizing public schools rather than even mentioning the implications for democracy of turning over publicly funded institutions to be exploited by the corporate sector. See John Greenwald, "School for Profit," *Time* (March 20, 2000), 56–57. For an extensive discussion of the dangers to democracy posed by public school privatization see Kenneth J. Saltman, *Collateral Damage: Corporatizing Public Schools—A Threat to Democracy* (Lanham, MD, and Boulder, CO: Rowman & Littlefield. 2000). See also, Henry A. Giroux, *Stealing Innocence: Youth Corporate Power and the Politics of Culture* (New York: St. Martin's Press, 2000) and Alex Molnar, *Giving Kids the Business: The Commercialization of America's School* (Boulder, CO: Westview, 1996).
3. For a brilliant discussion of the political use of childhood innocence, see Henry A. Giroux, *The Mouse that Roared: Disney and the End of Innocence* (Lanham, MD and Boulder, CO: Rowman & Littlefield, 1999).
4. For an excellent analysis of this phenomenon in relation to the broader privatization of the public sector and of mass media, see Robert McChesney, *Rich Media, Poor Democracy* (Urbana, IL: University of Illinois Press, 1999). David Cromwell notes that the oil industry, not merely a few companies, are engaged in funding and distributing pro-oil corporate curriculum ("Oil Propaganda Wars." *Z Magazine*, March 2000, 7–8).
5. This package also includes aid to Kosovo and Peru, condemned by the Clinton administration for its fraudulent presidential elections.
6. For an in-depth history of how U.S. drug eradication efforts in the region have helped to build up South and Central American intelligence operations that have routinely instituted torture and corruption, see Peter Dale Scott and Jonathan Marshall, *Cocaine Politics: Drug, Armies, and the CIA in Central America*, 2nd ed. (Berkeley, Los Angeles, London: University of California Press, 1991, 1998). The authors here cite as an example the Peruvian agency SIN (National Intelligence Service) which was created by the CIA and whose agents were trained by the CIA. SIN was headed by the now-infamous Vladimiro Montesinos who was revealed as the terrorizing spook behind much of the corruption in Alberto Fujimori's regime. Though Montecino's acceptance of bribes became a mark of his immorality in a spectacle circulated in the international press in 2000, prompting Fujimori's resignation by FAX from Japan, the same sort of outrage was never directed towards what Scott and Marshall have documented as Montecino's undisputed ties to the drug cartels in Colombia and other places (x-xi).
7. Not mentioned here is the proportion of now taxable large assets that are associated with the drug trade.
8. "Paul Reyes, commander of the FARC, met with Richard Grasso, chairman of the New York Stock Exchange, who explained to the guerrilla leader how markets worked. As the two figures embraced in this rebel-controlled area demilitarized by the government, Grasso told Reyes that Colombia would benefit from increased global investment and that he hoped that this meeting would mark the beginning of a new relationship between the FARC and the United States" (Peter McLaren, *Che Guevara, Paulo Friere, and the Pedagogy of Revolution* (Lanham, MD and Boulder, CO: Rowman & Littlefield, 2000), 70).

9. This wasn't the first time this particular river was made into a polluted site by oil-related industries. There's a history here. "Virulently antiunion employers, epitomized by Henry Ford, retained their own strikebreaking 'security forces.'" During the Communist-led Ford Hunger March of unemployed workers in March 1932, Ford's men shot to death four workers at the gates of the huge River Rouge complex. After more than seventy thousand sympathizers attended the funeral march, Ford and other employers responded by purging and blacklisting thousands of suspected radicals from their plants." (William M. Adler. *Molly's Job: A Story of Life and Work on the Global Assembly Line* (New York: Scribner, 2000), 104–105).

10. Martin S. Fridson, *How to be a Billionaire: Proven Strategies from the Titans of Wealth* (New York: John Wiley & Sons, 2000), 148–50. "Subpoenas and fines for harassment of competitors and price-fixing dogged Waste Management during its spectacular growth period… [R]egulators and prosecutors relentlessly investigated Waste Management, inspired by previous revelations of organized crime's control of commercial waste hauling in southern New York and northern New Jersey…. Not only his business strategies, but also his financial practices generated criticism. Observers objected to the prices he paid in certain acquisitions, arguing that they exceeded industry norms…Huizenga also had to endure the accusation that the companies he created through consolidation fared poorly after he left the scene…. Finally, critics lambasted Huizenga's practice of acquiring businesses for stock," etc.

11. Noam Chomsky in *Breaking Free: The Transformative Power of Critical Pedagogy*, Pepi Leistyna and Stephen Sherblom, Eds. *Harvard Educational Review*, 1996, 111.

12. Amoco is hardly the first corporation to appropriate progressive methodology in a way that jettisons critical social transformation as an underlying ideal. Disney's Celebration, Florida schools exemplify this corruption: see Henry A. Giroux, *The Mouse That Roared* (Lanham, MD and Boulder, CO: Rowman & Littlefield, 1999). As Donald Lazere has argued, "[M]any…Freireans…have failed to perceive that the political right has coopted their ideas to depict its own social camp, even in its most powerful, privileged, and prejudiced sectors, as meriting the same level of pluralistic encouragement of self-esteem and expression of feelings accorded the least privileged groups. Some such students expect teachers to make them feel good about being bigots, like Rush Limbaugh does—and some teachers… gladly comply" (Donald Lazere. "Spellmeyer's Naive Populism," *CCC 48* (May 1997: 291)).

13. Monsanto is the main sponsor of this exhibit. Other sponsors include ConAgra, National Science Foundation, The Fort James Foundation, Chicago Park District, Abbott Laboratories, Pfizer Foundation, Prince Charitable Trusts, Service/Master Company, Marion S. Searle/Searle Family Trust, and the Chicago Board of Trade Foundation.

14. "'PCB is a persistent chemical which builds up in the environment. It, therefore, should not be allowed to escape…' —Monsanto, 1972" (Beiles, 2000, p. 19).

REFERENCES

Atwell, Nancie. 1998. *In the Middle: New Understandings About Writing, Reading, and Learning.* Portsmouth, NH: Heinemann.

Beiles, Nancy. 2000. "What Monsanto Knew." *The Nation* (20 May): 18–22.

Cooper, Mark. 2001. "Plan Colombia: Wrong Issue, Wrong Enemy, Wrong Country." *The Nation* (19 March): 14.

Cromwell, David. 2000. "Oil Propaganda Wars." *Z-Magazine:* 8.

Delacourte, Justin. 2001. "Human Rights and Military Aid for Colombia: With "Friends" Like the Senate Democrats, Who Needs Enemies?" *Z-Net.* Available: www.lbbs.org/ZNETTOPnoanimation.html

Friedman, Thomas. 1999. *The Lexus and the Olive Tree.* New York: Farrar Strauss Giroux.

Friere, Paulo. 1970/1993. *Pedagogy of the Oppressed,* trans. M Bergman Ramos. New York: Continuum.

Giroux, Henry. 2001. *Public Spaces, Private Lives: Beyond the Culture of Cynicism.* Lanham: Roman & Littlefield.

Grieder, William. 1997. *One World, Ready or Not: The Manic Logic of Global Capitalism,* New York: Touchstone.

Grieder, William. 2000. "The Last Farm Crisis." *The Nation* (20 November): 15.

Haraway, Donna J. 1997. *Modest Witness@Second Millenium.FemaleMan Meets OncoMouse: Feminism and Technoscience.* New York and London: Routledge.

Harvey, David. 1996. *Justice, Nature and the Geography of Difference.* Maiden, MA and Oxford, UK: Blackwell.

Herman, Edward, and Cecilia Zarate-Laun. 1999. "Globalization and Instability: The Case of Colombia." *Z-Net.* Available: www.Ibbs.org/ZNETPOP noanimation.html

Molnar, Alex. 1996. *Giving Kids the Business: The Commercialization of America's School.* Boulder, CO: Westview.

Pardo, Steve. 1999. "River Rouge Fears Explosion: City Sues BP/Amoco in Effort to Clean Up Sewers and Avoid Repeat of 1988 Blast." *The Detroit News* (30 November): D3.

Press, Eyal. 1999. "Texaco on Trial." *The Nation* (31 May): 11–16.

Ries, Al, and Laura Ries. 1999. *The 22 Immutable Laws of Branding.* New York: HarperBusiness.

Robbins, Carla Anne. 2000. "How Bogota Wooed Washington to Open New War on Cocaine." *The Wall Street Journal* (23 June): A12.

Ross, Andrew. 2000. "The Mental Labor Problem." *Social Text 63* (Summer): 1–31.

Taussig, Michael. 1987. *Shamanism, Colonialism and the Wild Man: A Study in Terror and Healing.* Chicago and London: University of Chicago Press.

Zarate-Laun, Cecilia. 1999. "Crossroads of War and Biodiversity: CIA, Cocaine, and Death Squads" (with the Eco-Solidarity Working Group). *Covert Action Quarterly* (Fall-Winter): 16–17.

Zarate-Laun, Cecilia. 2001. "Introduction to the Putumayo: The U.S.-Assisted War in Colombia." *Z-Net* (February). Available: www.lbbs.org/Zmag/articles/ feb011aun.htm

15

From *Pedagogy of the Oppressed*

PAULO FREIRE

A CAREFUL ANALYSIS of the teacher-student relationship at any level, inside or outside the school, reveals its fundamentally *narrative* character. This relationship involves a narrating Subject (the teacher) and patient, listening objects (the students). The contents, whether values or empirical dimensions of reality, tend in the process of being narrated to become lifeless and petrified. Education is suffering from narration sickness.

The teacher talks about reality as if it were motionless, static, compartmentalized, and predictable. Or else he expounds on a topic completely alien to the existential experience of the students. His task is to "fill" the students with the contents of his narration—contents which are detached from reality, disconnected from the totality that engendered them and could give them significance. Words are emptied of their concreteness and become a hollow, alienated, and alienating verbosity.

The outstanding characteristic of this narrative education, then, is the sonority of words, not their transforming power. "Four times four is sixteen; the capital of Pará is Belém." The student records, memorizes, and repeats these phrases without perceiving what four times four really means, or realizing the true significance of "capital" in the affirmation "the capital of Pará is Belém," that is, what Belém means for Pará" and what Pará means for Brazil.

Narration (with the teacher as narrator) leads the students to memorize mechanically the narrated content. Worse yet, it turns them into "containers," into "receptacles" to be "filled" by the teacher. The more completely she fills the receptacles, the better a teacher she is. The more meekly the receptacles permit themselves to be filled, the better students they are.

Education thus becomes an act of depositing, in which the students are the depositories and the teacher is the depositor. Instead of communicating, the teacher issues communiqués and makes deposits which the students patiently receive, memorize, and repeat. This is the "banking" concept of education, in which the scope of action allowed to the students extends only as far as receiving, filing, and storing the deposits. They do, it is true, have the opportunity to become collectors or cataloguers of the things they store. But in the last analysis, it is the people themselves who are filed away through the lack of creativity, transformation, and knowledge in this (at best) misguided system. For apart from inquiry, apart from the praxis, individuals cannot be truly human. Knowledge emerges only through invention and re-invention, through the restless, impatient, continuing, hopeful inquiry human beings pursue in the world, with the world, and with each other.

In the banking concept of education, knowledge is a gift bestowed by those who consider themselves knowledgeable upon those whom they consider to know nothing. Projecting an absolute ignorance onto others, a characteristic of the ideology of oppression, negates education and knowledge as processes of inquiry. The teacher presents himself to his students as their necessary opposite; by considering their ignorance absolute, he justifies his own existence. The students, alienated like the slave in the Hegelian dialectic, accept their ignorance as justifying the teacher's existence—but, unlike the slave, they never discover that they educate the teacher.

The *raison d'être* of libertarian education, on the other hand, lies in its drive towards reconciliation. Education must begin with the solution of the teacher-student contradiction, by reconciling the poles of the contradiction so that both are simultaneously teachers *and* students.

This solution is not (nor can it be) found in the banking concept. On the contrary, banking education maintains and even stimulates the contradiction through the following attitudes and practices, which mirror oppressive society as a whole:

(a) the teacher teaches and the students are taught;
(b) the teacher knows everything and the students know nothing;
(c) the teacher thinks and the students are thought about;
(d) the teacher talks and the students listen—meekly;
(e) the teacher disciplines and the students are disciplined;
(f) the teacher chooses and enforces his choice, and the students comply;
(g) the teacher acts and the students have the illusion of acting through the action of the teacher;
(h) the teacher chooses the program content, and the students (who were not consulted) adapt to it;
(i) the teacher confuses the authority of knowledge with his or her own professional authority, which she and he sets in opposition to the freedom of the students;
(j) the teacher is the Subject of the learning process, while the pupils are mere objects.

It is not surprising that the banking concept of education regards men as adaptable, manageable beings. The more students work at storing the deposits entrusted to them, the less they develop the critical consciousness which would result from their intervention in the world as transformers of that world. The more completely they accept the passive role imposed on them, the more they tend simply to adapt to the world as it is and to the fragmented view of reality deposited in them.

The capability of banking education to minimize or annul the students' creative power and to stimulate their credulity serves the interests of the oppressors, who care neither to have the world revealed nor to see it transformed. The oppressors use their "humanitarianism" to preserve a profitable situation. Thus they react almost instinctively against any experiment in education which stimulates the critical faculties and is not content with a partial view of reality but always seeks out the ties which link one point to another and one problem to another.

Indeed, the interests of the oppressors lie in "changing the consciousness of the oppressed, not the situation which oppresses them";[1] for the more the oppressed can be led to adapt to that situation, the more easily they can be dominated. To achieve this end, the oppressors use the banking concept of education in conjunction with a paternalistic social action apparatus, within which the oppressed receive the euphemistic title of "welfare recipients." They are treated as individual cases, as marginal persons who deviate from the general configuration of a "good, organized, and just" society. The oppressed are regarded as the pathology of the healthy society, which must therefore adjust these "incompetent and lazy" folk to its own patterns by changing their mentality. These marginals need to be "integrated," "incorporated" into the healthy society that they have "forsaken."

The truth is, however, that the oppressed are not "marginals," are not people living "outside" society. They have always been "inside"—inside the structure which made them "beings for others." The solution is not to "integrate" them into the structure of oppression, but to transform that structure so that they can become "beings for themselves." Such transformation, of course, would undermine the oppressors' purposes; hence their utilization of the banking concept of education to avoid the threat of student *conscientização*.

The banking approach to adult education, for example, will never propose to students that they critically consider reality. It will deal instead with such vital questions as whether Roger gave green grass to the goat, and insist upon the importance of learning that, on the contrary, Roger gave green grass to the rabbit. The "humanism" of the banking approach masks the effort to turn women and men into automatons—the very negation of their ontological vocation to be more fully human.

Those who use the banking approach, knowingly or unknowingly (for there are innumerable well-intentioned bank-clerk teachers who do not realize that they are serving only to dehumanize), fail to perceive that the deposits themselves contain contradictions about reality. But, sooner or later, these contradictions may lead formerly passive students to turn against their domestication and the attempt to domesticate reality. They may discover through existential experience that their present way of life is irreconcilable with their vocation to become fully human. They may perceive through their relations with reality that reality is really a *process*, undergoing constant transformation. If men and women are searchers and their ontological vocation is humanization, sooner or later they may perceive the contradiction in which banking education seeks to maintain them, and then engage themselves in the struggle for their liberation.

But the humanist, revolutionary educator cannot wait for this possibility to materialize. From the outset, her efforts must coincide with those of the students to engage in critical thinking and the quest for mutual humanization. His efforts must be imbued with a profound trust in people and their creative power. To achieve this, they must be partners of the students in their relations with them.

The banking concept does not admit to such partnership—and necessarily so. To resolve the teacher-student contradiction, to exchange the role of depositor, prescriber, domesticator, for the role of student among students would be to undermine the power of oppression and serve the cause of liberation.

Implicit in the banking concept is the assumption of a dichotomy between human beings and the world: a person is merely *in* the world, not *with* the world or with others;

the individual is spectator, not re-creator. In this view, the person is not a conscious being (*corpo consciente*); he or she is rather the possessor of *a* consciousness: an empty "mind" passively open to the reception of deposits of reality from the world outside. For example, my desk, my books, my coffee cup, all the objects before me—as bits of the world which surround me—would be "inside" me, exactly as I am inside my study right now. This view makes no distinction between being accessible to consciousness and entering consciousness. The distinction, however, is essential: the objects which surround me are simply accessible to my consciousness, not located within it. I am aware of them, but they are not inside me.

It follows logically from the banking notion of consciousness that the educator's role is to regulate the way the world "enters into" the students. The teacher's task is to organize a process which already occurs spontaneously, to "fill" the students by making deposits of information which he or she considers to constitute true knowledge.[2] And since people "receive" the world as passive entities, education should make them more passive still, and adapt them to the world. The educated individual is the adapted person, because she or he is better "fit" for the world. Translated into practice, this concept is well suited to the purposes of the oppressors, whose tranquility rests on how well people fit the world the oppressors have created, and how little they question it.

The more completely the majority adapt to the purposes which the dominant minority prescribe for them (thereby depriving them of the right to their own purposes), the more easily the minority can continue to prescribe. The theory and practice of banking education serve this end quite efficiently. Verbalistic lessons, reading requirements,[3] the methods for evaluating "knowledge," the distance between the teacher and the taught, the criteria for promotion: everything in this ready-to-wear approach serves to obviate thinking.

The bank-clerk educator does not realize that there is no true security in his hypertrophied role, that one must seek to live *with* others in solidarity. One cannot impose oneself, nor even merely co-exist with one's students. Solidarity requires true communication, and the concept by which such an educator is guided fears and proscribes communication.

Yet only through communication can human life hold meaning. The teacher's thinking is authenticated only by the authenticity of the students' thinking. The teacher cannot think for her students, nor can she impose her thought on them. Authentic thinking, thinking that is concerned about *reality*, does not take place in ivory tower isolation, but only in communication. If it is true that thought has meaning only when generated by action upon the world, the subordination of students to teachers becomes impossible.

Because banking education begins with a false understanding of men and women as objects, it cannot promote the development of what Fromm calls "biophily," but instead produces its opposite: "necrophily."

> While life is characterized by growth in a structured, functional manner, the necrophilous person loves all that does not grow, all that is mechanical. The necrophilous person is driven by the desire to transform the organic into the inorganic, to approach life mechanically, as if all living persons were things.... Memory, rather than experience; having, rather than being, is what counts: The necrophilous person can relate to an object—a flower or a person—only if he possesses it; hence a threat to his possession is a threat to himself; if he loses possession he loses contact with the world.... He loves control, and in the act of controlling he kills life.[4]

Oppression—overwhelming control—is necrophilic; it is nourished by love of death, not life. The banking concept of education, which serves the interests of oppression, is also necrophilic. Based on a mechanistic, static, naturalistic, spatialized view of consciousness, it transforms students into receiving objects. It attempts to control thinking and action, leads women and men to adjust to the world, and inhibits their creative power.

When their efforts to act responsibly are frustrated, when they find themselves unable to use their faculties, people suffer. "This suffering due to impotence is rooted in the very fact that the human equilibrium has been disturbed."[5] But the inability to act which causes people's anguish also causes them to reject their impotence, by attempting

> ...to restore [their] capacity to act. But can [they], and how? One way is to submit to and identify with a person or group having power. By this symbolic participation in another person's life, [men have] the illusion of acting, when in reality [they] only submit to and become a part of those who act.[6]

Populist manifestations perhaps best exemplify this type of behavior by the oppressed, who, by identifying with charismatic leaders, come to feel that they themselves are active and effective. The rebellion they express as they emerge in the historical process is motivated by that desire to act effectively. The dominant elites consider the remedy to be more domination and repression, carried out in the name of freedom, order, and social peace (that is, the peace of the elites). Thus they can condemn—logically, from their point of view—"the violence of a strike by workers and [can] call upon the state in the same breath to use violence in putting down the strike."[7]

Education as the exercise of domination stimulates the credulity of students, with the ideological intent (often not perceived by educators) of indoctrinating them to adapt to the world of oppression. This accusation is not made in the naïve hope that the dominant elites will thereby simply abandon the practice. Its objective is to call the attention of true humanists to the fact that they cannot use banking educational methods in the pursuit of liberation, for they would only negate that very pursuit. Nor may a revolutionary society inherit these methods from an oppressor society. The revolutionary society which practices banking education is either misguided or mistrusting of people. In either event, it is threatened by the specter of reaction.

Unfortunately, those who espouse the cause of liberation are themselves surrounded and influenced by the climate which generates the banking concept, and often do not perceive its true significance or its dehumanizing power. Paradoxically, then, they utilize this same instrument of alienation in what they consider an effort to liberate. Indeed, some "revolutionaries" brand as "innocents," "dreamers," or even "reactionaries" those who would challenge this educational practice. But one does not liberate people by alienating them. Authentic liberation—the process of humanization—is not another deposit to be made in men. Liberation is a praxis: the action and reflection of men and women upon their world in order to transform it. Those truly committed to the cause of liberation can accept neither the mechanistic concept of consciousness as an empty vessel to be filled, nor the use of banking methods of domination (propaganda, slogans—deposits) in the name of liberation.

Those truly committed to liberation must reject the banking concept in its entirety, adopting instead a concept of women and men as conscious beings, and consciousness as consciousness intent upon the world. They must abandon the educational goal of deposit-making and replace it with the posing of the problems of human beings in their relations with the world. "Problem-posing" education, responding to the essence of consciousness—*intentionality*—rejects communiqués and embodies communication. It epitomizes the special characteristic of consciousness: being *conscious of,* not only as intent on objects but as turned in upon itself in a Jasperian "split"—consciousness as consciousness *of* consciousness.

Liberating education consists in acts of cognition, not transferrals of information. It is a learning situation in which the cognizable object (far from being the end of the cognitive act) intermediates the cognitive actors—teacher on the one hand and students on the other. Accordingly, the practice of problem-posing education entails at the outset that the teacher-student contradiction to be resolved. Dialogical relations—indispensable to the capacity of cognitive actors to cooperate in perceiving the same cognizable object—are otherwise impossible.

Indeed, problem-posing education, which breaks with the vertical patterns characteristic of banking education, can fulfill its function as the practice of freedom only if it can overcome the above contradiction. Through dialogue, the teacher-of-the-students and the students-of-the-teacher cease to exist and a new term emerges: teacher-student with students-teachers. The teacher is no longer merely the-one-who-teaches, but one who is himself taught in dialogue with the students, who in turn while being taught also teach. They become jointly responsible for a process in which all grow. In this process, arguments based on "authority" are no longer valid; in order to function, authority must be *on the side of* freedom, not *against* it. Here, no one teaches another, nor is anyone self-taught. People teach each other, mediated by the world, by the cognizable objects which in banking education are "owned" by the teacher.

The banking concept (with its tendency to dichotomize everything) distinguishes two stages in the action of the educator. During the first, he cognizes a cognizable object while he prepares his lessons in his study or his laboratory; during the second, he expounds to his students about that object. The students are not called upon to know, but to memorize the contents narrated by the teacher. Nor do the students practice any act of cognition, since the object towards which that act should be directed is the property of the teacher rather than a medium evoking the critical reflection of both teacher and students. Hence in the name of the "preservation of culture and knowledge" we have a system which achieves neither true knowledge nor true culture.

The problem-posing method does not dichotomize the activity of the teacher-student: she is not "cognitive" at one point and "narrative" at another. She is always "cognitive," whether preparing a project or engaging in dialogue with the students. He does not regard cognizable objects as his private property, but as the object of reflection by himself and the students. In this way, the problem-posing educator constantly re-forms his reflections in the reflection of the students. The students—no longer docile listeners—are now critical co-investigators in dialogue with the teacher. The teacher presents the material to the students for their consideration, and re-considers her earlier considerations as the students express their own. The role of the problem-posing educator is to create, together with the students, the conditions under which knowledge at the level of the *doxa* is superseded by true knowledge, at the level of the *logos*.

Whereas banking education anesthetizes and inhibits creative power, problem-posing education involves a constant unveiling of reality. The former attempts to maintain the *submersion* of consciousness; the latter strives for the *emergence* of consciousness and *critical intervention* in reality.

Students, as they are increasingly posed with problems relating to themselves in the world and with the world, will feel increasingly challenged and obliged to respond to that challenge. Because they apprehend the challenge as interrelated to other problems within a total context, not as a theoretical question, the resulting comprehension tends to be increasingly critical and thus constantly less alienated. Their response to the challenge evokes new challenges, followed by new understandings; and gradually the students come to regard themselves as committed.

Education as the practice of freedom—as opposed to education as the practice of domination—denies that man is abstract, isolated, independent, and unattached to the world; it also denies that the world exists as a reality apart from people. Authentic reflection considers neither abstract man nor the world without people, but people in their relations with the world. In these relations consciousness and world are simultaneous: consciousness neither precedes the world nor follows it.

> La conscience et le monde sont dormés d'un même coup: extérieur par essence à la conscience, le monde est, par essence relatif à elle.[8]

In one of our culture circles in Chile, the group was discussing (based on a codification[9]) the anthropological concept of culture. In the midst of the discussion, a peasant who by banking standards was completely ignorant said: "Now I see that without man there is no world." When the educator responded: "Let's say, for the sake of argument, that all the men on earth were to die, but that the earth itself remained, together with trees, birds, animals, rivers, seas, the stars …wouldn't all this be a world?" "Oh no," the peasant replied emphatically. "There would be no one to say: 'This is a world'."

The peasant wished to express the idea that there would be lacking the consciousness of the world which necessarily implies the world of consciousness. *I* cannot exist without a *non-I*. In turn, the *not-I* depends on that existence. The world which brings consciousness into existence becomes the world *of* that consciousness. Hence, the previously cited affirmation of Sartre: "*La conscience et le monde sont dormés d'un même coup.*"

As women and men, simultaneously reflecting on themselves and on the world, increase the scope of their perception, they begin to direct their observations towards previously inconspicuous phenomena:

> In perception properly so-called, as an explicit awareness [*Gewahren*], I am turned towards the object, to the paper, for instance. I apprehend it as being this here and now. The apprehension is a singling out, every object having a background in experience. Around and about the paper lie books, pencils, inkwell, and so forth, and these in a certain sense are also "perceived", perceptually there, in the "field of intuition"; but whilst I was turned towards the paper there was no turning in their direction, nor any apprehending of them, not even in a secondary sense. They appeared and yet were not singled out, were not posited on their own account. Every perception of a thing has such a zone of background intuitions or background awareness, if "intuiting" already includes the state of being turned towards, and this also is a

"conscious experience", or more briefly a "consciousness of" all indeed that in point of fact lies in the co-perceived objective background.[10]

That which had existed objectively but had not been perceived in its deeper implications (if indeed it was perceived at all) begins to "stand out," assuming the character of a problem and therefore of challenge. Thus, men and women begin to single out elements from their "background awareness" and to reflect upon them. These elements are now objects of their consideration, and, as such, objects of their action and cognition.

In problem-posing education, people develop their power to perceive critically *the way they exist* in the world *with which* and *in which* they find themselves; they come to see the world not as a static reality, but as a reality in process, in transformation. Although the dialectical relations of women and men with the world exist independently of how these relations are perceived (or whether or not they are perceived at all), it is also true that the form of action they adopt is to a large extent a function of how they perceive themselves in the world. Hence, the teacher-student and the students-teachers reflect simultaneously on themselves and the world without dichotomizing this reflection from action, and thus establish an authentic form of thought and action.

Once again, the two educational concepts and practices under analysis come into conflict. Banking education (for obvious reasons) attempts, by mythicizing reality, to conceal certain facts which explain the way human beings exist in the world; problem-posing education sets itself the task of demythologizing. Banking education resists dialogue; problem-posing education regards dialogue as indispensable to the act of cognition which unveils reality. Banking education treats students as objects of assistance; problem-posing education makes them critical thinkers. Banking education inhibits creativity and domesticates (although it cannot completely destroy) the *intentionality* of consciousness by isolating consciousness from the world, thereby denying people their ontological and historical vocation of becoming more fully human. Problem-posing education bases itself on creativity and stimulates true reflection and action upon reality, thereby responding to the vocation of persons as beings who are authentic only when engaged in inquiry and creative transformation. In sum: banking theory and practice, as immobilizing and fixation forces, fail to acknowledge men and women as historical beings; problem-posing theory and practice take the people's historicity as their starting point.

Problem-posing education affirms men and women as beings in the process of *becoming* —as unfinished, uncompleted beings in and with a likewise unfinished reality. Indeed, in contrast to other animals who are unfinished, but not historical, people know themselves to be unfinished; they are aware of their incompletion. In this incompletion and this awareness lie the very roots of education as an exclusively human manifestation. The unfinished character of human beings and the transformational character of reality necessitate that education be an ongoing activity.

Education is thus constantly remade in the praxis. In order to *be*, it must *become*. Its "duration" (in the Bergsonian meaning of the word) is found in the interplay of the opposites *permanence* and *change*. The banking method emphasizes permanence and becomes reactionary; problem-posing education—which accepts neither a "well-behaved" present nor a predetermined future—roots itself in the dynamic present and becomes revolutionary.

Problem-posing education is revolutionary futurity. Hence it is prophetic (and, as such, hopeful). Hence, it corresponds to the historical nature of humankind. Hence, it affirms women and men as beings who transcend themselves, who move forward and look ahead, for whom immobility represents a fatal threat, for whom looking at the past must only be a means of understanding more clearly what and who they are so that they can more wisely build the future. Hence, it identifies with the movement which engages people as beings aware of their incompletion—an historical movement which has its point of departure, its Subjects and its objective.

The point of departure of the movement lies in the people themselves. But since people do not exist apart from the world, apart from reality, the movement must begin with the human-world relationship. Accordingly, the point of departure must always be with men and women in the "here and now," which constitutes the situation within which they are submerged, from which they emerge, and in which they intervene. Only by starting from this situation—which determines their perception of it—can they begin to move. To do this authentically they must perceive their state not as fated and unalterable, but merely as limiting—and therefore challenging.

Whereas the banking method directly or indirectly reinforces men's fatalistic perception of their situation, the problem-posing method presents this very situation to them as a problem. As the situation becomes the object of their cognition, the naïve or magical perception which produced their fatalism gives way to perception which is able to perceive itself even as it perceives reality, and can thus be critically objective about that reality.

A deepened consciousness of their situation leads people to apprehend that situation as an historical reality susceptible of transformation. Resignation gives way to the drive for transformation and inquiry, over which men feel themselves to be in control. If people, as historical beings necessarily engaged with other people in a movement of inquiry, did not control that movement, it would be (and is) a violation of their humanity. Any situation in which some individuals prevent others from engaging in the process of inquiry is one of violence. The means used are not important; to alienate human beings from their own decision-making is to change them into objects.

This movement of inquiry must be directed towards humanization—the people's historical vocation. The pursuit of full humanity, however, cannot be carried out in isolation or individualism, but only in fellowship and solidarity; therefore it cannot unfold in the antagonistic relations between oppressors and oppressed. No one can be authentically human while he prevents others from being so. Attempting *to be more* human, individualistically, leads to *having more*, egotistically, a form of dehumanization. Not that it is not fundamental *to have* in order *to be* human. Precisely because it *is* necessary, some men's *having* must not be allowed to constitute an obstacle to others' *having*, must not consolidate the power of the former to crush the latter.

Problem-posing education, as a humanist and liberating praxis, posits as fundamental that the people subjected to domination must fight for their emancipation. To that end, it enables teachers and students to become Subjects of the educational process by overcoming authoritarianism and an alienating intellectualism; it also enables people to overcome their false perception of reality. The world—no longer something to be described with deceptive words—becomes the object of that transforming action by men and women which results in their humanization.

Problem-posing education does not and cannot serve the interests of the oppressor. No oppressive order could permit the oppressed to begin to question: Why? While only a revolutionary society can carry out this education in systematic terms, the revolutionary leaders need not take full power before they can employ the method. In the revolutionary process, the leaders cannot utilize the banking method as an interim measure, justified on grounds of expediency, with the intention of *later* behaving in a genuinely revolutionary fashion. They must be revolutionary—that is to say, dialogical—from the outset.

NOTES

1. Simone de Beauvoir, *La Pensée de Drotte, Aujord'hui* (Paris); ST, *El Pensamiento politico de la Derecha* (Buenos Aires, 1963), p. 34.
2. This concept corresponds to what Sartre calls the "digestive" or "nutritive" concept of education, in which knowledge is "fed" by the teacher to the students to "fill them out." See Jean-Paul Sartre, "Une idée fundamentale de la phénomeno-logie de Husserl: L'intentionauté," *Situations I* (Paris, 1947).
3. For example, some professors specify in their reading lists that a book should be read from pages 10 to 15—and do this to "help" their students!
4. E. Fromm, *The Heart of Man: Its Genius for Good and Evil* (New York, 1964), p. 41.
5. *Ibid.*, p. 31.
6. *Ibid.*
7. Reinhold Niebuhr, *Moral Man and Immoral Society* (New York, 1960), p. 130.
8. Sartre, *op. cit.*, p. 32.
9. See chapter 3.—Translator's note.
10. Edmund Husserl, *Ideas—General Introduction to Pure Phenomenology* (London, 1969), pp. 105–106.

Suggested Readings
for Further Study

Apple, M. (2001). *Educating the "Right" way: Markets, standards, God and inequality.* New York: RoutledgeFalmer.

Beane, J. (1999). Middle schools under siege: Points of attack, *Middle School Journal, 30*(4), 3–9.

Beane, J. (1999). Middle schools under siege: Responding to the attack, *Middle School Journal* 30(4), 3–6.

Carnegie Foundation Task Force on Education on Economic Growth (1983). *Action for excellence.* Denver: Education Commission of the States.

Chomsky, N. (2002). The function of schools, In Mitchell, P., & Schoeffel, J. (Eds.) *Understanding power: The indispensable Chomsky* (pp. 233–248). New York: The New Press.

Chomsky, N. (2003). Prospects on democracy, In Otero, C. P. (Ed.) *Chomsky on democracy and education* (pp. 236–261). New York: RoutledgeFalmer.

Clark, S., & Clark, D. (1994). *Restructuring the middle level school.* Albany, NY: State University of New York.

Cuban, L. (1992). What happens to reforms that last? The case of the junior high school. *American Educational Research Journal, 29*(2), 227–251.

Dickinson, T. (Ed.) (2001). *Reinventing the middle school.* New York: RoutledgeFalmer.

Felner, R., Jackson, A., Kasak, D., Mulhall, P., Brand, S., & Flowers, N. (1997). The impact of school reform for the middle years, *Phi Delta Kappan, 78*(7), 528–532, 541–550.

Freire, P. (1994). *Pedagogy of hope: Reliving pedagogy of the oppressed.* New York: Continuum International Publishing Group.

Freire, P. (2000). *Pedagogy of freedom: Ethics, democracy, and civic courage.* Lanham, MA: Rowman & Littlefield.

Gay, G. (1994). Coming of age ethnically: Teaching young adolescents of color, *Theory Into Practice, 33*(3), 149–155.

George, P. S., Alexander, W. M., & Bushnell, D. (1998). *Handbook for middle school teaching* (2nd ed.). New York: Longman.

Giroux, H. (1983). *Theory and resistance in education.* Westport, CT: Bergin & Garvey.

Gould, S. (1981/1996). On eugenics, testing, and IQ. In *The mismeasure of man* (pp. 367–390). New York: W.W. Norton.

Kasak, D. (1998). Flexible organizational structures. This we believe … and now we must act, *Middle School Journal, 29*(5), 56–59.

Kozol, J. (1992). *Savage Inequalities.* New York: Harper Perennial.

Lipman, P. (2004). *High stakes education: Inequality, globalization, and urban school reform.* New York: RoutledgeFalmer.

Lipsitz, J., Mizzel, M., Jackson, A. W., and Austin, L. (1997). Speaking with one voice, *Phi Delta Kappan, 78*(7), 533–540.

Lounsbury, J. (1996). Key characteristics of middle level schools, *ERIC,* pp. 1–3; (2000). The middle school movement: "A charge to keep," *ERIC,* pp. 1–2.

Lounsbury, J. (1996). Personalizing the high schools: Lessons learned in the middle, *NASSP Bulletin,* pp. 1–5.

National Middle School Association. (2003). *This we believe: Successful schools for young adolescents.* Westerville, OH: National Middle School Association.

NMSA Research Committee (2003). *Research and resources in support of 'This We Believe.'* Westerville, OH: National Middle School Association.

Saltman, K. (2000). *Collateral damage: Corporatizing public schools: A threat to democracy.* Lanham, MA: Rowman & Littlefield.

Saltman, K., & Gabbard, D. (2003). *Education as enforcement: The militarization and corporatization of schools.* New York: RoutledgeFalmer.

Scales, P. (2003). *Other people's kids: Social expectations and American adults' involvement with children and adolescents.* New York: Kluwer Academic.

Slattery, P. (1999). The excluded middle: Postmodern conceptions of the middle school. In Walley, C., & Gerrick, W. (Eds.). *Affirming middle grades education.* Boston, MA: Allyn & Bacon.

Spring, J. (1972). *Education and the rise of the corporate state.* Boston, MA: Beacon Press.

Spring, J. (1998). *Education and the rise of the global economy.* Mahwah, NJ: Lawrence Erlbaum Associates.

III

THE CONSTRUCTION OF IDENTITY

Kenneth J. Saltman

The term identity refers ... to ... a *subjective sense of an invigorating sameness* and *continuity* ... located *in the core of the individual* and yet also *in the core of his communal culture.* (Erikson, 1968, pp. 19, 22)

   The concept of identity ... is therefore not an essentialist, but a strategic and positional one ... this concept of identity does *not* signal that stable core of the self, unfolding from beginning to end through all the vicissitudes of history without change.... Identities are about questions of using the resources of history, language, and culture in the process of becoming rather than being: not "who we are" or "where we came from," so much as what we might become, how we have been represented and how that bears on how we might represent ourselves.... Identities are constructed within, not outside, discourse ... produced in specific historical and institutional sites within specific discursive formations and practices.... Identities are constructed through, not outside, difference ... this entails the radically disturbing recognition that it is only through the relation to the Other, the relation to what it is not, to precisely what it lacks, to what has been called its *constitutive outside* that the "positive" meaning of any term—this its "identity"—can be constructed. (Hall, 1996, pp. 3–4)

What is identity and what is its relevance for early adolescence? Erik Erikson gave new meaning to the concept of identity as reflected in the quote above. In his psychosocial theory of human development, he presents identity versus identity confusion as the normative social crisis that characterizes adolescence as a distinctive period in the lifespan (1968). It is through his work that identity formation has been deemed the pivotal developmental task for adolescents, as they traverse the path from childhood to adulthood. As such, it is a primary focus of attention in middle level theory and practice, directed toward that goal of supporting youth in forming a healthy identity. In contrast, Stuart Hall's quote presents a decisively critical perspective on identity that is grounded in cultural studies. He discusses the construction of social identities as a dynamic, ever-changing discursive, representational process through which differential self-other meanings are mutually forged, contested, and altered throughout historical time. Erikson's and Hall's views foreground the chapters in this section that reflect different theoretical perspectives on the psychic and social origins of identity, and consider the implications of these views for social life.

Although Stuart Hall's critical perspective embeds the meaning-making process of identity construction in the cultural practices and dynamics of social life, and Erikson's theory is based on the premise that identity is both a social and psychological construction, the prevailing view in traditional circles is that identity is an individual, internal endeavor for youth, facilitated by well-meaning parents, teachers, and other adults.

Early writings on adolescence, such as G. Stanley Hall's, suggested that this developmental period was defined by a crisis of individual development informed by a social crisis, the advent of industrialization. For Hall, the advent of modern industrial society threatened the nervous energy of youth thereby imperiling the development of the human race. Although Hall's thought was grounded in racism, sexism, and bad science (see Bederman section I, chapter 3), he nonetheless viewed the connection between the self and society as inextricably interwoven (as Moran's excerpt on the invention of the sexual adolescent explains in section I, chapter 7). Subsequent writers on adolescence and middle level education retained the idea that adolescence was a time marked by crisis. However, this crisis began to be defined by individual versus social processes and by internal versus external dynamics of conflict. The concept of adolescence and the process of identity formation became suffused with the traditional view in classical psychoanalysis that adolescents traverse a personal, internal, psychosexual conflicts (Freud, 1905; Blos, 1962), and with the burgeoning ideology of individualism and the notion of the "self-made man" that accompanied emergent industrial capitalism in the early 19th century. Increasingly ... individualized phenomenon, subject to personal choice and effort, as well as to internal motivation and conflict. Increasingly adolescent identity development came to be viewed as an individualized phenomenon, subject to personal choice and effort, as well as to internal motivation and conflict.

Identity formation is not just a matter of individual decision making about "what I'm going to be." Identity is not simply an individual creation, nor merely a self-contained individual process, nor a "natural unfolding" of the self. Rather, individuals are positioned in a larger constellation of social relationships, as well as in the larger social order of hierarchical relationships, which contribute to the creation of particular social identities and related meanings. It is important to distinguish between simply understanding identity as "a formation" versus "a construction." Construction implies that there are many other forces at work and that something is being dynamically created in a social context, rather than merely unfolding in isolation. It recognizes that identity is an active, fluid, social meaning-making process.

We challenge the view in much academic literature, and in popular discourse, that treats children as if they are not active participants in the dynamics of inequality in society, and as if their ideologies and life trajectories are not shaped by their participation in these social processes. The operative assumption has been that youth do not create, contest, or internalize meaning about relations of power nor are their identities shaped by the relations of power or their interactive relationships with others. Implicit is the view that children and youth are not intellectually, socially, or emotionally sophisticated enough to make sense of their place in the various social arenas. Although children and youth are making sense of their social worlds from birth, Piaget's work on stages of cognitive development is often erroneously used to justify the omission of these issues in discussions with youth in schools and other settings even though they are already thinking about these things. Our concern as educators is with how people can be positioned in ways that they develop democratic identities and learn to participate in democratic social relationships in schools, communities, and society at large.

The chapters in this section focus on the issue of identity, because of its central role in defining and shaping this stage of adolescence. These chapters present different theoretical perspectives regarding the psychological and social origins of and processes involved in the formation and construction of individual and social identities. They consider the social meanings that are created and contested across various dimensions of identity along the intersecting lines of race, gender, class, language diversity, and sexuality. The compilation of traditional and critical texts in this section include theoretical and ethnographic texts drawn from psychoanalysis, critical psychology, sociology, and cultural studies, which address the complexity of the process of identity formation and construction. The readings highlight the role of schools and other institutions in the creation and contestation of particular social identities, and raise questions about the subjective processes that inform the dynamics of this human meaning-making process.

The early texts in this section increasingly complicate notions of identity and the myriad of potential processes that are at play. The texts also entertain dialogue about the significance of different theoretical perspectives on identity, as they inform popular culture, the affect construction of marginalized social identities, explain and justify or excuse societal inequalities, or chart the path to liberatory practices in schools and other institutions. These texts also entertain consideration of the implications of particular views on identity and their origins for related policies and practices instituted in middle schools.

The readings in this section offer a critical perspective on identity development at the middle level and illustrate ways in which the critical perspectives here differ from more common approaches. As Erik Erikson elaborates in chapter 16, a psychosocial identity is formed throughout an individual's life, and individual identity formation is thoroughly interwoven with the social context. Much literature on adolescence, youth, and middle level education presumes that identity is "found" at this transitional period. Identity, for Erikson is formed in the core of the individual but also in the core of his or her communal culture. The self is thus socially situated. For Erikson, the balance between identity and identity confusion is in motion or in process throughout the lifespan, although adolescence is the pivotal time for its formation, and stabilization.

Chapters 17 and 18 by Ward and Brown, like Erikson highlight the construction of identity through the interplay between the individual and the social. If identity is socially-situated then some of the forces at play in forming identity include class, race, ethnicity, gender, sex, age, language, and nation. In chapter 17, Janie Ward's ethnographic study examines the ways in which African American adolescents negotiate racial identity in the context of a wealthy white private school. Through her interviews and experiences with the girls, she addresses the powerful role that African American parents play in preparing their daughters for the inevitable encounters with institutional racism in school and society. She examines the ways in which the girls forge strong, positive meanings about themselves in the context of experiencing different messages about race and class in the school environs, as well as in the broader culture. She argues for an understanding of the challenges faced by youth in resisting essentialist meanings about race, and the responsibilities that lie at the feet of educational institutions in disrupting destructive policies, practices, and cultural norms.

In chapter 18, Brown does a comparative race- and class-based analysis of the differential financial, material, and curricular resources, the militarized, "repressive" versus privileged, "democratic" school practices and culture that exist in poor African American and wealthy European American public schools. She examines shifts in the economy and the state apparatus, of which schools are a part, as these complex forces dynamically contribute to the creation of particular social identities and life trajectories for the youth in the two schools. She considers the ideological formations that have historically justified the educational and social practices that support unequal relations of power in society, and argues for liberatory educational practices that promote critical consciousness and new life options for youth.

There is an important difference in the ways that these authors conceive of the relationship between the individual and the social. For example, many noncritical writers on middle level treat subjugated identities of social class, race, and gender as "risk factors" for individuals in the social context. Problematically, this presumes that the privileged position within these categories is the norm, the benchmark, or the ideal against which other identities are to be judged. When subjugated identities are assumed to be "risk factors" at best, they are presumed to be at best overcome. Perhaps most importantly, within such a deficit model of identity, the knowledge that working-class, non-White, and nonmale students bring to the classroom is presumed by official and implicit curricula to be inferior and in need of overcoming. Self-contained identity formation is viewed as an internal, voluntary process, which ultimately excuses society's role in creating and maintaining particular trajectories for youth across racial and class lines. These authors in this section contribute important ways of thinking about identity that differ from more common approaches.

Stuart Hall's discussion of culture and identity in chapter 19 foregrounds the critical approach to identity here by emphasizing that culture is about shared meanings that are not only "in the head." Differences and parallels are evident in Hall's critical view and the psychoanalytic, sociocultural perspective of Erikson. Cultural meanings, as Hall states, "organize and regulate social practices, influence our conduct and consequently have real, practical effects" (Hall, 1997, p. 3). For Hall, cultural meanings in the form of symbols and broader public discourses organize social life. Meaning is produced at multiple sites on what he calls the "circuit of culture." In part, the importance of this is Hall's emphasis on the ways that language, knowledge, meaning, and identities are saturated by power relations. For Hall, different people and institutions have different amounts of power to produce meanings and influence interpretive practices. Meaning, which is constantly being produced and exchanged by multiple meaning-making forces, including school, mass media, home, community, religion, and the state, not only gives us a sense of our own identity but also informs our sense of our relations to others, marks out group boundaries, and places individuals within social hierarchies. This way of thinking about identity through shared and negotiated meanings accords with a democratic pedagogy that views knowledge as made by learners rather than merely received. Hence, particular meanings constructed about groups as inherent qualities in texts and other venues reveals the relationship between knowledge and authority. Power relations determine who is in a position to circulate particular meanings that reinforce social inequality. The social conditions surrounding this meaning-making process also provide a context for others to contest and negotiate those meanings in the practical life. This presumes that what knowledge and whose knowledge matters is something to be negotiated and deliberated over, and questioned rather than merely received either by supposed experts or standardized tests and curricula.

Such an approach to identity also opens new ways of thinking about how teachers as meaning-makers can contribute to constructing student identities in ways that are more democratic, critical, egalitarian, and just. Ferguson's discussion of black masculinity in schools in chapter 20 is a case in point. She emphasizes that the relationship between the securing of order in school and the making of identities is seldom addressed. For Ferguson, a central question educators must face is how "the social hierarchy of society is recreated by the school." Like Stuart Hall, Ferguson emphasizes how the meaning of symbols, including affect, style, manners, expressiveness, and language, is struggled over by different groups but is also wielded like weapons to enforce a cultural order that has very real material, economic, and political effects on people in institutions like schools. Like Enora Brown's chapter, this chapter is particularly important for calling into question widespread beliefs about discipline that justify punitive treatment of students rather than approaches to learning that take seriously the relationship of youth identity to broader questions of what makes knowledge meaningful for students, power, and politics. It highlights another dimension of the relationship between the construction of social identities and the social and economic structures of inequality that characterize public schools and are inherent in capitalism. As Brown's chapter illustrates, the critical perspective on identity recognizes the extent to which the construction of identity contributes to the stratification of youth and their tracking into particular life trajectories and social identities that maintain the social order.

Like Ferguson, in chapter 21 Stacey Lee emphasizes the ways that meanings about non-White youth are produced, distributed, and consumed and how this effects the formation of youth identities. Lee's highlighting of the model minority stereotype of Asians emphasizes that all too often discussions about race simplify it into a matter of black and white. Such misrepresentations for Lee silence and marginalize diverse ethnicities into a single "racial/panethnic" group. As Lee argues, this is hardly innocent as such erasure of difference functions not only to mis-recognize Asian Americans but also to deny poverty and illiteracy among Asians, while simultaneously justifying the scapegoating of African Americans. Lee's discussion emphasizes the ways meanings about Asian Americans are largely produced by corporate mass media and yet such meanings influence how Asian Americans are treated in schools and by other state institutions.

Particular social meanings are created and contested around sexuality as a dimension of identity. The issue of adolescent homosexuality is a case in point. Many school personnel shun, ignore, and/or by default or design contribute to the stimatization of youth who are marginalized as a result of their sexual orientation. Anderson in chapter 22, highlights both developmental and social issues that should be considered for gay and lesbian youth. His discussion is based on the premise that youth are stigmatized, that homophobia is a problem, and that these issues are necessary, important, and discussable topics for middle school personnel that will support youth development and should help to create democratic life spaces for youth in schools. Although not in this volume, Peter McLaren's discussion on schooling and gay identity raises precisely this question: "How can teachers work together in the interests of developing a critical subjectivity among themselves and their students that can begin to rehabilitate the pathological development of homophobic discourses in current school policy and practice?" (1995, p. 109). More broadly, McLaren goes on to ask how can the particular social relations of homosexuality be taken up critically by teachers in relation to the politics of difference, the ideological myth of heterosexuality, and the moral obligation to the other? His discussion illuminates Stuart Hall's critical view of identity and advocates for more democratic ways of constructing youth identities.

Julia Hall, Angela Valenzuela, and Donaldo Macedo each take up a particular dimension of identity related to race, class, and ethnicity. Julia Hall's discussion in chapter 23 on working-class White girls in a deindustrialized town examines the impact of those social forces on the construction of their working-class female identities in that context. Issues of family, social relations, school experiences, and racial dynamics are addressed in this chapter based on Bourdieu's reproduction theory. As such, Julia Hall examines the ways in which social and economic realities frame and reproduce particular social identities and relationships.

In chapter 24, Angela Valenzuela examines the social forces that contribute to divisions amongst Mexican American youth, considers the varied meanings of "Mexican-ness" that are created, negotiated and contested in schools, and highlights differential forms of consciousness amongst immigrant and U.S.-born Mexican youth that are forged through practices and policies in schools. Students' comments illuminate Valenzuela's analysis of the "politics of difference" and the significance of language, i.e., speaking Spanish, for Mexican youths' sense of Mexican idnetity, strivings towards biculturalism or cultural assimilation. She illustrates ways in which the school's rules, language policies, and devaluation of Spanish are divisive and institutionalize inequality by marginalizing immigrant youth and privileging those who are U.S.-born.

Finally, in chapter 25 Donaldo Macedo examines the origins of the English Only Movement and critically analyzes its colonizing role for those who do not speak English. He discusses the economic and social function of the movement, its implications for the quality of life for the non-English speaking, the ideological roots and justifications for this view, and the social imperatives to resist this movement. Further, he examines this movement's function in the construction of particular social identities along language lines, and the ways in which this privileging of English instantiates social and economic hierarchies both within and outside of the U.S. borders. He challenges all to oppose this movement, to engage a new concept of literacy, to acknowledge the relations of power that are operating in this movement, and to take up a position that is emancipatory and embraces the socio-cultural and liberatory strivings of those most oppressed.

QUESTIONS FOR REFLECTION AND DIALOGUE

1. How is a critical perspective on identity at the middle level different from a noncritical perspective?
2. How do the readings in the section contribute to a critical middle level education?
3. How do the perspectives on identity here differ from the way identity is commonly discussed?
4. How do the various authors conceive of identity as related to community, politics, and power?
5. How do the authors think differently about the centrality of identity development for adolescents?
6. How do Erik Erikson and Stuart Hall conceive of identification differently? Why might this matter?
7. What are the social, cultural, or economic implications for different ways of conceiving of identity?
8. Could different ways of thinking about identity result in very different policies for schools or in schools?
9. How would the understandings of identity presented here inform pedagogical decisions in schools? In public education as a whole?

REFERENCES

Blos, P. (1962). *On adolescence. A psychoanalytic interpretation.* New York: Free Press.

Erikson, E. (1968). *Identity: Youth and crisis.* New York: W. W. Norton & Co.

Hall, G. S. (1904). *Adolescence.* New York: D. Appleton & Co.

Hall, S. (Ed.) (1997). *Representation: Cultural representation and signifying practices* (Culture, Media, and Identitites, Vol. 2). Thousand Oaks, CA: Sage Publishers.

Hall, S. (1966). Introduction: Who needs identity? In S. Hall & P. duGay (Eds.) *Questions of cultural identity.* Thousand Oaks, CA: Sage Publishers.

McLaren, P. (1995). Moral panic, schooling, and gay identity: Critical pedagogy and the politics of resistance, In G. Unks (Ed.) *The gay teen: Educational practice and theory for lesbian, gay, and bisexual adolescents.* New York: Routledge.

16

Identity: Youth and Crisis

Erik H. Erikson

Before we try to understand the meaning of the present-day echo of our terms, let me take a long look back to our professional and conceptual ancestors. Today when the term identity refers, more often than not, to something noisily demonstrative, to a more or less desperate "quest," or to an almost deliberately confused "search" let me present two formulations which assert strongly what identity feels like when you become aware of the fact that you do undoubtedly *have* one.

My two witnesses are bearded and patriarchal founding fathers of the psychologies on which our thinking on identity is based. As a *subjective sense* of an *invigorating sameness* and *continuity*, what I would call a sense of identity seems to me best described by William James in a letter to his wife:[1]

> A man's character is discernible in the mental or moral attitude in which, when it came upon him, he felt himself most deeply and intensely active and alive. At such moments there is a voice inside which speaks and says: "*This* is the real me!"

Such experience always includes

> ... an element of active tension, of holding my own, as it were, and trusting outward things to perform their part so as to make it a full harmony, but without any *guaranty* that they will. Make it a guaranty ... and the attitude immediately becomes to my consciousness stagnant and stingless. Take away the guaranty, and I feel (provided I am *ueberhaupt* in vigorous condition) a sort of deep enthusiastic bliss, of bitter willingness to do and suffer anything ... and which, although it is a mere mood or emotion to which I can give no form in words, authenticates itself to me as the deepest principle of all active and theoretic determination which I possess ...

James uses the word "character," but I am taking the liberty of claiming that he describes a sense of identity, and that he does so in a way which can in principle be experienced by any man. To him it is both mental and moral in the sense of those "moral philosophy" days, and he experiences it as something that "comes upon you" as a recognition, almost as a surprise rather than as something strenuously "quested" after. It is an active tension (rather than a paralyzing question)—a tension which, furthermore, must create a challenge "without guaranty" rather than one dissipated in a clamor for certainty. But let us remember in passing that James was in his thirties when he wrote this, that in his youth he had faced and articulated an "identity crisis" of honest and desperate depth, and that he became *the* Psychologist-Philosopher of American Pragmatism only after having experimented with a variety of cultural, philosophic, and national identity elements: the use in the middle of his declaration of the untranslatable German word "*ueberhaupt*" is probably an echo of his conflictful student days in Europe.

One can study in James's life history a protracted identity crisis as well as the emergence of a "self-made" identity in the new and expansive American civilization. We will repeatedly come back to James, but for the sake of further definition, let us now turn to a statement which asserts a unity of *personal and cultural* identity rooted in an ancient people's fate. In an address to the Society of B'nai B'rith in Vienna in 1926,[2] Sigmund Freud said:

> What bound me to Jewry was (I am ashamed to admit) neither faith nor national pride, for I have always been an unbeliever and was brought up without any religion though not without a respect for what are called the "ethical" standards of human civilization. Whenever I felt an inclination to national enthusiasm I strove to suppress it as being harmful and wrong, alarmed by the warning examples of the peoples among whom we Jews live. But plenty of other things remained over to make the attraction of Jewry and Jews irresistible—many obscure emotional forces, which were the more powerful the less they could be expressed in words, as well as a clear consciousness of inner identity, the safe privacy of a common mental construction. And beyond this there was a perception that it was to my Jewish nature alone that I owed two characteristics that had become indispensable to me in the difficult course of my life. Because I was a Jew I found myself free from many prejudices which restricted others in the use of their intellect; and as a Jew I was prepared to join the Opposition, and to do without agreement with the "compact majority."

No translation ever does justice to the distinctive choice of words in Freud's German original. "Obscure emotional forces" are *"dunkle Gefuehlsmaechte"*; the "safe privacy of a common mental construction" is *"die Heimlichkeit der inneren Konstruktion"*—not just "mental," then, and certainly not "private," but a deep communality known only to those who shared in it, and only expressible in words more mythical than conceptual.

These fundamental statements were taken not from theoretical works, but from special communications: a letter to his wife from a man who married late, an address to his "brothers" by an original observer long isolated in his profession. But in all their poetic spontaneity they are the products of trained minds and therefore exemplify the main dimensions of a positive sense of identity almost systematically. Trained minds of genius, of course, have a special identity and special identity problems often leading to a protracted crisis at the onset of their careers. Yet we must rely on them for formulating initially what we can then proceed to observe as universally human.

This is the only time Freud used the term identity in a more than casual way and, in fact, in a most central ethnic sense. And as we would expect of him, he inescapably points to some of those aspects of the matter which I called sinister and yet vital—the more vital, in fact, "the less they could be expressed in words." For Freud's "consciousness of inner identity" includes a sense of bitter pride preserved by his dispersed and often despised people throughout a long history of persecution. It is anchored in a particular (here intellectual) gift which had victoriously emerged from the hostile limitation of opportunities. At the same time, Freud contrasts the *positive identity* of a fearless freedom of thinking with a *negative* trait in "the peoples among whom we Jews live," namely, "prejudices which restrict others in the use of their intellect." It dawns on us, then, that one person's or group's identity may be relative to another's, and that the pride of gaining a strong identity may signify an inner emancipation from a more dominant group identity, such as that of the "compact majority." An exquisite triumph is suggested in the claim that the same historical development which restricted the prejudiced majority in the free use of their intellect made the isolated minority sturdier in intellectual matters. To all this, we must come back when discussing race relations.[3]

And Freud goes farther. He admits in passing that he had to suppress in himself an inclination toward "national enthusiasm" such as was common for "the peoples among whom we Jews live." Again, as in James's case, only a study of Freud's youthful enthusiasms could show how he came to leave behind other aspirations in favor of the ideology of applying the methods of natural science to the study of psychological "forces of dignity." It is in Freud's dreams, incidentally, that we have a superb record of his suppressed (or what James called "abandoned," or even "murdered") selves—for our "negative identity" haunts us at night.[4]

The two statements and the lives behind them serve to establish a few dimensions of identity and, at the same time, help to explain why the problem is so all-pervasive and yet so hard to grasp: for we deal with a process "located" *in the core of the individual* and yet also *in the core of his communal culture*, a process which establishes, in fact, the identity of those two identities. If we should now pause and state a few minimum requirements for fathoming the complexity of identity we should have to begin by saying something like this (and let us take our time in saying it): in psychological terms, identity formation employs a process of simultaneous reflection and observation, a process taking place on all levels of mental functioning, by which the individual judges himself in the light of what he perceives to be the way in which others judge him in comparison to themselves and to a typology significant to them; while he judges their way of judging him in the light of how he perceives himself in comparison to them and to types that have become relevant to him. This process is, luckily, and necessarily, for the most part unconscious except where inner conditions and outer circumstances combine to aggravate a painful, or elated, "identity-consciousness."

Furthermore, the process described is always changing and developing: at its best it is a process of increasing differentiation, and it becomes ever more inclusive as the individual grows aware of a widening circle of others significant to him, from the maternal person to "mankind." The process "begins" somewhere in the first true "meeting" of mother and baby as two persons who can touch and recognize each other,[5] and it does not "end" until a man's power of mutual affirmation wanes. As pointed out, however, the process has its normative crisis in adolescence, and is in many ways determined by what went before and determines much that follows. And finally, in discussing identity, as we now see, we cannot separate personal growth and communal change, nor can we separate (as I tried to demonstrate in *Young Man Luther*) the identity crisis in individual life and contemporary crises in historical development because the two help to define each other and are truly relative to each other. In fact, the whole interplay between the psychological and the social, the developmental and the historical, for which identity formation is of prototypal significance, could be conceptualized only as a kind of *psychosocial relativity.* A weighty matter then: certainly mere "roles" played interchangeably, mere self-conscious "appearances," or mere strenuous "postures" cannot possibly be the real thing, although they may be dominant aspects of what today is called the "search for identity."

In view of all this, it would be obviously wrong to let some terms of personology and of social psychology often identified with identity or identity confusion—terms such as self-conception, self-imagery, or self-esteem, on the one hand, and role ambiguity, role conflict, or role loss, on the other—take over the area to be studied, although teamwork methods are, at the moment, the best approach in this general area. What these approaches as yet lack, however, is a theory of human development which attempts to come closer to something by finding out wherefrom and whereto it develops. For identity is never "established" as an "achievement" in the form of a personality armor, or of anything static and unchangeable.

The traditional psychoanalytic method, on the other hand, cannot quite grasp identity because it has not developed terms to conceptualize the environment. Certain habits of psychoanalytic theorizing, habits of designating the environment as "outer world" or "object world," cannot take account of the environment as a pervasive actuality. The German ethologists introduced the word "*Umwelt*" to denote not merely an environment which surrounds you, but which is also in you. And indeed, from the point of view of development, "former" environments are forever in us; and since we live in a continuous process of making the present "former" we never—not even as a newborn—meet any environment as a person who never had an environment. One methodological precondition, then, for grasping identity would be a psychoanalysis sophisticated enough to include the environment; the other would be a social psychology which is psychoanalytically sophisticated; together they would obviously institute a new field which would have to create its own historical sophistication. In the meantime, we can only try to see where a historical instance or a bit of normative development, a fragment of case history, or an event in a biography becomes clearer when something like identity development is assumed to exist. And, of course, it helps to note down in detail what and why and how an item seems to become clearer.

But once we accept a historical perspective, we face the probability that the quotations which I have offered as a massive motto are really tied to a kind of identity formation highly dependent on cultural conditions of a sedentary middle class. True, both James and Freud belonged to the middle class of the early industrial era which migrated from country to city or from city to city, and James, of course, was the grandson of an immigrant. Nevertheless, their homes and their studies, their academic and their clinical associations were, even when revolutionary in scientific matters, highly stable in their morals and ideals. It may well be that what "you can take for granted" (a phrase which Freud used in order to characterize his attitude toward morality) also determines what chances you can fruitfully take with it. And chances they took, the revolutionary minds of the middle class of the nineteenth century: Darwin, by making man's very humanity relative to his animal ancestry; Marx, by exposing the middle-class mind itself as class-bound; and Freud, by making our ideals and our very consciousness relative to an unconscious mental life.

Since then there have been national wars, political revolutions, and moral rebellions which have shaken the traditional foundations of all human identity. If we wish to find witnesses to a radically different awareness of the relation of positive and negative identity, we only have to change our historical perspective and look to the Negro writers in this country today. For what if there is nothing in the hopes of generations past nor in the accessible resources of the contemporary community which would help to overcome the negative image held up to a minority by the "compact majority"? Then, so it seems, the creative individual must accept the negative identity as the very base line of recovery. And so we have in our American Negro writers the almost ritualized affirmation of "inaudibil-ity," "invisibility," "namelessness," "facelessness"—a "void of faceless faces, of soundless voices lying outside history," as Ralph Ellison puts it. But the responsible Negro writers continue to write and write strongly, for fiction even in acknowledging the depth of noth-ingness can contribute to something akin to a collective recovery.[6] This, as we shall see, is a universal trend among the exploited. It is no coincidence that one of the most telling autobiographic documents of India's liberation as a nation also bears the "negative" title *Autobiography of an Unknown Indian.* No wonder that in young people not inclined toward literary reflection, such deepseated negative identities can be reabsorbed only by a turn to militancy, if not transient violence.

There are many formulations of what constitutes a "healthy" personality in an adult. But if we take up only one—in this case, Marie Jahoda's definition, according to which a healthy personality *actively masters* his environment, shows a certain *unity of personality*, and is able to *perceive* the world and himself *correctly*[7]—it is clear that all of these criteria are relative to the child's cognitive and social development. In fact, we may say that child-hood is defined by their initial absence and by their gradual development in complex steps of increasing differentiation. How, then, does a vital personality grow or, as it were, accrue from the successive stages of the increasing capacity to adapt to life's necessities—with some vital enthusiasm to spare?

Whenever we try to understand growth, it is well to remember the *epigenetic principle* which is derived from the growth of organisms *in utero*. Somewhat generalized, this prin-ciple states that anything that grows has a ground plan, and that out of this ground plan the parts arise, each part having its time of special ascendancy, until all parts have arisen to form a functioning whole. This, obviously, is true for fetal development where each part of the organism has its critical time of ascendance or danger of defect. At birth the baby leaves the chemical exchange of the womb for the social exchange system of his society, where his gradually increasing capacities meet the opportunities and limitations of his culture. How the maturing organism continues to unfold, not by developing new organs but by means of a prescribed sequence of locomotor, sensory, and social capacities, is described in the child-development literature. As pointed out, psychoanalysis has given us an understanding of the more idiosyncratic experiences, and especially the inner conflicts, which constitute the manner in which an individual becomes a distinct personality. But here, too, it is important to realize that in the sequence of his most personal experiences the healthy child, given a reasonable amount of proper guidance, can be trusted to obey inner laws of development, laws which create a succession of potentialities for significant interaction with those persons who tend and respond to him and those institutions which are ready for him. While such interaction varies from culture to culture, it must remain within "the proper rate and the proper sequence" which governs all epigenesis. Personality, therefore, can be said to develop according to steps predetermined in the human organism's readiness to be driven toward, to be aware of, and to interact with a widening radius of significant individuals and institutions.

It is for this reason that, in the presentation of stages in the development of the personality, we employ an epigenetic diagram analogous to the one employed in *Childhood and Society* for an analysis of Freud's psychosexual stages.[8] It is, in fact, an implicit purpose of this presentation to bridge the theory of infantile sexuality (without repeating it here in detail) and our knowledge of the child's physical and social growth.

The diagram is presented [here]. The double-lined squares signify both a sequence of stages and a gradual development of component parts; in other words, the diagram formalizes a progression through time of a differentiation of parts. This indicates (1) that each item of the vital personality to be discussed its systematically related to all others and that they all depend on the proper development in the proper sequence of each item; and (2) that each item exists in some form before "its" decisive and critical time normally arrives.

If I say, for example, that a sense of basic trust is the first component of mental vitality to develop in life, a sense of autonomous will the second, and a sense of initiative the third, the diagram expresses a number of fundamental relations that exist among the three components, as well as a few fundamental facts for each.

Each comes to its ascendance, meets its crisis, and finds its lasting solution in ways to be described here, toward the end of the stages mentioned. All of them exist in the beginning in some form, although we do not make a point of this fact, and we shall not confuse things by calling these components different names at earlier or later stages. A baby may show something like "autonomy" from the beginning, for example, in the particular way in which he angrily tries to wriggle his hand free when tightly held. However, under normal conditions, it is not until the second year that he begins to experience the whole critical alternative between being an autonomous creature and being a dependent one, and it is not until then that he is ready for a specifically new encounter with his environment. The environment, in turn, now feels called upon to convey to him its particular ideas and concepts of autonomy in ways decisively contributing to his personal character, his relative efficiency, and the strength of his vitality.

It is this encounter, together with the resulting crisis, which is to be described for each stage. Each stage becomes a crisis because incipient growth and awareness in a new part function go together with a shift in instinctual energy and yet also cause a specific vulnerability in that part. One of the most difficult questions to decide, therefore, is whether or not a child at a given stage is weak or strong. Perhaps it would be best to say that he is always vulnerable in some respects and completely oblivious and insensitive in others, but that at the same time he is unbelievably persistent in the same respects in which he is vulnerable. It must be added that the baby's weakness gives him power; out of his very dependence and weakness he makes signs to which his environment, if it is

	1	2	3	4	5	6	7	8
VIII								INTEGRITY vs. DESPAIR
VII							GENERATIVITY vs. STAGNATION	
VI						INTIMACY vs. ISOLATION		
V	Temporal Perspective vs. Time Confusion	Self-Certainty vs. Self-Consciousness	Role Experimentation vs. Role Fixation	Apprenticeship vs. Work Paralysis	IDENTITY vs. IDENTITY CONFUSION	Sexual Polarization vs. Bisexual Confusion	Leader and Followership vs. Authority Confusion	Ideological Commitment vs. Confusion of Values
IV				INDUSTRY vs. INFERIORITY	Task Identification vs. Sense of Futility			
III			INITIATIVE vs. GUILT		Anticipation of Roles vs. Role Inhibition			
II		AUTONOMY vs. SHAME, DOUBT			Will to Be Oneself vs. Self-Doubt			
I	TRUST vs. MISTRUST				Mutual Recognition vs. Autlatic Isolation			

guided well by a responsiveness combining "instinctive" and traditional patterns, is peculiarly sensitive. A baby's presence exerts a consistent and persistent domination over the outer and inner lives of every member of a household. Because these members must reorient themselves to accommodate his presence, they must also grow as individuals and as a group. It is as true to say that babies control and bring up their families as it is to say the converse. A family can bring up a baby only by being brought up by him. His growth consists of a series of challenges to them to serve his newly developing potentialities for social interaction.

Each successive step, then, is a potential crisis because of a radical change in perspective. Crisis is used here in a developmental sense to connote not a threat of catastrophe, but a turning point, a crucial period of increased vulnerability and heightened potential, and therefore, the ontogenetic source of generational strength and maladjustment. The most radical change of all, from intrauterine to extrauterine life, comes at the very beginning of life. But in postnatal existence, too, such radical adjustments of perspective as lying relaxed, sitting firmly, and running fast must all be accomplished in their own good time. With them, the interpersonal perspective also changes rapidly and often radically, as is testified by the proximity in time of such opposites as "not letting mother out of sight" and "wanting to be independent." Thus, different capacities use different opportunities to become full-grown components of the ever-new configuration that is the growing personality.

· · ·

As technological advances put more and more time between early school life and the young person's final access to specialized work, the stage of adolescing becomes an even more marked and conscious period and, as it has always been in some cultures in some periods, almost a way of life between childhood and adulthood. Thus in the later school years young people, beset with the physiological revolution of their genital maturation and the uncertainty of the adult roles ahead, seem much concerned with faddish attempts at establishing an adolescent subculture with what looks like a final rather than a transitory or, in fact, initial identity formation. They are sometimes morbidly, often curiously, preoccupied with what they appear to be in the eyes of others as compared with what they feel they are, and with the question of how to connect the roles and skills cultivated earlier with the ideal prototypes of the day. In their search for a new sense of continuity and sameness, which must now include sexual maturity, some adolescents have to come to grips again with crises of earlier years before they can install lasting idols and ideals as guardians of a final identity. They need, above all, a moratorium for the integration of the identity elements ascribed in the foregoing to the childhood stages: only that now a larger unit, vague in its outline and yet immediate in its demands, replaces the childhood milieu—"society." A review of these elements is also a list of adolescent problems.

If the earliest stage bequeathed to the identity crisis an important need for trust in one-self and in others, then clearly the adolescent looks most fervently for men and ideas to have *faith* in, which also means men and ideas in whose service it would seem worth while to prove oneself trustworthy. (This will be discussed further in the chapter on fidelity.) At the same time, however, the adolescent fears a foolish, all too trusting commitment, and will, paradoxically, express his need for faith in loud and cynical mistrust.

If the second stage established the necessity of being defined by what one can *will* freely, then the adolescent now looks for an opportunity to decide with free assent on one of the available or unavoidable avenues of duty and service, and at the same time is mortally afraid of being forced into activities in which he would feel exposed to ridicule or self-doubt. This, too, can lead to a paradox, namely, that he would rather act shamelessly in the eyes of his elders, out of free choice, than be forced into activities which would be shameful in his own eyes or in those of his peers.

If an unlimited *imagination* as to what one *might* become is the heritage of the play age, then the adolescent's willingness to put his trust in those peers and leading, or misleading, elders who will give imaginative, if not illusory, scope to his aspirations is only too obvious. By the same token, he objects violently to all "pedantic" limitations on his self-images and will be ready to settle by loud accusation all his guiltiness over the excessiveness of his ambition.

Finally, if the desire to make something work, and to make it work well, is the gain of the school age, then the choice of an occupation assumes a significance beyond the question of remuneration and status. It is for this reason that some adolescents prefer not to work at all for a while rather than be forced into an otherwise promising career which would offer success without the satisfaction of functioning with unique excellence.

In any given period in history, then, that part of youth will have the most affirmatively exciting time of it which finds itself in the wave of a technological, economic, or ideological trend seemingly promising all that youthful vitality could ask for.

Adolescence, therefore, is least "stormy" in that segment of youth which is gifted and well trained in the pursuit of expanding technological trends, and thus able to identify with new roles of competency and invention and to accept a more implicit ideological outlook. Where this is not given, the adolescent mind becomes a more explicitly ideological one, by which we mean one searching for some inspiring unification of tradition or anticipated techniques, ideas, and ideals. And, indeed, it is the ideological potential of a society which speaks most clearly to the adolescent who is so eager to be affirmed by peers, to be confirmed by teachers, and to be inspired by worth-while "ways of life." On the other hand, should a young person feel that the environment tries to deprive him too radically of all the forms of expression which permit him to develop and integrate the next step, he may resist with the wild strength encountered in animals who are suddenly forced to defend their lives. For, indeed, in the social jungle of human existence there is no feeling of being alive without a sense of identity.

Having come this far, I would like to give one example (and I consider it representative in structure) of the individual way in which a young person, given some leeway, may utilize a traditional way of life for dealing with a remnant of negative identity. I had known Jill before her puberty, when she was rather obese and showed many "oral" traits of voracity and dependency while she also was a tomboy and bitterly envious of her brothers and in rivalry with them. But she was intelligent and always had an air about her (as did her mother) which seemed to promise that things would turn out all right. And, indeed, she straightened out and up, became very attractive, an easy leader in any group, and, to many, a model of young girlhood. As a clinician, I watched and wondered what she would do with that voraciousness and with the rivalry which she had displayed earlier. Could it be that such things are simply absorbed in fortuitous growth?

Then one autumn in her late teens, Jill did not return to college from the ranch out West where she had spent the summer. She had asked her parents to let her stay. Simply out of liberality and confidence, they granted her this moratorium and returned East.

That winter Jill specialized in taking care of newborn colts, and would get up at any time during a winter night to bottle feed the most needy animals. Having apparently acquired a certain satisfaction within herself, as well as astonished recognition from the cowboys, she returned home and reassumed her place. I felt that she had found and hung on to an opportunity to do actively and for others what she had always yearned to have done for her, as she had once demonstrated by overeating: she had learned to feed needy young mouths. But she did so in a context which, in turning passive into active, also turned a former symptom into a social act.

One might say that she turned "maternal" but it was a maternalism such as cowboys must and do display; and, of course, she did it all in jeans. This brought recognition "from man to man" as well as from man to woman, and beyond that the confirmation of her optimism, that is, her feeling that something could be done that felt like her, was useful and worth while, and was in line with an ideological trend where is still made immediate practical sense.

Such self-chosen "therapies" depend, of course, on the leeway given in the right spirit at the right time, and this depends on a great variety of circumstances. I intend to publish similar fragments from the lives of children in greater detail at some future date; let this example stand for the countless observations in everyday life, where the resourcefulness of young people proves itself when the conditions are right.

The estrangement of this stage is *identity confusion,* which will be elaborated in clinical and biographic detail in the next chapter. For the moment, we will accept Biff's formulation in Arthur Miller's *Death of a Salesman:* "I just can't take hold, Mom, I can't take hold of some kind of a life." Where such a dilemma is based on a strong previous doubt of one's ethnic and sexual identity, or where role confusion joins a hopelessness of long standing, delinquent and "borderline" psychotic episodes are not uncommon. Youth after youth, bewildered by the incapacity to assume a role forced on him by the inexorable standardization of American adolescence, runs away in one form or another, dropping out of school, leaving jobs, staying out all night, or withdrawing into bizarre and inaccessible moods. Once "delinquent," his greatest need and often his only salvation is the refusal on the part of older friends, advisers, and judiciary personnel to type him further by pat diagnoses and social judgments which ignore the special dynamic conditions of adolescence. It is here, as we shall see in greater detail, that the concept of identity confusion is of practical clinical value, for if they are diagnosed and treated correctly, seemingly psychotic and criminal incidents do not have the same fatal significance which they may have at other ages.

In general it is the inability to settle on an occupational identity which most disturbs young people. To keep themselves together they temporarily overidentify with the heroes of cliques and crowds to the point of an apparently complete loss of individuality. Yet in this stage not even "falling in love" is entirely, or even primarily, a sexual matter. To a considerable extent adolescent love is an attempt to arrive at a definition of one's identity by projecting one's diffused self-image on another and by seeing it thus reflected and gradually clarified. This is why so much of young love is conversation. On the other hand, clarification can also be sought by destructive means. Young people can become remarkably clannish, intolerant, and cruel in their exclusion of others who are "different," in skin color or cultural background, in tastes and gifts, and often in entirely petty *[sic]* of dress and gesture arbitrarily selected as the signs of an in-grouper or out-grouper. It is important to understand in principle (which does not mean to condone in all of its manifestations) that such intolerance may be, for a while, a necessary defense against a sense of identity loss. This is unavoidable at a time of life when the body changes its proportions radically, when genital puberty floods body and imagination with all manner of impulses, when intimacy with the other sex approaches and is, on occasion, forced on the young person, and when the immediate future confronts one with too many conflicting possibilities and choices. Adolescents not only help one another temporarily through such discomfort by forming cliques and stereotyping themselves, their ideals, and their enemies; they also insistently test each other's capacity for sustaining loyalties in the midst of inevitable conflicts of values.

The readiness for such testing helps to explain the appeal of simple and cruel totalitarian doctrines among the youth of such countries and classes as have lost or are losing their group identities—feudal, agrarian, tribal, or national. The democracies are faced with the job of winning these grim youths by convincingly demonstrating to them—by living it—that a democratic identity can be strong and yet tolerant, judicious and still determined. But industrial democracy poses special problems in that it insists on self-made identities ready to grasp many chances and ready to adjust to the changing necessities of booms and busts, of peace and war, of migration and determined sedentary life. Democracy, therefore, must present its adolescents with ideals which can be shared by young people of many backgrounds, and which emphasize autonomy in the form of independence and initiative in the form of constructive work. These promises, however, are not easy to fulfill in increasingly complex and centralized systems of industrial, economic, and political organization, systems which increasingly neglect the "self-made" ideology still flaunted in oratory. This is hard on many young Americans because their whole upbringing has made the development of a self-reliant personality dependent on a certain degree of choice, a sustained hope for an individual chance, and a firm commitment to the freedom of self-realization.

We are speaking here not merely of high privileges and lofty ideals but of psychological necessities. For the social institution which is the guardian of identity *is* what we have called *ideology*. One may see in ideology also the imagery of an aristocracy in its widest possible sense, which connotes that within a defined world image and a given course of history the best people will come to rule and rule will develop the best in people. In order not to become cynically or apathetically lost, young people must somehow be able to convince themselves that those who succeed in their anticipated adult world thereby shoulder the obligation of being best. For it is through their ideology that social systems enter into the fiber of the next generation and attempt to absorb into their lifeblood the rejuvenative power of youth. Adolescence is thus a vital regenerator in the process of social evolution, for youth can offer its loyalties and energies both to the conservation of that which continues to feel true and to the revolutionary correction of that which has lost its regenerative significance.

We can study the identity crisis also in the lives of creative individuals who could resolve it for themselves only by offering to their contemporaries a new model of resolution such as that expressed in works of art or in original deeds, and who furthermore are eager to tell us all about it in diaries, letters, and self representations. And even as the neuroses of a given period reflect the ever-present inner chaos of man's existence in a new way, the creative crises point to the period's unique solutions.

We will in the next chapter present in greater detail what we have learned of these specialized individual crises. But there is a third manifestation of the remnants of infantilism and adolescence in man: it is the pooling of the individual crises in transitory upheavals amounting to collective "hysterias." Where there are voluble leaders their creative crises and the latent crises of their followers can be at least studied with the help of our assumptions —and of their writings. More elusive are spontaneous group developments not attributable to a leader. And it will, at any rate, not be helpful to call mass irrationalities by clinical names. It would be impossible to diagnose clinically how much hysteria is present in a young nun participating in an epidemic of convulsive spells or how much perverse "sadism" in a young Nazi commanded to participate in massive parades or in mass killings. So we can point only most tentatively to certain similarities between individual crises and group behavior in order to indicate that in a given period of history they are in an obscure contact with each other.

But before we submerge ourselves in the clinical and biographic evidence for what we call identity confusion, we will take a look beyond the identity crisis. The words "beyond identity," of course, could be understood in two ways, both essential for the problem. They could mean that there is more to man's core than identity, that there is in fact in each individual an "I," an observing center of awareness and of volition, which can transcend and must survive the *psychosocial identity* which is our concern in this book. In some ways, as we will see, a sometimes precocious self-transcendence seems to be felt strongly in a transient manner in youth, as if a pure identity had to be kept free from psychosocial encroachment. And yet no man (except a man aflame and dying like Keats, who could speak of identity in words which secured him immediate fame) can transcend himself in youth. We will speak later of the transcendence of identity. In the following "beyond identity" means life after adolescence and the uses of identity and, indeed, the return of some forms of identity crisis in the later stages of the life cycle.

• • •

Linguistically as well as psychologically, identity and identification have common roots. Is identity, then, the mere sum of earlier identifications, or is it merely an additional set of identifications?

The limited usefulness of the mechanism of identification becomes obvious at once if we consider the fact that none of the identifications of childhood (which in our patients stand out in such morbid elaboration and mutual contradiction) could, if merely added up, result in a functioning personality. True, we usually believe that the task of psychotherapy is the replacement of morbid and excessive identifications by more desirable ones. But as every cure attests, "more desirable" identifications at the same time tend to be quietly subordinated to a new, unique Gestalt which is more than the sum of its parts. The fact is that identification as a mechanism is of limited usefulness. Children at different stages of their development identify with those part aspects of people by which they themselves are most immediately affected, whether in reality or fantasy. Their identifications with parents, for example, center in certain overvalued and ill-understood body parts, capacities, and role appearances. These part aspects, furthermore, are favored not because of their social acceptability (they often are everything but the parents' most adjusted attributes) but by the nature of infantile fantasy which only gradually gives way to more realistic judgment.

In later childhood the individual is faced with a comprehensible hierarchy of roles, from the younger siblings to the grandparents and whoever else belongs to the wider family. All through childhood this gives him some kind of a set of expectations as to what he is going to be when he grows older, and very small children identity with a number of people in a number of respects and establish a kind of hierarchy of expectations which then seeks "verification" later in life. That is why cultural and historical change can prove so traumatic to identify formation: it can break up the inner consistency of a child's hierarchy of expectations.

If we consider introjection, identification, and identity formation to be the steps by which the ego grows in ever more mature interplay with the available models, the following psychosocial schedule suggests itself.

The mechanism of *introjection* (the primitive "incorporation" of another's image) depends for its integration on the satisfactory mutuality between the mothering adult(s) and the mothered child. Only the experience of such initial mutuality provides a safe pole of self-feeling from which the child can reach out for the other pole: his first love "objects."

The fate of childhood *identifications,* in turn, depends on the child's satisfactory interaction with trustworthy representatives of a meaningful hierarchy of roles as provided by the generations living together in some form of family.

Identity formation, finally, begins where the usefulness of identification ends. It arises from the selective repudiation and mutual assimilation of childhood identifications and their absorption in a new configuration, which, in turn, is dependent on the process by which a society (often through subsocieties) identifies the young individual, recognizing him as somebody who had to become the way he is and who, being the way he is, is taken for granted. The community, often not without some initial mistrust, gives such recognition with a display of surprise and pleasure in making the acquaintance of a newly emerging individual. For the community in turn feels "recognized" by the individual who cares to ask for recognition; it can, by the same token, feel deeply—and vengefully—rejected by the individual who does not seem to care.

A community's ways of *identifying* the *individual,* then, meet more or less successfully the individual's ways of identifying himself with others. If the young person is "recognized" at a critical moment as one who arouses displeasure and discomfort, the community sometimes seems to suggest to the young person that he change in ways that to him do not add up to anything "identical with himself." To the community, the desirable change is nevertheless conceived of as a mere matter of good will or of will power ("he could if he wanted to") while resistance to such change is perceived as a matter of bad will or, indeed, of inferiority, hereditary or otherwise. Thus the community often underestimates to what extent a long, intricate childhood history has restricted a youth's further choice of identity change, and also to what extent the community could, if it only would, still help to determine a youth's destiny within these choices.

All through childhood tentative crystallizations of identity take place which make the individual feel and believe (to begin with the most conscious aspect of the matter) as if he approximately knew who he was—only to find that such self-certainty ever again falls prey to the discontinuities of development itself. An example would be the discontinuity between the demands made in a given milieu on a little boy and those made on a "big boy" who, in turn, may well wonder why he was first made to believe that to be little is admirable, only to be forced to exchange this more effortless status for the special obligations of one who is "big now." Such discontinuities can, at any time, amount to a crisis and demand a decisive and strategic repatterning of action, leading to compromises which can be compensated for only by a consistently accruing sense of the practicability and feasibility of such increasing commitment. The cute, or ferocious, or good small boy who becomes a studious, or gentlemanly, or tough big boy must be able—and must be enabled—to combine both sets of values in a recognized identity which permits him, in work and play and in official and intimate behavior, to be (and to let others be) a combination of a big boy and a little boy.

The community supports such development to the extent that it permits the child, at each step, to orient himself toward a complete "life plan" with a hierarchical order of roles as represented by individuals of different ages. Family, neighborhood, and school provide contact and experimental identification with younger and older children and with young and old adults. A child, in the multiplicity of successive and tentative identifications, thus begins early to build up expectations of what it will be like to be older and what it will feel like to have been younger—expectations which become part of an identity as they are, step by step, verified in decisive experiences of psychosocial "fittedness."

The final identity, then, as fixed at the end of adolescence, is superordinated to any single identification with individuals of the past: it includes all significant identifications, but it also alters them in order to make a unique and reasonably coherent whole of them.

NOTES

1. *The Letters of William James,* edited by Henry James (his son), Vol. I, Boston: The Atlantic Monthly Press, 1920, p. 199.
2. Sigmund Freud, "Address to the Society of B'nai B'rith" [1926], *Standard Edition,* 20:273, London: Hogarth Press, 1959.
3. See Chapter VIII.
4. See Chapter IV, section 5.
5. Joan M. Erikson, "Eye to Eye," *The Man Made Object,* Gyorgy Kepes (ed.), New York: Braziller, 1966.
6. See Chapter VIII.
7. Marie Jahoda, "Toward A Social Psychology of Mental Health," *Symposium on the Healthy Personality,* Supplement II: Problems of Infancy and Childhood, Transactions of Fourth Conference, March, 1950, M. J. E. Benn (ed.), New York: Josiah Macy, Jr. Foundation, 1950.
8. See Erik H. Erikson, *Childhood and Society,* 2nd ed., New York: W.W. Norton, 1963, Part I.

17

Racial Identity Formation and Transformation

JANIE VICTORIA WARD

Editor's Note: Dr. Ward participated in all four years of the Emma Willard School study as an interviewer. In this chapter she discusses issues of racial identity formation of a group of young minority women who were participants in the study. Because the author, a black woman, interviewed nearly all of the minority women, a same-sex, same-race match between interviewer and interviewee was achieved.

IN A RECENT study of black adolescents' self-concept and academic achievement, Signithia Fordham presents an analysis of the tension felt by some students between group identity and academic success. She asks if racelessness, the tactic adopted by a number of high achieving black students, is a "pragmatic strategy or a Pyrrhic victory" (Fordham 1988; see also Fordham and Ogbu 1986). She describes students torn between an individualistic ethos encouraged by school officials and a collectivistic ethos promoted by peers. For some black students, doing well in school is equated with "selling out" or becoming non-black; thus for them, "the burden of acting white" was too high a price to pay for academic success.

This chapter presents a very different relationship between group identity and adolescent development. Listening to the voices of a small group of academically successful black adolescent women exploring the meaning of race in their lives reveals how racial identity formation, personal commitment, and academic achievement can successfully converge during the high school years. This chapter has implications for understanding the psychosocial development of black adolescents, particularly black females, and for creating positive and nurturing educational environments for minority students in racially isolated settings.

Between the years 1981 and 1985, when this research project took place, a minimum of thirty-eight and a maximum of fifty-one minority students attended Emma Willard School. Of this number approximately twenty-four were from American ethnic and racial minorities. These children were primarily black American, but several originated from other countries, including the Caribbean Islands and Africa. Over the four-year period a total of seven minority girls were interviewed.[1] From these seven girls, twenty interviews were generated, and they provide the data analyzed in this paper.

The minority students received the same interview questions as the majority students. Both groups were asked self-description and morality questions. In addition the interviewers asked the students to explore their significant relationships and solicited their opinions about growing up female. Following the formal interview, which usually lasted from one to two hours, the interviewers asked the minority students the following questions regarding their racial identities: What does it mean to you to be a black woman? How has the meaning changed for you over the years? What do you think being black will mean to you in the future?

With very few exceptions, discussions of race and race-related topics presented themselves throughout the entire interview session. However, data analysis of the girls' reflections on the meaning and role that race plays in their lives were mentioned primarily in response to the aforementioned specific queries.

Background information was not collected on the young women, although some information was shared during the interview sessions; thus data about socioeconomic status and factors related to individual family histories are incomplete. The purpose of this chapter is to focus not on individual cases, but on general themes that seemed to recur in the data when racial identity and race-related events were discussed.

Although specific data were not compiled, two major background factors affecting the lives of the young black women should be acknowledged. First, several girls grew up in family settings with ethnic origins other than black American (including Caribbean, Hispanic, and biracial families). Often these students volunteered comparisons of their past experiences with those of black American students they knew, pointing out both similarities and differences. Studies of black family life have focused on the life-styles, beliefs, and practices of black American families, and most of the research cited in this paper reflects this orientation. The early developmental paths followed by Emma Willard's black girls may have differed slightly given their multiculturality and subsequent intraracial differences in family socialization.

A second commonality in the girls' backgrounds was attained anecdotally. Very few of the young women grew up in predominantly black neighborhoods. Many described themselves as suburbanites in black spillover communities; most had spent at least part, if not all, of their childhood in mixed, or predominantly white, neighborhoods. Previous schooling reflected this fact as well. Only two students recalled attending an academic institution with large numbers of black or other minority students. In conversations with these girls, this aspect of their childhoods stood out. Although they were in small numbers at Emma Willard, their "minority" status (in terms of numbers) was by no means new to them. All of the young women had previously experienced racial isolation either in their integrated communities, where there might have been two or three other black families, or in their schools, in which more than two black children per class was rare. Therefore, for this group growing up and being educated in racially isolated settings was the norm. The choice to send a child away to boarding school is difficult for any family and is perhaps harder still for families in which minority of color is involved. It would seem that these earlier "minority" educational experiences helped to prepare both parent and child for what was later to come.

The seven black girls interviewed at length over the four-year study represent both the diversity and similarities evident in the nation's black communities. Several were children of immigrants, and a few were born outside of this country. For two students, Spanish was the primary language spoken at home. However varied the life experiences of the past, strong commonalities exist among members of the black diaspora. This is manifest most clearly in the fact that blacks residing in the United States must all share the common social experience of racism and discrimination. In this nation, the visibility of one's skin color and of other physical traits associated with socially devalued groups marks individuals as "targets" for subordination and discrimination by members of the white society. Thus the most striking commonality among blacks is the oppression they share based solely on the meanings attributed to the color of one's skin.

The research presented in this paper provides empirical evidence from a small sample of black female adolescents of what some psychologists have called the developmental process of black identity formation. The research seeks to illuminate how young women integrate their race-related experiences of the past with their present-day reality. The connections between patterns of family socialization, beliefs, attitudes, and values developed and adopted over time—and the girls' own subjective understanding of the role that race plays in their lives—will be made more clear.

BRIEF THEORETICAL OVERVIEW

This work is placed within two existing bodies of literature: First, the exhaustive research explicating the process of identity formation for adolescents in general and second, the current understandings of racial identity formation and its significance and implications during the adolescent years.

Erikson's concept of identity formation has been central to the literature on adolescent development (1950, 1956, 1968). He states that adolescence has as its most fundamental task the establishment of a sense of identity. To understand development, one must understand the context in which one lives. The process of identity formation is psychosocial, which refers both to the continuity of self over time and to one's relationship to society. Central to the experience of adolescence is the cognitive ability to take the self as object and to reflect upon the relationship between self and society. The adolescent is thus able to see the self as the self is seen by others. Erikson ties identity formation to ideology, that is, a necessary simplification of beliefs. Adolescence is a period of renegotiation—of social relationships and power dynamics—and often demands a redefinition of the self. Standing at the threshold of adulthood, the interplay between who I am and what I believe may lead the teen to reject the prevailing truths of childhood, constructing in their place new truths that affirm the emerging sense of one's identity and one's status in the world.

The effort to understand identity formation in black adolescents is incomplete without an appreciation of the concept of racial identity. Psychologists argue that a stable concept of self both as an individual as well as a group member (black) is essential to the healthy growth and development of the black self (Comer and Poussaint 1975; Cross 1971, 1978, 1980; Ladner 1978). Through racial identity, the group's way of organizing experience is transmitted to and internalized by the child (Barnes 1980). While so often neglected or confused in the literature, this integration of the individual's personal identity with one's racial identity is a necessary and inevitable developmental task of growing up black in white America.

During adolescence, he need to identify strongly with a sense of peoplehood or a shared social identity is heightened by a consciousness of belonging to a specific group that is characteristically different from other groups. Black teens often begin to question the relevancy of using a white norm for self measurement. To be black takes on new and powerful meanings—meanings that hold social and political significance to who one is and who one believes one should become.[2] As the black child sees herself as others see her, she knows that she is viewed in this society as a member of a devalued group. Transmitted daily to black children are messages that black people are undesirable, inadequate, and inferior. Therefore, if she is black, she is undesirable, inadequate, and inferior. In the face of glaring contradictions between the black experience as non-blacks believe it to be, and the black experience that the black adolescent knows it to be, the task becomes one in which the black child must unravel the faulty and dangerous attacks upon her identity, both individual and group. While some black children fall victim to these attempts to demean and destroy a positive sense of self, many studies show that blacks do not believe the negative stereotypes about themselves nor do they believe that they are inferior to whites (Powell 1982).

This movement beyond an internalization of racial subservience to racial pride begins first with a conscious confrontation with one's racial identity. Resolution of the so-called identity crisis of youth requires that all adolescents proclaim "I am not" as the first step to defining what I am. To the initial stages of the identity process the black adolescent, all too familiar with the demeaning stereotypes held about her and her racial group, must add "I am not what you believe black people to be, *and I am black*." Herein lie the necessary statements of repudiation and affirmation. The black adolescent must reject white society's negative evaluation and must construct an identity that includes one's blackness as positively valued and desired. For blacks, identity formation is a necessary rebirth in one's own terms. If this process of positive identification with the black reference group, despite its devalued status, is not completed and internalized, identity formation will be at risk. The process of repudiation, a casting off of the racially based negative perceptions of others, lays the groundwork for the formation of a positive self-concept.

Growing up black dictates the necessity to negotiate discriminatory and oppressive conditions. It means having to face daily injustice inflicted simply on the basis of skin color. And it means having to live among and interact with people who may seek to hurt you. Some psychologists argue that black children who enter an alien, isolating environment with their self-esteem intact, should have little trouble withstanding the assaults against their budding personality. Yet being and becoming black is seldom an easy experience.

THE RACIAL IDENTITY INTERVIEW

It is not surprising that all of the young black women at Emma Willard remembered and shared past personal experiences where they had been made painfully aware of themselves as racially different from whites. Many years have passed since a brownie troop leader, upon discovering a parent of one of her brownies was black, dismissed the girl from the troop, justifying her decision on the child's lack of "brownie spirit." And the recollection of a teacher who made her resentment of a little black girl's academic achievement very clear, although it has long since lost its initial sting, remains sharp memory. "There was a time

[when] I said, Gosh, it would be so much easier if I were white," explained Ann as she remembered the name calling and teasing she was forced to endure. She could still recall the psychic energy required to be always on the defensive, trying desperately to find words to fire back that would make her attacker feel as bad as she. As she grew older, resentment turned to understanding, and her anger to pity and resignation. Numerous incidents similar to these were now an acknowledged part of the girls' personal histories and served to lay the foundation upon which their racial identities were built.

To no other question in the racial identity interview was there a more uniform response than to the question, What does it mean to be a black woman? "It means it's going to be hard" was a prediction echoed by all. Even the sheltered experience of Emma Willard was not enough to convince the young women that life after Emma would be anything similar to life in the school. For a few of the girls, the impact of the consequence of being black and female evolved over time: "… now I see that sometimes you really are knocked down just because you are black, and I have come to accept that and learn to deal with it." For others the focus on diligence was projected into the work world, where these black women could already imagine obstacles to be overcome. As one says, "I will always have to work harder. I would have that pressure, and I would be watched, you know." Explained another: "I will have to be better than another, say, a white woman who is, who would be my equal in terms of qualifications. I will have to do something that will be one step better than her … because you've got two strikes against you: You're a woman and you're black." This awareness of double jeopardy, because of the additive effect of gender and race, served to heighten levels of introspection and self-examination. In the process, some young women uncovered personal fortitude beneath the struggle.

> I really think you have to understand who you are better, because there are going to be experiences that are really going to try your strength as a human being. And I think you need a very strong inner strength. [But] we have always worked, and we have always had to be strong. And I think that is a historical strength.…

Psychologist Diane Slaughter concurred when she wrote. "Black women must see [their liberation] through an assessment of what the black experience in this nation and abroad has been." This historical analysis is crucial to the black woman's sense of self and empowerment.

Expressions of racial pride were also repeated from interview to interview. Maria represented these sentiments well when she proclaimed:

> There's a lot of heritage and culture behind all of that. I have to be very proud of that, and I'm not saying you have to fight for it … but you have to be willing to make your stand. It's a very important part of any culture today, and it shouldn't be just brushed aside.

The articulations of racial pride and proactive orientation toward racial barriers heard from Emma Willard's young black women align with Bowman and Howard's study of socialization and achievement in black youth. In their study differential patterns by gender were noted, suggesting that within black families there is a greater emphasis on racial pride in the socialization of girls. This contrasts with a greater emphasis on racial barriers for boys (Bowman and Howard 1985). The young black women at Emma Willard spoke often of feeling both good about their race and personally strengthened by their racial status.

Most of the women interviewed seemed to have brought to Emma Willard the skills necessary to survive and flourish in a predominantly white academic setting. The strong family background of each of these girls was instrumental in preparing the adolescents for what they would encounter.

What lessons are learned and what role do black families play in helping their children negotiate the persistent dynamics of racism and discrimination? Many researchers have attempted to elucidate a theoretical framework for describing black families. Given that black people are not a monolithic group in either their attitudes or their ways of expressing them, and given that there are a variety of ways of adapting to the American system of race relations, the functional approach to studying black family life suggests that families possess a distinct culture and strength that enables them to survive in racist America.

Through socialization the child learns what she needs to know about the world, how things are, and the skills necessary to cope and succeed. The task of the black family has been to provide a sense of identity and historical continuity by instilling in its offspring a sense of racial purpose and pride, thereby preparing its children to live among white people without becoming white people (Ladner 1971, 1978). Black families socialize their children to acquire the attitudes, values, and appropriate patterns of interaction conducive to their social and political environment. These include age and sex roles (which historically have been necessarily flexible in the black community), as well as the racial roles of resistance, suspicion, and caution (Nobles 1980, 1981). If power is the ability to define phenomena, then the black family and community play a crucial role in the interpretation of race relations and in the invention of strategies necessary to prevail. What one chooses depends on the way that one perceives the problem, and how one perceives the problem depends on where one stands. Black families prepare black children for the onslaught of negation they must endure by providing the positive feelings and self-confidence underlying what it means to be a black person and a member of the black race.

Whether they were being teased or being painfully ignored, all of the girls who had reported past experiences of discrimination also reported that they brought the incidents home for discussion. Parents had the task of interpreting the incident for the child, explaining the confusing and painful aspects of being singled out and demeaned. Learning to live with the heartache of being discriminated against and the knowledge that such events could and would occur again is not easy. These are very difficult lessons to be transmitted to the black child.

Nearly all of the girls interviewed acknowledged that the information they received about how to deal with race came from within the family. "Our family talks about it [racism] … and how to deal with it" was the most common response. One girl elaborates:

> Like sometimes when something happens and it really bothers me, I'll talk to my mother or my sister and say: 'Somebody said something and I'm trying to decide whether they meant it or if they didn't know what they were saying and it just came out.' So we'll talk about it then. But its the type of thing where my whole family … like we know it's there. And if somebody had trouble dealing with it, then we talk about it and try and help them. Otherwise it's just like, whoa, you just ignore it and do the stuff you can.

Parents also have the responsibility of interpreting race-related incidents for children who don't yet fully understand these dynamics. Several students described family discussions of racial events in which sensitive subtleties of racial content were carefully dissected and reviewed. This served a dual purpose. First, it gave the child criteria for determining malice, and it helped the child determine what action was then appropriate for retribution or reconciliation. Finally, students described sophisticated coping techniques that were developed to help the child make sense of painful personal attacks and maintain self-worth and value. Rose recalled that her father would say, "We all know the reason behind this. But don't dwell on it, just forget about it." Thus when messages of white society say "you can't," the well-functioning black family and community stand ready to counter such messages with those that say, You can, we have, we will.

To understand the formation and transformation of racial identity in the young black women of Emma Willard, one must understand the context in which they were living during the four-year study. At any given time they represented less than twenty percent of the student population. During the years of the study there were never more than two black faculty members employed at the school at any given point. Thus, should a race-related event erupt on campus, black students rarely have adult blacks to help negotiate its outcome. Two-thirds of Emma Willard's students, the boarding population, live, sleep, and eat with one another, (including all of the young women in this sample), and although from time to time tempers may flare, the close proximity of the setting forces the young women to become adept at interpersonal understanding and conflict resolution. The black women interviewed all expressed great satisfaction with their choice to attend Emma Willard and most spoke fondly of the friendships they had forged with both white and black students. Learning about race and race relations did not stop just because the young women had left their families and communities behind. The education continued on Emma's campus, in the classrooms and in the dormitories.

Black students learned a great deal about themselves and the meaning that race would play in their lives through their interactions with white students. "I'm a comfortable black friend," Vera noted ironically, describing how her background, articulateness, and even lighter skin color made her very acceptable to white friends (see Okazawa-Rey, Robinson, and Ward 1987). Susan repeated this observation, "If you are a light black person, people will react differently to you than if you are my color." She told the author, "It's as if they can see you more clearly …," suggesting that the closer blacks look and act like whites, the easier they can be imagined as equals. Susan acknowledged that she falls victim to similarly narrowed perceptions herself: "I think I see myself as a black person in a predominantly white school, just because I don't know the people. They come off first as white and then I get to know them and then the color disappears." A number of students mentioned their awareness of differences between themselves and their white counterparts, citing most often family financial status, differing tastes in music, and differing childrearing practices, particularly those involving discipline. Nevertheless for the most part, the young black women described themselves as very similar to their white friends in terms of goals, attitudes, and desires. At the same time they all acknowledged that the color of their skin created for them a different reality than for whites. The philosophy of Emma Willard is to promote and encourage individuality, Alice explained, yet when a problem occurred black students received a very mixed message from whites in school. In her view: "We're always on display … always being watched and when one of you slip up, they say that the black community slipped up…. We are all looked at as one large grouping." This double-talk —you're different, but you're the same—was unsettling to the young women interviewed, and it reinforced their belief that in the minds of white America, the blacks' individual identity and group identity would always be enmeshed.

Because the girls were interviewed at different ages and at differing stages of maturation and self-awareness, their comments offer an interesting array of perspectives regarding specific incidents in which white students, letting their guard drop, allowed their true feelings to show. In these moments of insensitivity, black students learned who their friends really were and whom they could trust. Overall the most striking indictment was a shared observation that their white friends were lamentably ignorant about racial differences. Some incidents were merely annoying, such as when white students would ask questions about how black women groom their hair. ("Come back someday when I'm hyperactive and need something to talk about and I will tell you," was one interviewee's exasperated reply.) Other stories describing comments heard from white students speaking about race from outdated and stereotypic notions of black American behavior, reflected a much deeper level of unenlightenment, and the young black women interviewed expressed shock and anger that such misinformation was allowed to persist.

Accurate racial knowledge, they felt, was terribly onesided, where black students knew far more about their white friends than the whites knew of blacks.[3] Attempts to educate were met with uneven success. According to the black women interviewed, part of the problem was the general hesitation white students expressed when discussions of race would arise. Explained Rose:

> Some of the girls are afraid of discussing … racial differences for fear that either they will offend me … what they don't understand is … I won't get upset if they are speaking out of pure ignorance … I will enlighten them. But I guess people are very afraid to face differences here. And what it could mean to them. It's a very fragile status quo. They guard it with their lives, just don't want to discuss it.

Maria added: "… they still think you might rob them in the night sort of thing, they are not comfortable with you yet. [They wonder], Did your brother mug me on the subway?" Distrust, fear, and apathy were cited as major factors preventing honest communication between the races. By virtue of being the color of the majority, white students could afford to make race a less significant aspect of their existence. The black students, however, knew that they live in a society that causes different outcomes for blacks and whites, and this simple fact had forged a wedge between the young women, which for some could not be overcome.

At a time when defining one's self-concept is crucial, integration reinforces the notion that black children are different. One black looking back on his student days recalls: "At that age you want to fit in with people around you. The last thing you want to do is stand out. The trouble is you do stand out. The education you get makes you stand out" (Perkins in Anson 1987, 41). Social integration and affluence can separate minority children from the racial ties, extended kinship networks, and folklore of ethnic culture and these must be replaced with something of equal value (Powell 1982). When peer acceptance is dependent upon how white-like one is, says psychiatrist Gloria Powell, then education becomes a subtractive process, a relinquishing of cultural self-identity. Black students in predominantly white settings are often living biculturally, straddling at least two worlds: black and white.

During adolescence, it can become increasingly difficult to separate one's own values and identity from those of the majority culture. Sometimes blacks and whites view the same circumstance from entirely different perspectives, causing a perceptual clash that begs for one's position to be affirmed. For several of the young women interviewed, Emma Willard's minority student population totaled more black students than they had been exposed to in the past. Barbara reflected, "I was always in such a white man's world. I thought maybe there was something more." At Emma Willard, Barbara was able to find more young women like herself, and to her particular delight, more high-powered ambitious young black women to whom she could relate. Barbara explains, "Most of them hold powerful positions in the school. They are not just back in the distance and everything." Eventually Barbara became one of those powerful black students, rising through the years to hold a key position in the school's black student organization (BSEW).

Black student organizations often fulfill the need to come to terms with racial and ethnic differences, by way of self- and group identity. Often such organizations can provide needed social support as the adolescents struggle with the complicated issues of identity, inclusion and exclusion, and intragroup differences. Many times it is in these settings that black students learn the most about themselves and about other blacks. When Emma Willard's black students came together in their group, they described a discovery of self through mutual recognition and connection. "I found a part of myself at BSEW," Mary recalled as she looked back on the day she first decided to join the group formally. In listening to Mary and others it was clear that the black women in BSEW shared tremendous affection and concern for the welfare of one another. During the years of this study, along with their formal activities, BSEW brought the girls together to help one another negotiate the Emma Willard way of life, to share beauty tips, to discuss racial incidents, and to talk about boys.

Male companionship is of course important to Emma Willard's young women, but issues around dating and relationships with men can be particularly perplexing for black women growing up outside the mainstream of their racial community. Along with never-ending conversations about young men, intraracial differences and similarities were often the topic of all-night discussions. Not everyone made sense of racial concerns in the same way, and, the girls discovered, not everyone was up to the challenge of being black. Black students learned a great deal about the many ways in which one can be a black woman from other black students. The neighborhood "oreos," black people who were ashamed of their heritage, were analyzed, criticized, and summarily denounced. And the occasional student who adopted a "blacker than thou" stance toward the others was similarly rebuked. Students described BSEW as safe and supportive, a place where confidence was kept, where students could feel free to share thoughts, feelings, and fears in an atmosphere of acceptance, camaraderie, and understanding.

Finally, BSEW provided an environment in which young black women could have the opportunity to recognize and participate in leadership activities. Two of the girls interviewed eventually held leadership positions at Emma Willard (in either BSEW or the school government), of which they spoke fondly and with tremendous pride. Ultimately these organizations figured prominently in the young women's development. First, students learned the difficulty and tremendous responsibility of leading others. "Dealing with people of your own race, you always expect them to somehow be behind you, and still it is the same amount of work and the same amount of hassle," Helen exclaimed. In large part, education is the process of helping students gain a degree of control over their lives in the present and in the future. Through her activities with BSEW, Helen was offered the chance to make a difference in her social environment. While the results of her efforts are unknown, the satisfaction she expressed and the lessons she learned about interpersonal negotiation, diplomacy, and tact were invaluable. Effective leadership demands that decisions regarding direction and purpose are made carefully. She explained:

> I think the black community really [must] have a sense of why am I here. What can I be doing, what is our purpose? We really have to put maybe a little more thought [into it], because whatever you go into may be that much harder for you, and you are going to have to make sure it is what you really want and what you really want to do. It's not easy to back away sometimes.

Even more revealing from the discussions of leadership was the manner in which service to others affected the young women's developing sense of self. Several students discovered that through community activities, whether they be on campus with BSEW or school government, or off campus with, for example, the local Big Sister organization, they could express their newly formed sense of social commitment. These students saw themselves as having a role to play in improving the lives of others, and especially in the development and the strengthening of black communities. It is not surprising that the young women who took on these extracurricular activities were the same girls who spoke most passionately about oppression, discrimination, and the desire for a better society. Most of the black students interviewed acknowledged the sacrifice (economic and otherwise) made by their parents in order for them to attend Emma Willard. An education at Emma Willard was indeed a privilege and, these young women believed, with that privilege came an obligation to give something back in return.

It has been said that to be born black and female is to start with two strikes against you. The convergence of these two gender and racial identities has been assumed to create an overwhelming dilemma not easily overcome. Yet from these data it is evident that the process of being and becoming black provides young women with three essential opportunities for growth. First, there is an opportunity for role negation—the repudiation of both race- and gender-based stereotypes. Second, there is an opportunity to create a new and personally defined identity in one's own terms. And third, when opportunities for leadership are provided, there's a chance to effect change in one's social environment by developing and pursuing one's personal commitments.

IMPLICATIONS

The purpose of this essay was to illuminate the formation and transformation of racial identity in a small group of black adolescent females attending Emma Willard School. Most of the focus was on the psychological experiences faced by these young women. The path that their development followed, however, was greatly influenced by the social context in which it was unfolding. Sometimes educational institutions, in the effort to assimilate minority students, follow a norm of promoting sameness, thus ignoring differences. This posture may encourage minority students to reject their ethnic identity and the unique qualities of being black. When education is seen as an estrangement from who one is, or is seen as an effort to disconnect the student from where she came, neither education nor integration will be served.

Predominantly white educational institutions, such as Emma Willard, may strive to be aware of and respectful toward racial differences. As is clear from these data, the implication of these differences for the psychological and social development of minority adolescents constitutes an important focus of research. While teachers and administrators of the school may not share the same cultural perspectives as the families of minority children, the school has a clear role to play in the developmental process. Teachers and administrators seeking to be supportive of this venture toward identity development and self-understanding can help students make sense of who they are and where they are going. In particular, they can help students make sense of what they see in the world; specifically the major social inequities in the United States and the evidence of racism and sexism. These are important educational lessons for children of all colors, but even more critical for black women. Research suggests that for females, issues of attachment and connection are of primary concern (Gilligan 1982), and for black females, the orientation toward racial pride and continuity begins early in life. Here, too, adults in predominantly white school settings have a role to play in helping minority students aspire while still maintaining connection with their racial and ethnic communities.

Ultimately, the young women interviewed over the four-year period ended up feeling that rather than being overwhelmed and disheartened by the double burden of being black and female, they felt fortunate to have an opportunity to reject negative stereotypes of black women, and to create and sustain in its place a positive racial identity. The process of racial identity formation encouraged them to decide upon who one is and what one will stand for. Especially through the pursuit of leadership opportunities, the young black women of Emma Willard gained a sense of personal efficacy and a commitment to acting in the public sphere. This serendipitous finding is indeed intriguing and suggests directions for future research.

NOTES

1. The interviews of the seven minority students occurred in the following manner. Two were interviewed only once, one was interviewed twice, one was interviewed three times, one was interviewed four times, and two were interviewed five times. While all of the black women were interviewed at least once by the author, two were interviewed by other (nonblack) interviewers on three occasions. In all cases, even when the girls were interviewed by someone else in the Harvard Group, the questions about racial identity were posed and discussed with the author. Most of the quotations used in this paper come from responses to that category of question; however, the question about self-description and leadership generated a number of usable comments. Following the interview sessions, only one tape was determined to be inaudible and unusable. The data presented in this paper comes from twenty interviews, the total of transcribable interviews of all the minority students.

2. Elsewhere I have analyzed five separate models of what psychologists and psychiatrists have described as black identity development (Ward 1984). These theoretical interpretations include a psycho-dynamic approach (Grier and Cobbs 1968), a developmental model (Thomas 1971 and Cross 1971), a

racial/cultural group orientation model (Nobles 1980) and a longitudinal, in-depth interview and analysis approach (Ladner 1971).

3. Jean Baker Miller, in *Towards a New Psychology of Women* from the Beacon Press in Boston, 1976, offers an excellent discussion of socio-political knowledge—black/white, male/female, subordinate/dominant relationships.

REFERENCES

Anson, R. S. 1987. *Best Intentions: The Education and Killing of Edmund Perry.* New York: Random House.

Barnes, E. 1972. "The Black Community as the Source of Positive Self-Concept for Black Children: A Theoretical Perspective in Black Psychology." In *Black Psychology,* edited by R. Jones. New York: Harper and Row.

Bowman, P., and C. Howard. 1985. Race-related socialization, motivation and academic achievement: A study of black youths in three generation families. *Journal of the American Academy of Child Psychiatry* 24 (2) 134–41.

Comer, J. and A. Poussaint. 1975. *Black Child Care.* New York: Pocket Books.

Cross, W. July 1971. The Negro to black conversion experience: Towards a psychology of black liberation. *Black World* 20, no. 9, 13–27.

——. 1978. Models of psychological nigrescence: A literature review. *Journal of Black Psychology* 5: 13–31.

——. 1980. "Black Identity: Rediscovering the Distinction between Personal Identity and Reference Group Orientation." New York: Africana Studies and Research Center, Cornell University.

Erikson, E. 1950. *Childhood and Society.* New York: W. W. Norton.

——. 1956. The problem of ego identity. *Journal of the American Psychoanalytic Association* 4: 56–121.

——. October 1964. A memorandum on identity and Negro youth. *Journal of Social Issues* 10:4, 29–42.

——. 1968. *Identity, Youth and Crisis.* New York: W. W. Norton.

Fordham, S., and J. Ogbu. 1986. Black students' school success: Coping with the burden of acting white. *The Urban Review* 18: 3, 176–206.

Gay, G. May 1978. Ethnic identity in early adolescence: Some implications for institutional reform. *Educational Leadership,* p. 649–55.

Gilligan, C. 1982. *In a Different Voice.* Cambridge, Mass: Harvard University Press.

Grier, W., and P. Cobbs. 1968. *Black Rage.* New York: Basic Books.

Jones, R. 1980. *Black Psychology,* 2nd Ed. New York: Harper and Row.

Ladner, J. 1971. *Tomorrow's Tomorrow: The Black Woman.* New York: Doubleday.

——. 1978. *Mixed Families: Adopting Across Racial Boundaries.* New York: Doubleday.

Nobles, W. 1981. "African-American Family Life: An Instrument of Culture." In *Black Families,* edited by H. P. McAdoo. Beverly Hills, Calif.: Sage Press.

——. 1980. "African Philosophy: Foundations for Black Psychology." In *Black Psychology,* edited by R. Jones, New York: Harper and Row.

Okazawa-Rey, M., T. Robinson and J. Ward. 1987. "Black Women and the Politics of Skin Color and Hair." In *Women, Power and Therapy: Issues for Women,* edited by M. Braude. New York: The Haworth Press.

Powell, G. 1982. "School Desegregation and Self-Concept Among Junior High School Students." In *The Afro-American Family: Assessment Treatment and Research Issues,* edited by B. Bass. G. Wyatt, and G Powell. New York: Grune and Stratton.

Slaughter, D. February 1972. Becoming an Afro-American woman. *School Review,* 299–318.

Thomas, C. 1971. *Boys Know More.* Beverly Hills, Calif.: Glencoe Press.

Ward J. January 1984. Racial identity formation and transformation: A literature review. Unpublished Qualifying Paper, Harvard Graduate School of Education.

18

Freedom for Some, Discipline for "Others": The Structure of Inequity in Education

ENORA R. BROWN

LOCKDOWN IS BECOMING the pervasive reality for working-class youth in public schools that resemble prisons or military camps rather than sites of learning and critical thought. In these schools, replete with metal detectors, armed guards, and periodic searches, poor youth, especially African American and other youth of color, are being subjected to increasing levels of physical and psychological surveillance, confinement, and regimentation. The physical restrictions imposed within the school walls are complemented by national policies and practices in education, such as school uniforms, more stringent, standardized forms of rote education, and JROTC, which signify the need for discipline, obedience, and conformity. This growing *culture of militarism* is being created/cultivated predominantly within grossly underfunded, tax-based schools of color in poor communities. Since youth identities in these communities are discursively constructed as underachieving, violent-prone, education-aversive youth (i.e., the dregs of society, who are in need of discipline and restraint), the imposition and presence of enforcement policies to "civilize their untamed spirits" seems merited and natural.

Conversely, public schools for wealthy youth resemble *palatial edifices*, adorned with all of the resources that constitute sites for learning, critical inquiry, and fluid social interchange. These schools are located on spacious grounds and are equipped with state-of-the-art facilities in comfortable, resource-rich environs that encourage the freedom of mobility and thought to discover, problem-solve, and create. The physical breadth and expanse of these public schools for predominantly wealthy white youth are complemented by national policies, such as the privatization of public education, the standards movement (e.g., major overhaul of the Scholastic Aptitude Tests [SAT's]), and advanced math/science/technology curricula that signify inherited privilege and institutionalized entitlement and promote independent thought, analysis, and creativity. This *culture of privilege* is expanding within schools that are brimming over with tax-based funds and supplemental resources from wealthy resident families. Since youth identities in these communities are discursively constructed as smart achievers and as the thoughtful professionals and cultured leaders of the future, the plentiful resources and relaxed, but rigorous learning environments seem to be the natural outgrowth of their self-directed, responsible, inquisitive, and creative spirits.

Polarized along social class and racial lines, public schools in poor, working-class and wealthy upper-class communities are *public* places whose fusion of space and experience are imbued with differential meanings[1] about the freedoms to which wealthy or poor youth are "entitled" and the consequent breadth of future life options that are available to them. These places constitute the physical space where particular social, economic, political, and psychic relationships are forged, nurtured, and contested. Public schools are sources of identity, constituted within webs of power relations that frame the choices and aspirations of youth. While the dominant discourse portrays these schools as the "natural" product of the values, capacities, and rights or residents in each community, it will be argued here that these schools are structurally embedded in, and historically constituted through, dynamic postindustrial, global economic, and political relationships. As such, the edifices *stand for/represent a* polarized and interdependent relationship between the upper class and the working class, the relative valuation of these classes in the dominant culture, and the "rightful" inherited identity positions of their youth in the existing social order. Shrouded in an ideology of individual choice, social Darwinism, and national unity, these schools reflects the intersubjective meanings created through the differential ways in which people live their lives in disparate communities.

This chapter will examine the differences between two public schools—Mountainview Township and Groundview Technical High schools—as they manifest historical institutional inequities in the public education system, which are exacerbated and codified by current national policies (i.e., *corporate privatization and domestic militarization of schools*) and are reified and justified by current ideological formulations about the "nature" or essentialized identities of the youth in these different contexts. First, comparative portraits will be presented of the current *financial and material resources* available, the *curricular and pedagogical experiences* provided, and the *social relationships* fostered within the divergent school cultures. The significance of the observed differences and the dynamic interplay of these dimensions of the educational experience within each school will be discussed as they "validate" the meritocratic justification for inequity in education, and as they influence the futures that youth envision, the paths they "choose," and the stations in life that are readily available.

Second, the historic roots of these school differences will be examined through an analysis of the political struggles for public education for the exslaves that accompanied the ascendance of industrialization after the Civil War.[2] This analysis is based on the overarching premise that the disparate quality of education in wealthy–poor racialized schools is organically linked to the economy. It will provide insight into the structural reproduction and function of social class and racial inequities in education.[3] Further, this chapter will discuss the significance of *current economic crises*,[4] including the seismic shift that a burgeoning information technology and robotics are introducing into the national economy,[5] along with the wholesale movement of industrial capital to cheaper global markets,[6] and the *corresponding political repression* exercised through legislative and judicial policies and practices.[7] These developments in economic and political life have ushered in corresponding efforts to privatize public education and militarize schools in poor communities to support corporations' perennial search for new markets for profit and to thwart the inevitable resistance and rebellion of those displaced within a postindustrial economy. This analysis will posit the view that the introduction of robotics and gradual emergence of laborless production is creating a dramatic shift in the national/global economy that *requires* drastic changes in the state apparatus,[8] especially in public education, in order to support changes in the existing social order.

It is in this context that the dominant culture's ideological tools have intensified to justify the intensifying polarization of wealth, to scapegoat racial, and ethnic sectors of the population as source of worsening economic and social conditions, and to redefine democracy as "individual, private choice," a first step in restructuring public education. This chapter will conclude by addressing the crucial role of critical pedagogy in educators' work to promote analytic understandings of the dynamics that undergird social inequity in education in order to guide our thinking and human agency in fostering social change.

MOUNTAINVIEW: FREEDOM TO BECOME

Bourdieu posits that institutions' monopolized appropriation of and methodical failure to transfer cultural capital and other instruments necessary for success in the dominant culture will instantiate their exclusive ownership and that of the culture as a whole in hands of the ruling class.[9] Concordantly, Spears states that the rigorous quality of education at elite institutions prepares those students for their inherited leadership roles in society with concordant ideological underpinnings, and that the absence of comparable educational experiences for students at nonelite institutions mitigates against creativity and poor students' ideological investment in a critical examination of oppression that would challenge the existing social order and their position within it.[10] Mountainview Township High School exemplifies wealthy schools within an educational system that systematically transmits the instruments of appropriation to local affluent students, who are being prepared to inherit and fulfill leadership positions in the dominant culture.

The sprawling public high school campus of Mountainview Township High School is located in an affluent Chicago suburb. It is blanketed with a lush landscaped lawn that is adorned with winding tree-lined paths that lead to seven strategically placed, spacious, modern glass and stone buildings. The picturesque, well-maintained campus has a large track field and other sport-specific courts and athletic fields. It has an adjoining faculty-student parking lot that is within walking distance of the shopping district, replete with quaint shops, restaurants, and businesses. Mountainview is nestled near a commercial thoroughfare that connects local shoreline communities whose $500,000 to $1,000,000–plus homes are comfortably adjoined by wooded areas and jogging paths. This school campus is the site for the academic, cultural, athletic, social, and civic pursuits of over three thousand ninth-through twelfth-grade students in the adjacent wealthy communities.

Upon entering Mountainview High School, one is struck by the expansive marble hallways, lined with windowseats beneath large windows that overlook the campus grounds and allow natural light to bathe the art-lined hallways. Students, casually dressed in non-descript jeans and designer clothes, freely and comfortably walk through the hall, and perch on window ledges to read or engage in conversation with friends. Running slightly late for class, students are gently encouraged by staff to "Hurry along." They are unburdened by the threat of a detention slip and classroom doors are left ajar for their late arrival. Individual administrative offices are spacious, well-furnished, inviting spaces that support the ongoing work of the school and comfortably accommodate visitors. Classrooms are awash with natural light and equipped with advanced technology and audiovisual equipment. Plentiful seating is available for students and teachers to engage in flexibly arranged discussions and a myriad of learning experiences to a background of quiet music. What a conducive environment for learning, thinking, and creating with others. On this open campus, students freely eat and drink in class and go home for lunch.

The various wings of each building reflect the range of academic and cocurricular experiences from which students may design "majors" and interdisciplinary courses of study. In addition to the wing devoted exclusively to fine arts, other academic spaces include: state-of-the-art computers, science, technology, and language labs, a theater and performing arts department, student-run radio and cable television stations, music facilities, news bureau, multiple gymnasiums, swimming pool and accessories, dance studio, Nautilus exercise room and equipment, an expansive library housing thousands of volumes, a cuisine-plentiful lunchroom, a student lounge, and an art gallery. National and international trips provide rich off-site learning experiences for student interests in marine biology, geology, and family support for social/intellectual inquiry.

Mountainview resembles a small liberal arts college with over three hundred multilevel, discipline-based academic courses, including advanced placement, from which students fashion their schedules. Courses include: mathematics, speech and drama, modern/classical languages, technology education, business education, social work, social studies, music, science, multicultural studies, gourmet cooking, interior and graphic design. Soccer, lacrosse, polo, fencing, and field hockey are a few of the sports that complement the usual array of athletic endeavors. In addition, there are over one hundred clubs and interest groups, from bridge to rugby and global exchange, from social service and AIDS coalition, to poetry, and cheerleading. The range of academic and cocurricular experiences, along with a counselor for every twenty-two students undergirds the vision and actuality of a 95 percent college-bound student population.

Who inhabits this space called Mountainview? Almost 88 percent of the students are European American, about 9 percent are Asian American, less than 2 percent are Latino American, and less than 1 percent are African American. Almost 97 percent of the students graduate and less than 1 percent are from low-income families. About 93 percent of the teachers are European American, less than 3 percent Asian American about 2 percent Latino, and approximately 1 percent African American. Eighty percent of the teachers have masters degrees and salaries average over $75,000. On the basis of local property taxes, over $15,000 is provided for each student.[11] For the youth in this community, Mountainview is *their space*, and hence *their place*. It is where *they* belong. The *socialized* choices, options, and freedoms that they experience and create in *their* school and community transmit and foster the creation of cultural capital that will prepare these youth to be the future CEO, facile owners, and manipulators of emergent information technology, architects of public policy, and nimble consumers and promoters of "high culture." These youth expect material wealth from the profits of today and will step into *their* place, their future, in the world.

GROUNDVIEW HIGH: DISCIPLINE TO CONSTRICT

> The action of the school, whose effect is unequal among children from different classes, and whose success varies considerably among those upon whom it has an effect, tends to reinforce and to consecrate by its sanctions the initial inequalities.[12]

Educational institutions play a pivotal role in forging *aspirations* and structuring *choice* for youth through the daily actions and practices in schools that sanction and codify existent social and economic inequities. Groundview Technical High School exemplifies schools within an educational system that instantiates limited options for and validates the constricted vision of youth in this poor community. The aspirations of youth, both wealthy and poor, reflect their "internalization of objective probabilities" and inform their life choices (i.e., material expressions of their efforts to reach what is attainable).[13] Their "choices" are not those of "autonomous moral agents acting in an existential vacuum," but rather are created and exercised through the dynamic interplay of social, psychic, political, and economic forces.[14] As students at Groundview make sense of the dynamic interplay of forces evident in the school's physical environs, public school policies and practices, and their own lived experiences, they insightfully deduce the prospects for their future, for their survival.

Groundview Technical High School is located in a poor urban Chicago community twenty-five miles from Mountainview. Its grounds consist of an imposing, self-contained faded red brick four-story building, in considerable disrepair, with an adjoining, uninhabitable, concrete court. The school consumes an entire square block and is bracketed by trash-strewn patches of wilted grass and a variegated concrete sidewalk in a working-class community. The smokestack structure is barely distinguishable from the worn vacant public housing buildings that stand nearby, and blends in with the rugged deteriorating landscape and the ceaseless traffic and fumes of the adjoining busy intersections. This eighty-five-year-old building is the site for close to three thousand ninth- through twelfth-grade students in the surrounding crowded urban community. Like other neighborhoods on "this side of town," this community was intentionally cut off from the nearby commercial and residential areas by the strategic positioning of a racial barrier—one of the nation's largest interstate highways.

One is welcomed into the physical structure of Groundview in a manner quite different from that of Mountainview. Upon entering the heavy steel doors of the school's main entrance, one is immediately greeted by two armed policemen and metal detectors, whose presence is as imposing as the red brick, crumbling structure of the school. This reception typically generates considerable tension and wariness and does *not* have the "ring of freedom." Students clad in black and white uniforms are herded/filed into the school with their picture IDs and class schedule, and must pass through the metal detectors to ensure that there are no weapons on school grounds. Students must wear their IDs and class schedules around their necks throughout the day, so that they may be policed/monitored upon entry into the lunchroom and other school checkpoints. The drably painted, relatively bare walls lead down dimly lit, dingy hallways, whose overhead buzzing fluorescent lighting is compromised by some boarded-up windows and noticeable fixtures in disrepair. The deteriorating physical structure reveals the lack of attention and funds devoted to the condition of the school and its inhabitants.

Students are exhorted by guards not to linger in the hallways or exceed the four minutes allotted for them to move between classes. After the bell has rung, students are not permitted in the hallways without a written excuse, and tardiness is punishable by detention. The halls are for swift transitions to and from class or other destinations. Tarrying is not allowed. This social practice is enforced by the presence of guards in all of the corridors and by the absence of any space for students to comfortably congregate, to have a leisurely chat with friends, or to sit and read a book. The one place where students may congregate is in the lunchroom. The "closed campus policy" at Groundview prohibits students from leaving the school for lunch once they have entered in the morning. The policy is reinforced by the presence of metal detectors at all entrances and exits throughout the building and the pending threat of suspension if students fail to comply. Rules are made and strictly enforced, with the expectation that students will follow them to avoid sanction. After passing through this checkpoint, one arrives at the administrative office, a room of ample size with cramped, limited space for staff. Visitors who come to the school stand at a counter, sing in, and receive pleasant assistance from staff behind their desks. The classrooms and connecting corridors built for 2,500 students barely accommodate the 3,000 students enrolled.

There are no well-equipped academic spaces for students' interests or choice in various disciplines of study (e.g., the humanities or social sciences). There is a metal shop, a wood shop, and cosmetology room to prepare students for particular skilled trades. There is a locked room full of woodshop and carpentry equipment in the school, but it is inaccessible to students, since staff members are not available to operate the equipment. There is one gymnasium and one computer in the sparsely-volumed library, which is often locked, as are student bathrooms. There is no theater, music area, pool, or exercise equipment, no science equipment and few books to share during class. The State of Illinois's required courses are available in the areas of English, history, mathematics, some sciences, and a few courses for elective credits to fulfill graduation requirements. The absence of current texts, equipment, or operative library for students' learning is synchronous with their "skilled" preparation for work, if any, in marginal service industries.

In the classrooms, students are seated at old desks and in some classes, as many as twenty-five students are crammed around four small tables. Few classes are fueled with engaging conversation between students and teacher. Most students are "busied" to the point of obvious boredom with ditto sheets or scripted lessons for recall and rote comprehension and are often engaged by teachers with directives and discordant communications. Frustration, disdain, contempt, and helplessness are apparent. Over two hundred students are assigned to a school counselor and few students are college-bound.

In contrast to Mountainview's fine arts wing or technology lab, Groundview in recent years has created a separate and distinct wing that is devoted to the Junior Reserve Office Training Corp (JROTC). It is a privileged space, inhabitable only by those who are enrolled, and is increasingly becoming a major component of the school's emergent curriculum and character as a site of military discipline. The JROTC hallways are adorned with military memorabilia, pictures of generals, scenes from past wars, and traditional patriotic images and symbols. This wing is equipped with many up-to-date computers and ample space for students to study. Students are allowed to move freely from place to place and to make choices about courses of study. Imbued with hopes for further education, these youth are being prepared to enter the disciplined ranks of the armed forces and to serve on the front lines of this nation's international skirmishes.

Who inhabits this space called Groundview? One hundred percent of the students are African American, over 93 percent are from low-income families, and less than 50 percent of the students graduate from high school. Forty-five percent of the teachers are European American, 40 percent African American, 11 percent Latino, 2 percent Asian American, and almost 3 percent Native American. Forty-five percent of the teachers have masters degrees and salaries average $50,000, one-half and one-third less that [sic] those at Mountainview, respectively. Students at Groundview receive half of the financial investment per student that students at Mountainview receive. On the basis of the property taxes in this community, $7,800 is spent on each student to ensure his or her place and space in the social order and the continuation of a well-oiled tracking system of inequity.[15]

For the youth in this part of the city, one gets the sense that they are *contained, confined, restricted,* and *monitored* in a space that *does not* feel like *their place.* There is no sense of ownership. It is where they are, but not where they belong. The paltry curriculum, physical restrictions, closed options, structure, discipline, control, and order, imposed "for their own good"[16] in prison-like schools, are preparing them for a place, at the lowest rung of the job market, in jail, or in chronic/permanent unemployment.

CURRICULAR PREPARATION FOR THE FUTURE: BUSINESS OR MILITARY?

The differences between the two Chicago area high schools are stark. The disparate financial and material resources, curricular and pedagogical experiences, and physical and social environs create different cultures or webs of meaning that are constitutive of particular social identity positions in society. Of particular interest are the *new* curricular offerings at each school. The burgeoning JROTC, vocational curricula at Groundview and the expansive college- and business-prep academic curricula at Mountainview are indicative of the social identities that are being forged for these youth and the proscribed future positions as adults in society for which they are being prepared.

At Mountainview, the extensive new programs of study are in electronics, robotics, digital and laser technology, computer science and programming, globalization, culture and Eastern languages. These cutting-edge areas of inquiry complement long-standing curricula in business (e.g., the economy, stockmarket, politics), engineering, interdisciplinary studies, advanced math, and science, and are burgeoning disciplines that will thrive on the knowledge constructed in the twenty-first century. These programs of study will support the profound and rapid economic shift from industrialization to robotics and electronic/information technology in a global market,[17] reinforce the digital divide, and secure the social class position of these students as they are prepared for leadership in business and the political, economic, and cultural centers worldwide. The school provides the opportunity for these students to produce and appreciate various forms of popular culture (e.g., videos, film, literature, music, drama), and to study the cultural meanings that are being negotiated around the globe. Armed with "technical knowledge" and cultural understanding, students at this elite public institution are being socialized to be arbiters of corporate capital. Their cultural capital will "confirm… their monopoly of the instruments of appropriation of the dominant culture and thus their monopoly of the culture."[18] Students at Mountainview have the most to gain from the continuation of the current social order.

JROTC is the "privileged" field of study at Groundview. Military enlistment is being marketed heavily in poor communities, especially those of color. Under the guise of enhancing students' educational opportunities, JROTC promises a less than glorious, uplifting future for these youth. JROTC takes $50,000 per year from each school budget, substitutes some important academic subjects for JROTC courses, and may hire teachers that are not certified in the subjects they teach.[19] With current efforts to privatize public education, the corporatization of the educational curriculum (i.e., courses of study tailored to corporate interests and profit) is being realized.[20] While JROTC is promoted as a program that will afford poor youth a career, a "way out," the Veterans Administration reports that veterans earn less than non-veterans, and that one-third are homeless and 20 percent are in prison.[21] Though 54 percent of the nation's JROTC participants and 50 percent of the front line troops of the military are people of color, few are likely to receive technical training and are thus more likely to be unemployed when they get out.[22] So much for the army motto: "Be all that you can be."

The proliferation of JROTC programs and the presence of military schools in Chicago reflects the current surge of militarism in poor communities, especially those that are African American and Latino. Students, at Groundview and other working-class communities are being channeled into the military to protect the global interests of corporate capital and the future CEOs from Mountainview. As former Secretary of Defense Dick Cheney stated, "The reason to have a military is to be prepared to fight and win wars. That is our basic fundamental mission. The military is not a social welfare agency. It's not a job program."[23] Retired Rear General Eugene J. Carroll, deputy director of the Center for Defense Information states, "It is appalling that the Pentagon is selling a military training program as a remedy for intractable social and economic problems in inner cities. Surely, its real motive is to inculcate a positive attitude toward military service at a very early age, thus creating a storehouse of potential recruits."[24]

The nationwide declination of troop strength and pending war over oil in the Middle east has prompted massive efforts to recruit from certain communities. The armed forces have added $1.5 million to their $95 million advertising budget to recruit youth enlistees. Though humor-laced advertisements for students and parents encourage youth to stay in school so that they may enter the army,[25] youth from the nation's Groundviews are not responding to this call to the military as enthusiastically as anticipated. To mask the marginal success of recruitment efforts, New York State's Army National Guard's systematically inflated troop strength figures in the 1990s.[26] For the first time since the Vietnam War, the Pentagon has extended active duty for 15,000 reserve troops from twelve months to two years, jeopardizing enlistees' salaries and employment stability.[27]

The marketing of JROTC programs in poor African American and Latino communities comes at a time when major changes in the nationally administered, standardized Scholastic Aptitude Test are under way. By 2005, the SATs will be overhauled to include a writing exam, grammar questions, a critical reading exam in history, the humanities, science, and so forth, and an extended math exam based on advanced math covered in three years of high school. Ostensibly, these changes will better align exams with the 97 percent of college-bound students that take higher-level math.[28] They will also structurally exclude Groundview students, whose school is on probation, provides scripted instruction, and has a graduation rate below 50 percent, and will fuel the adage: "College isn't for everyone."

The SAT overhaul and an addition of $8–12 to the $26 registration fee will affect school curricula and systemically constrict the already narrow band of high school students who will be able to afford or be adequately prepared to take the SAT exam or attend college.[29]

There is little question about which students are being tracked to become CEOs in business and which are being tracked to *serve and protect* corporate capital's interests in the military. The systematic implementation of such grossly unequal new programs of study adds new meaning to the idea of "choice" and reveals the powerful role of schools in reproducing and normalizing existent social class inequities. The divergent qualities of "freedom" and "constraint" at the two schools reflect interdependent, carefully maintained socialization processes necessary for students' future positions in society.[30] While dominant culture ideology champions the aspirations and accomplishments of youth as products of individual will, family values, and personal vision, it masks the powerful role of social, economic, and political forces in codifying and justifying the hierarchical positions occupied by youth across social class and racial lines.

While some from Groundview may "make it" in spite of the odds and are to be lauded for overcoming the obstacles, this portrait does not lend itself to a celebration of resilience and does not discount the many heroic and subtle forms of resistance exercised by marginalized youth to create new possibilities. Neither do these portraits suggest that social and economic relationships are unidirectional, deterministically creating mindless drones that blindly assume their stations in life. Rather, these portraits were designed to unequivocally render visible the pervasive, *evolving* structure of inequity, privilege, and discrimination in education that has unjustly benefited/damaged youth and to critique an educational system that prohibits success for the many and enables success for very few.

The disparities between Mountainview and Groundview are not new to public education, but may be traced back to the mid-nineteenth century. In 1857, African American leaders fought against the gross difference between the $16 spent on each white student in schools, which were "splendid, almost palatial edifices, with manifold comforts, conveniences, and elegancies," and the lone penny spent on African American students, whose school buildings were "dark and cheerless" in "environs full of vice and filth."[31] Similarly, Kozol's poignant accounts in 1991 document the funding-based *structural continuity of inequity* in education for white, wealthy youth and working-class youth of color.[32] Race and class disparities in public education historically have been linked to the oppression of the working poor and the economic interests of industrial and corporate capital. As the driving needs of the capital have changed and economic relations have shifted with technological innovation, there have been related changes in the state apparatus and political infrastructure that are manifested in public education. The following sections will examine some continuities and discontinuities in the fundamental relationship between major shifts in the economic social order and relations of production (i.e., rise of the industrial economy and the information-driven economy), that have been accompanied by repressive political measures and have ushered in requisite changes in public education.

HISTORICAL ROOTS AND SIGNIFICANCE OF THE DIFFERENCE
The current inequities and related injustices in public education are deeply rooted in the sociohistorical, economic, and political structures of this country and serve an indispensable

social function in maintaining and perpetuating the social order. *Industrialization created an economic necessity for universal public education*, which in turn, has been both an instrument of oppression and the maintenance of a two-tiered system in this country and a tool of liberation for democracy. In *The Education of Blacks in the South, 1860–1935*, Anderson examines the inextricable link between late nineteenth and early twentieth-century industrialization and mass schooling as a "means to produce efficient and contented labor and as a socialization process to instill in black and white children an acceptance of the southern racial hierarchy"[33] and the pivotal role of racial division in maintaining the burgeoning Northern industrial capitalists' control over white striking workers. For wealthy whites, universal public education would promote social stability, production efficiency, and economic prosperity.

Ex-slaves were the first native Southerners to struggle for universal, state-supported public education in the *classical liberal tradition,* in defense of emancipation and against the planters' regime.[34] However, "white architects of black education," a contingent of Northern and Southern white entrepreneurs, social scientists, and philanthropists, crafted a special form of *industrial education* for blacks to substitute older, cruder methods of socialization, coercion, and control and to support the demand for an efficient, organized agricultural sector to supplement the emergent industrial nation's trade with England.[35] The "architects" advocacy and financial support for an industrial education for blacks and classical liberal education for whites afforded marginal material and psychological privilege to white workers (i.e., racial privilege would compensate for their social class disadvantage). This stratified public education would address the educational and ideological needs of a growing industrial society, while subjugating black and white laborers in relation to the owners of wealth. William Baldwin, Northern philanthropist and universal public education advocate, states:

> The potential economic value of the Negro population properly educated is infinite and incalculable…. Time has proven that he is best fitted to perform the heavy labor…. This will permit the southern white laborer to perform the more expert labor, and to leave the fields, the mines, and the simpler trades for the Negro.[36]
>
> The union of white labor, well organized, will raise the wages beyond a reasonable point, and then the battle will be fought, and the Negro will be put in at a less wage, and the labor union will either have to come down in wages, or Negro labor will be employed.[37]
>
> Except in the rarest of instances, I am bitterly opposed to the so-called higher education of Negroes.[38]

Baldwin's and other advocates' financial support for public education was contingent on a brand of industrial education for blacks (i.e., Hampton-Tuskegee Idea), that was not equivalent to higher education for whites, and would divide the working poor in the interests of the burgeoning industrial capitalists.[39] These conditions informed the structure, social practices, and justificatory ideology of emergent separate, unequal education, and reflect Bourdieu and Passeron's analysis that the "neutral" face of public education, as social equalizer, conceals its dynamic contribution to the reproduction of class structure, with its attendant privileges and relations of power.[40] W.E.B. DuBois, noted African American scholar and advocate, understood both the emancipatory possibilities of public education and enslaving function of race-class stratified education. Thus, he vigorously opposed the limited goal of industrial or classical education and argued for higher education that would promote blacks' strident moves toward equality and not compromise the working poor.[41]

While support for universal public education was integral to the ongoing struggle for democracy, the architects' economic motices wereniether noble nor altruistic, and dovetailed with those of Southern white planters who opposed public education. Though the opponents relied ton "illiterate exploited agricultural laborers" and feared that education would fuel workers' economic and political aspirations, both agreed on black disfranchisement, segregation, and economic subordination.[42] During reconstruction, the architects "ignored" opponents' funding of widespread vigilante violence by the Ku Klux Klan and other terrorist groups to force freedmen and freed women back to slave status, to secure a wedge between them and poor whites, and to reestablish the rule of white slave-owning oligarchy.[43] The architects and opponents of public education strove to protect the economic interests of the wealthy through both legal and extralegal forms of coercion. In concert, the industrial education "for" and the reign of terror against blacks served to maintain the social and economic order.

This legacy of race-class inequity reveals *structural and ideological continuities* between past practices and the current relationship between Groundview Technical and Mountainview Township High Schools. First, Groundview's curricula resembles the industrial education model designed for ex-slaves, which prepares poor African American youth to take on the "simpler trades." The "higher education" is reserved for the white propertied class at Mountainview to prepare them with expertise for leadership. In addition, the bifurcated forms of public education and the divergent cultural capital afforded different race-class groupings mitigate against current fears that education will "inflate workers' economic and political aspirations." While the "nonelite" education at Groundview does not encourage poor African American youth to document or question their oppression, the transmission of power and privilege at Mountainview fosters students' investment in the existing social order. Third, the ascendant culture of militarism in poor schools of color hearkens back to the legal and extralegal forms of coercion used by the early advocates and opponents of public education imbued with the warning, "Stay in your place." The surveillance, confinement, discipoline, and systemic violence in poor schools is reminiscent of earlier efforts to deter freedmen's and freed women's resistance to forced labor and their struggle for the freedoms afforded whites.

There is continuity. What prevails is a two-tiered educational system maintained by systemic efforts to quell the stirrings of poor youth of color. While today's postindustrial economic and political configurations do not mirror those that existed during the post–Civil War days of the late nineteenth century, the fundamental disparity between the wealthy and the poor characterizes current relationships within global capitalism.[44] There is discontinuity. The ascendance of an information-based, electronics-driven postindustrial economy has ushered in a new era that is reshaping the political and educational landscape, creating more pronounced forms of structural inequity and attendant forms of repression.

THE ECONOMY AND THE STATE

The rise of industrial capitalism laid the foundation for structural inequities in universal public education. In this postindustrial era, what economic and political conditions are structuring, altering, or dismantling public education? Do current inequities in education and the cultures of militarism and privilege, in turn, serve certain economic interests? These questions flow from the premise of a fundamental, synergistic relationship between *the economy and the state*. The *base* (i.e., social relations and the tools, skills, technology that constitute the process of production to meet human needs) is both reflected in and protected, organized, and strengthened by a corresponding *superstructure* (i.e., political state apparatus or societal laws, institutions, and ideological formations).[45] While some have disavowed the validity of this structural relationship on the basis of economic determinism or the exclusion of human agency, this perspective, even in the postindustrial era, provides a lens through which complex, often contradictory processes of social life may be understood. While Engels did posit the economic necessity of societal development, he discussed the base and superstructure as a dynamic, *bidirectional*, and interdependent relationship between the economy and the state and emphasized the inherent, indispensable role of humans in shaping history.[46]

Complementarily, Althusser's treatise on the state apparatus highlights the interdependent roles of ideology and repression within the superstructure. The Repressive State Apparatus (RSA) (i.e., the government, administration, army, police, courts, and prisons) and Ideological State Apparatus (ISA) (i.e., religious, educational, family, legal, poligical, trade union, communications, and cultural) function to maintain and support capitalist relations of production. While the RSA and ISA function primarily by repression and ideology, respectively, each contains elements of the other (i.e., the RSA can function ideologically, the ISA repressively).[47] In mature capitalism the educational ideological system is the dominant apparatus within the ISA. "Thus ... Schools ... use suitable methods of punishment, expulsion, selection, etc., to 'discipline' not only their shepherds, but also their flocks."[48] The theological constructs, base and superstructure, and repressive and ideological arms of the state apparatus are valuable analytical tools for examining the dynamic, nonlinear processes that constitute societal change. The next sections address the emergence of automation and corresponding rise of domestic militarism as profound changes in base and superstructure that contextualize the privatization of public education and militarization in schools bolstering structural inequity.

FROM INDUSTRIAL PRODUCTION TO AUTOMATION AND ROBOTICS

The introduction of new technologies under certain conditions precipitates qualitative leaps in the scale of production and gradually changes the nature of social and political life.[49] The innovation of the steam engine and electric motor in the late 1800s launched the Industrial Revolution, transforming society from an agricultural to financial industrial economy.[50] Electromechanics enabled the creation of *labor-saving devices* for efficient routinized, mass production that far exceeded the limits imposed by the manual labor of the individual artisan, cottage industry, or chattel slavery. The mechanization of Southern agriculture and centralization of large-scale, assembly-line production severely disrupted agrarian life and forced laborers to migrate to the nation's cities. The social nature of production in industry reconfigured the nation's economy, transferring its hub from declining rural to thriving urban financial centers.[51]

Just as electromechanics forged the ascendance of industrial capitalist production, so has the emergence of microelectronic technology catalyzed the digital revolution, forging a postindustrial, information-driven economy. The invention of the microchip in 1971 harkened the incipient overthrow of the reign of electromechanics in industrial production, transforming as economy based on mechanical labor to an information-driven global economy based on automation and robotics.[52] Microchips could record and play back human activity in small, affordable computers, eclipsing the labor-saving devices of industrialization, with the epochal introduction of *labor-replacing devices.*[53] Replete with the cumulative knowledge, skills, and efforts of human activity, computers, robotics, digital telecommunications, and biotechnology can create, manage, and monitor goods and services for human consumption and survival.

The automation of production is precipitating an unprecedented reorganization of society and permanently altering the forms and nature of work, as robotics and the independent commodification of information and knowledge are replacing the sale of labor power and decentering human activity in the productive process. Some project that the perpetual production of innovation (i.e., "new knowledge for making goods")[54] and cyber factories, consisting of a "web of intelligent machines," will be the source of profit, and shift the role of humans to more autonomous, decentralized, supervisory functions.[55] With the further bifurcation of manual and intellectual work, hierarchies of knowledge production occupations are anticipated. High/low paid technical/professional workers may increasingly design, compose, and alter instructions for machines, as others' intellectual work (e.g., engineers, architects), is deskilled through computer software.

Laborless production is permeating every aspect of economic life (e.g., agriculture, medicine, law, construction, automobile, steel, and wood production, telecommunications, commodities trading, education, transportation, retail, clerical work, space travel, oceanography, government agencies, social services, insurance, libraries, computer programming, and so forth).[56] Internet shopping by manufacturers for raw materials is affecting supply and demand, pricing, marketing, inflation and global labor markets.[57] Computerized systems allow technicians in the U.S. to control production in low-wage shops abroad. Tasks may be performed well beyond human capacity.

In mining, computer-operated systems command/monitor the excavation of over one hundred tons of coal an hour by massive whirling drills, the production of an army of shovels, drills, and trucks, and the transport of 240 tons of rock by one truck and driver, with prospects for fully operated coal mines via satellite. These and other advancements in the steel and automotive industries have increased profits and reduced the workforce by 21 percent since 1997.[58]

In agriculture, computerized controllers and navigation systems provide precision farming via satellites to pinpoint specific fertilizer, pesticide, and water needs of crops. Digitalized infrared photography identifies problem areas undetectable by the human eye, resulting in earlier, targeted diagnosis and treatment of produce. Increasingly, $160,000 robotic sanitized cow milking systems are being used by large farmer/owners, who anticipate major profits from 10–15 percent increases in production and decreases in the number of hired farm workers.[59]

Nanotechnology (the science of molecule-sized devices) is revolutionizing medicine, computing, and food supplies, through small machines that grab and rearrange individual atoms.[60] Nanomedicine has produced a DNA computer, which in the future will provide noninvasive surgery, detect and destroy disease-causing agents, and synthesize drug treatment, through the ingestion of nanobots.[61] Nanofood supplies will synthesize food molecularly and, in the right hands, *could* prevent starvation and clean up toxic waste on an atomic level.[62] IBM's data-storage technology holds the equivalent of two hundred CD-ROM's on a postage stamp-sized surface, and projections for nanocomputing are supercomputers the size of a drop of water.[63] The miniaturization of electronics has created far-reaching possibilities for humans to meet their needs. However, contention surrounds this domain (e.g., genetic engineering) as patents threaten to privatize knowledge for profit or egregious violations of human dignity, which retards progress in medical science that is vital to the improvement of the human condition.[64]

The military's well-funded, aggressive pursuit of large, top-down automation has produced robots that are central to "DDD" work (i.e., "Duty, Dull, and Dangerous" tasks), including spy satellite surveillance and scout-search-destroy missions. Unmanned cars, planes, trucks, cruise missiles, and "smart bombs" perform many functions in robotic war via computer- operated systems. Robotocists have produced protein-based solar connected combat helmets, which mimic the surrounding environment and are difficult to detect electronically, and exoskeletons, which are prosthetic suits that carry soldiers' weapons and supplies. Robotunas support efforts to create swift submarines and do research on the ocean deep. Prospects for robots that "think and walk" range from domestic service to law enforcement and military combat.[65] The notion of Robocop is not far-fetched.

Technological developments have had a profound effect on the global economy and are pivotal in the unending cycle of economic crises inherent to capitalism. As international corporations introduce labor-replacing devices, "downsize," and export factories to cheaper labor markets to maximize profits, blue- and white-collar workers are expunged from the workplace. From 1960–92, workers employed in the steel industry declined from 600,000 to less than 200,000; half of the jobs in the auto industry were lost; machine tools/ electrical machinery decreased by 40 percent.[66] In 1982, 1,287,000 jobs were lost to plant closings and layoffs, augmented in 1987 with merger-induced layoffs in banking.[67] Steadily, average unemployment has risen, from 4.9 percent between 1956–73, to 7.2 percent between 1974–87, and poverty in 1994 had not been as high since 1961.[68] Increasingly, workers are relegated to temporary, part-time, or contractual jobs without benefits, disguising the 12 percent unemployment rate and swelling the ranks of the "working poor" and permanently unemployed.[69]

As consumers worldwide are less able to buy goods, corporations increase layoffs and technological innovations to cut costs, and thrust the impoverished abroad further into slave-like subsistence. The cycle of massive overproduction and underconsumption of commodities, competitive capital expansion/consolidation, and structural unemployment, endemic to capitalism, is exacerbated and accelerated by automated laborless production. Polarized redistribution of the nation's wealth results, from 1967–92, in the wealthiest white families' incomes increasing twenty-fold, and the poorest black families' incomes decreasing fortyfold.[70] The full impact of corporate efforts to mask years of declining profits (e.g., Enron, Tyco, WorldCom scandals, and ensuing bankruptcies), unprecedented layoffs, and continual automation of the workplace, has yet to be seen.

Under these conditions of plenty, the livelihood and survival of many are at stake. Some blame technology for the unbridled propulsion toward the "end of work," for distorted and unethical uses of technology, and for "the declining significance of humans." These critics overlook the profound contribution that human innovation makes to humanity, if used as an instrument for human need, rather than for private profit.

Under these conditions, the financial arbiters of global capital scapegoat the disenfranchised as the cause of the crisis. They seek new methods of control, new forms for the state apparatus to accommodate the changing economic relations, and new ways to stem the rising tide of disillusionment and resistance that the "grotesque international inequities of wealth" produce. Hence, domestic militarism, armed with its ideological weapons, arises to sustain the social order.

DOMESTIC MILITARIZATION

> The state apparatus… i.e. the police, the courts, the prisons; but also the army … intervenes directly as a supplementary repressive force in the last instance.[71]
>
> The Repressive State Apparatus functions massively and predominantly *by repression* (including physical repression), while functioning secondarily by ideology…. The Ideological State Apparatuses function massively and predominantly *by ideology,* but they also function secondarily by repression, even if ultimately … this is very attenuated and concealed, even symbolic.[72]

In *Lockdown America: Police and Prisons in the Age of Crisis,* Parenti provides an insightful historical analysis of the successive wave of repressive legislative, political, and institutional measures, adopted from 1968 to the 1990s, that were coterminous with the wave of economic crises and reflect the dual function of the state through ideology and force. The mid-1960s were characterized by social activism in factories, schools, and communities and urban rebellions following the civil rights and anti–Vietnam war movement.[73] Simultaneously, drugs were invidiously infused in the military in Vietnam and in urban communities, serving to narcotize emergent restlessness and disillusion. Though the government instituted many ameliorative, short-lived social programs, the emergent ideological shift to *law and order* was pronounced, sustained preparation for ensuing repressive measures. This shift culminated in the 1968 Omnibus Crime Control and Safe Streets Act, initiating the erosion of civil liberties (e.g., wiretapping and dilution of Miranda Rights), and $3.55 billion for the Law Enforcement Assistance Administration (LEAA)in 1970 to bolster local and state police training and equipment.[74] Through the SAs' twin arms —ideology and force—the law and order campaign and passage of repressive legislative measures reasserted social control over social reform.

With the advent of microelectronics and exodus of factories and local businesses from thriving urban centers in the 1970s and 1980s, industrialization, unemployment, and competition from cheap labor abroad grew, putting labor unions in jeopardy. in 1979, a frontal attack on unions was made with the aggressive, divisive firing of eleven thousand striking air traffic controllers, wage freeze, and deregulation of the industry. This chastening, repressive move within the ISA against organized labor and rhetorical blame for rising costs and fewer jobs on unions, along with Reagan's incisive tax cuts for the wealthy, positioned the government solidly behind corporate interests. From 1965–92, a group of manufacturers moved 1,800 plants to Mexico, employing 500,000 workers, and from 1980–85, close to 2.3 million jobs were lost forever.[75] Thus, the bargaining position of labor and the right to strike were simultaneously compromised for workers, and the state reestablished the primacy of corporate control.

Illegal drug use and sale escalated in declining cities, as class polarization, white flight, and the concentration of urban poverty among people of color grew. Increased violence, local rivalries for profits from the drug economy, and thousands of arrests were symptomatic of rampant unemployment and desperation. This social and economic deterioration swole the ranks of the cast-off populations, deemed "social junk" (e.g., addicts and mentally ill) and "social dynamite" (e.g., displaced workers). Parenti argues that the growing "surplus population" had to be contained or subjugated through brute force to destabilize a potentially rebellious, cast-off population of displaced workers and to mask the illusory health of the national economy.[76] Conditions were ripe to scapegoat the "racial other," one of the state's indispensable ideological weapons of deflection. Through the discourse in popular culture and other venues, "inner" cities became synonymous with violence, drugs, and African American and Latino youth, which served as "proof" of the inefficacy of social programs. This view ideologically presaged the roll-back of the social programs of the 1970s and "a new wave of criminal justice crackdown."[77] Though "crime control" was marginally related to crime, it was presented as a means to contain the "dangerous classes" and accompanied the simultaneous resurgence of vigilante organizations, and extra-legal terror.[78]

As part of the war on drugs, the 1984 Comprehensive Crime Control Act sanctioned the denial of bail and federal parole and increased the fines.[79] The Anti-Drug Abuse Act of 1986 and 1998 imposed higher sentences on the use of crack cocaine (cheaper and more prevalent in communities of color) than on cocaine power (more expensive and prevalent in white upscale communities), and sanctioned the death penalty for tag-alongs in drug-related felonies and (un)intentional killings.[80] These "legal" measures institutionalized inequity in the judicial system's sentencing and imprisonment processes and the disproportionate incarceration of poor people of color. They masked the prevalence of drug use in affluent, white communities, contributed to the demonization of African Americans and Latinos, which provided ideological justification for increased state repression, violence, and containment in these communities (e.g., police brutality, racial profiling). As the legislative arm of the ISA legalized inequity, the RSA's court system forced incarceration based on race and class, and in turn, reaffirmed demonizing, scapegoating discourses within the ISA.

The ideological and repressive aspects of domestic militarism have surfaced primarily through the legal, judicial, and law enforcement apparatuses of the state. The institutionally sanctioned militarization of public housing in Chicago, designed to be massive intern/containment centers in impoverished communities, was new terrain for the state, bringing surveillance and law enforcement to the homes of the poor. Though allocated funds for building upkeep were diverted for years from residents, resources for containment and surveillance appeared rapidly (i.e., security, ID cards, metal detectors, police, electronic surveillance, and "Clean Sweeps").[81] Though the history of fiscal mismanagement contributed to the rapid deterioration of the buildings, it was ascribed to residents' criminality, uncleanliness, and disregard for property. This justified the need for residential imprisonment and paved the way for the needed demolition of public highrises, but brought about massive displacement of successive generations of permanently unemployed people of color. The repressive and ideological arms of the state have been unrelenting in implementing domestic militarism and have hit those on the bottom of the economic rung the hardest. The successive array of legislative and law enforcement measures serve as a defense against the resistance of the "surplus populations" and the devastating social ills that result from inadequate means to live. They paved the way for the state's reliance on more stringent repressive apparatuses—the prison system and the military.

The massive expansion of the prison-industrial complex, a lucrative entity, is at the center of domestic militarism and corporate privatization of public services. As the criminalization of the poor escalates, the prison industry is housing the cast-offs, employing the unemployed in cities devastated by deindustrialization, and creating profits for private corporations. Based on third-grade reading scores, the projected needs for prison construction are increasingly daily. The prison population has doubled since 1978, running 15 percent over capacity, due to the imprisonment of "offenders" who historically have received alternative sentences.[82] The current annual budget is over $25 billion, far exceeding that of welfare, 1 percent of the GNP.[83] Consistent with the pattern of structural inequity, of the 6.6 million people in prisons, 63 percent are African American, 25 percent is Latino.[84] They are incarcerated with adult inmates 12–25 times more often that are white youth.[85] Arrests are increasing for illegal drug use and driving under the influence of alcohol, signaling the shrinking life options and demoralizing efforts to "ease the pain."

The prison system plays a clear role in the discipline and forced containment of inmates, exercised through cell life, prison guards, SWAT commandos, and violence. Its ideological function surfaces by examining the prison system's role in the provision of free labor, enabled by the Federal Prison industries Enhancement Act (PIE) of 1979.[86] In this era of economic retrenchment, the captive prison population is a prime source of free/cheap labor, legitimated by their "need for rehabilitation." Though private corporations have taken advantage of prison labor, it has been unprofitable, due to limited space, threat of law suits, public relations concerns about prison-made products, the imposition of prison procedures on the work process, and poor quality of work due to prisoners' resistance.[87] Though prison labor is not profitable, the repressive function that prisons serve is complemented by their ideological function of reassuring the public that the "wayward and morally depraved" are being rehabilitated, that their tax dollars are being efficiently used, and that they are safe from the "dangerous classes." The removal of libraries, educational programs, and exercise rooms from prisons signals a return of the view that prisons are for retribution and punishment, not for rehabilitation of society's cast-offs. The domestic militarism escalates with the unprecedented extension of surveillance and the military into civilian life.

The tragic events of September 11 have forever changed life in the United States and its relationship to the international community, economically and politically. The economy was further wounded, as exemplified in the airline industry, and American confidence in the market waned as further layoffs occurred. The personal and national vulnerability created on that day has forged national unity and a pervasive underlying current of fear. The threat of terrorism in the midst of a deepening recession contributed to the invocation of Operation TIPS (Terrorism Information and Prevention System) to establish networks of public workers, "worker corps," to report "any suspicious activities" observed. Now neighbors and civilian workers will serve as an auxiliary arm of the state.[88] In an effort to further stem the tide of terrorism, plans are under way to revamp the Posse Comitatus Act of 1898, which severely restricted the military's right to participate in domestic defense.[89] The overhaul of this Act will allow the military to act as a law enforcement body within the nation's borders. Visions of tanks in the nation's streets are not far-fetched, and the threatened loss of civil liberties embodied in the sweeping terms of the legislation has evoked outcries from the American population to *preserve democracy in order to defend it.*

IDEOLOGY AND REPRESSION IN EDUCATION

The rise in domestic militarism that is reflected in legislation, the criminal justice system, the military, and institutional policies, and that functions dually through ideology and force, complements the economic restructuring and deepening crisis of the world economy. As such, it provides the context for commensurate shifts in education. There has been a glaring reversal in government policy in providing or guaranteeing services that were once considered entitlements and requisite supports for a decent quality of life. Health care, education, welfare, social security, and other social programs that supported the maintenance of the workers' capacity to work are being replaced by programs of control or being subjected to corporate privatization. The public face of welfare-to-work, managed care in medicine, and educational vouchers belie less noble intentions than efforts to improve self sufficiency, curtail insurance abuse, or enhance individual choice.

This significant shift signals the SA's "response" to the economic crisis and new conditions of laborless production.[90] By cutting costs in social programs, and more importantly by divesting in the livelihood and survival of the masses of working people, the state is supporting the consolidation of corporate capital. Plagued by declining profits and the redundancy of labor in production, privatization provides an excellent opportunity for financiers to commodify public spheres of services, including public education. More insidious, however, is the idea that with increasing automation, the maintenance of workers, who are irrelevant to the production process and creation of the nation's wealth, is no longer a priority. The general population and the cast-offs in the economy bear the brunt of these developments. In this context, the dismantling of public education becomes an "economic necessity" for the arbiters of power.

The neoliberal promotion of "market" choice, repositions individual/private rights over the common good in order to justify corporate privatization and school vouchers. The promotion of "market choice" is cojoined with the drive toward standardization as the means to regulate variations in the educational marketplace (i.e., the quality of schools from which to choose and the quality of education provided for students).[91] Ostensibly, corporate privatization will promote equity and increase accountability, flexibility, and local control for failing schools through competition and the efficient use of resources, and standardized testing will even the playing field. In fact, *privatization redirects public funds for private accumulation.* It allows the government to abdicate its social responsibility to educate youth, and reduces education to a privately owned commodity of corporations, whose consumers are students, subject to the fluctuations of the market (i.e., the financial resource needs of their sponsors). "Schoolchoice" and the imposition of a national curriculum and standardized testing will exacerbate existing inequities hidden in the structures of public education.

The construction of "choice" as the property of autonomous moral agents is far from reality in its conception and execution. Students' use of vouchers at their school of choice is a fallacy, as efforts to implement the Leave no Child Behind Act (NCLB) Act of 2001 illustrate. Frustrated parents, boards of education, and policymakers are chafing under a plan that cannot work. There are insufficient transfer schools to serve the 3.5 million students in failing schools.[92] In Illinois, of the 124,000 eligible students, 1,200 were granted transfers.[93] The geographic distance between differential property tax–based schools precludes travel for most students in poor communities, and some magnet schools and others have "chosen" not to accept school transfers or have set preclusive standards for student admittance. While some poor and middle-income students may use vouchers to attend religious or adjacent community schools, or escape the "inner city," the overwhelming demand for and obstacles to voucher use in "good" schools are prohibitive. However, the wealthy may use vouchers, money from the public sector's poorly funded schools, to subsidize their private education. Disguised as an entitlement for all, vouchers and other forms of "choice" will benefit very few.

The surge of militarism in schools mirrors the national trend toward domestic militarism. True to form, the poor are targeted, especially those of color, who are expendable in the workforce. While Ph.D.s are being hired to teach wealthy youth, Troops to Teachers is preparing retired military personnel on a "fast track" for certification in education administration, to provide "leadership" and structure in "at-risk" schools. While specialized magnet schools are being built in cities for some, disciplinary schools are being constructed for others. The CEO of Philadelphia Public Schools, Paul Vallas, is contracting $7 million with private firms to create alternative disciplinary schools for "violent" youth, and to set up widespread Saturday detention, in-school suspension, and community service for nonviolent disruptive youth.[94] These programs to end bad behavior after one infraction further demonize urban youth as guilty offenders and institutionally serve as "halfway" houses to jail, contributing to the fivefold (500 percent) increase in African American men's incarceration in the past twenty years, versus a mere 23 percent increase in their college enrollment.[95]

As evidenced at Groundview, the presence of metal detectors and police for student protection not only contains the "dangerous classes," but prepares them for their proscribed place in the new economy—prison or the military. The culture of militarism and pronounced presence of force in schools supports Althusser's notion that both repression and ideology are operative within the ISA, as each arm of the state, containing elements of the other, is used as necessary to support or push forward the existing social order. Expulsion, punishment, selection, and discipline complement the ideological function of schools. This overt repression is accompanied by a defunct curriculum and inadequate resources that deprive youth of their human desire to think, explore, and create. It conveys a powerful ideological message to the students and the broader culture: "This is your worth." The absence of resources seems to "fit" the essential qualities of the youth and justifies the institutional inequity.

The repressive and ideological aspects of the culture of militarism support the renegotiation of boundaries for Groundview youths' anticipated role in a postindustrial society. At Mountainview, the ideological aspects of the culture of privilege are not supplemented by force, but are complemented by proscriptive practices and polices that socialize students "to be free" to fulfill their complementary role in the emergent economy, as the privileged.[96] As such the policies and practices in the educational system play a vital role in the maintenance and in the restructuring of society.

CONCLUSION

> Every society is really governed by hidden laws, by upspoken but profound assumptions on the part of the people, and ours is no exception.… The time has come, God knows, for us to examine ourselves, but we can only do this if we are willing to free ourselves of the myth of America and try to find out what is really happening here.[97]

The restructuring of a postindustrial economy is well under way, accompanied by the emergence of domestic materialism throughout society. This process is also evident in education with the privatization of public education and introduction of militarism to poor schools. On the one hand, the present examination paints a bleak picture of increased polarization between the poor and wealthy, declining schools, and efforts by the state to protect corporate capital's interests through ideology and force. On the other hand, it addresses the powerful dual historical role of education as a site of struggle, in both maintaining structural inequities in society and in promoting major changes in economic, social, and political lives. Education has both enslaving and emancipatory possibilities, especially during this period of economic restructuring and rapid change in our social life, and may, in turn, forge new ways of thinking about social life.

Educators have a crucial role to play in countering the domestic militarism and privatization in schools and society at large, both ideologically and practically. It is incumbent upon educators to examine, wrestle with, and strive to understand the historically embedded, social, economic, ideological, and political realities that exist, so that our efforts to promote change will be well-guided. By examining the motive forces of the economy, the state, and social life in all of its forms, we may arrive at critical analyses to guide our strivings for an educational system and quality of life across race and class that disrupt structural inequity and affirm our basic humanity. In this sense, education across multiple contexts is *a key*—a vehicle in the informed process of change.

Most important, we must challenge the corrosive ideologies and institutional practices that constrain the possibilities for youth, by changing the objective probabilities before them. Toward this end, we must struggle to preserve democracy and to ensure a quality education for all youth across racial and class lines. We must strive to create schools and other sites of learning that nurture the natural strivings of youth/humans to explore, think, inquire, discover, create, and innovate. Central to this work is our role in providing a forum for students to critically examine their immediate realities and the broader questions that have bearing on their lives through multiple texts. Our struggle *against inequity* requires thoughtful examination in educational contexts that will contribute to the preparation of successive educators' participation in the *struggle for humanity*.

NOTES

A substantially different version of this chapter appeared in *The School Field: International Journal of Theory and Research in Education*, XII (3/4), Autumn 2001, pp. 91–109.

1. Robert Friedland, "Space, Place, and Modernity," *A Journal of Reviews: Contemporary Sociology* 21, no. 1 (1992): 8–36.
2. James Anderson, *The Education of Blacks in the South*, 1860–1935 (Chapel Hill, N.C.: University of North Carolina Press, 1988).
3. Pierre Bourdieu, "Cultural Reproduction in Education, Society, and Culture," in *Power and Ideology in Education,* edited by J. Karabel and H. Halsey (London: Sage, 1977).

4. Michael Apple and Christopher Jenks, "American Realities: Poverty, Economy, and Education," in *Cultural Politics and Education,* edited by M. Apple (New York: Teachers College Press, 1996); Christian Parenti, *Lockdown America* (New York: Verso, 1999); Jim Davis, Thomas Hirschl, and Michael Stack, eds., *Cutting Edge: Technology, Information, Capitalism, and Social Revolution* (New York: Verso, 1997).

5. Davis, Hirschl, and Stack, *Cutting Edge.*

6. Richard Appelbaum, "Multiculturalism and Flexibility: Some New Directions in Global Capitalism," in *Mapping Multiculturalism,* edited by Avery F. Gordon and Christopher Newfield (Minneapolis, Minn.: University of Minnesota Press, 1996).

7. Parenti, *Lockdown America.*

8. Louis Althusser, *Lenin and Philosophy and Other Essays* (New York: Monthly Review Press, 1971).

9. Bourdieu, *Cultural Reproduction,* 494.

10. Arthur Spears, "Race and Ideology: An Introduction," in *Race and Ideology: Language, Symbolism and Popular Culture* (Detroit: Wayne State University Press, 1999), 42.

11. Illinois State Board of Education Report Card, 2000 (isbe.net).

12. Bourdieu, *Cultural Reproduction,* 493.

13. Jay MacLeod, *Ain't No Makin' It: Aspirations in a Low-income Neighborhood* (Boulder, Colo.: Westview Press, 1987), 19.

14. Michael Dyson, "Growing Up Under Fire: Boyz N the Hood and the Agony of the Black Man in America," *Tikkun* 6, no. 5 (November–December 1991): 74–78.

15. Illinois State Board of Education Report Card, 2000.

16. Alice Miller, *For Your Own Good: Hidden Cruelty in Child-Rearing and the Roots of Violence* (New York: Doubleday, 1983).

17. Guglielmo Carchedi, "High-Tech Hype: Promises and Realities of Technology in the Twenty-first Century," in *Cutting Edge: Technology, Information, Capitalism, and Social Revolution,* edited by Jim Davis, Thomas Hirschl and Michael Stack (New York: Verso, 1997), 73–86.

18. Bourdieu, *Cultural Reproduction,* 494.

19. "Military Industrial: JROTC Is a Recruiting Program for Dead-End Military Jobs," available at www.schoolsnotjails.com (March 29, 2001): 1.

20. Kenneth J. Saltman, *Collateral Damage: Corporatizing Public Schools—A Threat to Democracy* (Lanham, Md.: Rowman & Littlefield, 2000), x.

21. "Military Industrial," 2.

22. Ibid., 2.

23. "Military Industrial," 1.

24. Ibid., 3.

25. Allison Fass, "Advertising: The Army Is Helping to Pay for a 'Stay in School' Campaign," *New York Times* (June 25, 2002): C6.

26. Richard Perez-Pena, "Report Says Enrollment in Guard Was Inflated," *New York Times* (June 29, 2002), A13.

27. Dave Moniz, "15,000 Reserves to Serve 2nd Year: Longest Call-Ups Since Vietnam," *USA Today* (August 26, 2002): 2.

28. Tamar Lewin, "College Board Announces an Overhaul for the SAT," *New York Times*(June 28, 2002): A1; Sean Cavanagh, "Overhauled SAT Could Shake Up School Curricula," *Education Week* (July 10, 2002).

29. Ibid., 3.

30. Noam Chomsky, "Intellectuals and Social Change," in *Understanding Power: The Indispensable Chomsky,* edited by Peter Mitchell and John Schoeffel (New York: New Press, 2002), 236.

31. Linda Darling-Hammond, "Inequality and Access to Knowledge," in *Handbook of Research on Multicultural Education,* edited by James A. Banks and Cherry A. Banks (New York: Macmillan), 466 (citing D. Tyack, *The One Best System*).

32. Jonathan Kozol, *Savage Inequalities: Children in America's Schools* (New York: Harper Perennial).

33. Anderson, *The Education of Blacks,* 27.

34. Ibid., 4–8.

35. Ibid., 89.

36. Baldwin quoted in Anderson, 1988, 82.

37. Ibid., 91.

38. Ibid., 247.

39. Ibid., 33–78. Anderson examines the origins of this particular form of industrial education and the controversy that surfaced between W. E. B. DuBois and Booker T. Washington, and Northern philanthropists and Southern planters.

40. Pierre Bourdieu and Jean-Claude Passeron, *Reproduction in Education, Society, and Culture,* 2nd ed. (London: Sage, 1970).

41. W. E. B. DuBois, "Does the Negro Need Separate Schools," *Journal of Negro Education* 4 (July 1935): 328–35.

42. Anderson, *The Education of Blacks in the South,* 81.

43. Howard Zinn, *A People's History of the United States* (New York: Harper Perennial 1980), 198.

44. Apple and Zenk, "American Realities: Poverty, Economy, and Education," 71.

45. Althusser, *Lenin and Philosophy,* 137–42.

46. Frederick Engels, "Letter to Joseph Bloch," (September 21, 1890): 12–14.

47. Althusser, *Lenin and Philosophy,* 142–143.

48. Ibid., 145.

49. Thomas Hirschl, "Structural Unemployment and the Qualitative Transformation of Capitalism," in *Cutting Edge: Technology, Information, Capitalism, and Social Revolution,* edited by Jim Davis, Thomas Hirschl, and Michael Stack (New York: Verso, 1997), 157–74.

50. Ibid., 158.

51. Jared Diamond, *Guns, Germs, and Steel* (New York: W.W. Norton, 1999).

52. Hirschl, "Structural Unemployment" 159.

53. Jim Davis and Michael Stack, "The Digital Advantage," in Davis, Hirschl, and Stack, *Cutting Edge: Techonology, Information, Capitalism, and Social Revolution,* edited by Jim Davis, Thomas Hirschl, and Michael Stack (New York: Verso, 1997, 121–44.

54. Tessa Morris-Suzuki, Robots and Capitalism, in *Cutting Edge: Technology, Information, Capitalism, and Social Revolution,* edited by Jim Davis, Thomas Hirschl, and Michael Stack (New York: Verso, 1997, 13 28.

55. "The Cyber Factory: A Web of Intelligent Machines," available at www.globaltechnoscan.com, 1–5.

56. Ibid.

57. Michael Casey, "Internet Changes the Face of Supply and Demand," *Wall Street Journal* (October 18, 1999): A4, 3Q.

58. Michael M. Phillips, "Business of Mining Gets a Lot Less Basic," *New York Times* (March 18, 1997): B13.

59. Marc Levy, "Robots Do the Milking On Some Farms," Associated Press, March 1, 2002.

60. Jesse Berst, "What's Next: Nanotechnology Promises Big Changes by Getting Small," (August 2, 2000), available at www.zdnet.com/anchordesk.

61. Patricia Reaney, "Scientists Build Tiny Computer from DNA," *India News: World* (November 22, 2001).

62. Ibid.

63. Ibid.

64. Jonathan King, "The Biotechnology Revolution: Self-Replicating Factories and the Ownership of Life Forms," in *Cutting Edge: Technology, Information, Capitalism, and Social Revolution,* edited by Jim Davis, Thomas Hirschl, and Michael Stack (New York: Verso, 1997, 145–56.

65. The Science Channel, "Technology Circuit: The Digital Domain," June 25, 2002.

66. Stanley Aronowitz and William DiFazio, *The Jobless Future: Sci-Tech and the Dogma of Work* (Minneapolis: University of Minnesota Press, 1994), 48.

67. Ibid., 2.

68. Hirschl, "Structural Unemployment," 161; Davis and Stack, "The Digital Advantage," 137.

69. Hirschl, 2.

70. Apple and Zenk, "American Realities," 72–73. In 1992, 80 percent of people were earning less than half the national income, and 20 percent of the wealthiest had almost 50 percent.

71. Althusser, 137.

72. Ibid., 145.

73. Parenti, *Lockdown America*, 4.

74. Ibid., 8–11.

75. Ibid., 42.

76. Ibid., 45.

77. Ibid., 44.

78. Noam Chomsky, *Rogue States: The Rule of Force in World Affairs* (Cambridge, Mass.: Southend Press, 2000), 153.

79. Parenti, *Lockdown America*, 50.

80. Ibid., 57–61.

81. Ibid., 59.

82. David B. Kopel, "Prison Blues: How America's Foolish Sentencing Policies Endanger Public Safety," *Policy Analysis* 208 (May 17, 1994), available at www.cato.org/pubs/pas/pa-208.html. "Race and Incarceration in the United States: Human Rights Watch Press Backgrounder" (February 27, 2002), 1–3, www.hrw.org/backgrounder/usa/race.

83. Ibid., Kopel, 4.

84. Fox Butterfield, "Study Finds Big Increase in Black Men as Inmates since 1980," *New York Times* (August 28, 2002), available at www.hrw.org/backgrounder/usa/race, 1; Jonathan D. Salant, "6.6 Million Under Nation's Correctional System," *Florida Times-Union* (August 26, 2002), 1.

85. Butterfield, "Study Finds Big Increase," 1.

86. Parenti, *Lockdown America*, 230.

87. Ibid., 233–35.

88. Adam Clymer, "Security and Liberty: Worker Corps to be Formed to Report Odd Activity," *New York Times* (July 25, 2002).

89. Eliabeth Becker, "Bush Seeks to Review Military's Home Role," *Chicago Tribune* (July 16, 2002): 1; Tribune New Services, "Ridge Calls for Study of Military's Home Role," *Chicago Tribune*, 22 July 2002, np.

90. Hirschl, "Structural Unemployment," 168.

91. Michael Apple, *Educating the "Right" Way: Markets, Standards, God, and Inequality* (New York: Routledge, 2001) 75.

92. Stephanie Banchero and Michael Martinez, "Federal School Reform Stumbles: Confusion Reigns Over Choice Plan," *Chicago Tribune* (August 28, 2002): 1.

93. Diana Jean Schemo, "Few Exercise New Right to Leave Failing Schools," *New York Times* (August 28, 2002), 1.

94. Susan Snyder, "Vallas: No Shuffling of Violent Students," *Philadelphia Inquirer* (August 22, 2002): 1.

95. Butterfield, 1.

96. Chomsky, *Intellectuals and Social Change*, 236–237.

97. Baldwin, 1961/1989, p. 11.

19

From *Representation: Cultural Representations and Signifying Practices*

Stuart Hall

___

INTRODUCTION

THE CHAPTERS IN this volume all deal, in different ways, with the question of representation. This is one of the central practices which produce culture and a key 'moment' in what has been called the 'circuit of culture' (see du Gay, Hall et al., 1997). But what does representation have to do with 'culture': what is the connection between them? To put it simply, culture is about 'shared meanings'. Now, language is the privileged medium in which we 'make sense' of things, in which meaning is produced and exchanged. Meanings can only be shared through our common access to language. So language is central to meaning and culture and has always been regarded as the key repository of cultural values and meanings.

But how does language construct meanings? How does it sustain the dialogue between participants which enables them to build up a culture of shared understandings and so interpret the world in roughly the same ways? Language is able to do this because it operates as a *representational system*. In language, we use signs and symbols—whether they are sounds, written words, electronically produced images, musical notes, even objects—to stand for or represent to other people our concepts, ideas and feelings. Language is one of the 'media' through which thoughts, ideas and feelings are represented in a culture. Representation through language is therefore central to the processes by which meaning is produced. This is the basic, underlying idea which underpins all six chapters in this book. Each chapter examines 'the production and circulation of meaning through language' in different ways, in relation to different examples, different areas of social practice. Together, these chapters push forward and develop our understanding of how representation actually *works*.

'Culture' is one of the most difficult concepts in the human and social sciences and there are many different ways of defining it. In more traditional definitions of the term, culture is said to embody the 'best that has been thought and said' in a society. It is the sum of the great ideas, as represented in the classic works of literature, painting, music and philosophy—the 'high culture' of an age. Belonging to the same frame of reference, but more 'modern' in its associations, is the use of 'culture' to refer to the widely distributed forms of popular music, publishing, art, design and literature, or the activities of leisure-time and entertainment, which make up the everyday lives of the majority of 'ordinary people'—what is called the 'mass culture' or the 'popular culture' of an age. High culture versus popular culture was, for many years, the classic way of framing the debate about culture—the terms carrying a powerfully evaluative charge (roughly, high = good; popular = debased). In recent years, and in a more 'social science' context, the word 'culture' is used to refer to whatever is distinctive about the 'way of life' of a people, community, nation or social group. This has come to be known as the 'anthropological' definition. Alternatively, the word can be used to describe the 'shared values' of a group or of society—which is like the anthropological definition, only with a more sociological emphasis. You will find traces of all these meanings somewhere in this book. However, as its title suggests, 'culture' is usually being used in these chapters in a somewhat different, more specialized way.

What has come to be called the 'cultural turn' in the social and human sciences, especially in cultural studies and the sociology of culture, has tended to emphasize the importance of *meaning* to the definition of culture. Culture, it is argued, is not so much a set of *things*—novels and paintings or TV programmes and comics—as a process, a set of *practices*. Primarily, culture is concerned with the production and the exchange of mean-ings—the 'giving and taking of meaning'—between the members of a society or group. To say that two people belong to the same culture is to say that they interpret the world in roughly the same ways and can express themselves, their thoughts and feelings about the world, in ways which will be understood by each other. Thus culture depends on its partic-ipants interpreting meaningfully what is happening around them, and 'making sense' of the world, in broadly similar ways.

This focus on 'shared meanings' may sometimes make culture sound too unitary and too cognitive. In any culture, there is always a great diversity of meanings about any topic, and more than one way of interpreting or representing it. Also, culture is about feelings, attachments and emotions as well as concepts and ideas. The expression on my face 'says something' about who I am (identity) and what I am feeling (emotions) and what group I feel I belong to (attachment), which can be 'read' and understood by other people, even if I didn't intend deliberately to communicate anything as formal as 'a message', and even if the other person couldn't give a very logical account of how s/he came to understand what I was 'saying'. Above all, cultural meanings are not only 'in the head'. They organize and reg-ulate social practices, influence our conduct and consequently have real, practical effects.

The emphasis on cultural practices is important. It is participants in a culture who give meaning to people, objects and events. Things 'in themselves' rarely if ever have any one, single, fixed and unchanging meaning. Even something as obvious as a stone can be a stone, a boundary marker or a piece of sculpture, depending on *what it means*—that is, within a certain context of use, within what the philosophers call different 'language games' (i.e. the language of boundaries, the language of sculpture, and so on). It is by our use of things, and what we say, think and feel about them—how we represent them—that we *give them a meaning*. In part, we give objects, people and events meaning by the frame-works of interpretation which we bring to them. In part, we give things meaning by how we use them, or integrate them into our everyday practices. It is our use of a pile of bricks and mortar which makes it a 'house'; and what we feel, think or say about it that makes a 'house' a 'home'. In part, we give things meaning by how we *represent* them—the words we use about them, the stories we tell about them, the images of them we produce, the emotions we associate with them, the ways we classify and conceptualize them, the values we place on them. Culture, we may say, is involved in all those practices which are not simply genetically programmed into us—like the jerk of the knee when tapped—but which carry meaning and value for us, which need to be *meaningfully interpreted* by others, or which *depend on meaning* for their effective operation. Culture, in this sense, permeates all of society. It is what distinguishes the 'human' element in social life from what is simply biologically driven. Its study underlines the crucial role of the *symbolic* domain at the very heart of social life.

Where is meaning produced? Our 'circuit of culture' suggests that, in fact, meanings are produced at several different sites and circulated through several different processes or practices (the cultural circuit). Meaning is that gives us a sense of our own identity, of who we are and with whom we 'belong'—so it is tied up with questions of how culture is used to mark out and maintain identity within and difference between groups (which is the main focus of Woodward, ed., 1997). Meaning is constantly being produced and exchanged in every personal and social interaction in which we take part. In a sense, this is the most privileged, though often the most neglected, site of culture and meaning. It is also produced in a variety of different *media*; especially, these days, in the modern mass media, the means of global communication, by complex technologies, which circulate meanings between different cultures on a scale and with a speed hitherto unknown in history. (This is the focus of du Gay, ed., 1997.) meaning is also produced whenever we express ourselves in, make use of, consume or appropriate cultural 'things'; that is, when we incorporate them in different ways into the everyday rituals and practices of daily life and in this way give them value or significance. Or when we weave narratives, stories—and fantasies—around them. (This is the focus of Mackay, ed., 1997.) Meanings also regulate and organize our conduct and practices—they help to set the rules, norms and conventions by which social life is ordered and governed. They are also, therefore, what those who wish to govern and regulate the conduct and ideas of others seek to structure and shape. (This is the focus of Thompson, ed., 1997.) In other words, the question of meaning arises in relation to *all* the different moments or practices in our 'cultural circuit'—in the construction of identity and the marking of difference, in production and consumption, as well as in the regulation of social conduct. However, in all these instances, and at all these different institutional sites, one of the privileged 'media' through which meaning is produced and circulated is *language*.

So, in this book, where we take up in depth the first element in our 'circuit of culture', we start with this question of meaning, language and representation. Members of the same culture must share sets of concepts, images and ideas which enable them to think and feel about the world, and thus to interpret the world, in roughly similar ways. They must share, broadly speaking, the same 'cultural codes'. In this sense, thinking and feeling are themselves 'systems of representation', in which our concepts, images and emotions 'stand for' or represent, in our mental life, things which are or may be 'out there' in the world. Similarly, in order to *communicate* these meanings to other people, the participants to any meaningful exchange must also be able to use the same linguistic codes—they must, in a very broad sense, 'speak the same language'. This does not mean that they must all, literally, speak German or French or Chinese. Nor does it mean that they understand perfectly what anyone who speaks the same language is saying. We mean 'language' here in a much wider sense. Our partners must speak enough of the same language to be able to 'translate' what 'you' say into what 'I' understand, and vice versa. They must also be able to read visual images in roughly similar ways. They must be familiar with broadly the same ways of producing sounds to make what they would both recognize as 'music'. They must all interpret body language and facial expressions in broadly similar ways. And they must know to translate their feelings and ideas into these various languages. Meaning is a dialogue—always only partially understood, always an unequal exchange.

Why do we refer to all these different ways of producing and communicating meaning as 'languages' or as 'working like languages'? How do languages work? The simple answer is that languages work *through representation*. They are 'systems of representation'. Essentially, we can say that all these practices 'work like languages', *not* because they are all written or spoken (they are not), but because they all use some element to stand for or represent what we want to say, to express or communicate a thought, concept, idea or feeling. Spoken language uses sounds, written language uses words, musical language uses notes on a scale, the 'language of the body' uses physical gesture, the fashion industry uses items of clothing, the language of facial expression uses ways of arranging one's features, television uses digitally or electronically produced dots on a screen, traffic lights use red, green and amber—to 'say something'. These elements—sounds, words, notes, gestures, expressions, cloths—are part of our natural and material world; but their importance for language is not what they *are* but what they *do*, their function. They construct meaning and transmit it. They signify. They don't have any clear meaning *in themselves*. Rather, they are the vehicles or media which *carry meaning* because they operate as *symbols*, which stand for or represent (i.e. symbolize) the meanings we wish to communicate. To use another metaphor, they function as *signs*. Signs stand for or *represent* our concepts, ideas and feelings in such a way as to enable others to 'read', decode or interpret their meaning in roughly the same way that we do.

Language, in this sense, is a signifying practice. Any representational system which functions in this way can be thought of as working, broadly speaking, according to the principles of representation through language. Thus photography is a representational system, using images on light-sensitive paper to communicate photographic meaning about a particular person, event or scene. Exhibition or display in a museum or gallery can also be thought of as 'like a language', since it uses objects on display to produce certain meanings about the subject-matter of the exhibition. Music is 'like a language' in so far as it uses musical notes to communicate feelings and ideas, even if these are very abstract, and do not refer in any obvious way to the 'real world'. (Music has been called 'the most noise conveying the least information'.) But turning up at football matches with banners and slogans, with faces and bodies painted in certain colours or inscribed with certain symbols, can also be thought of as 'like a language'—in so far as it is a symbolic practice which gives meaning or expression to the idea of belonging to a national culture, or identification with one's local community. It is part of the language of national identity, a discourse of national belongingness. Representation, here, is closely tied up with both identity and knowledge. Indeed, it is difficult to know what 'being English', or indeed French, German, South African or Japanese, *means* outside of all the ways in which our ideas and images of national identity or national cultures have been represented. Without these 'signifying' systems, we could not take on such identities (or indeed reject them) and consequently could not build up or sustain that common 'life-world' which we call a culture.

So it is through culture and language *in this sense* that the production and circulation of meaning takes place. The conventional view used to be that 'things' exist in the material and natural world; that their material or natural characteristics are what determines or constitutes them; and that they have a perfectly clear meaning, *outside* of how they are represented. Representation, in this view, is a process of secondary importance, which enters into the field only after things have been fully formed and their meaning constituted. But since the 'cultural turn' in the human and social sciences, meaning is thought to be *produced*—constructed—rather than simply 'found'. Consequently, in what has come to be called a 'social constructionist approach', representation is conceived as entering into the very constitution of things; and thus culture is conceptualized as a primary or 'constitutive' process, as important as the economic or material 'base' in shaping social subjects and historical events—not merely a reflection of the world after the event.

'Language' therefore provides one general model of how culture and representation work, especially in what has come to be known as the *semiotic* approach—*semiotics* being the study or 'science of signs' and their general role as vehicles of meaning in culture. In more recent years, this preoccupation with meaning has taken a different turn, being more concerned, not with the detail of how 'language' works, but with the broader role of *discourse* in culture. Discourses are ways of referring to or constructing knowledge about a particular topic of practice: a cluster (or *formation*) of ideas, images and practices, which provide ways of talking about, forms of knowledge and conduct associated with, a particular topic, social activity or institutional site in society. These *discursive formations*, as they are known, define what is and is not appropriate in our formulation of, and our practices in relation to, a particular subject or site of social activity; what knowledge is considered useful, relevant and 'true' in that context; and what sorts of persons or 'subjects' embody its characteristics. 'Discursive' has become the general term used to refer to any approach in which meaning, representation and culture are considered to be constitutive.

There are some similarities, but also some major differences, between the *semiotic* and the *discursive* approaches, which are developed in the chapters which follow. One important difference is that the *semiotic* approach is concerned with the *how* of representation, with how language produces meaning—what has been called its 'poetics'; whereas the *discursive* approach is more concerned with the *effects* and *consequences* of representation—its 'politics'. It examines not only how language and representation produce meaning, but how the knowledge which a particular discourse produces connects with power, regulates conduct, makes up or constructs identities and subjectivities, and defines the way certain things are represented, thought about, practised and studied. The emphasis in the *discursive* approach is always on the historical specificity of a particular form or 'regime' of representation: not on 'language' as a general concern, but on specific *languages* or meanings, and how they are deployed at particular times, in particular places. It points us towards greater historical specificity—the way representational practices operate in concrete historical situations, in actual practice.

The general use of language and discourse as models of how culture, meaning and representation work, and the 'discursive turn' in the social and cultural sciences which has followed, is one of the most significant shifts of direction in our knowledge of society which has occurred in recent years. The discussion around these two versions of 'constructionism'—the semiotic and discursive approaches—is threaded through and developed in the six chapters which follow. The 'discursive turn' has not, of course, gone uncontested. You will find questions raised about this approach and critiques offered, as well as different variants of the position explored, by the different authors in this volume. Elsewhere in this series (in Mackay, ed., 1997, for example) alternative approaches are explored, which adopt a more 'creative', expressive or performative approach to meaning, questioning, for example, whether it makes sense to think of music as 'working like a language'. However, by and large, with some variations, the chapters in this book adopt a broadly 'constructionist' approach to representation and meaning.

• • •

It is worth emphasizing that there is no single or 'correct' answer to the question, 'What does this image mean?' or 'What is this ad saying?' Since there is no law which can guarantee that things will have 'one, true meaning', or that meanings won't change over time, work in this area in bound to be interpretative—a debate between, not who is 'right' and who is 'wrong', but between equally plausible, though sometimes competing and contested, meanings and interpretations. The best way to 'settle' such contested readings is to look again at the concrete example and to try to justify one's 'reading' in detail in relation to the actual practices and forms of signification used, and what meanings they seem to you to be producing.

One soon discovers that meaning is not straightforward or transparent, and does not survive intact the passage through representation. It is a slippery customer, changing and shifting with context, usage and historical circumstances. It is therefore never finally fixed. It is always putting off or 'deferring' its rendezvous with Absolute Truth. It is always being negotiated and inflected, to resonate with new situations. It is often contested, and sometimes bitterly fought over. There are always different circuits of meaning circulating in any culture at the same time, overlapping discursive formations, from which we draw to create meaning or to express what we think.

Moreover, we do not have a straightforward, rational or instrumental relationship to meanings. They mobilize powerful feelings and emotions, of both a positive and negative kind. We feel their contradictory pull, their ambivalence. They sometimes call our very identities into question. We struggle over them because they matter—and these are contests from which serious consequences can flow. They define what is 'normal', who belongs—and therefore, who is excluded. They are deeply inscribed in relations of power. Think of how profoundly our lives are shaped, depending on which meanings of male/female, black/white, rich/poor, gay/straight, young/old, citizen/alien, are in play in which circumstances. Meanings are often organized into sharply opposed binaries or opposites. However, these binaries are constantly being undermined, as representations interact with one another, substituting for each other, displacing one another along an unending chain. Our material interests and our bodies can be called to account, and differently implicated, depending on how meaning is given and taken, constructed and interpreted in different situations. But equally engaged are our fears and fantasies, the sentiments of desire and revulsion, of ambivalence and aggression. The more we look into this process of representation, the more complex it becomes to describe adequately or explain—which is why the various chapters enlist a variety of theories and concepts, to help us unlock its secrets.

The embodying of concepts, ideas and emotions in a symbolic form which can be transmitted and meaningfully interpreted is what we mean by 'the practices of representation'. Meaning must enter the domain of these practices, if it is to circulate effectively within a culture. And it cannot be considered to have completed its 'passage' around the cultural circuit until it has been 'decoded' or intelligibly received at another point in the chain. Languages, then, is the property of neither the sender nor the receiver of meanings. It is the shared cultural 'space' in which the production of meaning through language— that is, representation—takes place. The receiver of messages and meanings is not a passive screen on which the original meaning is accurately and transparently projected. The 'taking of meaning' is as much a signifying practice as the 'putting into meaning'. Speaker and hearer or writer and reader are active participants in a process which—since they often exchange roles—is always double-sided, always interactive. Representation functions less like the model of a one-way transmitter and more like the model of a dialogue—it is, as they say, *dialogic*. What sustains this 'dialogue' is the presence of shared cultural codes, which cannot guarantee that meanings will remain stable forever—though attempting to fix meaning is exactly why *power* intervenes in *discourse*. But, even when power is circulating through meaning and knowledge, the codes only work if they are to some degree shared, at least to the extent that they make effective 'translation' between 'speakers' possible. We should perhaps learn to think of meaning less in terms of 'accuracy' and 'truth' and more in terms of effective exchange—a process of *translation*, which facilitates cultural communication while always recognizing the persistence of difference and power between 'speakers' within the same cultural circuit.

• • •

WHY DOES 'DIFFERENCE' MATTER?

Before we analyse any more examples, let us examine some of the underlying issues posed by our first question. Why does 'difference' matter—how can we explain this fascination with 'otherness'? What theoretical arguments can we draw on to help us unpack this question?

Questions of 'difference' have come to the fore in cultural studies in recent decades and been addressed in different ways by different disciplines. In this section, we briefly consider *four* such theoretical accounts. As we discuss them, think back to the examples we have just analysed. In each, we start by showing how important 'difference' is—by considering what is said to be its positive aspect. But we follow this by some of the more negative aspects of 'difference'. Putting these two together suggests why 'difference' is both necessary and dangerous.

1

The first account comes from linguistics—from the sort of approach associated with Saussure and the use of language as a model of how culture works, which was discussed in Chapter 1. The main argument advanced here is that *'difference' matters because it is essential to meaning; without it, meaning could not exist.* You may remember from Chapter 1 the example of *white/black*. We know what *black* means, Saussure argued, not because there is some essence of 'blackness' but because we can contrast it with its opposite— *white*. Meaning, he argued, is relational. It is the '*difference*' between *white* and *black* which signifies, which carries meaning. Carl Lewis in that photo can represent 'femininity' or the 'feminine' side of masculinity because he can mark his '*difference*' from the traditional stereotypes of black masculinity by using the *red shoes* as a signifier. This principle holds for broader concepts too. We know what it is to be 'British', not only because of certain national characteristics, but also because we can mark its 'difference' from its 'others'— 'Britishness' is not-French, not-American, not-German, not-Pakistani, not-Jamaican and so on. This enables Linford Christie to signify his 'Britishness' (by the flag) while contesting (by his black skin) that 'Britishness' must always mean 'whiteness'. Again, 'difference' signifies. It carries a message.

So meaning depends on the difference between opposites. However, when we discussed this argument in Chapter 1, we recognized that, though binary oppositions—*white/black, day/night, masculine/feminine, British/alien*—have the great value of capturing the diversity of the world within their either/or extremes, they are also a rather crude and reductionist way of establishing meaning. For example, in so-called black-and-white photography, there is actually no pure 'black' or 'white', only varying shades of grey. 'Black' shades imperceptibly into 'white', just as men have *both* 'masculine' and 'feminine' sides to their nature; and Linford Christie certainly wants to affirm the possibility of being both 'black' *and* 'British' though the normal definition of 'Britishness' assumes that it is white.

Thus, while we do not seem able to do without them, binary oppositions are also open to the charge of being reductionist and over-simplified—swallowing up all distinctions in their rather rigid two-part structure. What is more, as the philosopher Jacques Derrida has argued, there are very few neutral binary oppositions. One pole of the binary, he argues, is usually the dominant one, the one which includes the other within its field of operations. There is always a relation of power between the poles of a binary opposition (Derrida, 1974). We should really write, **white**/*black*, **men**/*women*, **masculine**/*feminine*, **upper class**/*lower class*, **British**/*alien* to capture this power dimension in discourse.

2

The second explanation also comes from theories of language, but from a somewhat different school to that represented by Saussure. *The argument here is that we need 'difference' because we can only construct meaning through a dialogue with the 'Other'*. The great Russian linguist and critic, Mikhail Bakhtin, who fell foul of the Stalinist regime in the 1940s, studied language, not (as the Saussureans did) as an objective system, but in terms of how meaning is sustained in the *dialogue* between two or more speakers. Meaning, Bakhtin argued, does not belong to any one speaker. It arises in the give-and-take between different speakers. 'The word in language is half someone else's. It becomes 'one's own' only when … the speaker appropriates the word, adapting it to his own semantic expressive intention. Prior to this … the word does not exist in a neutral or impersonal language … rather it exist in other people's mouths, serving other people's intentions: it is from there that one must take the word and make it one's own' (Bakhtin, 1981 [1935], pp. 293–4). Bakhtin and his collaborator, Volosinov, believed that this enabled us to enter into a struggle over meaning, breaking one set of associations and giving words a new inflection. Meaning, Bakhtin argued, is established through dialogue—it is fundamentally *dialogic*. Everything we say and mean is modified by the interaction and interplay with another person. Meaning arises through the 'difference' between the participants in any dialogue. *The 'Other', in short, is essential to meaning.*

This is the positive side of Bakhtin's theory. The negative side is, of course, that therefore meaning cannot be fixed and that one group can never be completely in charge of meaning. What it means to be 'British' or 'Russian' or 'Jamaican' cannot be entirely controlled by the British, Russians or Jamaicans, but is always up for grabs, always being negotiated, in the dialogue between these national cultures and their 'others'. Thus it has been argued that you cannot know what it meant to be 'British' in the nineteenth century until you know what the British thought of Jamaica, their prize colony in the Caribbean, or Ireland, and more disconcertingly, *what the Jamaicans or the Irish thought of them ...* (C. Hall; 1994).

3

The third kind of explanation is anthropological, and you have already met it in du Gay, Hall et al. (1997). *The argument here is that culture depends on giving things meaning by assigning them to different positions within a classificatory system. The marking of 'difference' is thus the basis of that symbolic order which we call culture.* Mary Douglas, following the classic work on symbolic systems by the French sociologist, Emile Durkheim, and the later studies of mythology by the French anthropologist, Claude Lévi-Strauss, argues that social groups impose meaning on their world by ordering and organizing things into classificatory systems (Douglas, 1966). Binary oppositions are crucial for all classification, because one must establish a clear difference between things in order to classify them. Faced with different kinds of food, Lévi-Strauss argued (1979), one way of giving them meaning is to start by dividing them into two groups—those which are eaten 'raw' and those eaten 'cooked'. Of course, you can also classify food into 'vegetables' and 'fruit'; or into those which are eaten as 'starters' and those which are eaten as 'desserts'; or those which are served up at dinner and those which are eaten at a sacred feast or the communion table. Here, again, 'difference' is fundamental to cultural meaning.

However, it can also give rise to negative feelings and practices. Mary Douglas argues that what really disturbs cultural order is when things turn up in the wrong category; or when things fail to fit any category—such as a substance like mercury, which is a metal but also a liquid, or a social group like mixed-race *mulattoes* who are neither 'white' nor 'black' but float ambiguously in some unstable, dangerous, hybrid zone of indeterminacy in-between (Stallybrass and White, 1986). Stable cultures require things to stay in their appointed place. Symbolic boundaries keep the categories 'pure', giving cultures their unique meaning and identity. What unsettles culture is 'matter out of place'—the breaking of our unwritten rules and codes. Dirt in the garden is fine, but dirt in one's bedroom is 'matter out of place'—a sign of pollution, of symbolic boundaries being transgressed, of taboos broken. What we do with 'matter out of place' is to sweep it up, throw it out, restore the place to order, bring back the normal state of affairs. The retreat of many cultures towards 'closure' against foreigners, intruders, aliens and 'others' is part of the same process of purification (Kristeva, 1982). According to this argument, then, *symbolic boundaries are central to all culture. Marking 'difference' leads us, symbolically, to close ranks, shore up culture and to stigmatize and expel anything which is defined as impure, abnormal. However, paradoxically, it also makes 'difference' powerful, strangely attractive precisely because it is forbidden, taboo, threatening to cultural order.* Thus, 'what is socially peripheral is often symbolically centred' (Babcock, 1978, p. 32).

4

The fourth kind of explanation is psychoanalytic and relates to the role of 'difference' in our psychic life. *The argument here is that the 'Other' is fundamental to the constitution of the self, to us as subjects, and to sexual identity.* According to Freud, the consolidation of our definitions of 'self' and of our sexual identities depends on the way we are formed as subjects, especially in relation to that stage of early development which he called the Oedipus complex (after the Oedipus story in Greek myth). A unified sense of oneself as a subject and one's sexual identity—Freud argued—are not fixed in the very young child. However, according to Freud's version of the Oedipus myth, at a certain point the boy develops an unconscious erotic attraction to the Mother, but finds the Father barring his way to 'satisfaction'. However, when he discovers that women do not have a penis, he assumes that his Mother was punished by castration, and that he might be punished in the same way if he persists with his unconscious desire. In fear, he switches his identification to his old 'rival', the Father, thereby taking on the beginnings of an identification with a masculine identity. The girl child identifies the opposite way—with the Father. But she cannot 'be' him, since she lacks the penis. She can only 'win' him by being willing, unconsciously, to bear a man's child—thereby taking up and identifying with the Mother's role, and 'becoming feminine'.

This model of how *sexual 'difference'* begins to be assumed in very young children has been strongly contested. Many people have questioned its speculative character. On the other hand, it has been very influential, as well as extensively amended by later analysts. The French psychoanalyst, Jacques Lacan (1977), for example, went further than Freud, arguing that the child has no sense of itself as a subject separate from its mother until it sees itself in a mirror, or as if mirrored in the way it is looked at by the Mother. Through identification, 'it desires the object of her desire, thus focusing its libido on itself' (see Segal, 1997). It is this reflection from outside oneself, or what Lacan calls the 'look from the place of the other', during 'the mirror stage', which allows the child for the first time to recognize itself as a unified subject, relate to the outside world, to the 'Other', develop language and take on a sexual identity. (Lacan actually says, 'mis-recognize itself', since he believes the subject can never be fully unified.) Melanie Klein (1957), on the other hand, argued that the young child copes with this problem of a lack of a stable self by splitting its unconscious image of and identification with the Mother into its 'good' and 'bad' parts, internalizing some aspects, and projecting others on to the outside world. The common element in all these different versions of Freud is the role which is given by these different theorists to the 'Other' in subjective development. Subjectivity can only arise and a sense of 'self' be formed through the symbolic and unconscious relations which the young child forges with a significant 'Other' which is outside—i.e. different from—itself.

At first sight, these psychoanalytic accounts seem to be positive in their implications for 'difference'. Our subjectivities, they argue, depend on our unconscious relations with significant others. However, there are also negative implications. The psychoanalytic perspective assumes that there is no such thing as a given, stable inner core to 'the self' or to identity. Psychically, we are never fully unified as subjects. Our subjetivities are formed through this troubled, never-completed, unconscious dialogue with—this internalization of—the 'Other'. It is formed in relation to something which completes us but which—since it lies outside us—we in some way always lack.

What's more, they say, this troubling split or division within subjectivity can never be fully healed. Some indeed see this as one of the main sources of neurosis in adults. Others see psychic problems arising from the splitting between the 'good' and 'bad' parts of the self—being pursued internally by the 'bad' aspects one has taken into oneself, or alternatively, projecting on to others the 'bad' feelings one cannot deal with. Frantz Fanon (referred to earlier), who used psychoanalytic theory in his explanation of racism, argued (1986/1952) that much racial stereotyping and violence arose from the refusal of the white 'Other' to give recognition 'from the place of the other', to the black person (see Bhabha, 1986b; Hall, 1996).

These debates about 'difference' and the 'Other' have been introduced because the chapter draws selectively on all of them in the course of analysing racial representation. It is not necessary at this stage for you to prefer one explanation of 'difference' over others, or to choose between them. They are not mutually exclusive since they refer to very different levels of analysis—the linguistic, the social, the cultural and the psychic levels respectively. However, there are two general points to note at this stage. First, from many different directions, and within many different disciplines, this question of 'difference' and 'otherness' has come to play an increasingly significant role. Secondly, 'difference' is **ambivalent**. It can be both positive and negative. It is both necessary for the production of meaning, the formation of language and culture, for social identities and a subjective sense of the self as a sexed subject—and at the same time, it is threatening, a site of danger, of negative feelings, of splitting, hostility and aggression towards the 'Other'. In what follows, you should always bear in mind this ambivalent character of 'difference', its divided legacy.

• • •

STEREOTYPING AS A SIGNIFYING PRACTICE

Before we pursue this argument, however, we need to reflect further on how this racialized regime of representation actually works. Essentially, this involves examining more deeply the set of representational practices known as **stereotyping**. So far, we have considered the essentializing, reductionist and naturalizing effects of stereotyping. Stereotyping reduces people to a few, simple, essential characteristics, which are represented as fixed by Nature. Here, we examine four further aspects: (a) the construction of 'otherness' and exclusion; (b) stereotyping and power; (c) the role of fantasy; and (d) fetishism.

Stereotyping as a signifying practice is central to the representation of racial difference. But what is a stereotype? How does it actually work? In his essay on 'Stereotyping', Richard Dyer (1977) makes an important distinction between *typing* and *stereotyping*. He argues that, without the use of *types*, it would be difficult, if not impossible, to make sense of the world. We understand the world by referring individual objects, people or events in our heads to the general classificatory schemes into which—according to our culture—they fit. Thus we 'decode' a flat object on legs on which we place things as a 'table'. We may never have seen that kind of 'table' before, but we have a general concept or category of 'table' in our heads, into which we 'fit' the particular objects we perceive or encounter. In other words, we understand 'the particular' in terms of its 'type'. We deploy what Alfred Schutz called *typifications*. In this sense, 'typing' is essential to the production of meaning (an argument we made earlier in Chapter 1).

Richard Dyer argues that we are always 'making sense' of things in terms of some wider categories. Thus, for example, we come to 'know' something about a person by thinking of the *roles* which he or she performs: is he/she a parent, a child, a worker, a lover, boss, or an old age pensioner? We assign him/her to the *membership* of different groups, according to class, gender, age group, nationality, 'race', linguistic group, sexual preference and so on. We order him/her in terms of *personality type*—is he/she a happy, serious, depressed, scatter-brained, over-active kind of person? Our picture of who the person 'is' is built up out of the information we accumulate from positioning him/her within these different orders of typification. In broad terms, then, 'a *type* is any simple, vivid, memorable, easily grasped and widely recognized characterization in which a few traits are foregrounded and change or "development" is kept to a minimum' (Dyer, 1977, p. 28).

What, then, is the difference between a *type* and a *stereotype*? *Stereotypes* get hold of the few 'simple, vivid, memorable, easily grasped and widely recognized' characteristics about a person, *reduce* everything about the person to those traits, *exaggerate* and *simplify* them, and *fix* them without change or development to eternity. This is the process we described earlier. So the first point is—*stereotyping reduces, essentializes, naturalizes and fixes 'difference'.*

Secondly, *stereotyping deploys a strategy of 'splitting'*. It divides the normal and the acceptable from the abnormal and the unacceptable. It then *excludes* or *expels* everything which does not fit, which is different. Dyer argues that 'a system of social- and stereo-types refers to what is, as it were, within and beyond the pale of normalcy [i.e. behaviour which is accepted as 'normal' in any culture]. Types are instances which indicate those who live by the rules of society (social types) and those who the rules are designed to exclude (stereotypes). For this reason, stereotypes are also more rigid than social types.... [B]oundaries ... must be clearly delineated and so stereotypes, one of the mechanisms of boundary maintenance, are characteristically fixed, clear-cut, unalterable' (ibid., p. 29). So, *another feature of stereotyping is its practice of 'closure' and exclusion. It symbolically fixes boundaries, and excludes everything which does not belong.*

Stereotyping, in other words, is part of the maintenance of social and symbolic order. It sets up a symbolic frontier between the 'normal' and the 'deviant', the 'normal' and the 'pathological', the 'acceptable' and the 'unacceptable', what 'belongs' and what does not or is 'Other', between 'insiders' and 'outsiders', Us and Them. It facilitates the 'binding' or bonding together of all of Us who are 'normal' into one 'imagined community'; and it sends into symbolic exile all of Them—'the Others'—who are in some way different—'beyond the pale'. Mary Douglas (1966), for example, argued that whatever is 'out of place' is considered as polluted, dangerous, taboo. Negative feelings cluster around it. It must be symbolically excluded if the 'purity' of the culture is to be restored. The feminist theorist, Julia Kristeva, calls such expelled or excluded groups, 'abjected' (from the Latin meaning, literally, 'thrown out') (Kristeva, 1982).

The third point is that *stereotyping tends to occur where there are gross inequalities of power.* Power is usually directed against the subordinate or excluded group. One aspect of this power, according to Dyer, is *ethnocentrism*—'the application of the norms of one's own culture to that of others' (Brown, 1965, p. 183). Again, remember Derrida's argument that, between binary oppositions like Us/Them, 'we are not dealing with ... peaceful coexistence ... but rather with a violent hierarchy. One of the two terms governs ... the other or has the upper hand' (1972, p. 41).

In short, stereotyping is what Foucault called a 'power/knowledge' sort of game. It classifies people according to a norm and constructs the excluded as 'other'. Interestingly, it is also what Gramsci would have called an aspect of the struggle for hegemony. As Dyer observes, 'The establishment of normalcy (i.e. what is accepted as 'normal') through social-and stereo-types is one aspect of the habit of ruling groups ... to attempt to fashion the whole of society according to their own world view, value system, sensibility and ideology. So right is this world view for the ruling groups that they make it appear (as it *does* appear to them) as 'natural' and 'inevitable'—and for everyone—and, in so far as they succeed, they establish their hegemony' (Dyer, 1977, p. 30). Hegemony is a form of power based on leadership by a group in many fields of activity at once, so that its ascendancy commands widespread consent and appears natural and inevitable.

REPRESENTATION, DIFFERENCE AND POWER

Within stereotyping, then, we have established a connection between representation, difference and power. However, we need to probe the nature of this *power* more fully. We often think of power in terms of direct physical coercion or constraint. However, we have also spoken, for example, of power *in representation*; power to mark, assign and classify; of *symbolic* power; of *ritualized* expulsion. Power, it seems, has to be understood here, not only in terms of economic exploitation and physical coercion, but also in broader cultural or symbolic terms, including the power to represent someone or something in a certain way—within a certain 'regime of representation'. It includes the exercise of *symbolic power* through representational practices. Stereotyping is a key element in this exercise of symbolic violence.

In his study of how Europe constructed a stereotypical image of 'the Orient', Edward Said (1978) argues that, far from simply reflecting what the countries of the Near East were actually like, 'Orientalism' was the *discourse* 'by which European culture was able to manage—and even produce—the Orient politically, sociologically, militarily, ideologically, scientifically and imaginatively during the post-Enlightenment period'. Within the framework of western hegemony over the Orient, he says, there emerged a new object of knowledge—'a complex Orient suitable for study in the academy, for display in the museum, for reconstruction in the colonial office, for theoretical illustration in anthropological, biological, linguistic, racial and historical theses about mankind and the universe, for instances of economic and sociological theories of development, revolution, cultural personalities, national or religious character' (pp. 7–8). This form of power is closely connected with knowledge, or with the practices of what Foucault called 'power/knowledge'.

REFERENCES

Babcock, B. (1978) *The Reversible World: symbolic inversion in art and society,* Ithaca, NY, Cornell University Press.

Bailey, D. (1988) 'Rethinking black representation' in *Ten/8*, No. 31, Birmingham.

Bakhtin, M. (1981) *The Dialogic Imagination*, Austin, University of Texas. First published 1935.

Barthes, R. (1977) 'Rhetoric of the image' in *Image–Music–Text*, Glasgow, Fontana.

Bhabha, H. (1986a) '"The Other question' in *Literature, Politics and Theory*, London, Methuen.

Bhabha, H. (1986b) 'Foreword' to Fanon, F., *Black Skin, White Masks*, London, Pluto Press.

Bogle, D. (1973) *Toms, Coons, Mulattoes, Mammies and Bucks: an interpretative history of blacks in American films*, New York, Viking Press.

Brown, R. (1965) *Social Psychology*, London/New York, Macmillan.

Cripps, T. (1978) *Black Film as Genre*, Bloomington, IN, Indiana University Press.

Davis, A. (1983) *Women, Race and Class*, New York, Random House.

Derrida, J. (1972) *Positions*, Chicago, IL, University of Chicago Press.

Diawara, M. (ed.) (1993) *Black American Cinema*, New York, Routledge.

Douglas, M. (1966) *Purity and Danger*, London, Routledge & Kegan Paul.

du Gay, P. (ed.) (1997) *Production of Culture/Cultures of Production*, London, Sage/The Open University (Book 4 in this series).

du Gay, P., Hall, S., Janes, L., Mackay, H. and Negus, K. (1997) *Doing Cultural Studies: the story of the Sony Walkman*, London, Sage/The Open University (Book 1 in this series).

Dyer, R. (ed.) (1977) *Gays and Film*, London, British Film Institute.

Dyer, R. (1986) *Heavenly Bodies*, Basingstoke, Macmillan/BFI.

Fanon, F. (1986) *Black Skin, White Masks*, London, Pluto Press. First published 1952.

Fernando, S. (1992) 'Blackened Images' in Bailey, D. A. and Hall, S. (eds) *Critical Decade, Ten/8*, Vol. 2, No. 2, Birmingham.

Frederickson, G. (1987) *The Black Image in the White Mind*, Hanover, NH, Wesleyan University Press.

Freud, S. (1977) 'Fetishism' in *On Sexualities*, Pelican Freud Library, Vol. 7, Harmondsworth, Penguin. First published 1927.

Gaines, J. (1993) 'Fire and desire: race, melodrama and Oscar Mischeaux' in Diawara, M. (ed.).

Gates, H. L. (1988) *The Signifying Monkey*, Oxford, Oxford University Press.

Gilman, S. (1985) *Difference and Pathology*, Ithaca, NY, Cornell University Press.

Green, D. (1984) 'Classified subjects: photography and anthropology—the technology of power', *Ten/8*, No. 14, Birmingham.

Hall, C. (1994) *White, Male and Middle Class*, Cambridge, Polity Press.

Hall, S. (1972) 'Determinations of news photographs' in *Working Papers in Cultural Studies No. 3*, Birmingham, University of Birmingham.

Hall, S. (ed.) (1977) *Representation: cultural representations and signifying practices*, London, Sage/The Open University (Book 2 in this series).

Hall, S. (1981) 'The whites of their eyes' in Brunt, R. (ed.) *Silver Linings*, London, Lawrence and Wishart.

Hall, S. (1996) 'The after-life of Frantz Fanon' in Read, A. (ed.) *The Fact of Blackness: Frantz Fanon and visual representation*, Seattle, WA, Bay Press.

hooks, b. (1992) *Black Looks: race and representation*, Boston, MA, South End Press.

Jordan, W. (1968) *White Over Black*, Chapel Hill, NC, University of North Carolina Press.

Klein, M. (1957) *Envy and Gratitude*, New York, Delta.

Kristeva, J. (1982) *Powers of Horror*, New York, Columbia University Press.

Lacan, J. (1977) *Écrits*, London, Tavistock.

Leab, D. (1976) *From Sambo to Superspade*, New York, Houghton Mifflin.

Lévi-Strauss, C. (1970) *The Raw and the Cooked*, London, Cape.

Lindfors, B. (unpublished) 'The Hottentot Venus and other African attractions'.

Long, E. (1774) *History of Jamaica*, London, Lowdnes.

Mackay, H. (ed.) (1997) *Consumption and Everyday Life*, London, Sage/The Open University (Book 5 in this series).

Mackenzie, J. (ed.) (1986) *Imperialism and Popular Culture*, Manchester, Manchester University Press.

McClintock, A. (1995) *Imperial Leather*, London, Routledge.

Mercer, K. (ed.) (1994) *Welcome to the Jungle*, London, Routledge.

Mercer, K. (1994a) 'Reading racial fetishism' in Mercer, K. (ed.).

Mercer, K. and Julien, I. (1994) 'Black masculinity and the politics of race' in Mercer, K. (ed).

Morton, P. (1991) *Disfigured Images*, New York, Praeger and Greenwood Press.

Richards, T. (1990) *The Commodity Culture of Victorian Britain*, London, Verso.

Riefenstahl, L. (1976) *The Last of the Nuba*, London, Collins.

Said, E. (1978) *Orientalism*, Harmondsworth, Penguin.

Segal, L. (1997) 'Sexualities', Chapter 4 in Woodward, K. (ed.) *Identity and Difference*, London, Sage/The Open University (Book 3 in this series).

Stallybrass, P. and White, A. (1986) *The Politics and Poetics of Transgression*, London, Methuen.

Staples, R. (1982) *Black Masculinity: the black man's role in American society*, San Francisco, CA, Black Scholar Press.

Thompson, K. (ed.) (1997) *Media and Cultural Regulation*, London, Sage/The Open University (Book 6 in this series).

Wallace, M. (1979) *Black Macho*, London, Calder.

Wallace, M. (1993) 'Race, gender and psychoanalysis in forties films' in Diawara, M. (ed.).

Woodward, K. (ed.) (1997) *Identity and Difference*, London Sage/The Open University (Book 3 in this series).

20

From *Bad Boys: Public Schools in the Making of Black Male Masculinity*

ANN ARNETT FERGUSON

SCHOOL RULES

This is the "banking" concept of education, in which the scope of action allowed to the students extends only as far as receiving, filing, and storing the deposits. They do, it is true, have the opportunity to become collectors or cataloguers of the things they store. But in the last analysis, it is men themselves who are filed away through the lack of creativity, transformation, and knowledge in this (at best) misguided system. For apart from inquiry, apart from praxis, men cannot be truly human. Knowledge emerges only through invention and reinvention, through the restless, impatient, continuing, hopeful inquiry men pursue in the world, with the world, and with each other.

—PAULO FREIRE, *PEDAGOGY OF THE OPPRESSED*

I am in school to learn.
I pledge to accept responsibility
for myself and my school work.
I pledge to accept responsibility
for my actions toward parents,
teachers, and my schoolmates.

—ROSA PARKS SCHOOL PLEDGE

School as a Sorting System

SCHOOL RULES GOVERN and regulate children's bodily, linguistic, and emotional expression. They are an essential element of the sorting and ranking technologies of an educational system that is organized around the search for and establishment of a ranked difference among children. This system is designed to produce a hierarchy: a few individuals who are valorized as "gifted" at the top and a large number who are stigmatized as failures at the bottom. School rules operate along with other elements of the formal curriculum such as standardized tests and grades to produce this ordered difference among children.

Since this is not the prevailing assumption about the goal of education in our society, we must turn to alternative views of schooling for a theoretical explanation of the process of how social difference is created and reproduced in schools. One view is that of "radical schooling" theorists, and the other is that of the poststructuralist Michel Foucault. In contrast to the widely held liberal belief that schools are meritocratic and that through them individuals regardless of their social, economic, or ethnic background are able to realize their potential and achieve economic and social mobility, these alternative perspectives presume schooling to be a system for sorting and ranking students to take a particular place in the existing social hierarchy.

Radical Schooling Theory

The radical perspective assumes that educational institutions are organized around and reflect the interests of dominant groups in the society; that the function of school is to reproduce the current inequities of our social, political, and economic system. It proposes that the crucial element for creating and reproducing social inequality is a "hidden curriculum" that includes such taken-for-granted components of instruction as differences in modes of social control and the regulation of relations of authority,[1] and the valorization of certain forms of linguistic and cultural expression.[2] This hidden curriculum reflects the "cultural hegemony" of the dominant class and works to reinforce and reproduce that dominance by exacerbating and multiplying—rather than diminishing or eliminating—the "inequalities" children bring from home and neighborhood to school.

Pierre Bourdieu is representative of this school of thought. He argues that schools embody the class interests and ideology of the dominant class, which has the power to impose its views, standards, and cultural forms—its "cultural capital"—as superior. Thus the ruling class is able to systematically enforce the social distinctions of its own lifestyle and tastes as superior standards to be universally aspired to. This imposition is effected through the exercise of "symbolic violence," the painful, damaging, mortal wounds inflicted by the wielding of words, symbols, standards.

Bourdieu's concept of "symbolic violence" is particularly useful for an examination of punishment practices as symbolic enforcers of a cultural hegemony in the hidden curriculum. He directs our attention to the manner in which this type of violence operates through taken-for-granted notions of the form and content of "proper" behavior overlooked by liberal notions of schooling. For example, "politeness," in his view, "contains a politics, a practical immediate recognition of social classifications and of hierarchies between the sexes, the generations, the classes, etc."[3] This example of the politics of politeness is one I will develop to demonstrate the way the social hierarchy of society is recreated by the school: how manners, style, body language, and oral expressiveness influence the application of school rules and ultimately come to define and label African American students and condemn them to the bottom rung of the social order.

Foucault's Theory of Disciplinary Power

Foucault's concepts of normalization and of normalizing judgments are also fruitful theoretical starting points for grounding the discussion of how power works through punishment. Though schooling is at the center of a vast social science investigation of socialization processes, most studies focus on classroom organization and interaction, on curriculum or on analysis of texts. In cases where discipline is the subject of inquiry, the salient issue typically becomes one of effective classroom management and style of social control for children.[4] Punishment as a mechanism in a process of social differentiation is generally neglected in this research.

One reason for this emphasis is the role that school discipline is assumed to play in the learning process. Conformity to rules is treated by school adults as the essential prior condition for any classroom learning to take place. Furthermore, rules bear the weight of moral authority. Rules governing children are seen as the basis of order, the bedrock of respect on which that order stands. Rules are spoken about as inherently neutral, impartially exercised, and impervious to individual feelings and personal responses. The question of how order is obtained, at whose expense, the messages this "order" bears, and the role that it plays in the regulation and production of social identities is rarely addressed.

Foucault provides an alternative approach to the function of discipline in institutions like schools. He conceptualizes discipline broadly as the mechanism for a new mode of domination that constitutes us as *individuals* with a specific perception of our identity and potential that appears natural rather than the product of relations of power. The disciplinary techniques of the school actively produce individual social identities of "good," "bad," "gifted," "having potential," "troubled," and "troublesome," rather than ferret them out and reveal them as they "naturally" exist. The objective of this mode of power is the production of people who are docile workers, self-regulating and self-disciplined.

Foucault asserts that normalizing judgments made through the allocation of reward and punishment are the most powerful instruments of this disciplinary power, whose function is not to suppress unwanted behavior or to reform it, but to

> refer individual actions to a whole that is at once a field of comparison, a space of differentiation…. It measures in quantitative terms and hierarchizes in terms of value the abilities, the level, the "nature" of individuals. It introduces through this "value-giving" measure, the constraint of a conformity that must be achieved. Lastly, it traces the limit that will define difference in relation to all other differences, the external frontier of the abnormal…. [It] compares, differentiates, hierarchizes, homogenizes, excludes. In short, it *normalizes.*[5]

So, school rules operate as instruments of normalization. Children are sorted, evaluated, ranked, compared on the basis of (mis)behaviour: what they do that violates, conforms to, school rules.

Foucault argues that disciplinary control is a modern mode of power that comes into existence with the formation of the bourgeois democratic state as a technique of regulation particularly suited to a form of governance predicated on the idea of formal equality. Under this type of regime, our status in a hierarchical system is no longer formally ascribed by birth but appears to be derived from how we measure up with regard to institutionally generated norms. "Each individual receives as his status his own individuality, in which he is linked by his status to the features, the measurements, the gaps, the 'marks' that characterize him and make him a 'case.'"[6] We come to know who we are in the world, and we are known by others, through our socially constituted "individual" difference rather than through an ascribed status such as class or race. In contemporary United States, disciplinary power becomes a particularly relevant technique of regulation and identity formation in a desegregated school system in which status once ascribed on the basis of racial superiority and inferiority is no longer legitimate grounds for granting or denying access to resources or attainment of skills.

Individualization is accomplished in institutions through a proliferation of surveillance and assessment techniques. In school, routine practices of classification, the ranking of academic performance through tests and grades, psychological screening measures, the distribution of rewards and punishment construct the "truth" of who we are.

We turn now to look at some of the mechanisms of the school that classify, compare, evaluate, and rank children through standardized tests and scores based on the official, academic curriculum. Though the official curriculum is not the subject of this study, I offer a brief overview because, as I will argue, there is a strong relationship between the hidden curriculum and the formal academic one, between a teacher's subjective evaluations of students' character and behavior and the kinds of classrooms they end up in. A disproportionate number of the kids who are in the remedial, low-track classrooms are those getting in trouble. A number of studies indicate that the placement of kids in high- or low-track groups or classrooms within schools is not simply the result of test scores of student achievement but is influenced by such things as teachers' perceptions of student appearance, behavior, and social background.[7] My objective is to suggest several ways in which to look at the interaction between objective standards and subjective modes of interpretation.

The Official Curriculum
Within Rosa Parks School, Children are formally classified and sorted into classrooms on the basis of age (grade level) and on the basis of race or ethnicity. The official explanation for this sorting is that it is to maintain a racial balance in classrooms and in the system in general. This racial balance, however, is not replicated in the special pullout programs for kids who deviate from the academic norms of the school system.

Children at Rosa Parks are sorted and ranked on the basis of tests of academic and psychological "capacity" as well as through the discipline system of the school. They are rank-ordered in relation to each other and to national norms on the basis of tests. At one end of this range of potential, ability, and talent are those who fall into the category of Gifted and Talented (GATE), the vast majority of whom are white. At the other end of the spectrum are students who are below average, failing, "at risk." The overwhelming majority are poor and black. In the final analysis, low-skill classrooms and supplementary programs like PALS are the place in school occupied by blacks, while enriched, innovative programs are largely the province of white kids.

These observations support Hochschild's findings that classrooms in schools with official desegregation policies are more racially segregated than schools in general, suggesting the existence of inequitable disciplinary practices and the segregation of blacks and whites into different "tracks."[8] She argues that for this reason it is important to look behind the official accounting of racial equity in school districts and follow sorting practices into the classrooms.

$$\cdots$$

Getting in Trouble: Regulating the Self
Body Trouble
Adults constantly monitor what the body of the child is saying to them, using the grammar of demeanor, posture, proper gesture. A certain humbling of the body, a certain

expression of submission, a certain obeisance toward power must be displayed in order to get off without a penalty or, next best, to get the minimum. Movements of eyes, head, placement of arms, hands, and feet can be the cause of the escalation of trouble. Face to face with adult power, children's bodies should not jiggle, jounce, rock back and forth, twist, slouch, shrug shoulders, or turn away. In interactions with school adults, children are expected to make and maintain eye contact. Looking away, down at the ground, or off in the distance is considered a sign of insubordination. Hands must be held at the side hanging down loosely, limply, not on hips (an expression of aggression) or in pockets (a sign of insolence and disrespect). A certain fearfulness is desirable, but must be displayed with sincerity, without any cockiness. Bodies have to actively express respect for adult authority: if they are too rigid they give off a sign rebelliousness or insincerity. Any one or any combination of those movements could violate the "Be courteous, cooperative" rule.

In the classroom, teachers demand bodies be arranged in certain positions before work can begin: sit up straight, both feet on the floor, hands off the desk, eyes in front toward teacher, or down on the desk. Bodies must be properly arranged both individually and as a group before they can erupt from the classroom to play. They must organize themselves into neat lines before they can enter or exit from classrooms, though lines become raggedy as soon as teachers move ahead or lag behind.

Bodies can move too fast or too slow. Running in the hallway is forbidden. Moving too slowly in the classroom from task to task can get you in trouble, so can opening one's desk and getting out the required textbook in slow motion, or going over to the pencil sharpener and taking too long to sharpen the pencil. These things in themselves do not call for disciplinary action, but become the occasion for an intervention by the teacher that can escalate into real trouble.

Adult bodies physically symbolize power in the school. For one, difference in body size between adults and most elementary school kids is still enormous. Adult bodies loom over children in moments of trouble. Most disturbing, however, is the way that this embodiment of fearsome power is specifically signaled by the presence of the adult black men in the school; their size and appearance speak volumes in punishment. The bodies of the adult black men come to stand in for the physical power that lies behind the verbal reprimands to which school authority is limited. Three of the five African American men working with children in the school are responsible for discipline. Each has impressive physiques, as if body size is a part of the job description. The figure whose job it is to strike fear in the hearts of children in school is epitomized by the intimidating physical presence of the African American male. Yet, these same men, guardians of law and order in the school, may become suspicious, dangerous characters in the eyes of ordinary citizens on the streets outside. The constant here is the fixing of meaning in the connection between black male bodies and fear.

Trouble and Emotion: "Attitude"

Whether the emotional expressions of children are proper displays of feeling or punishable acts is a matter of adult interpretation. Expressions of anger, outbursts of temper, tears of disappointment, while not against the rules, are potential moments of trouble. Many of the infractions coded as disruption, defiance, or disrespect—or sometimes as all three—seemed to emanate from the display of emotions by children, the performance of self in this relation of power described by the popular expression *attitude*. These generally involved interactions where children are seen as challenging adult authority and power. Girls committed approximately 40 percent of these infractions to boys' 60 percent; the vast majority were African American.

Adult descriptions of infractions on the referrals often invoked their reading of the tone of the exchange as expressed through children's body language and nonverbal forms of communication. Here is how a teacher documented one incident of defiance: "James was doing math, so I asked him to return Lashawn's geography book. The third time I asked he did it, but gave me a look that said, 'you bitch....' I cannot let this sort of action pass unnoticed." James's punishment was a cooling-off period in the Punishing Room. This was also the consequence for a girl who "responded very disrespectfully. Tone of voice, words used, body language, unwilling to acknowledge misbehavior, shoves blame back on teacher." Another girl got detention because, as the student specialist wrote, "She was 'moving' her mouth while P.E. teacher was talking." Another girl received after-school detention for a "sassy mouth, standing with attitude, walking away when I called to her in the 6th grade line at lunch." The same girl got two days of in-house detention for "disruption in class, disrespectual [*sic*] and defiant when spoken to. Mouthy and had an attitude." A white girl was sent to cool off in the Punishing Room after she was charged with "defiance; flapping & pouting; slamming drawers, called Sharon a bitch."

What is most significant for us here is that readings of "defiant attitude" are often deciphered through a racialized key. Gilmore's study of literacy achievement in predominately low-income, urban black elementary school students corroborates this point.[9] He found that many of the most crucial social interactions in school settings were highly charged with emotion and regularly interpreted by teachers in terms of students' "attitude."[10] He documents how African American pupils' expression of feeling in confrontations with authority figures in school often involved a bodily display of "stylized sulking" as a face-saving device. For girls, this included a sound such as "humpf" followed by chin held high, closed eyelids, and movement of the head upward and to the side. For boys, the display involved hands crossed at the chest, legs spread wide, head down, and gestures such as a desk pushed away. Both black and white teachers perceive these displays as threatening, as denoting a specifically black communicative style that they interpreted as showing a "bad attitude" by demonstrating the child's refusal to align himself with the school's standards, choosing instead to identify with what they considered a black lower-class style. Gilmore found that teachers used these displays as a measure of students' academic potential and that teacher judgments about this kind of "attitude" weighed heavily when decisions about placement in special honors classes were being made, even outweighing more "objective" measures such as demonstrated academic achievement.[11]

Whether these ways of displaying emotion do or do not conform to the acceptable rules for comportment in school is not the main issue here. What I want to foreground with this example is the exercise of symbolic violence and the relationship between a hidden or noncognitive form of assessment and an official one. Cultural modes of emotional display by kids become significant factors in decisions by adults about their academic potential and influence decisions teachers make about the kinds of academic programs in which they will be placed. These are the kind of emotional displays, for example, that can also be the basis for placement in Special Day Classes or for denying access to enrichment classes.

Moments of discipline are also occasions when adults act emotionally, when the appearance of distance and control slips. I observed the way the adults' need to act the part of outrage or shock with the body seemed to stir up real expressions of feeling in them. This performance is something slightly shameful that must be guarded, kept private, protected from too much outside observation. Later, I was especially aware of how these displays entered into early considerations about allowing me to observe in the relatively private, hidden, space of the Punishing Room.

The Troublemakers almost by definition were characterized by school adults as defiant and disrespectful. At the same time, the boys are conscious of how adults often let go and lose control in moments of discipline. They charged that the teachers treated kids rudely, with no respect. They expressed strong feelings of resentment of the asymmetrical power relations that existed between the adults and themselves. They pointed to the different rules of demeanor and "attitude" that apply to the teachers.

Trey: You see the teachers talk about us having an attitude problem, but then they do have one too.

Ann: The teachers do? How?

Trey: They think that just because we're younger than them, they're older—they can have attitude with us or something. They think it's all right to treat us anyway they want.

Ann: An example?

Trey: The way they talk to us. Like they yelling up in your face and pointing at you—and you want to do that back and you get in trouble. But they don't want that done to them. *No!* They think they're *it*.

Horace told a story that for him exemplified the one-sidedness of the respect exchange:

> The math teacher kept calling me by my last name but everybody else by their first name. He was getting on my nerves. [Horace's last name is Budd, so calling him by his last name did have a special twist.] I asked him about five times to stop doing it but he just kept on. He also called people names like *retard*. Then he was writing on the board—we was all laughing because he had a "murphy" [his pants were caught in the back of his crotch]. Everyone was laughing but the teacher said, "Budd, you're going to be the first one out of this class. Get out right now." Then I just stayed out of the classroom till the whole second period was over.

Trey's observation that adults are rude to kids in school and Horace's example are not a distortion of reality in order to cast their own behavior in a good light. I witnessed the discourteous, harassing treatment of pupils by some of the school adults. This verbal disparagement and the harsh dressing-down of kids was carried out in the name of school discipline required by certain kinds of children; it was seen as an essential weapon, given the circumstances, in the creation and maintenance of order. It was typically unleashed against children who were black, poor, and already labeled as trouble; students whose parents had little power or credibility, who would come in and complain about how their kids were being treated.

For Troublemakers, this lack of reciprocity of respect and display of "attitude" on the part of the teachers is an important structuring element of the conditions of schoolwork that has consequences both for their interactions with adults as well as with their peers. I discovered that other research investigating teacher-student relations documented the way that pupils' feelings about disrespectful behavior on the part of teachers prompted reciprocation on their part: teachers who were uncivil were treated in kind.[12]

While the relations of power and the lack of respect for pupils by school adults was articulated as a source of real anger and emotion by the Troublemakers, the sense of resentment was not echoed by the Schoolboys, who generally did not engage in power struggles with the teachers. The Schoolboys, however, were conscious of the "work" they do to produce an identity that was unimpeachable. Though they described behavior that they engaged in that was technically rule breaking, they conform to the teacher's description of the ideal pupil who follows orders without argument or questions. They talked about the work they do to stay out of trouble. The performance of obedience and management of impression is a key element in this work. Martin, one of the Schoolboys, talked about the enactment of obedience. When I asked him how he managed to stay away from the Punishing Room, he replied: "Just kinda like what the teacher says—I just do it real quick." Martin knows that it is more than merely following orders. Keisha, after all, was following orders when she got in trouble in the hallway. Orders must be followed "real quick" without hesitation and sincerely played. It is not just doing what one is told but the visible commitment to the idea of following orders that is important. Martin understands that the speed of compliance demonstrates the unthinking impulse to obey; hesitation implies that perhaps a decision is being taken about whether to obey or not and is seen as a clear challenge to relations of power.

Clothes, Language, and Identities

The school has unwritten rules about clothing that remain informal so that they can deal as required with the coming and going of youth style. The policing of clothing at Rosa Parks is most vigilant around boys' style of dress. Certain articles of clothing have become identified by school as signals of rebellion, uncontrollability, of gang membership. The school reads male expression through clothing as the harbinger of more dangerous expressions, as if the representation of the thing is the thing itself.

Baseball caps, especially worn back to front and slightly angled, are a particularly powerful object in the contest of power between adults and children in the school. The unwritten rule is that caps are allowed before and after school and during the recesses. Many teachers ignore the rule as petty but call it into action at some point as an instrument of asserting dominance. This illustration from my field notes is an example of what I mean.

> I have come to talk to Jamal's teacher at recess. He is going out the door, football in hand as I enter, but the teacher calls him back because I am there. He is wearing his cap pulled low on his forehead. He looks dismayed at the delay and asks how long it will be. The teacher seems furious at this question. "Don't you ever dare ask me how long I'm going to keep you or you'll be in here for the whole lunch period." He slouches into a seat. She continues to harangue: "Take that hat off! I want to see your eyes." He pulls it off slowly.

Some of the fundamental aspects of presentation and performance of self, such as language, as well as some of the more changeable and passing, such as style, can get a child in trouble. Language, like bodies, is important in conveying sincerity and deference. Style of address is a signal for adults to either escalate the demand for obedience or permit safe passage. For example, a "yeah" rather than "Yes, Mr. or Mrs.—" is considered cheeky. Mumbling in response to something an adult asks is also taken as possible insubordination and is usually followed with further interrogation to ascertain the intention.

The use of Black English, the mother's tongue, rather than "standard" English will get an African American child in trouble. This is true at the level of the formal curriculum as well as in terms of more subjective judgments about how its usage reflects on individual intelligence and cultural deficiency. All the reading, all tests, all communications with and of power are supposed to take place in Standard English. The whole lexicon of home and street, the way the children tell their lives to themselves and others must be squeezed into this standard. When you create yourself through words, the official language of power must be used in order to be rewarded directly or indirectly.

A defiant, challenging, oppositional body; dramatic, emotional expressions; a rich, complex nonstandard vocabulary establish the "outer limits" in a field of comparison in which the desired norm is a docile bodily presence and the intonation and homogeneous syntax of Standard English. This outer limit is exemplified by the black child: the closer to whiteness, to the norm of bodies, language, emotion, the more these children *are* self-disciplined and acceptable members of the institution.

I have been looking at relations of power in this discussion of school rules as if the only axis along which these operate is that of adult and child: adult policing of the boundaries and children's incursions into the territory and privileges of being "grown up." It is easy to run afoul of the rules, to get in trouble. The rules govern not just the surfaces of the time and spaces of school but also deep, personal structures: self-expression and the proper display of feeling. It is clear that there is an enormous amount of interpretation, of reading of the meaning of personal, as well as cultural, forms of communication, that takes place in exchanges between adults and children.

I have only briefly mentioned how race might make a difference in the exercise of rules. Yet the statistics that I have presented suggest that though all children may be up to their eyeballs in this sea of adult rules, the overwhelming majority of those who get in trouble in school are African American males.

How race is used as a filter in the interpretive work of making judgments about the implications of children's behavior is the subject of chapter 4. I will examine the racialized images, beliefs, and expectations that frame teacher appraisals of black children, in general, and African American boys, in particular. It is crucial to emphasize here that I am not concerned with investigating *individual* teacher's racial attitudes, but institutional discourses and practices. As a whole, teachers at Rosa Parks School seemed genuinely convinced of the racially blind impartial nature of their practices. Schoolwide there were efforts made to infuse assemblies, classroom, and curriculum with "multicultural' programs. This is one reason why it seems imperative to lay out the processes by which well-intentioned individuals actually and actively reproduce systems of oppression through institutional practices and symbolic forms of violence.

NAUGHTY BY NATURE

> What are little boys made of?
> What are little boys made of?
> Frogs and snails
> And puppy-dogs' tails,
> That's what little boys are made of.

—*Oxford Dictionary of Nursery Rhymes*

> What makes the presence and control of the police tolerable for the population, if not fear of the criminal?

—Michel Foucault, *Power/Knowledge*

> In order for me to live, I decided very early that some mistake had been made somewhere. I was not a "nigger" even though you called me one.… I had to realize when I was very young that I was none of those things that I was told I was. I was not, for example, happy. I never touched a watermelon for all kinds of reasons. I had been invented by white people, and I knew enough about life by this time to understand that whatever you invent, whatever you project, that is you! So where we are now is that a whole country of people believe I'm a "nigger" and I don't.

—James Baldwin, "A Talk to Teachers"

Two representations of black masculinity are widespread in society and school today. They are the images of the African American male as a criminal and as an endangered species. These images are routinely used as resources to interpret and explain behavior by teachers at Rosa Parks School when they make punishment decisions. An ensemble of historical meanings and their social effects is contained within these images.

The image of the black male criminal is more familiar because of its prevalence in the print and electronic media as well as in scholarly work. The headlines of newspaper articles and magazines sound the alarm dramatically as the presence of black males in public spaces has come to signify danger and a threat to personal safety. But this is not just media hype. Bleak statistics give substance to the figure of the criminal. Black males are disproportionately in jails: they make up 6 percent of the population of the United States, but 45 percent of the inmates in state and federal prisons; they are imprisoned at six times the rate of whites.[13] In the state of California, one-third of African American men in their twenties are in prison, on parole, or on probation, in contrast to 5 percent of white males in the same age group. This is nearly five times the number who attend four-year colleges in the state.[14] The mortality rate for African American boys fourteen years of age and under is approximately 50 percent higher than for the comparable group of white male youth, with the leading cause of death being homicide.[15]

The second image, that of the black male as an endangered species, is one which has largely emanated from African American social scientists and journalists who are deeply concerned about the criminalization and high mortality rate among African American youth.[16] It represents him as being marginalized to the point of oblivion. While this discourse emanates from a sympathetic perspective, in the final analysis the focus is all too often on individual maladaptive behavior and black mothering practices as the problem rather than on the social structure in which this endangerment occurs.

These two cultural representations are rooted in actual material conditions and reflect existing social conditions and relations that they appear to sum up for us. They are lodged in theories, in commonsense understandings of self in relation to others in the world as well as in popular culture and the media. But they are condensations, extrapolations, that emphasize certain elements and gloss over others. They represent a narrow selection from the multiplicity, the heterogeneity of actual relations in society.

Since both of these images come to be used for identifying classification, and decision making by teachers at Rosa Parks School, it is necessary to analyze the manner in which these images, or cultural representations of difference, are produced through a racial discursive formation. Then we can explain how they are utilized by teachers in the exercise of school rules to produce a context in which African American boys become more visible, more culpable as "rule-breakers."

A central element of a racist discursive formation is the production of subjects as essentially different by virtue of their "race." Historically the circulation of images that represent this difference has been a powerful technique in this production.[17] Specifically, blacks have been represented as essentially different from whites, as the constitutive Other that regulates and confirms "whiteness." Images of Africans as savage animalistic, subhuman without history or culture—the diametric opposite of that of Europeans—rationalized and perpetuated a system of slavery. After slavery was abolished, images of people of Africa: descent as hypersexual, shiftless, lazy, and of inferior intellect, legitimated a system that continued to deny rights of citizenship to blacks on the basis of race difference. This regime of truth about race was articulated through scientific experiments and "discoveries," law, social custom, popular culture, folklore, and common sense. And for three hundred years, from the seventeenth century to the middle of the twentieth century, this racial distinction was policed through open and unrestrained physical violence. The enforcement of race difference was conscious, overt, and institutionalized.

In the contemporary period, the production of a racial Other and the constitution and regulation of racial difference has worked increasingly through mass-produced images that are omnipresent in our lives. At this moment in time it is through culture—or culturalism[18]—that difference is primarily asserted. This modern-day form for producing racism specifically operates through symbolic violence and representations of Blackness that circulate through the mass media, cinematic images and popular music, rather than through the legal forms of the past. The representational becomes a potent vehicle for the transmission of racial meanings that reproduce relations of difference, of division, and of power. These "controlling images" make "racism, sexism, and poverty appear to be natural, normal, and an inevitable part of everyday life."[19]

Cultural Representations of "Difference"

The behavior of African American boys in school is perceived by adults at Rosa Parks School through a filter of overlapping representations of three socially invented categories of "difference": age, gender, and race. These are grounded in the commonsense, taken-for-granted notion that existing social divisions reflect biological and natural dispositional differences among humans: so children are essentially different from adults, males from females, blacks from whites.[20] At the intersection of this complex of subject positions are African American boys who are doubly displaced: as black children, they are not seen as childlike but adultified; as black males, they are denied the masculine dispensation constituting white males as being "naturally naughty" and are discerned as willfully bad. Let us look more closely at this displacement.

The dominant cultural representation of childhood is as closer to nature, as less social, less human. Childhood is assumed to be a stage of development; culture, morality, sociability is written on children in an unfolding process by adults (who are seen as fully "developed," made by culture not nature) in institutions like family and school. On the one hand, children are assumed to be dissembling, devious, because they are more egocentric. On the other hand, there is an attribution of innocence to their wrongdoing. In both cases, this is understood to be a temporary condition, a stage prior to maturity. So they must be socialized to fully understand the meaning of their acts.

The language used to describe "children in general" by educators illustrates this paradox. At one districtwide workshop for adult school volunteers that I attended, children were described by the classroom teacher running the workshop as being "like little plants, they need attention, they gobble it up." Later in the session, the same presenter invoked the other dominant representation of children as devious, manipulative, and powerful. "They'll run a number on you. They're little lawyers, con artists, manipulators—and they usually win. They're good at it. Their strategy is to get you off task. They pull you into their whirlwind."

These two versions of childhood express the contradictory qualities that adults map onto their interactions with children in general. The first description of children as "little plants," childhood as identical with nature, is embedded in the ideology of childhood. The second version that presents children as powerful, as self-centered, with an agenda and purpose of their own, arises out of the experience adults have exercising authority over children. In actual relations of power, in a twist, as children become the objects of control, they become devious "con artists" and adults become innocent, pristine in relation to them. In both instances, childhood has been constructed as different in essence from adulthood, as a phase of biological, psychological, and social development with predictable attributes.

Even though we treat it this way, the category "child" does not describe and contain a homogeneous and naturally occurring group of individuals at a certain stage of human development. The social meaning of childhood has changed profoundly over time.[21] What it means to be a child varies dramatically by virtue of location in cross-cutting categories of class, gender, and race.[22]

Historically, the existence of African American children has been constituted differently through economic practices, the law, social policy, and visual imagery. This difference has been projected in an ensemble of images of black youth as not childlike. In the early decades of this century, representations of black children as pickaninnies depicted them as verminlike, voracious, dirty, grinning, animal-like savages. They were also depicted as the laugh-provoking butt of aggressive, predatory behavior; natural victims, therefore victimizable. An example of this was their depiction in popular lore as "alligator bait." Objects such as postcards, souvenir spoons, letter-openers and cigar-box labels were decorated with figures of half-naked black children vainly attempting to escape the open toothy jaws of hungry alligators.[23]

Today's representations of black children still bear traces of these earlier depictions. The media demonization of very young black boys who are charged with committing serious crimes is one example. In these cases there is rarely the collective soul-searching for answers to the question of how "kids like this" could have committed these acts that occurs when white kids are involved. Rather, the answer to the question seems to be inherent in the disposition of the kids themselves.[24] The image of the young black male as an endangered species revitalizes the animalistic trope. Positioned as part of nature, his essence is described through language otherwise reserved for wildlife that has been decimated to the point of extinction. Characterized as a "species," they are cut off from other members of family and community and isolated as a form of prey.

There is continuity, but there is a significant new twist to the image. The endangered species and the criminal are mirror images. Either as criminal perpetrator or as endangered victim, contemporary imagery proclaims black males to be responsible for their fate. The discourse of individual choice and responsibility elides the social and economic context and locates predation as coming from within. It is their own maladaptive and inappropriate behavior that causes African Americans to self-destruct. As an endangered species, they are stuck in an obsolete stage of social evolution, unable to adapt to the present. As criminals, they are a threat to themselves, to each other, as well as to society in general.

As black children's behavior is refracted through the lens of these two cultural images, it is "adultified." By this I mean their transgressions are made to take on a sinister, intentional, fully conscious tone that is stripped of any element of childish naïveté. The discourse of childhood as an unfolding developmental stage in the life cycle is displaced in this mode of framing school trouble. Adultification is visible in the way African American elementary school pupils are talked about by school adults.

One of the teachers, a white woman who prided herself on the multicultural emphasis in her classroom, invoked the image of African American children as "looters" in lamenting the disappearance of books from the class library. This characterization is especially meaningful because her statement, which was made at the end of the school year that had included the riots in Los Angeles, invoked that event as a framework for making children's behavior intelligible.

> I've lost so many library books this term. There are quite a few kids who don't have any books at home, so I let them borrow them. I didn't sign them out because I thought I could trust the kids. I sent a letter home to parents asking them to look for them and turn them in. But none have come in. I just don't feel the same. *It's just like the looting in Los Angeles.*

By identifying those who don't have books at home as "looters," the teacher has excluded the white children in the class, who all come, from more middle-class backgrounds so, it is assumed, "have books at home." In the case of the African American kids, what might be interpreted as the careless behavior of children is displaced by images of adult acts of theft that conjure up violence and mayhem. The African American children in this teacher's classroom and their families are seen not in relation to images of childhood, but in relation to the television images of crowds rampaging through South Central Los Angeles in the aftermath of the verdict of the police officers who beat Rodney King. Through this frame, the children embody a willful, destructive, and irrational disregard for property rather than simple carelessness. Racial difference is mediated through culturalism: blacks are understood as a group undifferentiated by age or status with the proclivity and values to disregard the rights and welfare of others.

Adultification is a central mechanism in the interpretive framing of gender roles. African American girls are constituted as different through this process. A notion of sexual passivity and innocence that prevails for white female children is displaced by the image of African American females as sexual beings: as immanent mothers, girlfriends, and sexual partners of the boys in the room.[25] Though these girls may be strong, assertive, or troublesome, teachers evaluate their potential in ways that attribute to them an inevitable, potent sexuality that flares up early and that, according to one teacher, lets them permit men to run all over them, to take advantage of them. An incident in the Punishing Room that I recorded in my field notes made visible the way that adult perceptions of youthful behavior were filtered through racial representations. African American boys and girls who misbehaved were not just breaking a rule out of high spirits and needing to be chastised for the act, but were adultified, gendered figures whose futures were already inscribed and foreclosed within a racial order:

> Two girls, Adila and a friend, burst into the room followed by Miss Benton a black sixth-grade teacher and a group of five African American boys from her class. Miss Benton is yelling at the girls because they have been jumping in the hallway and one has knocked down part of a display on the bulletin board which she and her class put up the day before. She is yelling at the two girls about how they're wasting time. This is what she says: "You're doing exactly what they want you to do. You're playing into their hands. Look at me! Next year they're going to be tracking you."
>
> One of the girls asks her rather sullenly who "they" is.
>
> Miss Benton is furious. "Society, that's who. You should be leading the class, not fooling around jumping around in the hallway. Someone has to give pride to the community. All the black men are on drugs, or in jail, or killing each other. Someone has got to hold it together. And the women have to do it. And you're jumping up and down in the hallway."
>
> I wonder what the black boys who have followed in the wake of the drama make of this assessment of their future, seeming already etched in stone. The teacher's words to the girls are supposed to inspire them to leadership. The message for the boys is a dispiriting one.

Tracks have already been laid down for sixth-grade girls towards specifically feminized responsibility (and, what is more prevalent, blame) for the welfare of the community, while males are bound for jail as a consequence of their own socially and self-destructive acts.

There is a second displacement from the norm in the representation of black males. The hegemonic, cultural image of the essential "nature" of males is that they are different from females in the meaning of their acts. Boys will be boys: they are mischievous, they get into trouble, they can stand up for themselves. This vision of masculinity is rooted in the notion of an essential sex difference based on biology, hormones, uncontrollable urges, true personalities. Boys are naturally more physical, more active. Boys are naughty by *nature*. There is something suspect about the boy who is "too docile," "like a girl." As a result, rule breaking on the part of boys is looked at as something-they-cannot-help, a natural expression of masculinity in a civilizing process.

This incitement of boys to be "boylike" is deeply inscribed in our mainstream culture, winning hearts and stirring imaginations in the way that the pale counterpart, the obedient boy, does not. Fiedler, in an examination of textual representations of iconic childhood figures in U.S. literature, registers the "Good Bad Boy" and the "Good Good Boy" as cultural tropes of masculinities:

> What then is the difference between the Good Good Boy and the Good Bad Boy, between Sid Sawyer, let us say, and Tom? The Good Good Boy does what his mother must pretend that she wants him to do: obey, conform; the Good Bad Boy does what she really wants him to do: deceive, break her heart a little, be forgiven.[26]

An example of this celebration of Good Bad Boy behavior, even when at the risk of order, is the way that one of the student specialists at Rosa Parks School introduced a group of boys in his classroom to a new student:

Teacher: Hey, they're thugs! Hoodlums! Hooligans! Gangsters! Stay away from these guys.
Boy (acting tough): Yeah, we're tough.
Teacher (really having fun): You ain't as tough as a slice of wet white bread!
Boy (sidling up to the teacher chest puffed out): I'm tougher than you.
Teacher: Okay! Go on! These are a bunch of great guys.
The newcomer looks at home.

African American boys are not accorded the masculine dispensation of being "naturally" naughty. Instead the school reads their expression and display of masculine naughtiness as a sign of an inherent vicious, insubordinate nature that as a threat to order must be controlled. Consequently, school adults view any display of masculine mettle on the part of these boys through body language or verbal rejoinders as a sign of insubordination. In confrontation with adults, what is required from them is a performance of absolute docility that goes against the grain of masculinity. Black boys are expected to internalize a ritual obeisance in such exchanges so that the performance of docility appears to come naturally. According to the vice principal, "These children have to learn not to talk back. They must know that if the adult says you're wrong, then you're wrong. They must not resist, must go along with it, and take their punishment," he says.

This is not a lesson that all children are required to learn, however. The disciplining of the body within school rules has specific race and gender overtones. For black boys, the enactment of docility is a preparation for adult racialized survival rituals of which the African American adults in the school are especially cognizant. For African American boys bodily forms of expressiveness have repercussions in the world outside the chain-link fence of the school. The body must be taught to endure humiliation in preparation for future enactments of submission. The vice principal articulated the racialized texture of decorum when he deplored one of the Troublemakers, Lamar's, propensity to talk back and argue with teachers.

Lamar had been late getting into line at the end of recess, and the teacher had taken away his football. Lamar argued and so the teacher gave him detention. Mr. Russell spelled out what an African American male needed to learn about confrontations with power.

> Look, I've told him before about getting into these show-down situations—where he either has to show off to save face, then if he doesn't get his way then he goes wild. He won't get away with it in this school. Not with me, not with Mr. Harmon. But I know he's going to try it somewhere outside and it's going to get him in *real* trouble. He has to learn to ignore, to walk away, not to get into power struggles.

Mr. Russell's objective is to hammer into Lamar's head what he believes is the essential lesson for young black males to learn if they are to get anywhere in life: to act out obeisance is to survive. The specter of the Rodney King beating by the Los Angeles Police Department provided the backdrop for this conversation, as the trial of the police officers had just begun. The defense lawyer for the LAPD was arguing that Rodney King could have stopped the beating at any time if he had chosen.

This apprehension of black boys as inherently different both in terms of character and of their place in the social order is a crucial factor in teacher disciplinary practices.

Getting a Reputation

Children are sorted into categories of "educability" as they get a reputation among the adults as troubled, troubling, or troublemakers. They are not only identified as problems, as "at-risk" by the classroom teacher, but gain schoolwide reputations as stories about their exploits are publicly shared by school adults in the staff room, at staff meetings, and at in-service training sessions. Horror stories circulate through the school adult network so that children's reputations precede them into classrooms and follow them from school to school. I pointed out earlier how Horace's name was invoked at a staff meeting as a benchmark of misbehavior against which other boys would be judged. As in: "That child's a problem. But he's not a Horace."

Once a reputation has been established, the boy's behavior is usually refigured within a framework that is no longer about childish misdemeanors but comes to be an ominous portent of things to come. They are tagged with futures: "He's on the fast track to San Quentin Prison," and "That one has a jail-cell with his name on it." For several reasons, these boys are more likely to be singled out and punished than other children. They are more closely watched. They are more likely to be seen as intentionally doing wrong than a boy who is considered to be a Good Bad Boy. Teachers are more likely to use the "moral principle" in determining whether to call attention to misdemeanors because "at-risk" children need discipline, but also as an example to the group, especially to other African American boys who are "endangered." The possibility of contagion must be eliminated. Those with reputations must be isolated, kept away from the others. Kids are told to stay away from them: "You know what will happen if you go over there." In the case of boys with reputations, minor infractions are more likely to escalate into major punishments.

Unsalvageable Students

In the range of normalizing judgments, there is a group of African American boys identified by school personnel as, in the words of a teacher, "unsalvageable." This term and the condition it speaks to is specifically about masculinity. School personnel argue over whether these unsalvageable boys should be given access even to the special programs designed for those who are failing in school. Should resources, defined as scarce, be wasted on these boys for whom there is no hope? Should energy and money be put instead into children who can be saved? I have heard teachers argue on both sides of the question. These "boys for whom there is no hope" get caught up in the school's punishment system: surveillance, isolation, detention, and ever more severe punishment.

These are children who are not children. These are boys who are already men. So a discourse that positions masculinity as "naturally" naughty is reframed for African American boys around racialized representations of gendered subjects. They come to stand as if already adult, bearers of adult fates inscribed within a racial order.

NOTES

1. Bowles and Gintis, *Schooling in Capitalist America.*
2. Bourdieu and Passeron, *Reproduction*; Basil Bernstein, *Towards a Theory of Educational Transmission*, vol. 3 of *Class, Codes, and Control* (London: Routledge and Kegan Paul, 1974).
3. Pierre Bourdieu, "The Economics of Linguistic Exchanges," *Social Science Information* 26, no. 6 (1977): 646.
4. See, for example, Delwyn Tattum, ed., *Management of Disruptive Pupil Behavior in Schools* (New York: John Wiley and Sons, 1986).
5. Michel Foucault, *Discipline and Punish*, translated from the French by Alan Sheridan (New York: Vintage, 1979), 183.
6. Ibid., 192.
7. For example, David H. Hargreaves, Stephen K. Hester, and Frank J. Mellor, eds., *Deviance in Classrooms* (London: Routledge and Kegan Paul, 1975); Perry Gilmore, "'Gimme Room': School Resistance, Attitude, and Access to Literacy," *Journal of Education* 167, no. 1 (1985); Helen Gouldner, *Teachers' Pets, Troublemakers, and Nobodies: Black Children in Elementary School* (Westport, Conn.: Greenwood Press, 1978).
8. Jennifer L. Hochschild, *The New American Dilemma: Liberal Democracy and School Desegregation* (New Haven: Yale University Press, 1984), 31.
9. Gilmore, "Gimme Room."
10. Ibid., 114.
11. Ibid., 112.
12. P. Marsh, E. Rosser, and R. Harre, *The Rules of Disorder* (London: Routledge and Kegan Paul, 1978). This disregard on the part of adults also had an effect on interaction between peers. Ray Rist observed that kindergarten children identified by the teacher as high achievers began to model their own relationship with the children identified as lows after that of the teacher. He recorded a number of interchanges in the classroom in which the highs belittled the lows. For example, "When I asked Lilly [low group] what it was she was drawing, she replied, 'A parachute.' Frank [high group] interrupted and said, 'Lilly can't draw nothin'." Ray C. Rist, *The Urban School: A Factory for Failure, a Study of Education in American Society* (Cambridge: MIT Press, 1973), 174.
13. *New York Times*, September 13, 1994, 1.
14. *Los Angeles Times*, November 2, 1990, 3.
15. G. Jaynes and R. Williams Jr., eds., *A Common Destiny: Blacks in American Society* (Washington, D.C.: National Academic Press, 1989), 405, 498.
16. See, for example, Jewelle Taylor Gibbs, "Young Black Males in America: Endangered, Embittered, and Embattled," in Jewelle Taylor Gibbs et al., *Young, Black, and Male in America: An Endangered Species* (New York: Auburn House, 1988); Richard Majors and Janet Mancini Billson, *Cool Pose: The Dilemmas of Black Manhood in America* (New York: Lexington Press, 1992); Jawanza Kunjufu, *Countering the Conspiracy to Destroy Black Boys*, 2 vols. (Chicago: African American Images, 1985).
17. See, for example, W. E. B. DuBois, *Souls of Black Folk* (1903; reprint, New York: Bantam, 1989); Frantz Fanon, *Black Skins, White Masks*, trans. Charles Lam Markmann (New York: Grove Press, 1967);

Stuart Hall, "The Rediscovery of 'Ideology': Return of the Repressed in Media Studies," in *Culture, Society, and the Media*, ed. Michael Gurevitch et al. (New York: Methuen, 1982); Leith Mullings, "Images, Ideology, and Women of Color," in *Women of Color in U.S. Society*, ed. Maxine Baca Zinn and Bonnie Thornton Dill (Philadelphia: Temple University Press, 1994); Edward Said, *Orientalism* (New York: Vintage, 1978).

18. Gilroy, *Small Acts*, 24, argues that "the culturalism of the new racism has gone hand in hand with a definition of race as a matter of difference rather than a question of hierarchy."

19. Collins, *Black Feminist Thought*, 68.

20. While many of the staff at Rosa Parks School would agree at an abstract level that social divisions of gender and race are culturally and historically produced, their actual talk about these social distinctions as well as their everyday expectations, perceptions, and interactions affirm the notion that these categories reflect intrinsic, *real* differences.

21. See, for example, Phillipe Ariès, *Centuries of Childhood: A Social History of Family Life* (New York: Vintage, 1962).

22. Thorne, *Gender Play*; and Valerie Polakow, *Lives on the Edge: Single Mothers and Their Children in the Other America* (Chicago: University of Chicago Press, 1993).

23. Patricia Turner, *Ceramic Uncles and Celluloid Mammies: Black Images and Their Influence on Culture* (New York: Anchor, 1994), 36.

24. A particularly racist and pernicious example of this was the statement by the administrator of the Alcohol, Drug Abuse, and Mental Health Administration, Dr. Frederick K. Goodwin, who stated without any qualms: "If you look, for example, at male monkeys, especially in the wild, roughly half of them survive until adulthood. The other half die by violence. That is the natural way of it for males, to knock each other off and, in fact, there are some interesting evolutionary implications.... The same hyper aggressive monkeys who kill each other are also hyper sexual, so they copulate more and therefore they reproduce more to offset the fact that half of them are dying." He then drew an analogy with the "high impact [of] inner city areas with the loss of some of the civilizing evolutionary things that we have built up.... Maybe it isn't just the careless use of the word when people call certain areas of certain cities, jungles." Quoted in Jerome G. Miller, *Search and Destroy: African American Males in the Criminal Justice System* (New York: Cambridge University Press, 1996), 212–13.

25. The consensus among teachers in the school about educational inequity focuses on sexism. Many of the teachers speak seriously and openly about their concern that girls are being treated differently than boys in school: girls are neglected in the curriculum, overlooked in classrooms, underencouraged academically, and harassed by boys. A number of recent studies support the concern that even the well-intentioned teacher tends to spend less classroom time with girls because boys demand so much of their attention. These studies generally gloss over racial difference as well as make the assumption that *quantity* rather than *quality* of attention is the key factor in fostering positive sense of self in academic setting. See, for example, Myra Sadker and David Sadker, *Failing at Fairness: How America's Schools Cheat Girls* (New York: C. Scribner's Sons, 1994). Linda Grant looks at both race and gender as she examines the roles that first- and second-grade African American girls play in desegregated classrooms. She finds that African American girls and white girls are positioned quite differently vis-à-vis teachers. In the classrooms she observed, white girls were called upon to play an academic role in comparison with African American girls, who were cast in the role of teacher's helpers, in monitoring and controlling other kids in the room, and as intermediaries between peers. She concluded that black girls were encouraged in stereotypical female adult roles that stress service and nurture, while white girls were encouraged to press toward high academic achievement. Most important for this study, Grant mentions in passing that black boys in the room receive the most consistent negative attention and were assessed as having a lower academic ability than any other group by teachers. See Linda Grant, "Helpers, Enforcers, and Go-Betweens: Black Females in Elementary School Classrooms," in *Women of Color in U.S. Society*, ed. Maxine Baca Zinn and Bonnie Thornton Dill (Philadelphia: University of Pennsylvania Press, 1994).

26. Leslie A. Fiedler, *Love and Death in the American Novel* (New York: Criterion, 1960), 267.

21

Asian Americans: The Absent/Silenced/Model Minority

Stacey Lee

DISCOURSES OF EXCLUSION: THE ABSENT VOICE(S) OF ASIAN AMERICA

In the United States discussions of race are generally framed in term of blacks and whites. Despite the fact that Asian Americans have been on the mainland of the United states for more than 150 years, Asians are still regarded as "strangers from a different shore" (Takaki, 1989) and voices from Asian America are excluded from the mainstream discourse on race. Two recent books that perpetuate the black and white discourse on race are Studs Terkel's *Race: How Whites and Blacks Think and Feel About the American Obsession* (1992) and Andrew Hacker's *Two Nations: Black and White, Separate, Hostile, Unequal* (1992). Although both books mention other racial groups, the authors define race relations in black and white terms (Winant, 1993). In his reasons for excluding Asians from his discussion of race, Hacker (1992) suggests that, due to the stellar achievements of Asian Americans, Asians may soon be considered to be white. The widespread popularity of these books suggests that many Americans have been influenced by the black and white view of race.

Because of the black and white discourse of race, most Americans do not view Asian Americans as legitimate racial minorities. Given this thinking, when institutions think about increasing racial diversity, they often focus on African Americans and sometimes on Latinos. Asians, on the other hand, are not seen as people who add to racial diversity, and thus they are largely absent from the discourse of diversity. For example, in constructing categories for minority scholarships and in recruiting minority students for admission, many universities exclude Chinese, Japanese, and Korean Americans. In her research on the controversy surrounding Asian Americans in higher education, Takagi (1992) found that Asian American students were "at odds with university goals of diversity, in terms of either, and sometimes both, academic achievement and racial mix of the student body" (p.81).

The reasons given for excluding Asian American perspectives from discussions of race fall into three categories. The first category includes explanations that center around the argument that there are not enough Asian Americans to warrant consideration. At a recent lecture on race in higher education, I was struck by the fact that the researcher had designed her research without consideration of Asian Americans. Her study, which examined attrition and retention rates across racial groups, included three categories for students: black/African American, Hispanic, and white. When asked whether she included students of Asian descent in her study, she responded by saying that there were not enough Asians in her study to constitute a separate category and that where there were Asians, they had been subsumed under the category of whites and others. Ironically, one of the states included in her study was California, a state in which 14% of the higher education enrollment in 1993 was Asian American.[1] In 1982, Betty Waki, a Japanese American art teacher in the Houston Unified School District, was classified as white because the system did not recognize Asians as a racial category. Her racial status denied, Ms. Waki subsequently lost her job because there were too many "white" art teachers in the district (Omi, 1992).

Another reason that Asian Americans are excluded from the discourse on race in the United States is that Asian Americans are perceived to be unassimilable foreigners as opposed to American minorities. The image that Asians are always foreign(ers) has been perpetuated by the Orientalist discourse which holds that there are innate differences between the East and the West (Cheung, 1993; Said, 1979). The Orientalist discourse suggests that an Asian person can never become an American. Rudyard Kipling's phrase, "East is East, and West is West, and never the twain shall meet," expresses this sentiment. Thus, regardless of the number of generations an Asian American person's family has been in the United States, he or she has probably been asked: "What country are you from?" In my experience as a third-generation Asian American woman, I have fielded many questions concerning my origins. When I tell people that I am from California, most respond by asking yet another question: "But where are you really from?" Their response to me suggests an unwillingness to accept me or any Asian as American. The persistent image of Asians as foreigners/outsiders implies that Asians are not legitimate members of U.S. society. This image silences Asian Americans by denying them "the right to say anything except words of gratitude and praise about America" (E. H. Kim, 1993a, p. 223).

Related to the image that Asians are foreigners is the fact that Asians in the United States are often seen as immigrants as opposed to minorities. In writing about differential educational achievement across minority groups. John Ogbu (1987, 1991) has perpetuated this distinction. According to his framework, which I will discuss in Chapter 3, Asians in the United States are immigrants, while African Americans are domestic minorities or involuntary minorities. While some Asians in the United States are immigrants, others are refugees, and still others have been here for numerous generations. Thus we are left wondering if Asians ever cease being immigrants. Are second-, third-, and fourth-generation Asian Americans still immigrants?

The final and perhaps most insidious reason given for excluding Asian voices from the discourse of race is the stereotype that Asians do not have any problems (i.e., they are model minorities). In the minds of most Americans, minorities like African Americans, Latinos, and Native Americans are minorities precisely because they experience disproportionate levels of poverty and educational underachievement. The model minority stereotype suggests that Asian Americans are "outwhiting whites" and have overcome discrimination to be more successful than whites. Ironically, this reason for excluding Asians from the discussion of race (i.e., that they are model minorities) is the very way in which Asian Americans receive the most attention in the discourse on race (E. H. Kim,

1993b). That is, when Asians are included in the discourse on race it is usually to talk about their "success." Asian Americans are described as hardworking entrepreneurs who are doing well economically (e.g., Korean merchants), and they are described as hardworking students who excel in math and science (e.g., Asian American whiz kids). While Asian Americans are stereotyped as model minorities, other racial minorities are stereotyped in overtly negative ways. In describing the 1980s discourse on race in the United States, Sleeter (1993) writes:

> The media frequently connected African Americans and Latinos with social problems that many Americans regarded as the result of moral depravity: drug use, teen pregnancy, and unemployment. Asian Americans are hailed as the "model minority" portrayed as achieving success in the U.S. through hard work and family cohesiveness (Suzuki, 1979), following the same route to success that many whites believed their ancestors followed. (p. 160)

Thus, within the model minority discourse, Asian Americans represent the "good" race and African Americans represent the "bad" race. Asian Americans represent the hope and possibility of the American dream.

MODEL MINORITY STEREOTYPE AS A HEGEMONIC DEVICE

By describing Asian Americans as model minorities, the diverse and complex experiences of Asian Americans remain hidden. Instead of seeing different Asian ethnicities as being separate and distinct, the model minority stereotype lumps diverse Asian ethnicities into one racial/panethnic group. This representation silences the multiple voices of Asian Americans, thereby creating a monolithic monotone. In addition, by painting Asian Americans as a homogeneous group, the model minority stereotype erases ethnic, cultural, social-class, gender, language, sexual, generational, achievement, and other differences. Furthermore, by describing Asian Americans as model minorities, the dominant group is imposing a categorical label on Asian Americans. Espiritu (1992) writes:

> An imposed category ignores subgroup boundaries, lumping together diverse peoples in a single, expanded "ethnic" framework. Individuals so categorized may have nothing in common except that which the categorizer uses to distinguish them. (p. 6)

The stereotype suggests that all Asians are the same because they all experience success. Thus the stereotype denies the poverty and illiteracy in Asian Americans communities (U.S. Commission on Civil Rights, 1992). In addition to silencing the wide range of Asian American experiences, the stereotype silences that fact that Asian Americans experience racism (Chun, 1980; Kwong, 1987; Suzuki, 1980; Takaki, 1989).

As a hegemonic device, the model minority stereotype maintains the dominance of whites in the racial hierarchy by diverting attention away from racial inequality and by setting standards for how minorities should behave. The model minority stereotype emerged during the 1960s in the midst of the civil rights era. Critics of the stereotype argue that the press began to popularize the stereotype of Asians as model minorities in order to silence the charges of racial injustice being made by African Americans and other minorities (Osajima, 1988; Sue & Kitano, 1973). Prior to this period, Asian Americans had often been stereotyped as devious, inscrutable, unassimilable, and in other overtly negative ways.

Articles that chronicled the success of Asian Americans began to appear in the popular press in the mid- 1960s. In December of 1966, *U.S. News & World Report* published an article lauding the success of Chinese Americans. The author wrote, "At a time when it is being proposed that hundreds of billions be spent to uplift Negroes and other minorities, the nation's 300,000 Chinese Americans are moving ahead on their own—with no help from anyone" ("Success Story," 1966, p. 73). The article went on to praise the good citizenship of Chinese Americans and the safety of Chinatowns.

The prescriptive nature of the model minority stereotype is striking in this 1966 article. Chinese Americans were singled out as good citizens precisely because that status quo saw them as the quiet minority who did not actively challenge the existing system. That is to say, Chinese Americans and other Asian Americans were seen as model minorities because they were believed to be quiet/silent and hardworking people who achieved success without depending on the government. In reflecting on how Asian Americans have been characterized, Filipina fiction writer Jessica Hagedorn (1993) writes, "In our perceived American character we are completely nonthreatening. We don't complain. We endure humiliation. We are almost inhuman in our patience. We never get angry" (pp. xxii–xxiii). Within the model minority discourse, "good" minorities, like "good" women, are silent (Cheung, 1993). "Good" minorities know their place within the system and do not challenge the existing system. *U.S. News & World Report* implied that other minority groups should model their behavior after Chinese Americans rather than spending their time protesting inequality. Thus Asian Americans were included in discussions of race in order to exclude/silence the voices of African Americans.

During the 1980s the model minority stereotype reached beyond Chinese and Japanese Americans to include Southeast Asians as well. In his analysis of the evolution of the model minority stereotype, Osajima (1988) asserts that, although the popular press began to recognize the potential negative implications of the model minority stereotype during the 1980s, it continued to portray Asian Americans as exemplary minorities who gain success through sheer effort and determination. The cover story for *Time*'s August 31, 1987, issue illustrates Osajima's point. The article, "The New Whiz Kids: Why Asian Americans Are Doing So Well, and What It Costs Them," lauded the academic achievement of Asian American students (Brand, 1987). It included stories of Southeast Asian refugees who overcame extreme obstacles to achieve academic success. In the author's words, "By almost every educational gauge, young Asian Americans are soaring" (p. 42). Once again, Asian Americans are depicted as brave, silent, and long-suffering people. The implicit message is that individual effort will be rewarded by success and that failure is the fate of those who do not adhere to the value of hard work. During my research, one of my earliest cues to the significance of the model minority stereotype for Asian American students' identities was that Asian American students repeatedly mentioned that they had read the aforementioned "Whiz Kid" article.

The model minority stereotype of Asian Americans is alive and well in the 1990s. The popular press and public figures from the New Right and neoconservative movements have continued to hold up examples of Asian American success as evidence that minorities can succeed in the United States (Hamamoto, 1992). Herrnstein and Murray's *The Bell Curve: Intelligence and Class Structure in American Life* (1994) once again casts Asian Americans as model minorities and African Americans as inferior. In the traditional family rhetoric espoused by neoconservatives and the New Right, Asian American families have been singled out as examples of old-fashioned, tight-knit families (Hamamoto, 1992; Palumbo-Liu, 1994). The stereotypic functional Asian American family is contrasted with the stereotypic dysfunctional black family headed by a single black mother on welfare. In his attack on political correctness and affirmative action programs, D'Souza (1992) argues that Asian Americans are a deserving minority being hurt by affirmative action programs. According to D'Souza, Asian American "success" is being punished, while African American or Latino "failure" is being rewarded.

In the 1992 riots that followed the Rodney King trial, the model minority image of Asian Americans was once again paraded across TV screens and newspaper headlines. This time Korean Americans were held up as legitimate victims who bravely sought to protect their private property. The conservative press represented Korean Americans as stand-ins for white, middle-class America. Korean Americans were depicted as hardworking, self-made immigrants whose property was threatened by the unlawful anger of black America. Palumbo-Li (1994) argues that, in the media coverage, "Korean-Americans were represented as the frontline forces of the white bourgeoisie," and he also argues that Korean Americans literally served as a "buffer-zone between the core of a multiethnic ghetto, and white, middle-class America" (p. 371). Asians were once again used as hegemonic devices to support notions of meritocracy and individualism. To sad irony, however, was that even while Asians were being used by the mainstream press to support dominant-group interests, Asian immigrants were abandoned in their time of need (Cho, 1993). Caught in the buffer-zone between blacks and whites, Asian Americans suffered significant losses.

In all of its permutations, the model minority stereotype has been used to support the status quo and the ideologies of meritocracy and individualism. Supporters of the model minority stereotype use Asian American success to delegitimize claims of inequality made by other racial minorities. According to the model minority discourse, Asian Americans prove that social mobility is possible for all those who are willing to work. Asian Americans are represented as examples of upward mobility through individual effort. Charges of racial inequality are met with stories of Asian American success, thereby reifying notions of equal opportunity and meritocracy (Chun, 1980; Hurh & Kim, 1989). As L. M. Wong (1993) notes:

> Asian Americans have embodied the liberal image of the acculturated racialized minority who have made it in white society. They are "useful" to those who are at the nadir [sic] of the stratification because they provide the "legitimate" and "correct" ways of social mobility. (p. 24)

Implicit in the argument that equal opportunity exists is the fact that the system is freed of any responsibility for inequality. According to this argument, if minorities (i.e., African Americans and Latinos) fail, they have only themselves to blame (Hurh & Kim, 1989). This victim blaming was clear in the 1966 *U.S. News & World Report* article.

Apple and Weis (1983) have written that "hegemony requires the consent of the dominated majority" (p. 19). Asian Americans who seek acceptance by the dominant group may try to emulate model minority behavior. At Academic High, many Asian American students willingly embraced the model minority stereotype. I would argue that their embrace of the model minority representation was partially motivated by the fact that the characterization of Asian Americans as model minorities seems positive and even flattering when compared with the stereotypes of other racial minorities. Furthermore, Asian American students at Academic High were often rewarded with teachers' praise and high grades for performing like model minorities. In their attempts to live up to the model minority standards, many Asian American students censured their own experiences and voices. Self-silencing and the uncritical acceptance of the model minority stereotype represent Asian American consent to hegemony. Black in the 1970s, Frank Chin and Jeffery Chan (1971) referred to this kind of behavior as the acceptance of "racist love." They write, "If the system works, the stereotypes assigned to the various races are accepted by the races themselves as reality, as fact, and racist love reigns" (p. 65). Although the majority of Asian American students at Academic High School spoke proudly of being stereotyped as model minorities and even engaged in the self-silencing of their experiences, there were Asian American students who actively resisted the conditions of the model minority stereotype.

As noted earlier, the model minority stereotype takes attention off the white majority by pitting Asian Americans against African Americans. When Asian Americans and African Americans engage in interracial competition/tension, they are consenting to hegemony. While Asian Americans and African Americans are fighting among themselves, the racial barriers that limit Asian Americans and African Americans remain unchallenged. The resentment that the model minority stereotype engenders contributed to the racial tension in the 1992 riots in Los Angeles. Although there was evidence of tension between Asian Americans and African Americans at Academic High, there was also evidence of resistance to the model minority construction of race. There were a few Asian Americans and African Americans who attempted to build a coalition of racial minorities to deconstruct white dominance. I examine both consensus and resistance to the hegemonic discourse of the model minority stereotype.

NOTE

1. According to the California Postsecondary Education Commission (1995), in the Fall of 1993, 36,111 of the 122,271 undergraduate students enrolled in the University of California system, 47,468 of the 262,492 undergraduate students enrolled in the California State University system, and 146,006 of the 1,074,174 undergraduate students enrolled in California community colleges were categorized as Asian/Pacific Islanders or Filipinos.

REFERENCES

Apple, M. W., & Weis, L. (1983). Ideology and practice in schooling : A political and conceptual introduction. In M. W. Apple & L. Weis (Eds.), *Ideology and practice in schooling* (pp. 3–33). Philadelphia: Temple University Press.

Brand, D. 1987, August 31). The new whiz kids. *Time*, 130(9), 42–51.

Cheung, K. (1990). The woman warrior versus the Chinaman pacific: Must a Chinese American critic choose between feminism and heroism? In M. Hirsch & E. F. Keller (Eds.), *Conflicts in feminism* (pp. 234–251). New York: Routledge.

Cheung, K. (1993). *Articulate silences: Hisaye Yamamoto, Maxine Hong Kingston, Joy Kogawa.* Ithaca, NY: Cornell University Press.

Chin, F., & Chan, J. P. (1971). Racist love. In R. Kostelanetz (Ed.), *Seeing through shuck* (pp. 65–79). New York: Ballantine.

Cho, S. K. (1993). Korean Americans vs. African Americans: Conflict and construction. In R. Gooding-Williams (Ed.), *Reading Rodney King/reading urban uprising* (pp. 196–211). New York: Routledge.

Chun, K. (1980, Winter/Spring). The myth of Asian American success and its educational ramifications. *IRCD Bulletin*, pp. 1–12.

D'Souza, D. (1992). *Illiberal education: The Politics of race and sex on campus.* New York: Vintage.

Espiritu, Y. L. (1992). *Asian American panethnicity: Bridging institutions and identities.* Philadelphia: Temple University Press.

Hacker, A. (1992). *Two nations: Black and white, separate, hostile, unequal* New York: Ballantine.

Hagedorn, J. (1993). Introduction. In J. Hagedorn (Ed.), *Charlie Chan is dead: An anthology of contemporary Asian American fiction* (pp. xxi–xxx). New York: Penguin.

Hamamoto, D. (1992). The contemporary Asian American family on television. *Amerasia Journal*, 18(2), 35–53.

Herrnstein, R. J., & Murray, C. (1994). *The bell curve: Intelligence and class structure in American life.* New York: Free Press.

Hurh, W. M., & Kim, K. C.(1989). The success image of Asian-Americans: Its validity, and its practical and theoretical implications. *Ethnic and Racial Studies*, 12(4), 512–538.

Kim, E. H. (1993a). Home is where the *han* is: A Korean American perspective on the Los Angeles upheavals. In R. Gooding-Williams (Ed.), *Reading Rodney King/reading urban uprising* (pp. 215–235). New York: Routledge.

Kim, E. H. (1993b). Preface. In J. Hagedorn (Ed.), *Charlie Chan is dead: An anthology of contemporary Asian American fiction* (pp. vii–xiv). New York: Penguin.

Kwong, P. (1987).*The new Chinatown.* New York: Hill & Wang.

Ogbu, J. U. (1987). Variability in minority school performance: A problem in search of an explanation. *Anthropology & Education Quarterly*, 18(4), 312–334.

Ogbu, J. U. (1991). Immigrant and involuntary minorities in comparative perspective. In M. Gibson & J. U. Ogbu (Eds.), *Minority status and schooling: A comparative study of immigrant and involuntary minorities* (pp. 3–33). New York: Garland.

Osajima, K. (1988). Asian Americans as the model minority: An analysis of the popular press image in the 1960s and 1980s. In G. Y. Okihiro, S. Hune, A. A. Hansen, & J. M. Liu (Eds.), *Reflections on shattered windows: Promises and prospects for Asian American studies* (pp. 165–174). Pullman: Washington State University Press.

Palumbo-Liu, D. (1994). Los Angeles, Asians, and perverse ventriloquisms: On the functions of Asian America in the recent American imaginary. *Public Culture*, 6, 365–381.

Said, E. W. (1979). *Orientalism*, New York: Vintage.

Sleeter, C. E. (1993). How white teachers construct race. In C. McCarthy & W. Crichlow (Eds.), *Race, identity, and representation in education* (pp. 157–171). New York: Routledge.

Success story of one minority group in the U.S. (1966, December 26). *U.S. News & World Report*, pp. 73–78.

Sue, S., & Kitano, H. H. L. (1973). Stereotypes as a measure of success. *Journal of Social Issues*, 29(2), 83–98.

Suzuki, R. H. (1979). Education and the socialization of Asian Americans: A revisionist analysis of the "model minority" thesis. In R. Endo, S. Sue, & N. N. Wagner (Eds.), *Asian-Americans: Social and psychological perspectives* (Vol. 2, pp. 155–175). Ben Lomond, CA: Science and Behavior Books.

Takagi, D. Y. (1992). *The retreat from race: Asian American admissions and racial politics.* New Brunswick, NJ: Rutgers University Press.

Takaki, R. (1989). *Strangers from a different shore: A history of Asian Americans.* New York: Penguin.

Terkel, S. (1992). *Race: How blacks and whites think and feel about the American obsession.* New York: New Press.

U.S. Commission on Civil Rights. (1992). *Civil rights issues facing Asian Americans in the 1990s.* Washington, DC: Author.

Winant, H. (1993). Amazing race: Recent writing on racial politics and theory. *Socialist Review*, 23(2), 161–183.

Wong, L. M. (1993, November). *Shifting identities and fixing hierarchies: Whiteness and the myth of the model minority.* Paper presented at the conference for the American Education Studies Association, Chicago.

22

Lesbian and Gay Adolescents: Social and Developmental Considerations

Dennis A. Anderson

A GREAT NUMBER of teenagers have had, or will have, homosexual experiences. In our society, homosexual behavior among adolescents is quite common (Kinsey, Pomeroy, and Martin, 1948; Kinsey, Pomeroy, Martin and Gebhard, 1953; Rutter, 1980) and includes incidental homosexual activities of otherwise predominantly heterosexually–oriented adolescents. There are, however, adolescents who have already identified themselves as predominantly homosexual, or who will later come to so identify themselves. For these adolescents, social and emotional development during adolescence are likely to differ in significant ways.

There is almost no prospective research on the development of sexual orientation. Most of our information comes from adult lesbians, gay men, and heterosexual adults recalling their past. From this data, models of homosexual identity formation have been described by several different authors (Troiden, 1988; Cass, 1990). The studies of gay and lesbian adolescents seem to confirm that a similar process is taking place (Boxer, Cook, and Herdt, 1989).

HOMOSEXUAL AROUSAL AND BEHAVIOR

According to reports of adult lesbians and gay men, the onset of homosexual arousal, homosexual erotic imagery, and homosexual romantic attachment occurs during adolescence. A majority have these experiences before fifteen years of age (Saghir and Robins, 1973). Gay males tend to be aware of their same-sex attractions somewhat earlier (twelve to fourteen years) than do lesbians (fourteen to sixteen years). A recent study of gay and lesbian adolescents of fourteen to twenty-one years, found the average age of first homosexual fantasies to be similar for both males and females, 11.2 and 11.9 years, respectively (Boxer, Cook, and Herdt, 1989).

HOMOSEXUAL EXPERIENCES

Gay males, on average, experience significant physical homosexual contact (including body-body contact, manual-genital contact, or oral-genital contact) about five years earlier than do lesbians. Saghir and Robins (1973) found that only twenty-four percent of the lesbians had such contact by fifteen years of age, with an increase to fifty-three percent by age nineteen, compared to over eighty percent of the gay males having such experiences by age fifteen. While there is wide individual variation, gay males tend to begin homosexual activity during early or mid-adolescence (Bell, et al., 1981; McDonald, 1982; Troiden, 1979), while lesbian females tend to begin similar activity around age twenty (Bell, et al., 1981). Thus, males are much more likely to act on their homosexual feelings soon after recognizing them than are females who may not begin homosexual behavior for many years after their awareness of homosexual attractions. In the study of gay and lesbian adolescents discussed above (Boxer, Cook, and Herdt, 1989), the differences in age of first physical homosexual experience were in a similar direction. The average age of first homosexual experience was 13.1 years for the gay boys and 15.2 years for the lesbian girls.

For many adolescents, homosexual activity is not merely incidental sex play or experimentation; rather it is an outward expression of an internal homosexual orientation which includes homosexual imagery, arousal, and romantic attachments. The term *homosexual orientation* is defined here as a "consistent pattern of sexual arousal toward persons of the same gender encompassing fantasy, conscious attractions, emotional and romantic feelings, and sexual behaviors" (Remafedi, 1987).

HETEROSEXUAL EXPERIENCES

It is important to realize that gay and lesbian teenagers frequently begin or continue heterosexual activity despite an awareness of their homosexual orientation. Both lesbian women and gay men report doing a good deal of heterosexual dating in their adolescent years. Heterosexual arousal and experience may precede or follow homosexual experiences, but the majority of lesbian women have had a heterosexual experience by their adult years. About half of lesbian women have experienced heterosexual emotional attachments before age twenty in addition to their homosexual attractions, and more than two-thirds reported experiencing heterosexual sexual arousal. A third had actually had intercourse by age twenty, a number similar to that for heterosexual women (Saghir and Robins, 1973). In the more recent Chicago study of lesbian and gay teens, three-quarters had experienced heterosexual intercourse (Boxer, Cook, and Herdt, 1989). Compared to gay men, more lesbians had experienced heterosexual intercourse by their adult years.

AWARENESS OF HOMOEROTICISM

An organized subjective awareness of experiences as "homosexual" may be lacking in early adolescents, who are cognitively immature and for whom development has just begun to allow longitudinal understanding of their personal history and its implications for their future. Studies of older cohorts show that lesbians self-identify as homosexual in their early twenties, whereas gay males more frequently self-identify in their early twenties, whereas gay males more frequently self-identify in their late teens or earlier (Saghir and Robins, 1973; Bell, et al., 1981; Chapman and Brannock, 1987; Dank, 1971; Woodman and Lenna, 1980). There is evidence that teenagers are now self-labeling at earlier ages than they did in the past (Offer and Boxer, 1991), perhaps because of secular changes in our society which allow more discussion of homosexuality, more public and media presentations of gay and lesbian persons, and more visibility of gay and lesbian people in all walks of life.

Gay or lesbian teenagers usually report that between ages twelve and fourteen they first realize that they are much more sexually attracted to persons of their own sex, even though they may not yet self-label as gay or lesbian. Most teenagers who acknowledge a predominantly homosexual arousal pattern realize almost immediately that words such as "gay" and "homosexual," or derogatory terms are applied to persons with such feelings. Most also report that they have felt somehow different for many years, sometimes beginning in early childhood, but they usually did not relate these feelings to their concept of homosexuality. In Bell, et al.'s study, three-quarters of lesbian women felt "sexually different" by the time they were age eighteen, whereas a much smaller minority of heterosexual women ever felt that way. The boys labeled their "sexual different" feeling as *homosexuality* considerably earlier that girls (Bell, et al., 1981). Gay adult males report the onset of "self-labeling as homosexual" close to the time of becoming aware of homosexual feelings in early adolescence. On the other hand, the age at which lesbians label this feeling of difference "homosexual" increases gradually through the adolescent years, with half self-labeling by age eighteen and most of the rest by their late twenties (Bell, et al., 1981; Saghir and Robins, 1973; Woodman and Lenna, 1980).

Most often, awareness of their homosexuality comes suddenly for adolescents—even for those gay or lesbian teenagers who may have frequently participated in homosexual sex or have had homoerotic experiences earlier in adolescence or childhood. There are many reasons why homosexual adolescents or even preadolescents come to such a seemingly sudden realization of their sexual orientation. Aside from the frequent use, during preadolescence or early adolescence, of denial to ward off the anxiety caused by homoerotic feelings or experiences, many adolescents only gain the cognitive capacity for abstract thought and formal reasoning which enables them to integrate the experiences they have had in the past with their current situation at this stage of development. Further, sexual arousal to particular stimuli, erotic imagery, masturbation, and romantic attachment all increase dramatically as puberty begins, and they are likely to be homosexual in content. In the social arena, gay and lesbian adolescents now see their peers become more interested in opposite-sex relationships and heterosocial activities, in marked contrast to their own indifference to these pursuits.

Whatever the experiences that lead to the growing personal awareness of their homosexuality, most gay and lesbian adolescents can vividly recall a period of intense anxiety when they first realized that they suddenly belonged to a group of people that is often vehemently despised. For the adolescent, an identity crisis occurs. It can be understood as the conflict produced by the juxtaposition of the negative ideas about homosexuality that were learned throughout childhood with the new awareness of homosexual attractions and identity that is developing. This suddenness of homosexual self-recognition contrasts with the lengthy process of actually coming to understand and accept one's sexuality, a process that takes years. This crisis of self-concept occurs because the gay adolescent senses a sudden involuntary joining to a stigmatized group. The stigma occurs because of homophobia, an unreasonable or irrational fear or hatred of homosexuals or homosexuality (Weinberg, 1972), which has been internalized during childhood. Homophobic attitudes may occur not only within individuals, as internalized homophobia, but also within organizations and the society at large, as institutionalized homophobia (Hencken, 1982). The gay or lesbian adolescent may have few resources available to get information about homosexuality. Little information is formally presented in a balanced and unbiased manner in most schools, and most reading materials that an adolescent may seek are likely to be censored, inaccurate, or blatantly homophobic. Another difficulty that gay and lesbian teenagers have in dealing with their homosexuality in adaptive ways in the absence of positive role models. Gay and lesbian teens do not see the same diversity of adults with whom to identify as heterosexual adolescents do, because so many lesbian and gay adults do not publicly acknowledge their sexual orientation. This is a particularly acute problem in the school setting, where gay and lesbian staff may experience the need to completely hide their sexual orientation, or may be unwilling to provide guidance or to support advocacy for lesbian or gay students out of fear of being suspected to be homosexual.

The teenager's management of the experienced stigma and internalized homophobia is crucial to the gay or lesbian adolescent's social and emotional development, and is crucial for school personnel to understand. Homosexual adolescents initially make one of three choices in dealing with their newly acknowledged feelings: (a) try to change them; (b) continue to hide them; or (c) accept them (Martin, 1982). These three strategies usually follow each other sequentially, but this is not invariable. Maylon (1981) reminds us that for some homosexual adolescents the initial reaction is one of denial of same-sex desires or suppression of these desires, with a developmental moratorium through which heterosexual norms are accommodated. This is followed, perhaps years later, with psychological and social integration of the homosexual orientation. Some individuals spend years—or decades—repressing their homosexual orientation while repeatedly engaging in homosexual behavior. From the time they first acknowledge their homosexuality, most gay adolescents go though a period when they attempt to change their sexual orientation or, at least, they hope these feeling will go away. For young persons, the incorrect notion that all or most homosexuals possess traits of the opposite sex is particularly prevalent. Many gay or lesbian teenagers will attempt to provide self-remedies by accentuating gender-typical behavior while avoiding any behavior which may be considered more typical of the opposite sex, or even just gender-neutral. Boys may walk with a swagger, engage in compulsive bodybuilding, or display aggressive, overassertive, or even antisocial behavior, while girls may dress in very feminine clothes, wear excessive amounts of makeup, or use exaggerated gestures. Both sexes may frantically pursue heterosexual dating and heterosexual activity, sometimes with the goal of pregnancy so as to have powerful evidence with which to claim heterosexuality. Masturbation is often avoided, or accompanied with tremendous guilt, because of the homosexual fantasies which occur. Associations with same-sex peers may be terminated or avoided because of the erotic feelings and anxiety-laden temptations that are aroused or because of the anxiety which accompanies the fear of discovery as the relationship develops. Most commonly, attempts are made to use sheer will and self-recrimination to suppress homoerotic thoughts and feelings.

This is often an extremely lonely time of gay and lesbian adolescents, especially for younger adolescents or preadolescents who are cognitively and affectively not equipped to effectively manage these issues. The developmentally normal egocentrism of early adolescence causes all adolescents to feel as though they are at the center of others' attention; they often believe that others are observing them, and that others are almost able to read their thoughts (Elkind, 1978), or "find them out" through their body language and interactions. At this time gay or lesbian adolescents feel very vulnerable to the potential for rejection or antihomosexual bias.* Certain endeavors—for which the adolescent may have considerable talent but which run counter to peer group ideals of gender appropriate interests, such as dramatics, singing, dance, or the creative arts for boys, or athletics or mechanical arts for girls—are sometimes purposely avoided. In some settings, academic achievement itself may be viewed as unmasculine behavior, and it is thus avoided by a boy who is attempting to maintain a positive image amongst his peers. The self-conscious, almost constant internal dialogue that develops may have marked deleterious effects upon personal relationships, particularly on the development of intimacy and friendship. Gay and lesbian adolescents are forever monitoring themselves: "Am I standing too close? Is my voice too high? Do I appear too happy to see him/her?" Activities that should be spontaneous expressions of affection or happiness become self-consciously controlled behavior or moments of agonizing fear or uncertainty. Particularly painful moments of many gay or lesbian adolescents are hearing an antihomosexual joke or seeing another individual being ridiculed or called some epithet which is commonly applied to homosexual persons. It is not unusual for a gay or lesbian adolescent to join in such activities in order to maintain his or her own "cover." Often, in order to avoid drawing attention to themselves, they will not associate in their schools with other students whom they believe to be gay or lesbian.

The experience of the adolescent whose homosexuality becomes known or is highly suspected varies. Name-calling, baiting, and practical jokes are common in all schools. Physical assault sometimes does occur, not to mention the more subtle but powerful forms of social ostracism. Exceptionally popular individuals or those who are successful in high status activities may not suffer as much harassment, but if they are not open about their sexual orientation, they may experience extreme anxiety about the prospect of discovery and loss of social status. Staff within schools determine to a great extent the atmosphere regarding homophobic bias. In many settings, derogatory statements about homosexuals, or antihomosexual epithets, go unchallenged where similar remarks of a racist nature would clearly not be tolerated.

COMING OUT TO OTHERS AND DEVELOPING A LESBIAN OR GAY IDENTITY

Studies suggest that an adolescent goes through a number of stages in coming to terms with a lesbian or gay identity. A lesbian or gay adolescent is likely initially to be aware of feelings of being different, sometimes dating back to early childhood. They then become aware of being attracted to others of the same sex. This has been described as a time of sensitization (Troiden, 1979). In an effort to understand her- or himself, the adolescent may have both homosexual and heterosexual experiences. This can be a time of confusion for the adolescent. Development of a same-sex love relationship, and disclosure to nonhomosexual peers and family are the final stages, indicating commitment to a lesbian or gay identity (Troiden, 1989). For many lesbians, this final stage of "coming out" to nonhomosexuals may occur many years after homosexual self-definition and same-sex love relationships have occurred. The same is true for gay men, but the available data suggest again that the entire process may occur at earlier ages for men than for women (Troiden, 1988).

CROSS-GENDER BEHAVIOR

Contrary to the common stereotypes, most homosexual adolescents do not exhibit gender-deviant behavior. Some gay or lesbian adolescents may, however, display extreme gender-deviant behavior. This includes cross-dressing in a provocative or defiant manner in situations which they perceive as hostile to their homosexual orientation. This is a defense against threatened self-esteem, and it can be viewed as an identification with the cultural or peer group gender-role expectations for homosexuals. Similar adaptations have been noted in individuals from extremely strict religious backgrounds where crossdressing or even transsexualism may be a defense against homosexuality (Hellman, Green, Gray and Williams, 1981). In some ethnic minority groups, especially Hispanic cultures or others with rigidly dichotomized sex-role differences between the feminine and the *macho*, there appears to be a greater tendency for homosexual adolescents to display more extreme gender-deviant behavior. In fact, those Latino homosexual male adolescents who conform to the social role of the effeminate *maricon* are more likely to be tolerated and less subject to violent harassment than are young homosexuals displaying more typically masculine behavior. Many gay adolescents who do cross-dress gradually drop this behavior once they are exposed to a gay peer group (Hetrick and Martin, 1988). In such gay peer groups, the dominant cultural expectations for cross-gender role behavior for homosexuals are experienced with less force.

PEER RELATIONSHIPS

The peer group provides the context for the formation of a personal identity which incorporates the various needs, values, and proclivities of the adolescent. Most adolescents realize that the expression of homosexual feelings within the dominant peer group, where there is tremendous pressure to conform to heterosexual norms, will result in alienation from peers at best, and violence at worst. Withholding important personal information and suppression of his or her genuine interests results in the elaboration of a false persona in order to gain peer acceptance or to maintain status. This psychosexual duality exacts a high cost in vigilance, self-loathing, and the elaboration of defenses to contain the chronic anxiety which this situation produces. This state inhibits a variety of important social interactions. The most destructive is the restriction of opportunities which promote the capacity to engage in erotic and nonerotic intimate relationships. Adolescents in this situation who are afforded the luxury of a relatively prolonged adolescence, such as college, may have the opportunity to complete the tasks of adolescence. For others, however, a premature foreclosure of identity development—during a period where much internalized homophobia has not been worked through—can result in a very long and unnecessarily painful "coming-out" process.

Gay and lesbian adolescents, whether they have "come out" or continue to hide, experience much of the heterosocial and explicitly, or implicitly, homophobic aspects of adolescent life as extremely isolating. Adolescence is a period of heightened awareness of sexuality, and gay and lesbian adolescents are apt to become frustrated by the variety of heterosexual and heterosocial outlets that are available to others while there are so few outlets available to them. To some gay and lesbian adolescents, the experience of watching boys and girls in school walk hand in hand down the hallway, while their own desires must be kept secret, produces feelings of rage and sadness that are difficult to resolve. In addition to having no opportunity to experience social interactions with gay or lesbian peers, there is little likelihood that they will see gay or lesbian adult role models in their day-to-day lives. Low self esteem, academic inhibition, truancy, substance abuse, social withdrawal, depressed mood, and suicidal ideation are not unusual, and may be difficult to differentiate from depressive disorders. It is not surprising that gay and lesbian adolescents, wanting involvement in a peer group that accepts them and offers the possibility of establishing intimate relationships, often begin to search for other gay persons. Gay and lesbian teenagers in large cities may call telephone hotlines, search for gay newspapers, or contact agencies that serve gay people. Gay boys are much more likely than lesbian girls to travel to areas where they believe gay people are to be found to have sexual encounters (Paroski, 1987). Unfortunately, this search may take the adolescent to areas where they are placed at risk (Roesler and Deisher, 1972), An adolescent who is lonely and sexually frustrated may interpret the release of tension, the supportive environment, and the physical affection of another person as love, an assumption which likely is premature. It is also possible for gay adolescents to feel so comfortable in the first gay supportive environment that they find that a premature foreclosure around a particular kind of lifestyle within the gay and lesbian community may follow.

In most large cities there are a variety of gay and lesbian services, but many of these are directed to adults and actively exclude gay youth because of their fear of reprisals if they serve young people. Services specifically for gay and lesbian youth are being developed throughout the country, and at least one national directory of services has been published (Hetrick-Martin Institute, 1992). Of course, in small towns or rural areas, none of these services are available. In large cities it is extremely difficult, and in most parts of the country it is impossible, for gay adolescents to succeed in meeting other gay adolescents in a positive and supportive environment.

SUMMARY

The proscriptions against homosexuality remain strong within the adolescent's world, especially the *early* adolescent world. Gay and lesbian adolescents whose sexual orientation is self-recognized typically experience intense conflicts with their social environment, particularly in the school environment. Adolescents who hide their sexual orientation from others expend enormous amounts of energy monitoring and restricting their interactions with others. The process of coming out often has deleterious effects on family life, peer relationships, and the development of intimate relationships with others. When school personnel encounter them, gay or lesbian adolescents may be at any stage of self-acknowledgment regarding their homosexuality. This acknowledgment may range from no awareness of their homosexuality, to full awareness and active hiding of it, to being publicly out of the closet and managing to develop a supportive social network. Staff or policies that trivialize the adolescent's homoerotic feelings, or view the behavior as a mere phase of normal development that will pass, are likely to do great damage to the self-concept of the homosexually-oriented teenager. Recognizing the complexity of the individual, family, and social dynamics of adolescent development can be invaluable to gay, lesbian, and "straight" students alike.

REFERENCES

Bell, A. P., Weinberg, and M. S., Hammersmith, S. D. (1981). *Sexual Preference: Its Development in Men and Women.* Bloomington, IN: Indian University Press.
Boxer, A. M., Cook, J. A., and Herdt, G. (1989). "First Homosexual and Heterosexual Experiences Reported by Gay and Lesbian Youth in an Urban Community." Presented at the *Annual Meeting of the American Sociological Association*, August, San Francisco. CA.

Cass, V. C. (1990). "The Implications of Homosexual Identity Formation for the Kinsey Model and Scale of Sexual Preference." In *Homosexuality/Heterosexuality: Concepts of Sexual Orientation*. D. P. McWhirter, S. A. Sanders, and J. M. Reinisch, eds. New York: Oxford University Press.

Chapman, B. E. and Brannock, J. C. (1987). "Proposed Model of Lesbian Identity Development: An Empirical Examination." *Journal of Homosexuality, 14*, pp. 69–80.

Dank, B. M. (1971). "Coming Out in the Gay World." *Psychiatry, 34*, pp. 180–197.

Elkind, D. (1978). *The Child's Reality*: *Three Developmental Themes*. Hillsdale, NJ: Etlbaum.

Hellman, R. E., Green, R., Gray, J. L., and Williams, K. (1981). "Childhood Sexual Identity, Childhood Religiosity, and Homophobia as Influences in the Development of Transsexualism, Homosexuality, and Heterosexuality." *Archives of General Psychiatry, 38*, pp. 910–915.

Hencken, J. (1982). "Homosexuality and Psychoanalysis: Toward a Mutual Understanding." In *Homosexuality: Social, Psychological and Biological Issues*. P. W. Weinrich, Jr., ed. Beverly Hills, CA: Sage.

Hetrick, E. S. and Martin, A. D. (1988). "Developmental Issues and their Resolution for Gay and Lesbian Adolescents." In *Integrated Identity for Gay Men and Lesbians: Psycho-Therapeutic Approaches for Emotional Well-Being*. E. Coleman, ed. New York: Harrington Park Press.

Hetrick-Martin Institute (1992). *You Are Not Alone: National Lesbian, Gay and Bisexual Youth Organization Directory, Spring*, 1993. New York: Hetrick Martin Institute.

Kinsey, A. C., Pomeroy, W. B., and Martin, C. E. (1948). *Sexual Behavior in the Human Male*. Philadelphia, PA: W.B. Saunders Co.

Kinsey, A. C., Pomeroy, W. B., Martin, C. E., and Gebhard, P. H. (1953). *Sexual Behavior in the Human Female*. Philadelphia, PA: W.B. Saunders Co.

Martin, A. D. (1982). "Learning to Hide: The Socialization of the Gay Adolescent." *Adolescent Psychiatry, 10*, pp. 52–65.

Maylon, A. K. (1981). "The Homosexual Adolescent: Development Issues and Social Bias." *Child Welfare, 60*, pp. 321–329.

McDonald, G. J. (1982). "Individual Differences in the Coming Out process for Gay Men: Implications for Theoretical Models." *Journal of Homosexuality, 8*, pp. 47–60.

Offer, D. and Boxer, A. M. (1991). "Normal Adolescent Development: Empirical Research Findings." In *Child and Adolescent Psychiatry: A Comprehensive Textbook*. M. Lewis, ed. Baltimore, MD: Williams and Wilkins.

Paroski, P. A. (1987). "Health Care Delivery and the Concerns of Gay and Lesbian Adolescents." *Journal of Adolescent Health Care, 8*, pp. 188–92.

Remafedi, G. (1987). "Adolescent Homosexuality: Psychosocial and Medical Implications." *Pediatrics, 79*, pp. 331–337.

Roesler, T. and Deisher, R. W. (1972). "Youthful Male Homosexuality: Homosexual Experience and the Process of Developing Homosexual Identity in Males Aged 16 to 22 Years." *Journal of the American Medical Association, 219*, pp. 1018–1023.

Rutter, M. (1980). "Psychosexual Development." In *Developmental Psychiatry*. M. Rutter, ed. Washington: American Psychiatric Press.

Saghir, M. T. and Robins, E. (1973). *Male and Female Homosexuality: A Comprehensive Investigation*. Baltimore, MD: Williams and Wilkins Company.

Troiden, R. R. (1979). "Becoming Homosexual: A Model of Gay Identity Acquisition." *Psychiatry, 42*, pp. 362–373.

——. (1988). "Homosexual Identity Development." *Journal of Adolescent Health Care, 9*, pp. 105–13.

——. (1989). "The Formation of Homosexual Identities." In *Gay and Lesbian Youth*. G. Herdt, ed. New York: Harrington Park Press.

Weinberg, G. (1972). *Society and the Healthy Homosexual*. New York: Anchor.

Woodman, N. and Lenna, H. (1980). *Counseling with Gay Men and Women*. San Francisco: Jossey-Bass.

23

Canal Town Girls

JULIA HALL

IN THIS CHAPTER, I focus on emerging female identity among the poor white Canal Town girls. Female identity among these girls surfaces in relation to that of the constructed white male and in respect to that of the male and female "other." In terms of the future, the white girls are envisioning lives in which, by charting a course of secondary education, they hope to procure jobs and self-sufficiency. However, as their narrations indicate, such plans are fueled with the hope that by living independent lives as single career women, they will bypass the domestic violence that rips through their lives and those of their mothers. As they position African American males and Puerto Rican males and females as inferior and on the margins of what is acceptable behavior, these white girls locate themselves at the center of Canal Town life, coded white and superior.[1] This exploration of white female meaning making evidences processes among individual girls that are, for the most part, quite similar. This can likely be attributed to the exclusivity of the peer culture and the fact that these females rarely travel outside the neighborhood.

During the past fifteen years, much work has been done on girls and women at school (Valli, 1988; Holland & Eisenhart, 1990; Weis, 1990; Raissiguier, 1994). Such ethnographic research has uncovered ways in which schools serve to reinforce a gender hierarchy whereby males are considered dominant as compared to females. By not challenging patriarchal dominance in the larger society, it has been argued that schools perpetuate such relations. Also explored in such studies is the formation of female youth cultures, and how these cultures are connected to broader structural inequalities (McRobbie, 1978; Smith, 1988). While all of this work is important in terms of understanding the ways in which institutions contribute to unequal outcomes for females, as well as the ways in which the cultures produced by girls and women contribute to these outcomes, the issue of violence as embedded in these arrangements remains unexplored.

Michelle Fine and Lois Weis have examined this theme as it boldly emerged in their data on the lives of poor and working class white adult women and the production of identity (1998). My studies have been informed by such work, and like these researchers, I did not set out to examine domestic violence in the lives of poor white girls. Knowing about such abuse, however, paved the way for me to listen carefully to this guarded secret. While it is widely argued that violence in the home appears across social classes, it is now generally understood there is more such abuse among poor and working class families.

It has also been found that white working class women experience more abuse as compared to working class women from other cultural backgrounds, and are more apt to treat their abuse as a carefully guarded secret.[2]

Another aspect of the construction of white adolescent female identity that emerges in the poor white Canal Town girl data includes expressed racism toward those from culturally oppressed groups. This finding contradicts existing work, in which a component of only white male identity formation depended upon denigration of the racial "other" (Weis, 1990; Fine et al., 1997). In earlier studies on females, white working class girls primarily elaborate identities around immediate, but historically inscribed gender struggles (McRobbie 1978; Weis, 1990). Although the white Canal Town girls do not patrol racial borders to the extent of white males in the literature, they *do* narrate lives that are being compromised by what they believe to be the deviant actions of those of African and Puerto Rican descent. As I conducted these interviews in the neighborhood community center, I attribute the girls' open discussion about racist attitudes to the informal and predominantly white site in which they have come to make my acquaintance, and to the fact that they had known me for more than a year prior to being interviewed. Since as compared to the streets and the school, the Center is seen by these white girls as a sanctioned or safe space, they may feel they do not have to be guarded.

JOBS AND CAREERS

Similar to the white Freeway females (Weis, 1990), the Canal Town girls do not narrate a marginalized wage labor identity. Instead, for both groups of females, securing a job or a career is a central goal. As the white Canal Town girls are only in middle school, their plans for the future may not yet be as specific or thought-out as those of the Freeway high school juniors. The point is that when asked to describe what they want their lives to look like after high school, the white Canal Town girls stress going to college and/or obtaining a good job, and like the Freeway females, only mention marriage or family after being asked.

Christina: I want to be a doctor.… I'll have to go to college for a long time.… I don't know where I'll go [to college], hopefully around here.… I'm not sure what type of doctor, but I'm thinking of the kind that delivers babies.

Hannah: I want to be a leader and not a follower.… I want to be a teacher in Canal Town because I never want to leave here.… I want to go to [local] community college, like my sister, learn about teaching little kids.… I definitely want to be a teacher.

Katie: I want to be a scientist; I just love math.… I want to stay [in Canal Town]. If I live someplace else I won't be comfortable.… I'm shy.… I want to work with, like, chemicals, test-tubes.

Lisa: I probably see myself as an educated person with a good job. The one thing I hate to see myself as is to grow up being a drunk person or a homeless person on the streets.… I would like most of all to be an artist, you know, with my own studio.… I'm going to start with cosmetology when I go to _____ [local high school], and then take it from there.

Erin: I'd like to go into carpentry. I already help my dad fix stuff, like the table … I just want to be a carpenter. I want to go to college and also be a carpenter which is something you don't got to go to school for; you just become one.… It's just what I want to be.

All of these young girls envision further education in their future, but most do not yet have a clear sense of which school they hope to attend or how long they plan to go.[3] Christina is the only one who talks about a career that absolutely requires a four-year degree and beyond, while it is uncertain whether Hannah, Katie, Lisa, or Erin might pursue their goals by obtaining a two- or four-year degree. Christina, Katie, and Erin intend "nontraditional" careers in male-dominant fields, while Lisa and Katie choose those which are typically female. Lisa seems the least committed to any career, and tells me she is encouraged by her guidance counselor to sign up for the female-dominated occupation, cosmetology, in high school. Due to their young ages, any of these girls may switch ideas about careers a number of times, yet when asked about the future, all of them focus their energies on the single pursuit of furthering their schooling and landing a job. Worth noting, Lisa says she worries about being homeless, which is likely a chronic fear among poor youth.

The white girls of Canal Town are the daughters of presently poor adults. The girls' grandparents, however, were part of the working class tradition of laborers in which the men brought home a family wage (Smith, 1987). The girls report that none of their parents continued their education beyond high school and a few did not graduate from grade twelve. College, these girls say, is not really an option that is discussed much at home. Perhaps Hannah has the clearest idea of where she would like to go to school because she is the only girl who I worked with that has an older sibling enrolled in an institution of higher education. Hannah's sister attends a nearby community college and studies interior design, a circumstance that likely influenced her little sister's plans. Interestingly, three of the females indicate that although they want to break out of cycles of dependence and have careers, they do not want to leave Canal Town— whether for school or work.

Although the importance of a job/career is emerging within poor white Canal Town girl identity, it cannot be determined whether these girls will follow through on their plans for further education/training. The outlook is not promising, as all but a few of their older siblings are negotiating lives riddled with substance abuse and early pregnancies, and conversations with the principal of the area high school reveal that very few local teenagers are enrolling in any form of advanced studies. Weis (1990) indicates that, based on an analysis of high school transcript dissemination by participants in her study, some of the white Freeway girls were sending their scholastic records to those schools which, to a certain extent, reflected their expressed desires for the future. However, an even larger number of these females did not apply to any institutions of higher learning, despite the centrality of job/career surfacing in their interviews.

Even though the Canal Town girls view education as important in obtaining their goals, to a certain extent, they both accept and reject academic culture and knowledge while in school. Similar to the white Freeway females (Weis, 1990), I observed that on a daily basis while in class, the white Canal Town girls copy homework, pass notes, and read magazines/books, or in other words, participate in the form rather than the content of schooling. In a small number of instances, these females also display resentment toward school authority. Weis delineates that the resentment exerted toward institutional authority as seen in previous ethnographies is typically male and is linked to the historical contestation between capital and workers. Because, historically, white women mostly labored in the private sphere or in a pool of marginalized wage labor, they did not directly engage in such struggles. Weis, therefore, explains it is not surprising that the white Freeway females did not exhibit expressed resentment. Although during the interviews at the Center, a few of the white Canal Town girls do evidence contempt for school authority, this resentment revolves around something completely different—the notion of racial privileging.

> *Erin:* My Spanish teacher is racist. She lets the Puerto Ricans do whatever they want to do. And the white girls are just out of it. The white kids have to do all the work. Like when this one girl [Puerto Rican] would say, "I'm not taking Spanish," the teacher would be like, "Okay." And when I asked if I had to do an assignment she would say "yes." And then I would say, "What about her [Puerto Rican girl]?" and the teacher would say, "Oh, she doesn't have to do that work." I told Ruby [white, elderly activities coordinator at the Center], and she went and talked to the teacher. Ruby has had to do this a couple of times the past couple of years or so.
>
> *Katie:* The teachers here like Puerto Ricans better than whites.… They [Puerto Ricans] get away with murder while we [white students] are made to do more work and are blamed when things go wrong.

Anger seemingly directed toward authority actually represents an overall emerging sense of racism among the white Canal Town girls. According to Erin and Katie, teachers favor the Puerto Rican students, while those who are white are given more work and are being unfairly blamed for problems within the school. That these girls view race as an issue around which to exhibit anger is a salient point, and will be elaborated upon later.

FAMILY

The Canal Town girls, like the older white working class females of Freeway (Weis, 1990), view jobs and careers as a central part of their futures, which is in vivid contrast to young women in previous studies (McRobbie, 1978; Valli, 1988; Raissiguier, 1994). But while the Freeway females mention the desire for marriage and family in their futures only after they financially secure themselves through education and entrance into the public world of paid work, with the exception of Lisa, most of the Canal Town girls contend they do not wish to have husbands, homes, and/or families at all. Rather, the Canal Town girls reveal they are looking to the life of a single career woman as a way to circumvent the abuse which they see inscribed in future families/relationships with men. In constructing identities, it quickly becomes clear that seeking refuge from domestic violence plays a big role. For many of these girls, the future includes avoiding marriage and family altogether and getting a job so they can rely upon themselves.

> *Christina:* I don't want to be married because if I was married my husband would want a kid. I don't want to have a kid because its father may not treat us right … hitting and stuff.… There's not enough for everybody, and the kid shouldn't have to suffer.… I want to always stay in Canal Town … live alone.… At least I know trouble here when I see it.
>
> *Hannah:* I don't want to get married and be told to stay at home … and be someone's punching bag.… I'll get a one-bedroom apartment and live alone and just try to be the best teacher I can be.
>
> *Katie:* I can't see myself being with a guy because they don't know how to not hit … that's, like, why I don't want to be married or have, like, a kid.… I'm going to go to school and be something really good.

Lisa: I guess I sort of want to be married, but I want to be free at the same time, and that's not going to happen. I won't be able to do what I want if I'm married.… He's got to treat me good and respect me for who I am and not for what he wants me to be, and not for what I did in the past … not a lot of hitting.… I just don't know if that exists.… I'd rather live by myself, focus on a career.

Elizabeth: I don't know yet [if I want to marry]. With the problems that happen, you never know. A person can act nice before you marry them, and then after they can be mean to you. They have all the power. They can make us do everything. My uncle is as lazy as hell. He makes my mom go to the store all the time. He makes us walk. My mom likes it, but I hate it.… We don't have a car, but he gets cable and my mom pays for it. He makes my mom pay for all the bills. We get our clothes from other people, but he buys his new.… I don't know if it's fair to have kids. If you don't put your kids first, you shouldn't bring them into the world.… If I get married, It will be to someone who's intelligent, willing to help, someone who doesn't drink, and someone who isn't violent.… I don't think it exists, so I want to just get a good job and live alone.

The Freeway (Weis, 1990) females say they desire careers so they do not have to depend upon a demanding husband. They also say they want to be prepared in the event of divorce or a husband's job loss. The girls of Canal Town, however, articulate they are not simply devising career-oriented plans to escape a patriarchal-dominant home. Rather, these girls specifically say they view a job as the ticket to a life free of abuse. By concentrating energies on the world of work instead of family, some of the girls feel they can spare bringing children into the world, whom they feel often bear the burnt of the problems of adults. As Elizabeth resolves, "If I get married it will be to someone … who doesn't drink, and [to] someone who isn't violent.… I don't think it exists, so I want to just get a good job and live alone."

While the Canal Town girls say they want to live as independent women in the public sphere, they are effectively developing such identities in response to violent men. By dreaming of living single, self-sufficient lives in the hopes of sidestepping violence, as will be seen, these females are not holding males accountable for abusive behavior. Males and their symbolic and material dominance cannot simply be erased from life, particularly when goals are to enter the public world of paid work. At this point in time, with little contact with institutions of higher education and careers outside Canal Town, many of these girls envision themselves continuing to live inside this sometimes violent neighborhood in which they are being raised.

DOMESTIC VIOLENCE

In present research on the conditions of poor and working class white women's lives, Weis et al. (1997) make a distinction between "settled lives" women, who exist in what appear to be stable, intact family structures, and "hard living" women, who move from household to household, partake of public assistance when needed, have less education, and have more low paying employment.[4] Both groups of women, however, negotiate lives saturated with domestic violence, the only difference being that "hard living" women exit from their homes and make their troubles public. Weis et al. raise concerns about the futures of these females, as the guiding philosophy of the federal government is to cut public assistance, thereby pushing family members deeper into private spaces, many of which are unhealthy.[5]

Considering the findings of Weis et al. (1997), it is crucial to begin to understand what life if like for the daughters of such white females, some of whom often have no choice but to ride along these supposed cycles of abuse.[6] Among the Canal Town girls, eight out of the nine depict lives which can be described as "hard living," while only Erin lives a seemingly "settled" life. When these young girls are asked to describe their neighborhood, they soon begin to tell stories of women being abused at the hands of men.

Erin: It's a pretty good place to live.… There's lots of auto crashes, drunk people. Lots of people go to the bars on Friday and Saturday and get blasted. They're always messing with people. Some guy is always getting kicked out of the bar for fighting. Guys are mostly fighting with their girlfriends and are getting kicked out for punching so they continue to fight in the street; I see it from my bedroom window, only the girl mostly gets beat up really bad.

Christina: There's lots of violence in this neighborhood. Like there's this couple that's always fighting. When the guy gets mad he hits her. It happens upstairs in their house. She's thrown the coffee pot at him and the toaster, they [coffeepot and toaster] landed in the street.… I saw it while walking by.… The guy would show off all the time in front of his friends. One day when he was hitting her she just punched him back and told him she wasn't going to live with him anymore. He used to hit her hard. She used to cry but she would still go out with him. She said she loved him too much to dump him. A lot of people go back.

Hannah: It's overall a nice neighborhood.… There's like a lot of physical and mental abuse that goes on. Just lots of yelling. I know one mother that calls her daughter a slut. She tells her, "You're not worth anything; you're a slut." … There's one family where the mother's boyfriend sexually abused her little girl, and stuff like that. The girl was like 7, and, like, he's still with them. The mother didn't care.… It's like fathers and boyfriends beat on the kids. They [mothers] don't take a stand. They don't say, "Well, you know that's my daughter" or "that's my son." It's like they don't care. They think that they're just to sit down and be home … they just sleep all day or watch TV. Some of them drink all day and are high and spend a lot of time sleeping it off.

Rosie: My neighborhood's quiet sometimes. It's a nice neighborhood, I guess. Sometimes it could be violent.… Like there was my mom's friend who came over once with bruises all over. Her boyfriend beat her up because she had a guy from downstairs come up to her house. The boyfriend got real mad and he was going to kill her because he was jealous. I didn't see the fight but I saw her. She looked like a purple people eater.… There's this one girl who got beat by her boyfriend. She did drugs and had another boyfriend, and the first boyfriend found out and got jealous. Violence is pretty much common in people's lives. About 95 percent of the world is angry. They attack things or litter, abuse people, and do other bad things like rape or kill. It's just the way it is.

Even though the community is seen as "a pretty good place to live" and "overall a nice neighborhood," the girls' descriptions of residency quickly devolve into stories of violence—mostly violence directed toward women by men in both public and private spaces. As Erin—who lives across the street from a tavern—watches out the window from her second-story flat, it is a normal occurrence for men to hit women in public sites, such as in a bar or on the street. As Christina walks through her neighborhood, she observes that violence also exists between men and women behind the closed doors of homes. Christina also notes that women often return to their abusive partners. Hannah distinguishes between different types of abuse—physical and mental—and gives examples of abuse between mothers and boyfriends, daughters and sons.[7] Rosie, it can be argued, is so desensitized to abuse that she humorously recalls how a badly beaten friend of her mother resembled a "purple people eater." In Rosie's view, "about 95 percent of the world is angry.... It's just the way it is."

Although these girls may look at abuse differently, they all are quick to recognize violence as a defining feature of their community. Missing in these perspectives, however, is the recognition that men are accountable for their abusive behavior. Instead, some girls blame women for letting males hit them and for returning to violent relationships. It is as if they are of the opinion that it is acceptable or normal for males to abuse females, and that it is the women's duty to negotiate their way around this violence. Hannah, for instance, is very critical of many neighborhood mothers who she feels are not putting their children's needs first. The data also indicate that violence is not necessarily hidden or kept a secret in Canal Town. Rather, despite their young ages, these white girls have heard of abuse in a variety of contexts and forms, and, according to their narrations, females in this community do not always endure their violence in isolation. Rosie, for example, reveals that a neighborhood woman sought refuge with her mother after a severe beating.

For these females, abuse does not just exist in public places and in the private dwellings of others. Violence also occurs in their own homes. Similar to poor and working class adult white women (Weis et al., 1997), in talking about personal experiences with abuse, the white girls typically contextualize violence as part of the past, as "things are better now." The younger females, though, are not as consistent in packaging such events in history. For instance, Elizabeth and Sally shift from present to past in describing the abuse in their homes. Many white Canal Town girls recall chilling vignettes of unbridled rage that pattern their upbringing.

Elizabeth: I want my mother's boyfriend to stop drinking so much. He drinks a lot. Like a sink full of beer cans, because his friends come over a lot too. They bring over cases and he usually gets drunk off a 12-pack.... Like every other day he will start screaming and blaming things on my sister, me, and my mom. My mom tells him, "No, it's not our fault." He forgets a lot too, like what he did with his money, or where he puts his pens and pencils. He starts screaming at us because he thinks we take them. The house has to be a certain way. If one thing is out of place, he'll hit us or lock us in the closet for a while, until my mom screams so much he lets us out ... but things are better now.

Sally: I used to think of myself as a zero, like I was nothing. I was stupid; I couldn't do anything.... I don't anymore, because we're all done with the violence in my house.... I've tried to keep it out since I was a kid.... My mom and John [mother's boyfriend] will argue over the littlest things. My mom is someone who is a violent person too. Sometimes she hits us, or he does. Then she would take a shower and we would get all dressed up, and we would all go out somewhere. After something bad would happen, she would try to make it better. She's a real fun person.... We're really close. We make cookies together and breakfast together.

Anne: My mom and her boyfriend constantly fight because they drink. When I was little I remember being in my bed. I was sleeping, only my other sisters came and woke me up because my mom and her boyfriend were fighting. We [Anne and sisters] started crying. I was screaming. My sisters were trying to calm me down. Our door was above the staircase and you could see the front door. I just had visions of me running out the door to get help because I was so scared. My oldest sister was like 9 or 10, and I had to go the bathroom and we only have one and it was downstairs. She sneaked me downstairs and into the kitchen and there was glasses smashed all over, there were plants under water, the phone cord was under water in the kitchen sink. It was just a wreck everywhere. But most of all, there were streams of blood mixing in with the water, on the floor, on the walls.

Rosie: I remember one Christmas my mom and my uncle were fighting. I escaped out the window to get help for my mom. We were living on the bottom floor at the time. I didn't have time to take a coat or mittens, I just grabbed my goldfish bowl.… I think it was because I didn't want to ever go back there. I immediately ran to the Center but it was closed, being like three in the morning or something. So I just ran around the neighborhood and water was splashing out of my goldfish bowl, and the fish were dying, and I was freezing, and I couldn't even scream anymore.

As these narrations indicate, domestic violence patterns the lives of these young poor girls.[8] In a moment of desperation Rosie seeks refuge at the Center, but it has long closed for the night. Mom can offer little salvation as she is often drunk, violent herself, or powerless as the man in her life is on an abusive rampage. As they escape into the icy night or are locked in closets, these girls have little recourse from the extreme and terrifying conditions which govern their lives. In Sally's case, her mother is also violent, yet is thought of as making up for that abuse by involving her daughter in family-style activities. Sally learns, therefore, not to see or feel pain. Given these accounts, it is easy to conclude that the effects of domestic violence are not something that can be contained at home, and the data indicate that exposure to abuse profoundly shapes the girls' behavior in other places. Such as school.

Elizabeth: About twice a month they [mom and boyfriend] fight. But not that far apart. Last time he [boyfriend] smacked me, I had a red hand on my face. I walked around with a red hand on my face, only I wouldn't let anybody see it.… I skipped school and the Center for, like, three days so no one would ask me about it.… I hid in my closet until you could barely see it. Then when I went back to school, I stayed real quiet because I didn't want people to look at me, notice the hand on my face.

Christina: When I had a boyfriend he [father] got so mad at me. He told me I wasn't allowed to have a boyfriend. I didn't know that because he never told me. He said that if he ever saw him again I would get my ass kicked. So one day he heard that Robbie [boyfriend] walked me to school. Well, he [father] came over that night and pulled down my pants and whipped me with his belt. I was bloody and the next day full of bruises. But I hurt more from being embarrassed to have my pants pulled down at my age. It hurt to sit all day long at school; that's all I could concentrate on. I couldn't go to the nurse because then she would find out. Nobody knew how I hurt under my clothes. I couldn't go to gym because people would find out, so I skipped. I hid in the bathroom but got picked up by the hall monitor who accused me of skipping gym to smoke. I just got so mad when I heard this, I pushed her [monitor] away from me and yelled. I was out of control with anger when they were dragging me down to the principal's. I got suspended for a week and had to talk to a school psychologist for two weeks about how bad smoking is for your health.

Rosie: My mom got money from her boyfriend for my school pictures, and when they came back, he saw them as I was getting ready for school … he threw them and said that I messed up my hair. But I got up an hour early that day to fix it, I remember, only my hair just flattened, not on purpose. He got real mad and picked up a lamp and threw it at her and it hit her but I tried to block it and got hit too. It fell on the floor all in pieces. She was crying because she was hurt and because he left and I was crying because I knew she would let him come back. So we were both crying, picking up the glass. Then I walked to school and I didn't open up my mouth once all day because I thought I would cry if I did.

Anne: Sometimes at school I just avoid teachers because they might feel sorry for me because they might see, like, bruises or something.… Sometimes I act bad so they won't feel sorry for me, then if they see a bruise or something they would think I deserved it. I would rather have them think that than getting the principal or nurse.

These glimpses into the lives of the Canal Town girls indicate that children from violent homes are learning at very young ages how to negotiate lives that are enmeshed in a web of overwhelming circumstances. Elizabeth talks about how her mother's boyfriend blames her and her mother and sister for all that is wrong, while Rosie gets hit with a lamp while trying to protect her mother. As they devise ways to conceal their bruises, they each face their pain alone. Elizabeth skips school and seeks shelter from the world in the same closet in which she is punished by her mother's boyfriend. Christina is choked on her anger and pain and separates herself from school activity only to become embroiled in another set of problems. As Rosie quietly sits through class, her physical and mental pain renders her completely disengaged from academic and social life at school. Anne deliberately acts bad to distract teachers from focusing on her scars of abuse.

In their analysis of domestic violence in the lives of poor and working class white women and the potential effects such abuse may have on their children, Weis and Fine (1996) review a substantial body of mostly quantitative literature in which such dimensions are explored. The narrations of the white Canal Town girls reflect findings in much of the existing research. As these girls evidence, abuse at home makes it difficult to concentrate in school, and the hurt, anger, and fear that they harbor inside often renders them silent, which also corroborates other studies (Elkind, 1984; Jaffee, Wolf, & Wilson, 1990). According to Afulayan (1993), some children blame themselves for the abuse, and skip school to protect a parent from the abuser, while other children become ill from worry. Depression, sleep disturbances, suicidal tendencies, and low self-esteem are other symptoms exhibited by children living in violent homes (Reid, Kavanaugh & Baldwin, 1987; Hughes, 1988).

All of the Canal Town girls reveal they spend incredible energy on keeping their abuse a secret while in school. This "culture of concealment" is likely in response to a number of fears, including fear of public embarrassment, fear of further angering an abuser, and/or fear that families will be torn apart by authorities. While observing the females at school, I noticed that, on a few occasions, some of the girls sustained bruises that perhaps could not be so easily hidden under long sleeves and turtlenecks. One day, for example, Christina came to school wearing an excessive amount of eye makeup, which was noticeable, considering she usually did not wear any. While talking to her outside after school, I realized that this was probably an attempt to conceal a black eye, which could clearly be seen in the harsh light of day.

Interestingly, I did not hear any talk of domestic violence at school—critical or otherwise. This finding parallels the poor and working class white women in the study of Weis et al.

(1997) who also were silent about the abuse in their lives, which was similarly not interrupted by schools, the legal system, and so forth. While at school, it did not seem to me that any of the girls sought help from their white female peers, teachers, or anyone else in coping with abuse. Instead, in the space of the school, a code of silence surrounding domestic violence prevailed, even though the white girls articulate an awareness of others' abuse throughout Canal Town. Not once did I hear students or teachers query others about violence or raise concern, nor was abuse even mentioned as a social problem in classes in which human behavior was discussed. Even on the day that Christina came to school attempting to camouflage a bruised eye, I did not observe a teacher pull her aside to talk, nor did I hear her friends ask her if she was alright. Dragged by their families from one violent situation to the next, it is remarkable that these girls are, for the most part, able to get through the school day, go home, and come back again "tomorrow."

•••

NOTES

1. The white Canal Town girls do not express the amount of contempt for African American females that they do for African American males. This is not to suggest these white girls are not racist toward African American females. In the confines of this study, however, the focus is on expressed anger about males of African American descent, and is linked, in part, to the stereotype of the sexual perpetrator.

2. My work has been greatly influenced by the work of Lois Weis and Michelle Fine and their recent findings from their large-scale Spencer Foundation project designed to capture narrations of poor and working class white, Latina/Latino, and African American young adults as to what their lives have been like since leaving high school (1998). Some of the points in this paragraph have been conceptualized by Weis and Fine.

3. In her analysis of the white Freeway females' desires for further education, Weis (1990) notes that although statisticians who report on national trends often contend that today, more than 50 percent of high school graduates directly enroll in further education, the high number of students in her analysis who say they plan to go on for advanced studies does not necessarily reflect such numbers. Weis clarifies that such reports are often manipulated by "educational inflation," in which enrollment in four-year institutions, community colleges, and other tertiary-level schools—such as business institutes and cosmetology courses—are collapsed into one category.

4. Authors borrow categories from Howell (1972).

5. Weis et al. (1997) assert that the poor and working class white women in their study are involved in "meaningful networks" such as church groups and literacy centers, and as a result, do not necessarily reflect the experiences of those females who are most disengaged. Similarly, as the white Canal Town females are all regular participants in the neighbourhood community center, they do not speak for those white girls that do not have "supportive" institutional connections.

6. Weis, Fine, and Marusza-Hall (1998) contend that the so-called cycle of violence may indeed be encouraged by living in a violent household, but, alternatively, may be largely produced because the violence goes unacknowledged, uninterrupted, and actively neglected by educators, clergy, family, neighbors, and friends.

7. This sophisticated way of looking at abuse is likely attributed to the extremely close relationship Hannah has with Ruby, who also serves as an informal counselor to these white youth.

8. Although the history of abuse in families and the frequency with which it occurs cannot be determined given the data, as Weis and Fine (1996) explain, if abuse was part of a parent's past, it will likely affect their parenting style and thus their children, even if there are no present instances of abuse.

9. I will further explore this point in Chapter 6.

10. In Proweller's (1995) exploration of the construction of female peer cultures in an upper-middle-class single-sex school, contextualized intersections of race and class generate a "polite" language of race which obscures any substantial discussion of structural inequity.

11. The authors contend that this more fluid sense of race exists in other Latin American countries, as does racism. In fact, Moore (1988) argues that racism in Cuba has historically rested upon the denigration of Africans.

12. I was not present during this discussion.

13. Personal communication with city bilingual education director, 1996.

REFERENCES

Afulayan, J. (1993). Consequences of domestic violence on elementary school education. *Child and Family Therapy*, 15 (3), 55–58.

Ani, M. (1994). *Yurugu: An African-centered critique of European cultural thought and behavior.* Trenton, NJ: African World Press.

Butler, J. (1993). *Bodies that matter: On the discursive limits of "sex."* New York: Routledge.

Carby, H. (1982). White women listen! Black feminism and the boundaries of sisterhood. In *The empire strikes back: Race and racism in 70s Britain.* Birmingham: The Center for Contemporary Cultural Studies.

Elkind, P. (1984). *All grown up and no place to go.* Reading, MA: Addison Wesley.

Fine, M., & Weis, L. (1998). *Voices of hope and despair.* New York: Beacon Press.

Fine, M., Weis, L., Addelston, J., & Maruszsa-Hall, J. (1997). (In)secure times: Constructing white working class masculine identities in the late 20th century. *Gender & Society, 11*, 52–68.

Holland, D., & Eisenhart, M. (1990). *Educated in romance: Women, achievement, and college culture.* Chicago: University of Chicago Press.

Hosmer, G. (1880). *Physiognomy of Buffalo. Publications of the Buffalo Historical Society.*

Howell, J. (1972). *Hard living on Clay Street: Portraits of blue collar families.* New York: Anchor Books.

Hughes, H. (1988). Psychological and behavioral correlates of family violence in child witnesses and victims. *American Journal of Orthopsychiatry, 58*, 77–90.

Jaffe, P., Wolfe, S., & Wilson, S. (1990). *Children of battered women.* Newbury, Park: Sage.

McRobbie, A. (1978). Working class girls and the culture of femininity. In *The University of Birmingham, Center for Contemporary Cultural Studies: Women take issue.* London: Hutchinson.

Moore, C. (1988). *Castro, the Blacks, and Africa.* Center for Afro-American Studies: University of California, Los Angeles.

Proweller, A. (1995). *Inside absence: An ethnography of female identity construction in an upper middle-class youth culture.* Unpublished doctoral dissertation, State University of New York at Buffalo.

Raissiguier, C. (1994). *Becoming women, becoming workers: Identity formation in a French vocational school.* Albany: State University of New York Press.

Reid, J., Kavanaugh, B., & Baldwin, J. (1987). Abusive parents' perception of child problem behavior: An example of paternal violence. *Journal of Abnormal Child Psychology, 15*, 451–466.

Smith, D. (1988). Femininity as discourse. In L. Roman, E. Christian-Smith, & E. Ellsworth, (Eds.). *Becoming feminine: The politics of popular culture.* London: The Falmer Press.

Smith, D. (1987). *The everyday world as problematic: A feminist sociology.* Boston: Northeastern University Press.

Valli, L. (1988). Gender identity and the technology of office education. In L. Weis (Ed.). *Class, race, and gender in American education.* Albany: State University of New York Press.

Weis, L., Maruszsa-Hall, J., & Fine, M. (1998). Out of the cupboard: Domestic violence and white poor and working class girls and women. *British Journal of Sociology of Education, 19 (1)*, 53–73.

Weis, L., Centrie, C., Valentin-Juarbe, J., & Fine, M. (1997). "It's a small frog that will never leave Puerto Rico": Men and the struggle for place in the U.S. In M. Fine & L. Weis (Eds.). *Voices of hope and despair.* Boston: Beacon Press.

Weis, L., & Fine, M. (1996). *"The teacher would call me 'piggy,' 'smelly,' 'dirty,' names like that: Prying open a discussion of domestic violence for educators."* Unpublished manuscript.

Weis, L., Fine, M., Proweller, A., Bertram, C., & Marusza-Hall, J. (1996). I've slept in clothes long enough: Excavating the sounds of domestic violence among women in the white working class. *Urban Review, 30 (1)*, 43–62.

Weis, L. (1990). *Working class without work:* New York: Routledge.

Willis, P. (1977). *Learning to labor: How working class kids get working class jobs.* New York: Columbia University Press.

Wilson, W. (1990). *The truly disadvantaged: The inner city, the underclass and public policy.* Chicago: University of Chicago Press.

24

Subtractive Schooling and Divisions Among Youth

Angela Valenzuela

Many social forces contribute to the divisions that exist among youth at Seguín. This chapter focuses on the important role that subtractive schooling plays in deepening these divisions and undermining opportunities for cross-generational relationships.[1] The discussion amplifies current conceptualizations in the literature regarding the process of cultural assimilation (e.g., Vigil 1997) by highlighting the school—or more pointedly, the schooling process—as a powerful, state-sanctioned instrument of cultural de-identification, or de-Mexicanization. The chapter has three main parts. I begin by recounting a classroom experience that reveals how *Mexicanidad* ("Mexican-ness") is not only a negotiated identity but a point of contention. The classroom discussion highlights the existence of divergent forms of consciousness among Mexican youth, on the one hand, and helps illuminate the school's role in perpetuating these divergences, on the other.

The experiences of Mexican youth provide a unique opportunity to extend McCarthy's (1993) analysis of the "politics of difference" to a group whose internal differences are routinely masked by such inclusive terms as "Hispanic," "Latino," or "involuntary minority" (Ogbu's [1991, 1994] term). McCarthy argues that researchers who study subordinate groups in educational settings would more accurately account for observed educational outcomes if they paid greater attention to the "multivocal, multiaccented nature of human subjectivity and the genuinely polysemic nature of minority/majority relations in education and society" (p. 337). He maintains that what separates minorities from each other, as well as from majority whites, are their distinct needs, interests, desires, and identities. These differences inevitably surface in educational settings because groups do not share an identical consciousness.

McCarthy's (1993) injunction to accord greater attention to human subjectivity is especially important in the case of Mexican immigrant youth, whose schooling experiences demonstrate that schools may be simultaneously subjectively additive and objectively subtractive. That is, immigrant youth may acquire useful skills and knowledge but at the cost of losing significant cultural resources, including a rich and positive sense of group identification. Olsen's (1997) ethnographic study in a northern California high school observes this problematic as well. This subjective experience gains added significance when one considers that the history of public schooling for U.S.-Mexicans shows schools to be key sites for both ethnic conflict and the production of minority status (San Miguel 1987, forthcoming; Spring 1997). Moreover, that immigrants become an "ethnic minority" within one or two generations, challenges McCarthy's unexamined assumption that minority status is neatly a priori or exogenous to schooling.

According immigrant subjectivity serious attention requires reframing racial and ethnic differences: they are more than "stock" that individuals possess, manipulate, and bring to bear on institutional life. These differences are dynamically linked to a larger historic process of subtractive cultural assimilation, more commonly known as Americanization (Hernández-Chávez 1988; Bartolomé 1994). So, when we examine the day-to-day school lives of Mexican youth, it is important to recognize that these experiences unfold against a much larger backdrop that is neither neutral nor benign.[2]

In the second section of this chapter, I use documentary data and evidence gathered from participant observation to examine Seguín High's subtractively assimilationist practices. The discussion highlights the institutional impediments to a more additive, culture-affirming vision of schooling and furthers the thesis that schooling subtracts resources from youth. I demonstrate how the structure of both the Spanish language and English as a Second Language (ESL) programs neglect the needs of Spanish-language youth. These programs provide an illusion of inclusion, but the institutional message they convey is that Spanish is a second-rate language and that the goals of bilingualism and biculturalism are neither worthwhile nor expedient (Valdés 1998).

In the last section, I return to the group interview data to investigate attitudinal differences among immigrant, mixed-generation, and U.S.-born friendship groups. This analysis reveals how attitudinal differences in the areas of culture, language, and identity underlie the social cleavages that exist between groups. Mixed-generation youth groups who share in a bilingual and bicultural identity appear to have the most balanced and favorable attitudes toward their immigrant and U.S.-born peers. Their statements contrast markedly from their peers located in immigrant and U.S.-born groups. While immigrants see U.S.-born youth as "too Americanized" and as negligent for succumbing to the corrosive influences of the dominant culture, U.S.-born youth are either hostile or reticent, evading the subject of immigrants. I conclude by suggesting how the capacity of individuals to manipulate their ethnic identity in educational settings is largely mediated by a schooling process aimed at divesting youth of their *Mexicanidad.*

RELATIONSHIPS AND THE "POLITICS OF DIFFERENCE"

The following account of a discussion in a sophomore English class helps concretize the meaning of McCarthy's "politics of difference." The exchange makes clear the contested nature of the relationship between the Spanish language and a Mexican identity. It also shows the students' divergent conceptualizations of the term "Mexican." Finally, the episode described below brings into clearer focus the effects of subtractive schooling on relationships among youth and between youth and adults.

One September morning, I came across a teacher named Mr. Perry from the English Department. He was only temporarily employed at Seguín, "subbing" until the principal could find a permanent replacement. He recognized me as "the person from Rice," and he asked whether I would be willing to be a role model and talk to his students—whom he described as a "lively bunch"—about college. Since he was behind on his grading, he also confessed that he could use the break that my visit would provide. I agreed to talk to the class.

There were about twenty students present, all sophomores. It was a "low-turnout day," according to Mr. Perry. After reviewing his students' homework assignments, he introduced me to the class. I talked for a few minutes, encouraging the students to consider going to college and explaining about college admissions requirements. Then, an immigrant student named Aarón spoke up.

"How well do students have to know English for college?" he asked in a heavy accent, and with a long blade of grass lodged between his teeth.

I told him that being able to read and write English rather than speaking it especially well is what is most important. Aarón said that his counselor had discouraged him from taking Spanish because he already knew it, so he was wondering if he was wasting his time taking Spanish classes. I told him that any class that helps students read and write well, regardless of the language, is good preparation for college.

Aarón's friend, Michael, who was sitting next to him, told the class, smiling, "I'm teaching him English."

"Good, and your friend helps you keep up with your Spanish, too," I suggested.

"Naw, I don't speak Spanish," Michael responded.

Aarón interjected, "He does. He just say he don't."

Turning to Aarón, Michael gave him a sour look. "Just because I speak it *un poquito* ("a little") doesn't mean I speak it."

"He does, Miss. He does. I heard him," Aarón insisted, still with the blade of grass in his mouth.

Aarón then punched Michael's sholder and Michael responded in kind, missing Aarón, who had dodged the punch by jerking his desk away. The desk tilted dangerously, teetering on a single leg for a split-second until Aarón wrestled it to the ground.

"Stupid!" Michael hissed, stonefaced as his classmates all burst into laughter.

Mr. Perry, who until then had been shuffling through papers on his desk, stopped and peered at the boys. "Okay, guys," he admonished them. "Settle down."

Despite the touchiness of the subject, I decided to pursue the language issue after the class had calmed down.

Empathizing with Michael, I said, "Look, I understand how it can be real hard when people expect you to know Spanish when you don't and especially when you haven't even been encouraged to hold onto it. And I'm writing about these things because this is a Mexican school where what language you speak is a big deal. So help me understand what you go through."

At first, everyone was silent. Then Jamail, the only African American male in the class, spoke up.

"I … I think it's hard for the immigrants here who don't know English because everyone expects them to know English," he offered, in a slow, thoughtful way. "In my classes, if no one translates for them, too bad. I couldn't do what they do."

A female student, who was filing her brightly polished red nails said, pointing first to me and then to Jamail, "Okay, so now I'm confused. You're saying some are expected to know Spanish and then you're saying some are expected to know English, two different things?"

Jamail explained, "I am expected to know English only."

Smiling, Aarón muttered loudly under his breath, "*Porque eres Negro.*" ("Because you're black.") This was somehow funny to the rest of the class.

"No, seriously," I protested, addressing the young woman with the red nails. "You raised a good question."

An impatient Aarón clarified, "Teachers want Mexicans to know English. Mexicans want Mexicans to know Spanish."

As Michael began to stew in his seat, the closeness of his relationship with Aarón became even more apparent to me.

"Look, we talked about this already, Aarón," he said testily. "I can be Mexican and not know Spanish. I hate anyone to think that just because I am darker than Jamail over there, that I have to speak Spanish."

Again, the other students laughed, including Jamail, whose complexion was lighter than Michael's. Aarón peered toward the corner of the room where another friend and ally, an immigrant male, sat frowning at Michael's comment.

Speaking more assuredly, Aarón declared, "That's not Mexican. You're a Chicano!"

"So, I'm a Chicano *and* Mexican," Michael retorted. " So I'm both!"

"Hey, hey, Michael. Chill!" Jamail coaxed. Several students chuckled, but most were listening intently as the discussion became more serious.

Then, from the furthest corner of the room, a young girl named Annalisa began to speak in a high-pitched, nasal tone. At first, her voice trembling, she produced only garbled words. The teacher put down his papers to listen to her. Annalisa paused, stared at the floor, and took a deep breath. Recovering from her false start, she began to describe a recent trip she had taken with her family to visit relatives in Mexico. She spoke of cousins who knew only Spanish and the difficulties she had in communicating with them because of her own lack of fluency. The most poignant statement she made was that her cousins referred to her as a *gringa* (white female) because of her poor command of Spanish.

"And I ain't no *gringa*," she told the class, still looking down at the floor. "They laughed when I said I was Mexican. And they said I lived in *Gringo-landia.*"

Her classmates sat in silence until, dragging the consonants in his words, Jamail asked quietly, "Wh-what's th-that?"

It means '*Gringo*-land' or America—the land where white people live," I explained.

"Ohhhh," he whispered.

Turning to Annalisa, I asked her if she had told her cousins that she felt insulted by their comments. She replied that because she had just met them and because she wanted them to think well of her and her family, she felt that she could not reveal how truly miserable they had made her feel. Instead, she smiled and laughed along with them, pretending that everything was fine.

"I don't like feeling this way," Annalisa continued, summing up her reactions to the trip, "but I feel like I never want to go back to Mexico to see them again."

Jenny, a student wearing three sets of gold hoop earrings of different sizes in her ears, suggested to Annalisa that maybe her cousins were jealous because she lived in the United States and they didn't.

"Maybe," Annalisa conceded, "but that still don't give 'em no right.…"

"No, it don't" Jenny agreed, interrupting, "but that's how I deal with it when my *güelito* (grandfather) says not to speak Spanish if me and my sisters are going to speak it all *pocho*. I just always think he's jealous or something. He lives half a year with us, the other half in Mexico. I think he wishes we were all Mexican … Mexican only, 'cause he tells me and my sisters we're *'americanizadas'* ('Americanized'). I guess 'cause we listen to heavy metal and wear black or 'cause I got my ears this way." (Some students laugh.) For real I heard him say *agringadas* ('whitened' women) about us one time. And that made me mad! Super mad! I'd hit anybody else who told me that! (More laughter.) Maybe I'm not Mexican. Maybe I'm just brown. But I sure ain't *agringada!*

Annalisa nodded slowly and sadly, the edges of her lips turned downward.

Trying to comfort Annalisa, who continued staring at the classroom floor, as if her ability to remain in control depended on her fixed gaze, Mr. Perry spoke up.

"Dear," he began, "I'm sorry they were mean to you, but can you help me understand just a little bit.… Uh, you *are* American and, uh, is it the word *gringo* or *gringo-landia* that hurt the most?"

In a frustrated tone, Michael replied for Annalisa. He told the teacher that the issue was not that Annalisa didn't think of herself as American, but that she was being told that she was not Mexican.

"Oh. Uh, you do think of yourself as American, then?" Mr. Perry questioned, failing to appreciate both the importance and the complexity of the identity issues with which the students were struggling.

"Of course," Annalisa replied, despondently.

At this point, all of the students paused. They looked at their teacher, disappointment and disgust apparent on every face. Some students shook their heads in disbelief.

Embarrassed, Mr. Perry apologized. "Okay, I'm sorry. I'm learning, too.…"

Ignoring the teacher, Jamail pointed to Aarón and began to verbalize what he had just learned by listening to his classmates. "So you be like her cousin when you tell Michael that he not Mexican. And Annalisa and Michael be mad because their family be Mexican even if they don't speak Spanish."

All heads in the classroom nodded approvingly.

"That's right, man," Michael confirmed, "and that's why I get mad at you, Aarón."

Flicking the blade of grass in the air like a tiny airplane, Aarón announced, " *'Ta 'ueno, 'ta 'ueno, ese* [Okay, okay, man] you Mexican, me Mexican, we all Mexican."

"You can't never be serious, man," Mechael complained, rolling his eyes at Aarón's response.

Noticeably proud of his ability to grasp the meaning of the discussion, Jamail instructed Aarón, "So lay off on Michael, dude. Michael be Mexican and that's that."

That comment made Michael crack his second smile that morning. Aarón shrugged his shoulders as he began to collect his things. The bell rang, and the students rushed off to lunch with smiles on their faces, including Annalisa, who also looked relieved.

"The spotlight's tough, but you did good," I told her as she walked past me.

Still silent, she offered me a parting smile.

The relation of language to identity was the heart of the discussion. Aarón sees Spanish fluency and a Mexican identity as inseparable. As Annalisa's story shows, for Mexican Americans, this is a psychically threatening stance. Annalisa has to be Mexican because she knows that she is not white. She, Jenny, and Michael must also rely on their lived experience as "Mexicans" in order to legitimate their claim to a Mexican cultural identity. Within this brand of *Mexicanidad*, the presumed association between the ability to speak Spanish and the possession of a Mexican identity is relaxed. To not relax this presumption is to invite anomie or total normlessness and alienation.[3] Aarón's distance from the U.S.-Mexican experience accounts for his flippant attitude toward his friend Michael.

First-generation immigrants like Aarón have trouble understanding the psychology of marginal, ethnic minority youth who identify as much with the term "Mexican" as they do with other self-identifiers like "Mexican American," and to a lesser extent, "Chicana/o" and "Hispanic."[4] Two factors are responsible for this lack of understanding. First, because many immigrants are preoccupied with acquiring fluency in the dominant language and culture, elaborating a Mexican identity in the United States seems regressive. Second, immigrants like Aarón have trouble seeing beyond their framework of *Mexicanidad* as a national identity, inextricably linked to Mexico. For Michael, Annalisa, and most U.S.-born youth, such a narrow, geographically based definition defies the word's common, everyday use. In their social world, *Mexicanidad* is an ethnic minority experience that has evolved (and continues to evolve) in relation to the dominant culture (Ogbu 1991, 1994).

From what I could tell, Aarón was one of only a few immigrants in the class. He was thus not in an ideal position to insist on what was, in his mind, the "correct" use of the term "Mexican." Consequently, the ethnicized, particularistic definition embraced by his Mexican American classmates prevailed.

Another theme that emerges from the student's exchange is the importance of the ability to speak Spanish and to speak it well. This is an extremely sensitive issue in the U.S. Mexican community. Accordingly, Trueba (1993) asserts,

> Language is one of the most powerful human resources needed to maintain a sense of self-identity and self-fulfillment. Without a full command of one's own language, ethnic identity, the sharing of fundamental cultural values and norms, the social context of interpersonal communication that guides interactional understandings and the feeling of belonging within a group are not possible. (p. 259)

As young adults, Michael and Annalisa are finding themselves held individually responsible for what is, in fact, a pressing collective issue—the "loss" of their language and the experience of marginality that follows from their poor command of Spanish. As the spheres of these teenagers' intimate social relationships widen to include Mexicans from Mexico, their inability to speak Spanish well leaves them vulnerable to derisive labeling and a particularly painful form of teasing. Their very identity as Mexicans is challenged when friends or relatives refer to them dismissively as "*gringa*," "*agringada*," "*pocho*," or "*americanizada*."

Jenny apparently has attained psychic equilibrium in her own experiences with similar forms of humiliation by concluding, at least for the time being, that the problem lies not with her, but with her grandfather, whom she views as being resentful of the fact that he is not an American himself. Jenny deflects the pain of her grandfather's remarks by substituting anger for shame, guilt, or remorse, and she suggests that Annalisa might find a similar approach constructive when dealing with her relatives. Despite their short-term usefulness, however, depression, anger, and defensive cultural posturing are limited and counterproductive responses if the ultimate goal is genuine dialogue and understanding. In the absence of sustained efforts toward cross-generational communication and solidarity, relationships—even intimate, family-based ones—are at risk.

Were youth to experience a politics of shared material or cultural interests, the mirror image of the politics of difference, their relationships would likely improve. They might even redirect their emotions and focus on the role of the school's assimilationist curriculum in promoting the confusion and conflict that surrounds their sense of identity. Such a reorientation would not only embody their collective interests but would also link them to the U.S.-Mexican community's broader historical struggle for equal educational opportunity (San Miguel 1987; Rosales 1996). Mr. Perry's disconnectedness from the most basic elements of the students' social and cultural world, however, indicates how difficult it would likely be to achieve this type of revised, politicized understanding at Seguín.

One reason Mr. Perry's insensitivity seemed especially striking was that it emerged at the very same time as Jamail's understanding of his peers' predicament perceptively deepened. Each time the discussion flagged, it was Jamail who came to the rescue. His questioning and prodding gave the exchange the impetus it needed to eventually assume a life of its own. Although he had no apparent emotional investment in any particular perspective on the relation of language to identity, Jamail quickly picked up on the social cues that signaled the need for a sensitive handling of the situation. He was so adept that he not only lowered his voice at appropriate moments, he also came through at the end with a fitting sanction of Aarón's behavior. In addition to the obvious fact that Jamail was a careful and skillful listener, I suspect that his experience as a racial minority and as a student in a virtually all-Mexican school contributed to his acute sensitivity to the delicate nature of the discussion. With his use of the Ebonics be-verb, "be Mexican," Jamail further invites a transborder interpretation of *Mexicanidad* as ever-present, embodying past, present, and future. He and Mr. Perry had become privy to a discussion rarely held publicly—much less between immigrant and U.S.-born youth—wherein the cultural "dirty laundry" was exposed.

Unlike Jamail, Mr. Perry did seem to feel that he had a stake in the outcome of the discussion. He had an emotional investment in Annalisa seeing herself as an "American." This personal agenda prevented him from being able to listen to what his students were saying—so much so that he disrupted the logical flow of the conversation (which Michael then brought back into line). The possibility that one could possess a bicultural identity appeared to be a wholly new, and disorienting, idea for him. His comments to me after class about being in the minority at the school led me to conclude that he felt defensive about the references to white people in the discussion. Further revealing his distance from the Mexican community was his numerical rather than political interpretation of the word "minority." The East End Mexican community exerts precious little control over the curriculum and process of schooling. While Mr. Perry should not be held up to a higher standard than regular, full-time faculty at Seguín, his lack of sophistication encapsulates problems endemic among the permanent, mostly non-Latino, faculty.

Mr. Perry's shallow, knee-jerk analysis of *Mexicanidad* was of great concern to me initially, but a conversation that I held with him later showed that he had grown significantly from the experience. He said that he had made the classroom discussion into the basis for a writing assignment that he then reinforced with more discussion. The title of the new assignment was "Being Mexican." He asked each student to write about what she/he thought it meant to be Mexican. Since some students did not identify with that term, preferring instead "Mexican American" or "Chicano," he allowed them to substitute the term that they believed best defined them. (Jamial wrote an essay on being African American.) Mr. Perry said that he had learned that "Mexican" was the most popular term among the students in his classroom, "no matter whether you're immigrant or homegrown."

According to Michael, in a follow-up discussion I had with him, all the students thought the assignment was "cool, especially the discussion part." Given the sensitive nature of the identity issue, Mr. Perry's students' eagerness to write down and continue to talk more or less publicly about their Mexican-ness deserves attention. Their response may signal just how badly youth need to use one another as sounding boards. The experience perhaps brought some closure to some of the healing that our discussion seemed to initiate. That these students are willing to write and talk for and in front of the likes of Mr. Perry, suggests possibilities for even greater openness in classes run by more culturally attuned teachers. Seguín high school classrooms could more regularly provide a positive forum for discussion. In speculating on my role, I feel that my presence helped Mr. Perry build on the interchange. My ethnicity not only helped give legitimacy to students' identity-related concerns, it also helped create a space for pedagogical action. My guess is that in the absence of shared understandings, an assignment on such a highly personal issue would require much more preparation.

Although many youths at Seguín are bicultural and bilingual, verbally proficient in two languages, they still tend to divide along generational lines, divisions which in turn signify differences in their levels of cultural assimilation. This situation is mediated by a host of schooling practices, to which I now turn.

SUBTRACTIVE SCHOOLING

"No Spanish" rules were a ubiquitous feature of U.S.-Mexican schooling through the early 1970s (Rosales 1981; San Miguel 1987). They have been abolished, but Mexican youth continue to be subjected on a daily basis to subtle, negative messages that undermine the worth of their unique culture and history. In sum, the structure of Seguín's curriculum is designed to divest youth of their Mexican identities and to impede the prospects for fully vested bilingualism and biculturalism. The single and only occasionally taught course on Mexican American history aptly reflects the students' marginalized status in the formal curriculum.

On a more personal level, students' cultural identities are systematically derogated and diminished. Stripped of their usual appearance, youth entering Seguín get "disinfected" of their identifications in a way that bears striking resemblance to the prisoners and mental patients in Goffman's essays on asylums and other total institutions (1977). ESL youth, for example, are regarded as "limited English proficient" rather than as "Spanish dominant" or as potentially bilingual.[5] Their fluency in Spanish is construed as a "barrier" that needs to be overcome. Indeed, school personnel frequently insist that once "the language barrier" is finally eliminated, Seguín's dismal achievement record will disappear as well. The belief in English as the ultimate panacea is so strong that it outweighs the hard evidence confronting classroom teachers every day: the overwhelming majority of U.S.-born, monolingual, English-speaking youth in Seguín's regular track do not now, have not in the past, and likely will not in the future prosper academically.

Another routine way in which the everyday flow of school life erodes the importance of cultural identity is through the casual revisions that faculty and staff make in students' first or last names. At every turn, even well-meaning teachers "adapt" their students' names: "Loreto" becomes "Laredo"; "Azucena" is transformed into "Suzy." Because teachers and other school personnel typically lack familiarity with stress rules in Spanish, last names are especially vulnerable to linguistic butchering. Even names that are common throughout the Southwest, like Martinez and and Perez, are mispronounced as MART-i-nez and Pe-REZ (instead of Mart-I-nez and PE-rez). Schooling under these conditions can thus be characterized as a mortification of the self in Goffman's terms—that is, as a leaving off and a taking on.

Analyses of three years' accumulation of documents provided by the school reveal a generalized pattern of cultural insensitivity. For instance, the only passage in the 84-page staff handbook that explicitly acknowledges the prevalence of Spanish-speakers among the student body is a single guideline intended only for the teacher whose job it is to discipline students. This sentence, found in the section that discusses the on-campus suspension policy and regulations, reads, "Rules will be posted in the center in English and Spanish." Similar instructions for counselors, teachers, nurses, or librarians do not exist. Not even in the section on homework policy—that encourages teachers to be resourceful and inventive with their assignments—are teachers advised to build on students' cultural backgrounds and experiences.

Another peculiarity of the staff handbook is its failure to mention, let alone quote, the school's purported commitment to multilingual literacy embodied in its mission statement:

> The graduates of Seguín High School will be able to participate, compete, and communicate effectively in an ever-changing multilingual world.[6]

With few students ever graduating, this statement is strikingly disconnected from what actually occurs at Seguín. In a school where English is the privileged medium of instruction in both curricular and extracurricular, faculty-sponsored activities, the sincerity of the commitment to producing multilingual students hardly seems credible.[7] The word, "multilingual," sounds suspiciously ambitious when Seguín has yet to deal effectively with its *bicultural* student body.

The student handbook has never been printed in Spanish. Moreover, despite the school's burgeoning Spanish-dominant population, the handbook makes no mention of the English as a Second Language (ESL) program. Instead, curriculum program information, which informs students about the number of credits required for graduation, is limited to youth who are enrolled in the "Regular" and "Advanced" high school programs (euphemisms for "tracks"). Thus, the type of schooling trajectory to expect or to work toward if one is a Spanish-dominant ESL student is not specified. Nor, at the other end of the spectrum, is any mention made of how to get into the school's honors program. Though all students are instructed to discuss their school plans with their pre-assigned school counselor, most students know that *no* counselor, pre-assigned or otherwise, will actually be available for such a discussion.

Another egregious handbook "oversight" regards the Texas Assessment of Academic Skills (TAAS) test. The handbook informs students that in addition to the minimum required credits for graduation, they must also pass this state-mandated exit exam. What it does not say is that the TAAS test is available only in English. Thus, students are not forewarned that their success or failure on the exam may turn more on their relative fluency in the English language than on their command of academic material. Given that large segments of the student population are not English-dominant, withholding this kind of information can spell last-minute failure for otherwise capable youth.

The subtractive elements in the school's curriculum have not gone unnoticed by all teachers. There are a few persistent faculty—most, but certainly not all of whom are Latino—who have promoted awareness of how the extant curriculum fails to build on students' skills, knowledge, and cultural background. Ms. Martinez, a Spanish language teacher, is especially active in this regard. She has developed a set of sound-bite responses to the many teachers who have questioned her additive philosophy. For instance, to the frequent query about why students in high school need Spanish courses at all, she typically replies, "For the same reasons you take English every year throughout middle and high school."

Through her work on various departmental and administrative committees, Ms. Martinez has focused on bringing about three interrelated policy changes: a separate Spanish Department, greater flexibility in the course assignment process for ESL youth, and improved linguistic assessment of Spanish-speaking youth. These recommendations critique the "blind" bureaucratic processes that obstruct the academic progress of all Mexican youth, but especially of Spanish-dominant students.

Departmental autonomy for Spanish would help avert the curricular mishandling of students that follows directly from conceptualizing Spanish as a "foreign language." The issue is quite simple to Ms. Martinez, who curtly states, "Spanish is foreign to people who don't speak Spanish." Her additive vision of schooling is clear in the following exchange we had in fall 1994:

> *Ms. Martinez.* In an ideal world, this school to me should be a bilingual high school where every student who walks out the door with a diploma … should be literate in English and Spanish … speak, comprehend, read, and write.
> *AV.* Are there any high schools like that anywhere?
> *Ms. Martinez.* I've never heard of one, but the students in this building have that ability, I think, and nobody is building on that asset.

Her sentiments are shared by a Latina ESL faculty member whom I had interviewed only days earlier. According to this teacher, one consequence of locating Spanish in the Foreign Language Department is that Mexican students are treated as any other immigrant group originating from distant lands, meaning that course offerings do not correspond to their needs. Because organizationally, Spanish is conceived as similar to such "foreign languages" as French and German, the majority of the courses are offered at the beginning and intermediate levels. Very few advanced Spanish-language courses exist. Rather than designing the program with the school's large number of native speakers in mind, Seguín's first- and second-year Spanish curriculum subjects students to material that insults their abilities. Taking beginning Spanish means repeating such elementary phrases as "*Yo me llamo María*" ("My name is *María*"), "*Tú te llamas José*" ("Your name is *José*"). According to both teachers, even students whose linguistic competence is more passive than active —that is, they understand but speak little Spanish—are ill-served by this kind of approach. A passively bilingual individual possesses much greater linguistic knowledge and ability than another individual exposed to the language for their first time. Since almost every student at Seguín is either a native speaker of Spanish or an active or passive bilingual, the school's Spanish program ill-serves all, though not even-handedly.

Many of the language teachers find ways to creatively circumvent the deficiencies of the curriculum. But this always entails working around their bureaucratically assigned text-books, since these invariably fail to correspond to their students' actual skill levels. Teachers of Spanish-dominant youth must spend their own money on materials if they wish to compensate for the curriculum's deficiencies. Thus, in very concrete ways, schooling subtracts resources from teachers, as well.[8]

Since support for a separate Spanish Department has not been forthcoming, Ms. Martinez and other faculty have requested that counselors exercise greater flexibility in the assignment process to make current offerings more relevant. For example, if students have taken advanced courses in Spanish, say as students in Mexico, they should be able to skip beginning Spanish and perhaps even intermediate-level courses and begin with advanced Spanish. According to existing guidelines, students who are genuinely interested in developing their first-language skills must weather many semesters of elementary-level Spanish before engaging advanced subject matter. This penalty, of course, is highest for students whose levels of educational attainment in Mexico are also high. According to Ms. Martinez, counselors should be able to suspend course-sequencing conventions to match students' actual skill levels. While they have this authority, they never exercise it:

> We express our concerns at the end of each spring semester. The summer comes, and by fall, the counselors continue doing what they've always done. It's like Spanish IA always has to be first, then IB and always in that order.

Ms. Martinez is well aware of the wider significance of her suggestions. Were they implemented, a major shift in the academic program would occur. An upside-down curricular pyramid would result, with far fewer beginning courses and many more advanced-level courses in Spanish. As Ms. Martinez indicates, because of the social distance between school personnel and the student body, it is difficult to persuade decision-makers of the importance of this kind of restructuring. Change would require a leap of faith that has so far not been forthcoming.[9] She attributes counselors' and administrators' obstinacy both to their reluctance to take on the logistical problems that restructuring Spanish classes would entail and to their failure to comprehend the relationship between first- and second-language development:

> One of the major problems is that many of the counselors are not bilingual and don't understand the importance of the first-language development of the students and they send them with good intentions to the classes they think [are best] or wherever there's room. They don't have a choice many times. They just send them wherever there's space for another body.... Students are not learning as much as they could when they are in the wrong class.

Even when placement decisions are "rationally" executed, they are typically based on crude measures. One is the school's home language survey, which asks students to report which language is predominant at home; the other measure is test score data from a language test administered before the student entered high school (typically, the test is given in middle school). Because the former index measures speaking ability rather than reading and writing abilities and the latter is frequently outdated, placement errors abound and the ESL program experiences huge fluctuations in size. For instance, between spring 1992 and fall 1993, the ESL program dropped from 600 to a total of 300 youth.

Clearly, with counselors carrying caseloads of 300-plus students each, expediency rules in placement decisions. However, as I discovered when I talked to Ms. Cardenas, who was at the time Seguín's only Spanish-speaking Latina counselor, other factors may play a role as well. Ms. Cardenas' advisees spanned a wide range, including all grade levels, ESL students, and regular track youth. She set her own priorities; that these sometimes resulted in a dismissive attitude toward ESL students and others was simply a hard fact of life. She explained her approach this way:

> What it is, is like everybody else…. Everybody wants their … their own student and they demand that we stop everybody else for stuff and take care of them and I think that's a problem. That they [ESL teachers] want us to, you know, handle the ESL students like they're number one. I mean, they're their priority. To me, every student is priority. I start with the seniors. To me they're the priorities because they have to … hurry up and graduate. And I work from seniors down, and if ESL runs in between there, I work on ESL. To me ESL and regular are exactly the same. I don't treat them [differently] or give anybody any preference. And that's what they [ESL staff] want.

This privileging of the graduating seniors over all others is universally employed by Seguín counselors and dates back at least to the October 1989 walkout (see chapter 2). Because undue curricular mishandling of youth in the privileged rungs of the curriculum contributed to the walkout, counselors either learned or were reminded about which segments of the student body were the most important for them to "protect."

Ms. Cardenas' seemingly merciless stance may be traced directly to her unenviable structural position as the only Mexican American, Spanish-speaking counselor at the school. A classic "token," she found herself constantly in a double-bind. If she failed to conform to the bureaucratic culture and expectations of the counseling department, she would risk being ostracized by her fellow counselors. However, conforming to counselors' practices was certain to make her a pariah in her own community of Mexican teachers, parents, and students. Over time, her "choice" to side with the counselors made her persona non grata at Seguín, especially among several vocal Latina ESL and vocational teachers who complained to the principal that she was dismissive toward their students. Ms. Cardenas lasted only three years in her position before the principal asked her to leave. A formal complaint to the principal from an ESL vocational teacher who felt that her students' needs were unduly neglected—alongside other similar complaints from other faculty—appeared to have influenced the principal's decision.

In a conversation I had with her weeks after her dismissal, Ms. Cardenas made clear how unprepared she had been for what befell her. "I can't believe this happened," she said, still shocked by the turn of events. "I did everything just like I thought I was supposed to." The contradictory aspects of token status were apparent in her account. Her experience suggests that if for no reason other than to mitigate the pressures toward conformity, instituting an ethnically balanced counselors' office would promote a more just working and decision-making environment.

The assessment of Spanish-dominant youth is the third issue that often brings Ms. Martinez into conflict with school counselors. Ms. Martinez maintains that through diagnostic testing, teachers can help students raise their test scores because they can apportion their instructional time to target those areas where students need the most help. Although such testing is supposed to be routine, the chaos that characterizes the beginning of each new school year at Seguín results in a systematic failure to test ESL students. Ms. Martinez concludes that the kinds of changes she has advocated will never come about in the absence of effective school-, district-, and state-level leadership.

Finally, Seguín subtracts resources from youth in ways that are directly related to how the state of Texas views the purpose and goals of its school-based ESL program. ESL is designed to impart to non-native English-speakers sufficient verbal and written skills to effectuate their transition into an all-English curriculum within a three-year time period. This transitional ideology (see note 2) translates into the organizational practice of segregating Spanish speaking students from English-speaking ones. Hence, layered over the school's academic tracking system is a "cultural tracking" system. I am not advocating the removal of immigrants' much-needed (though often deficient) school-administered language support systems. I do wish, however, to point out several key consequences of cultural tracking.

By obstructing possibilities for fully vested bilingualism and biculturalism at the individual and collective levels, cultural tracking creates and reinforces divisions among youth. These divisions encourage U.S.-born youth to nurture a false sense of superiority and to equate the ESL program and, by extension, Mexican immigrants and the Spanish language, with second-class status. Cultural tracking thus stigmatizes immigrant youth. These divisions also influence the level of social capital students possess in their peer groups (see chapter 4). Finally, cultural tracking restricts immigrants' achievement potential by limiting the courses offered within the cultural track to those taught in the general academic tract: honors-track ESL courses do not exist. "Graduation" out of the ESL track is thus always horizontal into the regular tract (see Valdés [1998], Olsen [1997], and Romo and Falbo [1996] for other similar critiques of ESL tracking).

In more specific terms, cultural tracking at Seguín means that Spanish-dominant students take ESL language courses that focus on developing their conversational skills in English. Because these courses focus on oral fluency, there is not enough attention to writing, reading, comprehension, or to academic vocabulary (see Olsen 1997, who expresses similar concerns about the ESL curriculum). If these students are lucky, however, they may get placed in ESL content-area courses. Content-area ESL courses cover the same material taught in the regular track curriculum, but the former are taught by ESL-certified teachers skilled at working with Spanish-speaking populations and trained in ESL methodologies like cooperative learning, the use of manipulatives, whole-language learning techniques, and so forth. These courses are referred to as "ESL-Math," ESL-U.S. History," and so on. However, because the "proper" number of content-area ESL courses the school offers is a continually contested issue, such courses are always in short supply.[10]

Moreover, since none of these courses is offered at an honors' level, immigrant youth are denied yet again the opportunity to achieve at an advanced academic level. While academic tracking is itself problematic, in the context of Seguín's tracking system, it is additionally so because cultural, nonacademic criteria block Spanish-dominant students' access to the honors program. However benign in conception and intention, programs that result in cultural tracking curtail youths' achievement potential and foster divisions among them.

• • •

CONCLUSION

One type of response that I received from U.S.-born youth groups remains to be examined: reticence. I found this silence on the subject of immigrants difficult to understand. These students' attitudes contrast markedly with that of their counterparts in generationally mixed groups, who readily mentioned clear advantages they derived from opportunities to nurture and expand their bilingual and bicultural competencies. The U.S.-born youths' silence lends support to the complaint registered by so many immigrant youth that this group is oblivious to their experiences.

Before accepting that conclusion, I re-analyzed the data, bearing in mind three rival interpretations. First, these students may have perceived my questions as a subtle way of accusing them of being discriminatory toward or prejudiced against immigrants. Second, these group members were truly equalitarian, and thus saw immigrant youth as no different from themselves, as all on an equal plane. Third, and I believe most likely, the subject of immigrants is an extremely sensitive and potentially volatile topic that inhibits open and honest discussion.

Contradicting the first interpretation, students in immigrant and mixed-generation groups never responded evasively to this line of questioning. Their respective tenuous and inclusive statuses precluded the possibility that they would be characterized as either discriminatory or prejudicial. However, supporting this interpretation was the off-handed, casual tones that marked the responses of U.S.-born youth. It wouldn't be the first time that they react differently to the same stimuli. Consider the following examples from the group interviews:

"Immigrants are no different from anybody else. There's good ones and bad ones." "People are people. What's there to talk about?" "I hate people to say some are more Mexican than others. That doesn't get us anywhere. God made us all equal." Even to a direct question I asked one particular group about the divisions that exist among youth generally, two students answered, respectively, "I wouldn't change a thing," and "We leave people alone if they leave us alone."

The most overtly equalitarian statement expressed above—"God made us all equal"—follows an acknowledgment of the politics of difference implicit in the allegation that some people can be "more Mexican" than others. The "we-they" distinction expressed by another student implies the "othering" of Mexican immigrants. The otherwise more neutral statements seem more like attempts to forestall further discussion rather than to promote lofty equalitarian ideals.

Evidence from the most overtly hostile U.S.-born groups suggests that the subject of immigrants is an extremely sensitive and potentially volatile topic. If students have not had the opportunity to discuss their feelings, opinions, and attitudes among themselves, a logical tendency would be to sidestep the issue by minimizing differences and providing curt responses. The complexity of the situation makes it difficult to conclude that youth in U.S.-born youth groups are simply oblivious. Their reticence may instead represent a covert form of the politics of difference that even my questioning could not jostle.

In conclusion, Seguín participates in the politics of difference whenever youth are deprived of the opportunity to openly evaluate and discuss the differences in social identities reflected among them. As discussed in the previous chapter, the development of divergent identities helps sustain the social decapitalization of U.S.-born youth. When immigrant youth become unavailable either as friends or as potential sources of academic support, U.S.-born youth are shut off from the pro-school, achievement-oriented ethos that prevails among so many of them. They also get divorced from the feedback loops that could alter their more ambivalent or antagonistic attitudes toward immigrants. Expressed positively, when one considers the bi-national experience that characterizes immigrant youth and their families, then having them as part of one's intimate network promises opportunities for life-enriching moments or even life-changing growth at such a critical point in young people's lives. Many such opportunities should exist, especially when the forging of meaningful connections is a realizable goal with a community that is nearly as close to its indigenous roots as it is to its immigrant history. However joyful or painful, the lessons learned and the discoveries made at the crossroads exceed by far anything that could be gleaned from a state-adopted text. An authentically caring pedagogy is optimally centered around such understandings.

Immigrant youth lose, too, from these politics of difference. They have little or no opportunity to fully understand or empathize with their U.S.-born counterparts' implicit critique of schooling. Perhaps more than they can imagine, the attitudes and behaviors of U.S.-born youth are governed by culturally shared criteria. With their *educación* model of schooling, they reject not education, but the content of their education and the way it is offered to them. They particularly resist the school's investment in their cultural and linguistic divestment, something that immigrant youth would do well to apprehend. When the organization of schooling deprives youth of historically derived understandings and the interpretive skills with which to assess these intergenerational cross-currents, divisions and misunderstandings can be expected to prevail.

NOTES

1. Broader societal forces certainly affect the attitudes that immigrant and U.S.-born youth hold toward each other. For example, Rodriguez and Nuñez's (1986) research among adult Mexican Americans and undocumented workers in the labor force shows the impact of each group's distinctive location in the occupational structure on the social distance between them and on their mutually critical perceptions.

2. For example, the Texas Bilingual Education Code (See. 29.051 State Policy) rejects bilingualism as a goal: "English is the basic language of this state. Public schools are responsible for providing a full opportunity for all students to become competent in speaking, reading, writing, and comprehending the English language." See also chapter 2 for a review of some of the most important historical and contemporary social, political, and economic factors shaping students' experiences at Seguín High.

3. For Mexican American girls, gender becomes an additional basis for marginality, although that issue was not raised during the classroom discussion. On average, females outperform males academically in each generation. However, as discussed in chapter 1, they are no more likely than males to see teachers as caring or to describe the school climate as favorable. Hence, good grades do not necessarily forestall marginality among regular-track youth.

In my research, it was females' withdrawal in the classroom that emerged as the primary indicator of their marginality. Indeed, Mexican American girls' silence and their hesitancy to speak up was a common complaint among Seguín teachers. Faculty often attributed this withdrawal either to the presence of males in the classroom or to Mexican culture, which allegedly inculcates passivity. Regardless of what they saw as the basis for their female students' disengagement, some teachers, as Linda's account (see chapter 4) makes clear, take advantage of the girls' compliance. However, since I did not focus my inquiry on gender and classroom dynamics, my findings in this area are somewhat limited (but see Orenstein [1994] and Olsen [1997] for an investigation of Latina female marginality).

4. Immigrants tend to refer to Mexican Americans as either "Chicano" or "Chicana," depending on whether they are male or female, respectively. *"México-Americano"* is another term immigrants used. As an identifier *for* Mexican Americans, "Chicana/o" may be popular among immigrants because the Mexican media popularized the term after it appeared in the title of several movies.

5. Rumbaut (1994) observed a correlation between self-esteem and being labeled "limited English proficient." Olsen's (1997) ethnographic data also reveal the powerful, negative impact of being an "ESLer" on immigrants' self-esteem.

6. Beginning in fall 1995, the mission statement was inserted into the teacher's handbook. Revised by Assistant Principal Ana Luera, the statement now reads: "The mission of Juan N. Seguín High School is to provide students with academic and technological excellence and social and emotional support in preparation as twenty-first century Americans." Note how the original reference to a multilingual world was subtracted.

7. The history of the school's mission statement helps account for its wording. It was drafted in the aftermath of the 1989 walkout due to the efforts of Ms. Martinez, a Mexican American Spanish teacher who headed the curriculum committee at the time. The walkout gave her and several other sympathetic faculty the political leverage necessary to write the statement. In light of Ms. Martinez's persistent efforts to alter the school's curriculum, the mission statement doubled as her critique of Seguín, on the one hand, and her emancipatory vision of education, on the other.

8. Because of limited school resources, many teachers are forced to draw from their personal reserves to enhance their ability to teach. An interesting question for future research is whether such spending varies according to the extent to which teachers perceive schooling as subtractive. A corollary question is whether a teacher's perception of schooling as subtractive is mediated by her/his academic field's location in the curriculum. It is conceivable that Spanish or ESL teachers not only see schooling as more subtractive than do their counterparts in other departments, but that they also spend more of their money as a percentage of their total income.

9. Partly following from Ms. Martinez's efforts, five classes of Spanish for native speakers (of Spanish) were eventually offered in 1991. In 1996, Honors Spanish was offered at Seguín for the first time in its history.

10. In 1993–94, for example, following the advice of the Math Department chair, the head counselor and head registrar in charge of the master schedule took it upon themselves to eliminate all ESL-Math courses. The chair's advice and the administration's response infuriated the two Latina math teachers, who ended up getting many of the ESL students rerouted to their classes anyway because the non-ESL math teachers were at a complete loss in having to contend with unprecedented numbers of students with whom they could not communicate (see Valdés [1998] for a comparable situation she came across in her research).

11. The Spanish and ESL clubs are the only exceptions to this rule.

12. I have visited many East End churches and have observed in each the same kind of divisions between immigrants and U.S.-born members. In fact, one large church I belonged to for several years dissolved along generational lines. This is a ubiquitous issue in Latino churches. Half of the church congregation prefers an exclusively Spanish service while the other half prefers either a bilingual or an exclusively English-speaking service. Moreover, the latter two options are often preferred within the context of Mexican or Latino church membership for cultural reasons. That is, they can more easily impart their religious beliefs and values to the next generation when members' experiences and cultural values are shared. However, there are also many people like these young women who attend either predominantly Anglo or integrated churches.

REFERENCES

Bartolomé, Lilia I. 1994. Beyond the methods fetish: Toward a humanizing pedagogy. *Harvard Educational Review* 64: 173–94.

Goffman, Erving. 1977. *Asylums: Essays on the Social Situation of Mental Patients and Other Inmates.* Garden City, N.Y.: Anchor Books.

Hernández-Chávez, Eduardo. 1988. Language policy and language rights in the United States. In *Minority Education: From Shame to Struggle*, by Tove Skutnabb-Kangas and James Cummins. Clevedon, Canada: Multilingual Matters 40.

McCarthy, Cameron, 1993. Beyond the poverty of theory in race relations: Nonsynchrony and social difference in education. In *Beyond Silenced Voices: Class, Race, and Gender in the United States Schools*, edited by Lois Weis and Michelle Fine. Albany: State University of New York Press.

Ogbu, John. 1974. *The Next Generation: An Ethnography of Education in an Urban Neighborhood.* Orlando, Fla.: Academic Press.

——. 1991. Immigrant and involuntary minorities in comparative perspective. In *Minority Status and Schooling: A Comparative Study of Immigrant and Involuntary Minorities*, edited by Margaret A. Gibson and John U. Ogbu. New York: Garland Publishing.

——. 1993. Frameworks-variability in minority school performance: A problem in search of an explanation. In *Minority Education: Anthropological Perspectives*, edited by Evelyn Jacob and Cathie Jordan. Norwood, N.J.: Ablex.

Olsen, Laurie, 1997. *Made in America: Immigrant Students in our Public Schools.* New York: The New Press.

Orenstein, Peggy. 1994. *School Girls: Young Women, Self-Esteem, and the Confidence Gap.* New York: Doubleday.

Rodriguez, Nestor P., and Rogelio T. Nuñez. 1986. An exploration of factors that contribute to differentiation between Chicanos and indocumentados. In *Mexican Immigrants and Mexican Americans: An Evolving Relation*, edited by Harley Browning and Rodolfo de la Garza. Austin: CMAS University of Texas Press.

Romo, Harriett D. 1985. The Mexican origin population's differing perceptions of their children's schooling. In *The Mexican American Experience: An Interdisciplinary Anthology*, edited by Rodolfo de la Garza et al. Austin: University of Texas Press.

Romo, Harriett D., and Toni Falbo. 1996. *Latino High School Graduation: Defying the Odds.* Austin: University of Texas Press.

Rosales, F. Arturo. 1996. *Chicano! The History of the Mexican American Civil Rights Movement.* Houston, Tex.: Arte Público Press.

——. 1981. Mexicans in Houston: The struggle to survive, 1908–1975. *The Houston Review: History and Culture of the Gulf Coast* 3: 224–48.

Rumbaut, Rubén G. 1994. The crucible within: Ethnic identity, self-esteem, and segmented assimilation among children of immigrants. *International Migration Review* 28: 748–94.

San Miguel, Guadalupe. 1987. *"Let All of them Take Heed": Mexican Americans and the Campaign for Educational Equality in Texas, 1910–1981.* Austin: University of Texas Press.

——. Forthcoming. *"Brown, Brown, We're Not White, We're Brown": Identity and Activism in the Politics of Chicano School Reform in Houston, Texas, 1965–1980.* College Station: Texas A&M Press.

Trueba, Henry T. 1993. The relevance of theory on language and culture with pedagogical practices. In *Language and Culture in Learning: Teaching Spanish to Native Speakers of Spanish*, edited by Barbara J. Merino, Henry T. Trueba, and Fabián A. Samaniego. Washington, D.C.: The Falmer Press.

Valdés, Guadalupe. 1998. The world outside and inside schools: Language and immigrant children. *Educational Researcher* 27: 4–18.

Vigil, Diego. 1997. *Personas Mexicanas: Chicano High Schoolers in a Changing Los Angeles.* Fort Worth, Tex.: Harcourt Brace College Publishers.

25

English Only: The Tongue-Tying of America

Donaldo Macedo

During the past decade conservative educators such as ex-secretary of education William Bennett and Diane Ravitch have mounted an unrelenting attack on bilingual and multicultural education. These conservative educators tend to recycle old assumptions about the "melting pot theory" and our "common culture," assumptions designed primarily to maintain the status quo. Maintained is a status quo that functions as a cultural reproduction mechanism which systematically does not allow other cultural subjects, who are considered outside of the mainstream, to be present in history. These cultural subjects who are profiled as the "other" are but palely represented in history within our purportedly democratic society in the form of Black History Month, Puerto Rican Day, and so forth. This historical constriction was elegantly captured by an 11th-grade Vietnamese student in California:

> I was so excited when my history teacher talked about the Vietnam War. Now at last,
> I thought, now we will study about my country. We didn't really study it. Just for one day,
> though, my country was real again. (Olsen, 1988, p. 68)

The incessant attack on bilingual education which claims that it serves to tongue-tie students in their native language not only negates the multilingual and multicultural nature of U.S. society, but blindly ignores the empirical evidence that has been amply documented in support of bilingual education. An example of a truly tongue-tied America materialized when the ex-foreign minister of the Soviet Union, Mr. Eduard Shevardnadze, began to deliver a speech in Russian during a recent commencement ceremony at Boston University. The silence that ensued was so overwhelming that one could hear a pin drop. Over 99% of the audience was saved from their monolingualism thanks to the intervention of an interpreter. In fact, the present overdose of monolingualism and Anglocentrism that dominates the current educational debate not only contributes to a type of mind-tied America, but also is incapable of producing educators and leaders who can rethink what it means to prepare students to enter the ever-changing, multilingual, and multicultural world of the 21st century.

It is both academicallly dishonest and misleading to simply point to some failures of bilingual education without examining the lack of success of linguistic minority students within a larger context of a general failure of public education in major urban centers. Furthermore, the English Only position points to a pedagogy of exclusion that views the learning of English as education itself. English Only advocates fail to question under what conditions English will be taught and by whom. For example, immersing non-English-speaking students in English as a Second Language programs taught by untrained music, art, and social science teachers (as is the case in Massachusetts with the grandfather clause in ESL Certification) will hardly accomplish the avowed goals of the English Only Movement. The proponents of English Only also fail to raise two other fundamental questions. First, if English is the most effective educational language, how can we explain that over 60 million Americans are illiterate or functionally illiterate (Kozol, 1985, p. 4)? Second, if education solely in English can guarantee linguistic minorities a better future, as educators like William Bennett promise, why do the majority of Black Americans, whose ancestors have been speaking English for over 200 years, find themselves still relegated to ghettos?

I want to argue in this paper that the answer lies not in technical questions of whether English is a more viable language of instruction or the repetitive promise that it offers non-English-speaking students "full participation first in their school and later in American society" (Silber, 1991, p. 7). This positions assumes that English is in fact a superior language and that we live in a classless, race-blind society. I want to propose that decisions about how to educate non-English-speaking students cannot be reduced to issues of language, but rest in a full understanding of the ideological elements that generate and sustain linguistic, racial, and sex discrimination. That is, educators need to develop, as Henry Giroux has suggested, "a politics and pedagogy around a new language capable of acknowledging the multiple, contradictory, and complex subject positions people occupy within different social, cultural, and economic locations" (1991, p. 27). By shifting the linguistic issue to an ideological terrain we will challenge conservative educators to confront the Berlin Wall of racism, classism, and economic deprivation which characterizes the lived experiences of minorities in U.S. public schools. For example, J. Anthony Lukas succinctly captures the ideological elements that promote racism and segregation in schools in his analysis of desegregation in the Boston Public Schools. Lukas cites a trip to Charlestown High School, where a group of Black parents experienced firsthand the stark reality their children were destined to endure. Although the headmaster assured them that "violence, intimidation, or racial slurs would not be tolerated," they could not avoid the racial epithets on the walls: "Welcome Niggers," "Niggers Suck," "White Power," "KKK," "Bus is for Zulu," and "Be illiterate, fight busing." As those parents were boarding the bus, "they were met with jeers and catcalls 'go home niggers. Keep going all the way to Africa!'" This racial intolerance led one parent to reflect, "My god, what kind of hell am I sending my children into?" (Lukas, 1985, p. 282). What could her children learn at a school like that except to hate? Even though forced integration of schools in Boston exacerbated the racial tensions in the Boston Public Schools, one should not overlook the deep-seated racism that permeates all levels of the school structure. According to Lukas:

> Even after Elvira "Pixie" Paladino's election to The Boston School Committee [in 1975] she
> was heard muttering about "jungle bunnies" and "pickaninnies." And John "Bigga" Kerrigan

[head of the School Committee] prided himself on the unrestrained invective ("I may be a prick, but at least I'm a consistent prick"), particularly directed at Blacks ("savages") and the liberal media ("mother-fucking maggots") and Lem Tucker, a Black correspondent for ABC News, whom Kerrigan described as "one generation away from swinging in the trees," a remark he illustrated by assuming his hands upwards, and scratching his armpits. (Lukas, 1985, p. 282)

Against this landscape of violent racism perpetrated against racial minorities, and also against linguistic minorities, one can understand the reasons for the high dropout rate in the Boston public schools (approximately 50%). Perhaps racism and other ideological elements are part of a school reality which forces a high percentage of students to leave school, only later to be profiled by the very system as dropouts or "poor and unmotivated students." One could argue that the above incidents occurred during a tumultuous time of racial division in Boston's history, but I do not believe that we have learned a great deal from historically dangerous memories to the degree that our leaders continue to invite racial tensions as evidenced in the Willie Horton presidential campaign issue and the present quota for jobs as an invitation once again to racial divisiveness.

It is very curious that this new-found concern of English Only advocates for limited English proficiency students does not interrogate those very ideological elements that psychologically and emotionally harm these students far more than the mere fact that English may present itself as a temporary barrier to an effective education. It would be more socially constructive and beneficial if the zeal that propels the English Only movement were diverted toward social struggles designed to end violent racism and structures of poverty, homelessness, and family breakdown, among other social ills that characterize the lived experiences of minorities in the United States. If these social issues are not dealt with appropriately, it is naive to think that the acquisition of the English language alone will, somehow, magically eclipse the raw and cruel injustices and oppression perpetrated against the dispossessed class of minorities in the United States. According to Peter McLaren, these dispossessed minority students who

> populate urban settings in places such as Howard Beach, Ozone Park, El Barrio, are more likely to be forced to learn about Eastern Europe in ways set forth by neo-conservative multi-culturists than they are to learn about the Harlem Renaissance, Mexico, Africa, the Caribbean, or Aztec or Zulu culture. (McLaren, 1991, p. 7)

While arguing for the use of the students' native language in their educational development, I would like to make it very clear that the bilingual education goal should never be to restrict students to their own vernacular. This linguistic constriction inevitably leads to a linguistic ghetto. Educators must understand fully the broader meaning of the use of students' language as a requisite for their empowerment. That is, empowerment should never be limited to what Stanley Aronowitz describes as "the process of appreciating and loving oneself" (1985). In addition to this process, empowerment should also be a means that enables students" to interrogate and selectively appropriate those aspects of the dominant culture that will provide them with the basis for defining and transforming, rather than merely serving, the wider social order" (Giroux & McLaren, 1986, p. 17). This means that educators should understand the value of mastering the standard English language of the wider society. It is through the full appropriation of the standard English language that linguistic minority students find themselves linguistically empowered to engage in dialogue with various sectors of the wider society. What I must reiterate is that educators should never allow the limited proficient students' native language to be silenced by a distorted legitimation of the standard English language. Linguistic minority students' language should never be sacrified, since it is the only means through which they make sense of their own experience in the world.

Given the importance of the standard English language in the education of linguistic minority students, I must agree with the members of the Institute for Research in English Acquisition and Development when they quote Antonio Gramsci in their brochure:

> Without the mastery of the common standard version of the national language, one is inevitably destined to function only at the periphery of national life and, especially, outside the national and political mainstream. (READ, 1990)

But these English Only advocates fail to tell the other side of Antonio Gramsci's argument, which warns us:

> Each time that in one way or another, the question of language comes to the fore, that signifies that a series of other problems is about to emerge, the formation and enlarging of the ruling class, the necessity to establish more "intimate" and sure relations between the ruling groups and the popular masses, that is, the reorganization of cultural hegemony. (Gramsci, 1971, p. 16)

This selective selection of Gramsci's position on language points to the hidden curriculum with which the English Only movement seeks to promote a monolithic ideology. It is also part and parcel of an ongoing attempt at "reorganization of cultural hegemony" as evidenced by the unrelenting attack by conservative educators on multicultural education and curriculum diversity. The ideological force behind the call for a common culture can be measured by the words of syndicated columnist Pat Buchanan, who urged his fellow conservatives "to wage a cultural revolution in the 90's as sweeping as the political revolution of the 80's" (Giroux, 1991, p. 15). In other words, as Henry Giroux has shown, the conservative cultural revolution's

> more specific expressions have been manifest on a number of cultural fronts including schools, the art world, and the more blatant attacks aimed at rolling back the benefits constructed of civil rights and social welfare reforms constructed over the last three decades. What is being valorized in the dominant language of the culture industry is an undemocratic approach to social authority and a politically regressive move to reconstruct American life within the script of Eurocentrism, racism, and patriarchy. (Giroux, 1991, p. 15)

Derrick Z. Jackson, in his brilliant article "The End of the Second Reconstruction," lays bare the dominant conservative ideology that informs the present cultural hegemony when he argues that "From 1884 to 1914, more than 3,600 African-Americans were lynched. Lynching is passé today. AIDS, infant mortality, violence out of despair, and gutted public education do the same trick in inner cities neatly redlined by banks" (1991, p. 27). In contrast to the zeal for a common culture and English only, these conservative educators have remained ominously silent about forms of racism, inequality, subjugation, and exploitation that daily serve to wage symbolic and real violence against those children who by virtue of their language, race, ethnicity, class, or gender are not treated in schools with the dignity and respect all children warrant in a democracy. Instead of reconstituting education around an urban and cultural studies approach which takes the social, cultural, political, and economic divisions of education and everyday life as the primary categories for understanding contemporary schooling, conservative educators have recoiled in an attempt to salvage the status quo. That is, they try to keep the present unchanged even though, as Renato Constantino points out:

> Within the living present there are imperceptible changes which make the status quo a moving reality.... Thus a new policy based on the present as past and not on the present as future is backward for it is premised not on evolving conditions but on conditions that are already dying away. (1978, p. 201)

One such not so imperceptible change is the rapid growth of minority representation in the labor force. As such, the conservative leaders and educators are digging this country's economic grave by their continued failure to educate minorities. As Lew Ferlerger and Jay Mandle convincingly argue, "Unless the educational attainment of minority populations in the United States improves, the country's hopes for resuming high rates of growth and an increasing standard of living look increasingly dubious" (1991, p. 12).

In addition to the real threat to the economic fabric of the United States, the persistent call for English language only in education smacks of backwardness in the present conjuncture of our ever-changing multicultural and multilingual society. Furthermore, these conservative educators base their language policy argument on the premise that English education in this country is highly effective. On the contrary. As Patrick Courts clearly argues in his book *Literacy for Empowerment* (1991), English education is failing even middle-class and upper-class students. He argues that English reading and writing classes are mostly based on workbooks and grammar lessons, lessons which force students to "bark at print" or fill in the blanks. Students engage in grudgingly banal exercises such as practicing correct punctuation and writing sample business letters. Books used in their classes are, Courts points out, too often in the service of commercially prepared ditto sheets and workbooks. Courts's account suggests that most school programs do not take advantage of the language experiences that the majority of students have had before they reach school. These teachers become the victims of their own professional ideology when they delegitimize the language experiences that students bring with them into the classroom.

Courts's study is basically concerned with middle-class and upper-middle-class students unburdened by racial discrimination and poverty, students who have done well in elementary and high school settings and are now populating the university lecture halls and seminar rooms. If schools are failing these students, the situation does not bode well for those students less economically, socially, and politically advantaged. It is toward the linguistic minority students that I would like to turn my discussion now.

THE ROLE OF LANGUAGE IN THE EDUCATION OF LINGUISTIC MINORITY STUDENTS

Within the last two decades, the issue of bilingual education has taken on a heated importance among educators. Unfortunately, the debate that has emerged tends to recycle old assumptions and values regarding the meaning and usefulness of the students' native language in education. The notion that education of linguistic minority students is a matter of learning the standard English language still informs the vast majority of bilingual programs and manifests its logic in the renewed emphasis on technical reading and writing skills.

I want to reiterate in this paper that the education of linguistic minority students cannot be viewed as simply the development of skills aimed at acquiring the standard English language. English Only proponents seldom discuss the pedagogical structures that will enable these students to access other bodies of knowledge. Nor do they interrogate the quality of ESL instruction provided to the linguistic minority students and the adverse material conditions under which these students learn English. The view that teaching English constitutes education sustains a notion of ideology that systematically negates rather than makes meaningful the cultural experiences of the subordinate linguistic groups who are, by and large, the objects of its policies. For the education of linguistic minority students to become meaningful it has to be situated within a theory of cultural production and viewed as an integral part of the way in which people produce, transform, and reproduce meaning. Bilingual education, in this sense, must be seen as a medium that constitutes and affirms the historical and existential moments of lived culture. Hence, it is an eminently political phenomenon, and it must be analyzed within the context of a theory of power relations and an understanding of social and cultural reproduction and production. By "cultural reproduction" I refer to collective experiences that function in the interest of the dominant groups rather than in the interest of the oppressed groups that are objects of its policies. Bilingual education programs in the United States have been developed and implemented under the cultural reproduction model leading to a de facto neocolonial educational model. I use "cultural production" to refer to specific groups of people producing, mediating, and confirming the mutual ideological elements that merge from and reaffirm their daily lived experiences. In this case, such experiences are rooted in the interest of individual and collective self-determination. It is only through a cultural production model that we can achieve a truly democratic and liberatory educational experience. I will return to this issue later.

While the various debates in the past two decades may differ in their basic assumptions about the education of linguistic minority students, they all share one common feature: they all ignore the role of language as a major force in the construction of human subjectivities. That is, they ignore the way language may either confirm or deny the life histories and experiences of the people who use it.

The pedagogical and political implications in education programs for linguistic minority students are far-reaching and yet largely ignored. These programs, for example, often contradict a fundamental principle of reading, namely that students learn to read faster and with better comprehension when taught in their native tongue. The immediate recognition of familiar words and experiences enhances the development of a positive self-concept in children who are somewhat insecure about the status of their language and culture.

For this reason, and to be consistent with the plan to construct a democratic society free from vestiges of oppression, a minority literacy program must be rooted in the cultural capital of subordinate groups and have as its point of departure their own language.

Educators must develop radical pedagogical structures which provide students with the opportunity to use their own reality as a basis of literacy. This includes, obviously, the language they bring to the classroom. To do otherwise is to deny minority students the rights that lie at the core of a democratic education. The failure to base a literacy program on the minority students' language means that oppositional forces can neutralize the efforts of educators and political leaders to achieve decolonization of schooling. It is of tantamount importance that the incorporation of the minority language as the primary language of instruction in education of linguistic minority students be given top priority. It is through their own language that linguistic minority students will be able to reconstruct their history and their culture.

I want to argue that the minority language has to be understood within the theoretical framework that generates it. Put another way, the ultimate meaning and value of the minority language is not to be found by determining how systematic and rule-governed it is. We know that already. Its real meaning has to be understood through the assumptions that govern it, and it has to be understood via the social, political, and ideological relations to which it points. Generally speaking, this issue of effectiveness and validity often hides the true role of language in the maintenance of the values and interests of the dominant class. In other words, the issue of effectiveness and validity becomes a mask that obfuscates questions about the social, political, and ideological order within which the minority language exists.

If an emancipatory and critical education program is to be developed in the United States for linguistic minority students in which they become "subjects" rather than "objects," educators must understand the productive quality of language. James Donald puts it this way:

> I take language to be productive rather than reflective of social reality. This means calling into question the assumption that we, as speaking subjects, simply use language to organize and express our ideas and experiences. On the contrary, language is one of the most important social practices through which we come to experience ourselves as subjects.… My point here is that once we get beyond the idea of language as no more than a medium of communication, as a tool equally and neutrally available to all parties in cultural exchanges, then we can begin to examine language both as a practice of signification and also as a site for culture struggle and as a mechanism which produces antagonistic relations between different social groups. (Donald, 1982, p. 44)

It is to the antagonistic relationship between the minority and dominant speakers that I want to turn now. The antagonistic nature of the minority language has never been fully explored. In order to more clearly discuss this issue of antagonism, I will use Donald's distinction between oppressed language and repressed language. Using Donald's categories, the "negative" way of posing the minority language question is to view it in terms of oppression—that is, seeing the minority language as "lacking" the dominant standard features which usually serve as a point of reference for the minority language. By far the most common questions concerning the minority language in the United States are posed from the oppression perspective. The alternative view of the minority language is that it is repressed in the standard dominant language. In this view, minority language as a repressed language could, if spoken, challenge the privileged standard linguistic dominance. Educators have failed to recognize the "positive" promise and antagonistic nature of the minority language. It is precisely on these dimensions that educators must demystify the standard dominant language and the old assumptions about its inherent superiority. Educators must develop liberatory and critical bilingual programs informed by a radical pedagogy so that the minority language will cease to provide its speakers the experience of subordination and, moreover, may be brandished as a weapon of resistance to the dominance of the dominant standard language of the curriculum.

In this sense, the students' language is the only means by which they can develop their own voice, a prerequisite to the development of a positive sense of self-worth. As Giroux elegantly states, the students' voice "is the discursive means to make themselves 'heard' and to define themselves as active authors of their worlds"(Giroux & McLaren, 1986, p. 235). The authorship of one's own world also implies the use of one's own language, and relates to what Mikhail Bakhtin describes as "retelling a story in one's own words" (Giroux & McLaren, 1986, p. 235).

A DEMOCRATIC AND LIBERATORY EDUCATION FOR LINGUISTIC MINORITY STUDENTS

In the maintaining a certain coherence with the educational plan to reconstruct new and more democratic educational programs for linguistic minority students, educators and political leaders need to create a new school grounded in a new educational praxis, expressing different concepts of education consonant with the principles of a democratic, multicultural, and multilingual society. In order for this to happen, the first step is to identify the objectives of the inherent colonial education that informs the majority of bilingual programs in the United States. Next, it is necessary to analyze how colonialist methods used by the dominant schools function, legitimize the Anglocentric values and meaning, and at the same time negate the history, culture, and language practices of the majority of linguistic minority students. The new school, so it is argued, must also be informed by a radical bilingual pedagogy, which would make concrete such values as solidarity, social responsibility, and creativity. In the democratic development of bilingual programs rooted in a liberatory ideology, linguistic minority students become "subjects" rather than mere "objects" to be assimilated blindly into an often hostile dominant "common" culture. A democratic and liberatory education needs to move away from traditional approaches, which emphasize the acquisition of mechanical basic skills while divorcing education from its ideological and historical contexts. In attempting to meet this goal, it purposely must reject the conservative principles embedded in the English Only movement I have discussed earlier. Unfortunately, many bilingual programs sometimes unknowingly reproduce one common feature of the traditional approaches to education by ignoring the important relationship between language and the cultural capital of the students at whom bilingual education is aimed. The result is the development of bilingual programs whose basic assumptions are at odds with the democratic spirit that launched them.

Bilingual program development must be largely based on the notion of a democratic and liberatory education, in which education is viewed "as one of the major vehicles by which 'oppressed' people are able to participate in the sociohistorical transformation of their society" (Walmsley, 1981, p. 74). Bilingual education, in this sense, is grounded in a critical reflection of the cultural capital of the oppressed. It becomes a vehicle by which linguistic minority students are equipped with the necessary tools to reappropriate their history, culture, and language practices. It is, thus, a way to enable the linguistic minority students to reclaim "those historical and existential experiences that are devalued in every-day life by the dominant culture in order to be both validated and critically understood" (Giroux, 1983, p. 226). To do otherwise is to deny these students their very democratic rights. In fact, the criticism that bilingual and multicultural education unwisely question the traditions and values of our so-called "common culture" as suggested by Kenneth T. Jackson (1991) is both antidemocratic and academically dishonest. Multicultural education and curriculum diversity did not create the S & L scandal, the Iran-Contra debacle, or the extortion of minority properties by banks, the stewards of the "common culture," who charged minorities exorbitant loan-sharking interest rates. Multicultural education and curriculum diversity did not force Joachim Maitre, dean of the College of Communication at Boston University, to choose the hypocritical moral high ground to excoriate the popular culture's "bleak moral content," all the while plagiarizing 15 paragraphs of a conservative comrade's text.

The learning of English language skills alone will not enable linguistic minority students to acquire the critical tools "to awaken and liberate them from their mystified and distorted views of themselves and their world" (Giroux, 1983, p. 226). For example, speaking English has not enabled African-Americans to change this society's practice of jailing more Blacks than even South Africa, and this society spending over 7 billion dollars to keep African-American men in jail while spending only 1 billion dollars educating Black males (Black, 1991).

Educators must understand the all-encompassing role the dominant ideology has played in this mystification and distortion of our so-called "common culture" and our "common language." They must also recognize the antagonistic relationship between the "common culture" and those who, by virtue of their race, language, ethnicity, and gender, have been relegated to the margins. Finally, educators must develop bilingual programs based on the theory of cultural production. In other words, linguistic minority students must be provided the opportunity to become actors in the reconstruction of a more democratic and just society. In short, education conducted in English only is alienating to linguistic minority students, since it denies them the fundamental tools for reflection, critical thinking, and social interaction. Without the cultivation of their native language, and robbed of the opportunity for reflection and critical thinking, linguistic minority students find themselves unable to re-create their culture and history. Without the reappropriation of their culture, the valorization of their lived experiences, English Only supporters' vacuous promise that the English language will guarantee students "full participation first in their school and later in American society" (Silber, 1991, p. 7) can hardly be a reality.

REFERENCES

Aronowitz, S. (1985, May). "Why should Johnny read." *Village Voice Literary Supplement,* p. 13.
Black, C. (1991, January 13). Paying the high price for being the world's no. 1 jailor. *Boston Sunday Globe,* p. 67.
Constantino, R. (1928). *Neocolonial identity and counter consciousness.* London: Merlin Press.

Courts, P. (1991). *Literacy for empowerment.* South Hadley, MA: Bergin & Garvey.

Donald, J. (1982). Language, literacy, and schooling. In *The state and popular culture.* Milton Keynes: Open University Culture Unit.

Ferlerger, L., & Mandle, J. (1991). *African-Americans and the future of the U.S. economy.* Unpublished manuscript.

Giroux, H. A. (1983). *Theory and resistance: A pedagogy for the opposition.* South Hadley, MA: Bergin & Garvey.

Giroux, H. (1991). *Border crossings: Cultural workers and the politics of education.* New York: Routledge.

Giroux, H. A. & McLaren, P. (1986). Teacher education and the politics of engagement: The case for democratic schooling. *Harvard Educational Review, 56*(3), 213–238.

Gramsci, A. (1971). *Selections from Prison Notebooks,* (Ed. and Trans. Quinten Hoare & Geoffrey Smith). New York: International Publishers.

Jackson, D. (1991, December 8). The end of the second Reconstruction. *Boston Globe,* p. 27.

Jackson, K. T. (1991, July 7). Cited in a *Boston Sunday Globe* editorial.

Kozol, J. (1985). *Illiterate America,* New York: Doubleday Anchor.

Lukas, J. A. (1985). *Common ground.* New York: Alfred A. Knopf.

McLaren, P. (1991). Critical pedagogy: Constructing an arch of social dreaming and a doorway to hope. *Journal of Education, 173*(1), 9–34.

Olsen, L. (1988). *Crossing the schoolhouse border: Immigrant students and the California public schools.* San Francisco: California Tomorrow.

Silber, J. (1991, May). *Boston University Commencement Catalogue.*

Walmsley, S. (1981). On the purpose and content of secondary reading programs: Educational and ideological perspectives. *Curriculum Inquiry, 11,* 73–79.

Suggested Readings for Further Study

Bettie, J. (2003). *Women without class: Girls, race, and identity*. Berkeley, CA: University of California Press.

Bickmore, K. (1999). Why discuss sexuality in elementary school? In Letts, W., IV, & Sears, J. (Eds.), *Queering elementary education: Advancing the dialogue about sexualities and schooling*. Lanham, MD: Rowman & Littlefield.

Bordo, S. (1993). Hunger as ideology. In *Unbearable Weight*. Berkeley, CA: University of California Press.

Brown, E. (2001). Human development and the social structure. In Watkins, W., Lewis, J., & Chou, V., *Race and Education* (pp. 128–139). Boston, MA: Allyn & Bacon.

Clark, K. B., & Clark, M. P. (1939). The development of consciousness of self and the emergence of racial identity in Negro preschool children. *Journal of Social Psychology, 10*, 591–599.

Dehyle, D. (1995). Navajo youth and Anglo racism: Cultural integrity and resistance, *Harvard Educational Review, 65*(3), 403–445.

Dehyle, D. (1998). From break dancing to heavy metal: Navajo youth, resistance, and identity, *Youth and Society, 30*(1), 3–32.

Driscoll, C. (2002). *Girls: Feminine adolescence in popular culture and cultural theory* (pp. 53–57, 62–69, 73–77). New York: Columbia University Press.

Fine, M. (1992). Sexuality, schooling, and adolescent females: The missing discourse of desire. In Fine, M. (Ed.), *Disruptive voices* (pp. 31–59). Ann Arbor, MI: The University of Michigan Press.

Fordham, S. (1996). *Blacked out: Dilemmas of race, identity, and success at Capital High*. Chicago, IL: University of Chicago Press.

Gaines, D. (1992). *Teenage wasteland: Suburbia's dead end kids*. New York: HarperPerennial.

Gilbert, P., & Taylor, S. (1991). *Fashioning the feminine: Girls, popular culture, and schooling*. North Sydney, Australia: Allen & Urwin.

Giroux, H. (1992). *Border crossings* (pp. 180–206). New York: Routledge.

Giroux, H. (1996) *Fugitive cultures: Race, violence, and youth*. New York: Routledge.

Giroux, H. (2002). The politics of pedagogy, gender and whiteness in "Dangerous Minds." In Giroux, H. (Ed.), *Breaking into the movies: Film and the culture of politics* (pp. 136–169). Malden, MA: Blackwell.

Goodman, R. T. (2004). *World, Class, and Women: Global literature, education, and feminism*. New York: RoutledgeFalmer.

Hall, S. (1996). Who needs identity? In Hall, S., & duGay, P. (Eds.), *Questions of identity*. Thousand Oaks, CA: Sage.

Henry, A. (1998). "Speaking up" and "speaking out": Examining "voice" in a reading/writing program with adolescent African Caribbean girls, *Journal of Literacy Research, 30*(2), 233–252.

Ladner, J. (1970). *Tomorrow's tomorrow: The Black woman*. Lincoln: University of Nebraska Press.

Leadbeater, B., & Way, N. (1996). *Urban girls: Resisting stereotypes, creating identities*. New York: New York University Press.

Letts, W., IV, & Sears, J. (Eds.) (1999). *Queering elementary education: Advancing the dialogue about sexualities and schooling*. Lanham, MD: Rowman & Littlefield.

Manning, L. (2002). *Developmentally appropriate middle level schools*. Wheaton, MD: Association for Childhood Education International.

McLaren, P. (1995) Moral panic, schooling, and gay identity, *High School Journal, 77*(1 or 2), (University of North Carolina Press).

McRobbie, A. (1991). *Feminism and youth culture: From 'Jackie' to 'Just Seventeen.'* Boston, MA: Unwin Hyman.

Morrison, D. (1997). *American Indian studies: An interdisciplinary approach to contemporary issues*. New York: Peter Lang.

Parker, S., Nichter, M., Nichter, M., Vuckovic, N., Sims, C., & Ritenbaugh, C. (1995). Body image and weight concerns among African American and white adolescent females: Differences that make a difference, *Human Organization, 54*(2), 103–114.

Saltman, K. (2000). Coca Cola and the commercialism of public schools, In *Collateral damage* (pp. 57–73). Lanham, MD: Rowman & Littlefield.

Sipe, P. (2004). Newjack: Teaching in a failing middle school, *Harvard Educational Review, 74*(3), p. 330–339.

Spencer, M. B. (1982). Personal and group identity of Black children: An alternative synthesis. *Genetic Psychology Monographs, 106*, 59–84.

Spencer, M. B. (1983). Black children's race awareness, racial attitudes, and self-concept: A reinterpretation. *Journal of Child Psychology and Psychiatry, 25*(3), 433–441.

Spencer, M. B. (1983). Children's cultural values and parental child rearing strategies. *Developmental Psychology, 3*, 351–370.

Spencer, M. B. (2000). Identity, achievement orientation, and race: "Lessons learned about the normative developmental experiences of African American males." In Watkins, W., Lewis, J., & Chou, V. (Eds.), *Race and education: The roles of history and society in education African American students* (pp. 100–127). Needham Heights, MA: Allyn & Bacon.

Unks, G. (1995). *The gay teen: Educational practice and theory for lesbian, gay, and bisexual adolescents.* New York: Routledge.

Ward, J. (2000). Raising resisters: The role of truth-telling in the psychological development of African American girls. In Weis, L., & Fine, M. (Eds.), *Construction sites: Excavating race, class and gender among urban youth.* New York: Teachers College Press.

Willis, P. (1977). *Learning to labor: How working class kids get working class jobs.* New York: Columbia University Press.

IV

CURRICULUM, ASSESSMENT, AND CRITICAL PEDAGOGY

Enora R. Brown

Teaching and learning should be a process of inquiry, of critique: it should also be a process of constructing, of building a social imagination that works within a language of hope. (McLaren, 1989, p. 197)

THE ORIGINAL *TURNING Points* report published in 1989 by the Carnegie Corporation was revised and released 11 years later in 2000, in the midst of the burgeoning standards movement, a year before the No Child Left Behind Act of 2001 (NCLBA) institutionalized this "educational reform." Although the revision of *Turning Points* preceded the official adoption of national educational policy represented by the NCLBA, there are changes in the report's recommendations from 1989 (see Executive Summary of *Turning Points* report, chapter 10 in section II) to 2000. Substantial changes to the recommendations about curriculum and the teaching-learning process in middle schools are commensurate with the national thrust toward standardization, accountability, and privatization, cornerstones of the educational reforms that threaten the quality of middle schools and the survival of public education. These changes subvert the possibility of creating a curriculum based on critical inquiry, constructed knowledge, and social imagination, as espoused in the opening quote. The revised recommendations in the *Turning Points* 2000 report, Educating Adolescents in the 21st Century, are as follows:

1. Teach a curriculum grounded in rigorous, public academic standards for what students should know and be able to do, relevant to the concerns of adolescents and based on how students learn best.
2. Use instructional methods designed to prepare all students to achieve higher standards and become lifelong learners.
3. Staff middle grades schools with teachers who are expert at teaching young adolescents, and engage teachers in ongoing, targeted professional development opportunities.
4. Organize relationships for learning to create a climate of intellectual development and a caring community of shared educational purpose.
5. Govern democratically, through direct or representative participation by all school staff members, the adults who know the students best.
6. Provide a safe and healthy school environment as part of improving academic performance and developing caring and ethical citizens.
7. Involve parents and communities in supporting student learning and healthy development. (p. 23)

While these recommendations were ostensibly designed to "ensure success for every student" (p. 25), they not only run counter to those in the original document in 1989 (see chapter 10, section II), but also undermine the 14 goals and characteristics of successful middle schools identified by the National Middle School Association in *This We Believe* (NMSA, 2003, p. 7; see introduction to Section II). Despite the apparent conflict between the revised recommendations and the NMSA position statement, it is interesting to note that there are some leading advocates within the National Middle School Association who acknowledge "remarkable parallels between the design elements in Turning Points 2000 and the characteristics of developmentally responsive middle level schools … [which] illustrates the points of agreement about the important elements that are required to ensure success for every student" (Erb, 2001). The "adaptive" versus liberatory response to the standards movement has profound implications for the direction and strength or vulnerability of middle level education, for the quality, goals, and value of learning for youth, and for insuring all youth equitable life options.

The chapters in Section IV focus on curriculum and assessment in middle school, with particular emphasis on the construction and use of knowledge directed toward social justice in middle schools and society. Critical theoretical and conceptual readings chart the direction for educators to develop integrated curriculum and assessment in schools. Other experiential texts are written by educators who implemented liberatory, problem-posing curricula, and alternatives to assessment, that counter the current thrust of the standards movement and other forms of education designed to stultify and domesticate the consciousness of learners (Freire, 1970/1933). These narrative analyses by educators-as-agents-of-change capture their experiences in implementing innovative curricula and advocating for programmatic change in middle schools, and are illustrative of the possibilities and surmountable challenges faced in transforming the educational processes within middle schools and changing the institutionalized nature of education on a national level. Social equality and justice are goals that are not only commensurate with teaching and learning in middle schools, but are also woven into the very purpose and function of education as an emancipatory process toward the realization for all of humanity.

The excerpt of the revised recommendations from the Carnegie Corporation's *Turning Points* report (2000) illustrates the pervasive influence of corporate-sponsored national educational "reforms" for standards and accountability on current middle school policy and practice. As the revisions illustrate, standards and quantifiable measures have become the outcomes of success and are at the heart of this new policy statement. Additionally, the commitment to eliminate tracking to "ensure the success for all students" and the stated goal to empower teachers and administrators have been removed, and there is equivocal commitment to the creation of small schools. These changes reflect the rallying of corporations like Carnegie and other sociopolitical forces, as they respond to fissures in the economy, and make recuperative efforts to invest in education, by revamping and privatizing public education. It is an effort to shift authority over knowledge to those in power, while simultaneously denying this aim, or the dire consequences to youth, especially poor and those of color, subjected to the banking approach to education directly determined by corporate interests. It is in this climate that the curricular tenets of the middle school concept are faced with the challenge of responding to these assaults on viable educational processes and determining how to maintain the valued elements of quality education for youth. In contrast to the first three sections of the *Critical Reader*, the readings in this final section begin with progressive and critical readings about curriculum and assessment in middle level education. In some way, each creates possibilities for teachers and teacher educators to consider ways of doing things differently in their pedagogical practices with middle school students and prospective teachers.

The first chapter in this section, chapter 26, is by James A. Beane, an advocate and scholar who has written extensively on the nature and content of curriculum for middle school youth. His problem-centered, integrated curriculum for democratic education work has set a new standard for middle school curriculum. Starting with an overview of the history of integrated curriculum, Beane clarifies its conceptual differences from interdisciplinary or core curricula. He dispels commonly held notions about integrated curricula through an examination of its four components—the integration of experiences, social life, knowledge, and curriculum design—its organization around the self and social problems, and its aim to promote democratic practice in schools. He considers the inhibitory role of discipline-based knowledge in public schooling and in the solving of real problems, and the function of academic disciplines in creating differential cultural capital for members of society and maintaining existent power relationships among groups. He presents a conceptual framework and discusses the power of organizing middle school curricula with students around consensually determined social problems and issues of personal significance, and of implementing this model through innovative projects and activities. He argues that the integrative curriculum will foster student investment in the learning process and prepare students to participate with others in solving social problems thoughtfully and intelligently in a democratic society.

Peter McLaren's chapter follows with a pivotal discussion of critical pedagogy. Grounded in critical theory, he provides a theoretical framework based on his discussion of concepts such as: the social construction of knowledge, different forms of knowledge, the relationship between knowledge and power, and the role of discourse or discursive practices in knowledge production. In chapter 27, he examines the significance of curriculum as a form of cultural politics, and the role of the "hidden curriculum" in the tacit construction of knowledge in schools. Throughout, he argues that unexamined knowledge produced in school curricula maintain dominant culture discourses, and serve to reproduce social and economic inequalities that exist in society and in schools. However, McLaren notes that integrated curriculum and critical pedagogy can resist and create new perspectives, alternate meanings, and tranformative social practices that shift the relations of power undergirding privilege and inequality. McLaren's work presents a clear conceptual rationale and imperative for educators to investigate the values, beliefs, and taken-for-granted truths that pervade education and move toward quality education and decent lives for all youth. Both Beane's and McLaren's chapters lay the theoretical and conceptual foundation for the next critical analyses of curricular experiences by educators in middle school classrooms.

Jean Anyon, in chapter 28, presents a unique critical analysis of social studies curricula, textbooks, and teacher attitudes about students from different social classes. She illustrates the social class basis of the curricula, teachers' views about the "appropriate curriculum" for working class, middle class, and upper class elementary and middle school youth, and students' reactions to their curricular experiences. Through teacher interviews, textual analyses of the curricular materials and teacher instruction at five schools, she reveals differences in the content, orientation, and quality of the curricular texts across class and in teacher attitudes toward, expectations for, and judgments about students based on their social class. Anyon examines the implications of these curricular choices and class-based ideological orientations for the maintenance of social inequality in education, the cultivation of particular personal qualities in youth, and the tracking of the children of unskilled laborers and multinational corporate parents into their future stations in society's socioeconomic hierarchy. Her analysis addresses the varied use of class-based knowledge for youth to either reproduce the cultural capital and structural inequality or disrupt relations of power and promote democratic social transformation. Anyon's chapter complements chapters by Bowles and Gintis in Section II and by Brown in Section III, by illuminating the relationship between the curriculum and the structure and function of public education.

In chapter 29, Eric Gutstein chronicles his work as a university professor, teaching mathematics from a social justice perspective in an urban Latino middle school, and examines the ways in which students use mathematics to understand the complexity of social justice issues. Using the text Mathematics in Context related to the National Council of Teachers of Mathematics (NCTM) standards as the basis for developing his work, Gutstein organizes a critical mathematics education curricula around real-world projects, such as housing discrimination, racial profiling, the war expenditures and our tax dollars, distribution of wealth, differences in educational achievement along racial, class, and gender lines. His Freirian "pedagogy of questioning" and his ardent reflections from a sociocultural perspective about his role as a white male educator of Latino students are evident in transcripted classroom dialogue and promote his explicit goal to address a range of struggles for emancipation. Through collaborative inquiry, students develop their mathematical power, experience its lifetime value for real-life problem solving, gain greater social consciousness, and a sense of personal agency and their own social identities. This chapter demonstrates how educators can thoughtfully draw from and transform "traditional materials," prepare students for the "gatekeeping" exercise of standardized testing, and simultaneously, guide them in examining, challenging, and transforming educational and societal inequalities.

Melinda Fine examines the dynamics that emerge in her middle school classroom through the discussion of controversial issues in chapter 30. Through interviews and self-reflective observations, she chronicles the challenges and possibilities that teachers and students face as they strive to address emotionally charged social and political issues in a community that is diverse on racial and class lines. She chronicles the class discussions throughout an interdisciplinary social studies unit, Facing History and Ourselves, focusing on the Holocaust, with the aim of fostering critical thinking, multiple perspectives, and moral decision making. Fine documents teachers' discomfort with conflict, the curriculum, the content of students' discussion, the eruption of arguments, and the thinking that evolves throughout the unit. She challenges the myth of students' unreadiness to discuss controversial, difficult topics, and demonstrates their ability, willingness, and thwarted desire to discuss issues that they are thinking about. Fine emphasizes the importance of creating safe spaces for dialogue, of being prepared for ambiguity, conflict, and emotions that naturally arise in discussions around issues about which people care passionately. Fine argues for extensive efforts to be made to engage students in dialogue and projects that prepare them to handle social and political differences constructively and to become advocates for true societal democracy.

Kathe Jervis, in chapter 31, illustrates the ways in which the class- and race-based ideology in the dominant culture pervade and frame teachers' ideologies, the standard curriculum, and students' experiences in a diverse, progressive middle school. She examines forms of racism that emerge in the classroom and are made apparent through student questions. Jervis chronicles teachers' silence in response to racism, their efforts to deny racial meanings that frame their pedagogical practices and interactions with youth, and the impact of unexamined assumptions on curriculum, teachers' racial interactions with and assessments of students, and relationships among school personnel. This chapter illustrates the subtle, but powerful forms of racism that need focused attention beyond the creation of integrated school communities. Jervis emphasizes the need for institutional financial support, professional development for teachers, and other supports for students facing racism in school and society. Her chapter presents a perspective that complements Ferguson's analysis of the racial construction of black boys' masculinity (see chapter 20, section III). The readings by Melinda Fine and Kathe Jervis reveal the successes and challenges faced in implementing innovative, liberatory curricula in middle school classrooms, and reveal the competence of middle school youth in posing or handling difficult issues of power, race, and social inequality that are traditionally omitted from classrooms and standard curricular texts. They raise complex social issues that are relevant to the current and future lives of students.

The concluding chapter in this section by Linda McNeil addresses the destructive long-term effects of national reforms for standardization and accountability on the quality and nature of teaching and learning and on youth, especially African American and Latino youth, and on the widening societal gap along race and class lines. In chapter 32, McNeil deconstructs the justificatory myth that standards will "bring students up to par," demonstrates their role in exacerbating and stabilizing class- and race-based tracking of youth in the public education system, and criticizes the technicization of education and deintellectualization of the general population. She examines the origins of social inequality in education and the role of standardization and accountability in maintaining structures of privilege and race and class stratification.

McNeil examines the day-to-day retrogressive impact of standardization on classroom practices and experiences in schools, i.e., the promotion of teachers' defensive teaching. Teachers reduce requirements to avert opposition and gain compliance, omit or mystify curricular content for students, and fragment or grossly oversimplify course content. As a result, she found teachers defensive, students disengaged, and reciprocally, teachers' intensified control. The downward cycle of student disengagement and teachers' intensified control is the inevitable manifestation of standardization and accountability at the point of the teaching and learning process. McNeil's incisive analysis is crucial for an understanding of the immediate and long-term effects of structural reform that destroys the emancipatory goals and purposes of education sought by all students, parents, and educators alike. She calls for all to examine these realities, to expose ideological or structural impingements, and to "roll back" initiatives that promise success for all children, but function as acts of violence against the youth in this country. The compilation of readings in this section provides insights into the complex relationships that exist among curricula, pedagogy, and constructions of youth identities, and into the role of education in promoting student learning and social change.

QUESTIONS FOR REFLECTION AND DIALOGUE

1. What are the implications of the changes in the *Turning Points* report recommendations made from 1989 to 2000, for middle school classrooms, for the future of public education?
2. What is the relationship between knowledge and power? What is the hidden curriculum and how does it function in education? How is it possible to investigate and reveal hidden curricula in curricular texts and teaching?
3. How is integrated curricula liberatory in ways interdisciplinary curricula is not? What social issues could be the focus of educational experiences?
4. What are the principles that guide Gutstein's social justice math curriculum? What possibilities and challenges does this liberatory curriculum bring to students?
5. Examine the teachers' responses to the conflicts that arose around the Holocaust curriculum in Melinda Fine's article. Is the goal of education to share all views equally? If so, how? If not, why? Does free speech support democracy?
6. Discuss the value of engaging students in dialogue about politically and emotionally charged issues. How does a critical pedagogy facilitate this and create emancipatory possibilities for students?
7. What are the subtle, but powerful forms of racism that surfaced in Jervis's chapter? Why is racism ignored by white teachers and what is the impact on youth of color? What implications does this have for you?
8. How might liberatory education for youth facilitate institutional or structural changes in society and create real social transformation?

REFERENCES

Erb, T. (2001). *This we believe … and now we must act.* Westerville, OH: National Middle School Association.
Freire, P. (1970/1993). *Pedagogy of the oppressed.* New York: Continuum.

Jackson, A., & Davis, G. (2000). *Turning points 2000: Educating adolescents in the 21st century.* Report of Carnegie Corporation of New York, New York: Teachers College Press.

McLaren, P. (1989) *Life in schools: An introduction to critical pedagogy in the foundations of education.* New York: Longman.

National Middle School Association (2003). *This we believe: Successful schools for young adolescents.* Westerville, OH: National Middle School Association.

26

A Special Kind of Unity

James A. Beane

SUPPOSE THAT WE are going to work with a group of students on a unit about "Environmental Issues," including major concepts or "big ideas" such as conservation, pollution, politics, and economics. What kinds of experiences might best help young people address these issues? To explore the concept of conservation, students might work on school or community recycling programs, make recommendations for resource conservation after studying waste patterns in the school or community, and/or carry out a multimedia campaign to encourage conservation and recycling in the school and community. To explore the concept of politics and the environment, they could carry out a survey in the school and community regarding attitudes toward issues such as recycling or land use, prepare exhibits that display competing viewpoints about environmental issues, and/or research how debates about environmental issues have changed over time. To explore the concept of pollution, they might test water or soil from nearby sources, survey businesses and industries about efforts to reduce pollution, and/or prepare exhibits on various kinds of pollution.

Having completed our work on that unit, suppose we next organize a unit on "Living in the Future," with related concepts such as technology, living spaces, health, and others. Here students could conduct a survey on beliefs held by peers about the future, tabulate the results, compare them to other forecasts, and prepare research reports. Or they might look at technological, recreational, entertainment, or social trends and develop forecasts or scenarios for the future of one or more of those areas. Or they could research past forecasts made for our own times to see if they actually occurred. Or they might develop recommendations for the future of their local communities in areas such as population, health, recreation, transportation, conservation, and so on. Or they could study the effects of aging on facial features to imagine how they might look when they are older.

Now, it does not take much more than a cursory reading of those examples to see how the young people involved in them would be engaged with an enormous range of knowledge, from information to values, and including content and skills from several disciplines of knowledge. Yet in the process of describing activities to address various concepts, I did not categorize them by various subject areas. Instead, knowledge was integrated in the context of the "environment" and "future" themes and the activities within them. In those contexts, moreover, knowledge took on an immediate importance and purpose. In this case, the answer to the usual student questions about why certain skills or concepts have to be learned is not "to prepare for some future" but to do what needs to be done *now*.

This classroom scenario has several distinguishing features. Its organizing centers are significant problems or issues that connect the school curriculum with the larger world. The organizing centers serve as a context for unifying knowledge. Knowledge, in turn, is developed as it is instrumentally applied to exploring the organizing centers. So organized, the curriculum and the knowledge it engages are more accessible and meaningful for young people and thus more likely to help them expand their understanding of themselves and their world. Of course, all curriculum designs claim to create connections of some kind or another—with the past, with the community, across subjects, and so on. But here is a curriculum design that seeks connections in all directions, and because of that special kind of unity, it is given the name *curriculum integration*.

Philosophers and educators have always been concerned with "integration" inasmuch as that term connotes the tension involved in part-whole relationships. In the 1800s the idea of integration in relation to schools was focused on the school's role in promoting social unity, or "social integration," especially as the idea of common, public schools gained ascendance. In the late 1800s, followers of the German educator Johann Herbart developed ideas about correlation of subjects that were sometimes referred to as "integration of studies." By the mid-1920s, however, "integration" had assumed a new meaning as organismic, and Gestalt psychologists had introduced the concept of an integrated personality and described processes by which people supposedly sought unity among their behaviors and values, between self and environment, and so on. It was this meaning of "integration," explored in a 1927 dissertation by Meredith Smith, that helped shape a crucial question: *Are certain curriculum organizations or approaches more likely than others to assist young people with the processes of personal and social integration*? Responses to that question took three directions.

One response suggested that the process of integration would be facilitated by a child-centered curriculum that drew its direction and organization from the child's interests, experiences, and "development." One example of this was the "activity curriculum" in which children were encouraged to draw their own conclusions from activities that involved observation, hands-on experimentation, and the like (Kilpatrick, 1934). Another was the "experience curriculum" in which teachers and students cooperatively planned activities around real-life situations with skills and concepts learned from carrying out the activities (Hopkins, 1941). Advocates claimed that these approaches aided integration by their focus on the students' own ways of organizing their ideas and experiences.

They also insisted that integration was something that people must do for themselves. For this reason they advised that the term not be used in relation to adult efforts to reorganize school subjects. Nevertheless, another response came from educators who were already interested in correlations across various subject areas and who often referred to those correlations as an "integrated curriculum." This response suggested that students were more likely to learn subject matter if it was organized into generalized concepts that cut across the fragmenting boundaries of separate subjects. So, for example, two subjects might be brought together in a "broad-fields approach" course such as humanities, skills might be reinforced across two subjects such as science and mathematics, or fragmented parts of a discipline might be "fused" to form a broad subject such as social studies (Hopkins, 1941).

Still another response to the question about integration and curriculum came from those progressives whose interests were focused on social issues and the concept of social integration. These educators supported the idea of personal integration and creative individuality but saw them as aspects of a democratic society rather than ends in themselves. Thus they questioned whether a completely child-centered curriculum would be truly integrative if it focused only on the individual process of integration and did not explicitly address the process of social integration. After all, the argument went, schools were supposed to be concerned with social improvement and the common good. Moreover, the "real life" with which the curriculum was supposed to correspond involves social as well as personal concerns (DeBoer, 1936). With a focus on social issues, advocates of this response framed what one called "the democratic integration process" by which the process of organizing experience and knowledge around social issues and situations might be done by groups as well as individuals (Cary, 1937). Thus the term *integration*, usually associated with psychology and knowledge organization, was also part of the movement for democratic education, including the popular problem-centered "core" curriculum (Rugg, 1936, 1939; Hopkins, 1941; Macdonald, 1971).

Given the treatment of curriculum integration in recent literature, speeches, and workshops, some people might find this brief historical sketch surprising. Current talk about curriculum integration is almost completely historical, suggesting alternately that it is rooted in reforms of the 1960s or that it is a recent "fad" that began in the late 1980s. Furthermore, the same current talk almost always implies that curriculum integration is simply a matter of rearranging lesson plans as overlaps among subject areas are identified. Neither interpretation is true, of course, but the fact that both are widely believed has seriously limited discussions about curriculum integration and the scope of its use in schools.

DIMENSIONS OF CURRICULUM INTEGRATION

As it is meant to be, curriculum integration involves four major aspects: the integration of experiences, social integration, the integration of knowledge, and integration as a curriculum design. By looking inside each of these, it is possible to imagine how all are brought together—"integrated," as it were—in a comprehensive theory of curriculum integration that is more significant and promising than the curriculum arrangements that are incorrectly identified as "integration" in too many current discussions.

Integration of Experiences

The ideas that people have about themselves and their world—their perceptions, beliefs, values, and so on—are constructed out of their experiences. What we learn from reflecting on our experiences becomes a resource for dealing with problems, issues, and other situations, both personal and social, as they arise in the future. These experiences, and the schemes of meaning we construct out of them, do not simply sit in our minds as static, hardened categories. Instead they are fluid and dynamic meanings that may be organized one way for dealing with one issue, another way for a second issue, and so on. This kind of learning involves having constructive, reflective experiences that not only broaden and deepen our present understandings of ourselves and our world but that also are "learned" in such a way that they may be carried forward and put to use in new situations (Dressel, 1958). In short, what I will call *integrative learning* involves experiences that literally become part of us—unforgettable learning experiences. Such learning involves integration in two ways: first, as new experiences are "integrated" into our schemes of meaning and, second, as we organize or "integrate" past experience to help us in new problem situations.

The crucial issue with regard to this theory is, of course, how to organize curriculum experiences and the knowledge they engage in such a way that young people may most easily integrate them into their schemes of meaning and carry them forward. Iran-Nejad, McKeachie, and Berliner (1990) suggest that too many educators believe that "simplification" of (or access to) knowledge is best achieved by presenting it in small bits and pieces. But a growing body of research suggests that access is most likely through "integration" of details, that is, by organizing through "whole ideas." They put it this way:

> The more meaningful, the more deeply or elaboratively processed, the more situated in context, and the more rooted in cultural, background, meta-cognitive, and personal knowledge an event is, the more readily it is understood, learned, and remembered. (p. 511)

In too many cases, the notion of learning that schools seem to promote is quite different from this. Instead of seeking meaningful integration of experience and knowledge, both are treated as a kind of "capital" for accumulation and cultural ornamentation. Knowledge is dispensed with the idea that it is to be stored away for future use, either to hand back in the form of test answers or displayed when the occasion suggests. If this seems too harsh, how else do we explain the responses young people get when they say, "Why do we have to learn this?" "Because you will need it for the test," their teachers reply. Or "for next year." Or, depending on the moment, "for college or middle school, or high school, or work." Or "You'll find out later in life." Dewey (1938), whose concept of experience and education the theory of integration follows, put the matter this way:

> Almost everyone has had occasion to look back upon his school days and wonder what has become of the knowledge he was supposed to have amassed during his years of schooling … but it was so segregated when it was acquired and hence is so disconnected from the rest of experience that it is not available under the actual conditions of life. (p. 48)

Social Integration

Among the important purposes for schools in a democratic society is that of providing common or shared educational experiences for young people with diverse characteristics and backgrounds. The idea of such experiences has long been tied to the concept of integration through emphasis on a curriculum that promotes some sense of common values or a "common good" (Smith, 1927; Childs & Dewey, 1933; Rugg, 1936; Hopkins, 1941; Hanna, 1946; Beane, 1980). The portion of the school program devoted to this purpose of "social integration" has often been referred to as "general education" because it is meant for all young people regardless of background or aspirations. It is this general education that is the site of debates over what ought to be required of all students or what all young people should "know."

While most people seem to think general education should amount to a collection of required subjects, many educators and activists committed to social reform have called for other types of arrangements. Most prominent among these has been a curriculum organized around personal and social issues, collaboratively planned and carried out by teachers and students together, and committed to the integration of knowledge. These kinds of arrangements are promoted not simply because they make knowledge more accessible for young people but because they help to create democratic classroom settings as a context for social integration.

For example, the use of a problem-centered curriculum follows from the idea that the democratic way of life involves collaborative work on common social issues. The participation of young people in curriculum planning follows from the democratic concept of participatory, collaborative governance and decision making. The inclusion of personal issues alongside social problems follows from the democratic possibility of integrating self and social interest. And, as we will soon see, the integration of knowledge follows from the idea of the democratic use of knowledge as an instrument for intelligent problem solving (B. Smith, Stanley, & Shores, 1950).

No doubt some would argue that ideas like social integration are simply an anachronism among the late-twentieth-century identity movements that seem to defy the very concept of shared educational experiences. Setting aside the fact that progressive visions of general education recognized that individuals would take away different meanings from a common experience, that argument would imply that social integration and the related idea of democratic schools were once tried on a large scale but eventually became irrelevant. The sad fact is that both social integration and democratic practice have largely eluded the schools. Worse yet, the schools and their traditional curriculum organization have too often been among the persistent sources of inequity and "disintegration" found across the whole society.

However, it is possible to identify both past and present examples of democratic schools in action. Not surprisingly, these accounts almost always involve the concept of social integration (usually in the form of attempts at developing "classroom communities"), the integration of school and community life, and the use of problem-centered, integrative curriculum designs (e.g., Apple & Beane, 1995; Wood, 1992; Zapf, 1959). It is in this context of democratic social integration that we see the most powerful use of the concept of curriculum integration. Yet that context is rarely included in popular talk about curriculum integration today. This is not really surprising given the nearly complete lack of historical grounding in such talk or the fact that attempts at democratic social integration are more complicated than prepackaged "integrated units" and certainly more dangerous politically.

Integration of Knowledge

When used in relation to curriculum, *integration* also refers to a theory of the organization and uses of knowledge. Imagine for the moment that we are confronted with some problem or puzzling situation in our lives. How do we approach the situation? Do we stop and ask ourselves which part of the situation is language arts, or music, or mathematics, or history, or art? I don't think so. Instead we take on the problem or situation using whatever knowledge is appropriate or pertinent without regard for subject-area lines. And if the problem or situation is significant enough to us, we are willing and anxious to seek out needed knowledge that we do not already have. In this way, we come to understand and use knowledge not in terms of the differentiated compartments by which it is labeled in school, but rather as it is "integrated" in the context of the real problems and issues.

The isolation and fragmentation of knowledge is part of the deep structures of schooling. This is evident in the subject-specific curriculum documents, schedules, and other artifacts of middle and high schools and in the separate subject/skill schedule in so many elementary school classrooms. This latter point is important because it is too often assumed that the elementary school curriculum is not as subject-defined as that of the middle and high schools. Yet the structure of a self-contained elementary school classroom, like the structure of "interdisciplinary" teams in middle and high schools, too often hides a schedule in which the first hour is for language arts, the second for arithmetic, the third for another area, and so on.

When the integration of knowledge is advocated in schools, it is usually argued on grounds that it makes knowledge more accessible or more meaningful by bringing it out of separate subject compartments and placing it in contexts that will supposedly make more sense to young people. As we have already seen, a growing body of research evidence suggests that such "contextualizing" of knowledge does make it more accessible, especially when those contexts are linked to the life experiences of young people. Important as this is, however, it is not the only argument for the integration of knowledge in curriculum organization.

Knowledge is a dynamic instrument for individuals and groups to use in approaching issues in their lives. In that sense knowledge is a kind of power, since it helps give people some measure of control over their own lives. When knowledge is seen simply as a collection of bits and pieces of information and skill organized by separate subjects or disciplines of knowledge, its uses and its power are confined by their boundaries and thus diminished. For example, the definition of problems and the means of addressing them are limited to what is known and deemed problematic within a particular subject or discipline. When we understand knowledge as integrated, we are free to define problems as broadly as they are in real life and to use a wide range of knowledge to address them.

Moreover, as I will argue more fully later, one among many criticisms of the separate-subject approach is that it largely includes only the knowledge that reflects the interests of high-culture social and academic elites. Since the separate-subject division of knowledge focuses only on topics within the subjects themselves, other kinds of issues and knowledge are prevented from entering into the planned curriculum (Bernstein, 1975). On the other hand, when we organize the curriculum around self and social issues and draw upon knowledge that is relevant to those issues, knowledge that is part of everyday life as well as what is often called "popular culture" also enter the curriculum. The addition of everyday and popular knowledge not only brings new meanings to the curriculum but also fresh viewpoints, since it frequently reflects interests and understandings of a broader spectrum of the society than do the school subjects.

When what counts for worthwhile knowledge is confined to that annointed by scholars in academic disciplines and others of the dominant culture, organized in ways that are convenient to them, and presented as a kind of "capital" accumulated for some future time or for cultural ornamentation, two things happen. First, young people are led to believe that important knowledge is abstract from their lives. Second, they are deprived of the possibility of learning to organize and use knowledge in relation to issues that concern them. Educators thus become implicated in an education that is not only narrow and incomplete, but unethical.

Thinking in this way about the integration of knowledge and its uses as an instrument for addressing real problems is one sign of a deeper meaning behind the idea of curriculum integration, namely, its possibilities for helping to bring democracy to life in schools (Bellack & Kliebard, 1971; Apple & Beane, 1995). While the idea of democratic schools is usually taken only to mean the use of participatory decision making, its extended meaning includes attending to the issues, problems, and concerns that confront the larger democratic society. This aspect of the democratic way of life involves the right, obligation, and power of people to seek intelligent solutions to the problems that face them, individually and collectively. And for this purpose, the integration of knowledge is especially suited.

Integration as a Curriculum Design

The fourth way in which the term *integration* is used is to refer to a particular kind of curriculum design. As we saw earlier, the design named "curriculum integration" has several features that, when taken together, distinguish it from other approaches. First, the curriculum is organized around problems and issues that are of personal and social significance in the real world. Second, learning experiences in relation to the organizing center are planned so as to integrate pertinent knowledge in the context of the organizing centers. Third, knowledge is developed and used to address the organizing center currently under study rather than to prepare for some later test or grade level. Finally, emphasis is placed on substantive projects and other activities that involve real application of knowledge, thus increasing the possibility for young people to integrate curriculum experiences into their schemes of meaning *and* to experience the democratic process of problem solving.

To these features, I would now add one more that has long been associated with the concept of integration in the curriculum, namely, the participation of students in curriculum planning (e.g., Hopkins, 1941). If integrative learning is a serious intention, it is important to know how young people might frame the issues and concerns that are used to organize the curriculum as well as what experiences they believe might help them learn. It is hard to imagine how adults might find about how any particular group of young people view these matters without somehow consulting them directly. Just as importantly, since curriculum integration is tied to the larger concept of democratic education, the matter of student participation in planning their own experiences must eventually become a crucial aspect of the design.

This definition of curriculum integration as a curriculum design may surprise some educators who, in workshops and professional literature, have seen the term applied generically to any approach beyond the strict separate-subject curriculum. Unfortunately, such confusion over terminology has surrounded the concept of integration in the curriculum since the 1930s and, as we shall see next, continues today.

ELSEWHERE BEYOND THE SEPARATE SUBJECTS

In the present round of interest in curriculum integration, two issues not only confuse its meaning but also threaten to undermine its use in schools. The first is the misapplication of the term *integration* to what is actually a "multidisciplinary" curriculum. The second is confusion over the sources of organizing centers or themes that are used in curriculum integration.

Multidisciplinary and Other Approaches

Curriculum integration is obviously quite different from the separate-subject approach that has dominated schools for so long. It is also different from other arrangements and designs that are, to some extent, beyond the strict separate-subject approach and to which the term *curriculum integration* is often misapplied. For example, the term has been used in attempts at reassembling fragmented pieces of a discipline of knowledge, such as creating social studies out of history and geography or whole language out of fragmented language arts. It has also been used with regard to addressing things such as thinking, writing, and valuing across subject areas. One might argue semantically that the word *integration* is technically acceptable in these situations, but this is clearly not what has been meant historically by "curriculum integration."

Another way in which the term *integration* is used is in relation to "the integrated day," a method used in some British primary schools since the 1960s (Jacobs, 1989). In this case, children are given a say in the order of events during the schoolday and the amount of time devoted to each. However, as Paul Hirst (1974) pointed out:

> That pupils plan how long they devote to something and the sequence of things they will do is perfectly compatible with a highly subject structured curriculum. An integrated day may, or equally may not, involve an integrated curriculum. (p. 133)

Those uses aside, the greatest confusion has to do with a very different curriculum design that is often, and mistakenly, labeled as "curriculum integration" but would more accurately be called "multidisciplinary" or "multisubject." One way of illustrating the difference between these approaches is to contrast the ways in which they are planned. In curriculum integration, planning begins with a central theme and proceeds outward through identification of big ideas or concepts related to the theme and activities that might be used to explore them. This planning is done without regard for subject-area lines since the overriding purpose is to explore the theme itself. In a multidisciplinary or multisubject approach, planning begins with recognition of the identities of various subjects as well as important content and skills that are to be mastered within them. A theme is then identified (often from within one or another subject) and approached through the question, "What can each subject contribute to the theme?" In this way, the identities of the separate subjects are retained in the selection of content to be used, and students still rotate from one subject to another as content and/ or skills from each are correlated to the theme. Moreover, though the subjects are taught in relation to the theme, the overriding purpose is still the mastery of content and skills from the subjects involved. In this sense, the theme is really a secondary matter.

The fact is that the multidisciplinary approach to curriculum is really not very far removed from the separate-subject one. Again, even as planning around an organizing center proceeds, the identities of the separate subjects are retained (J. H. Young, 1991/ 1992). And as multidisciplinary units are carried out, students still experience a daily round of separate subjects in which the teachers more or less attempt to relate subject areas to the organizing center. This is very different from curriculum integration, in which students move from one activity or project to another, each one involving knowledge from multiple sources. But more than this, the two approaches, multidisciplinary and integration, are distinguished by deeper differences. Like the separate-subject approach, the multidisciplinary one still begins and ends with the subject-based content and skills while curriculum integration begins and ends with the problem- and issue-centered organizing centers (Bellack & Kliebard, 1971). Along the way, these organizing centers also contextualize knowledge and give it significant purpose. Because the multidisciplinary approach begins with content and skills, knowledge is fixed in predetermined sequences, while integration recognizes external knowledge but sequences it by relevance to the problem at hand.

Distinguishing between curriculum integration and multidisciplinary arrangements is not merely a semantic game; in fact, it is crucial for a very practical reason. Since curriculum designs beyond the separate-subject approach are so unfamiliar to most people, including most teachers, it is important that they understand the fullest range of alternatives. If multi-disciplinary arrangements are mistakenly named as "curriculum integration," then the discussion of alternatives may stop before the possibility of real curriculum integration is made known. As discussions about curriculum organization develop and labels multiply, a pretty reliable way to figure which is which is to check for the root word *discipline*, which refers to the differentiated categories of knowledge that subjects represent. Where that root word is used—*multidisciplinary, interdisciplinary, cross-disciplinary,* and so on—something other than curriculum integration, usually a realignment of the existing subjects, is almost always intended.

I do not want to demean the multidisciplinary approach to curriculum here. In fact, its use has brought dramatic progress in many schools. As teachers have carried out multidisciplinary units, they have been more likely to use culminating activities that are project-centered and that call for the use of knowledge from all subject areas involved. In planning such units, teachers of different subjects frequently discover that they cover common skills and concepts. This often leads to simultaneous teaching of those skills and concepts in the subjects involved and the use of common assignments to show students connections between subjects. Since any such connections are likely to help students to some extent, multidisciplinary discussions across different subjects are very important. And in most middle and high schools where teachers in different subject departments often barely know each other, such discussions are nothing short of miraculous (Siskin & little, 1995; National Association of Secondary School Principals, 1996).

It is worth noting that subject-loyal teachers frequently rebel more over contrived use of their areas in multidisciplinary arrangements than over the prospect of a real integration of knowledge. This is probably due to the fact that multidisciplinary arrangements retain the identities of subjects and, therefore, imply no changes in content coverage or sequence. In moving away from subject identities, the idea of really integrating knowledge reduces the need for contrived arrangements. As Dewey (1900/1915) advised:

> All studies grow out of relations in the one great common world. When the child lives in varied but concrete and active relationship to this common world, his studies are naturally unified. It will no longer be a problem to correlate studies. The teacher will not have to resort to all sorts of devices to weave a little arithmetic into the history lesson, and the like. Relate the school to life, and all studies are of necessity correlated. (p. 32)

Understanding these differences may also help us to clarify another issue in current discussions about alternatives to the separate-subject approach. I refer here to popular attempts to describe many alternatives, each with its own finely shaded description. This proliferation of "types," usually set along a continuum, has in some ways overly complicated the field. Beyond that deeply structured, separate-subject design, the crucial question is this: As we create new designs, will we or won't we attempt to retain the identity of the separate subjects? If yes, then the resulting design will be multidisciplinary. If no, if we are willing to let go of those distinctions, we may find our way to curriculum integration. While there may be many shades and variations within them, when it comes to the fate of subject matter, there really are but these two alternatives.

Organizing Centers

As interest in alternatives to the strict separate-subject approach has grown, it has become fashionable to claim that "Our school is using a thematic approach." While this may seem like a good thing on the face of it, such a claim raises the question of where the themes come from and how they are identified. The fact is that there are several sources of curriculum organizing centers beyond the separate subjects, and in the matter of integration, some are more promising than others.

One source of organizing centers is topics that are already contained within the separate subjects and covered in that approach to curriculum. Here, for example, are such topics as "Colonial Living," "Metrics," "Transportation," "Myths and Legends," or "The Middle Ages." The use of topics from within the existing curriculum, particularly historical periods, has been prominent at the elementary and middle school levels for years and is now of growing interest to high school educators. Obviously such organizing centers are popular largely because of their familiarity and the implication that the usual content will still be covered.

Another source is social problems or issues, such as "Conflict," "The Environment," "Living in the Future," or "Education." Social problems have been used as organizing centers by progressive educators for years, but others often shy away from them because such themes shift the focus from covering content to solving problems and because they may seem controversial in the conservative context of many schools.

A third source is the issues and concerns of young people themselves, including such issues as "Getting Along With Peers," "Life in School," "Choosing a Personal Future," or "Who Am I?" The concerns of young people are often used as organizing centers for set-aside arrangements of "affective education," such as advisory programs. This is at least partly because many educators simply cannot imagine that the agendas of young people themselves could or should have a place at the center of the curriculum.

A fourth source is what we might call "appealing topics," such as "Dinosaurs," "Apples," or "Teddy Bears." Topics like these have been popular at the elementary school level and to some extent in middle schools, and they usually involve projects and other interesting activities. However, the use of this source always raises two questions. One has to do with whether such topics have enough significance to warrant the amount of time devoted to them (Edelsky, Altmeyer, & Flores, 1991). The other question concerns to whom, exactly, the topics are supposed to be "appealing," the students or the teacher. One case to which this question might apply, for example, is the currently popular use of the 1960s as a theme, a decade in which many of today's teachers just happened to have spent their own adolescence.

A fifth source is process-oriented concepts, such as "Change," "Systems," or "Cycles." These concepts are different from the other sources in that they are about processes that apply to virtually everything rather than about a particular topic. This source of themes is somewhat puzzling since curriculum organizing centers are intended to provide students with concrete unity and coherence. Perhaps it is the fact that process concepts seem to apply to everything that makes them popular among those seeking a way to invite colleagues beyond the separate-subject approach. This may also be why they are most often used in relation to multidisciplinary arrangements. The problem with process-oriented concepts is that in applying to almost everything, they are not about anything in particular. For this reason they might be useful as strands within more concrete themes, but not as themes themselves.

Any of these types of organizing centers can be used with either a multidisciplinary approach or curriculum integration, *if we define the latter simply as a matter of disregarding subject-area lines in planning.* However, if we understand curriculum integration in terms of its larger meaning and implications, then the concerns of young people and social issues emerge as the sources most clearly tied to integration. After all, personal and social concerns are quite literally the "stuff" of life and likely to be the organizing schemes young people already use for knowledge and experience. Thus the familiarity and recurrence of such organizing centers may make "integration" all the more probable and meaningful. As Dressel (1958) suggested:

> Perhaps the extent to which a student perceives his own personal pattern of educational experiences as interrelated among themselves and as related to the problems and experiences presently and probably to be engaged in outside of school has more to do with the encouragement of integrative growth than any other single factor. (p. 21)

In the end, organizing centers that are not related to significant self and social issues may be interesting, fun, exciting, and even likely contexts for correlating separate-subject content, but they will not do if we really mean to engage in curriculum integration. William Smith (1935) put the whole matter this way:

> In order to be real, a learning situation must meet cenain conditions: (1) It must revolve about problems which are germane to youth; (2) it must be concerned with vital and crucial aspects to the world in which youth is learning to live; and (3) it must call for dynamic and creative behavior on the part of the learner. A sound curriculum would thus consist of a succession of natural and vital units of experience, each centering about a real problem, each drawing upon subject-matter as needed, irrespective of boundary lines, and each eventuating in growth in capacity to live. The development of such a curriculum obviously calls for more than bringing subjects together into friendly relations under one teacher or, by way of so-called correlation, under several teachers. The essence of integration lies in the use of subject-matter by the learner rather than by teachers. It is a dynamic and creative process. (p. 270)

THE CURRENT INTEREST

The 1990s have been marked by a renewed interest in curriculum integration. Why this is so is a matter of some curiosity, especially since the general mood of this era is decidedly not in the direction of a progressive movement such as the one in which curriculum integration was initiated. However, a number of factors have converged to give the idea of integration some serious momentum.

First among these factors is growing support for curriculum arrangements that involve application of knowledge rather than merely memorization and accumulation. The move away from simple accumulation has support among a somewhat odd mix of advocates, including educators disenchanted with low-level learning and bored students, business leaders interested in applied knowledge skills such as problem solving, various groups calling for higher standards and more challenging content, and evaluation specialists concerned about authentic assessment.

A second factor is interest in new ideas about how the brain supposedly functions in learning. According to widely reported research, the brain processes information through patterns and connections with an emphasis on coherence rather than fragmentation (Macdonald, 1971; Caine & Caine, 1991; Sylwester, 1995). Those who advocate integration from this research claim that the more knowledge is unified, the more it is "brain-compatible" and, therefore, more accessible for learning. Interestingly, in the 1930s round of interest in integration, Hopkins (1941) and others warned that there could be no guarantee that any organization of knowledge by adults would necessarily be compatible with the integrative processes of young people. The new research suggests that this earlier admonition may have been somewhat overstated in that even correlation alone seems to make knowledge more accessible for students.

A third factor is the emerging sense that knowledge is neither fixed nor universal. I refer here to the postmodern and poststructural fascination with multiple meanings of language and action, and with the idea that knowledge is socially constructed. In the late twentieth century, it is getting increasingly hard to think of an answer to the question of what knowledge is of most worth when nothing is more certain than uncertainty, when yesterday's truth is repealed by today's discovery, which, in turn, is clearly in danger of tomorrow's breakthrough. As a curriculum approach that made its living off the claim of having all the answers (and the right questions), the separate-subject approach has never been on shakier epistemological grounds.

Related to this third factor is the recognition among a growing number of scholars that problems of real significance cannot be solved out of a single discipline of knowledge and, therefore, that it is increasingly necessary to look at the world across disciplines (Klein, 1990). For example, how is it that problems in the environment, in human relations, in medical ethics, and so on can be resolved by work within a single area? The answer is that they cannot. And what is the sense of having a curriculum that acts as though such problems are not on the minds of the young or that their consideration must begin with mastering a smattering of isolated facts from different subject areas rather than with the problems themselves.

A fourth factor is the continuing presence of those educators who maintain a serious interest in progressive educational ideas. This group would include, for example, advocates of "whole-learning" arrangements, such as whole language, unit teaching, thematic curriculum, and problem- and project-centered methods. It would also include those who recognize the social problem focus and the instrumental uses of knowledge in curriculum integration as an aspect of democratic education (Apple & Beane, 1995). And, too, it would include representatives of subject-area associations and projects, including in mathematics and science, who have called for ending fragmentation within their areas and connecting them to larger problems and issues.

In naming this collection of supportive factors, I am not claiming that all individuals or groups associated with any one of them support curriculum integration as I have described it. For example, the attitudes and skills that business leaders want schools to promote may fit well with the applied knowledge and project aspects of curriculum integration but not necessarily with ideas like the critical use of knowledge or the emphasis on economic equity within democratic social integration. Similarly, the concept of democratic social integration is likely to be entirely distasteful for those postmodernists who would argue that democracy is about difference rather than unity. As a collection, however, those supportive factors generally contribute to a climate in which it is possible for those who are interested in real curriculum integration to pursue their work. Moreover, the fact that there are multiple sources of support means that there may be many positions from which people will find their way to curriculum integration.

Ironically, many educators today like to speak of change in terms of "paradigm shifts" they have made or are trying to make. Such shifts most often seem to involve things like changing the school schedule, more sharply defining outcomes of schooling, or coming up with new methods of assessment. I understand the meaning of paradigm shift to entail a change in viewpoint so fundamental that much of what is currently taken for granted is now called into question or rendered irrelevant or wrong (Kuhn, 1962). So defined, it is hard to take the kinds of changes just mentioned as paradigm shifts. These, like most of the changes usually associated with "restructuring," ask only about "how" we do things and leave alone more fundamental questions about "what" we do and "why."

Curriculum integration centers the curriculum on life itself rather than on the mastery of fragmented information within the boundaries of subject areas. It works off a view of learning as the continuous integration of new knowledge and experience so as to deepen and broaden our understanding of ourselves and our world. Its focus is on life as it is lived now rather than on preparation for some later life or level of schooling. It serves the young people for whom the curriculum is intended rather than the specialized interests of adults. It concerns the active analysis and construction of meanings rather than merely assuming the validity of others' meanings. And it brings the idea of democracy to life through its problem-centered focus, its uses of knowledge, and its participatory framing. Described this way, curriculum integration involves something more like a real paradigm shift than what has usually passed for such.

REFERENCES

Apple, Michael W., & Beane, James A. (Eds.). (1995). *Democratic schools.* Alexandria, VA: Association for Supervision and Curriculum Development.

Beane, James A. (1980). The general education we need. *Educational Leadership, 37*(4), 307–308.

Bellack, Arno A., & Kliebard, Herbert M. (1971), Curriculum for integration of disciplines. In Lee C. Deighton (Ed.), *The encyclopedia of education* (pp. 585–590). New York: Macmillan.

Bernstein, Basil. (1975). *Class, codes, and control: Vol. 3. Towards a theory of educational transmissions* (2nd ed.) London: Routledge & Kegan Paul.

Caine, Renata, & Caine, Geoffrey. (1991). *Teaching and the human brain.* Alexandria, VA: Association for Supervision and Curriculum Development.

Cary, M. E. (1937). *Integration and the high school curriculum.* Unpublished doctoral dissertation, Ohio State University, Columbus.

Childs, John L., & Dewey, John. (1933). The social-economic situation and education. In William H. Kilpatrick et al., *The educational frontier* (pp. 32–72). New York: Century.

DeBoer, Jon. J. (1936). Integration: A return to first principles. *School and Society, 43,* 246–253.

Dewey, John. (1915). *The school and society* (rev. ed.). Chicago: University of Chicago Press. (Original work published 1900).

Dewey, John. (1938). *Experience and education.* Bloomington, IN: Kappa Delta Pi.

Dressel, Paul L. (1958). The meaning and significance of integration. In Nelson B. Henry (Ed.), *The integration of educational experiences,* 57th Yearbook of the National Society for the Study of Education, Part II (pp. 3–25). Chicago: University of Chicago Press.

Edelsky. Carole, Altmeyer, Bess, & Flores, Barbara. (1991). *Whole language: What's the difference?* Portsmouth, NH: Heineman.

Hanna, Paul R. (1946). Education for the larger community. *Educational Leadership, 4*(2), 27–33.

Hirst, Paul. (1974). *Knowledge and the curriculum.* London: Routledge & Kegan Paul.

Hopkins, L. Thomas. (1941). *Interaction: The democratic process.* New York: Heath.

Iran-Nejad, Asghar, McKeachie, Wilbert J., & Berliner, David C. (1990). The multisource nature of learning: An introduction. *Review of Educational Research, 60,* 509–515.

Jacobs, Heidi Hayes (Ed.). (1989). *Interdisciplinary curriculum: Design and implementation.* Alexandria, VA: Association for Supervision and Curriculum Development.

Kilpatrick, William H. (1934). The essentials of the activity movement. *Progressive Education, 11,* 346–359.

Klein, Julie Thompson. (1990). *Interdisciplinarity: History, theory, and practice.* Detroit: Wayne State University Press.

Kuhn, Thomas S. (1962). *The structure of scientific revolutions.* Chicago: University of Chicago Press.

Macdonald, James B. (1971). Curriculum integration. In Lee C. Deighton (Ed.), *The encyclopedia of education* (pp. 590–593). New York: Macmillan.

National Association of Secondary School Principals. (1996). *Breaking ranks: Changing an American institution.* Reston, VA: Author.

Rugg, Harold. (1936). *American life and the school curriculum.* Boston: Ginn.

Rugg, Harold (Ed.). (1939). *Democracy and the curriculum.* 3rd Yearbook of the John Dewey Society. New York: Appleton-Century.

Siskin, Leslie Santee, & Little, Judith Warren. (1995). *The subjects in question: Departmental organization and the high school.* New York: Teachers College Press.

Smith, B. Othanel, Stanley, William O., & Shores, J. H. (1950). *Fundamentals of curriculum development.* New York: Harcourt, Brace, & World.

Smith, Meredith. (1927). *Education and the integration of behavior* (Contributions to Education, No. 261). New York, Teachers College, Columbia University.

Smith, William A. (1935). Integration: Potentially the most significant forward step in the history of secondary education. *California Journal of Secondary Education, 10,* 269–272.

Sylwester, Robert. (1995). *A celebration of neurons.* Alexandria, VA: Association for Supervision and Curriculum Development.

Wood, George H. (1992). *Schools that work.* New York: Dutton.

Young, Jean Helen. (1991/1992). Curriculum integration: Perceptions of pre-service teachers. *Action in Teacher Education, 13*(4), 1–9.

Zapf, Rosalind M. (1959). *Democratic processes in the classroom.* Englewood Cliffs, NJ: Prentice Hall.

27

Critical Pedagogy and the Social Construction of Knowledge

PETER MCLAREN

CRITICAL EDUCATIONAL THEORISTS view school knowledge as historically and socially rooted and interest bound. Knowledge acquired in school—or anywhere, for that matter—is never neutral or objective but is ordered and structured in particular ways; its emphases and exclusions partake of a silent logic. Knowledge is a *social construction* deeply rooted in a nexus of power relations. When critical theorists claim that knowledge is socially constructed, they mean that it is the product of agreement or consent between individuals who live out particular social relations (e.g., of class, race, and gender) and who live in particular junctures in time. To claim that knowledge is socially constructed usually means that the world we live in is constructed symbolically by the mind through social interaction with others and is heavily dependent on culture, context, custom, and historical specificity. There is no ideal, autonomous, pristine, or aboriginal world to which our social constructions necessarily correspond; there is always a referential field in which symbols are situated. And this particular referential field (e.g., language, culture, place, time) will influence how symbols generate meaning. There is no pure subjective insight. We do not stand *before* the social world; we live *in the midst* of it. As we seek the meaning of events we seek the meaning of the social. We can now raise certain questions with respect to the social construction of knowledge, such as: why do women and minorities often view social issues differently than white males? Why are teachers more likely to value the opinions of a middle-class white male student, for instance, than those of a black female?

Critical pedagogy asks how and why knowledge gets constructed the way it does, and how and why some constructions of reality are legitimated and celebrated by the dominant culture while others clearly are not. Critical pedagogy asks how our everyday commonsense understandings—our social constructions or "subjectivities"—get produced and lived out. In other words, what are the *social functions* of knowledge? The crucial factor here is that some forms of knowledge have more power and legitimacy than others. For instance, in many schools in the United States, science and math curricula are favored over the liberal arts. This can be explained by the link between the needs of big business to compete in world markets and the imperatives of the new reform movement to bring "excellence" back to the schools. Certain types of knowledge legitimate certain gender, class, and racial interests. Whose interests does this knowledge serve? Who gets excluded as a result? Who is marginalized?

Let's put this in the form of further questions: What is the relationship between social class and knowledge taught in school? Why do we value scientific knowledge over informal knowledge? Why do we have teachers using "standard English"? Why is the public still unlikely to vote for a woman or a black for president? How does school knowledge reinforce stereotypes about women, minorities, and disadvantaged peoples? What accounts for some knowledge having high status (as in the great works of philosophers or scientists) while the practical knowledge of ordinary people or marginalized or subjugated groups is often discredited and devalued? Why do we learn about the great 'men' in history and spend less time learning about the contributions of women and minorities and the struggles of people in lower economic classes? Why don't we learn more about the American labor movement? How and why are certain types of knowledge used to reinforce dominant ideologies, which in turn serve to mask unjust power relations among certain groups in society?

FORMS OF KNOWLEDGE

Critical pedagogy follows a distinction regarding forms of knowledge posited by the German social theorist Jürgen Habermas.[1] Let's examine this concept in the context of classroom teaching. Mainstream educators who work primarily within liberal and conservative educational ideologies emphasize technical knowledge (similar to Giroux's *productive knowledge*): Knowledge is that which can be measured and quantified. Technical knowledge is based on the natural sciences, uses hypothetico-deductive or empirical analytical methods, and is evaluated by, among other things, intelligence quotients, reading scores, and SAT results, all of which are used by educators to sort, regulate, and control students.

A second type, *practical knowledge*, aims to enlighten individuals so they can shape their daily actions in the world. Practical knowledge is generally acquired through *describing and analyzing social situations historically or developmentally*, and is geared toward helping individuals understand social events that are ongoing and situational. The liberal educational researcher who undertakes fieldwork in a school in order to evaluate student behavior and interaction acquires practical knowledge, for instance. This type of knowledge is not usually generated numerically or by submitting data to some kind of statistical instrument.

The critical educator, however, is most interested in what Habermas calls *emancipatory knowledge* (similar to Giroux's *directive knowledge*), which attempts to reconcile and transcend the opposition between technical and practical knowledge. Emancipatory knowledge helps us understand how social relationships are distorted and manipulated by relations of power and privilege. It also aims at creating the conditions under which irrationality, domination, and oppression can be overcome and transformed through deliberative, collective action. In short, it creates the foundation for social justice, equality, and empowerment.

CRITICAL PEDAGOGY AND THE POWER/KNOWLEDGE RELATION

Critical pedagogy is fundamentally concerned with understanding the relationship between power and knowledge. The dominant curriculum separates knowledge from the issue of power and treats it in an unabashedly technical manner; knowledge is seen in overwhelmingly instrumental terms as something to be mastered. That knowledge is always an ideological construction linked to particular interests and social relations generally receives little consideration in education programs.

The work of the French philosopher Michel Foucault is crucial in understanding the socially constructed nature of truth and its inscription in knowledge/power relations. Foucault's concept of "power/knowledge" extends the notion of power beyond its conventional use by philosophers and social theorists who, like American John Dewey, have understood power as "the sum of conditions available for bringing the desirable end into existence."[2] For Foucault, power comes from everywhere, from above and from below; it is "always already there" and is inextricably implicated in the micro-relations of domination and resistance.

DISCOURSE

Power relations are inscribed in what Foucault refers to as *discourse* or a family of concepts. Discourses are made up of discursive practices that he describes as

> a body of anonymous, historical rules, always determined in the time and space that have defined a given period, and for a given social, economic, geographical, or linguistic area, the conditions of operation of the enunciative function.[3]

Discursive practices, then, *refer to the rules by which discourses are formed, rules that govern what can be said and what must remain unsaid, who can speak with authority and who must listen.* Social and political institutions, such as schools and penal institutions, are governed by discursive practices.

> Discursive practices are not purely and simply ways of producing discourse. They are embodied in technical processes, in institutions, in patterns for general behavior, in forms of transmission and diffusion, and pedagogical forms which, at once, impose and maintain them.[4]

For education, discourse can be defined as a "regulated system of statements" that establish differences between fields and theories of teacher education; it is "not simply words but is embodied in the practice of institutions, patterns of behavior, and in forms of pedagogy."[5]

From this perspective, we can consider *dominant* discourses (those produced by the dominant culture) as "regimes of truth," as general economies of power/knowledge, or as multiple forms of constraint. In a classroom setting, dominant educational discourses determine what books we may use, what classroom approaches we should employ (mastery learning, Socratic method, etc.), and what values and beliefs we should transmit to our students.

For instance, neo-conservative discourses on language in the classroom would view working-class speech as undersocialized or deprived. Liberal discourse would view such speech as merely different. Similarly, to be culturally literate within a conservative discourse is to acquire basic information on American culture (dates of battles, passages of the Constitution, etc.). Conservative discourse focuses mostly on the works of "great men." A liberal discourse on cultural literacy includes knowledge generated from the perspective of women and minorities. A *critical* discourse focuses on the interests and assumptions that inform the generation of knowledge itself. A critical discourse is also self-critical and deconstructs dominant discourses the moment they are ready to achieve hegemony. A critical discourse can, for instance, explain how high status knowledge (the great works of the Western world) can be used to teach concepts that reinforce the status quo. Discourses and discursive practices influence how we live our lives as conscious thinking subjects. They shape our subjectivities (our ways of understanding in relation to the world) because it is only in language and through discourse that social reality can be given meaning. Not all discourses are given the same weight, as some will account for and justify the appropriateness of the status quo and others will provide a context for resisting social and institutional practices.[6]

This follows our earlier discussion that knowledge (truth) is socially constructed, culturally mediated, and historically situated. Cleo Cherryholmes suggests that "dominant discourses determine what counts are true, important, relevant, and what gets spoken. Discourses are generated and governed by rules and power."[7] Truth cannot be spoken in the absence of power relations, and each relation necessarily speaks its own truth. Foucault removes truth from the realm of the absolute; truth is understood only as changes in the determination of what can count as true.

> Truth is a thing of this world: it is produced only by virtue of multiple forms of constraint. And it induces regular effects of power. Each society has its regime of truth, its 'general politics' of truth: that is, the types of discourse which it accepts and makes function as true; the mechanisms and instances which enable one to distinguish true and false statements, the means by which each is sanctioned; the techniques and procedures accorded value in the acquisition of truth; the status of those who are charged with saying what counts as true.[8]

In Foucault's view, truth (educational truth, scientific truth, religious truth, legal truth, or whatever) must not be understood as a set of "discovered laws" that exist outside power/knowledge relations and which somehow correspond with the "real." We cannot "know" truth except through its "effects." Truth is not *relative* (in the sense of "truths" proclaimed by various individuals and societies are all equal in their effects) but is *relational* (statements considered "true" are dependent upon history, cultural context, and relations of power operative in a given society, discipline, institution, etc.). The crucial question here is that if truth is *relational* and not *absolute*, what criteria can we use to guide our actions in the world? Critical educators argue that *praxis* (informed actions) must be guided by *phronesis* (the disposition to act truly and rightly). This means, in critical terms, that actions and knowledge must be directed at eliminating pain, oppression, and inequality, and at promoting justice and freedom.

Lawrence Grossberg speaks to the critical perspective on truth and theory when he argues

> the truth of a theory can only be defined by its ability to intervene into, to give us a different and perhaps better ability to come to grips with, the relations that constitute its context. If neither history nor texts speak its own truth, truth has to be won; and it is, consequently, inseparable from relations of power.[9]

An understanding of the power/knowledge relationship raises important issues regarding what kinds of theories educators should work with and what knowledge they can provide in order to empower students. *Empowerment* means not only helping students to understand and engage the world around them, but also enabling them to exercise the kind of courage needed to change the social order where necessary. Teachers need to recognize that *power relations correspond to forms of school knowledge that distort understanding and produce what is commonly accepted as "truth."* Critical educators argue that knowledge should be analyzed on the basis of whether it is oppressive and exploitative, and not on the basis of whether it is "true." For example, what kind of knowledge do we construct about women and minority groups in school texts? Do the texts we use in class promote stereotypical views that reinforce racist, sexist, and patriarchal attitudes? How do we treat the knowledge that working-class students bring to class discussions and schoolwork? Do we unwittingly devalue such knowledge and thereby disconfirm the voices of these students?

Knowledge should be examined not only for the ways in which it might misrepresent or mediate social reality, but also for the ways in which it actually reflects the daily struggle of people's lives. We must understand that knowledge not only distorts reality, but also provides grounds for understanding the actual conditions that inform everyday life. Teachers, then, should examine knowledge both for the way it misrepresents or marginalizes particular views of the world and for the way it provides a deeper understanding of how the student's world is actually constructed. Knowledge acquired in classrooms should help students participate in vital issues that affect their experience on a daily level rather than simply enshrine the values of business pragmatism. School knowledge should have a more emancipatory goal than churning out workers (human capital) and helping schools become the citadel of corporate ideology.[10] School knowledge should help create the conditions productive for student self-determination in the larger society.

CRITICAL PEDAGOGY AND THE CURRICULUM

From the perspective of critical educational theorists, the curriculum represents much more than a program of study, a classroom text, or a course syllabus. Rather, it represents the *introduction to a particular form of life; it serves in part to prepare students for dominant or subordinate positions in the existing society.*[11] The curriculum favors certain forms of knowledge over others and affirms the dreams, desires, and values of select groups of students over other groups, often discriminatorily on the basis of race, class, and gender. In general, critical educational theorists are concerned with how descriptions, discussions, and representations in textbooks, curriculum materials, course content, and social relations embodied in classroom practices benefit dominant groups and exclude subordinate ones. In this regard, they often refer to the *hidden curriculum.*

THE HIDDEN CURRICULUM

The *hidden curriculum* refers to *the unintended outcomes of the schooling process.* Critical educators recognize that schools shape students both through standardized learning situations, and through other agendas including rules of conduct, classroom organization, and the informal pedagogical procedures used by teachers with specific groups of students.[12] The hidden curriculum also includes teaching and learning styles that are emphasized in the classroom, the messages that get transmitted to the student by the total physical and instructional environment, governance structures, teacher expectations, and grading procedures.

The hidden curriculum deals with the tacit ways in which knowledge and behavior get constructed, outside the usual course materials and formally scheduled lessons. It is a part of the bureaucratic and managerial "press" of the school—the combined forces by which students are induced to comply with dominant ideologies and social practices related to authority, behavior, and morality. Does the principal expel school offenders or just verbally upbraid them? Is the ethos of the office inviting or hostile? Do the administration and teachers show respect for each other and for the students on a regular basis? Answers to these questions help define the hidden curriculum, which refers then, to the *non-subject-related* sets of behaviors produced in students.

Often, the hidden curriculum displaces the professed educational ideals and goals of the classroom teacher or school. We know, for example, that teachers unconsciously give more intellectual attention, praise, and academic help to boys than to girls. A study reported in *Psychology Today* suggests that stereotypes of garrulous and gossipy women are so strong that when groups of administrators and teachers are shown films of classroom discussion and asked who is talking more, the teachers overwhelmingly chose the girls. In reality, however, the boys in the film "out talk" the girls at a ratio of three to one. The same study also suggests that teachers behave differently depending on whether boys or girls respond during classroom discussions. When boys call out comments without raising their hands, for instance, teachers generally accept their answers; girls, however, are reprimanded for the same behavior. The hidden message is "Boys should be academically aggressive while girls should remain composed and passive." In addition, teachers are twice as likely to give male students detailed instructions on how to do things for themselves; with female students, however, teachers are more likely to do the task for them instead. Not surprisingly, the boys are being taught independence and the girls dependency.[13]

Classroom sexism as a function of the hidden curriculum results in the unwitting and unintended granting of power and privilege to men over women and accounts for many of the following outcomes:

- Although girls start school ahead of boys in reading and basic computation, by the time they graduate from high school, boys have higher SAT scores in both areas.
- By high school, some girls are less committed to careers, although their grades and achievement-test scores may be as good as boys. Many girls' interests turn to marriage or stereotypically female jobs. Some women may feel that men disapprove of women using their intelligence.
- Girls are less likely to take math and science courses and to participate in special or gifted programs in these subjects, even if they have a talent for them. They are also more likely to believe that they are incapable of pursuing math and science in college and to avoid the subjects.
- Girls are more likely to attribute failure to internal factors, such as ability, rather than to external factors, such as luck.

The sexist communication game is played at work, as well as at school. As reported in numerous studies it goes like this:

- Men speak more often and frequently interrupt women.
- Listeners recall more from male speakers than from female speakers, even when both use a similar speaking style and cover identical content.

- Women participate less actively in conversation. They do more smiling and gazing; they're more often the passive bystanders in professional and social conversations among peers.
- Women often transform declarative statements into tentative comments. This is accomplished by using qualifiers ("kind of" or "I guess") and by adding tag questions ("This is a good movie, isn't it?"). These tentative patterns weaken impact and signal a lack of power and influence.[14]

Of course, most teachers try hard not to be sexist. The hidden curriculum continues to operate, however, despite what the overt curriculum prescribes. The hidden curriculum can be effectively compared to what Australian educator Doug White calls the *multinational curriculum*. For White,

> [T]he multinational curriculum is the curriculum of disembodied universals, of the mind as an information-processing machine, of concepts and skills without moral and social judgment but with enormous manipulative power. That curriculum proposed the elevation of abstract skills over particular content, of universal cognitive principles over the actual conditions of life.[15]

White reminds us that no curriculum, policy, or program is ideologically or politically innocent, and that the concept of the curriculum is inextricably related to issues of social class, culture, gender, and power. This is, of course, not the way curriculum is traditionally understood and discussed in teacher education. The hidden curriculum, then, refers to learning outcomes not openly acknowledged to learners. But we must remember that not all values, attitudes, or patterns of behavior that are by-products of the hidden curriculum in educational settings are necessarily bad. The point is to identify the structural and political assumptions upon which the hidden curriculum rests and to attempt to change the institutional arrangements of the classroom so as to offset the most undemocratic and oppressive outcomes.

CURRICULUM AS A FORM OF CULTURAL POLITICS

Critical educational theorists view curriculum as a form of *cultural politics*, that is, as a part of the sociocultural dimension of the schooling process. The term cultural politics permits the educational theorist to highlight the political consequences of interaction between teachers and students who come from dominant and subordinate cultures. To view the curriculum as a form of cultural politics *assumes that the social, cultural, political and economic dimensions are the primary categories for understanding contemporary schooling.*[16]

School life is understood not as a unitary, monolithic, and ironclad system of rules and regulations, but as a cultural terrain characterized by varying degrees of accommodation, contestation, and resistance. Furthermore, school life is understood as a plurality of conflicting languages and struggles, a place where classroom and street-corner cultures collide and where teachers, students, and school administrators often differ as to how school experiences and practices are to be defined and understood.

This curriculum perspective creates conditions for the student's self-empowerment as an active political and moral subject. I am using the term *empowerment* to refer to the process through which students learn to critically appropriate knowledge existing outside their immediate experience in order to broaden their understanding of themselves, the world, and the possibilities of transforming the taken-for-granted assumptions about the way we live. Stanley Aronowitz has described one aspect of empowerment as "the process of appreciating and loving oneself;"[17] empowerment is gained from knowledge and social relations that dignify one's own history, language, and cultural traditions. But empowerment means more than self-confirmation. It also refers to the process by which students learn to question and selectively appropriate those aspects of the dominant culture that will provide them with the basis for defining and transforming, rather than merely serving, the wider social order.

Basing a curriculum on cultural politics consists of linking critical social theory to a set of stipulated practices through which teachers can dismantle and critically examine dominant educational and cultural traditions. Many of these traditions have fallen prey to an *instrumental rationality* (a way of looking at the world in which "ends" are subordinated to questions of "means" and in which "facts" are separated from questions of "value") that either limits or ignores democratic ideals and principles. Critical theorists want particularly to develop a language of critique and demystification that can be used to analyze those latent interests and ideologies that work to socialize students in a manner compatible with the dominant culture. Of equal concern, however, is the creation of alternative teaching practices capable of empowering students both inside and outside of schools.

NOTES

1. See Jurgen Habermas, *Knowledge and Human Interests*, trans. J. J. Shapiro (London: Heinemann, 1972); see also Jurgen Habermas, *Theory and Practice*, trans. J. Viertel (London: Heinemann, 1974). As cited in Kemmis and Fitzclarence, *Curriculum Theorizing*, 70–72.
2. John Dewey, in J. Ratner (Ed.) *Intelligence in the Modern World. John Dewey's Philosophy* (New York: The Modern Library, 1939), 784. See also Michael Foucault *Power/Knowledge*, in C. Gordon (Ed.), (L. Marshall, J. Mepham, and K. Spoer, Trans.), *Selected Interviews and Other Writings 1972–77* (New York: Pantheon, 1980), 187.
3. Michael Foucault, *The Archaeology of Knowledge* (New York: Harper Colophon Books, 1972), 117.
4. Michael Foucault *Power/Knowledge*, in *Writings 1972–77* (New York: Pantheon, 1980), 200.
5. Richard Smith and Anna Zantiotis, "Teacher Education, Cultural Politics, and the Avant-Garde," in H. Giroux and P. McLaren (Eds.), *Schooling and the Politics of Culture* (Albany, NY: SUNY Press, in press), 123.
6. See Chris Weedon, *Feminist Practice and Post-Structuralist Theory* (Oxford: Basil-Blackwell, 1987).
7. Cleo Cherryholmes, "The Social Project of Curriculum: A Postructural Analysis," *American Journal of Education* (in press): 21.
8. Foucault, *Power/Knowledge*, 131.
9. Lawrence Grossberg, "History, Politics and Postmodernism: Stuart Hall and Cultural Studies," *Journal of Communication Inquiry* 10, 2 (1987): 73.
10. For more about the relationship of power and knowledge, see Kathy Borman and Joel Spring, *Schools in Central Cities* (New York: Longman, 1984); Henry Giroux, "Public Education and the Discourse of Possibility: Rethinking the New Conservative Left Educational Theory," *News for Teachers of Political Science* 44 (1985, Winter): 13–15.
11. See Doug White, "After the Divided Curriculum," *The Victorian Teacher* 7 (1983, March); Giroux and McLaren, "Teacher Education and the Politics of Engagement," 228.
12. See the wide range of articles in H. Giroux and D. Purple (Eds.), *The Hidden Curriculum and Moral Education: Deception or Discovery?* (Berkeley, CA: McCutchen Publishing Corp., 1983).
13. Myra Sadkev and David Sadkev, "Sexism in the Schoolroom of the 80's," *Psychology Today* (1985, March): 55–57.

14. Sadkev and Sadkev, "Sexism in the Schoolroom," 56–57. Also, the 1980 *Nova* television program, *The Pinks and the Blues* (WGBH, Boston), summarized by Anthony Wilden. "In the Penal Colony: The Body as the Discourse of the Other," *Semtiotica*, 54 1/2 (1985): 73–76.

15. White, "After the Divided Curriculum," 6–9.

16. Giroux and McLaren, "Teacher Education and the Politics of Engagement," 228–229.

17. Stanley Aronowitz, "Schooling, Popular Culture, and the Post-Industrial Society: Peter McLaren Interviews Stanley Aronowitz," *Orbit* (1986): 17, 18.

28

Social Class and School Knowledge

Jean Anyon

When Max Weber and Karl Marx suggested that there were identifiable and socially meaningful differences in the educational knowledge made available to literati and peasant, aristocrat and laborer, they were of course discussing earlier societies. Recent scholarship in political economy and sociology of knowledge has also argued, however, that in advanced industrial societies such as Canada and the U.S., where the class structure is relatively fluid, students of different social class backgrounds are still likely to be exposed to qualitatively different types of educational knowledge. Students from higher social class backgrounds may be exposed to legal, medical, or managerial knowledge, for example, while those of the working classes may be offered a more "practical" curriculum (e.g., clerical knowledge, vocational training) (Rosenbaum 1976; Karabel 1972; Bowles and Gintis 1976). It is said that such social class differences in secondary and postsecondary education are a conserving force in modern societies, an important aspect of the reproduction of unequal class structures (Karabel and Halsey 1977; Apple 1979; Young and Whitty 1977).

The present article examines data on school knowledge collected in a case study of five elementary schools in contrasting social class settings in two school districts in New Jersey. The data suggest, and the article will argue, that while there were similarities in curriculum topics and materials, there were also subtle as well as dramatic differences in the curriculum and the curriculum-in-use among the schools. The study reveals that even in an elementary school context, where there is fairly "standardized" curriculum, social stratification of knowledge is possible. The differences that were identified among the schools suggest as well that rather than being simply conserving or "reproductive," school knowledge embodies contradictions that have profound implications for social change. The reproductive and nonreproductive possibilities of school knowledge involve theoretical implications of the data and will be delineated after the data have been presented.

METHODOLOGY

Data on the nature and distribution of school knowledge were gathered in an investigation of curriculum, pedagogy, and pupil evaluation practices in five elementary schools differentiated by social class.[1] The methods used to gather data were classroom observation;

informal and formal interview of students, teachers, principals, and district administrative staff; and assessment of curriculum and other materials in each classroom and school. Classroom data to be reported here are drawn primarily from the fifth and second grades in each school. All schools but one departmentalize at the fifth-grade level, and with the exception of the school that does not, where only one fifth-grade teacher agreed to be observed, in all schools two or three fifth-grade teachers and two second-grade teachers were observed and interviewed. All but one of the teachers in the study had taught for more than four years. The fifth grade in each school was observed by the investigator for ten three-hour periods, and the second grade was observed for two three-hour periods. Formal interviews were carried out during lunchtime, and before and after school. Data were gathered between September 15, 1978, and June 20, 1979.

For purposes of this study, social class is considered as a series of relationships to several aspects of the process in society by which goods, services, and culture are produced. That is, while one's occupational status and income level contribute to one's social class, they do not define it. Contributing as well are one's relationships to the system of ownership of physical and cultural capital, to the structure of authority at work and in society, and to the content and process of one's own work activity. For example, members of the capitalist class participate in ownership of the apparatus of production in society, while many middle-class and most working-class persons do not; capitalists and affluent professional persons have more access to decision-making power in work institutions and in society than do many middle-class and most working-class people; capitalist and professional work activity often involves more creativity, conceptualization, and autonomy than do the jobs of most middle-class and working-class people in, say, civil service (the bureaucracy) or industry. One's relationships to all three of these aspects of production (to the systems of ownership and authority, and to work itself) determine one's social class. All three relationships are necessary and no single one is sufficient for determining a relation to the process of production in society.[2]

The terminology defining social classes and differentiating the schools in this study is to be understood in a technical sense, as reflected in the process by which the sample of schools was selected. Thus, the schools in this study were differentiated not only by income level as an indicator of parent access to capital, but also by the kind of *work* that characterized the majority of parents in each school.

The first three schools were in a medium-size city district in northern New Jersey, and the final two were in a nearby New Jersey suburban district. In each of three city schools, approximately 85% of the students were white. In the fourth school, 90% were white, and in the last school, all were white.

The first two schools are designated *working-class schools*, because the majority of the students' fathers (and approximately one-third of their mothers) were in unskilled or semiskilled occupations, with somewhat less than one-third of the fathers being skilled workers. Most family money incomes were at or below $12,000 during the period of the study, as were 38.6% of all U.S. families (U.S. Bureau of the Census 1979, p. 2, Table A). The third school is designated the *middle-class school*, although because of residence patterns the parents were a mixture of highly skilled, well-paid blue collar and white collar workers, as well as those with traditional middle-class occupations such as public school teachers, social workers, accountants, and middle-managers. There were also several local doctors and town merchants among the parents. Most family money incomes were between $13,000 and $25,000 during the period of the study, as were 38.9% of all U.S. families (U.S. Bureau of the Census 1979, p. 2, Table A).

The fourth school is designated the *affluent professional school,* because the bulk of the students' fathers were highly-paid doctors such as cardiologists; television or advertising executives; interior designers; or other affluent professionals. While there were a few families less affluent than the majority (e.g., the families of the superintendent of schools and of several professors at nearby universities, as well as several working-class families), there were also a few families who were more affluent. The majority of family money incomes were between $40,000 and $80,000 during the period of the study, as were approximately 7% of all U.S. families.[3]

The final school is called the *executive elite school.* The majority of pupils' fathers in this school were vice presidents or more advanced corporate executives in U.S. -based multinational corporations or financial firms on Wall Street. Most family money incomes were over $100,000 during the period of the study, as were less than 1% of U.S. families (see Smith and Franklin 1974).

SOCIAL CLASS AND SCHOOL KNOWLEDGE

There were several similarities in curriculum among the schools in this study. (Indeed, all schools were subject to the same state requirements). All schools used the same math textbook and series throughout the elementary grades (*Mathematics Around Us*, Scott Foresman, 1978). In language arts, both district courses of study included punctuation, sentence types and structure, grammar, and some writing exercises. In all fifth grades there was at least one box of an individualized reading program available; all classes had a basal reading series available, and two of the five schools (middle-class and executive elite) had the same basal reading series available in several grades of the school (*The Holt Basic Reading System,* Holt, Rinehart and Winston, 1977).

The schools did, however, use different social studies and science textbooks and materials, but there were several curriculum similarities among them. For example, all social studies books exhibited what I have called elsewhere "key ideas" in United States social studies content (Anyon 1979a): a positive and overtly stated valuing of American political democracy and freedom, American "progress," industry, and technology (see also Fox and Hess 1972; FitzGerald 1979; and Anyon 1978, 1979b). The natural science textbooks and program materials in both districts were similar in that they emphasized empirical investigation as the basis of scientific understanding, the use by students of processes of observation and experimentation, and "the scientific method."

Despite curriculum similarities, there were substantial differences in knowledge among the schools. The following sections of this article present and discuss data on these differences. Data from each social setting include significant information on the school, the teachers, and the community; what school personnel said, in interviews, about school knowledge; evidence from the curriculum and the curriculum-in-use in several content areas (e.g., math, science, social studies); and what students expressed concerning school knowledge and its meaning for them. A dominant theme emerged in each social setting, and these are also presented and briefly discussed.

Working-Class Schools

On the streets surrounding each school are small wooden frame houses. Many have small front porches and most date from the first decade of this century. The streets are clean, but there are no trees on the streets near either school. A railroad track separates the neighborhoods of each school from the rest of the town. One of the schools was constructed in 1912, the other in 1919. No additions have been built onto either school, but there are two trailers (for the second grades) in one asphalt playground. The rooms in the schools are sparsely furnished. There are no clocks in any of the classrooms. The halls and rooms are clean. The school population is heterogeneous as to white ethnic group composition, and there are small but growing Hispanic and black populations. Neither principal knows the history of his or her school building.

Approximately one-third of the teachers in each school were born in the city and lived there, but most are from "uptown," a different section. Most graduated from local state teachers colleges and were young; many were single. There were more male teachers in the working-class schools than in the other schools of this study.

One male teacher characterized his school as a "tough" school and said he had been nervous when they told him he would be teaching there. He said he felt better after the principal had told him, "Just do your best. If they learn to add and subtract, that's a bonus. If not, don't worry about it." A second-grade teacher stated to me that she did not mind teaching in this school because it was "easy," compared to many other schools. She said that she would not want to teach in the district's school for the "gifted and talented." "You have to work too hard. I have a friend who teaches there and she goes in early every *day*. She's always doing something special." Another second-grade teacher said that the children in her school were getting "dumber" as the years went by. She also said, "I would *never* teach in the suburbs. The parents there think their kids are God's gift. Although, some parents *here* are beginning to think they have rights, too." One day a fifth-grade teacher brought into the teachers' room a box of cards labeled "Diacritic Reading." A sixth-grade teacher looked at the box, laughed, and said, "Are you kidding? *I* can hardly read that!" The face of the woman who had brought the box reddened, and she turned the box over so that the title was not visible.

What School Personnel Said About School Knowledge

I asked the two fifth- and two second-grade teachers in each school what knowledge was most appropriate for the children in their classes. Most spoke of school knowledge in terms of facts and simple skills. One fifth-grade teacher said, for example, "What these children need is the basics." When I asked her what the basics were, she said, "The three Rs—simple skills." When I asked why, she responded, "They're lazy. I hate to categorize them, but they're lazy." Another fifth-grade teacher said, "Take social studies. History is a fact-oriented subject. But I really don't do much. I do map skills, though. It's practical—it's good for measuring and it's math." A fifth-grade teacher in the other school said she did social studies by putting notes on the board which the children then copied. I asked why she did that, and she said, "Because the children in this school don't *know* anything about the U.S., so you can't teach them much." The male fifth-grade teacher in this school said, "You can't teach these kids anything. Their parents don't take care about them, and they're not interested." A second-grade teacher when asked what was important knowledge for her students said, "Well, we keep them *busy*."

Evidence from the Curriculum and the Curriculum-in-Use

Mathematical knowledge was often restricted to the procedures or steps to be followed in order to add, subtract, multiply, or divide. All schools in the district use the same math text. It has numerous pages which are explicitly intended as departures from the mechanics of such skills as adding and subtracting. These pages call for mathematical reasoning, inferrence, pattern identification, or ratio setup, for example. One of the fifth-grade teachers called these pages "the thinking pages" and said she "rarely" uses them. "They're too hard." She concentrates, she said, "on the basics." That is, "how you multiply and divide." The fifth-grade math teacher in the other working-class school said, "These pages are for creativity—they're the extras." She uses them "sometimes."

A common feature of classroom mathematics in both working-class schools was that a large portion of what the children were asked to carry out procedures, the purposes of which were often unexplained, and which were seemingly unconnected to thought processes or decision making of their own. An example of this type of instruction was when one of the fifth-grade teachers led the children through a series of steps to make a one-inch grid on their papers without telling them that they were making a one-inch grid or that it would be used to study scale. She said, "Take your ruler. Put it across the top. Make a mark at every number. Then move your ruler down the bottom. Now, put it across the bottom. Now make a mark on top of every number. Now draw a line from…." At this point, one student said that she had a faster way to do it and the teacher said, "No, you don't; you don't even know what I'm making yet. Do it this way, or it's wrong." After the students had made the lines up and down and across the page, the teacher said she wanted them to make a figure by connecting some dots, measure the figure, using the scale of one inch equals one mile, and then cut it out. After she had led them through these steps, she said, "Don't cut until I check it."

Teachers in each school in the district are given a choice of the social studies text they want to use. The texts chosen by the fifth-grade teachers in the working-class schools contained less information, fewer inquiry or independent research activities, and more of an emphasis on social studies knowledge as facts to be remembered than the texts used in any other school of this study. In one of the working-class schools the fifth-grade teachers chose *The American Nation: Adventure in Freedom* (Follet 1975).This text is "designed for educationally deficient secondary school students" (teachers guide, p. 3). It is written on a sixth-to-seventh-grade level. It was intended for "low ability students … who often exhibit environmental deficiencies … and social and emotional problems" (teachers guide, p. 3). A striking characteristic of the textbook is the paucity of information. The book is intended as a year's work; it is divided into 16 "lessons." There are one to four paragraphs of history in each lesson, a vocabulary drill, and a review and skills exercise in each to check "recall and retention." The teacher's guide explains the sparsity of information by saying that an important criterion of teaching materials for "educationally deficient students" is that "[e]xtraneous subject matter and excessive details should be eliminated in order to present subjects and concepts that are important and also within the[ir] comprehension range…" (p. 39). The teachers guide also states that "It ought to be said at the outset that students with educational deficiencies are not always able to succeed in an inquiry lesson that places great demands on them" (p. 20). Rather, "The students feel secure in doing routine tasks" (p. 8). "You should follow fairly regular patterns from day to day so that the students do not become confused or distracted" (p. 8). The students should be "conditioned" to make "organized responses" (p. 11). The students should be "trained in the techniques of assembling information…" (p. 16). "Tests should seek to determine the students' retention to factual matter and their reading and comprehension" (p. 23).[4]

The textbook chosen by the fifth-grade teachers in the other working class school is *Your Country and Mine* (1969 edition) in Ginn's Tiegs Adams series. This textbook is not explicitly designed for any particular type of students. It is not an inquiry text; it is fact oriented. Two of three evaluative activities at the end of each chapter are "Do you know?" (asking for facts in 84% of the cases), and "See if your remember" (asking for recall—filling in the blanks or matching). A third activity involved, in approximately 60% of the cases, reading a map.

The social studies knowledge in these schools was the least "honest" about U.S. society. There was less mention of potentially controversial topics than in other series in other schools. Both texts refer to the economic system as a "free enterprise" system. There are five paragraphs on minority and women's rights and history in one text and ten in the other. (As we will see, this is considerably less than discussions of these topics in books used in other schools in this study.) As in most U.S. history texts, however, (Anyon 1979b; FitzGerald 1979) there is contained in both texts the history of powerful groups—political parties and leaders, military systems, business, technology, industry. There is little information on the working class in either book—four pages in one book and two in the other discuss labor history. Neither text attempts to identify interests workers have in common, nor discusses the situations of economic and social conflict in which workers exist.

Social studies instruction commonly involved carrying out tasks such as copying teacher's notes, answering textbook questions, or coloring and assembling paper cutouts. For example, in the school where the second book was available, the fifth grade teacher had purchased a supplemental booklet from Instructo entitled *The Fabulous Fifty States.* Each day she put information from the booklet in outline form on the board and the children copied it. The type of information did not vary: the name of the state, its abbreviation, state capital, nickname of the state, its main products, main business, and a "fabulous fact" (e.g., "Idaho grew 27 billion potatoes in one year. That's enough potatoes for each man, woman, and …"). As the children finished copying the sentences, the teacher erased them and wrote more. Children would occasionally go to the front of the classroom and pull down the wall map in order to locate the states they were studying, and the teacher did not dissuade them. But I never saw her refer to the map; nor did I hear her make other than perfunctory remarks concerning the information the children were copying. Occasionally, the children colored in a ditto (also from an Instructo booklet) and cut it out to make a stand-up figure of some sort (representing, for example, a man roping a cow in the Southwest). The teacher referred to these cutouts as social studies projects.

There were occasions when the teachers did seem to make attempts to go beyond simple facts and skills and to transmit more elaborate conceptual knowledge. Science instruction was often such a case, and the male fifth-grade teacher's use of the science textbook (*STEM*, Addison-Wesley, 1977) was in large measure such a symbolic gesture. He assigned the text, did demonstrations and "experiments," but, he said, "I don't do the tests [provided by the manual]. It's too depressing. They never get it, and they'll never *use* it!"

• • •

Executive Elite School

The school is a handsome Colonial-style building, with a large white portico on the front. It was originally built in 1929; an addition was added in 1949; a second in 1956, and a new library in 1972. The school sits back from the street on a broad lawn with several bushes and trees in front of it. The door has shiny brass trim, as do the principal's office and the teachers' lounge. Each classroom has polished oak cabinets with cut-glass doors. The windows of the classrooms sparkle. There is an alphalt play area in back, and beyond that two large grassy playing fields and a running track. The principal is involved, with some of the parents, in building a "tire playground." Most of the homes along the streets near the school are large estates, partially hidden by foliage and long driveways.

A recent state order to integrate the town's schools led to a Board of Education plan to bus students from a school which had the majority of the town's blacks and low-income whites. Some of the students were to be bused to the executive elite school. The plan was dropped after parents at the executive elite school threatened to pull their children out of the school and put them in private schools. As of this writing, all elementary schools in the town will be integrated except the executive elite school: there will be no busing; the school that is predominantly black and low income will be closed, and its students will walk to other schools (the closest it over a mile away). There will be no black or low-income children in the executive elite school. One of the teachers I was observing offered her reason for the parents' actions. She said, "It was class, not race. They [the parents in this school] didn't want *any* low-income kids here. They didn't want the discipline problems. And they didn't want the [achievement] scores lowered, to hold back their kids. I taught over there once," she said, referring to the school that would be closed, "and you can't teach them *anything*! They're flying all over the room. And their parents don't care about education. One father, he was a plumber, he said, 'well, if being a plumber is good enough for me, it's good enough for my son. What does he have to go to college for?'"[5]

Many of the teachers in the executive elite school are from middle- and upper-middle-class backgrounds. One older teacher spoke of her first year teaching, saying she loved it so much that she never even cashed her paychecks, just threw them in her drawer (she had been living with her parents). All the teachers are female except for the gym teacher. Most are married to professionals or to men in business (e.g., to a doctor, an insurance executive).

All teachers with whom I spoke regarded their students as of higher social status than themselves. One teacher contrasted the part of town she lived in with this one, saying she lived in a section like that of the [affluent professional] school which is "more mixed." Another teacher said, "These people are the successful ones. They know who they are; there is a class structure in this society and these people are at the top. And they know what they want for their kids. And some of them know where they came from—the ones who worked their way up." Another teacher said, "It's in their genes. They're handsome, you should see the fathers. They even *look* like executives!" A third-grade teacher said, "They're the successful ones. And some got that way through marriage." Said a first-grade teacher, "They're at the top, and they have breeding." "Breeding?" I asked. "It's a way of talking, dressing, even the mothers are well educated," she responded. "And they run the town!"

What School Personnel Said About School Knowledge

When I asked the two fifth-grade and two second-grade teachers in this school what knowledge was important for their students, most referred to intellectual processes such as reasoning and problem solving. One said, "They'll go to the best schools, and we have to prepare them." Another said, "It's not just academics; they need to learn to think. They will have important jobs, and they need to be able to think things through." When I asked a second-grade teacher who I was observing what was appropriate knowledge for her students, she said, "They need to learn the basics, we're going back to that now." "The basics?" I asked. "Yes, to think and write properly." Referring to science, a fifth-grade teacher said, "I try to get them to create an environment where they can solve problems—they manipulate variables and solve a problem."

The superintendent of schools, who has an Ed.D. from Harvard University, is attempting to institute a "Philosophy for Children Program" in the school, the purpose of which would be "to teach children to think and reason correctly, and to come up with valid conclusions."[6] The fifth-grade teachers in this school said they have been instructed by the superintendent to develop an "Olympics of the Mind"—a competition of "open-ended questions" for which there are no "set answers." (This would accompany the Field Olympics held by the fifth grades [in this and the affluent professional school] at the end of the year, at the end of their study of ancient Greece. The Field Olympics during this particular year included chariot races, a torch-lighting ceremony written by several children, and the culminating races to year-long competition in gym class track and field. Gold and silver medals were awarded.)

Evidence from the Curriculum and the Curriculum-in-Use

The fifth-grade teacher who teaches math said that her goal in this subject is the development of mathematical reasoning. She said the "demands" of "getting through the curriculum" do not leave her time to have the children "explore" with manipulables such as geoboards. She said she also tries to teach math as a "decision-making process." For example, presenting a new type of division problem to her class, she asks, "What's the *first* decision you'd make if presented with this kind of example? What is the first thing you'd *think*, Craig?" Craig says, "To find my first partial quotient." She responds, "Yes, that would be your first decision. How would you do that?" Craig explains, and then she says, "OK, we'll see how that works for you." She usually asks the children to explain why their answers are right or wrong, to explain how they know or how they found out an answer. She often says to her classes, "If you think logically [or rationally] about it, you can figure it out." Indeed, in every math class observed, she asked her class questions which required them to manipulate hypothetical variables to solve the problem.

Science is another subject in which intellectual process such as reasoning was stressed. The principal said that all teachers in the school are "required" to use a science program. The fifth- and sixth-grade teachers used the ESS. According to the principal, the rest of the teachers in the school use Science—A Process Approach (SAPA). SAPA was designed to present instruction that is "intellectually stimulating and scientifically authentic." It focuses on the processes involved in scientific reasoning, and there is a "progressive intellectual development with each process category." The children are expected to learn such things as how to infer internal mechanisms of plants, how to make and verify hypotheses about animal behavior, and how to perform experiments on the actions of gases.[7] A second-grade teacher I observed said she likes the program because "it's integrated and organized. And it tells you exactly what to do."

While this school used the same social studies series as the affluent professional school, social studies instruction in the classes I observed here was more academically (rigorously) organized than in the affluent professional school, followed more closely the discussion questions posed by the text, and involved a large amount of independent library research but very little creative or artistic project work. The fifth-grade social studies teacher said she based her instruction on discussion questions in the text and district study guides, and on activities provided by ten "individual study packets."

The fifth-grade social studies guide for the district was written by the former fifth-grade teacher in this school and the district social studies specialist. The former social studies teacher in this school also wrote the individual study packets of research and writing activities for the fifth-grade topics. (These were not available in the affluent professional school.) The district guide to the fifth-grade units on ancient Greece and Rome states the rationale for the course of study: "By an increased awareness of past problems and the human conditions which cause these problems, maybe we can prevent what Arnold Toynbee has pointed out, 'Nineteen of twenty-one civilizations have died from within and not by conquest from without. There were no bands playing and flags waving when these civilization decayed. It happened slowly, in the quiet and the dark when no one was aware' " (p. 2). The guide takes many of its questions and activities from the Allyn and Bacon Series.

Social studies knowledge was more sophisticated, complex, and analytical than in other schools. The social studies teacher I observed said she tried to have the children tackle the "important concepts." The following are examples of questions from the children's text that I heard discussed in class: "Greek comedies often poked fun at popular leaders. Would this be possible in a society that was not free? Can you think of any bad effects this might have? Any good effects?" "Look up the word 'imperialism,' What are some good and bad effects of imperialism?" (p. 41) "Were the Athenians wrong in condemning Socrates for his beliefs? Would you expect a person to be put to death for their ideas in a democracy? Explain" (p. 51). "There were two main classes in the early Roman republic. There were the noble, wealthy *Patricians*. There were the common people, or *plebs*. Would you expect these classes to get into quarrels? … Find out about the struggle between plebs and patricians in 494 B.C. The plebs went "on strike." What rights and protections did they get as a result?" (p. 80)

Social studies knowledge in this school also involved an explicit recognition of social class in ancient history. For example, the text identified, and the students discussed, what the text calls a "ruling class" in ancient society. In every chapter but two in the text on Greek and Roman civilization, there is the heading "Classes in Society" (with relevant concepts identified). Questions I heard discussed in the classroom included "What class conflicts occurred?" (*Greek and Roman Civilization*, p. 74) and "How was class structure affected by changes in property ownership after the Punic Wars?"(p. 74).

Not only textbooks but the individual study packets as well included an explicit recognition of social class. There were two fifth-grade packets for independent study of Latin America. One was on geography, and the other was called "Class and Culture." Sample questions follow: "Pretend you are a member of the upper class or lower class of Latin America. Write your "life story." Include the history of the group you are in. Where were you born? What were your ancestors and parents like? Will you always belong to this social class? What is your day-to-day life like?"

Scattered throughout the teacher's guide are references to other social classes, for instance, "the lower classes," "the common classes." For example, "Rule by the ignorant and easily swayed lower classes led to grave errors in judgment like the Syracusan expedition" (teachers guide, *Greek and Roman Civilization,* p. 55). "Whatever his political views, Pericles was no imitator of the 'common man.' It was precisely this restraint, control and rationality that made Pericles a valuable leader. Witness the conditions after his death, when 'common men' became leaders of Athens: the rationality, direction, and sensible restraint that had characterized policy in Pericles' day suddenly evaporated, leaving a splintered, chaotic, and impulsive Assembly in charge of formulating policy" (teachers guide, *Greek and Roman Civilization,* p. 39). [Interestingly, however, while the series is quite explicit about classes in ancient Greece and Rome (and Sumer), and a sixth-grade text called *The Challenge of Change* is quite explicit about the social class divisions in European history ("upper classes" were "the gentry, nobles, bishops"; the "middle classes" were "the Bourgoisie[sic] or merchants, tradesmen, yeoman farmers, lawyers, doctors and clergymen" and the "lower classes were small farmers, laborers, the poor") (p. 29), the textbook series does not discuss class in this fashion in the American history textbook it provides for fourth grade, and there is no division there of U.S. society into social classes.]

While classroom social studies knowledge tends to be *analytical*, neither text nor most social studies discussions were *critical* of the social class structure or distribution of wealth and power; rather, they gave it high value and a "naturalness," or "timelessness," going back, indeed, to ancient Greece. There were occasions, however, in the classroom of the fifth-grade teacher who teaches math, science, and health but not social studies, when class discussions were "almost" critical; that is, the teacher often asked the children *why* things were done or happened in a certain way, when that way appeared to be *irrational*. For example, after showing the class a film on the making of a Morton's "cream" pie almost entirely with chemicals, she asked, "Why do companies put chemicals in food when the natural ingredients are available?" The following excerpt of a discussion in this teacher's class provides a further example of her attempt to have her class give critical thought to a social problem. Strikes of newspaper workers, sanitationmen and truckers had been in the news. The children had just read for homework a story in their *Scholastic News* about a teachers'strike.[8]

T: OK, suppose I'm the manager and you ask me, and I won't give you a raise. Then what do you do? David?

S: Strikes are *not* a good idea: the public is always affected. Students don't learn if teachers strike.

S: Companies don't make profits if workers strike.

T: I'm asking you question to help you think this through, I'm not saying I'm not agreeing with you.

S: It goes both ways. Take the newspaper strike. A worker may have a family he or she has to support, but without newspapers, we don't know, as David said.

T: But what if you really feel …

S: (cuts off the teacher) If you really feel strongly, you should.

S: No. The students were hurt by the strike of the teachers. (He begins a monologue about how the teachers shouldn't strike because it hurts the public. The teacher finally calls on another student.)

S: Workers say, "I think I deserve a raise for building really good cars." But the managers are against strikes. They say, "Workers only work eight hours and I work twelve. Why *shouldn't* I get more?"

T: A lot of you are concerned about the public. But suppose you have a boss who really takes advantage of you. What then?

S: I'd probably try to find another job. I wouldn't stay with that creep!

T: I want you to think about this. We won't have time to discuss it; I'm the boss.

S: You're always the boss. (Laughter, teacher smiles).

T: I say, "Strike and I'll fire you. I don't need you…. I'm going to buy a machine!" Think about that. (They get up for lunch.)

Discussions like this one and indications that such discussions may go on in other rooms (e.g., intricate bulletin board displays of designs for home heating with solar power; school clothing and food drives; stories written about families who are poor and black; and district-run affirmative action and sexism awareness workshops for teachers) indicate that the school may play a politically liberalizing role in the children's upbringing. For example, the discussion the teacher and students had about strikes seems to have made some impression on them. During the discussion only one child came out in favor of strikes. One said to me on the playground at lunch, "Mrs. [B] was for strikes, but we weren't." Several weeks later when I was interviewing the children I asked all interviewees if they thought strikes were right or wrong. Only two children said strikes were wrong; three children said yes, strikes are right; and all the rest but one (14) said "It depends." The children who said it depended gave responses like the following: "They're right *and* wrong; it depends on how you do it. The union figured out a way to make picket lines legal, and that's wrong. But you can't fire all the people; you won't be good in the public eye and your product will go down. Then you'd go bankrupt and have to close the company for a while." "Well, it depends; it's OK if it's really gone too far, but the *idea* doesn't hit me too well. It's just a public disturbance." "They're right and wrong. Mrs. [B] said people *should* strike to get enough money. And most people in the class didn't agree with her. My parents said maybe the company can't give the workers more, and they should try to talk it out."[9]

• • •

CONCLUSION AND IMPLICATIONS

I would conclude that despite similarities in some curriculum topics and materials, there are profound differences in the curriculum and the curriculum-in-use in the sample of schools in this study. What counts as knowledge in the schools differs along dimensions of structure and content. The differences have been identified and discussed briefly in the foregoing sections; now they will be assessed for social and theoretical implications. The assessment will focus on reproductive and nonreproductive aspects of knowledge in each social-class setting. "Reproductive" will refer to aspects of school knowledge that contribute directly to the legitimation and perpetuation of ideologies, practices, and privileges constitutive of present economic and political structures. "Nonreproductive" knowledge is that which facilitates fundamental transformation of ideologies and practices on the basis of which objects, services, and ideas (and other cultural products) are produced, owned, distributed, and publicly evaluated. The present definition of social change as fundamental transformation transcends the goals of, but does not deny the importance of, humanitarian efforts and practices in institutions such as the school. As we shall see, however, the genesis of truly transformative activity is in the contradictions within and between social settings.

In the working class schools there are two aspects of school knowledge that are reproductive. First, and quite simply, students in these schools were not taught their own history—the history of the American working class and its situation of conflict with powerful business and political groups, e.g., its long history of dissent and struggle for economic dignity. Nor were these students taught to value the interests which they share with others who will be workers. What little social information they were exposed to appears to provide little or no conceptual or critical understanding of the world or of their situation in the world. Indeed, not knowing the history of their own group—its dissent and conflict—may produce a social amnesia or "forgetting" (Jacoby, 1975). Such "forgetting" by the working class has quietistic implications in the social arena and potentially reproductive consequences.

A second reproductive aspect of school knowledge in these working-class schools was the emphasis in curriculum and in classrooms on mechanical behaviors, as opposed to sustained conception. This is important to a reproduction of the division of labor at work and in society between those who plan and manage (e.g., technical professionals, executives) and the increasing percentage of the work force whose jobs entail primarily carrying out the policies, plans, and regulations of others. These working-class children were not offered what for them would be *cultural capital*—knowledge and skill at manipulating ideas and symbols in their own interest, e.g., historical knowledge and analysis that legitimates their dissent and furthers their own class in society and in social transformation.

These aspects of school knowledge in the working-class schools contribute to the reproduction of a group in society who may be without marketable knowledge; a reserve group of workers whose very existence, whose availability for hire, for example, when employed workers strike, serves to keep wages down and the work force disciplined. A reserve group is, of course, essential to capitalism because lower wages permit profit accumulation, which is necessary to the viability of firms, banks, state budgets and other bank-financed budgets of, one could argue, the entire system.

On the other hand, however, there is a major contradiction in school knowledge in these working-class schools, and from this may emerge a situation that is potentially socially transformative. Teacher control of students is a high priority in these schools, as in other schools. What the teachers attempted, in these two working-class schools, however, was *physical* control. There was little attempt to win the hearts and minds of these students. Now, our own era in history is one in which social control is achieved primarily through the dominant ideology and the perceived lack of ideological alternatives. But the working-class children in the schools studied here were taught very little of the ideology that is central to stable reproduction of the U.S. system, e.g., traditional bodies of knowledge that include the ideologies of an alleged lack of social alternatives to capitalist organization, patriotism and nationalism, faith in one's own chance of "making it big," and belief that the economy and polity are indeed designed in the interests of the average man and woman. In some cases, children in this study gave evidence that they had already rejected the ideologies of patriotism and of equal chances for themselves.

The absence of traditional bodies of knowledge and ideology may make these children vulnerable to alternative ideas; the children may be more open to ideas that support fundamental social change. Indeed, some of the children were already engaged in struggle against what was to them an exploitative group—the school teachers and administrators. They were struggling against the imposition of a foreign curriculum. They had "seen through" that system. The children's struggle, however, was destructive to themselves. Really *useful* knowledge for these students, e.g., honest "citizenship" education, would authenticate students' own meanings and give them skills to identify and analyze their own social class and to transform a situation that some already perceive is not in their own interest.

A social and theoretical implication of the education of the working-class students in this study, then, is that while a reserve pool of marginally employed workers is perhaps assured by modern schooling, ideological hegemony is not. Ideological hegemony is, rather, extremely tenuous, and the working class may be less ideologically secured than some other social groups. What is important is to make available to working-class students the cultural and ideological tools to begin to transform perspicacity into power.[10]

In the middle-class school, the children I observed were not taught the history of workers or of dissent, nor were they instructed to unify around common interests they will have as wage earners in a system in which many middle-class jobs are becoming increasingly like industrial and clerical jobs—mechanical and rote (for example, computer, technical, and social work; other service jobs; perhaps teaching; nursing and other formerly professional jobs). There were, however, distinguishing characteristics of knowledge in this middle-class school that are important primarily because of the social-class location of the families. For example, the notion of knowledge as originating in external and externally approved sources, as generated and validated by experts, may yield a passive stance before ideas and ideology and before the creation or legitimation of new ideas. This, of course, has implications of intellectual passivity, and ideological quietude. Moreover, school knowledge in the middle-class school was highly commodified. The reification of ideas and knowledge into given facts and "generalizations" that exist separately from one's biography or discovery contributes to the commodification of knowledge. It is true that knowledge in the working-class schools was reified as well. However, in order to be a commodity, a product must have some value in the market-place and must be perceived as having some value, or no one would "buy" it. That is, it must have an exchange value. Traditional conceptual or academic knowledge in the working-class schools is not perceived by many teachers or students as having exchange value in the marketplace, or workplace, of working-class jobs. Therefore, it does not have commodity status. In the social class position of the present middle-class school, however, the teachers and students perceive the knowledge to have market value: there is a perceived chance that if one can accumulate facts, information and "generalizations," one can exchange them for college entrance or for a white-collar (perhaps even professional) job. But as is true of all commodities, when one exchanges an object, one gives up its use for oneself. Furthermore, a commodity is useful only in an exchangeable, objectified form. Forms in which knowledge is useful for reflection, critical thought, or making sense do not generate as much value in the competition for college entrance and the majority of U.S. jobs.

Commodification of knowledge in the middle-class school is reproductive in part because it helps to legitimate and reproduce the ideology of production for consumption, for example, production of knowledge and other cultural products for the market rather than for personal use or for social transformation. (An actively consuming public is, of course, a material necessity in a capitalist system, and thus legitimation of the ideology of consumption—of production *for* consumption—has direct economic reproductive consequences as well.)

There is a second aspect of knowledge in the middle-class school that is reproductive. This is also a part of the apparent acceptance or belief in the possibility of success for oneself. It is a social fact of major importance that the U.S. middle class is a group whose recent history has shown rapidly decreasing economic stability for individual families. There is, thus, material reason for the reification of knowledge into accumulatable form and for the anxiety which the children manifest concerning tests, college, and jobs. For example, the amount of attention one must pay to "getting ahead" not only leaves little interest or time for critical attention, but it also actively fosters and strengthens belief in the ideologies of upward mobility and success. For example, "If I do not believe that there is a chance for me, and that I can succeed, why should I try so hard? Why go along?" I must *believe* in order to work hard; and to work hard increases the personal (psychological) necessity of my belief. So, the perception of social possibilities for the middle class hinted at in this study and the ideologized and reified school knowledge found in their schooling contribute not only to some of them "getting ahead," but to the production of a class with perhaps the highest degree of mystification and ideological internalization. This, of course, is reproductive.

There is, however, a potentially nonreproductive contradiction to be foreseen regarding school knowledge and the lives of these children. Many of those whose schooling and families have promised them a high reward for working hard and doing well will actually *not* succeed in the job market. This situation, after years of schooling in ideology and promises, may serve to generate cynicism or, more constructively, a critical view of the system. Also, the fact that many of these students will go to college may expose them to alternative ideas. They may be exposed to authors and professors who present alternative views and critical assessments of the social order. From this new knowledge and social perspective, they may, perhaps, be moved to utilize their own curiosity, to begin to use knowledge to question what is. Such questioning is a beginning of any socially transformative activity.

In the affluent professional school there are several aspects of school knowledge that are reproductive. First, the children are taught what is, for most of them, their own history— the history of the wealthy classes. They are taught that the power of their own group is legitimate. They are, as well, taught ways of expressing and using such ideas—that ideology—in their own interests. They are being provided with cultural capital. Indeed, the fact that the knowledge of their own group is socially prestigious knowledge enhances the exchange value of their knowledge as capital. Moreover, because many affluent professional jobs (doctor, lawyer, professor, scientist) still require conception and creativity and independent thought, many of the children in this school will be in the privileged position of having the *use* value of their knowledge (for personal creativity, for example) be at the same time its *exchange* value (for example, they will get paid for doing creative, conceptual work).

A second aspect of school knowledge that is reproductive here is its nascent empiricism (by empiricism I refer to the emphasis in adult science on basing knowledge on experience and on appearances, on observable data this experience produces.) As the basis for knowledge or explanations, empiricism is socially reproductive when it provides a framework for allegedly independent thought. Empiricism uses characteristics of observable data and characteristics of the observed relationships between data for its explanations; empiricism eschews explanations and analyses which are based on transcendent and nonempirical knowledge (see Bernstein 1978). This mode of inquiry thus uses categories and explanations that are confined to what already exists, to what can be observed. This mitigates against challenges to the necessity or naturalness of these categories and of what exists. School science programs and math manipulables make a small contribution, then, to the legitimation of empiricism as a way of seeking and testing knowledge, and to the acceptance of what is, as opposed to what could be. The programs are, in this case, a potential invisible boundary of the social thought of these children.

Accompanying the nascent empiricism in this affluent professional school is the emphasis on individual development as a primary goal of education (as opposed, for example, to the development of the priority of collective goals). A priority on personal expression, personal "meaning making" and the "construction of reality" mitigates against collectivistic values and meanings and solutions; it is thereby reproductive of values important to an individualistic, privately owned, and competitive economy.

Finally, the emphasis in the curriculum and classrooms on active use of concepts and ideas by students, as opposed to a stress on mechanics or rote behaviors, facilitates the perpetuation of an unequal division of labor in U.S. society, where some (these children?) will plan and others (working-class and middle-class children?) will have jobs that entail carrying out the plans.

There are, however, basic contradictions apparent in the school knowledge of these affluent professional children. In these conflicts one can see powerful implications for social transformation. For example, the contradiction between attempting as a student, and making sense as an adult, presumably later in one's professional creative labors, in a society where many things do *not* make sense and are irrational is a conflict which may generate political radicalism. such a conflict may lead to intellectuals who are highly critical of the system and who attempt to persuade others by disseminating their own views. Or, it may lead to political activism, to overt attempts to take physical action against perceived political and economic irrationalities, as, for example, the students in Students for a Democratic Society (SDS)—a radical, anti-Vietnam War Group—a majority of whom were from affluent professional families. Indeed, as Alvin Gouldner points out (1979), almost all leaders of social revolutions in the modern era have come from families of comparatively high standing in their society who were exposed to large amounts of cultural capital (e.g., Marx, Engels, the majority of the early Bolsheviks, Mao Tse-tung, Chou En-Lai, Ho Chi Minh, and Fidel Castro).

It is probably true that the conflict inherent in attempting to make sense in a world that is in many ways irrational is present for all children in all schools and social classes. What makes the conflict a potentially powerful force in the affluent professional school, however, is first the social-class position of these children, their cultural capital, and future access to information, power, and further cultural capital afforded to them by their social position. A second factor important here is the nature of their schooling. These children were told, and encouraged, more than the children in any other school to be creative, to think for themselves, and to make sense. It is indeed because of such encouragement to the young that the increasingly ideological notions of freedom and democracy can be turned back upon the economically and politically powerful and made into truly transformative demands.

Another contradiction to the school knowledge of these children that is nonreproductive is the contradiction between the value placed on creativity and personal decision making, and the systematic, increasingly rationalized nature of school and professional work in U. S. society. This conflict, already apparent in the use of science and reading programs in this school, is a contradiction that suggests possible later conflicts between the use and exchange values of knowledge in adult work, for example, between one's own creativity and the increasing rationalization and control of professional work by technology, bureaucratic trends, and centralization. It also suggests class conflict between affluent professionals, with their own interests and skills and relative power in the bureaucracy on one hand, and the capitalists, who are their "bosses" and who hold the purse strings, on the other. Conflict between the educated classes and the ruling class has long been a source of movement for social transformation. Indeed, as Gouldner (1979) reminds us, it has been this class—the educated, the intellectuals—who have, to date, taken control in periods of revolutionary upheaval, e.g., in the early Soviet Union and China. It is, then, important to provide the children of the affluent professional class with school knowledge that is not just conceptual, analytical, and expressive, but that, is also critical and collective. Such knowledge would foster responsiveness not only to the needs of individual "meaning making" and development, but to the development of a wider social collectivity that, not coincidentally, would affirm the needs of the working and middle classes as well.

The executive elite school offers cultural capital to its children, whose families as a class have the major portion of available physical capital in society. These children are taught the history of "ruling" groups, and that rule by the wealthy and aristocratic is rational and natural, going back, for example, to the Ancient Greeks. Such knowledge, is, for them, symbolic capital. They are provided with other kinds of symbolic capital as well—practice in manipulating socially prestigious language and concepts in systematic ways. They are told the importance of controlling ideas and given some insight into controlling ideas in their own (Western) culture. The fact that the culture of their social class is the dominant and most prestigious one enhances the exchange value or "worth" of their knowledge in the marketplace.

Some of these children had a fair amount of class consciousness, if this is defined as knowledge of themselves as part of a group in society and in history, and an appreciation of their own group's interests as opposing the interests of other groups in society (e.g., plebs, strikers). While class consciousness among the working classes is likely to be nonreproductive, such a consciousness among the capitalist class is, of course, likely to increase their efforts to win conflicts, to conserve culture, and to maintain their social position, e.g., to prevent what Toynbee said was the "decay of civilization from within."

School knowledge in the executive elite school was the most "honest" about society, U.S. social problems, and social irrationalities. It was sometimes expressive of liberal concerns, as well. Indeed, it came the closest to being socially critical. The children were given analytical and unsentimental insight into the system. Whereas, for example, middle-class children might see a pluralism of equal or competing ethnic cultures, the children of the executive elite might perceive social class and economic conflict. Thus, these children may be less ideologically mystified than, for example, the middle-class students. The executive elite students—in different and more socially profitable ways than the working-class students—may see more clearly through the rhetoric of nationalism and equal opportunity to the raw facts of class and class conflict.

There is a potential contradiction here in the "clarity" of understanding the system that may, in the particular context of the social-class position of these children, have transformative possibilities. This is the contradiction for them between the use and exchange values in their knowledge: the contradiction between using knowledge for pleasure and enjoying one's class privilege, for example, and the exchange value of knowledge when it must be used to maintain that privilege. Two particular characteristics that empower this contradiction for these children (because the contradiction does appear in weaker forms in other schools) are, first, that extreme pressure is necessary, and excruciating struggle is demanded in a capitalist political democracy to actually maintain one's position of economic power and privilege. To grow up in the modern capitalist class is not only to enjoy travel, luxury, good schools, and financial wealth; it is also to have to maintain power in the face of others competing with you, within an irrational economic system that is increasingly difficult to predict, manage, and control—not only in the U.S. but in a rebellious Third World, as well. To be the "best," one must continually "beat the best." This is severe pressure. Second, to be a powerful capitalist, one must cause suffering and actually exploit others. Indeed, one's wealth and power are possible only because there are others (e.g., a reserve "pool" of workers) who do not have power and resource. These two "facts of life" of "being a capitalist" mean that if one is not ideologically secured, one may reject these demands. In contrapuntal fashion, the pressures, the irrationalities, and the exploitative characteristics of one's role in the system may one day cause the system to be perceived as the enemy—to be destroyed, rather than exploited. One thinks, as examples, of ruling class "children" who have rejected their privileges for radical politics and who have attempted to destroy members of their own class (the Baader Meinhoff Group in Germany, the Red Brigades in Italy, or, indeed, the Weathermen in the U.S.). While such efforts at social transformation are violent and irrational and are not condoned, they must be acknowledged as nonreproductive in intent.

By situating school knowledge in its particular social location, we can see how it may contribute to contradictory social processes of conservation and transformation. We see the schools reproducing the tensions and conflicts of the larger society. It becomes apparent as well that an examination of only one social site may blur the distinctions and subtleties that a comparative study illuminates. That is, a social phenomenon may differ by social class; and indeed similar (or the same) phenomena may have different meanings in different social contexts.

This study has suggested, as well, that there are class conflicts in educational knowledge and its distribution. We can see class conflict in the struggle to impose the knowledge of powerful groups on the working class and in student resistance to this class-based curriculum. We can see class conflict in the contradictions within and between school knowledge and its economic and personal values, and in attempts to impose liberal public attitudes on children of the rich.

Class conflict in education is thus not dormant, nor a relic of an earlier era; nor is the outcome yet determined. No class is certain of victory, and ideological hegemony is not secure. Those who would struggle against ideological hegemony must not confuse working-class powerlessness with apathy, middle-class ideology with its inevitability, or ruling-class power and cultural capital with superior strength or intelligence. Just as blacks were not the happy-go-lucky fellows of former stereotypes, so the working class is not dull or acquiescent, and the rich are not complacent or secure. Indeed, perhaps the most important implication of the present study is that for those of us who are working to transform society, there is much to do, at all levels, in education.

NOTES

1. The study was funded by two grants from Rutgers University Research Council, whose generous support is hereby acknowledged.
2. For further discussion of social class in these terms, see Anyon (1980).
3. This figure is an estimate. According to the Bureau of the Census, only 2.6% of families in the United States had money incomes of $50,000 or over in 1977 (U.S. Bureau of the Census 1979, Table A p.2). For figures on income at these higher levels, see Smith and Franklin (1974).
4. One might assume from the social studies text chosen by these teachers that their students were somewhat retarded. In fact, the mean IQ of the fifth-grade children for whom the book was chosen was 102; the mean IQ of the fifth graders in the other working-class school was 104 (CBT, McGraw Hill, Short Form). [Mean IQ in the middle-class school fifth grades was 105; in the affluent professional, 117; and in the executive elite, 120 (Otis-Lennun).] (Seven fifth graders in the working-class fifth grades combined had IQs that indicated above-average intelligence: 129, 139, 125, 133, 126, 130, 128. One other boy had tested in the second grade as having an IQ of 140; on the fifth grade test his score was 120.) It is my opinion (contradicted after completion of the study by the two teachers to whom I offered it) that the reasons for choosing this book were first, its assumption of low ability in the students, and second, the fact that this assumption provides a rationale that makes teaching as work much easier: If the students cannot *do* anything but vocabulary drill and skill work, then we, as teachers, do not have to *plan* anything else. The teachers said they chose the book because it was "easy," and stressed "skills the children need."
5. My request to include in this study (i.e., in 1978–1979) the school that had the majority of the town's blacks and most of the low-income whites was denied by the Board of Education.
6. See Hugh Munby's (1979) critique of the program which appeared in *Curriculum Inquiry* 9:3.
7. The quote and descriptions are taken from Mayor's (1972) account. See also American Association for the Advancement of Science (1972).
8. An interesting contrast here is that during the same week, in one working-class fifth grade I saw copies of *My Weekly Reader* in several children's desks. On the cover were striking truck drivers, and the lead story asked, "Do workers have the right to strike?" (The article suggested that they did.) I asked the teacher if he had used that issue with his class and he said, "No, some of them did the puzzle, but they just throw it away."
9. During interviews of children in other schools I asked if they knew what strikes were (practically all did) and if they thought strikes were right or wrong. In the working-class schools 13 of 20 said yes, strikes were right ("people have the right to strike"); five said, "strikes are wrong"; two said "sometimes they're right." In the middle-class school seven said strikes were right; eight said strikes were wrong; and three said, "sometimes." In the affluent professional school two said strikes were "OK" and "Yes, they're all right"; eight said strikes were wrong, and nine said, "It depends."
10. It is interesting to note (as information that supports my interpretation of a "perspicacious" working class) that several academic surveys in the 1960s (reported in Zinn 1980) showed that in 1964 (before students and intellectuals had discovered the Vietnam War) and throughout the war, Americans with only a grade-school education were much stronger for withdrawal from the war than Americans with a college education. Zinn argues that "the regular polls, based on samplings, underestimated the opposition to the war among lower-class people" (p. 482). Just as the earliest anti-Vietnam protests came out of the Civil Rights movement as blacks began being drafted, so opposition was stronger earlier in working-class communities as young men from these communities were drafted.

REFERENCES

American Association for the Advancement of Science. *Science—a process approach: Purposes, accomplishments, expectations.* (AAAS Miscellaneous Publication no. 67-12, September 1967). Lexington, Mass.: American Association for the Advancement of Science, 1972.

Anyon, Jean. "Elementary social studies textbooks and legitimating knowledge." *Theory and Research in Social Education* 6, no. 3 (September 1978): 40–55.

——. "Education, social 'structure' and the power of individuals." *Theory and Research in Social Education* 7, no. 1 (Spring 1979): 49–60. (a)

——."Ideology and United States history textbooks." *Harvard Educational Review* 49, no. 3 (August 1979): 361–386. (b)

——. "Social class and the hidden curriculum of work." *Journal of Education* 162, no. 1 (Winter 1980): 67–92.

——. "Schools as agencies of social legitimation." *Journal of Curriculum Theorizing*, to appear.

Apple, Michael. *Ideology and curriculum.* Boston: Routledge and Kegan Paul, 1979.

Bernstein, Richard. *The restructuring of social and political theory.* Philadelphia: University of Pennsylvania Press. 1978.

Bowles, Samuel, and Gintis, Herbert. *Schooling in capitalist America: Educational reform and the contradictions of economic life.* New York: Basic Books, 1976.

Educational Development Center. *A working guide to the elementary science study.* Newton, Mass.: Educational Development Center, 1971.

Fttzgerald, Frances. *America revised.* Boston: Little, Brown, 1979.

Fox, Thomas, and Hess, Robert. *An analysis of social conflict in social studies textbooks.* Final Report, Project no. II–116. Washington, D.C.: United States Department of Health, Education and Welfare, 1972.

Giroux, Henry. "Schooling and the culture of positivism: Notes on the 'death' of history." *Educational Theory*, to appear.

Gouldner, Alvin. *The future of intellectuals and the rise of the new class.* New York: Seabury Press. 1979.

Hal, Christopher. "Elementary science study." In *The eighth report of the National Clearinghouse on Science and Mathematics Curricular Development,* edited by David Lockard. Baltimore, Md.: University of Maryland, 1972.

Jacoby, Russel I. *Social amnesia.* Boston: Beacon Press, 1975.

Karabel, Jerome. "Community colleges and social stratification." *Harvard Educational Review* 42, no. 4 (November 1972): 521–562.

——. and Halsey. A. H. *Power and ideology in education.* New York: Oxford University Press, 1977.

Mayor, John. "Science—a process approach." In *The eighth report of the National Clearinghouse on Science and Mathematics Curricular Development,* edited by David Lockard. Baltimore, Md.: University of Maryland, 1972.

Munby, Hugh. "Philosophy for children: An example of curriculum review and criticism." *Curriculum Inquiry* 9, no. 3 (Fall 1979): 229–249.

Rosenbaum, James. *Making inequality: The hidden curriculum of high school tracking.* New York: Wiley, 1976.

Smith, James, and Franklin, Stephan. "The concentration of personal wealth, 1922–1969." *American Economic Review* 64, no. 4 (May 1974): 162–167.

United States Bureau of the Gensus. "Money income in 1977 of families and persons in the United States." In *Current population reports*, Series P-60, no. 118. Washington, D.C.: United States Government Printing Office, 1979.

Young, Michael, and Whitty, Geoff. *Society, state and schooling.* Sussex, England: Falmer Press, 1977.

Zinn, Howard. A people's history of the United States. New York: Harper and Row, 1980.

29

Teaching and Learning Mathematics for Social Justice in an Urban, Latino School

Eric Gutstein

With every single thing about math that I learned came something else. Sometimes I learned more of other things instead of math. I learned to think of fairness, injustices and so forth everywhere I see numbers distorted in the world. Now my mind is opened to so many new things. I'm more independent and aware. I have learned to be strong in every way you can think of it. (Lupe, Grade 8)

LUPE WROTE THE above after almost 2 years in a mathematics class where a principal focus was on *teaching and learning mathematics for social justice*. But what does it mean to teach and learn mathematics for social justice? How might this take shape in the classroom? What is the relationship to a curriculum based on the National Council of Teachers of Mathematics [NCTM] *Principles and Standards for School Mathematics* (2000)? In this article I address these questions and describe a research project in which I was a middle-school mathematics teacher in an urban, Latino school. I have two purposes here: (a) to uncover and concretize components of teaching and learning mathematics for social justice and (b) to understand the relationship of a *Standards*-based curriculum to that process. I situate this study alongside NCTM's positions on equity and extend them, and I examine students' learning from the perspective of teaching for social justice and through the lens of the vision for school mathematics described in the NCTM's *Standards*. I also discuss students' changed dispositions toward mathematics and raise further research questions.

NCTM published the initial *Curriculum and Evaluation Standards for School Mathematics* over 10 years ago (NCTM, 1989) and declared equity to be an aim of mathematics education reform. The authors specified certain "new societal goals for education" (p. 3) and incorporated equity into the goal of *opportunity for all*. Although the *Curriculum Standards* did not explicitly define equity, it stated, "the social injustices of past schooling practices can no longer be tolerated.... Creating a just society in which women and various ethnic minorities enjoy equal opportunities and equitable treatment is no longer an issue" (p. 4). The authors also took a strong position against tracking: "we believe that current tracking procedures often are inequitable, and we challenge all to develop instructional activities and programs to address this issue directly" (p. 253). The *Curriculum Standards* embraced democratic citizenship with mathematical literacy as a key component.

One can, however, critique the *Curriculum Standards'* equity framework because the document was also largely about U.S. economic competitiveness and workforce preparation in a global context. One of the new societal goals of the *Curriculum Standards* (NCTM, 1989) was to develop "mathematically literate workers" (p. 3), situating equity within the context of economic productivity: "the educational system of the industrial age does not meet the economic needs of today" (p. 3) and "equity has become an *economic necessity*" (p. 4, my emphasis). It is not surprising that the document reflects multiple perspectives on equity, because it was developed and written by consensus. But to discuss equity from the perspective of U.S. economic competition is to diminish its moral imperative and urgency.

In the revised *Principles and Standards* (NCTM, 2000), equity had a more prominent focus and was not tied to economics. Of the six unifying principles in the document, equity is the first, thus demonstrating a deeper concern than in the original document. The revision reiterates the strong stand against tracking and other forms of differential curriculum and insists that all students have access to high-quality curriculum and technology and to highly qualified teachers with adequate resources and subject-matter knowledge. The point is made clearly that uniformly high expectations of students and strong supports are necessary to achieve equity. However, the document does not address what else might be necessary to attain equity, nor does it propose how to transform inequitable mathematics classrooms into equitable ones.

In his analysis of the 1989 *Curriculum Standards,* Apple (1992) raised several issues. He acknowledged the *Curriculum Standards'* primary intent—literacy for democratic citizenship—but pointed out that the intentions of its creators do not determine how others might use it. Apple placed the document within its sociopolitical context, that of unequal relations of power in society, and questioned whether literacy in the *Curriculum Standards* meant *functional literacy* (i.e., being able to read and do mathematics) or *critical literacy* (i.e., approaching knowledge critically, seeing social events in the interrelationships of their historical and political contexts, and acting in one's own interest as a conscious agent in and on the world [Freire, 1992; Macedo, 1994]). Apple raised questions of how to achieve the principal purpose outlined and implied in *both Standards* documents—a just society—and what are the specific roles that mathematics education can play in reaching that goal. Apple is not alone in raising these questions. Both Secada (1996) and Tate (1996) ask whether the *Curriculum Standards* might in fact exacerbate existing inequalities because students in schools with more opportunity to learn—more resources, more access to better qualified teachers and better curricula—might benefit more from the document than students in poorer communities and schools (Oakes, 1985, 1990).

Clearly these are complicated questions, and neither the *Standards* documents nor any other such document has the sole responsibility for answering them. But the documents further the struggle for equity by openly discussing these issues. Over the past 15 years, many mathematics educators have worked for equity in various theoretic and programmatic ways (e.g., Campbell, 1996; Frankenstein, 1995; Gutiérrez, in press; Khisty, 1995;

Moses & Cobb, 2001; Secada, 1991, 1996; Silver, Smith, & Nelson, 1995; Tate, 1995; Weissglass, 2000). Unfortunately, we are not much closer to achieving full equity in mathematics (nor anywhere else in society), despite important advances such as the reduction (but not elimination) of gender disparities. Some may argue about the size of, and trends in, the gaps, but the travesty of unequal experiences, opportunities, and outcomes between rich and poor and between whites and students of color is unarguable—equity is not here.

Although mathematics educators have worked in various ways to promote equity, little literature exists that documents efforts to teach mathematics as a specific tool for equity and social justice. Important exceptions do exist, notably Frankenstein's work (1987, 1989, 1991, 1995, 1997) and that of Skovsmose (1994a, 1994b). But how might teaching mathematics for social justice take shape in practice, and how might it advance the struggle for equity? One way to address this is to consider what teaching for social justice might mean in *any* context, independent of a specific discipline.

TEACHING FOR SOCIAL JUSTICE

An important principle of a social justice pedagogy is that students themselves are ultimately part of the solution to injustice, both as youth and as they grow into adulthood. To play this role, they need to understand more deeply the conditions of their lives and the sociopolitical dynamics of their world. Thus, teachers could pose questions to students to help them address and understand these issues. For example: Why are there so many gangs in your neighborhood, and why are so many bright and talented students dropping out and joining them? Why is the complexion of your neighbourhood changing, and what's behind those changes? As students begin to address questions that have meaning in their lives, they begin to understand the forces and institutions that shape their world and to pose their own questions. These processes of helping students understand, formulate, and address questions and develop analyses of their society are critical components of teaching for social justice and may be encapsulated as "developing socio political consciousness" or *conscientização*, as Freire (1992) called it. Without these tools, students cannot work for equity and social justice.

There is nothing unusual about wanting students to be socially aware. But although necessary, this may be insufficient for students to become actively involved in rectifying social inequalities. Freire (Freire & Macedo, 1987) spoke of *writing* the world (and not just understanding it), which meant, for him, to remedy unjust situations. To write the world, students also need a sense of *agency*, that is, a belief in themselves as people who can make a difference in the world, as ones who are makers of history. Educators working toward an equitable and just society can help students develop not only a sophisticated understanding of power relations in society but also the belief in themselves as conscious actors in the world. Helping young people develop a sense of personal and social agency can be an important step toward achieving equity.

Finally, teaching for social justice also includes helping students develop positive social and cultural identities by validating their language and culture and helping them uncover and understand their history (Murrell, 1997). This can be complicated and may be especially hard for teachers from cultural backgrounds that are different from those of their students. However, respecting and listening to—and learning from—children and adults who make up the school and community are essential to help students develop such identities (Delpit, 1988). Thus, a pedagogy for social justice has three main goals: helping students develop sociopolitical consciousness, a sense of agency, and positive social and cultural identities.

Ladson-Billings (1994) describes aspects of a liberatory education for African Americans, which may be extended to other marginalized students:

> Parents, teachers, and neighbors need to help arm African American children with the knowledge, skills, and attitude needed to struggle successfully against oppression. These, more than test scores, more than high grade-point averages, are the critical features of education for African Americans. If students are to be equipped to struggle against racism they need excellent skills from the basics of reading, writing, and math, to understanding history, thinking critically, solving problems, and making decisions. (pp. 139–140)

As Ladson-Billings points out, an emancipatory education does not neglect disciplinary knowledge. In fact, learning specific subjects such as mathematics can help one better understand the sociopolitical context of one's life. No one would argue that learning to read is unimportant in understanding society. Similarly, mathematics can be a valuable tool in deepening one's awareness. And conversely, becoming more interested in analyzing the conditions of one's community can motivate students to acquire more tools to further those investigations (MacLeod, 1991). These complementary and related components— making sense of sociopolitical contexts and learning subjects like mathematics and reading —are integral to a pedagogy of social justice. An education that provides students with the knowledge and dispositions to struggle against racism and other forms of oppression ultimately helps create a more just and equitable society.

It may be hard to imagine teaching mathematics for social justice because of the dearth of examples in the literature. There are several possible explanations for this, especially in public, K–12 schools. First, educational practices that involve students in discussions and actions that critique sources of knowledge, question institutional practices, and run counter to norms and power structures within society are potentially problematic and can threaten schools and authority. Teachers put themselves at genuine risk by raising such issues. Second, the pressure of high-stakes tests, so prevalent in urban districts and increasingly dominating the public school agenda in the United States, can cause teachers and administrators to shy away from such a pedagogy (Lipman & Gutstein, 2001). Third, the roots of mathematics education as a field stem from mathematics and psychology (Kilpatrick, 1992), and researchers have historically focused more on cognition than on sociocultural contexts (although this situation is changing [see Lerman, 2000]). And fourth, there is the common notion that mathematics is an "objective" science that is neutral and context free.

However, Frankenstein's work at the college level does offer a social-justice model (1991, 1995, 1997). She has taught for years, not youths who are essentially "captives" in highly regimented schools, but rather adults who have a fair amount of autonomy in their lives and educational choices. She provides examples of teaching mathematics for social justice, such as having students analyze military versus domestic expenditures to help them understand and critique societal fiscal priorities, and she demonstrates how it is possible for students to transform their awareness of society through mathematics classes.

Even outside of mathematics, there is limited research on actual K-12 classroom practices involving social justice pedagogy. (For some examples, see Bigelow, Christensen, Karp,

Miner, & Peterson, 1994; Bigelow, Harvey, Karp, & Miller, 2001; La Colectiva Intercambio, 1996; MacLeod, 1991; Sylvester, 1994.) Case studies of teaching for justice and equity in K-12 mathematics classrooms may help us understand critical features of such a pedagogy and some of the associated enabling and disabling conditions, and they may ultimately help us move toward a more just and equitable society.

This article spans almost 2 years in an urban, Latino public school where I tried to teach mathematics for social justice. In 1997–1998, I taught a seventh-grade mathematics class from November through the end of the school year, then moved with the class to eighth grade in 1998–1999. Here I describe aspects of my teaching (mainly my curriculum and, to a lesser extent, my pedagogy) and of my students' learning. My aim is to describe the context of the classroom, provide specific examples of how teaching mathematics for social justice took shape in my situation, and examine the interconnections of my teaching and students' learning, which were necessarily interwoven.[1] Thus, I describe my overall goals, the classroom environment and culture, and aspects of my curriculum and pedagogy, and I provide evidence for students' learning and changed dispositions.

As a teacher, my larger goals were the three I discussed above for teaching for social justice: to help develop students' social and political consciousness, their sense of agency, and their social and cultural identities. But I was a *mathematics* teacher, and so I had mathematics-specific objectives that were related to these larger goals. Therefore, I developed a series of 17 real-world mathematics projects that connected to students' lives and experiences. In this article, I focus on the relationship of the goal of developing sociopolitical consciousness to students' mathematics learning and dispositions. Elsewhere, I discuss helping students develop a sense of agency (Gutstein, 2002a) and positive social and cultural identities (Gutstein, 2002b).

First I discuss my research site and methodology. Then I provide an overview of my teaching goals, classroom, and pedagogy, and then describe the curricular components of my class. The next sections contain an explanation of the three mathematics-specific objectives I had for my students, followed by the interrelationship of the goals of teaching for social justice and the *Standards*-based curriculum. Throughout these sections, I interweave my data and analysis. I conclude the article with theoretical and practical implications and raise further questions about teaching for social justice and increasing equity in schools.

• • •

AN OVERVIEW OF MY CLASSROOM, PEDAGOGY, CURRICULUM, AND SPECIFIC MATHEMATICS OBJECTIVES

> The challenge we now face is how to create a curriculum filled with responsible social and political issues that will help students understand the complexity of such problems, help them develop and understand the role of mathematics in their resolution, and allow them, at the same time, to develop mathematical power. (Romberg, 1992, p. 435)

My three mathematics objectives related closely to Romberg's challenge and were all part of my larger goals in teaching for social justice. I wanted my students to use mathematics to understand—and potentially act on—their sociopolitical context (i.e., to *read the world* to develop mathematical power and in the process to transform their attitude toward

mathematics). Table 29.1 contains both the larger goals involved in teaching for social justice and also my mathematics-specific objectives, and it points out that the first larger goal
and first specific objective are essentially the same.

The first objective, understanding and acting on one's surroundings, can be referred to
as learning to "read the world" (Freire & Macedo, 1987). Reading the world is akin to
developing a sociopolitical consciousness of the conditions and context of one's life, but
I am speaking here of doing this with the *specific* use of mathematics. In my view, reading
the world with mathematics means to use mathematics to understand relations of power,
resource inequities, and disparate opportunities between different social groups and to
understand explicit discrimination based on race, class, gender, language, and other differences. Further, it means to dissect and deconstruct media and other forms of representation and to use mathematics to examine these various phenomena both in one's
immediate life and in the broader social world and to identify relationships and make
connections between them. I tried to help my students learn how to do this by having
them complete real-world projects in which mathematics was the primary analytical tool.
For example, I developed a project in which students analyzed racially disaggregated data
on traffic stops. The mathematical concepts of proportionality and expected value are
central to understanding racial profiling. Without grasping those concepts, it is hard to
realize that more African American and Latino drivers are stopped than one would
expect, and this disproportionality should lead one to examine the root causes of the
anomaly. Mathematics can be a vehicle that leads into a deeper consideration of the bases
of inequitable treatment.

Although I describe this elsewhere (Gutstein, 2002b), an important theme that
emerged from my analysis is that my students also began to examine more generally inequality and discrimination in their lives and society—and not just with mathematics. We
had discussions that started from mathematical investigations of, for example, housing
discrimination but then moved on to broader, related topics. We also discussed topics that
seemed to have little to do with mathematics but that then became grist for mathematical
explorations. I call this *going beyond the mathematics* (Gutstein, 2000).

From Freire's (Freire & Macedo, 1987) point of view, reading the world is inseparable
from *reading the word* (acquiring text literacy). He led mass literacy campaigns focused on
emancipation in Brazil as well as in newly independent African nations in the 1970s.
Freire's (1994) emphasis was on helping people develop literacy through reading their
worlds as a starting point:

> Anyone taking a literacy course for adults wants to learn to read and write sentences, phrases,
> words. However, the reading and writing of words comes by way of the reading of the world.

TABLE 30.1 Teaching Goals and Objectives

Goals of Teaching for Social Justice	Specific Mathematics-Related Objectives
Develop Sociopolitical Consciousness	Read the World Using Mathematics
Develop Sense of Agency	Develop Mathematical Power
Develop Positive Social/Identities	Change Dispositions Toward Cultural Mathematics

Reading the world is an antecedent act vis-à-vis the reading of the word. The teaching of the reading and writing of the word to a person missing the critical exercise of reading and rereading the world is, scientifically, politically, and pedagogically, crippled. (pp. 78–79)

In my case, reading the *word* refers to developing mathematical literacy and mathematical power.

My second mathematics-specific objective was to help my students develop mathematical power, to use Romberg's words. I embraced, and tried to actualize, the vision for school mathematics elaborated in the NCTM's *Standards.* I use the following from the *Principles and Standards* (NCTM, 2000) as a working definition of mathematical power.

Students confidently engage in complex mathematical tasks … draw on knowledge from a wide variety of mathematical topics, sometimes approaching the same problem from different mathematical perspectives or representing the mathematics in different ways until they find methods that enable them to make progress … are flexible and resourceful problem solvers … work productively and reflectively … communicate their ideas and results effectively … value mathematics and engage actively in learning it. (p. 3)

I used *Mathematics in Context (MiC)* (National Center for Research in Mathematical Sciences Education [NCRMSE] & Freudenthal Institute, 1997–1998) as the basis of my curriculum. *MiC* is a comprehensive curriculum for Grades 5–8 developed with funding from the National Science Foundation (NSF) and was one of 13 curricula whose development was funded by the NSF to help make the NCTM's *Standards* into a reality. Teaching *MiC* was a significant component of my class.

My third objective was that through the real-world projects, students would develop a profoundly different orientation toward mathematics than they had after years in public schools and would become more motivated to study and use it. Although my students used *MiC* the preceding 2 years, their previous teachers were new to the curriculum. By the students' accounts, my observations, and her own admission, their fifth-grade teacher lacked experience and confidence in teaching mathematics and taught very little *MiC.* Their sixty-grade teacher was knowledgeable about mathematics but felt the pressures of standardized tests and curriculum coverage and supplemented *MiC* a good deal (Gutstein, 1998); from my observations, she was a good traditional mathematics teacher. Thus, despite some exposure to *MiC,* when my students entered seventh grade, they had much of the typical and well-documented disposition with which most mathematics educators and teachers are familiar—mathematics as a rote-learned, decontextualized series of rules and procedures to memorize, regurgitate, and not understand.

My curriculum had two main components: *MiC* and a series of real-world projects. The basic curriculum was *MiC,*[2] on which we spent probably 75–80% of our time. *MiC* has 10 units per grade, although no class at Rivera ever completed that many. My students finished several units per year and also completed most of the assessments that come with the units. At the time, Rivera used *MiC* in mathematics classes in Grades 4–8.

MiC's philosophy is multifaceted (NCRMSE & Freudenthal Institute, 1998). Much is similar to that of the NCTM's *Standards,* such as the importance of valuing multiple strategies, the necessity of student interaction, and the assumption of different roles for students and teachers. *MiC* emphasizes that students gradually develop formal approaches to mathematics. "It is preferable that students use informal strategies that they understand rather than formal procedures that they do not understand" (p. 5), and that students should "reinvent significant mathematics." It also holds that mathematics is a product of human activity, that models help students develop mathematical understanding at different levels, and that real-world contexts are necessary for learning mathematics.

MiC's real-world contexts were particularly appropriate because I wanted my students to learn mathematics *meaningfully*, that is, to view mathematics as a relevant tool, connected to their lives and experiences, with which to make sense out of social phenomena. Researchers have reported various ways that teachers help students learn mathematics meaningfully. These include teaching mathematics in culturally relevant ways (Gutstein, Lipman, Hernández, & de los Reyes, 1997; Ladson-Billings, 1995a; Tate, 1995), teaching it in critically literate ways (Frankenstein, 1997), and using students' and their community's *funds of knowledge* to develop curriculum (Andrade, Carson, & González, 2001; González et al., 1993). However, although *MiC* uses real-life settings for *all* its contexts, my students felt that they could not relate that well to these settings (Gutstein, 1998). But even if my students felt that they could relate to the *MiC* settings, I still would have developed the real-world projects to incorporate issues of economic and racial discrimination and inequality, immigrant status, gentrification, and other examples of injustice facing them and their families on a daily basis. *MiC* contexts, though mostly likable and interesting according to my students, did not deal with these sorts of issues. Nonetheless, *MiC*'s real-world contexts were essential because they helped create a classroom culture in which other real-world contexts could be investigated.

Over the almost 2 years that I taught them, my students completed 17 real-world projects, lasting from a couple of days to a couple of weeks. Besides mathematics, all the projects included writing and interpreting data, graphs, pictures, maps, or text (often newspaper articles). In one way or another, virtually every project related to and built on my students' lived experiences as urban youth from immigrant, Latino, working-class families. For example, the following was part of the *Racism in Housing Data?* project. I gave students the data for the highest median house price in the area at the time (in 1997, the suburb of McFadden, $752,250) and asked them these questions:

How could you use mathematics to help answer whether racism has anything to do with the house prices in McFadden. Be detailed and specific!! Describe:

1. What mathematics would you use to answer that question.
2. How would you use the mathematics.
3. If you would collect any data to answer the question, explain *what* data you would collect and *why* you would collect that data.
4. Give examples of data that would cause you to believe that racism *is* involved in the McFadden housing price, and explain why you reached that conclusion based on the analysis of the data.
5. Give examples of data that would cause you to believe that racism *is not* involved in the McFadden housing price, and explain why you reached that conclusion based on the analysis of the data.

One week later, I assigned the second part of the project, in which I reproduced the students' various responses in summary form. I asked students to pick two of the responses, explain in writing why those were good data with which to analyze if racism was involved, and answer the question, "How can you use the data you picked out to know whether or not racism is involved?"

I intended these assignments to help students use mathematics to make sense of complex social questions. But just as using *MiC*—where all mathematics is from the world —does not guarantee by itself that students can use mathematics to analyze if racism is a factor in housing prices, similarly, projects like this do not either. A colleague of mine commented, referring to a project where students analyzed world maps and discovered that not all accurately represented reality (Gutstein, 2000, 2001), one does not just walk into a classroom with maps over the shoulder and expect students to create real meaning. How students construct meaning depends much on the teacher's pedagogy and on the classroom environment co-created by the teacher and students.

In my class we *normalized* politically taboo topics (Gutstein, 1999)—that is, we went beyond mathematics and discussed issues that mattered in students' lives. In particular, race, racism, discrimination, power, and justice became ordinary topics of conversation. Sometimes they were related to mathematics and sometimes not. Also, as students used mathematics to discover some vastly unfair things, many at times felt powerless. I had to learn how to help them reconcile feelings of "oh well, what can I do about it" with their increasing awareness of injustice. There was also my role as a white, male professional teaching Latino, working-class youth and trying (presumptuously?) to help them develop positive social and cultural identities. There were other issues, such as whether students wrote on their projects what they thought I wanted to hear and the influence of district and school contexts and the support of the principal. All of these issues and my attempts to deal with them are important but beyond the scope of this article. I discuss these further in (Gutstein, 1999, 2000, 2002a, 2002b).

READING THE WORLD USING MATHEMATICS

From a Freirean perspective, reading the *world* and reading the *word* are dialectically related and, ideally, reinforce each other. By reading the world, we become motivated to read the word better; by reading the word, we can better read the world. Of course, in practice, this is not always so straightforward. Freire worked with adults involved in social production who chose to learn to read. Some lived in newly independent nations, rebuilding their countries. Even among those in his native Brazil, many were working for social change. Power relations between teachers and students were generally equitable. However, middle school students in highly regimented, disciplined, urban schools where high-stakes tests and punitive structures reign do not necessarily approach math with the same openness. Furthermore, Freire (Freire & Macedo, 1987) advocated that active participation in transforming society be the context for learning to read the world and the word:

> Reading the world always precedes reading the word, and reading the word implies continually reading the world.… In a way, however, we can go further and say that reading the word is not preceded merely by reading the world, but by a certain form of *writing* it or *rewriting* it, that is, of transforming it by conscious, practical work. For me, this dynamic movement is central to the literacy process. (p. 35)

This too does not easily transfer to middle school students at Rivera. Nevertheless, even though my students did not share the actual life experiences or the specific outlook of the adults with whom Freire worked, they did begin to read the world using mathematics.

As a Freirean pedagogy (Freire, 1992) suggests, I did not try to have my students answer questions so much as raise them. Questions such as why females, students of color, and low-income students score lower on SAT and ACT exams are not easily answerable—and students did raise that question in one of our projects. I did not try to answer many questions like this—nor could I answer all their questions. And I did not want my students to accept any view without questioning it. I did share my own opinions with my students because I agreed with Freire's contention that progressive educators need to take the responsibility to dispel the notion that education can be the inactive transfer of inert knowledge and instead to promote the idea that all practice (including teaching) is inherently political. I take Freire (1994) to mean here that educators need to be explicit in their views while at the same time to respect the space for others to develop their own.

> [I]nasmuch as education of its very nature is directive and political, I must, without ever denying my dream or my utopia before the educands, respect them. To defend a thesis, a position, a preference, with earnestness, defend it rigorously, but passionately, as well, and at the same time to stimulate the contrary discourse, and respect the right to utter that discourse, is the best way to teach, first, the right to have our own ideas, even our duty to "quarrel" for them, for our dreams … and second, mutual respect (p. 78).

My criteria for evidence of reading the world included that students used mathematics as a tool to analyze social issues like racism and other forms of bias and to understand power relations and unequal resource allocation in society. I looked for signs that students used mathematics to scrutinize representations of reality (like maps) and to link them to issues of injustice. My criteria also included that students looked for relationships between various social issues we studied. Consistency of their ideas was less important, because the situations were complex and because middle school students are just beginning to more deeply form and articulate their ideas about the world.

One of our projects (from Peterson, 1995) involved simulating the distribution of world wealth by continents. I told students the number of people and the total wealth of each continent. The students found the percent each continent's population was of the world's population, and then using those percents we distributed ourselves randomly to each "continent" (area of the room). We then distributed the "wealth" of the world (two bags of cookies), using the same idea, to each continent and shared the cookies equally within the continent. Thus, the two students in North America each received a stack of 14   cookies, whereas the four of us in Africa shared the crumbs (literally) of 1 cookie. As a group, we compared the ratios of North America to Asia (1 ½ cookies per person) to Africa. Students saw that the average wealth of a North American was 56 times greater than that of an African. While students were genuinely shocked and upset to learn about the wealth inequity, Marsol went deeper in her analysis and presented it verbally in class. She later wrote:

And even if some continents have more wealth than others, that doesn't mean that the people in the continent all have the same amount of wealth. Some have no wealth at all, while others can have billions of dollars of wealth. If you look at Africa, there are 763 million people living there and they have 436.6 billion dollars in wealth. For all we know, one person might have 436.6 billion dollars in wealth and everybody else might not have any at all. Of course, we know this isn't so, but it just makes you realize that knowing how much wealth each continent has doesn't really tell you anything about how much wealth the people have on each continent. In the U.S., Bill Gates holds more money than anybody else, but if you divide the wealth by population, Bill would probably have an average amount of money and a homeless would have an average amount of wealth.

Her comment is a mathematical critique of the weakness of a one-number summary for a data set. It represents a relatively sophisticated understanding for a middle school student and forms an informal basis upon which to abstract more complicated mathematics. More important, it helped students deepen, in a concrete way, their understanding of wealth inequality *between* continents to include the idea of wealth inequality *within* a continent. Several students responded in their own writings to Marisol's point in class. Omar connected his own life experience to the world situation, and, using her framework, he drew an analogy between the world wealth inequality and the inequality between his hard-working parents and a well-paid, professional athlete:

What Marisol said on Friday was right on the spot. Not all the wealth is distributed equally. You may see some homeless guy looking for food but then the next moment, you see someone driving their brand new Mercedes convertible. For example, even the ones that aren't homeless. Our family makes somewhere in the neighbourhood of $40,000. I heard that Michael Jordan makes about $1,000 for every minute he plays. So that means that in 40 minutes he makes our whole family's earnings. While my parents work year round for that money. I really think Marisol hit [it] right on the money. I learned that lesson that plays a huge role in life.

I followed up this project with a related one a few months later where we considered the wealth distribution within the United States. Using data from Wolff (1995), we compared the financial wealth of the wealthiest 1% of the United States, the next 19%, and the bottom 80%. Before I gave the students the data, I asked them to guess the distribution. Every student was significantly off in her or his estimate and believed U.S. wealth to be more equitably distributed than it was. Students wrote what they thought about the subject before and after the activity, what they learned, how (specifically) they used mathematics, whether they could have understood the ideas without using mathematics, and how the activity made them feel. All but 3 of the 26 expressed that they learned a lot and gave specific examples; one of the three said she already knew how unevenly distributed the wealth was in the United States, but her estimate also was very wrong. Twenty three reported feelings including "shock," a strong sense of "unfairness" [many], "anger," "mad," "this is a really powerful situation," "bad and disturbed," "disappointed," "determined," [to change things], and "it makes me think a lot." Only one student reported feeling "nothing," one student did not understand the activity as evidenced by his report, and one felt "mixed" [because] "in a way I'm happy the U.S. is 'rich' because it gives people more opportunities (or at least it seems)," but she also wrote, "I still have questions about why this is like this and if we could ever change it."

I often explicitly asked students to make judgments about complex social situations on the basis of data. In the *Racism in Housing Data?* project, students responded in a variety of ways. Some of these were relatively straightforward applications of mathematics. For example, one student discussed how she would use mathematics to compare the percentages of different-race home owners in the community, as well as the prices that people of different races paid. However, she then went further mathematically and discussed racism within the context of changing prices over time and the size of the house:

> [A]lthough price, you can't be sure of, since the worth of things is going up and down. For example, if a White has a house that cost him $100,000 but he got it 30 years ago, and a Black just got a house for 200,000 a year ago, that wouldn't be racism. It would be racism if, let's say, a white family got the house 3 months ago and they paid 250,000 and then a Black family paid for a house 3 months ago but they paid $752,000 [the median house price for the suburb], that would be racism, unless the house of the Black people was 3 times as big. If there was no racism, it would be if the White family paid for the house $250,000 and the Black family paid $250,000, but both bought their houses 3 months ago. I reached my conclusion by looking at what time they bought it and at what price.

Another student used the criteria of salaries for different ethnicities and related that to changing neighbourhood demographics and rising taxes:

> There would be racism if the Latino average salaries are for example, $40,000 a year and the whites are $250,000 a year or more, and the builders are building more new houses in the Latino area so that Latinos' taxes would go up when people move in, thus making the Latinos move out, then it would be racism. It wouldn't be racism if the salaries of the whites and Latinos were about the same and the houses were being built on both Latino and whites' neighbourhoods.

Another student also discussed salaries, but with respect to house price and affordability:

> First I would find the price of a house in McFadden and a working-class Latino's annual income. Then I would divide the house's price to find the annual payment. Then I would take the income and subtract the cost of living (food, clothes, etc.) and compare the difference to the house's payments. If there is a large difference in the two, it is possible discrimination exists in the prices of McFadden because the price is impossible for most, if not all, working-class Latinos. I would say there was no racism involved if the prices were more affordable for minority groups.

Students also related McFadden's prices to other suburbs:

> Well, first of all, since McFadden is the most expensive suburb, what we could do to find out using math would be look at different suburbs. What I mean is that we look at other suburbs like Piedmont and others' prices, and depending on the average single-family house cost, we

could find out if it was racism or not. You see, because many Latinos live in Piedmont and other suburbs that aren't so expensive.

It is worthwhile to examine the complex issues students brought up. Some students contended that they could tell if racism was involved by looking at house prices by neighborhood. If the same house were higher priced in neighbourhoods of color, then racism existed—that is, prices were unfairly raised to make people of color pay more. However, other students claimed just the opposite! They stated that if house prices for the same houses were higher in white communities, this was racism because realtors knew that people of color could not afford as much and were keeping neighbourhoods white by raising house prices beyond what families of color could afford. From discussions like these, students began to appreciate that the answers were not simple and that mathematics played a role in trying to sort out difficult, real-world questions.

In another project, I asked students to examine 1997 SAT and ACT exam scores by race, gender, and social class. The project was particularly intense for students because Latinos and low-income students were on the bottom, and this raised significant questions about how to do this type of project without reinforcing negative stereotypes, depressing, or paralyzing students—and about my role (Gutstein, 1999, 2002a). In part 1, students made up three questions about the scores that could be answered with mathematics and explained how they would use math to answer them.

Part 2 read:

> The SAT is made by the Educational Testing Service (ETS). Look at the SAT data by income level and average score of all students. Write a one-page letter to ETS about that data, asking any questions you want and making any points you want to. Include a graph that shows the income level and average scores as a way to talk about and question the data.

Of the 21 students who completed the project, 5 interrelated class and race (e.g., "your data might not be correct because I know that race and income don't equal intelligence"). Eleven questioned the relationship of income and quality of education (e.g., "what if you have a really smart student that only has an income of $9,000 would he/she not get much of an education?") Three other raised the same issue solely about race (e.g., "How come whites and Asians get higher scores, yet everyone else gets lower scores. How does race affect your scores? Now I really want to know is there racism involved"). The remaining 2 suggested that effort could overcome the discrepancies (e.g., "All of these [low-income] people want to become doctors, lawyers, sports players, etc. So why are 'rich' smarter?") The majority reasoned that either whites or people with higher income (not necessarily mutually exclusive) got a better education, and better education led to higher SAT scores—but most could not explain why. Overall, there was the strong current that "the income of what you [ETS] put for every year has nothing to do with a person's mind."

In reading the responses, the main theme that emerges is students' efforts to make sense of an extremely complex situation. Their questions were genuine and came from their experiences as educationally disadvantaged and marginalized students who saw themselves in the data and wanted to know why. They learned that situations like these were complicated and that mathematical analyses could be entry points to learn about inequality.

NOTES

This research was partially funded by a University Research Council grant from DePaul University. I would like to acknowledge the appreciable help on earlier drafts of this article from Pauline Lipman and the *JRME* editorial staff as well as from the anonymous reviewers—and I want to thank the students of Diego Rivera School for their help as well.

1. Indeed, as Ladson-Billings (2001) points out, in Hebrew and other languages, teaching and learning are the same word, although I explicate them somewhat independently here.

2. I have worked closely with the developers of *MiC* over a number of years and was a consultant on the Teacher Resource and Implementation Guide (NCRMSE & Freudenthal Institute, 1998). I am also a member of the *MiC* consultants group.

REFERENCES

Anderson, G. L., Herr, K., & Nihlen, A. S. (Eds.). (1994). *Studying your own school: An educator's guide to qualitative practitioner research*. Thousand Oaks, CA: Corwin Press.

Andrade, R., Carson, C., & González, N. (2001). Creating links between home and school mathematics practices. In E. McIntyre, A. Rosebery, & N. González (Eds.), *Classroom diversity: Connecting curriculum to students' lives*. Portsmouth, NH: Heinemann.

Apple, M. (1992). Do the Standards go far enough? Power, policy, and practice in mathematics education. *Journal for Research in Mathematics Education, 23*, 412–431.

Bigelow, B., Christensen, L, Karp, S., Miner, B., & Peterson, B. (Eds.). (1994). *Rethinking our classrooms: Teaching for equity and justice*. Milwaukee, WI: Rethinking Schools, Ltd.

Bigelow, B., Harvey, B., Karp, S., & Miller, L. (Eds.). (2001). *Rethinking our classrooms, Volume 2: Teaching for equity and justice*. Milwaukee, WI: Rethinking Schools, Ltd.

Bishop, A. J. (1991). *Mathematical enculturation: A cultural perspective on mathematics education*. Dordrecht, The Netherlands: Kluwer.

Boaler, J. (1997). *Experiencing school mathematics: Teaching styles, sex, and setting*. Buckingham, England: Open University Press.

Boaler, J. (1998). Open and closed mathematics. *Journal for Research in Mathematics Education, 29*, 41–62.

Boaler, J. (2000). Exploring situated insights into research and learning. *Journal for Research in Mathematics Education, 31*, 113–119.

Campbell, P. F. (1996). Empowering children and teachers in the elementary mathematics classrooms of urban schools. *Urban Education, 30* 449–475.

Cochran-Smith, M., & Lytle, S. L. (1993). *Inside-outside: Teacher research and knowledge*. New York: Teachers College Press.

Delpit, L. (1988). The silenced dialogue: Power and pedagogy in educating other people's children. *Harvard Educational Review, 58*, 280–298.

Emerson, R. M., Fretz, R. I., & Shaw, L. L. (1995). *Writing ethnographic fieldnotes*. Chicago: University of Chicago Press.

Frankenstein, M. (1987). Critical mathematics education: An application of Paulo Freire's epistemology. In I. Shor *(Ed.)*, *Freire for the classroom: A sourcebook for liberatory teaching* (pp. 180–210). Portsmouth, NH: Boyton/Cook.

Frankenstein, M. (1989). *Relearning mathematics: A different third R—radical maths*. London: Free Association Books.

Frankenstein, M. (1991). Incorporating race, gender, and class issues into a critical mathematical literacy curriculum. *Journal of Negro Education, 59*, 336–359.

Frankenstein, M. (1995). Equity in mathematics education: Class in the world outside the class. In W. G. Secada, E. Fennema, & L. B. Adajian (Eds.), *New directions for equity in mathematics education* (pp. 165–190). Cambridge: Cambridge University Press.

Frankenstein, M. (1997). In addition to the mathematics: Including equity issues in the curriculum. In J. Trentacosta & M. Kenney (Eds.), *Multicultural and gender equity in the mathematics classroom* (pp. 10–22). Reston, VA: National Council of Teachers of Mathematics.

Freire, P. (1992). *Pedagogy of the oppressed*. (M. B. Ramos, Trans.). New York: Seabury Press.

Freire, P. (1994). *Pedagogy of hope.* New York: Continuum.

Freire, P., & Macedo, D. (1987). *Literacy: Reading the word and the world.* Westport, CT: Bergin & Garvey.

González, N., Moll, L. C., Floyd-Tenery, M., Rivera, A., Rendon, P., Gonzáles, R., et al. (1993). *Teacher research on funds of knowledge: Learning from households.* Tucson, AZ: National Center for Research on Cultural Diversity and Second Language Learning.

Gutiérrez, R. (in press). Enabling the practice of mathematics teachers in context: Toward a new equity research agenda. *Mathematics, Teaching, and Learning.*

Gutstein, E. (1998, April). *Lessons from adopting and adapting* Mathematics in Context, *a standards-based mathematics curriculum, in an urban, Latino, bilingual middle school.* Paper presented at the Annual Meeting of the American Educational Research Association, San Diego.

Gutstein, E. (1999, April). *Teaching mathematics for critical literacy in an urban, Latino classroom* Paper presented at the Annual Meeting of the American Educational Research Association, Montreal.

Gutstein, E. (2000, April). *When what you see is not what you get: Urban Latino students read the world with mathematics.* Paper presented at the Research Presession of the Annual Meeting of the National Council of Teachers of Mathematics, Chicago.

Gutstein, E. (2001). Math, maps, & misrepresentation. *Rethinking Schools, 15* (3), 6–7.

Gutstein, E. (2002a, April). *Roads toward equity in mathematics education: Helping students develop a sense of agency.* Paper presented at the Annual Meeting of the American Educational Research Association, New Orleans.

Gutstein, E. (2002b). *What else have we been lied to about? Using mathematics to read the world.* Manuscript in preparation.

Gutstein, E., Lipman, P., Hemández, P., & de los Reyes, R. (1997). Culturally relevant mathematics teaching in a Mexican American context. *Journal for Research in Mathematics Education, 28,* 709–737.

Hammersley, M., & Atkinson, P. (1983). *Ethnography: Principles in practice.* London: Tavistock Publications.

Khisty, L. L. (1995). Making inequality: Issues in language and meanings in mathematics teaching with Hispanic students. In W. G. Secada, E. Fennema, & L. B. Adajian (Eds.), *New directions for equity in mathematics instruction* (pp. 279–297). Cambridge: Cambridge University Press.

Kilpatrick, J. (1992). A history of research in mathematics education. In D. A. Grouws (Ed.), *Handbook of research on mathematics teaching and learning* (pp. 3–38). New York: Macmillan.

LaColectiva Intercambio (1996). Ways of looking, teaching, and learning: A tapestry of Latino collaborative projects. In C. E. Walsh (Ed.), *Education reform and social change: Multicultural voices, struggles, and visions* (pp. 95–122). Mahvah, NJ: Erlbaum.

Ladson-Billings, G. (1994). *The dreamkeepers.* San Francisco: Jossey-Bass.

Ladson-Billings, G. (1995a). Making mathematics meaningful in multicultural contexts. In W. G. Secada, E. Fennema, & L. B. Adajian (Eds.), *New directions for equity in mathematics education* (pp. 126–145). Cambridge: Cambridge University Press.

Ladson-Billing, G. (1995b). Toward a theory of culturally relevant pedagogy. *American Educational Research Journal, 32,* 465–491.

Ladson-Billings, G. (2001). *Crossing over to Canaan: The journey of new teachers in diverse classrooms.* San Francisco, Jossey-Bass.

Lave, J. (1988). *Cognition in practice: Mind, mathematics, and culture in everyday life.* Cambridge: Cambridge University Press.

Lave, J. & Wegner, E. (1991). *Situated learning: Legitimate peripheral participation.* New York: Cambridge University Press.

Lerman, S. (2000). The social turn in mathematics education research. In J. Boaler (Ed.), *Multiple perspectives on mathematics teaching and learning* (pp. 19–44). Westport, CT: Ablex.

Lipman, P., & Gutstein, E. (2001). Undermining the struggle for equity: A case study of a Chicago Latino/a school. *Race, Gender, and Class, 8,* 57–80.

Lubienski, S. T. (2000). Problem solving as a means toward mathematics for all: An exploratory look through a class lens. *Journal for Research in Mathematics Education, 31,* 454–482.

Macedo, D. (1994). *Literacies of power: What Americans are not allowed to know.* Boulder, CO: Westview.

MacLeod, J. (1991). Bridging street and school. *Journal of Negro Education, 60,* 260–275.

Moses, R. P. & Cobb, C. E., Jr. (2001). *Math literacy and civil rights.* Boston: Beacon Press.

Murrell, P. C., Jr. (1997). Digging again the family wells: A Freirean literacy framework as emancipatory pedagogy for African American children. In P. Freire, (Ed.), *Mentoring the mentor: A critical dialogue with Paulo Freire* (pp. 19–58). New York: Peter Lang Publishing.

National Center for Research in Mathematical Sciences Education (NCRMSE) & Freudenthal Institute. (1997–1998). *Mathematics in context: A connected curriculum for grades* 5–8. Chicago: Encyclopaedia Britannica Educational Corporation.

National Center for Research in Mathematical Sciences Education (NCRMSE) & Freudenthal Institute. (1998). *Teacher resource and implementation guide*. Chicago: Encyclopaedia Britannica Educational Corporation.

National Council of Teachers of Mathematics (1989). *Curriculum and evaluation standards for school mathematics*. Reston, VA: Author.

National Council of Teachers of Mathematics (2000). *Principles and standards for school mathematics*. Reston, VA: Author.

Nunes, T. (1992). Ethnomathematics and everyday cognition. In D. A. Grouws (Ed.), *Handbook of research on mathematics teaching and learning* (pp. 557–574). New York: Macmillan.

Oakes, J. (1985). *Keeping track: How schools structure inequality*. New Haven: Yale University Press.

Oakes, J. (1990). *Multiplying inequalities: The effect of race, social class, and tracking on opportunities to learn mathematics and science*. Santa Monica, CA: RAND.

Ogbu, J. U. (1987). Variability in minority school performance: A problem in search of an explanation. *Anthropology and Education Quarterly, 18,* 312–334.

Peterson, B. (1995). Teaching math across the curriculum: A 5th grade teacher battles "number numbness." *Rethinking Schools, 10 (1),* 1 & 4–5.

Romberg, T. A. (1992). Further thoughts on the Standards: A reaction to Apple. *Journal for Research in Mathematics Education, 23,* 432–437.

Romberg, T. A., Shafer, M., & Webb, N. (2000). *Study of the impact of Mathematics in Context on achievement*. Madison, WI: Wisconsin Center for Education Research, University of Wisconsin–Madison.

Secada, W. G. (1991). Diversity, equity, and cognitivist research. In E. Fennema, T. P. Carpenter, & S. J. Lamon (Eds.), *Integrating research on teaching and learning mathematics* (pp. 17–53). Albany, NY: State University of New York Press.

Secada, W. G. (1996). Urban students acquiring English and learning mathematics in the context of reform. *Urban Education, 30,* 422–448.

Silver, E. A., Smith, M. S., & Nelson, B. S. (1995). The QUASAR Project: Equity concerns meet mathematics education in the middle school. In W. G. Secada, E. Fennema, & L. B. Adajian (Eds.), *New directions for equity in mathematics education.* (pp. 9–56). Cambridge: Cambridge University Press.

Skovsmose, O. (1994a). Toward a critical mathematics education. *Educational Studies in Mathematics, 25,* 35–57.

Skovsmose, O. (1994b). *Toward a philosophy of critical mathematical education*. Boston: Kluwer Academic Publishers.

Sylvester, P. S. (1994). Teaching and practice. *Harvard Educational Review, 64,* 309–331.

Tate, W. F.(1995). Returning to the root: A culturally relevant approach to mathematics pedagogy. *Theory into Practice, 34,* 166–173.

Tate, W. F. (1996). Urban schools and mathematics reform: Implementing new standards. *Urban Education, 30,* 371–378.

Weissglass, J. (2000). No compromise on equity in mathematics education: Developing an infrastructure. In W. G. Secada (Ed.), *Changing the faces of mathematics: Perspectives on multiculturalism and gender equity* (pp. 5–24). Reston, VA: National Council of Teachers of Mathematics.

Wolff, E. N. (1995). *Top heavy: The increasing inequality of wealth in America and what can be done about it*. New York: The New Press.

30

"You Can't Just Say That the Only Ones Who Can Speak Are Those Who Agree With Your Position": Political Discourse in the Classroom

Melinda Fine

CAMBRIDGE, MASSACHUSETTS, LIES just across the Charles River from Boston. Known best for its stately, well-kept colonial homes and the ivy-clad brick buildings of Harvard University, this three-hundred-and-fifty year old city is generally perceived as a White, middle-class, intellectual enclave. While this perception is at least partially true, this densely packed city of almost 100,000 is in fact far more heterogeneous than its popular image suggests. One-fifth of all Cambridge residents are foreign-born, and one-half of these arrived during the past decade. A majority of the city's African Americans, as well as immigrants from Cape Verde, Brazil, Southeast Asia, Central America, and Haiti, tend to reside in neighborhoods that look quite different from the tree-lined streets and white-trimmed mansions surrounding Harvard University.

The Medgar Evers School is located in one of the poorer neighborhoods of Cambridge.[1] Here, mostly Black, Latino, Haitian, and Asian families live in multifamily homes that are usually close together, and often in need of paint or new siding. Many of Medgar Evers' students come from the large housing project just across the street; 44 percent of the student population qualifies for free or reduced-price lunches. Because of the city's desegregation program, however, the school's roughly six hundred K-8 students are more racially balanced than the neighborhood in which the school is located: in 1992–1993, the school was 43 percent White, 34 percent African American, 16 percent Asian, and 7 percent Latino.

Medgar Evers is a long, three-story, beige concrete building of irregular geometric design. Surrounded by few trees, the school appears cold and austere when viewed from the street. Once inside, however, one gets an entirely different impression. Classrooms, offices, the school library, and the auditorium spin off from an airy central space that is open from the third floor to the basement. Sunlight streams in through skylights on the school's slanted roof, infusing all three floors of the building with light. Terracotta-tiled floors, clean hallways, notices for bake sales and other school events, as well as abundant displays of student artwork make the school feel cheery and welcoming. An enormous map of the world hangs on a wall across from the school's central office. This map is covered with push pins, each connected to a string that leads to a flag representing the country pinpointed. "We have children and families in our school representing *at least* sixty-four countries of the world," a card next to the map states. "We want to encourage children to become familiar with the world map, to identify all of the countries of origin, and to help celebrate our diversity!"

I have visited a classroom in this school nearly every day for the past four months, acting as a participant/observer while carrying out research for my doctoral dissertation in education. I have come to study how the teacher and students in one classroom grapple with an interdisciplinary social studies unit called "Facing History and Ourselves."[2]

This program seeks to provide a model for teaching history in a way that helps students reflect critically upon a variety of contemporary social, moral, and political issues. It focuses on a specific historical period—the Nazi rise to power and the Holocaust—and guides students back and forth between an in-depth historical case study and reflection on the causes and consequences of present-day prejudice, intolerance, violence, and racism.[3]

Facing History's decision to use the Holocaust as a case study and a springboard for exploring contemporary issues is complex and merits some discussion. When middle school teachers in Brookline, Massachusetts, created Facing History and Ourselves in 1976, relatively few Holocaust curricula existed. Perceiving the Holocaust to be a watershed event of the twentieth century, these teachers felt that their students should, indeed, learn about such a critical historical moment. At the same time, however, they felt that the Holocaust's "meaning" to students must lie not only in understanding its unique historical dimensions, but also in grappling with its more generalizable lessons about human behavior. Historically examining the escalation of steps through which individuals living under Nazi rule were made to follow Hitler—from the use of propaganda to influence one's thinking, to the threats against one's economic and personal security, to the use of terror to compel obedience—course designers sought to help students identify how opportunities for resistance were gradually eroded with the demise of German democracy and the rise of a totalitarian state. Using historical understanding as a catalyst for more personal, critical reflection, they intended to foster students' awareness of the social conditions that can undermine democracy and promote their sense of moral and political responsibility as future citizens.

It might well be asked whether these goals could not also be achieved by undertaking a different, perhaps more relevant case study—of the Middle Passage (the transatlantic slave trade), for example, or the genocide of Native Americans. No doubt they could be. Program designers, teachers, and promoters do not argue that the Holocaust is the only genocide—or even the most important genocide—to teach about. In fact, Facing History has developed other curricular materials that deal more directly with these "closer-to-home" events, and the Facing History Resource Text includes a chapter on the Armenian Genocide.[4]

Program advocates do contend, however, that discussions about contemporary racism and violence may in fact be facilitated by focusing on a period of history more tangential to the cultural backgrounds of the course's ethnically diverse students. As Larry Myatt, a longtime teacher of the course and the director of an inner-city high school in Boston, says, Facing History offers "a way to talk about these issues in a *removed* way so that we don't hit people over the head with a two-by-four and say 'racism!' 'scapegoating!'"[5]

In keeping with the program's educational priorities, the semester-long curriculum is structured to move back and forth between a focus on "history" and a focus on "ourselves." Initial chapters of the program's resource book encourage thinking about universal questions of individual identity and social behavior. From here the course moves on to its more specific case study of prejudice and discrimination: an examination of the history of anti-semitism, beginning as far back as ancient Rome. Students undertake a rigorous, multifaceted study of German history from 1914 to 1945, examining, for example, the impact of Nazi racial policies in education and the workplace, the nature of propaganda, and the various roles played by victims, victimizers, and bystanders during the Third Reich. These lessons provide critical historical content and serve as structured exercises for thinking about the choices that individuals, groups, and nations faced with regard to action and resistance. These exercises, in turn, prepare students for later discussions about how they themselves can assume responsibility for protecting civil liberties and becoming active citizens.[6]

Facing History's complex intellectual content is undergirded by a pedagogical imperative: to foster perspective-taking, critical thinking, and moral decision-making among students. It is specifically geared toward adolescents who are developmentally engaged in a fierce (and somewhat contradictory) struggle to become distinct individuals *and* to fit in with their peers. These students, curriculum developers argue, have the most to gain from a course that "raises the problem of differing perspectives, competing truths, the need to understand motives and to consider the intentions and abilities of themselves and others."[7] Rather than shying away from the conflicts that are inevitably generated when a diverse group of adolescents work to clarify their own beliefs and values, teachers encourage students to view complexity and conflict as potentially conducive to personal growth and social exchange.

I chose to observe the implementation of Facing History and Ourselves in the Medgar Evers school for specific reasons—reasons undoubtedly operative in my interpretation of the course and, consequently, important to acknowledge here. First and foremost, I am a supporter of the program's goals. Educational efforts to foster moral and social responsibility are difficult undertakings, not only because of the conflictual nature of the material inevitably confronted with the students, but also because of the embattled position many such education programs—including Facing History—find themselves in today. I consider them socially necessary, nonetheless.

I also find compelling Facing History's claim that using historical subject matter somewhat tangential to the lives of racially diverse students may quite effectively reach and motivate students in multicultural urban settings. For this reason I have observed Facing History courses in several urban schools over the past few years, while completing my own doctoral work and serving as a research consultant to the Facing History organization.[8] My professional collaboration with Facing History has deepened my understanding of the program, but also demanded that I be vigilant in pushing myself to view its classroom practice in a critical light.

Consequently, while at the Medgar Evers school, I observed class daily for an eleven-week period. I hoped to learn how students and their teacher interpreted issues raised by the course, recognizing that their interpretations would no doubt shift during the semester and assuming, too, that they would at times produce conflict among classroom participants. I intended to describe how these conflicts were negotiated within the classroom.

To carry out my objectives, I felt that I needed to know as much as possible about the students, their teacher, and the school culture that surrounded the classroom study. I needed to have all classroom participants speak freely with me, and thus I needed to be known and trusted by them. These requirements dictated a qualitative, descriptive, phenomenological, and self-consciously personal approach to my subject, involving, among other things, participant/observation, in-class and post-class writing, lengthy individual interviews with students and their teacher, and ongoing review of students' written work.

My relations with the teacher and students were open and friendly. Over the course of the semester, I was invited to a bar mitzvah, sock hop, viola recital, and soccer match, and after the school year ended, I received a letter from one student asking me out to lunch. Since my intent was to get to know classroom participants and to let them get to know me, I never tried to hold myself aloof or maintain the stance of a completely distant, "objective" observer. Though I didn't, for the most part, participate actively in class discussion, I nonetheless tried to act in a style compatible with the school's "open" atmosphere. My constant, in-class writing was obvious to all present (in fact, students often teased me about how quickly I wrote), and I did comment on topics when asked by either the teacher or students. I also frequently asked, and was told, about students' basketball games, dances, baby-sitting, and dates. In turn, students asked and were told about me: that I was a teacher, an activist, and at that time a graduate student, and that I was writing a book about them.

I identify what I did and where I stand in relation to Facing History not to suggest that researcher "bias" qualifies the validity of my observations—as if some wholly neutral position were a preferable point of departure or even possible to attain. I believe all researchers stand in some relation to their subject; the reader simply deserves to know where I stand before watching these classroom events along with me.

• • •

It is an unseasonably hot day in May. The twenty-three students in Marysa Gonzalez's seventh/eighth-grade class sit fanning themselves with their spiral notebooks as late-morning sun pours into the classroom through a large, partially closed window on the far side of the room. Of the twelve girls and eleven boys in this room, six are African American, four are Asian, and thirteen are White, one of whom is a Latina. Nursing her latest sports injury, Jess limps to her seat clad in navy blue shorts and a University of Michigan tee-shirt. Abby sports a summer-bright turquoise shirt, matching socks, and white stretch pants. The top piece of her shoulder length, sandy-blond hair is pulled back in a clip, and her bangs remain loose and hanging. Sandra's clothing and hairstyle are almost identical. Alan and Josh each sport marginally punk hairdos. Alan wears an earring in his left ear. Chi-Ho's pressed, beige cotton shirt remains buttoned at both the neck and cuffs, and he removes his thick, black-rimmed glasses every now and then to wipe the sweat from his brow. Jamal and Amiri both wear oversized tee-shirts and baggy cotton pants.

The teacher, Marysa Gonzalez, searches intently through piles of paper on her desk. A handsome Latina in her late forties, her style is informal and unpretentious: she wears light khaki slacks, a loose-fitting red cotton shirt, and no makeup. Her long black hair, pulled back in a loose braid, is streaked with grey.

It is the eleventh and second-to-last week of the Facing History course. Using students' understanding of the Holocaust as a lens through which to approach more immediate concerns, Marysa focuses the remaining class discussions around contemporary political problems in order to highlight students' own social and political responsibilities. This way of bringing closure to the course is in keeping with the final chapter of the Facing History Resource Text:

> This curriculum must provide opportunities for students to explore the practical applications of freedom, which they have learned demand a constant struggle with difficult, controversial, and complex issues.... This history has taught that there is no one else to confront terrorism, ease the yoke and pain of racism, attack apathy, create and enforce just laws, and wage peace but *us*.... We believe that participating in decision-making about difficult and controversial issues gives practice in listening to different opinions, deciphering fact from opinion, confronting emotion and reason, negotiating, and problem-solving.[9]

Marysa circulates around the uncomfortably hot classroom handing out the syllabus for the week. Listing all reading and homework assignments for the next five days, the syllabus begins with a quote from radical community organizer Saul Alinsky, which is directly relevant to this week's discussion: "Change means movement, movement means friction, friction means heat, and heat means controversy. The only place where there is no friction is in outer space or a seminar on political action."

Intended as a comment upon political conflicts in the world at large, Alinsky's remark is equally telling about classroom dynamics. Over the next several days, students will view provocative documentary films about individuals and/or organizations holding controversial and differing political beliefs. These films (and related readings) are intended to impress upon students the importance of clarifying one's own political beliefs and raise complex questions about how a democratic and pluralistic society should best handle the conflicts generated by political diversity. In discussing these films, political differences within the classroom itself will be illuminated and debated, and dilemmas raised by the course's intellectual content will be mirrored in the lived curriculum of classroom dynamics.

From my perspective, these classroom dynamics reveal tensions about conflicting values and ideologies among teachers, students, and the Facing History curriculum itself, demonstrating the enormous complexity of the endeavor to catalyze critical, moral thinking among adolescent students. On the one hand, the Facing History program advocates bringing forth multiple points of view, developing students' understanding of multiple perspectives, and promoting tolerance among diverse peoples of often differing backgrounds. In the classes I have observed, teacher practice is to a considerable extent in keeping with these curricular values; teachers often actively engage with students of diverse political perspectives and encourage them to remain fair-minded and open to at least hearing alternative points of view. On the other hand, the program unequivocally rejects moral relativism, condemning social attitudes and beliefs that in any way repress or discriminate against individuals or social groups. Tensions inevitably arise when teachers and students differ in their feelings about which beliefs actually further or hinder these stated curricular objectives. Whose standards should determine what is morally "right" or "wrong"? Do these determinations align with an individual's own political beliefs? How should beliefs that some regard as "wrong" be handled in the classroom? What are the repercussions of silencing these viewpoints or, alternatively, allowing them to be voiced freely? As the recent controversy over New York City's "Children of the Rainbow" curriculum demonstrates, these questions are increasingly the subject of national educational debate.

Marysa and her students also clearly struggle with questions such as these. A close look at how they are dealt with here—within the safety of a trusted school community—may help to illuminate how they are negotiated within a broader social context. What follows, then, is a portrait of classroom life. It is intended not as an evaluative critique of the Facing History program's success or failure in meeting its stated goals, but rather as an analytic exploration of the dynamics encountered in attempting to do so. As a matter of both research inquiry and writing style, social science portraiture investigates, describes, and analyzes characters, settings, and events in context and in relation to one another, and is informed by an awareness of the researcher's own relationship with his or her subject.[10] Equally important, portraiture offers a style of writing designed to engage the reader in the particular experience described and, in so doing, give him or her a sense of a larger whole. I offer the following in the spirit of what the writer Eudora Welty has noted in another context: "One place comprehended can make us understand other places better."[11]

• • •

FRIDAY, MAY 11

"Remember yesterday? What did we see?" Marysa asks about a film in which the subject of political difference is raised. Sandra answers, "A story about a man who taught his students that the Holocaust never happened, and that Jews wanted to rule the world." Abby adds, "He also said that all the banks and the finances were controlled by Jewish people." "Yeah," agrees Alan, "he thought there was an international Jewish conspiracy."[12]

Students take turns passionately describing "Lessons in Hate," an early 1980s documentary about Jim Keegstra, a popular and charismatic mayor and teacher in a small town in Alberta, Canada, who taught anti-semitic beliefs to students for more than a decade. The film extensively documents Keegstra arguing that the Holocaust was a "hoax" that in no way singled out Jewish people. He also argues that the French revolution was a product of the "international Jewish conspiracy"; that John Wilkes Booth, the man who shot Abraham Lincoln, was a Jew; and that Jews caused the American Civil War. Young, vulnerable, and with little access to alternative beliefs or perspectives, Keegstra's students uncritically absorbed his teachings, or, in a few cases, adopted them ambivalently in order to receive a passing grade. More problematic still, Keegstra's statements were tacitly accepted by the school's principal and faculty, and by most of the town's council and citizens. When the mother of one student finally challenged Keegstra's teachings, she was vehemently opposed by members of her community. The school board eventually fired Keegstra, but not until after a long and difficult battle had been waged that painfully divided members of the small town.[13]

The Keegstra film raises questions about how a community can tolerate conflictual beliefs among its members while still maintaining cohesion. Showcasing the struggles experienced by both Keegstra and those who oppose him, it demonstrates how difficult it can be to stand up for one's beliefs, regardless of their content. After what they have read, seen, and been taught throughout the semester, Marysa's students are outraged that anyone could minimize the horror of the Holocaust, much less deny its very existence. Distancing themselves from their Canadian peers, some make disparaging remarks about Keegstra's seemingly docile and gullible students:

Abby: It seems like these people just *feed* on people who are torn apart. They just suck them up by providing them with an excuse to hate! They probably want to find a way to place the blame on someone else just to explain their own situation.

Marysa: Exactly! What's the vocabulary word which describes that? (Several students shout out, "scapegoating!") Well, what can you do to help people when they're in this condition? What can you do to turn their beliefs around?

Josh: Kill them!

Marysa: What?! Kill them?!

Josh: Yes. If they say those things, and if they start a war or something, you have to fight back.

Alan: But if you go out and fight these people, and you kill six hundred or seven hundred of them, it won't stop *anything*! More will just come and fight back!

Marysa: What I'm *really* trying to push is that this is not just a problem that happened in history, a long time ago—the Dark Ages, when I was born. These issues are *here*, in the present. And you're a part of it. You have to be aware of it so *you* are not brainwashed or indoctrinated in the future.

For the next several minutes, students discuss the apparent differences between their own multicultural community and Keegstra's ethnically homogeneous school and town. Marysa asks students to identify similarities between Nazi doctrine and what Keegstra taught, and Abby brings up the international Jewish conspiracy theme. Drawing this argument closer to home, Marysa suggests parallels between the historical claim that Jews have controlled the financial industry and the present-day fear that Japanese increasingly dominate the U.S. economy. Chi-Ho raises his hand and quietly drops a bombshell: "I think that a Jewish international conspiracy *does* exist, but not quite as much they say. So many people are talking about it, it must be some way true." "What?!" several students exclaim at once. Josh stares in disbelief at the boy who sits next to him, suddenly a stranger. Susie and Jess yell out in disbelief. Marysa responds in a strained but consciously even-tempered voice, "Chi-Ho, why do you think this?" Chi-Ho answers in a somewhat muffled voice, "I don't know, but I do." Marysa continues, "Don't you think that if there was a conspiracy it could have stopped the Holocaust?" "No, I don't," Chi-Ho replies, "because it's more recent. It's developed since the fifties only, I think." Marysa responds emphatically, "Chi-Ho, we need to talk!"

Animated one-on-one conversations spring up between students who sit next to each other in all corners of the room; the whole class seems to be buzzing. Abby raises her hand and (deliberately or not) turns up the heat several notches. She says, "I'm against what some people are doing with Israel, with the way it was established and with killing the Palestinians and everything. But that's different from an international Jewish conspiracy."

"*What* are you talking about?" Josh exclaims furiously. "We weren't even talking about that!" Sandra adds critically, "What are you against now, Abby?" Abby answers, "I'm against the way the country was set up." Marysa asks incredulously and slightly sarcastically, "The UN vote?" Abby replies, "Not that, but what happened to the Palestinian people *through* that. Elie Wiesel and people like that were involved, and millions of Palestinian people were massacred and forced to leave their homes, just like in the Holocaust."

All hell breaks loose. It seems like everyone begins yelling at Abby, and Chi-Ho's earlier remark is left by the wayside. Abby steadfastly holds her ground. Though her words remain strong and her claims unqualified, she slumps further and further into her seat with each new attack by her classmates. She strikes me as being both scared and defiant. Confused about historical facts, Josh defends the state of Israel.

Josh: They were *attacked* in an eight-day war!

Abby: Well, it's still not right to be killing people to set up a country!

Josh: That's exactly what *we* did to set up *our* country!

Abby: So? I'm against *that*, too! I don't believe in that either!

Sandra (becoming increasingly exasperated): Well, what *are* you for? What *do* you believe in?

(*Alison and Susie nod emphatically in agreement.*)

Abby (matter-of-factly): I believe in control by the people.

Marysa: But how do you determine which people should have control, Abby? In the film we saw, the Canadian teacher thinks he should have control, 'cause he thinks he's right. How are you going to decide who gets to speak and who doesn't?

Students debate the conundrum of free speech for the remaining few minutes of class. Though Marysa has (perhaps self-consciously) shifted discussion away from a contentious and personalized debate, the classroom atmosphere remains charged.

I am scheduled to interview Abby later on this same day. As students get ready for lunch, I watch Abby self-consciously gather her books, seeming proud yet uncomfortable about being isolated. Calling out to her, I suggest that we can discuss the points she has raised during our interview, if she is interested; she smiles appreciatively.

Sandra, Alison, and Angela note my overture and come up to speak with me on their way out of the room. "Look, I don't know much about the Jewish religion, or any religion, really," Sandra says, "but isn't it true that in the Bible it says that the land was originally Jewish land, and that's why they wanted it? Or, why didn't the Jewish people just go to a different country?"

I try to answer as best as I can, explaining that Jews, Christians, and Moslems have all lived on the land, and that all have laid claim to it at different periods of history. "But doesn't the Bible say that the Jews were there *first*?," Angela retorts, "and then the Moslems came when the Jews went to Egypt?" Trying to grant each group its legitimacy, I speak to the importance of finding contemporary political solutions to the problem. Seeing myself more as a participant/observer than an arbiter of divergent viewpoints, I refuse to choose sides despite the girls' best efforts to make me do so. The three girls head off for lunch less angry, but still visibly confused.

Josh leaves class upset by the comments made by both Abby and Chi-Ho. He speaks to Marysa for almost an hour after class, refusing to sit next to Chi-Ho and demanding that his seat be changed. In keeping with the curriculum's intent to foster students' ability to listen to alternative perspectives, Marysa tells me later:

> I tried to explain to Josh that Chi-Ho was the same person Josh thought he was before he made that statement. I told him that the way to respond to problems is not to refuse to speak to someone, but to talk together to try to figure it out and to help people to change their beliefs.

But "talking together" is not always easy. True to Alinsky's comment, "frictions" caused by Abby and Chi-Ho seem to circulate around the class as a whole (several students shout at Abby and Chi-Ho); between students and their teacher (Marysa expresses unequivocal disapproval of both students' comments); and, perhaps most poignantly, within students' individual relationships (friendships between Josh and Chi-Ho as well as Abby and Sandra are strained).

Marysa leaves class as upset as many of her students and uncertain about how to proceed. In fact, her confusion seems to have been manifest in her classroom dealings. Confronted with views she finds repugnant and even dangerous, she does, nevertheless, encourage students to remain open-minded, independent in their thinking, and respectful of difference. She even engages Abby and Chi-Ho in a critical debate, urging them to clarify their thinking and to defend their controversial points of view. At the same time, however, Marysa implicitly undermines the views of both of these students. By publicly acknowledging her disagreement with Abby and Chi-Ho, she uses her implicit authority as the "teacher" (the one empowered to design seating plans, assign homework and grades, and so forth) to undermine, rather than muzzle, these students' perspectives. Given the power differential between teacher and student, the critical debate between them is unevenly weighted.

For example, Marysa challenges Chi-Ho's remarks before the full classroom community, but then seeks to remove them from the public arena. "Chi-Ho, we need to talk," she says after only a brief exchange, simultaneously displacing disagreement to the private realm and suggesting that, once there, she will set the record straight. Moments later Marysa chooses not to intervene when several students jump on Abby, and her own questions of Abby sound slightly facetious. Finally, she eventually steers discussion away from the Middle East and toward freedom of speech in the midst of an unresolved debate.

Admittedly uncomfortable with the arguments raised and feeling unequipped to handle them, Marysa avails herself of her proximity to the Facing History and Ourselves national office and calls in staff member Steve Cohen to address the controversial issues raised by Abby and Chi-Ho. While I believe Marysa is making good use of an available resource, I also wonder whether she is bringing Steve in to quell controversy and, in essence, to set the record straight. A balding, wiry man in chinos and tennis shoes, Steve visits class a few days later.

MONDAY, MAY 14

"Why did Hitler choose to focus on the Jews?" Steve asks to open this morning's complex agenda. Alan replies, "He said that they were in charge of the money." Jess adds, "He said they were the people who put Germany in the economic state they were in." "Well, why did people believe it?" Steve continues. Abby says, "It's like that quote, 'If you tell a lie big enough and long enough, people will start to believe it.'" Steve asks, "Do you think that's true, from your own experience?" "Well, I've always been someone who doesn't like to just go along with what other people are saying," Abby replies, "but *yeah*, if you hear something long enough, it affects you … you kind of forget what your own principles are."

Steve bounces around the room, weaving around students' desks and speaking quickly in an animated voice that is often squeaky with excitement. Focusing directly on each student with whom he speaks, and referring to each by name, he engages the class in a discussion about how basic emotions and stereotypes take over when you "forget your own principles" and are "no longer able to think." "I want you to think about how stereotypes and propaganda work," Steve explains, "because, as you know, Hitler didn't invent anything new. Before Hitler, there was plenty of hatred of Jews." He continues with the following example:

> In the 1890s, a book appeared, and it was called … *Protocols of the Elders of Zion.* (Steve writes the title of the book on the board, and students copy it into their journals.) It appeared in Russian in 1890. And it explained that there was an *international* group of Jews who used to get together and meet in a Jewish cemetery in Prague, at night, and they would plan *everything* that was going to happen in the world. (Josh taps Chi-Ho on the shoulder, as if to suggest that he should listen closely.) This book was republished in England in 1919. It was republished in the United States in the 1920s—in a newspaper owned by Henry Ford, one of the two or three most important men in the country! In England it was published in *the* most important newspaper—the *Times* of London. And the most interesting thing about this book is—it's a fraud! It's complete nonsense! It's made up! (Josh again prods Chi-Ho and whispers something to him; Chi-Ho smiles awkwardly.)
>
> How do you know it's a fraud? Well, in the 1890s, this book was written by members of the Russian police force. (Steve writes "1890—Russian police force" hurriedly on the board.) And how do you know that? Well, because this book was actually *copied* (Steve's voice cracks in excitement) from a book that was written in 1864 in France that didn't blame *Jews*, but that said the ruler of France, Napoleon III, was trying to take over the world (he writes "Napoleon, 1864" on the board). And everywhere where Napoleon appears in *this* book (Steve points to the original text), the word *Jews* appears in this one (he points to the words "Elders of Zion"). Think about this for a second! A French book in 1864 was copied by the Russians in 1890. The British copied the Russians. And the Americans copied the British. And it's a complete fraud! It's hocus pocus! It's untrue! It's a *lie*. And millions and millions of people believed it. (Pause). How come?
>
> *Susie:* Because nobody told them any differently.
>
> *Alan:* Because they believed it was written by someone who knew!
>
> *Josh:* A lot of people want to blame somebody else for all of their problems.
>
> *Chi-Ho:* Because then you're not responsible for what happens to people.

"Exactly!" Steve exclaims. "There are a lot of things that happen that are really beyond our control. An idea like this says—even if it's someone you hate, *somebody* is in control. Somebody is in charge of what's going on. And even if things are lousy, it's nice to be able to say, it wouldn't be lousy if it weren't for, these bums. Let me show you how this happened in real life! This should take about five hours, but I'll do it in three minutes. You ready?" Students nod that they are.

For the next several minutes, Steve gives a remarkably clear and concise account of the infamous turn-of-the-century case in which Alfred Dreyfus, one of the few Jewish officers in the French Army, was falsely accused of giving military secrets to the Germans, convicted in two trials, and sentenced to prison on Devil's Island. "Many people said, 'How could Dreyfus have done it alone?' And others said, 'Aha, he didn't! He was part of this!' " (Steve points again to "Elders of Zion" on the board).

Abby asks, "Is that thing called the international Jewish conspiracy?" Steve explains: "In France, they called it the 'Syndicat.' And they referred to it as the 'international Jewish conspiracy.' There's a tremendous *power* in this kind of idea. Why were people so willing to believe it of Jews? Would they have believed it if this was … about Catholics? Would that have been popular in Europe?" "No," answers Sandra, "there are a lot of Catholics, so it wouldn't be as easy as singling out one Jew." Abby interjects, "What things you believe in will also depend upon the family you grow up in." Steve agrees, and draws the thorny issue of an international Jewish conspiracy to a close by reinforcing the curriculum's valuation of critical thinking. He says, "One of the things you're going to have to decide is whether you're going to believe what people say, or whether you're going to try to figure it out on your own."

Chi-Ho has remained conspicuously silent throughout this entire discussion. Often quiet in class, his behavior today is not unusual. Today's lecture, however, is given in response to his earlier remark, and it would seem to call for his participation. While only Josh makes a point of publicly acknowledging the connection between the previous class and today's by tugging at Chi-Ho's shirt-sleeve and whispering to him repeatedly, other students shoot furtive glances in Chi-Ho's direction. Chi-Ho seems to studiously ignore all meaningful looks. Though he appears to be listening throughout class and assiduously copies Steve's blackboard notes into his journal, he does not acknowledge that today's lecture was, however subtly, directed at him.

This is by no means the case with Abby when the second item on today's agenda is discussed. Referring to a set of maps of the pre- and post-World War I period, Steve shows how the world has changed since the fall of the Ottoman Empire. He points to the Middle East region and says: "There are White people, Black people, and Brown people living here. It's a whole Rainbow Coalition! After World War I, one of the major questions was—should people like this be able to rule *themselves*? And the winners of the war—France, Britain, and the United States—say 'No!' They give them independence with training wheels, and the winners of the war are gonna be the training wheels! These people end up living in countries which are *invented* after World War I. It's all a product of politics! Well, what kinds of problems might the 'training wheels' encounter?"

"They had to make sure the new boundaries wouldn't get people mad because they don't want to start another war," Alan answers thoughtfully. Nora adds, "They needed to keep people together with their own people so they'll be content." Drawing his finger across a large section of the map, Steve describes how Transjordan was ruled by the victorious British until 1948. "And who lived here?" he asks simply, pointing to Palestine. "Palestinians," Abby replies. Steve continues, asking, "Who were they, and what was their religion?" "They were Arabs," Abby responds. "They were Moslems, Jews, and Christians," corrects Steve. "To be a 'Palestinian' meant literally to live in Palestine. And they all lived under British rule."

For the next several minutes, Steve helps the class review what happened to Jews in the years leading up to and immediately following World War II. Josh remembers that Jews tried to get out of Europe, but often had no place to go. Angela believes many headed for Palestine because they had "religious ties there." Nora comments that it was often impossible to return to their homes because "they were taken by people, like their neighbors." Zeke adds that their possessions were taken, too.

"Lots of Jews live in detention camps for two or three years after the war," Steve explains. "The Jews in Palestine want the European Jews to come there, but the Arabs and Christians don't want them to. The British have control of Palestine and they don't know what to do with it. Since the British can't figure it out, they give the problem to the United Nations, which functions as an international government with representatives from different countries. This is the U.N.'s big moment! Well, in 1947 the U.N. votes to divide Palestine again, into a state for Jews and a state for non-Jews."

"Is this when the eight day war took place?" Josh interjects, reviving his previous comment. "No," Steve answers, "that took place later." Nora comments, "The U.N. is made up of representatives from all different countries, right? So, what did the Palestinian representative do?" Supportive and genuinely impressed, Steve exclaims, "That's a great question! There wasn't one, since Palestine was under British rule." "Well," Nora continues, "did the majority of the non-Jews in Palestine agree with the decision?" Steve responds, "Absolutely not! The majority of people were not happy. So in 1948 a war occurs—it's a small war compared to World War I and World War II—and in that war, the *Jewish* side of Palestine manages to survive, but the *non-Jewish* region gets taken—not by Israel, but by 'Transjordan.' … The Jewish part becomes Israel, but the non-Jewish part becomes Jordan and Egypt."

Abby is getting frustrated with Steve's version of history. She breaks in in a loud and exasperated voice, "But there was lots of violence between the Jews and non-Jews! A lot of people were killed! People were kicked off their homes. It was just like in the Holocaust!" Steve acknowledges the complexity of the situation, but is direct in his rebuttal. Calmly and with authority, he asserts, "That's not quite true; part of it's true, but it's *very* complex. There were broadcasts telling people to leave their land, and many people *wanted* to leave because they wanted to get away from the war. When the Israeli government came in, they didn't know what to do with the Arab land. The people that fled their homes *do* end up living in camps, but that was the choice of the Jordanians, not the Israelis."

Abby objects, saying, "But they shouldn't have had to leave in the first place!" "They *chose* to leave," Steve responds, "There's *no* question that this displaced people and that people lost their homes who didn't want to. But there's also *no* question that extermination was *not* the policy.… The other thing is that many Jews in these Arab countries also lost *their* homes. One of the things that happens in times of war is that international human rights are *completely* neglected. This should make us think very closely about the policies of international government—they're *not* extermination policies, but they're also not policies that make it very easy for people to live their lives in the way they would like to." Abby isn't satisfied. "But if the Palestinians hadn't been kicked off …" she begins. Steve breaks in, "Do you mean the Palestinian non-Jews?" Accommodating Steve's language,

Abby continues, "OK, if the Palestinian non-Jews hadn't been kicked off, why should they be so angry about not having their land?" "Oh, well! They've spent the past forty years living in camps and wanting to be on their parents' land!" Steve responds.

Most students have remained silent yet attentive during this exchange. Sandra sits close by Abby and does not come to her aid, despite Abby's frequent, beseeching looks in her direction. Josh only half-hides a smirk, seemingly pleased that Steve is taking Abby on. He now contributes to the discussion, "But there was another war!" and Steve replies, "There have been *lots* of wars. The tension Abby speaks to developed more after the land was taken in 1967. Many people believe that land should be exchanged for peace. There's a large Peace Now movement in Israel today saying that those territories should be given back to the Palestinian Arabs."

"But they *won* the war!" Josh repeats emphatically. "I learned that in Temple!" Steve responds by briefly highlighting different points of view within contemporary Israeli (Jewish) society. He is careful to distinguish between current policies and those on which the state was founded. Though he admits the existence of conflicting perspectives within contemporary Israeli society, he leaves less room for alternative interpretation when it comes to the founding of the state ("The tension Abby speaks to developed more after the land was taken in 1967," he says, and he suggests that Palestinians were not "kicked off" their land but "*chose*" to leave it). Though Steve is by no means alone in articulating this perspective (and in distinguishing it from current Israeli policies), it nonetheless reflects only one particular viewpoint in a complex and contentious historical debate.[14]

Some of Steve's other interventions are also grounded in a particular political stance. While acknowledging that the founding of the State of Israel was accompanied by some human rights violations, he denies that those violations were systematic or a matter of official policy. Moments later, he "corrects" Abby's language by recommending that she refer to Arabs as "Palestinian non-Jews"—a categorization that is itself not politically neutral, and arguably comparable to referring to Blacks as non-Whites or women as non-men. Like Marysa in the earlier classroom incident, Steve acts in somewhat contradictory ways, eliciting students' diverse viewpoints on the one hand while undermining the legitimacy of those with which he disagrees on the other.

Class nearly over, students begin to close their notebooks and put them inside their desks. Marysa and Steve turn to each other and begin speaking privately in the front of the room; they express pleasure and relief at having gotten through a potentially difficult session without drawing too much fire.

That neither Steve nor Marysa entirely transcended their own political beliefs in interpreting and responding to political differences within the classroom is not surprising; I would argue that no one can do so. These beliefs are a part of our internal make-up, as operative within these teachers as they are within my own interpretations of their practice. I did not leave my own political beliefs at the door when I entered the classroom; they were within me as I observed each class. These perspectives no doubt influenced how I interpreted classroom tensions between eliciting and muting student voice. As a Jewish woman strongly committed to a peaceful resolution of the Israeli-Palestinian conflict, I felt strongly opposed to Chi-Ho's remarks and to Abby's more extreme comments, even though I disagreed with how the teachers at times responded to both of these students.

Interviews conducted individually with Chi-Ho, Abby, Josh, and Sandra shortly after these classes took place support my interpretation of these classroom events as political in nature.[15] By "political" I mean to suggest not only the content of the classroom debate (in which a diversity of political views were expressed), but also the process by which it was negotiated (whereby controversial voices were silenced by those with greater authority and power). In these instances, power was exercised between students and their teachers; between Marysa and Steve; and among the students themselves. So, too, the relations among these players were hierarchical: some were given (or assumed) more authority to speak than others. And, depending on one's point of view, opposing positions were granted legitimacy or invalidated. In the process, some students felt silenced and subordinated, while others felt empowered and privileged.

In the course of our interviews, Chi-Ho and Abby express discomfort at feeling "unheard" and "misunderstood" in class, while Sandra and Josh enjoy the fact that these students were silenced. Expressing frustration with being "misunderstood," Chi-Ho remarks, [Josh] wouldn't listen! … [It felt] terrible … I was disappointed. I *really* think that Marysa didn't really listen to me very carefully, and, if she *did*, she would understand what I meant."

Abby's response to the classes under study is multifaceted. She initially admits to being confused by Steve's alternative reading of historical events and expresses concern for (what she imagines to be) *his* discomfort. Portraying *herself* as the agent of her silencing (rather than Steve), Abby notes:

> I *really* was confused by what he said, because, from what *I* had read (because my parents have a lot of books about that), it *really* was the total *opposite* of what he was saying. And, I mean, I *didn't* want to make a scene, so I didn't really, you know, say as much as I could have? I *didn't* want to totally contradict him, 'cause it would have made him feel uncomfortable. So I just kind of left it.

Moments later, however, Abby suggests that this self-censorship was not entirely voluntarily. Though she hesitantly adopts Steve's terminology, she nevertheless defends her own perspective and argues that he was unable to hear it:

> I thought about it a lot *during* and *afterwards* and, I *really* think that his point of view was *really, really* closed-minded! I mean, he thought about what I had to say, but he basically said it was totally wrong! … I was *trying to tell him* that from what *I've learned*, the situation between (pause) Palestinian non-Jews and the *Jews* was *very* oppressive, and one-sided, and it was really an awful situation! And he kind of *glorified* it in a way, and made it sound like it wasn't as violent as it really was!

While Abby eventually admits to having modified some of her own thinking in response to Steve, she seems frustrated that he has not done the same:

> I didn't really mean *millions* because there weren't that many Palestinian non-Jews in the country.… *He* was right, because I thought about it and it wasn't really *extermination*. But they *really* wanted them to move off that land! And it was *their* homeland in the first place! And I *meant* that by taking them out of their home, as the Nazis did with the Jews, they put

them in something that was like a *camp* where they weren't allowed to have any *human* rights that most people take for granted. I agree with him that the methods weren't exactly extermination but I *don't* agree with him when he says it wasn't as bad as in the *first* steps [of the Holocaust].

In contrast, neither Josh nor Sandra expresses discomfort with classroom dynamics, but they instead express pleasure in Steve's having silenced those with whom they disagree. Sandra notes with satisfaction, "When Steve came in and told Abby, 'You're wrong!' well, it was kind of funny, because she got like, *really mad*." Josh similarly notes, "Steve, he's great! He came in and he said this is total nonsense." Whispering "Don't tell her, but Abby talks a lot!" Josh takes pleasure in describing a contentious class in which his own beliefs reflect majority opinion while Abby's are seen as marginal. "I like when people make sure people know what's going on," he says later of Steve's also having put Chi-Ho in his place.

These excerpts suggest a confluence between my interpretation of classroom dynamics and students' experience of the course. Though students differed among themselves in their feelings about classroom dynamics, they shared my belief that both Marysa and Steve conveyed their own sense of "right" and "wrong" to the class and made sure, as Josh says, that "people know what's going on."

TUESDAY, MAY 15

The day after Steve Cohen's visit, students return to the issue of contemporary political conflicts as originally intended by the curricular text. Walking toward the back of the class with a videotape in hand, Marysa begins: "We've talked about the thirties and the forties, and we've seen a movie about something happening in Canada in the eighties. Now we're going to look at our own home, the U.S. This documentary film is about the Ku Klux Klan teaching kids *your* age.[16] Imagine if you grew up in a town, an all-Black town, say, and you *adored* your teacher, and he told you all about all the horrible things Whites did—many of which I think are true. Would it be easy to believe it?" "It would be real easy," Jamal answers without hesitation, " 'cause he'd be my role model." "That's why indoctrination is so scary," Marysa continues, "and so important to understand. If you hear something again and again from someone you believe in, and you don't hear anything else, even though it may be one person's perspective, you'll probably believe it.… So in a way the diversity around you here, and the strengths from the differences of opinion you hear, and the strengths of the educational system you're in, encourage you to question and to learn different points of view. Try to think about that while you're watching this." Marysa pops the video cassette into the VCR, Angela hits the lights, and students settle down to watch TV.

"Klan Youth Corps" is a 1982 film about how the Ku Klux Klan recruits and trains American youth. Filled with riveting footage of actual night-time cross-burning ceremonies and stirring appeals made by the Klan's Imperial Wizard, the film documents 10- to 17-year-olds receiving instruction in racist ideology. The Imperial Wizard implores, "We will kill. We will stand in the streets. We will do what we have to to stop the niggers and the communists, won't we?" A counselor warns preteens at a Klan Youth summer camp that "many of the things you read in school are not the truth—they're just lies." And row upon row of cleanly scrubbed White boys and girls stand at attention and recite the Klan Youth Corps pledge in unison: "I pledge to practice racial separation in all my social contacts and to keep my forced contacts with other races on a strictly business basis. I pledge to oppose the false teaching that all races are equal or the same. I pledge that I will immediately go to the aid of any White person being attacked physically or verbally by a person of another race. I pledge that I will fight for the complete separation of all races in America and I will recruit others to do the same." The film is as direct as it is unnerving.

Marysa stops the tape and hits "rewind," while Angela turns on the lights. "Why don't people arrest the KKK?" Alison immediately asks. "They're protected by the First Amendment," Marysa replies. "Also, in a small town like that, people aren't going to stand up to it 'cause they'll probably believe it!" comments Alan. "They can pass out literature and wear their robes," Marlene adds, "but until they kill someone, or get caught killing someone, you can't do anything." Nora comments, "I understand that they're protected by the First Amendment, but I also think that they might abuse it. You never know how far they'll go."

Acknowledging that there's a big controversy about this, Marysa mentions the case in which members of the American Nazi Party won the right to march in Skokie, Illinois, after having been defended by the ACLU on the grounds of freedom of speech. The proud son of a prominent civil liberties attorney, Josh corrects Marysa matter-of-factly: "Freedom to assemble." Marysa continues, putting forth the traditional civil liberties argument, "If you stop *them*, who decides the next group that cannot speak?" Abby and Marysa debate this point:

Abby: I think society should be able to decide who should not speak.

Marysa: But "society" can fluctuate from time to time, group to group.

Abby: But the majority of society is not in support of oppression.

Marysa: What about people under Hitler?

Abby: If Hitler hadn't had the right to free speech, people wouldn't have believed him!

Marysa: Where do you draw the line? How do you decide who can and who can't speak? The First Amendment protects *everybody's* rights.

Abby: But millions of people don't agree with them!

Marysa: Let's say we wouldn't let socialists or communists speak.

Abby: But they're not oppressing other people!

Marysa: Capitalists feel they are.

Abby (laughing): Well, they're *wrong*!

Marysa: Abby, there's a bit of tunnel vision here that we have to speak about. You can't just say that the only ones who can speak are those who agree with your position!

As in the case of the two earlier classes described, this resource film and the discussion that followed raises the dilemma of how a democratic community that values free speech, diversity, and the open exchange of ideas can fairly address unpopular, controversial, or "wrong" points of view. Should those who voice these views simply be silenced, as Abby believes with regard to the KKK and to others who hold "oppressive" beliefs? And as Marysa—the individual holding the most power within the class—rejoins, who should define what constitutes "oppression" and be empowered to enact this silencing? As we have seen, answers to these questions are no simpler to find in the microcosm of the classroom than they are in Skokie, Illinois. Students' experiences of how issues raised by the film are handled in the classroom are contradictory. On one hand, they talk about valuing open-mindedness, a plurality of opinions, and the importance of free expression; on the other, at times they seek closure to controversies and rest easier in being told which opinions are "right."

For example, Sandra pays Steve a high compliment consistent with her valuation of "keeping an open mind": "You know, Steve doesn't just read one book and say, 'Well, this one book is right,'" she tells me during our interview. "He's the kind of person who reads lots of things, in depth." She criticizes Abby, in contrast, for failing to do the same: "Abby, she's not having an open mind! She's just so set about what she wants to believe."

But while Sandra values open-mindedness in theory, she herself finds it difficult to sustain. Overwhelmed by the diversity of opinions offered on the Middle East, she asks me to provide closure to this contentious debate, saying, "There's that issue about how the people were moved out. And Abby says some of the same things that were used in the Holocaust were used *there*, like murdering people, and some women were raped. And, then Steve said that they were *asked* to leave, and they left voluntarily. So I don't know which to believe! Because Abby said she's read it in books, and that Steve just learned it in *conservative* books, and, see, I don't know! So who is more, who is *more right*?" Disquieted by my refusal to grant either position full legitimacy, she eventually consoles herself in the best pluralist tradition: "There could be Steve's point of view, and [Abby's] point of view, and then mix them together and there could be something that they could come to."

Josh's approach to the problem is negotiated differently. At first glance he seems desirous of silencing those with whom he disagrees. He argues for "killing" people who hold beliefs like those of Holocaust revisionist Jim Keegstra and he appears equally dismissive of Abby's point of view. A longtime friend of Chi-Ho's, however, he is torn between an impulse to shut his friend out altogether (as manifested in his desire to move his seat) and an impulse to engage him in struggle (as manifested in his ribbing of Chi-Ho in class). He ultimately supports the second position, though he clearly has difficulty doing so. Evoking the words of his much revered father, Josh says, "I've been taught that you do not start violence with people, and that the only way to prove yourself as a great person is to talk to people, to make them see that what they're saying is *so wrong*. This is what me and my father used to disagree on, but I'm beginning to believe him."

Abby seems to embody most dramatically the tensions between valuing open-mindedness and taking a clear moral stance. Reflecting the political priorities of her parents, she argues passionately in favor of social change and sees eliciting different points of view as essential to achieving it, saying, "I *really* believe that there needs to be some change in the world today! And I think a *really* important part of *change* is understanding what someone else is *thinking*.… If you just *come* out, *say* what you think, and give *no* regard to what the *other* person is thinking, then that will create anger. And *resentment*. And they won't really be open to change." Knowing that the points of view of her fellow classmates are important in this regard, Abby continues, "I'm usually one of the only ones who is really speaking up, and I *really* want to know what other people think about what I'm saying … so maybe I could either argue it out, and *really* try to tell them what my point of view was, or just hear what other people are thinking about.… Because if they don't *speak*, I'm totally, totally closed off from anything that they're thinking about."

But while Abby campaigns eloquently for lively debates in which multiple points of view are brought out into the open, she argues equally well against granting each view legitimacy. Far from falling into a relativist trap, she asserts, "I *do* believe that there is *always a right* thing! And a lot of people have the impression that it's just your *opinion*. And your point of view. And they don't really give a chance to have one be right. It's just always 'They should be able to say that because that's their *opinion*.' And I really, really *don't* agree with that!" Directly challenging the civil libertarian line promoted by Marysa in reference to the KKK, she charges, "I think that the *right* thing should always be promoted and the people who think *otherwise* should not be allowed to speak!"

• • •

Students' contradictory yearnings for both closure and openness may be irresolvably in tension. Teachers' efforts to foster tolerance for alternative perspectives may be similarly at odds with their efforts to promote moral thinking. The ambiguities, conflicts, and tensions that arose during these three classroom sessions demonstrate the enormous challenge of debating contemporary social and political issues in the classroom.

There are those who oppose interjecting contemporary issues into the classroom for precisely these reasons. Conservative activists like Phyllis Schlafly, for example, have in the past attacked the Facing History and Ourselves program precisely because it encourages adolescents to reflect critically on current social issues. Condemning the program in national public hearings in 1984, she charged that it (and other so-called "therapy education" initiatives) could "depress the child" by "forc[ing] [him] to confront adult problems which are too complex and unsuitable for his tender years."[17] By causing the child to be "emotionally and morally confused," they could, she felt, lead to the "high rates of teenage suicide, loneliness, premarital sex, and pregnancies" that plague contemporary society.[18]

The Department of Education's National Diffusion Network—an agency that reviews curricula and funds their dissemination—reflected Schlafly's concerns in 1986–1988 when it denied funds to the Facing History program. The Department's action sparked a Congressional hearing and heated debate among public-policy makers, educators, and other concerned citizens.[19]

But one need not look as far back as the mid-eighties to find opposition to classroom discourse on contemporary social and political debates. Only recently, the New York City Board of Education ousted Chancellor Joseph A. Fernandez, largely because of his support for initiatives that included AIDS education, condom distribution, and a curriculum that advocated tolerance for diverse social groups, including homosexuals. According to Carol Ann Gresser, the New York School Board's newly elected chair, parents were upset by Fernandez's promotion of a "social agenda" in the schools. "You can't bring into the classroom issues that haven't even been decided by the society," she said.[20]

I would argue exactly the opposite: one cannot possibly avoid bringing into the classroom issues over which society is still divided because students themselves are well aware of these issues and hungry to discuss them with their peers. The liveliness of the classroom sessions presented here testifies to students' investment in just such debates. While these students were at times discomfited by what transpired in class, they were also vitally invested, excited, and engaged in the struggle. Though Sandra begged for closure, she tolerated not getting it; though Josh demanded separation from Chi-Ho, he remained sitting next to his friend; though Marysa opposed Abby, she engaged with her in open debate; though Abby felt intimidated, she hung in and held her ground. In short, while tempers were high, feelings impassioned, and intellects fiercely engaged, the group never closed down or fell apart. Highly conscious of their differences and the fault lines that divide them on specific issues, the class remained a community throughout. Their ability to do so reflects the skill with which Marysa created an environment of relative trust and safety within the classroom, and Facing History's engendering of personal, critical reflection no doubt contributed to that effort. But the strengths and capacities that students bring with them into this or any other classroom—their hunger to sort out where they stand and their ripeness for engaging in just such debates—must also be taken into account.

Thus, though opponents may argue that the inevitable consequence of such classroom interactions is either political indoctrination or the promotion of moral relativism, I would contend that neither is a necessary outcome nor an accurate characterization. What does seem inevitable is ambiguity and conflict—on this point, at least, advocates and opponents both agree. But here, too, programs encouraging engagement with social, moral, and/or political issues may offer a possible passageway through trouble—not by denying conflict through positing an unproblematized, homogeneous ideal, but by helping students to take well-thought-out stands and to listen closely to each other. Hopefully, by doing so they will learn to tolerate more fully the conflicts they will inevitably encounter in the world beyond the classroom. At their best, what programs like Facing History and Ourselves may offer students is not a blueprint for creating a single ideal community, but practice in making webs between multiple ones. And that is essential to education in a democracy.

NOTES

1. At the request of school administrators, the names of the school and its students and teachers have been changed.
2. Information about this curriculum can be obtained from Facing History and Ourselves, 16 Hurd Road, Brookline, MA 02146 (617-232-1595). The organization develops and disseminates curricular materials and runs an extensive training program to prepare teachers to teach the curriculum.
3. Throughout this article, the term "Holocaust" is used to refer to the Nazi genocide of Jews.
4. See Alan Stoskopf and Margot Stern Strom, *Choosing to Participate: A Critical Examination of Citizenship in American History* (Brookline, MA: Facing History and Ourselves, 1990); Margot Strom and William Parsons, *Facing History and Ourselves: Holocaust and Human Behavior* (Watertown, MA: Intentional Educations, 1982).
5. See Melinda Fine, "Collaborative Innovations: Documentation of the Facing History and Ourselves Program at an Essential School," *Teachers College Record*, 94, No. 4 (1993), 776.
6. Strom and Parsons, *Facing History*.
7. Strom and Parsons, *Facing History*, p. 14.
8. See Melinda Fine, "Facing History and Ourselves: Portrait of a Classroom," Special Issue: "Whose Culture?" *Educational Leadership* (1991/1992), 44–49; Fine, "Collaborative Innovations," pp. 771–789; Melinda Fine, "The Politics and Practice of Moral Education: A Case Study of Facing History and Ourselves," Diss., Harvard Graduate School of Education, 1991; and Melinda Fine, *Habits of Mind: Struggling over Values in America's Classrooms* (San Francisco: Jossey-Bass, 1995).
9. Strom and Parsons, *Facing History*, pp. 383, 387.
10. See, for example, Sara Lawrence Lightfoot, *The Good High School: Portraits of Character and Culture* (New York: Basic Books, 1983). For an excellent discussion of the similarities and differences between portraiture and other forms of social science inquiry, see Marue Walizer, "Watch With Both Eyes: Narratives and Social Science: Sources of Insight into Teachers' Thinking," Diss., Harvard University Graduate School of Education, 1987, pp. 12–47, 101–129.
11. Eudora Welty, *The Eye of the Storm: Selected Essays and Reviews* (New York: Vintage Books, 1979), p. 129.

12. All quotations of in-class comments are from written notes taken while class was in session.

13. "Lessons in Hate," distributed by Intersection Associates, Cambridge, Massachusetts, and available through the Facing History and Ourselves Resource Library.

14. See, for example, Zachary Lockman, "Original Sin," in *Intifada: The Palestinian Uprising Against Israeli Occupation*, ed. Zachary Lockman and Joel Beinin (Boston: South End Press, 1989), pp. 185–204.

15. All interviews with students were tape-recorded. Students' verbal emphases are indicated in the text in italics.

16. "Klan Youth Corps," distributed by the Anti-Defamation League of B'nai B'rith, New York, New York, and available through the Facing History and Ourselves Resource Library in Brookline, Massachusetts.

17. Phyllis Schlafly, *Child Abuse in the Classroom* (Illinois: Pere Marquette Press, 1984), pp. 435–437.

18. Schlafly, *Child Abuse*, p. 12.

19. For a fuller discussion of this controversy, see Fine, *Dilemmas of Difference*.

20. "A Full-Time Volunteer," *New York Times*, May 13, 1993, p. B3.

31

"How Come There Are No Brothers on That List?": Hearing the Hard Questions All Children Ask

KATHE JERVIS

Bias, both conscious and unconscious, reflecting traditional and unexamined habits of thought, keeps up barriers that must come down if equal opportunity and non-discrimination are ever genuinely to become this country's law and practice.

—SUPREME COURT JUSTICE RUTH BADER GINSBURG IN *PENA V. ADERAND,* A 1995 DISSENTING OPINION ON AFFIRMATIVE ACTION

Teachers are in an ideal position … to attempt to get all of the issues on the table in order to initiate true dialogue. This can only be done, however, by seeking out those whose perspectives may differ most, by learning to give their words complete attention, by understanding one's own power, even if that power stems merely from being in the majority, by being unafraid to raise questions about discrimination and voicelessness with people of color, and to listen, no, to hear what they say.

—LISA DELPIT, *THE SILENCED DIALOGUE: POWER AND PEDAGOGY IN EDUCATING OTHER PEOPLE'S CHILDREN*

People who have no choice but to live their life in their black skins know racism when they see it. Racism is never subtle to the victim. Only White people say race doesn't matter.

—CARRIE MORRIS, PATHWAYS SCHOOL FACULTY MEMBER

WHEN I WAS hired to document the first year of a New York City public middle school, my job was to provide feedback and raise questions that would encourage more reflective practice, and then to write about the dilemmas facing this new school.[1] As I began this documentation at Pathways, as I am calling the school, I joined a faculty with whom I shared common values and a high degree of trust.[2] What I was to focus on was not set in stone; however, when I went over my notes at the end of the first year, the themes of race and ethnicity stood out prominently. Almost every incident that caught my eye seemed tinged by issues of equity, differences, and how children are known as part of their own cultures. Equally striking was that despite the faculty's expressed commitment to structures that supported equity and respected differences, my notes suggested that children's daily experience of race went undiscussed among the adults. I kept returning to how this school, which sought, according to its founding vision, "to enroll students with a diverse racial, economic, ethnic, and ability mix," in fact managed to avoid talking about race, even when events seemed to demand it.[3] I was further struck by how I, as a White staff member, had registered events without seeing them and had failed to understand earlier the meaning of what I had recorded.

Neither an evaluator nor a neutral observer, I was a documenter who was also fully engaged in working for the success of the school, and my role included staff responsibilities.[4] I had an advisory group that allowed me access to issues I might never have thought to raise were I not meeting with parents, reading student journals, and otherwise participating in the daily life of the school.[5] In addition to what I learned from my advisory, my data came from direct observations, interviews, casual conversations, faculty meeting notes, and school documents. I started with observations of children and actual events rather than the literature or theory.

My interpretation of selected school events begins in September 1990 and continues through June 1991. Though I have consciously tried to incorporate other faculty perspectives, this is my story, or at least one that I have shaped. Not everyone on the staff saw events the way I did. When a teacher asked me why I focused this article on race rather than on the development of curriculum at Pathways, I knew that what framed my question was not the burning issue for all faculty. I was in uncharted territory; race had not been a salient category in planning for the documentation. Racial boundaries provoke the deepest questions of personal identity and social structure, as well as the deepest silences, and an exploration of race is not what I or anyone else initially expected from this documentation. Only later, as I created written pictures of daily school life, did I notice how children's questions about race and ethnicity dropped from the faculty's collective memory as soon as the moment of questioning came to an end, and how everyone on the staff, including me, missed what children seemed to be asking: "Who am I in this school community?"

This blindness to racial issues in schools has complex causes and deep roots. This blindness caused Pathways faculty to overlook, deny, or ignore issues of power embedded in race. We did not question who talked honestly, or who listened to whom, nor did individuals look critically at why some children became more central to the school's agenda than others. Faculty of color often vented their concerns outside of formal meetings. In the meetings, according to my notes, the majority White faculty did not appear to question their own perspectives, or ask whether there was a need to see kids more clearly in terms of their race and culture or to consider alternative interpretations of behavior.

Personal silence about race is common, and institutions like Pathways are shaped as much by what does not happen as by what does. Pathways' handpicked faculty had plunged into the hard work of founding a new school without anticipating the need for any overt discussion of race, and ingrained dominant societal norms prevailed by default.

All schools take refuge in silence about race to some degree, and many educators are novices at constructing multicultural, integrated school settings (Grant & Secada, 1990).

What my documentation revealed is that racial issues were often invisible to the majority White faculty, or thought not to be about race. But like ultraviolet sun rays, damage from unexplored racial attitudes often appears long after the actual exposure. Building a successful integrated school means paying attention to people of color and attending to White racial attitudes before emergencies require it.

That society's problems play out in schools means that schools also offer an opportunity to open a dialogue about race and equality, yet this dialogue is never easy. At the heart of the story I am telling here is the striking ambiguity inherent in the individual incidents; people at Pathways disagreed about whether, and in what ways, events were racial. I have attempted to present enough details so readers can draw their own conclusions about what may be racial, adolescent, gender, happenstance, denial, or a mix of other factors that influence what happens in schools (McCarthy, 1993).

A lot occurred at Pathways that first year. Bringing into being an educational vision for sixth and seventh graders required instilling an ethos, setting standards, and establishing moral authority while simultaneously facing bureaucratic constraints, learning how to run a fire drill, and mollifying anxious parents. For this article, I set aside these monumental tasks and ignored many unique events that interacted with race. While readers may conclude from the incidents I have chosen to describe that Pathways faculty frequently got caught up in racial crises, that would be inaccurate and misleading.

DOCUMENTING RARELY HEARD STORIES

A colleague, Brenda Engel, influenced my approach to the work at Pathways. She makes a distinction between "documentation," which is a nonjudgmental and neutral selection of systematically collected documents reflecting a "complicated, many-faceted sequence of evens that has occurred over a period of time so that it may be examined at leisure," and a "documented account," in which the documents are used to support a thesis (Engel, 1975, p. 3). This article is an example of the latter; I have chosen particular incidents, teased out from a complex whole, to address what I feel goes on everywhere, even in the "best schools," as adults and children try to untangle the larger societal issues that play themselves out in schools.

One purpose of a documenter is to function as a mirror, helping to make practitioners aware of their own practice. In my experience, once all the particulars of any incident are written down—what exactly was said or done—it becomes harder for faculty to stay with comfortable, unreflective thinking. The racial dynamics at Pathways likely mirror what happens in many schools facing similar challenges. In this article, I explore these dynamics and call attention to the deep levels of awareness necessary to change previously unexamined behavior.

This article evolved as I circulated drafts to all the staff, taking their comments into account with each revision. Though faculty talk about race was rare at the time of the incidents recorded here, I have included many of their responses to what I wrote. That the faculty engaged with me in this documentation effort is a tribute to their honesty, good faith, and their willingness to learn from the work.

During the rewrites, colleagues, friends, and family also added information, took issue with my viewpoints, and challenged me to clarify meaning, teaching me all along. For me, this is one way of socially constructing knowledge. Writing this piece has been a struggle to transform a still incomplete learning experience into more solid personal understanding.

What follows are glimpses of daily life at Pathways that invite educators to think about how we can begin and sustain the hard conversations about race that will allow us to hear—really hear—our own, as well as our children's, questions.

Creating a New School

Located on the edge of Harlem in a nineteenth-century elementary school building that just happened to have a vacant top floor, Pathways opened with its facility in a state of terrible disrepair. "As I was walking up the steps for the first time, I felt like I had spiders crawling around in my stomach. How come the school is so dreadfully damaged with cracks? What have I gotten myself into?" seventh grader Hector Zelaya wrote on the first day. To reach Pathways, Hector and his peers had to traverse the barren playground with its netless basketball hoops, climb up the long flights of stairs, the last of which smelled of wet plaster, and skirt the large buckets positioned to catch the water that dripped through the roof whenever it rained. Even the district office liaison called the setting "a hostile environment." Yet the staff was thrilled. Unlike the anonymous, bureaucratic junior highs with escalating dropout rates and demoralized faculties so often depicted in the press, Pathways was founded by teachers excited about exercising their own autonomy in a small, personal community.[6] Hector, one of many children who responded to the faculty's excitement, ended his essay saying, "When I got to class I felt at home and my worries were over. Now I know it's not just the outside; its the inside and the people. I'm growing to like it on the first day and later on I'll love it (maybe)."

To build something where nothing existed before captured the founding director's imagination. Jan Palmer had not worked full time since before her oldest child was born. Her biological White and adopted Black children were now grown, and she was ready for the grueling hours that directing a school required. She was not even deterred by her temporary per diem status, which meant that her job showed up on the computer as a vacancy open to any high-seniority teacher.

Unlike a hiring system in which teachers are assigned to a school by a central office, alternative school directors have the luxury of hiring staff from among those applicants who wish to join their faculty. To select committed teachers who shared the values she considered crucial to founding a new school, Jan interviewed candidates, visited them on site, and invited them to observe her own classroom. She assessed their energy level, their willingness to work hard, and looked for evidence that children were at the center of their focus; too many worksheets, too much dependence on canned curriculum, or too much ego were grounds for rejection. As it turned out, none of the people she hired had weekend or after-school jobs, all were married, and all but the youngest had children. On the surface, we seemed more alike than different.

Nevertheless, we were a diverse staff. Don Jackson had previously taught for twenty years in "regular" junior highs, where he was often a minority White teacher. Carrie Morris, a seasoned African American teacher and former staff developer, was a twenty-year-plus veteran of the New York City Public Schools with more varied experience teaching children of all races than the rest of us. Bilingual, bicultural Lucy Lopez-Garcia, a Puerto Rican, moved comfortably within both Anglo and Latino cultures. A nursery school teacher only a few credits shy of a teaching credential, Lucy was delighted to work officially as an aide, but to function as a faculty member who was centrally important to colleagues, children, and parents in her role as an advisor and teacher of art. For Jim Serota, a White

Ivy League graduate who had worked in an inner-city after-school program for two years, this was his first teaching job. Marilyn Ross, another young, White, first-year teacher, joined the staff part time in October. For several years, Jan and I been colleagues at a small, integrated middle school. When she decided to start a new school, I saw it as an opportunity to capture the experience in writing, and we conceived this documentation project, which built on my previous descriptions of classrooms and my twenty years of teaching.

The staff agreed with the vision statement that "a good school for preadolescents maintains a diverse community to educate children for life in a democratic society," but no one thought that implementing this vision was going to be easy. As Carrie told the deputy superintendent, "You have to engineer life in a diverse group to make it work. You can't leave it—any of it—to chance." This integrated faculty actively sought out White students to create a diverse student body and, at the same time, took care to keep those students from dominating academically. Although the staff did not spend planning time explicitly talking about race, they did engineer a four-pronged effort designed to achieve a fair and equitable school. First, the school recruited a cohort of academically proficient Black and Latino students, whose presence as role models confounded the stereotype of integrated schools in which Whites remain at the top of the academic hierarchy. Referred by an organization that prepared students of color for independent schools, these high-powered entrants became academic stars. Second, faculty planned heterogeneous classes, which prevented labelling children by their academic proficiency or lack of it. Third, teachers created openings for all kinds of talents to surface. They carefully mixed race, age, and abilities of students in subject matter classes, advisories, and special projects that required various skills. Fourth, they modelled respectful appreciation of differences through a year-long social studies curriculum, "Coming to America," which attempted to honor contributions from a variety of cultures.

The school enrolled sixty-three students. Although children do not actually come in standard demographic slots, convention requires labeling their heritages. We categorized slightly more than one-third of the student body as Latino, slightly over one-third as African American, slightly less than one-third as White, and two students as Asian. All students spoke English; many were bilingual in English and Spanish. Forty-three children applied for either free lunch (if their family of four had an annual income of less than $16,500) or for reduced-fee lunch (family income of less than $23,000). Reading and math scores ranged from the eighth to the ninety-ninth-plus percentile. When school began, no faculty member had taught children so diverse along so many dimensions, nor had their students been in such mixed classrooms before.

Few mortals succeed in meeting their highest goals, including the founders of schools in the first year. The stories I tell about race may suggest that this new middle school didn't come close to providing a good place for children, which would not be true. That Pathways students loved to come to school is amply documented in the essays I asked them to write in October, February, and June. Sixth grader Marie Diaz's June list distills the satisfaction that many students expressed in their essays:

Some things that I like about Pathways are:

1. on trips teachers aren't always watching what you do
2. there's a lot of gossip going on
3. the teachers are very, very friendly.

4. if you have a problem they will talk to you about it.
5. teachers trust us
6. I like science because we get to experiment with things, not just read a science book and then write a paragraph about what you read.
7. they take us to a lot of trips.

Further evidence that Pathways children enjoyed school comes from the official records: On the same day that Marie wrote her essay, a board of education attendance auditor tallied the books and concluded that Pathways had one of the highest teacher and student attendance rates of any school in New York City.

The small size, the strong advisory system, the care with which the faculty observed children, and the trust the school inspired meant that students exposed their feelings and that faculty took note of them. Yet despite conscientious attention to equitable structures and the teachers' concerted efforts to know children well, students' talk about race often caught faculty off guard. When race surfaced at unplanned moments, children's questions went unaddressed.

"HE'S NOT ONE OF US, IS HE?": A CHILD'S FLEETING QUESTION

It is easy to see race as an issue in a school where, day after day, the students in the top tracks are White and the students in remedial classes are primarily children of color. It is harder to make meaning from conversational snatches that easily get lost in the sweep of school life. The following 30-second incident has buried in it a child's real question. From my notes the first week of school:

> It is the first afternoon together in the park and the first full day of school. Don, a teacher (White) organizes a football game. Duke, a sixth grader (White), literally mows down Sam (White) on the other team, violating the agreed upon rules. Several kids (African American) complain. Duke calls them "Schmucks," and angrily retreats, muttering under his breath about how he knows the rules because he has played football all his life. Another teacher (White) encourages them to "forget it" and get on with the game, but several kids (all races) from both teams go immediately to Carrie (African American). They are baffled by Duke's behavior, by his insistence that he was playing correctly, by his belief that he had the right to knock Sam down, and his verbal epithet, which these kids took to be a racial slur. Arnold (African American) puts his arm next to Carrie's, and says seriously, "He isn't one of us, is he?"
>
> "What do you mean?" Carrie says. Arnold replies, "You know, his skin isn't dark. He called us 'Smokes'." (Field notes, September 13)

"He isn't one of us, is he?" is a basic human way to categorize the world. The disintegration of this football game exemplifies the subtle ways race seeps into children's consciousness. Arnold, as he compared his arm to Carrie's, thought that he heard his classmate say "smokes," referring to his skin color. Arnold's question and its accompanying gesture have become, for me, emblematic of the complicated, ambiguous nature of race and racism.[7]

Arnold did not hear "schmucks," the Yiddish word of derision in general use, which I heard clearly, and it may not have been a familiar word to him. So while Duke's insult was not a "racist" slur, this exchange illustrates the way Arnold made sense of his newly integrated world. This incident confirmed for me that when adults and children do not know each other and understand even less about each other's cultural backgrounds, race easily becomes the most salient personal attribute. Ambiguous remarks fall into the most obvious category, which is skin color, especially when students see color in discriminatory terms.

Nothing is inherently odd about noticing race and skin color, but in this society they are fraught with hidden meanings. Misinformation and lack of knowledge about race can be a minefield when no acceptable forum exists to raise questions. Although Arnold had never been in the same classroom with Whites before, and Duke had never been a racial minority at school, we never thought to create such a forum at Pathways. As a staff we were unprepared for students' barely articulated questions about this new racial mix. Whether due to conscious avoidance or unconscious denial, or a mix of both, I never talked to either child about what happened, nor did Carrie and I discuss it with each other or think to bring it to a faculty meeting. Arnold's question remained unexplored and Duke's behavior went unexamined. Pathways' curriculum, which was explicitly meant to be "gender fair and multicultural," openly addressed the question, "Who am I and how did my ancestors come to America?" yet it did not provide a place for Arnold to consider the implications of what he really wanted to know: "He isn't one of us, is he?"

The faculty listened to students and encouraged them to articulate their feelings, which paid off in personal relationships and mutual trust, but what was left unsaid or ignored about racial and cultural identity left children with a powerfully negative message. "People identify others by their skin color before their cultural identity," Carrie said after she read a draft of this article, and lamented that "little is embedded in any school's curriculum that really speaks to these issues."

SERVANT OR SLAVE?

Before the staff was even in place, Pathways received a grant to hire a "playwright in residence" to teach all students "writers' workshop" twice weekly for six weeks. Jan hired Martin Cane, who came in mid-September to share his ideas with the faculty:

> Martin Cane, a young [White] playwright, arrived to meet the faculty. During the staff meeting, he explained how he is going to work: "First there will be a staged reading by professional actors of my own play. Putting on my play first means that I put myself on the line before I ask kids to do it. It is also a chance to have a common experience. Then kids will write scenes, from 2–10 pages and I will pick eight of them. The criteria for selection could be diversity of topic, how hard a kid worked, how passionate she is, how much of a breakthrough it is, or how much possibility it opens up for kids. After the scenes have been selected, professional actors will spend the day rehearsing plays with the student writers, and then there will be an all school event for families that night." (Field notes, September 12)

Faculty were impressed with Martin's values and program plans. In early October, he started teaching three sections of writers' workshop. His facility with language, his ability to provide students with instant phrases that got them unstuck, his energy and good actor's voice, and his swift pacing entranced me. After the first day, a sixth grader said about this master of language so skilled in releasing kids' imaginations, "That man sees things the rest of us don't see."

Martin's three back-to-back classes drained even his prodigious energy. Although the school tried to rearrange the schedule, Martin's own work prevented any shift. The emotions unleashed in his classes spilled out in unpredictable ways, especially when his energy ebbed. During the second week of Martin's program, he asked students to write about a scary emotion, and Bart, a White child, recalled an experience from several years earlier that still evoked his strong response. When Bart lived in South Africa, he found a poisonous snake in his garden, and he and a servant killed it. On hearing Bart read this story aloud, Sal, a Latino child, leapt up out of his chair and said, "You had slaves!" It was an accusation, not a question. Martin reddened, and said, "Servant is the word," and moved right on; this exchange took under thirty seconds.

Sal could not calm down, and after class he bullied Bart until a teacher intervened. Sal would not budge from his opinion that having a servant in South Africa meant that Bart's family was rich and owned slaves, both reasons to be hostile toward Bart. From that point on, this physically powerful child hectored the meeker Bart on many occasions.

Although this brief exchange between Sal and Bart appeared in my notes, and others witnessed it, we missed its racially loaded implications. We were inattentive to Sal and Bart when they most needed adult support to work through their strong feelings and to see the world through each others' eyes.

As a part-time, short-term artist-in-residence, Martin may have been the catalyst for this situation, but the regular faculty held the responsibility for helping children interpret it. If individual teachers are to see that children achieve a deeper understanding of class differences and racial issues, they need to generate opportunities for the whole faculty to discuss these topics among themselves. Had the school done so in this case, we might have seen that Sal needed a place to make his deep concerns about slavery explicit so that other students could recognize his perspective about the Black struggle in South Africa and come to understand what set him off. Faculty missed the chance to create such a forum. Instead, the only visible aftermath of this brief incident was Sal's continual picking on Bart, which then became an issue not of race, but of disciplining Sal for his "hot temper." It seems to me that adults' urge to curb unwanted behavior often shifts their focus from children to discipline, especially when rules can be invoked to cover situations, such as discussions of race, that make them uncomfortable.

"HOW COME THERE ARE NO BROTHERS ON THAT LIST?"
Once the students had completed their play scenes, Martin chose eight of them to be staged by professional actors. He carefully described his process of selection:

> I made choices by first reading all the plays without regard for racial diversity or kids who needed support. I put scenes in three piles—strong, maybes, and rejects. Those in the third pile either were unfinished, had no investment, were unclear, or had no conflict—a central aim of my teaching. Then I reread them to see if I made any mistakes, but didn't move any into the "strong" pile. Then I shaped the performance evening, looking for humor, strong emotion, and a variety of subjects. All three classes had to be represented. Only after I met those criteria did I look at individuals for racial and gender balance. I chose one child who

had come far and this would make a big difference to his growth. I couldn't help it that 6 out of the 8 selected plays were by girls. (Field notes, December 3)

On a Monday morning, two weeks after he had last taught, Martin returned to the first-period writing class, now overseen by regular Pathways faculty, and gave a moving intro-duction before announcing his final selections. He said with feeling, "My plays don't always get produced, and I have to accept that. It is part of being a playwright. I want you to know that when I tell you all of the plays were good, I really mean it. If I didn't believe the plays were good, I wouldn't say so." He named four children whose scenes were chosen and took them immediately to work with the professional actors. Other students quietly continued reading and writing.

Martin gave the same introduction to the second class, and took two children out. Only one boy, Derek, objected loudly, "My play was so fresh. It's not fair." Third period was dif-ferent. This noisy class, for which Martin had the least energy, still did good work. Martin gave a short, less heartfelt version of what he had said to the other classes. Without talking about himself or the quality of the plays, he said wearily that "choosing play scenes was hard," and named two authors, who left with him to rehearse. Both of these winners were White, although those chosen from the other classes were children of color. After Martin's departure, Marilyn, a White faculty member newly hired to teach the writers' workshop, introduced an assignment, but the kids were not with her. Amid some commotion in the back of the room, Jerome, an African American, said rather tentatively, but in a voice loud enough to make everyone listen, "It's not my question, but someone wants to know, 'how come there are no brothers on that list?'"

Above the noisy responses—everyone wanted an answer—Jan took over. In the room to help with the play scene logistics, she moved to the front of the class and began, "That is not true. The list is balanced." Pulling a list from her pocket, she read it aloud, naming an Asian and a Hispanic; when she got to Bianca, whose surname is Hispanic, she looked up and said, "Bianca is Hispanic." The class exploded. Everyone had something to say at the same time, and the voices got even louder before the crescendo peaked. For-getting the original question of why no Black boys were chosen from this class, kids shrieked: "Bianca told me she was Black!" "How could anyone who talks like that be Hispanic?" "She has a Black attitude." The kids were astonished that anyone thought Bianca was Hispanic. Bianca's heritage is extremely complex; she is the biological child of a Latino father and a White mother, and the foster child of African American parents. Her peers saw her as Black. They totally overlooked the fact that if she were Black, then the list included at least one Black person. Bianca was not in this section of writers' workshop, so she could not answer questions about her background. For the adults in the room, all we thought we knew about supporting children's need for self-identifica-tion went down the drain, and the issue raised by Jerome —"How come there are no brothers on that list?"—went with it.

Voices were getting still louder when Lisa, an African American, changed the subject, which generated even more heat. "Why did I do this play anyway if it wasn't chosen?" she protested. "I spent half a week thinking of a topic and the other half writing seven pages. A waste. A pure waste." She was raging. Her anger at not being chosen despite her hard work sent hot sparks into the room. Serena, a Latina, answered her articulately and passionately:

"Not everyone can be chosen. You still learn from writing." Energy whirled around the room and kids weren't in any state to listen. The period ended, mercifully for us, with a *deus ex machina* when two unplanned visitors arrived, almost as if in answer to our prayer for a diversion. Amid much chaos, the visitors offered us good wishes for our new school, and the class left for lunch. Jerome's question remained unanswered.

Although a child's whispered remark about the race of the winning playwrights should have alerted us to the conversation students were eager to have, we were more inclined to bury this uncomfortable 45-minute period in oblivion. Neither Jan, Marilyn, nor I brought it up informally or at any faculty meeting. The issues of children's racial and ethnic identity could have provided fertile ground for weeks of curriculum, but the pace of the day crowded out time for a topic that was hard for faculty to discuss and for which no particular space had been created within the school structure. Instead, we were embarrassed by a classroom eruption that took us beyond our own comfort level. To us, this noisy digression merely interfered with our pedagogical intentions, and we missed the opportunity for inquiry it might have provided. The issue of race as a factor in the selection process had disappeared from any formal discussion among children or faculty. The incident, however, did not end there.

The Pathways faculty worked hard to support children who struggled to find their own voices and act on their views. Lisa, still harboring strong feelings about why she wasn't selected, appropriately took this issue to her advisory, which wrote Martin the following letter:

12/3/90

To Mr. Martin Cane

In our Advisory we all discussed about how you chose the scenes for the plays.

1. I think we all understand that only a certain amount of people would be chosen. We all wish that we would be recognized for our work.
2. Before the plays were chosen you gave some people the idea that their plays were going to be chosen by giving them the idea that their work was Excellent.
3. What was the reason those people got chosen over the rest of us?

Lisa's initial outrage about how hard she worked on her play cut to the heart of the school's double message: We are inclusive until we decide to be exclusive. Lisa's concerns in class, mingled with the talk about race that charged the atmosphere, grew out of her sense of powerlessness when confronted with the subjectivity of the play scene selections. She regained some control by going to her advisory. The advisory's letter, a mature, logical response devoid of the intense feelings she expressed in class, lacked explicit mention of race, perhaps because word had spread that Martin's list was, in fact, racially balanced. On it were a Black boy, a Black girl, two Latinas, a White boy, a White girl, an Asian girl, and Bianca with her complex background. Since evidence disproved the contention that there were no brothers on the list, the original question slipped back underground.

Had we adults who witnessed these complicated feelings listened more carefully and been more attuned to the crucial importance of students' questions about race, we might have discussed the explosive class at the next faculty meeting. Then all of us, including

Lisa's advisor, who had not known about what happened, would have been better prepared to open conversations with children about racial exclusion and identity. Just because there was one brother on the list didn't mean the discussion should have ended.

Conversation about children's racial identity—so obviously ripe for exploration—never reappeared, at least not in any form that caught my attention. Only in hindsight did I see the possibilities for supporting children's understanding of their own heritages (Cohen, 1993). As for other fallout, a district colleague, one of our visitors who arrived in the midst of this classroom chaos, bruited it around that he was surprised discipline was so lax at Pathways. Such criticism was frequently leveled by adults in the school community when kids expressed volatile feelings about race, as in the struggle between Sal and Bart.

This incident might have been lost, except that I took notes. After I circulated a description of this episode to the staff as part of my first draft of this article, the faculty wondered what initially prompted LaTasha, an African American student, to question the composition of the play scene list, and what caused Jerome to repeat her question. Why didn't LaTasha ask her own question? Was hers a casual query, which then sparked Jerome's urgent need to know? Why had the issue of race not come up during class sooner? Gender issues had been debated heatedly in other classes since the beginning of the year, yet talk about race had been essentially absent. Lucy speculated that perhaps Pathways' emphasis on belonging to a new school community, conveyed in the much-repeated phrase "we are all pioneers together," may have felt to the children like a "melting pot" philosophy that discouraged rather than invited discussions of differences. Did kids not feel safe enough to ask hard personal questions until now? And, even more disturbing, how much energy did kids of color spend wondering what was safe to say in a White teacher's class (Delpit, 1990)?

Equally significant was the issue of selectivity. No one absorbed what Martin had said in September: "The hardest task is to provide an inclusive experience and then be exclusive about it." Although children and teachers knew only eight plays would be selected, the reality hadn't sunk in. The children felt misled and took the route available through race to express their discomfort with a White male who closed the gate on their aspirations to be selected. A more established school might—just might—have thought more about the consequences of competitiveness interjected by an outsider.

These three vignettes caught faculty off balance. The following two incidents, involving Duke, who "mowed down" Sam in a football game the first day of school, and Derek, who also singled himself out on the first day, are weightier, with more apparent long-term consequences for these students and the school. While the stories differ, both boys shared a deep uncertainty about their place in school, and neither ever became fully part of the Pathways community.

WHITES AS A MINORITY

Changing demographics have produced a relatively new phenomenon in public education: White students as a racial minority in urban schools. Pathways staff believes that integration is worth preserving, but even if it were not—as many families of color are beginning to say—public schools are open to every child and all children deserve to be part of the school community. Only in retrospect were faculty able to raise the question, How do we serve all children together in the same educational institution?

That first year, faculty assumed that enough White children at Pathways were comfortable so that little attention was paid to the issue of "minority" White children. Faculty were disinclined to talk about children whose White skin already gave them a privileged position in society. Jan said later that the particular White children who were struggling were "finding out that in this school they are not the aristocracy." Carrie added, "It's good for their souls," but she also pointed out that "White kids are paying the price of a discriminatory society, as are Black and Latino kids."

My notes about Duke's experience as a White student at Pathways highlight one example of what teachers face if they want to integrate all children in a school community. White children do experience fewer problems in society; "Duke will always be able to get a taxi in the middle of the night," Carrie reminded me. Nevertheless, Duke needed to find a place at school. These excerpts from my advisory notes early in the year show my own inadequate and tentative responses as I threw myself into unfamiliar territory:

> One of the Black kids brought his sketch pad from home full of magic marker cartoons, and explained that he does them by eye, not by tracing. Everyone admired the drawings. When he came to a black-faced Mickey Mouse, Duke said, "Hey Mickey Mouse isn't Black." Kids said emphatically, "Why not?" and Duke backed off.
>
> Then, Bianca read her book report on *The Miss USA Pageant*. In the course of it, she was asked: "How did you know how old the new Miss USA was?" She answered, "I bin knowing it." Duke snapped, "You can't say that. It's not right." I said, "It may not be standard English, but it is absolutely correct in Bianca's home language. It means she has known it for a long time." (Field notes, September 18)

Though Duke's two contributions to this advisory session were sharply rebuffed, I never thought to explain to him why his peers and I objected. My notes from that day include another incident:

> The next thing I knew Jose was yelling, "Fight in the gym." When I arrived in the gym, Michael (African American)—and Duke were indeed fighting. Michael, feeling the sting of Duke's behavior over the last few days, said to me, "I don't like the way he has an attitude with teachers." I took Duke—the more upset—into the office; teary-eyed and angry, he said, "I'm one of the few White boys here. I grew up in an upper class White community and I'm not taking anything from anybody." I was surprised to hear a child use the term "upper class" and ignored it, but I wondered if he assumed that he would be treated differently from others. I quoted Jan's line reminding him America is changing and he will be better prepared to be a leader if he learns how to get on in a diverse group. I reiterated emphatically that this has to be a safe place for everybody—no fights, no snap judgments about the way others speak or draw. He agreed and pulled himself together while I went off to explain to Michael that fights are not allowed, and that while we have to teach Duke a few things, it isn't his responsibility to change Duke's attitude by himself. Relieved that I did not call his mother, he said, "Thank you for this talk." (Field notes, September 18)

At the time, I wondered about Duke's sense of entitlement—what I knew about his neighborhood or his family background gave me no clue to how he understood his self-proclaimed socioeconomic status. To my knowledge, he was a regular middle-class kid. Yet I never addressed his feelings of superiority, nor did I recognize that uncertainty and fear about this new school might be the real issue for him. Instead, I pointed out that White children do face fewer problems in society and told Duke he would be better prepared for today's society if he learned to lead by experiencing life as a racial minority. My reaction reflects an unexamined assumption about White privilege, and is one reason why people of color oppose integration that historically focuses on benefits for White children (Foster, 1993; Ladson-Billings, 1994). While I impressed upon the boys our desire to make the Pathways community safe for everyone, and I thought I made sense talking to Michael about Duke's prejudices, it never occurred to me to sit them down to talk with each other.

On October ninth, Duke apparently told a Latino fifth grader from the elementary school downstairs to "bug off" (at least that is what he said in his sanitized version). He admitted the child's only provocation was to be in the way. The offended child had threatened to bring an older brother and his friends to the playground "for protection," and Pathways students standing nearby (all Black, except for one White friend of Duke's) had refused to get involved. Understandably sensing danger, they had gone immediately to the Pathways office to report what had happened. The dangerous feeling lingered for a few days and to straighten things out with the elementary school, the building principal met with this fifth grader and the Pathways students who had witnessed the challenge. From my notes:

> The principal lectured the Pathways' kids on how they were outsiders in the neighborhood and tried to get them to see how the elementary kids felt with new non-neighborhood kids on the playground. At first it seemed like her lecture only exacerbated the middle school kids' feelings of nervousness and Duke's feelings of being in the minority. In talking it over in our own staff meeting we concluded her message about outsiders is so basic to the neighborhood ethic that we have to take it seriously. It was decided that rather than have the building principal and Jan supervise the playground for the next two weeks ("Two ladies for protection—no way," the men on the faculty said), kids would just be sent home immediately after school. Don pointed out what everybody needed to remember: "Duke doesn't understand that talk connects up with action much more quickly in this neighborhood. Duke has a lot to learn." (Field notes, October 15)

Faculty continued to watch Duke. By the time of his self-evaluation, we saw some small progress. This mid-semester exercise asked students, "What are the most important things you have learned?" On his first draft, Duke answered "math facts." The next day, on his final draft, he wrote instead, "I learned a lot about other kids." By Thanksgiving he had stopped reacting negatively to differences—at least out loud. He still had few friends and hung out only with White males, even when their most obvious commonality was being White. At the parent conference following this self-evaluation, his father agreed with us about Duke's social growth: "Yeah, things are better. He doesn't come home with stories anymore about how he's the only one who knows anything and everyone else is dumb."

Duke and Carrie had a good relationship, though she had no compunction about describing him, out of his hearing, as a racist. She often said, "after all, he is a kid." At

Carrie's insistence, he stopped telling her offensive off-color jokes and apologized when she pointed out his arrogant behavior. He declared science with Carrie "my best subject." If given a choice in class with whom to work, he never chose a child of color. He did not socialize after school or join the basketball team, though he did play pickup games at lunch with racially mixed teams. He even played on the girls' kickball team when "they needed a good kicker." He knew a lot about baseball—statistics, history, strategy—but in the classroom Duke shared reluctantly and others listened equally reluctantly. He affected the student body very little, except that kids were aware of his racial attitudes, as shown in my notes from the spring:

> The kids are watching a slide show in preparation for the three day camping trip. The quality of attention borders on the disrespectful. Many in the audience have never been to camp—or even away from home overnight, and nervous tension is high. The slides, shown by the camp director, picture much younger children—all White. The (Black) boys on the back bench were loud and disruptive. One of them said derisively: "Look at all those Dukes up there." I was not meant to hear their remark and they didn't know that I did. When I reported this remark to the faculty, frankly thinking the kids had observed Duke well, Marilyn (White) rightly reminded me that, "If they had been White boys talking about a Black child, you wouldn't have hesitated for a minute to stop them." True. It never occurred to me to intervene. (It was easier for me to label Duke "racist" than initiate a hard conversation about "all those Dukes" with the boys on the back bench.) (Field notes, May 1)

Late in the spring, Duke began to talk about leaving Pathways. At first he said, "This school doesn't have enough extracurricular activities (though he never stayed for what they had), or that the "work isn't hard enough" (though I believed he didn't push himself to excel); finally, after some urging to be honest, he said it wasn't the school he didn't like, but he wanted to be where his friends were. In advisory, he did what was expected, joined games, and spoke when called on, but he was never central to the group. On a final assignment to write what was important about Pathways, he said:

> It's a small school. The teachers can get to know you better. They have time to work with you. In fact I think they get a little too personal. Like telling you to interact with people you don't really like instead of being with your friends. They worry too much about racism. They worry too much about your personal life instead of your academic life. I met a lot of nice people in my one year, but I really don't feel right here.

This essay matched what other children often noticed about Pathways' size and personal atmosphere. It also called attention to Duke's feelings of being separate and disconnected from the group. Late in the year, I tried to open a discussion with him about what I perceived as his narrowness in his choice of friends, and he didn't like it. Perhaps I didn't know how to talk about race effectively, and had not created enough openings during the year for him to say what was on his mind.

Whether Duke is biased because of family or societal attitudes or is merely unhappy with his minority status is not really the issue. If integrated schools are going to succeed, it is imperative to find a way to include "all those Dukes" in the community. Duke never became an accepting or acceptable member of Pathways. Jan willingly admitted that

"White children who come from the power structure with more experience and opportu-nities didn't get enough attention from us," while Carrie pointed out that "all children suf-fer from racism." The issues around White children may not be the most essential—children of color definitely pay a higher price for society's biases—but if public schools are to be successfully integrated, faculties will have to think harder about Whites as minorities, just as schools are now thinking harder about supporting children of color in predominantly White institutions.

For many White families, sending their children to schools where students are pre-dominantly children of color requires giving up a privileged status gained by virtue of their White skin (McIntosh, 1988). Basic to the problem is this statement overheard at the district office: "If the mix is one-third Black, one-third Hispanic, and one-third White, White parents see the school as two-thirds non-White." Pathways is deliberately trying to achieve that one-third, one-third, one-third ratio in order to maintain an inte-grated setting. As part of managing that ratio, faculty must do more to insure that White parents are willing partners.

From the viewpoint of justly allocating school resources of faculty time and attention, that expenditure does not seem fair. To call for a big investment of faculty energy might create the impression of giving more of a scarce school resource to the dominant group. Children of color need an equal share of teachers' energy. Even in a school that is respect-ful of difference, it takes time-consuming, committed, moral leadership to build a school community based on the agreement that we are all citizens in this society together. Cer-tainly, integration must be built on something other than a White, middle-class model for the benefit of Whites, as many Black families are now charging (Ladson-Billings, 1994). Yet, if White children are to learn to be comfortable when they number only a handful in a large group, they and their families will need this leadership. Such moral guidance to do what is right, rather than what is politically expedient for those in power, is not so easily given. My experience at Pathways and other schools suggests that many school communi-ties are not yet prepared for what that leadership might entail.

Veteran White teachers may have thought about educating the increasing numbers of children of color, albeit often in terms of assimilating them into White middle-class norms. Many White teachers—who have rarely been a numerical minority them-selves—have little empathy or knowledge about what would make the transition smoother for children who come from a predominantly White setting to a predominantly Black and Latino setting. I have already noted that the faculty made assumptions about White chil-dren's comfort levels. Indeed, it was easier for me to ignore Duke's lack of ease because he was White. In comparison with White faculty, Carrie's own racial experiences gave her more insight into Duke's minority status. Yet it was an unfair burden on Carrie to expect her to educate the faculty about race. White faculty already ask too much of faculty of color in interpreting students' behavior; this is work Whites must learn to do.

DO I HAVE A PLACE IN THIS SCHOOL?

The story of Derek's expulsion centers around the daunting challenge of educating other people's children as we would our own (Delpit, 1988). The "we" here refers to any of us who teach children across racial, ethnic, or class boundaries, which includes most teachers in today's urban settings. The background of this story is governance: Who sets the boundaries? Who is "the boss" of the school? What happens when standards of behavior are ignored or defied? In the foreground is Derek, who did not connect with enough Pathways adults to learn as we would like our own children to learn. The vision that every individual was valued faded when faculty seriously disagreed over Derek. Whether the staff used every means at their disposal to help him, and how they interpreted their responsibility or lack of it for Derek's predicament, is one of the story's unresolved and guilt-provoking themes. This story also calls attention to what happens when adults reach an impasse with a child who does not meet their standards of behavior.

Since Pathways faculty ostensibly shared the same values, governance by consensus worked fine when no one had passionate feelings, and the issues were not loaded. Congenial meetings, good parties, and genuine friendships cemented faculty bonds. But in a crisis—and no one knew what form it would take until it happened—the method of consensus failed. We had no practice with confrontation, no precedent for resolving heated arguments, and no way to talk at meetings about differing perceptions of each others' actions. As a result, consensus collapsed in a crisis around Derek. No one heard his unarticulated question: "Where is my place in this school?"

From the staff viewpoint, Derek was trouble. Even on the first day of school, when kids were on their best behavior, Derek stood out. In my journal notes of the first all-school meeting, I speculated: "Derek didn't wait to sit on the rug when everyone else did, nor did he want to line up by height for Don's game. Was his reluctance related to his being one of the shortest boys in the school?" Since that first day, this twelve-year-old African American boy could disrupt class merely by walking across the room on his way to the bathroom. He might provocatively pull his sweats up and down, or whack a child as he passed, which may have been an affectionate gesture, but was disruptive nonetheless. He frequently refused to engage in anything even vaguely academic, thus he never became competent enough at school work to demonstrate that he was making progress.

Over the year, Derek's disrespect for adults—at least the White adults—escalated. Or, perhaps the White adults disrespected Derek by interpreting his behavior though narrow lenses, causing events to escalate.[8] Something about Derek locked faculty into battle with him. Derek was not a "middle-class" kid.[9] He may not have been well understood by White faculty, who focused on his "attitude" and failed to see how he was setting himself up for school failure right before their eyes. We need to understand more about children like Derek who often push adults beyond their own limits, but we also need to recognize how those limits relate to culture, class, and race.

With no one looking carefully at anything about this child except his transgressions, Derek became increasingly lost to view. School structures and faculty support that might have helped him find his way were absent. Yet Pathways faculty did have structures for paying attention to individual children. Each month, we scheduled a Descriptive Review, an activity designed to build a community based on shared knowledge about children, which entailed an in-depth look at one particular child. For each Descriptive Review, the faculty chose children who caused them to "tear their hair out" or who raised particular linguistic or pedagogical issues.[10] Based on those criteria Derek qualified, but each month we chose children who appealed to us more than Derek.

Of all the faculty, only Carrie got on well with Derek. Her ability to hear the hard-to-ignore children who were often disliked by others served him well. When she asked in a strong throaty tone, "Darling, what are you doing?" Derek frequently stopped his misbehavior and apologized in his own distinctive deep voice. Though I did not teach him, I saw how Derek's behavior aggravated those who were not as clearly connected to him as Carrie was. In the minor contretemps that teachers deal with daily, Derek managed to resist adult eye contact ("Please look at me when I am talking"), continue the offending infraction ("I asked you once to stop drumming on the table!"), and draw his friends into his court of appeal ("I wasn't talking, was I?"). Not everyone was as able to set clear boundaries for him as Carrie was. Perhaps Carrie's more ready acceptance of children like Derek who tested adult authority prevented her from calling sooner than others might have for drastic measures. And maybe she absorbed and took care of so much of his particular misbehavior that the rest of the faculty didn't need to signal for help. In any case, until Derek got into hopeless confrontations with the rest of the faculty, attention to other children took precedence over his annoying behavior and undone homework.

Derek's first real blow-up with an adult came in January. Everyone acknowledged that Derek was the star player on the basketball team, though something of a "hot dogger." When a referee called a foul on him during a regular intramural game, Derek lost his temper and kicked over a trash can. Carrie calmed him down and the school imposed no sanctions. In retrospect, some faculty considered this tolerance of Derek's unsportsmanlike behavior an egregious error. Later Don said, "We should have suspended him right then."

Even though Don was particularly vexed by Derek's behavior with other faculty members, he and Derek had no particular tension in their relationship. Don's math classes were popular, well organized and executed, with high standards for all children's achievement, and Derek behaved in them. In October, Derek wrote a description of his new teachers, including Don: "My math teacher plays too much, but I like him. When he gets to business he's strict." Don pointed out, "He may not have always done his homework, but he never gave me trouble in math class."

But skirmishes with Derek did take place elsewhere, especially outside the school walls. Field trips became increasingly hard for him when he refused to obey adults other than Carrie, even for seemingly simple instructions like, "The museum guard said to put your lunch away." As the year progressed, Derek began to cause so much trouble that Jan started a written record on him, which included such phrases as, "resisted authority … shouted out … refused to follow directions."

No one challenged Don in formal meetings when he reminded us of Derek's charismatic influence over other children. A teacher with over twenty years' experience, Don had a district-wide reputation for excellence. Former students remembered his teaching. Don quickly saw through logistical dilemmas, and staff accepted his authoritative solutions. As the ranking White male on this newly constituted faculty, his strong deep voice carried weight. The director listened. When Don repeatedly said that "Derek didn't care about us or the school," no one disagreed, nor did they counter his assertion that "Derek had too much power." Later in the year, everyone agreed with his conclusion that "Derek was unpredictable and all of us were thrown off balance."

Yet in retrospect, we saw that Derek never got into fights with other kids, came to school on time, was a star in basketball, had a good relationship with his advisor, and had lots of friends. Both girls and boys jockeyed to be part of his group at lunch. His inability or unwillingness to do academic work should have singled him out early for special attention, but it didn't. Students with more visible needs climbed to the top of the agenda, and as the year proceeded, Derek's name never came up at a staff meeting in answer to the regular question: "Who are you worried about?" By early spring, his inappropriate behavior with adults obscured any attempt to figure out how to support his academic learning.

By mid-April, Derek's behavior had become intolerable. When teachers tried to reason with him, distract him, or isolate him, he resisted by turning away, cursing, shouting, and kicking. Jan was usually unperturbable, able to tolerate children's idiosyncrasies and even their occasional misbehavior. But Derek's particular intransigence, his refusal listen to adults, and the way he challenged them by resisting their requests broke down Jan's usually calm exterior. She could no longer see the twelve-year-old boy in front of her.

A crisis began to build on April 18th. From the school's "incident record":

> During gym, with no apparent provocation … Derek got angry. Carrie put her arm around him and started to talk to him, but he pulled away from her and hit a student who just happened to be behind him. Later in the office he threw his bookbag on the floor toward Jan, used the phone without permission, and was rude when told to hang up. (School records, April 18)

The crisis erupted on April nineteenth. Derek outraged the adults, first when he violated a serious school rule by returning twenty minutes late from lunch, and then when he interrupted an all-school meeting. At this meeting, planned by Carrie and the Student Advisory Council, students told their own stories of discrimination. From my notes:

> When Leonora tells a story, Derek yells, "No wonder they kicked you out of Woolworth's, you've got a dirty looking face." Sonia tells a story about how she, Erin, and Josie were on the subway in the Bronx and a policemen tore up Josie's Brooklyn bus pass. Derek shouts out, "What did you do?" Josie responds with where she was walking and Derek interrupts impatiently: "No, what did *you* do to make him tear up your bus pass?" He is agitated and can't be calmed down. Several stories later, Pam tells about gender bias she felt on the all school basketball team and Derek yells out that he doesn't think boys should have girls on this team. (Field notes, April 19)

Derek behaved as an audience of one, asking his own questions and injecting his opinions at will. The faculty cut him no slack. Carrie moved him off the floor and onto a chair immediately and, as she monitored the group, other adults took turns sitting next to him. At the time no one suggested that talk of discrimination against young Black males might have contributed to his agitated behavior. As someone who often stood out in a group, Derek may have easily identified with Leonora's panic and anger at being singled out. Derek's question, "What did you do?" was apt, but it went unheard as other than an unacknowledged interruption.

Right after the meeting, Jan asked Derek and several other boys to stay after school to account for their lateness. From her written description:

> Derek began to sing rather than listen. I asked him to leave the room and wait in the hall. He went instead to the gym and began to play basketball. When Don sent him back to the hall, he came into the classroom without permission, banged his bookbag on a desk, sat down

and began to talk to his detained friends. He cursed at me and then at Don and threatened us physically. We told him to wait in the hall and we consulted with Carrie. We all agreed he should be suspended. I asked Carrie to tell him. (School records, April 19)

As his advisor, Carrie was Derek's official advocate and the liaison between home and school. As Carrie and Jan stood together to decide Derek's fate, Carrie was visibly exasperated. She was tired enough of Derek's behavior not to argue his case. She agreed to the suspension and sat him down directly to tell him. From my notes:

About 3:00 Carrie and Derek sit down very close together on the stacked blue mats in the office. Derek is crying. As they lean their backs against the wall with their bodies almost touching, it seems a very personal contact. About 3:20, they stand up and Carrie says "Goodbye, you have to go home right now."

 Carrie then said to me that she told him she was going to call his mother, but not that he was suspended. She was moved by the talk with him. "I just can't suspend him until I talk to his mother." But rather than leaving, Derek went into the gym and began to play basketball. When Jan walked though the gym, she told him that since he was suspended, he should leave. Hearing that he was suspended, he lost control. He had a two-year-old tantrum with a twelve-year-old's vocabulary. He finally left, upset, but he left. (Field notes, April 19)

That was a public account. In my private journal I described Don's response to Derek's tantrum. I saw Derek as genuinely out of control, hence my comparison to a two-year-old. Derek's obscenities were hard to hear, but even harder for me to hear was Don's powerful White male voice saying to this distressed twelve-year-old: "Call the police. I'm going to call the police…. He is damaged goods." I had no idea what Derek absorbed in the midst of his own tantrum, but other teachers heard it. I was enraged, as were others, but no one, including me, took a public stand. Later, in the women's bathroom, several of us agreed that White males get away with a lot, but no one ever said anything directly to Don.

After Derek finally left that Friday afternoon, the faculty was worn down. His lateness from lunch, his resistance to the consequences, his worse than usual behavior in the meeting, and this last vivid outburst had taken their toll. Don and Jan decided to expel him rather than suspend him. Carrie did not argue for keeping him. She said with deep weariness, "Derek tries my soul," and wondered whether anything could be done to change his behavior.

On Saturday, Jan phoned each faculty member. Individual phone calls prevented faculty from hearing each other's deliberations, so it was harder to share their thinking, but it was the usual way faculty communicated on weekends and evenings. Don never wavered: "Derek is taking over this school and we can't have that." Faculty argued variously that you can't escalate a suspension to an expulsion over a weekend when the student was not at school; that it was morally wrong to accept Derek in the school community and then expel him without trying every option; that without due process or knowledge of the public school legal issues, expulsion was inadvisable; that expelling a child without warning is threatening to other children. Everyone did agree that Derek was a pain to have around. His mother was available only sporadically and his father even more rarely. If we could have magically pushed a button to send him to a better school where he got along with adults more easily, we would gladly have done it. Faculty agonized over where Derek could go, but Derek's options were limited, and even after the weekend, many of us felt Pathways was the best place for him to finish his sixth-grade year.

On Sunday night, the calls resulted in a plan created by Jan and Carrie for a Monday morning meeting with Derek and his parents. No expulsion, they agreed. But at the meeting, when Derek seemed to Jan to be unrepentant and lacking an understanding of his suspension, she decided on the spot to expel him. All the weekend talk about community, trust, and even the legal issues fell by the wayside in the face of Jan's reluctance to have Derek return to school. Afterwards, Jan said the school's inability to cope with Derek determined her decision, despite her Sunday-night intentions. Whatever caused Jan to lose faith in this child's possibilities, or the possibilities of Pathways, was in full gear at that meeting.

The school day proceeded as usual, but after school, the news of Derek's expulsion spread and feelings ran high. Faculty accepted the decision as a done deal, despite their discomfort with it. Carrie had vehemently opposed the expulsion in conversations with Jan, and admitted privately that she was startled and angry during the Monday morning meeting when Jan ignored their plans. She felt "Derek was contrite and near tears," but, she conceded, she would never, never contradict a director, especially in front of parents. Some faculty felt Jan heard only Don's view that expelling Derek was the right decision.

At the weekly staff meeting the next day, we mechanically dispensed with the regular agenda in thirty minutes in order to develop a written policy on suspension and expulsion that would prevent future lack of clarity. Given the uncertainties of a new institution, it was not surprising that faculty were so willing to set school-wide policy to cover discipline. Jan began by saying evenly and without affect:

> We need a policy for kids who are giving as trouble. I realize that somewhere last week I gave up on Derek. Something happened that made me not listen and I didn't realize it. There are things we didn't do. We didn't suggest counseling, we didn't suspend him, and we put up with things from him that we don't accept from others. (Field notes, April 23)

Jim wondered whether we should reconsider our decision to expel Derek or just move on. "I am still working on my feelings," he admitted, speaking for himself, but implicitly for the whole group. Don repeated his consistent position that whatever happened wouldn't have occurred if we only had had better rules, clearer discipline, and sharper boundaries for kids to know "what's what."

Jan and Don were still convinced expulsion was the correct decision. If a faculty could be characterized as depressed, this faculty was. The adults' anger and sadness mixed with Derek's classmates' surprise and confusion weakened everyone. Used to operating consensually, we had no experience openly disagreeing with Jan or with each other. Ousting Derek from the community made everyone feel badly, yet life with him had been undeniably hard. This decision brought to the surface differences in faculty values and assumptions about children, about schools, and about each other. The limits of the school's ability to support a difficult child were suddenly on view for everyone to see.

As usual, Don posed the question that framed the discussion: "What are the conditions for membership in this school community?" Marilyn, a first-year teacher, responded immediately, "You can think of communities that never expel members and ones that excommunicate. What kind of a community do we want to be?" The power of her question got lost as the talk returned to Derek. Carrie felt that Derek was more contrite at Monday's meeting than Jan's description portrayed. Considering the passionate feelings I heard her express in the halls, Carrie's tone at the staff meeting was moderate. She said evenly:

> I would rather err on the side of the child. The reason I didn't want to suspend Derek was because he'd be on the street all day or in the arcades. But after we accept kids, we have to include them and get them connected. We didn't act sooner because we had to get to other problems sooner. Derek's healthy. He defends himself. He's not resigned. That's a strength. In reality, it is easier not to have him, but are we being fair? (Field notes, April 23)

As much as Jan sympathized with the attempt to be fair, she wanted Derek gone—for reasons I believe even she did not understand at the time. Jan again reiterated that there had been no progress in Derek's understanding of his egregious behavior: "Derek couldn't retell what he did. It was not like he just left out chunks of the story, he didn't understand."

Don repeated what he had often said: "Derek is an incredibly powerful person. We cannot do anything for him. He is more powerful than we are." At 6 feet, 5 inches, Don's sheer physical presence is a factor in any meeting, and his forceful voice leaves nothing tentative about his contributions, whether he means them to be dogmatic or not. Softening his stance, Don added, "I feel a sense of failure, of course, but he did not respect us or care." No one presented any evidence to counter Don's statement. Not I or anyone else argued Derek's case. There was dead silence. Something intransigent in Don and Jan's position made it seem just as hard for me to get through to them as it was to discipline Derek on a field trip.

Jan then spoke in support of Don's opinion: "Kids have to be willing to listen, willing to change. There has to be a parent or an adult to work with." To which Carrie responded, without missing a beat, "But some kids don't have a parent and you have to work with that kid anyway."

The discussion returned to the need for a policy. Don pointed out, "The problem is not making a policy or writing it down, but in implementing it consistently. Discipline has to be consistent or it is nothing." At 5:05, Don stood up to signal that for him, the meeting was over.

After Don left, Carrie turned to me and said passionately what she did not say in the meeting: "Don's position disturbs me. You can't decide on boundaries and then expect kids to arrange themselves to fit. You can't have static boundaries when you work with children. Especially kids like Derek. I am still upset. You don't cut off a kid's finger when he touches the hot pie."

Talk about Derek went underground. The next day, when rehashing the staff meeting, Carrie observed, "We talked, but we didn't engage." Her perception matched mine. We agreed that the previous day's meeting was intense and fast paced and that faculty had differing perspectives; there was a little snapping, but no raised voices, no questioning, and no arguing. This unfinished incident left everyone tired and irritable. Underlying the tension was our inability to find a solution for Derek that worked for him and for us. The focus on a general policy kept the faculty distanced from Derek and obscured any recognition of his needs. Disagreement over the treatment of Derek prevented faculty from hearing this strong-voiced adolescent or each other. We retreated from the conflict.

It is easy to invoke society's hierarchies here: the unspoken constraints that kept a Black teacher from countering a White director or women from challenging male authority (Delpit, 1988; Fine, 1991). The small size of the faculty makes generalizing much like walking into quicksand, yet it is possible to see stereotyped power relations at work. In this case, Don, anticipating that his voice would be heard, repeatedly articulated his opinion and kept focused on translating it into action. Others did not challenge him, and those power relations became entangled with the issue of who speaks for an advisee. Carrie privately expressed feeling that Derek's fate was predetermined and that "I would be wasting my breath," which prevented her from advocating more strongly for his retention, even though she was his advisor. Her reluctance to speak on his behalf made it less likely that others would argue for him when she did not. Other teachers did not contradict Don when he described Derek's power to disrupt the school. Jan supported Don, since she felt the health of the school would suffer if Derek stayed. Don told me that because I did not teach Derek I could not know what other faculty faced, and his pointed logic reinforced whatever powerlessness I already felt. I and others remained mute. This interactive dynamic—Don and Jan expecting to have their opinions valued, and Carrie and I convinced that we would be dismissed —confirmed the conventional power relations between men and women, Blacks and Whites, directors and teachers.[11]

As Maxine Greene (1993) reminds us, "There are ways of speaking and telling that construct silences, create 'others,' invent gradations of social difference necessary for the identification of norms" (p. 216). Until we find another way, until power to speak is equalized and reciprocal so that *all* faculty can expect to be heard, children like Derek will not be well served.

School officials who set and legitimate boundaries have tremendous power over children's lives, and the interplay between institutional norms and individual adult's attitudes complicates what happens to students like Derek who do not meet standard expectations.[12] How to serve the Dereks of this world is not only an educational question, but also a political question that links power, discipline, and race. None of this speculation, all done in retrospect, could have helped us with Derek. Events occurred too quickly.

The following afternoon, the District Office guidance counselor phoned Jan to summon her to a meeting with Derek's parents. Jan took the call in the school office as Don and I sat nearby. From my notes:

> Jan was calm and not at all defensive. She apologized for her first year naivete, gave details of Derek's behavior, told how hard it was to reach his parents, and listened. She could have been ordering supplies for all the emotion in her voice. It soon became clear that expelling a child is not an option. Jan was asked to appear in the Central Office with an incident report to meet with Derek's family. On the phone she was gracious and accepting. Off the phone she was upset. Don said ominously, "Can you imagine what he'll be like if he knows we have no recourse to expulsion? He'll be uncontainable." (Field notes, April 24)

After the meeting with Derek's parents, Jan reported that Derek would be back. Expulsion was legally indefensible because Derek never had the two non-contiguous five-day suspensions, which the district requires.

Jan modelled decorum for the staff and kids. Derek came back without a fuss, and with an agreement *not* to go on any school field trips without his mother or father. His parents never participated, and since trips were a central part of the curriculum, Derek was often absent. His return was also predicated on foregoing the three-day overnight camping trip, leaving him out of the pre-trip excitement. His presence reminded everyone of the expulsion controversy, which undoubtedly affected his treatment by adults and children. Carrie took responsibility for his last two months. This excerpt from my notes shows Derek's better and worse days:

> Derek came back and was better. He still had to be spoken to at the City Fair [not technically a trip but a district-sponsored requirement]. Carrie had to speak to him four times and called his father immediately. She said she could not take him to the Central Park Challenge unless his father came. He said he would. On the day of the Challenge his father didn't show up and Derek was devastated. Carrie agreed to take him on the grounds that kids have to be in groups to learn how to behave. He was fine. When she talked to the mother about his father's not showing up, the mother said, "That's the story of Derek's life. He never shows up." (Field notes, May 15)

The decision to expel Derek was Jan's most naive decision of the year and, as she agrees, her biggest mistake. That she accepted Derek's return so readily and with such good grace helped rectify it, but Derek's place in the school community was already compromised and this experience took its toll on everyone. The next year, Derek's parents put him in Catholic school.

This child, who was caught in family and social circumstances beyond his control, called Pathways's basic values into question and brought faculty differences into focus. The last week in April I recorded in my journal that "I didn't take notes because it was too painful for everybody to see me carrying a notebook." In a number of small but perceptible ways that were tied to particular events surrounding Derek, our collegial bonds loosened. Don fell that Jan could have stopped Derek's misbehavior had she been a more powerful director. Carrie said that she couldn't stand Don talking negatively about children, as he sometimes did. Separated by these differences and by declining trust, faculty could no longer tap each other's knowledge or work out the human tangles.

Overall, the faculty poured astounding energy into educating children of all colors, and most children were treated as well as any parent would want. Black children are numerous enough at Pathways that it is hard to say that Derek's Blackness made it difficult for him to be treated respectfully by White faculty. But since Derek *is* Black, that fact cannot be divorced from his interactions with faculty. Some faculty thought Derek one of the most "difficult" students. In retrospect, it may have been easier—at least consciously—for White faculty to focus on his "attitude" rather than his race.

It is also hard to say whether Derek's Blackness affected Carrie's ability to connect with him. I cannot know whether her more solid relationship with Derek had anything to do with their shared race. She understood his strengths and his precarious stance in the world as a Black boy. Carrie included Derek in the school community and she didn't flinch at his misbehavior. But Derek needed more than what this one African American teacher could provide. Had Carrie felt less constrained by the dynamics described earlier, she might have convinced others that Derek was being shortchanged at school.

Dismissing Derek and other similar "problems" as too troubled for schools to educate is often easier than dealing with their difficulties, and many educators practice this kind of triage. Small schools should be particularly able to reach students like Derek, but these students must be known in all their complexity, not just as a thorn in the side of adults who have no investment in their lives. For such a promise of personalized schools to be fulfilled, faculties have to adopt Carrie's attitude about children. She often says, "When I am in a quandary about how to handle a child, I think 'What would I do if that child were my child?' and 'How would I want that child handled were my son or daughter in that situation?'" Parents have an urgency about their own children. We all need to feel the same urgency when we teach other people's children (Delpit, 1988).

FACULTY LEADERSHIP: "DOES WOOLWORTH'S DISCRIMINATE?"

In the spring, a spontaneous discussion on bias grew into a project involving every student at Pathways. The project originated in Advisory Council, Pathways's fledgling student government, and resulted in an all-school meeting on discrimination (the one where Derek so outraged the adults). Jan recounted how this topic arose in the first Advisory Council meeting:[13]

> After spring vacation, Carrie and I were all sitting around in a circle with about 12 kids, two from each advisory, and I asked, "What issues should we address here?"
>
> "Bias" Sudi answered. "People ask me to speak Chinese, even though I am Japanese. Or ask me about Korean green grocers as if I knew everything."
>
> Then older boys of color began to tell stories of how they were being treated in stores. "Racism," kids said. Carrie built on their responses by talking about the civil rights movement, fact finding, protests and sit ins. She said to me later, "These kids don't know history. They don't know how to protest. We have to do something." (Field notes, April 7)

While faculty managed to avoid talking about race by advocating more explicit rules and discipline policies, the students, under Carrie's leadership, confronted racial discrimination directly. After hearing kids' stories about police officers, store clerks, and the random person on the subway who said to Jessica's racially mixed group, "Whites shouldn't be with Black people," faculty readily agreed that teaching children to confront discrimination as they travelled around the city was essential to their well-being. Discussing circumstances facing children outside of school was clearly easier than discussing how race plays out in school with one another.

Every Thursday, during class time, and occasionally over pizza brought in for lunch, the Advisory Council met in Carrie's science classroom. The Council included three Whites, one Asian, four Hispanics, and four Blacks. Once the students decided to plan and practice for the all-school meeting on discrimination, Carrie proceeded. She had a clear goal, moved the discussion along at a pace that she dictated, elicited discussion from her questions, monitored the side conversations, noticed behavior beyond the norms, acted on some of it, and drew out the kids in order to help them understand what she wanted to teach:

1. A racist experience is anything that happens to you because of your race.
2. You can protect yourself against bias and not be diminished by it.

3. You can feel like a whole person after something unpleasant has happened to you.
4. Be careful what you call racist—not every discriminatory incident is racist. It might be against children, women, teenagers with loud voices, or teenagers in groups. Still people often discriminate against young boys of color who get stereotyped and judged by the color of their skin.

Carrie's entry into this teaching was through kids' shared stories. After hearing each story, she asked "How did you feel?" and "What recourse do you have?" By the second and third meeting, kids asked these questions themselves. At the end of every meeting, Carrie reminded kids of their belly button. "What is something that no one can take away from you? Your belly button is what holds you together. So when someone judges you unfairly, remember your belly button. No one can take that away from you. When you are angry have one thing that you can say that will pull you back together."

On April nineteenth, the Advisory Council sat on chairs in a circle surrounded by fifty children on the floor listening to their stories. The tone of this "fishbowl" was calm—except, as already described, for Derek. The largest boys struggled to keep their legs in a confined space, and this sensitive topic produced some nervous fidgeting, but students were interested in their classmates' dramatic, sometimes painful, stories:

> Lisa began: When Stella, Sudi and I were in Woolworth's looking around, a saleslady stopped us and asked, "Who's here with you?" When we told her we weren't here with any adults, she said, "Sit in a corner and write a list of what you want and then come back."
>
> Juan told a variation: I was with some friends standing in line at the Woolworth's cash register getting ready to pay for a notebook and some White guys were ahead of us. They paid, but when it was our turn, the man at the door came over and asked us to empty our pockets.
>
> Bianca followed: When Jessica, Ramona and I were in Woolworth's and Ramona was buying a water gun, Jerome, Arnold, and their friends wanted to come in with us. The guard let us in, but not the boys. (Field notes, April 19)

The take-home lesson from these stories was that it matters how children present themselves in public. Students noticed that their adolescent voices can be as threatening as their skin color. The biggest boys of color had the biggest problems. In addition to bringing patterns to the surface, this public forum allowed children to testify to their pain and hear the community respond sympathetically to their stories of hurtful devaluation and exclusion.

When the meeting broke up and students moved to their homerooms, the subsequent smaller group discussions about discrimination were both intimate and orderly. Serious talk flowed easily without any of the out-of-control rage that occurred in December during the (admittedly more immediate) discussion of "how come there are no brothers on that list?" The formal process of the large meeting showed respect for everyone's perspective. Faculty agreed with the aims of the meeting: to give children a chance to tell their stories and learn some strategies to confront discrimination. However, and this is still the heart of the matter, Carrie made this meeting happen.

All children at Pathways benefited from Carrie's charismatic personality, her commitment to academic achievement, her willingness to give freely of her time to kids (she preferred to have lunch with children rather than with adults), her consistency (if she said during class "see me later," she never forgot), her clear expectations (she insisted on complete sentences when children responded), and her scaffolding of what children needed to do as students (she practiced having them come into the room "like you have a purpose and something to do"). Yet it was Carrie's personal knowledge, her own experience with what children of color face, and her parenting of her own Black children that made it possible for her to run this assembly. Had she not been at Pathways, the assembly might never have happened.

Based on the Advisory Council assembly, Carrie developed an all-school project entitled "Does Woolworth's Discriminate?" Students conducted a controlled study on who was allowed to go into Woolworth's at lunchtime. They designed the study, set groups with different racial makeups into Woolworth's at different times to test Woolworth's "admission policy," analyzed the data, and extrapolated the findings beyond their original sample. Advisory Council members modeled role-playing in each Advisory so that children would learn a technique to help them understand different perspectives. Then all the children role-played how to approach and respond to various acts of discrimination. Carrie received a grant to help other teachers construct similar curricula. "Does Woolworth's Discriminate?" was a model for honest talk with kids. Based on issues they care about, this project recognized that students felt secure in their own school community, encouraged them to raise questions about their problematic status in the outside world, and gave them the means to seek answers, and develop actions to gain personal control.

As successful as this program was, programs do not eradicate racism; rather, beliefs and attitudes lead people to make changes. Individual transformation come through reflecting on values that underlie programs and actions. At Pathways, more fundamental change came from thinking together about Derek and Duke than from any of the programs, curriculum, or initial structures that the school set in place.

CONCLUSION

One lesson that could be taken from this selective account is that even in the "best schools, where faculty try hard to pay attention to individuals, Whites' blindness to race clouds their ability to notice what children are really saying about themselves and their identities. Safe spaces rarely exist in schools for adults or children to explore race, especially when Whites—who tend not to think of race all that often —determine the agendas, and teachers from other backgrounds become used to the absence of talk about race, or are convinced they will not be heard.

At Pathways, as in many schools, faculty members' personal backgrounds and assumptions about race, ethnicity, and class were little known to each other and not much explored. When school life went smoothly, our habits continued without examination. When conflicts arose, we had no way to untangle the knots. Faculty members need to be open with each other in order to have honest discussions. Such openness may not be possible in a new school, where the pace is like the title of John Adam's musical composition, *A Short Ride in a Fast Machine*. The first year in Pathways was exhilarating, but each day passed much too quickly to begin to have the extended discussions necessary to develop openness and honesty. Yet in no experience, even in an established school where a slower pace might allow for more conversational possibilities, race is often not well understood or thought to be a topic for discussion.

Talking honestly about racism may be the hardest thing faculties do in school. Racial issues in America are complex, full of strong feelings and equally strong denials; anyone who has sat around a table with adults who feel awkward and tentative about having these conversations knows this is so. The initial task for educators may be to figure out how to make these conversations commonplace. How to do this within the already overloaded school day is not easy. Without a commitment from every person to participate and trust that others will listen and change, the effort is futile.

Teachers at Pathways and elsewhere are often good at observing who is stuck in math, whose writing needs help, who needs more skill in reading comprehension. Good teaching entails such observations. But until teachers, especially White teachers, get in the habit of looking more closely at the nuances of race and seeing patterns, building up evidence to anchor their impressions, sharing their conclusions with one another, and examining their own racial attitudes, they will not learn enough to provide for all children.

Only as I wrote up these glimpses of school life did I begin to hear, really hear, Carrie say, "People who have no choice but to live their lives in their Black skins know racism when they see it. Racism is never subtle to the victim. Only White people say race doesn't matter." Certainly, in our society, Whites in power are more interested in downplaying race, and it is Whites who decide what is and what is not racist (Sleeter, 1993; Tatum, 1992). What I learned from Carrie prompted me to write this article.

Complicating the dialogue about race is the ambiguity inherent in racial issues. However, the point is not to get the right labels—often no clear answer exists as to what is a racial incident, or whether an event involves bias, and if it does, whether it is conscious or unconscious. The very fact that it is difficult to say what is and is not a racial issue both makes it easier to avoid a discussion of race and gives an added edge to any exchange. Participants disagree not only about the substance of an issue, but also about what they are talking about. This makes conversation even harder, and it takes a committed faculty to keep talking (Burbules & Rice, 1991; Henze, Lucas, & Scott, 1993; Murphy & Ucelli, 1989; Olson, 1991).

The incidents related here focus on what faculty didn't hear, didn't understand, or didn't choose to pursue. This account does not relate the many times faculty stuck with kids to work through differences or put energy into including children in the community. Just as Marie Diaz's essay stands for many kids' responses to school, let sixth grader Serena Martinez's interview with me at the end of the year speak for faculty effort and children's learning:

> Serena [on handling racial conflict]: Each teacher helps you a lot because if there is a little problem they make it a BIG DEAL and that helps. Even though at the beginning you think, "Oh this is boring; I don't want to do this because it's not going to change anything." Then you talk and you see the other side of the person and then you understand and then you know how they feel. Its nice when you talk it out…. At other schools after you have a fight with somebody, you don't resolve anything so there is still something in there and you still want to fight. Here you discuss the problems and you get to hear other people's sides. And you understand. (Taped interview, May 30)

This eloquent statement by a child confirms that not all opportunities to confront racial problems were missed. Carrie agreed: "When things arose, most individual racial incidents were handled well enough, quite well in fact. By that I mean kids understood their own responsibility and how it affected the outcome."

The staff learned from Derek's exile and Duke's withdrawal. Five years later, Pathways has become a stronger school for having lived through these serious missteps. In order to learn, faculties not only have to make mistakes, they also have to recognize them as mistakes. This documentation made what happened visible and discussable, and the following year the entire faculty began to talk about race more publicly. After the addition of more Latino and African American faculty, several outside researchers, and longer meetings with more overt conflict, this reflective faculty began to unlock the silences. Out of these experiences, several staff members have produced their own articles. More importantly, faculty now do better with the successors to Derek and Duke.

Attempts to educate *all* children in today's climate are fraught with pedagogical and social uncertainties that defy a single response. Many possible entry points exist, but developing structures for faculty members to reflect on their experiences and share their own perspectives is essential. Faculties need protected time during the day to talk, a willingness to question previously entrenched assumptions, and encouragement to be honest in collegial forums rather than in the hallways. As Lisa Delpit (1988) says, teachers need to be "unafraid to raise questions about discrimination and voicelessness with people of color, and listen, no, to *hear*, what they say" (p. 297). Connecting with each other and seeing the implications for educating children requires an alertness to what happens inside schools and out, a consciousness about how others see the world, a willingness to talk honestly, and a commitment to change the power relationships in the world.

When Whites in power don't hear the boiling lava that lies below the surface, they perpetuate silences about race. Then they are surprised when racial feelings erupt, although it is they who have paid no attention to the volcano.[14]

NOTES

1. This work was funded by the Aaron Diamond Foundation, which is not responsible for the thinking expressed here.
2. Despite their permission to use real names. I have changed both the name of the school and the names of the teachers to preserve their privacy. I have also changed the names and details of children and their parents.
3. Initially drafted by the founding director and polished by me, this vision statement explicitly committed the school to an integrated, untracked student body. Faculty agreed to it in principle when they came to work at the school.
4. Although my position as a part-time documenter allowed me time and distance to reflect on my work as a member of the staff at Pathways, mine was not the outside perspective of an academic researcher (a tradition in which I have not been trained). Throughout my teaching career and involvement in teacher-research communities, one of my purposes in writing about classrooms has been to make practice explicit for a larger audience. Ultimately, what I write also contributes to improving my own practice as well. For further discussion of my work, see Jervis, Carr, Lockhart, and Rogers (1996).
5. At Pathways, every adult had an advisory of nine or ten students. Advisories met four days a week for an hour to discuss school and non-school topics, read novels, celebrate birthdays, and sort out school experiences together. Advisors acted as liaisons with parents, advocated for advisees with other faculty, and talked individually to students about their progress and problems.
6. In New York City's thirty-two decentralized elementary and middle school/junior high districts, Mary Ann Raywid's (1990) definition of alternative schools applies: "Alternative schools are likely to be small; independently launched from program to program; separately operated without a great deal of

external oversight or district-level coordination; internally less differentiated than other schools as to status and role; and quite variable from one program to another" (p. 96). New York's alternative schools draw from the whole city, but they generally strive for mixed abilities and diversity. It is important to note that Pathways's autonomy is linked to its small size as well as to its status as an alternative school. A small faculty can more easily make up their own schedules, report cards, or curricula, and also decide to change them if they do not work well.

7. On the day of this incident in 1990, I recorded Arnold's words and gestures in my notebook. That night I typed up the incident, threw any my handwritten version, and forgot about it. Then in the fall of 1994, white sorting my files after yet another revision, I found one page of the original handwritten notes. On that page, but not in my typed notes, I had recorded that "a [White] teacher encouraged kids to 'forget it', when Arnold objected to Duke's behavior." In 1990, I had apparently "registered" that something, perhaps racial, went on between Arnold and Duke, but did not "see" that a White colleague urged kids to ignore it. Though somehow I knew to save that handwritten page, it took me years to understand, and then express, how White resistance to seeing, exemplified in my own actions as well as my colleague's advice to Arnold and Duke, is an enormously complicated aspect of racism.

8. See the chapter "African American Schoolchild in a Strange Land" in Janice Hale (1994) for a discussion of this interpretation.

9. See Knapp and Woolverton (1995) for a review of these issues.

10. Descriptive Review, developed by Patricia Carini and her colleagues in North Bennington, Vermont (Prospect Archive, 1986), is one method Pathways faculty used to help them understand children. In this process, a teacher collects, for presentation to other teachers, observations of one student's behaviors organized around a focusing question intended to illuminate some puzzling aspect of the child's school life. The presenting teacher describes the child fully, rendering physical gestures, temperament, relationships, interests, and approaches to formal academics in as detailed a way as possible. Other teachers ask questions to clarify the description. Then the group makes recommendations for practice. The underlying goal of a Descriptive Review is to describe a child as carefully as possible, to avoid evaluative judgments, and to develop strategies that build on the child's strengths.

11. Don's strongest reaction to my interpretation of this data was how he had not heard Carrie. "Was it really so hard for me to listen?" he asked. I noticed that the following year, when I attended several faculty meetings, he listened more carefully, and Carrie's voice became stronger. This may be a good example of documentation stimulating change.

12. For a discussion of standards, see Jervis and McDonald (1996).

13. Two representatives from each advisory were appointed by advisors or elected by advisories. That students came to the Council by different selection processes did not seem to be an issue, since they all felt it was an honor to serve. Carrie volunteered to oversee this Advisory Council. Jan, as director, worked with her, and I participated in the weekly meetings.

14. I would like to acknowledge Michelle Fine for suggesting this metaphor when she commented on a draft of this article.

REFERENCES

As is standard feminist practice, I have included first and last names of authors.

Burbules, Nicholas, & Rice, Suzanne. (1991). Dialogue across differences: Continuing the conversation. *Harvard Educational Review, 61,* 393–416.

Cohen, Jody. (1993). Constructing race at an urban high school: In their minds, their mouths, their hearts. In Lois Weis & Michelle Fine (Eds.), *Beyond silenced voices: Class, race and gender in United States schools* (pp. 289–308). Albany: State University of New York Press.

Delpit, Lisa. (1988). The silenced dialogue: Power and pedagogy in educating other people's children. *Harvard Educational Review, 58,* 280–298.

Delpit, Lisa. (1990). Seeing color: Review of *White Teacher. Hungry Mind Review, 15,* 4–5.

Engel, Brenda. (1975). *A handbook of documentation.* Grand Forks: University of North Dakota, North Dakota Study Group on Evaluation.

Fine, Michelle. (1991). *Framing dropouts: Notes on the politics of an urban public high school.* Albany: State University of New York Press.

Foster, Michele. (1993). Resisting racism: Personal testimonies of African-American teachers. In Lois Weis & Michelle Fine (Eds.), *Beyond silenced voices: Class, race, and gender in United States schools* (pp. 273–288). Albany: State University of New York Press.

Grant, Carl, & Secada, Walter. (1990). Preparing teachers for diversity. In W. R. Houston (Ed.). *Handbook of research on teacher education* (pp. 403–422). New York: Macmillan.

Greene, Maxine. (1993). Diversity and inclusion: Towards a curriculum for human beings. *Teachers College Record, 95,* 213–221.

Hale, Janice E. (1994). *Unbank the fire: Visions for the education of African American children.* Baltimore: Johns Hopkins University Press.

Henze, Rosemary, Lucas, Tamara, & Scott, Beverly. (1993, April). *Dancing with the monster: Teachers attempt to discuss power, racism, and privilege in education.* Paper presented at the annual meeting of the American Educational Research Association, New Orleans.

Jervis, Kathe, Carr, Emily, Lockhart, Patsy, & Rogers, Jane. (1996). Multiple entries to teacher inquiry: Dissolving the boundaries between research and teaching. In Linda Baker, Peter Afflerbach, & David Reinking (Eds.), *Developing engaged readers in school and home communities* (pp. 247–268). Mahwah, NJ: Lawrence Erlbaum.

Jervis, Kathe, & McDonald, Joseph. (1996). Standards: The philosophical monster in the classroom. *Phi Delta Kappan, 77,* 563–569.

Knapp, Michael S., & Woolverton, Sara. (1995). Social class and schooling. In James A. Banks & Cherry A. McGee Banks (Eds.), *Handbook of research on multicultural education* (pp. 548–569). New York: Macmillan.

Ladson-Billings, Gloria. (1994). *The dreamkeepers: Successful teachers of African American children.* San Francisco: Jossey-Bass.

McCarthy, Cameron. (1993). Beyond the poverty of theory in race relations: Nonsynchrony and social difference in education. In Lois Weis & Michelle Fine (Eds.), *Beyond silenced voices: Class, race, and gender in United States schools* (pp. 325–346). Albany: State University of New York Press.

McIntosh, Peggy. (1988). *White privilege and male privilege: A personal account of coming to see correspondences through work in women's studies* (Working Paper No. 189). Wellesley, MA: Wellesley College Center for Research on Women.

Murphy, Donald, & Ucelli, Juliet. (1989). Race, knowledge, and pedagogy: A Black-White teacher dialogue. *Holistic Education Review, 2*(4), 48–50.

Olson, Ruth Anne. (1991). *Language and race: Barriers to communicating a vision* (Reflective Paper No. 1). St. Paul, MN: Supporting Diversity in Schools.

Prospect Archive and Center for Education and Research. (1986). *The Prospect Center documentary processes.* North Bennington, VT: Author.

Raywid, Mary Ann. (1990). Successful schools of choice: Cottage industry benefits in large systems. *Educational Policy, 4*(2), 93–108.

Sleeter, Christine. (1993). White teachers construct race. In Cameron McCarthy & Warren Crichlow (Eds.), *Race, identity, and representation in education* (pp. 157–171). London: Routledge.

Tatum, Beverly Daniel. (1992). Talking about race, learning about racism: Application of racial identity development theory in the classroom. *Harvard Educational Review, 62,* 1–24.

32

Standardization, Defensive Teaching, and the Problems of Control

Linda M. McNeil

Standardization reduces the *quality and quantity of what is taught and learned in schools.* This immediate negative effect of standardization is the overwhelming finding of a study of schools where the imposition of standardized controls reduced the scope and quality of course content, diminished the role of teachers, and distanced students from active learning.

The long-term effects of standardization are even more damaging: *over the long term, standardization creates inequities, widening the gap between the quality of education for poor and minority youth and that of more privileged students.* The discriminatory effects of standardization are immediately evident in the reduction in both the quality and quantity of educational content for students who have historically scored low on standardized assessments. Over time, the longer standardized controls are in place, the wider the gap becomes as the system of testing and test preparation comes to substitute in minority schools for the curriculum available to more privileged students. These new structures of discrimination are being generated by the controls that began in the schools documented in this study and that in the succeeding years have become the dominant model of schooling in one of the nation's largest and most diverse states, Texas. This book documents the immediate educational costs to curriculum, teaching, and children when the controls were first introduced. It then analyzes their growing power to damage the education of all children, but particularly those who are African American and Latino.

In the name of improving educational quality and holding schools and school personnel more accountable for their professional practice, the state government enacted a set of standardized controls to monitor children's learning and teachers' classroom behavior. These controls arose outside the educational system, derived from pressures from the business establishment to fund only those educational expenses that contributed to measurable outcomes. They were implemented from the top of the state bureaucracy, through the district bureaucracies, and subsequently imposed on schools. The controls were set forth as "reforms." The activities they mandated were to be uniform, and the means of monitoring the activities were standardized scoring instruments. In the name of "equity," these reforms imposed a sameness. In the name of "objectivity" they relied on a narrow set of numerical indicators. These hierarchical reform systems seem upon first reading to be extreme, but over time they have become the model for increasingly hierarchical and pre-scriptive systems being promoted as improving education. More seriously, they have legit-imated "accountability" as the presiding metaphor in shifting the power relations governing public education.

The research reported in this volume did not begin as a study of the effects of state-level educational standardization. The findings are all the more powerful because, in fact, they were not expected. Nor were they sought. This research began as a search for organiza-tional models of schooling that provided structural support for authentic, engaged teach-ing and learning. The research was designed to study schools in which school knowledge was credible, in which teachers brought their own personal and professional knowledge into the classroom, and in which teachers and students entered into shared, authentic study of significant topics and ways of knowing. Analyzing such teaching and learning in its organizational context could shed light on the ways the structures of schooling can enhance, rather than impede, educational quality.

Teaching and learning widely regarded to be authentic, to be meaningful to the students and to their experiences beyond school, was found in a series of urban magnet schools. As exemplars of authentic teaching and learning, the magnet schools carry spe-cial importance because their students were predominantly minority, African American and Latino. These schools had been established to be of such high quality that they would serve a city as the vehicle for desegregation through voluntary cross-city student transfers. This book was intended to document the ways that curriculum and learning are constructed and made meaningful in schools whose organizational structure subor-dinates the credentialing function and other procedural and behavioral controls to teaching and learning. The magnet schools proved to be schools where teachers and stu-dents, free of the constraints of the state textbook adoption list and from state and local prescriptive rules governing curriculum, co-constructed rich academic environments in a multiracial setting.

During the collection of observational data in these magnet schools, while the data on authentic teaching and learning were quite persuasively accruing, the state enacted policies meant to "reform" all schools.[1] These policies brought all schools in the state under a cen-tralized system of prescriptive rules and standardized procedures for monitoring compli-ance. These exemplary magnet schools, serving racially diverse and in many cases poor students, were not exempt from the centralized controls.

As the controls were imposed, and the regulations increasingly standardized, the quality of teaching and learning at even these exemplary schools began to suffer. Teaching, curriculum, and students' roles in classrooms were transformed by the standardizations and by the categories of compliance they imposed. Within the observational data began to emerge phony curricula, reluctantly presented by teachers in class to conform to the forms of knowledge their students would encounter on centralized tests. The practice of teaching under these reforms shifted away from intellectual activity toward dispensing packaged fragments of information sent from an upper level of the bureaucracy. And the role of students as contributors to classroom discourse, as thinkers, as people who brought their personal stories and life experiences into the classroom, was silenced or severely circumscribed by the need for the class to "cover" a generic curriculum at a pace established by the district and the state for all the schools.

The magnet teachers and their students did not comply thoughtlessly with the new standardizations. Instead they struggled to hold onto school lessons that held credibility in the world outside schools, to lessons that sprang from teachers' passions and children's curiosities, to lessons that built a cumulative base of new understandings for these students, many of whom were counting on the magnet schools to open previously closed doors to college and careers. The work of resistance itself, however, took a toll on time, energies, and the activities that could not be salvaged as the controls became more tightly monitored.

CONTROLLING MYTHS

The myth of such controls is that they "bring up the bottom," that they are aimed at the lowest levels of performance. The myth further promotes the idea that "good schools" will not be affected and, conversely, that any school that is adversely affected by centralized controls must not have been a "good" school. The corollary holds for teachers: if teachers are negatively affected by standardized reforms, then they must have been the "weak" or "bad" teachers in need of reforming.

The following analysis shatters the myth that standardization improves education. It challenges the widespread notion that standardization equals, or leads to, "standards." What will be clear from a close-up analysis of the effects of standardization is that, in fact, *standardization undermines academic standards* and seriously limits opportunities for children to learn to a "high standard."

The issue of the confusion between standardization and "standards" is of critical importance because increasingly scores on individual students' standardized tests of academic skills and of the mastery of subject content carry with them serious consequences both for the students and for those who teach them. "High-stakes" decisions, such as grade placement and promotion (or retention), placement in highly stratified academic tracks, and even graduation are increasingly determined by students' scores on centrally imposed, commercial standardized tests. When they are used in "accountability systems," individual and aggregate student test scores are used as indirect measures of teachers' work, principals' "performance," and even of the overall quality of the school. Such practices are highly questionable and are prompting serious scrutiny by policymakers and testing professionals of the possible misuses of student tests (Heubert and Hauser 1999).

The ethical questions raised among testing experts regarding the use of standardized student tests for other purposes such as employee (teacher, principal) performance and school quality tend to be regarded by policymakers in heavily centralized states and districts as points requiring fine-tuning and, in fact, are often used as justification for extending tests to additional grade levels and subjects to "assure that the testing is as comprehensive as possible."[2]

The Texas case is important to study and to analyze at each level of implementation because it demonstrates the wide gulf between academic "standards" and the curricular content to which students have access under a highly centralized system of standardized testing. It is crucial to understand because it provides the first opportunity to examine how issues of quality and "high standards" become so easily co-opted by the similar language—but oppositional philosophy and opposite consequences—of standardization. The "high stakes" to the students, in the use of their scores to regulate an entire system, appear at first to be merely the decisions made about them individually—their promotion or graduation, for example. The schools described in this book in some detail demonstrate that what is ultimately at stake is the capacity to provide a substantive education that is not driven by, not stratified by, and not reduced by the kinds of standardized tests being increasingly adopted across the states under the guise of "raising standards."

That standardization is harmful to teaching and learning is not a new idea. Critique of the embodiment of technical mechanisms for transforming the power relations within schools and reordering the power relations that govern the larger role of school in society is the subject of a now comprehensive body of theory (Apple 1979, 1995, 1996; Apple and Oliver 1998; Beyer and Apple 1998a; Freire 1970, 1985, 1995; Giroux 1983, 1996; Greene 1978; McLaren and Gutierrez 1998; Sarason 1971, 1996; Wise 1979; Wrigley 1982; and others). Such critical scholarship, including critical cultural studies, studies in the political economy of schools, and critical analyses of pedagogy have emerged as bases upon which to examine the increasing technicizing of public education. At the macrolevel of theorizing, there is, within this body of scholarship, increased attention to and understanding of the conservative transformation of American public education through the use of technicist forms of power. In addition, fine-grained classroom studies, particularly in the area of the sociocultural linguistics and critical race studies, are documenting the linguistic and culturally subtractive effects of generic models of schooling on Spanish-dominant and other immigrant and minority children (Fordham and Ogbu 1986; Gutierrez and Larson 1994; Gutierrez, Rymes, and Larson 1995; Romo and Falbo 1996; Suarez-Orozco 1991; Valenzuela 1999).

This scholarship has been essential in creating frameworks for questioning the power relations that shape the role of the school in the larger society. In addition, through critical scholarship we have now an established tradition for examining the social and cultural origins of school knowledge, for raising questions about whose interests are served by educational institutions and whose interests and cultures are represented by the knowledge and ways of knowing institutionalized in schools. Critical studies have insisted that our understandings of schools and the educational practices within them not be limited to technical representations of the schools, their programs, or their students' performance. Our conceptualizations of the ways race, social class, social "place," gender, conflicting community histories, and competing definitions of schooling that all shape "schooling" for us are enriched by this growing literature.

Even within an increasingly complex and international body of scholarship, however, there are serious gaps. One of these is the absence of critical scholarship that carries theory into, or builds theory from, what goes on inside schools. And even more glaringly and ironically absent, given the role of critical scholarship in raising issues of power and power inequities, is the lack of up-close studies of systems of schooling. Jean Anyon's powerful book, *Ghetto Schooling: A Political Economy of Urban Educational Reform* (1997a), stands as an exception. This extraordinarily complex study examines the interrelation of race, local politics, local economics, and even the global economic forces that have over time "pauperized" urban education in a major U.S. city, Newark, New Jersey. Her study is exemplary for situating both the "problems" of urban schools and their potential to become educational for poor and minority children not merely in their internal structures ("Do they 'work'?"), but in the sociocultural contexts of their communities and in the economic and political forces beyond those communities that have over the years come to dominate the resources and political power available in support of these schools. Her analysis is especially powerful because it does not leave these forces at an abstract level, but rather concretizes particular groups, particular legislation, particular individuals' roles in the destruction and rebuilding of the civic capacity of a community to act on behalf of its schools.

Yet even this very detailed study stops at the classroom door. Its analysis of the factors inside schools that have over the years been damaged by increasingly racist and class-based resourcing of schools is descriptive of both the organizational factors (leverage over resources, teacher preparation, administrative authority) and programmatic components (availability of kindergarten, creation of alternative programs for children not well served by traditional schools). But this description and analysis are seen more from an organizational perspective and from the perspective of community constituencies working to reclaim the power to improve schools, rather than from children's experience of these and other aspects of schooling. We still have serious need of studies that not only get inside classrooms but also document from the inside out the ways increasingly differentiated power relations are changing systems of schooling and the ways those systems are shaping what is taught and learned.

It is critical scholarship, then, which gives us a lens for going beyond the appearance, slogans, and indicators, to examine the forces such as standardization that are increasingly shifting both school practice and the power relations shaping that practice. What has been missing from both the global theorizing and the microlevel studies from a critical perspective is an analysis of *how these standardizing forces play out through the system of schooling*: from the political forces shaping the policies, through the bureaucratic systems enacting the policies, to what children are taught and what they experience in the classrooms under these policy mandates. *Contradictions of Reform* provides the first such comprehensive analysis of a system of standardization and its educational consequences. It overcomes the silence in the critical literature about how standardization comes about, how the innocuous-sounding language of standardization ("high standards" and "accountability") comes to mask the reductions in academic quality, and how technical indicators ("objective measures") transform what is valued in teaching and curriculum. The analysis further fills the gap in the critical literature by situating the voices and experiences of particular teachers and students within a particular system, overcoming the tendency of global theorizing to portray a picture that, even if essentially correct, remains at such an abstract level that it lacks credibility to a broader public trying to understand its schools.

Contradictions of Reform looks firsthand at "best case" schools where teachers and highly diverse students, despite serious resource shortages, had been able within the context of a supportive organizational structure, to co-construct authentic educational experiences.

These schools are recorded here in extensive detail to demonstrate the complexity of creating and sustaining such educational programs and to give tangible evidence of the educational value to students when their classroom knowledge is credible and when the educational process involves the minds and knowledge base of the teachers and the minds and experiences of the students. The study then traces the ways standardized controls directly and negatively impact the teaching, curriculum, and role of students in those schools. These standardized controls are traced from their origins in the business leadership outside schools, through political trade-offs with the governor and legislature that silenced educators and forced them to accept a highly complex system of controls over their work in exchange for even very modest pay increments. The analysis then tracks the bureaucratic implementation of these controls, into "instruments of accountability," to measure teachers' classroom practice and the "outcomes" of children's learning. This systemic analysis, from corporate pressure to legislature to school bureaucracy to classroom, sheds new light on the harmful effects of policies that on the surface seem to be benign attempts to monitor educational quality and to assure that schools are run in a cost-effective manner. In reality these policies of standardization are decreasing the quality of teaching and learning in our schools, especially in the schools of poor and minority children. The analysis concludes with an examination of the longer-term effects of such systems of accountability; there is growing evidence that the institutionalization of standardization is widening the gap between poor and minority youth and their peers in more privileged schools.

The language of accountability seems, on a commonsense level, to be about professional practice that is responsible to the children and to the public. The language of standardization appears to denote equity, of assuring that all children receive the same education. Behind the usages of these terms in educational policy, however, is a far different political and pedagogical reality. "Accountability," as will be discussed in the last chapter, reifies both a resource dependency and a hierarchical power structure which maintains that dependency. It further undermines both the public voice in public schooling and the public role of schools in democratic life. "Standardization" equates sameness with equity in ways that mask pervasive and continuing inequalities. Taken together, the increasing use of *standardization,* prescriptive of educational programs, and *accountability,* equating educational accomplishment with outcomes measures, are restructuring public education in two critical ways. First is the shifting of decisions regarding teaching and learning away from communities and educational professionals and into the hands of technical experts following a political agenda to reduce democratic governance of schooling. Second (and particularly serious in its consequences for children in light of the success of the magnet schools in educating highly diverse students) is the restratification by class and race through highly technical systems governing the content and means of evaluation. The final chapter will show how the forms of control, which have their origins in the 1980s reforms, are now deeply entrenched and are not only reducing the overall quality of education but also dramatically widening the gap between poor and minority children's education and the education of more privileged youth.

Standardization in the form of legislated controls over testing and curriculum is an externalization of management controls arising from the bureaucratizing of schooling early in the twentieth century. Its derivations from within the organizational structures of schooling, rather than from theories of child development and learning, have traditionally signaled a separateness from teaching, learning, and curriculum. The perceived separateness between school organization and teaching and learning has been shown, however, to be misleading. Even where there are not in place formal controls over curriculum and teaching, there are, within bureaucratic school structures, imbedded controls.

These bureaucratic controls are not separate from the educational purposes of schooling; rather, they play an active role in determining the quality of teaching and the nature of what is taught.

DEFENSIVE TEACHING AND THE CONTRADICTIONS OF CONTROL

The public will to provide an education to all the citizens in a democracy carries with it issues of cost (Who will pay for such an education?) and governance (How will so many schools be organized and overseen?). It is one of the great ironies of American education that in order to provide a free public education to all its children, schools were created along the model of factory assembly lines in order to reduce the cost of schooling per child and assure millions of children of a diploma, a credential of school completion (Callahan 1962; Kliebard 1986; McNeil 1986). A school that is designed like a factory has a built-in contradiction: running a factory is tightly organized, highly routinized, and geared for the production of uniform products; educating children is complex, inefficient, idiosyncratic, uncertain, and open-ended. Historically, the two purposes of schooling, that is, educating children and running large-scale educational institutions, have been seen as separate domains. The one is aimed at nurturing individual children and equipping them with new knowledge and skills; the other focuses on processing aggregates of students through regularized requirements of the credentialing process. A bureaucratic school, or a school that is part of a bureaucratic system, is thus structured to be in conflict with itself (McNeil 1986, 3). And at the point of the tension—where the two oppositional forces intersect—are the children, the teacher, and the curriculum. How the tension is resolved will in large measure shape the quality of what is taught and learned in the school.

"When the school's organization becomes centered on managing and controlling, teachers and students take school less seriously." With this statement I summed up the analysis of schools and classrooms I wrote as the book, *Contradictions of Control: School Structure and School Knowledge*. To elaborate, I added, "They [teachers and students] fall into a ritual of teaching and learning that tends toward minimal standards and minimal effort. This sets off a vicious cycle. As students disengage from enthusiastic involvement in the learning process, administrators often see the disengagement as a control problem. They then increase their attention to managing students and teachers rather than supporting their instructional purpose" (McNeil 1986, xviii).

That earlier research study, an ethnographic analysis of the factors shaping what is taught in schools (McNeil 1986), revealed that the effects of bureaucratic controls on teaching and learning were not vague influences, but rather very concrete and visible transformations of course content and classroom interaction. That study, conducted in four high schools in the midwestern United States, revealed that behind overt symptoms of poor educational quality lie complicated organizational dynamics (McNeil 1988c). The nature of teachers' practice, the quality of course content and the level of students' engagement may not themselves be weaknesses, but may be symptoms that reflect teachers' and students' accommodations to priorities built into the organizational structure of the school.

Where teachers feel that they have no authority in the structure of the school, or where they see the school as emphasizing credentialing over the substance of schooling, they tend to create their own authority or their own efficiencies within the classroom by tightly controlling course content. They begin to teach a course content that I termed *school knowledge*, which serves the credentialing function of the school but which does not provide students with the rich knowledge of the subject fields nor with opportunities to build their own understandings of the subject.

As background for examining the authentic teaching and learning in the magnet schools, it is important to understand the very concrete ways in which teachers in the midwestern schools shaped school content in reaction to the schools' subordination of the educational goals to the goals of control and credentialing. Teachers who wanted their students to comply with course requirements often did so by reducing those requirements in order to gain minimal participation with minimal resistance. I termed this *defensive teaching* (McNeil 1986, ch. 7). Teachers who taught defensively, asking little from their students in order to satisfy institutional requirements with as little resistance and with as few inefficiencies as possible, tended to bracket their own personal knowledge from the treatment of the subject of the lesson. And they used strategies to silence student questions or (inefficient) discussions. These strategies bear reviewing because it is in part their absence from the magnet classrooms that so starkly shows the differences between teaching in a supportive organizational structure and teaching in a controlling environment.

First, teachers controlled content by *omission*. They tended to omit topics that were difficult to understand and or contemporary topics that would invite student discussion. They especially tended to omit subjects, or treatments of subjects, that were potentially controversial. Controversy, and passionate student discussion, might threaten the teacher's interpretation; interpretations that differed from the teacher's were seen as threatening teacher authority. One teacher even said he had eliminated student research papers because at a time of volatile political debate he found that students doing their own research could become "self-indoctrinated," that is, they came to their own interpretations of the subject (McNeil 1986, 172). At the least, controversy could disrupt the pacing of the coverage of the course material, causing the third-period class, for example, to lag behind the less talkative fourth-period class.

Teachers also maintained a controlling environment in their classes by *mystifying* course content. They mystified a topic by making it seem extremely important, but beyond the students' understanding. It was to be written in the notes for the test, but not understood. In economics class, topics like the Federal Reserve system or international monetary policies would be subjected to mystification; they would be mentioned but not elaborated upon, with the message that students need to recognize the term but leave the understanding of the subject to "the experts." (At times teachers also mystified topics about which *they* had little knowledge, willingly obscuring their students' access to the topic, rather than to learn on behalf of or in collaboration with their students.)

The information that was important to the content of the course, the content that teachers did want their students to learn, would be presented in the form of a list of facts (or names or dates or formulas or terminologies) to be memorized and repeated on tests. Complex subjects that were too essential to the course to be omitted (the Civil War, for example, in a history class; cell processes in biology; the effects of reagents in chemistry) would be reduced to lists and fragments of fact and transmitted by the teacher. In most cases, the lists were presented in a format that condensed and structured the course content into a consensus curriculum. One teacher explained that her job was to read the scholarly literature (in her case, "the historians") and distill the information into a list on which "all historians now agree." This *fragmentation* of course content tended to disembody the curriculum, divorcing it from the cultures and interests and prior knowledge of the students, from the teachers' knowledge of the subject, and from the epistemologies, the ways of knowing, within the subject itself. It also placed barriers between the knowledge as packaged for use in school and its relation to understandings of that subject within the cultural and practical knowledge outside schools. The origins of ideas, the shaping of interpretations, the possibility of inquiry into where this knowledge came from and how it was shaped by human experience were all absent from the curriculum. "School knowledge" was a priori what the teacher conveyed and students received to satisfy school requirements.

A fourth strategy these teachers used to control course content, and with it classroom interactions, was what I have termed *defensive simplification*. When teachers perceived that students had little interest in a lesson or that the difficulty in studying the lesson might cause students to resist the assignment, they made both the content of the assignment and the work students were to do as simple as possible. They minimized *anticipated* student resistance by simplifying course content and demanding little of students. This strategy was used when the topic was complex and in need of multiple explanations if all students were to understand; labor history might be reduced to a list of famous strikes, labor laws, management policies, and key labor leaders. The connections among these would go unexplained; they would simply be names on a list. Student assignments were reduced to taking notes on lectures, copying lists from the blackboard, filling in blanks on worksheets, and reading one or two pages on the subject. Extensive writing that called for student interpretations, for student research beyond the classroom, for engagement with text was absent from these classes—in stark contrast to the responsibilities that, as will be demonstrated, the magnet students assumed on a regular basis.

The thin academic content in these classes, surprising because these were known as "good schools," gave the impression that the teachers were undereducated in their subjects. Interviews with the teachers, however, revealed that they were well read, that they kept up in their fields, that they discussed literature and current events and new discoveries with their friends. They frequently talked with adults, in the teacher's lounge or over lunch, about complex ideas and about what they were learning from their personal reading and travels. When they came into the classroom, however, the subject they had discussed outside the classroom would be rendered unrecognizable when presented to their students as lists and facts. They rarely brought their personal knowledge, or their professional knowledge of their subjects, into the classroom (Shulman 1987); personal knowledge and school knowledge were for them quite separate. In interviews teachers explained that they feared that if the assignments (and treatment of course topics) were too complex, then students would not do the work. In addition, they feared that if students knew how complex the world is, particularly our economic institutions, then they would become cynical and discouraged about their futures and about "the system." They mistook their students' compliance for acceptance of what they were being taught.

Although most of the students in these middle-class, White schools sat quietly and appeared to be absorbing the information provided by their teachers (most of them passed the subjects), interviews with students at all achievement levels revealed that the students did not find the school knowledge credible. School was far from their only source of information; they had televisions, jobs, grandparents, and peers. They did not necessarily have sophisticated understandings of various subjects, but they knew that for some reason "they only tell you here what they want you to know." I had been in the schools for so many months before interviewing students that when we did sit down to talk, several expressed their concern that I might be taken in by the content of the lessons. They advised, "Don't believe what they tell you here," and then each would go on to tell of a school-supplied fact that was directly contradicted by a personal experience or by something learned from a job or a parent. (Some of the school-supplied information was more reliable than what they learned at their jobs or from their friends, but not having the opportunity in school to examine and to come to understandings of what was being taught, they assumed a greater credibility on the part of what they learned outside school.)

The students and teachers in these schools were meeting in an exchange to satisfy the bureaucratic requirements of schooling. The teachers recognized full well that if the school were smooth-running and few students failed their courses, then the administration would be pleased, and that any extra efforts—to develop an interesting curriculum, to assign and grade student research papers, to stay late to meet with students wanting extra help—would not only not be rewarded but also be disdained as unnecessary. The students knew that if they exerted at least minimum effort, then they would pass their required courses; if they ventured opinions and tried to start discussions, then they would be viewed as disruptive. (*Contradictions of Control* includes examples of student attempts to bring their own ideas into the classroom; one teacher lowered "class participation" grades if students tried to discuss).

In response to impersonal bureaucratic schools that emphasized the controlling and credentialing functions at the expense of the educative goals of schooling, teachers and students were engaged in a vicious cycle of lowering expectations. When teachers tightly controlled the curriculum, the students mentally disengaged; teachers saw student disengagement as the reason to tighten controls. When administrators saw teachers and students exerting so little effort, they saw the school as "out of control," and in response they tightened up administrative controls, issuing new directives and increasingly formalizing the hierarchical distances between the administration and the classroom. Within this cycle of lowering expectations, the school, for both teachers and students, begins to lose its legitimacy as a place for serious learning.

The *Contradictions of Control* schools held within them the potential for authentic teaching and learning. It was to be found not in merely changing the dispositions of individual teachers, but in breaking the cycle of lowering expectations set up when teachers teach defensively and students find school knowledge not worthy of their effort. Breaking this cycle within the traditional bureaucratic school structure, in which the credentialing and controlling processes of schooling so easily came to dominate the educational purposes of schooling, can be difficult. The teachers in the midwestern schools were not under legislated curriculum directives, nor was their pay tied to student test scores or compliance with standardized mandates. These teachers were not directly de-skilled by a regulatory context. They were participating in their own de-skilling by bracketing their personal knowledge when they entered the classroom and by using on their students the controlling practices they so resented from administrators.

One school stood out from the others as a school whose administrative structure was organized not to enforce rules and credentialling procedures, but to support teaching. That school (McNeil 1986, ch. 6) demonstrated that when the professional roles, resource allocations, and procedures of a school are organized in support of academics (rather than oppositional to "real teaching"), teachers feel supported to bring their best knowledge into the classroom. They are willing to take risks in incorporating into lessons their questions and uncertainties as well as their deep understandings of their subject. They are willing to let their students see them learning and asking questions (rather than controlling all discussion) and, in turn, they invite their students to make their own questions, interpretations, and partial understandings a vital part of the learning process. Seeing that school, where curriculum content was not "school knowledge," but was congruent with the knowledge that teachers held and with the subject as it is encountered in the world outside schools, raised the question of what other structures of schooling might foster authentic teaching and learning. Observing that school where scarce resources went first to instruction in a variety of imaginative ways, and where administrative personnel put their own time and efforts at the disposal of their faculties, raised the possibility of identifying other examples of schools structured to support educating children in ways consistent with their need to be nurtured and with their need to learn content whose purpose went far beyond building a record of grades and school credentials.

Contradictions of Control cut new theoretical ground for understanding the complex relationships between school organization and what is taught and learned. The wisdom that school administration and instruction are loosely linked domains was challenged by the clear evidence that a controlling administrative environment undermined teaching and learning by the responses it invoked in teachers and students.

The analysis presented here began with the selection of the magnet schools as counterexamples to the organizational de-skilling of teachers. These schools, as the next three chapters document, proved that schools can be organized in ways that do not put teachers in conflict with administrative purposes when they do their best teaching. They show that in a supportive environment, teachers will work alone and collaboratively to develop complex and up-to-date curricula, that they will tackle complex and controversial topics essential to their students' understandings, that they will struggle to find ways to make learning possible for all their students. The magnet schools carried many agendas as they were established and as they came to be the chief conduits to college for hundreds of minority youth in a city with a long history of discriminatory school practices. For this analysis, their benefit is in exemplifying the possibilities for authentic teaching and learning when schools are structured to foster learning rather than to process students or control them.

The success of the magnet schools in providing a substantive education for diverse urban students was jeopardized when a layer of organizational controls became state law (chapter 5). These controls, centralized and highly standardized, threatened the educational programs by imposing on the magnet school curricula magnified versions of the simplifications used by the midwestern teachers to limit their students' access to knowledge. The magnet teachers refused to be de-skilled, but as chapter 6 will dramatically record, the costs of new standardization policies fell heavily on their curricula and on their students and threatened to drive them out of public classrooms when remaining meant participating in the de-skilled teaching of "school knowledge."

The experiences of the students and teachers in the magnet schools under increasingly standardized controls raise serious questions about the purposes behind these controls. For educators, they also raise serious questions about the long-term effects of students whose entire educational experience is dominated by standardization. In chapter 7, I discuss those long-term effects, both on children and on the system of schooling. When standardization becomes institutionalized, and student testing comes to be used for monitoring "accountability" throughout a state's educational system, the negative effects fall most heavily on the poorest children, minority children whose entire school experience comes to be dominated by an attempt to raise their (historically low) test scores at any cost.

NOTES

1. A note on methodology: this study began as an analysis of the factors shaping curriculum in schools whose organizational and administrative structures were designed to support, rather than control, teaching and learning. For that analysis, daily observations in classrooms over the course of at least a semester in each school formed the primary data on curriculum and teaching. Interviews with teachers, students, administrators, and parents, and historical research into the schools and their programs, were conducted formally and informally at strategic points before, during, and following classroom observations. Interviews with central office administrators in the offices of curriculum, gifted-and-talented programs, magnet services, and evaluation and research provided key information on the administrative and legal contexts of the magnet schools during their formation and in the years leading up to and inclusive of the time of the study.

   Once the state-mandated reforms under House Bill 72 and related state education agency directives began to affect the schools, subsequent investigation was made into the role of the SCOPE committee, Perot's use of advisors, state implementation of the legislation, and the offices and structures through which these policies were implemented within the school district. Reviews of legislative and committee documents, correspondence, initial evaluation reports, administrative documents, and related materials from a wide range of observers and participants in the state-level reforms and district implementation were essential to the understanding of not only the content of the reforms but also the rationale being used at each level to justify their implementation. Interviews with several key shapers of these policies, both from outside and from within SCOPE and the state government, were extremely helpful in tracking how decisions were being made, and the assumptions of schooling on which they were based. (None of these sources was available to or known to the teachers being observed, who were receiving the directives as rules emanating from a higher but undesignated level in the bureaucracy.) Copies of district and state standardized tests and test-driven curricula and teacher assessment instruments from a number of years were examined. The schools have been followed for several years following the initial implementation of the curriculum directives and teacher assessment instrument, through the successive state test-driven programs, which have followed from the proficiencies, with site visits to the schools, periodic interviews with teachers and administrators, and information gathered through a wide association with these schools.

   The contemporary legacy of these early standardizations (especially in chapter 7) is analyzed here on the basis of extensive work with urban teachers and administrators through the teacher enhancement programs of the Rice University Center for Education, school visits and observations, analysis of TAAS-related materials from the state and the testing companies, interviews with teachers, conversations with a wide range of teachers and administrators, parents, and students, regarding the impact of the TAAS on classrooms, press coverage and district administrative bulletins related to the TAAS, and a variety of other formal and informal sources.

   To counter any tendency to generalize from an in-depth but relatively small data sample, or from individual occurrences, several correctives were built into the research. First, any outlier occurrences, for which there was not a pattern beyond those occurrences, were not deemed as "data" for the purpose of the overall analysis. (Individual occurrences held significance in themselves, but are not reported in this analysis unless they indicate a *pattern of teaching* and *of the effects of standardization* that go beyond that any one occurrence.) There is no reliance on "horror stories" for this analysis, in other words, or exceptional events. Second, at each step of data collection and interim analysis, counter examples to trends in the data have been actively sought. For example, when it became apparent that biology teachers were having to eliminate many of their lessons, particularly those that integrated biological concepts around hands-on phenomena such as student-built marine aquaria or a natural habitat, interviews were scheduled with biology teachers at other schools to determine whether this problem was specific to the magnet schools, or even these teachers, or whether these curricular deletions were widespread. Also, counter interpretations were investigated; for example, if a teacher was having to delete a portion of the curriculum, further research was conducted to see if factors other than the prescriptive testing had had an effect, perhaps a less visible effect.

The search for counter examples and counter interpretations is significant because this analysis is not a mere listing of problems or "unintended consequences" of an otherwise sanguine set of policies. As discussed in chapter 7, the negative effects of the standardizing policies have been their primary effects on classrooms and teaching, and their effects on the locus of control over schooling have become visible as, in fact, intended consequences, not circumstantial by-products.

2. This perspective has been reiterated by proponents of state testing, and the Texas Accountability System specifically, in public meetings and private discussions at which this researcher was present.

REFERENCES

Anyon, Jean. (1997a). *Ghetto Schooling: A Political Economy of Urban Educational Reform*. New York and London: Teachers College Press.

Apple, Michael W. (1979). *Ideology and Curriculum*. London: Routledge & Kegan Paul.

Apple, Michael W. (1995). *Education and Power*, 2d ed. New York: Routledge.

Apple, Michael W. (1996). *Cultural Politics and Education*. New York and London: Teachers College Press.

Apple, Michael W., and Anita Oliver. (1998). "Becoming Right" Education and the Formation of Conservative Movements. In Dennis Carlson and Michael W. Apple (eds.), *Power/Knowledge/Pedagogy: The Meaning of Democratic Education in Unsettling Times*. Boulder: Westview Press.

Beyer, Landon E. and Michael W. Apple. (1998a). *The Curriculum: Problems, Politics, and Possibilities*, 2nd ed. Albany: State University of New York Press.

Callahan, Raymond. (1962). *Education and the Cult of Efficiency*. Chicago: University of Chicago Press.

Fordham, S., and J. Ogbu. (1986). "Black Student's School Success: Coping with the Burden of 'Acting White'." *Urban Review* 18: 176–206.

Freire, Paulo. (1970). *Pedagogy of the Oppressed*. Translated by Myra Bergman Ramos. New York: Seabury.

Freire, Paulo. (1985). *The Politics of Education: Culture, Power and Liberation*. Translated by Donaldo Macedo. South Hadley: Mass.: Bergin and Garvey.

Freire, Paulo. (1995). *A Pedagogy of Hope*. New York: Continuum.

Giroux, Henry. (1983). *Critical Theory and Educational Practice*. Geelong, Victoria, Australia: Deakin University Press.

Giroux, Henry. (1996). *Pedagogy and the Politics of Hope*. Boudler: Westview Press.

Greene, Maxine. (1978). *Landscapes of Learning*. New York: Teachers College Press.

Gutierrez, K., B. Rymes, and J. Larson. (1995). "Script, Counterscript, and Underlife in the Classroom: *James Brown v. the Board of Education*." *Harvard Education Review* 65, no. 3: 445–71.

Huebert, Jay P., and Robert M. Hauser (eds.) (1999). *High Stakes: Testing for Tracking, Promotion, and Graduation*. Committee on Appropriate Test Use, Board on Testing and Assessment, Commission on Behavioral and Social Sciences and Education, and National Research Council. Washington, D.C.: National Academy Press.

Kliebard, Herbert M. (1986). *The Struggle for the American Curriculum*. New York and London: Routledge.

McLaren, Peter L., and Kris Gutierrex. (1998). "Global Politics and Local Antagonisms: Research and Practice as Dissent and Possibility." In Dennis Carlson and Michael W. Apple (eds.), *Power/Knowledge/ Pedagogy: The Meaning of Democratic Education in Unsettling Times*. Boulder: Westview Press.

McNeil, Linda M. (1986). *Contradictions of Control: School Structure and School Knowledge.* New York and London: Routledge.

McNeil, Linda M. (1988c). "Teacher Knowledge and the Organization of the School." A paper prepared for presentation at the "School Organization and Climate" session of the Annual Meeting of the American Educational Research Association, New Orleans.

Romo, Harriet D., and Toni Falbo. (1996). *Latino High School Graduation: Defying the Odds.* Austin: University of Texas Press.

Sarason, Seymour B. (1971). *The Culture of School and the Problem of Change.* Boston: Allyn and Bacon.

Sarason, Seymour B. (1996). *Revisiting the Culture of School and the Problem of Change.* New York and London: Teachers College Press.

Shulman, Lee. (1987). "Knowledge and Teaching: Foundations of the New Reform." *Harvard Education Review,* 57, no. 1 (February): 1–22.

Suarez-Orozco, Marcelo M. (1991). "Hispanic Immigrant Adaptation to Schooling." In Margaret A. Gibson and John U. Ogbu (eds.), *Minority Status and Schooling: A Comparative Study of Immigrant and Involuntary Minorities.* New York: Garland Publishing.

Valenzuela, Angela. (1999). *Subtractive Schooling: U.S.-Mexican Youth and the Politics of Caring.* Albany: State University of New York Press.

Wise, Arthur. (1979). *Legislated Learning: The Bureaucratization of the American Classroom.* Berkeley and Los Angeles: University of California Press.

Wrigley, Julia. (1982). *Class Politics and Public Schools: Chicago, 1900–1950.* New Brunswick, N.J.: Rutgers University Press.

Suggested Readings
for Further Study

Apple, M. (1979). *Ideology and curriculum.* New York: Routledge.

Bartolome, L. (1995). Beyond the methods fetish: Toward a humanizing pedagogy, *Harvard Educational Review, 65*(2), 173–194.

Beane, J. (1990). *Affect in the curriculum: Toward democracy, dignity, and diversity.* New York: Teachers College Press.

Beane, J. (1993). *A middle school curriculum: From rhetoric to reality.* Columbus, OH: National Middle School Association.

Beane, J., & Brodhagen, B. (2001). Teaching in middle schools. In Richardson, V. (Ed.) *Handbook of research on teaching* (pp. 1157–1174). Washington, DC: American Educational Research Association.

Butler, D., & Manning, M. (1998). *Assessing gender differences in young adolescents.* Olney, MD: Association for Childhood Education International.

Cochran-Smith, M. (1997). Color-blindness and basket-making are not the answers, *American Educational Research Journal, 32*(3), 493–522.

Darder, A., Baltodano, M., & Torres, R. (2003). *The critical pedagogy reader.* New York: Routledge.

Edelsky, C. (1996). *With literacy and justice for all: Rethinking the social in language and education.* Bristol, PA: Taylor & Francis.

Erb, T. (2001). *This we believe … and now we must act.* Westerville, OH: National Middle School Association.

Erb, T., & Dickinson, T. (1997). *The future of teaming.* Columbus, OH: National Middle School Association.

Giroux, H. (1992/2005) *Border crossings: Cultural workers and the politics of education* (2nd ed.). New York: Routledge.

Goodman, R., & Saltman, K. (2002). *Strangelove: OR how we learn to stop worrying and love the market.* Lanham, MA: Rowman & Littlefield.

Gould, S. (1981/1996). *The mismeasure of man.* New York: W. W. Norton.

Gutierrez, R. (2000). Is the multiculturalization of mathematics doing us more harm than good? In Mahalingam, R., & McCarthy, C. (Ed.) *Multicultural curriculum: New directions for social theory, practice, and policy.* New York: Routledge.

Hilliard, A. (2000). Standards: Decoy or quality control?, In Swope, K., & Miner, B. (Eds.) *Failing our kids: Why the testing craze won't fix our schools* (pp. 64–69). Milwaukee, WI: Rethinking Schools.

Irvin, J. (Ed.) *What current research says to the middle level practitioner.* Westerville, OH: National Middle School Association.

Khisty, L. (1995). Making inequality: Issues of language and meanings in mathematics teaching with Hispanic students. In Secada, W., Fennema, E., & Adajian, L. (Eds.). *New directions for equity in mathematics education* (pp. 279–297). New York: Cambridge University Press.

Kincheloe, J., & Steinberg, S. (1998). *Unauthorized methods: Strategies for critical teaching.* New York: Routledge.

Kohl, H. (1994). *"I won't learn from you": And other thoughts on creative maladjustment.* New York: The New Press.

Ladson-Billings, G. (1994). *Dreamkeepers: Successful teachers of African American children.* San Francisco, CA: Jossey Bass.

Ladson-Billings, G. (1999). Just what is critical race theory and what's it doing in a nice field like education? In Parker, L., Dehyle, D., & Villenas, S. (Eds.) *Race is … race isn't: Critical race theory and qualitative studies in education.* New York: HarperCollins.

Ladson-Billings, G. (2001). The power of pedagogy: Does teaching matter? In Watkins, W., Lewis, J., & Chou, V. (Eds.). *Race and education: The roles of history and society in education African American students* (pp. 73–88). Needham Heights, MA: Allyn & Bacon.

Ladson-Billings, G. (Ed.) (2003). *Critical race theory perspectives on social studies: The profession, policies, and curriculum.* Greenwich, CT: Information Age Publishing.

Lee, C. D. (2001). Unpacking culture, teaching and learning: A Response to 'The Power of pedagogy.' In Watkins, W., Lewis, J., & Chou, V. (Eds.). *Race and education: The roles of history and society in educating African American students* (pp. 89–99). Needham Heights, MA: Allyn & Bacon.

Leistyna, P. (2005). *Cultural studies from theory to action.* Malden, MA: Blackwell.

Leistyna, P., Woodrum, A., & Sherblom, S. (Eds.) (1996). *Breaking free: The transformative power of critical pedagogy.* Cambridge, MA: Harvard Educational Review.

Loewen, J. (1995). *Lies my teacher told me: Everything your American history textbook got wrong.* New York: Touchstone Press.

Lounsbury, J. (Ed.) (1992). *Connecting the curriculum through interdisciplinary instruction.* Columbus, OH: National Middle School Association.

Macedo, D. (1994). *Literacies of power.* Boulder, CO: Westview Press.

Macedo, D. (2003). *Hegemony of English.* Boulder, CO: Paradigm Press.

MacLeod, J. (1991). Bridging street and school, *Journal of Negro Education, 60*(3), 260–275.

McEwin, C. K., & Dickinson, T. (1997). Middle level teacher preparation and licensure. In Irvin, J. (Ed.). *What current research says to the middle level practitioner.* Westerville, OH: National Middle School Association.

McEwin, C., Dickinson, T., Erb, T., & Scales, P. (1997). Organizing principles for middle grades teacher preparation, *Teacher Education Quarterly, 24*(4), 9–20.

Oakes, J. (1998) Detracking for student achievement, *Educational Leadership, 55*(6), 38–41.

Oakes, J. (2000). Becoming good American schools: The struggle for civic virtue in educational reform, *Phi Delta Kappan, 81*(8), 568–575.

Peterson, B., & Neill, M. (2000). Alternatives to standardized tests. In Swope, K., & Miner, B. (Eds.) *Failing our kids: Why the testing craze won't fix our schools* (pp. 96–101). Milwaukee, WI: Rethinking Schools.

Sapon-Shevin, M. (1994). Cooperative learning in middle schools: What would it take to really do it right? *Theory Into Practice, 33*(3), 183–190.

Scales, P. C., & McEwin, C. K. (1994). *Growing pains: The making of America's middles school teachers.* Columbus, OH: National Middle School Association.

Schaafsma, D. (1993). *Eating on the street: Teaching literacy in a multicultural society.* Pittsburg, PA: University of Pittsburgh Press.

Spring, J. (1994/1997). *Deculturalization and the struggle for equality: A brief history of the education of dominated cultures in the United States.* New York: McGraw-Hill.

Stevenson, C. (1998/2000). *Teaching ten to fourteen year olds* (3rd ed.). Boston, MA: Allyn & Bacon.

Swope, K., & Miner, B. (Eds.) (2000). *Failing our kids: Why the testing craze won't fix our schools.* Milwaukee, WI: Rethinking Schools.

Walkerdine, V. (1998). *Counting girls out: Girls and mathematics.* London: Falmer Press.

Zinn, H. (1995). Why students should study history: An interview with Howard Zinn. In Levine, D., Lowe, R., Peterson, B., & Tenorio, R. (Eds.) *Rethinking schools: An agenda for change* (pp. 89–99). New York: The New Press.

Afterword

Mara Sapon–Shevin

My local high school implemented a passbook system that seemed dangerously reminiscent of South Africa or Nazi Germany. Students were required to be in possession of their passbooks at all times, and any adult was entitled to stop them at any point and demand to see their book. Failure to produce their passbook resulted in immediate disciplinary action. Each student was allowed only a certain number of bathroom passes per month, and when those were gone, well, they were just out of luck. And, at some times during the day, the bathrooms were simply "closed," and even those with valid passes were denied access. A student there commented, "I feel like I'm in prison, and I don't even know what my crime was." Sadly, her crime was her age, nothing more and nothing less. Who are these "young criminals" who must be treated like this?

No group of young people is as routinely maligned as adolescents. Mention in any social circle that you have teens or pre-teens and people roll their eyes and offer condolences. When my own daughters were this age, no one *ever* said, "Wow! How exciting to have children at that age. They're so full of life, energy and commitment. You must be having a wonderful time with them." Instead they offered sympathy, small tsk-tsk sounds and muttered, "Oh dear, you poor thing, you must have your hands full." Adolescence may be socially constructed, as this book argues, but rather than a social construction like "motherhood" which evokes smiles and sighs, adolescents tend to evoke suspicion, fear, and the perceived necessity of strict (often punitive) control.

This book demands that we look differently — critically — at the ways in which middle school age students have been constructed, mis/educated and controlled, usually with the putative reasoning that this is "for their own good." The authors ask us to think about the historical, political and economic contexts within which young people come of age and are taught their places in the world, and the role of the schools in this acculturation process. In this age of standards and high stakes testing, coupled with the current repressive political climate, there is real danger that adolescents will soon be firmly characterized exclusively by the language of risk, danger and threat rather than by a discourse of hope, possibility and growth.

What do we achieve by constructing adolescents as "trouble" or at best "incipient trouble"? Most distressingly, it means that we can dismiss students' views, silence their voices,

and disempower them completely with rigid rules and prescriptive policies. The consequences of such dismissal and disempowerment, however, have been shown to lead to devastating results for the young people themselves and for the greater society. Low
expectations, suspicion and silencing rarely produce engagement, high achievement and
commitment to the community. If we define good citizens as those who are docile, compliant, obedient and passive, then many of our current middle school practices are completely on target.

But what if we defined "good citizenship" consistent with Paulo Freire's notion of education, seeing our goal as raising students' consciousness of the oppressed so that they
could transform their own lives and society? What if, instead of the current standards
imposed by outside accreditation sources, we had middle school standards such as these?

- Every student will learn to think critically and question the relationships between
  knowledge, power and authority.
- Every student will demonstrate a commitment to civic participation and democratic
  social transformation.
- Every student will be able to identify instances of sexism, racism, homophobia, classism, ableism and religious oppression within their school and community.
- Every student will develop skills in identifying their own privilege and demonstrate
  multiple strategies for challenging oppressive behavior in others.
- Every student will be able to define and implement (when demanded) political
  change strategies such as letter writing campaigns, boycotting, civil disobedience, and
  public protest.

What if we truly believed that adolescents' passion for social justice, their impatience
with pretense and superficiality and their insistence on honesty and integrity could be
acknowledged, nurtured, and enlisted in the service of creating a more just society?

Three recent experiences with middle school and high school students have convinced
me that this is more than just a possibility. In Cleveland, seventh graders analyzed their
classroom, their school and their community in terms of accessibility for people with disabilities and then wrote letters to administrators, business owners and community politicians sharing their findings and elaborating needed changes. In 1994, I chaperoned middle
school and high school students from a group called "Youth Against Homophobia" to a
large Gay Rights' March in Washington, D.C. and observed extraordinary maturity, solidarity and responsibility. And, lastly, I have had the privilege of working with middle
school and high school students to develop curriculum for a program called "Endracism/
Endinjustice: Challenging Oppression, Building Allies," and then seen these students go on
to be student facilitators with their peers. Their commitment to do the hard work of creating social justice was inspiring.

What characterized each of these experiences was that the young people were actively
engaged in addressing something that they saw as unfair, as needing change, as incompati-
ble with their own sense of justice. And they were given the opportunities and skills to be
active participants in the change process. They participated with others of different ages in
projects in the "real world" and the results of their efforts were immediately visible. Treated
with dignity and respect, they consistently rose to the occasion. They were not asked to be

quiet or to refrain from critique. Rather they were encouraged to ask themselves and others, "How could the world be different? What can I do to make that happen?"

It lies within our power as educators and citizens to construct a different vision of adolescence and to create schools consistent with that vision. As a society we can ill-afford to continue treating adolescents as mini-prisoners within holding facilities, removed from the "real world" and segregated by age. We must provide chances for students to see themselves as meaningful participants in a rich, multicultural, diverse society, as change agents and as human beings worthy of our deepest respect and our profoundest kindness. This book is a beginning.

About the Editors

Enora R. Brown is an associate professor in the Department of Educational Policy Studies and Research at DePaul University where she teaches graduate and undergraduate courses on human development, middle school, and identity. She is the author of articles and book chapters on the subjects of human development, educational policy, and the politics of education with a focus on identity and race.

Kenneth J. Saltman is an assistant professor in the Department of Educational Policy Studies and Research at DePaul University where he teaches graduate and undergraduate courses on sociology of education, philosophy of education, and middle school. His books include *The Edison Schools: Corporate Schooling and the Assault on Public Education* (Routledge, 2005) *Education as Enforcement: the Militarization and Corporatization of Schools* (co-edited with David Gabbard, Routledge, 2003), and *Collateral Damage* (Rowman & Littlefield, 2000).

Permissions

Index